SECOND EDITION

Strategies of Qualitative Inquiry

INTERNATIONAL ADVISORY BOARD

Arthur P. Bochner
Communication,
University of South Florida

Ivan Brady
Anthropology, State University
of New York at Oswego

Julianne Cheek
Health,
University of South Australia

Patricia Clough
Sociology and Women's Studies,
the Graduate Center,
City University of New York

Yen Le Espiritu
Ethnic Studies,
University of California,
San Diego

Orlando Fals Borda
Sociology,
National University of Colombia

Michelle Fine
Social Psychology,
City University of New York

Davydd Greenwood
Anthropology,
Cornell University

Jaber F. Gubrium
Sociology,
University of Florida

Rosanna Hertz
Sociology and Women's Studies,
Wellesley College

Udo Kelle
Institute for Interdisciplinary Gerontology,
University of Vechta,
Germany

Anton Kuzel
Family Medicine,
Virginia Commonwealth University

Patti Lather
Education,
Ohio State University

Morten Levin
Sociology and Political Science,
Norwegian University
of Science and Technology

Meaghan Morris
Humanities and Social Science,
University of Technology, Sydney

Michael A. Olivas
Law,
University of Houston

Shulamit Reinharz
Sociology,
Brandeis University

James J. Scheurich
Education,
University of Texas at Austin

David Silverman
Sociology,
Goldsmith College, University of London

Linda Smircich
Management and Organization Studies,
University of Massachusetts–Amherst

Robert E. Stake
Education,
University of Illinois, Urbana-Champaign

Barbara Tedlock
Anthropology,
State University of New York at Buffalo

William G. Tierney
Education,
University of Southern California

Harry Wolcott
Education and Anthropology,
University of Oregon

SECOND EDITION

Strategies of Qualitative Inquiry

editors

NORMAN K. DENZIN
University of Illinois at Urbana-Champaign

YVONNA S. LINCOLN
Texas A&M University

SAGE Publications
International Educational and Professional Publisher
Thousand Oaks ■ London ■ New Delhi

H61. S8823   2003 c.2

Copyright © 2003 by Sage Publications, Inc.

All rights reserved. No part of this book may be reproduced or utilized in any form or by any means, electronic or mechanical, including photocopying, recording, or by any information storage and retrieval system, without permission in writing from the publisher.

For information:

Sage Publications, Inc.
2455 Teller Road
Thousand Oaks, California 91320
E-mail: order@sagepub.com

Sage Publications Ltd.
6 Bonhill Street
London EC2A 4PU
United Kingdom

Sage Publications India Pvt. Ltd.
B-42 Panchsheel Enclave
Post Box 4109
New Delhi 110-017 India

Printed in the United States of America

Library of Congress Cataloging-in-Publication Data

Strategies of qualitative inquiry / Norman K. Denzin, Yvonna S. Lincoln.—2nd ed.
        p. cm.
    Selections from the Handbook of qualitative research. 2nd ed.
    Includes bibliographical references and index.
    ISBN 0-7619-2691-7 (Paper)
    1. Social sciences-Methodology. 2. Social sciences-Research-Methodology.
I. Denzin, Norman K. II. Lincoln, Yvonna S. III. Handbook of qualitative research.
    H61 .S8823 2003
    300´.7´2—dc21   2002156612

Printed on acid-free paper

03 04 05 06 07 08 09 10 9 8 7 6 5 4 3 2 1

Acquiring Editor:	Margaret H. Seawell
Production Editor:	Claudia A. Hoffman
Typesetter:	Christina Hill
Indexer:	Molly Hall
Cover Designer:	Michelle Lee and Ravi Balasuriya
Cover Photograph:	C. A. Hoffman

Contents

Preface

◆ For over than three decades, a quiet methodological revolution has been taking place in the social sciences. A blurring of disciplinary boundaries has occurred. The social sciences and humanities have drawn closer together in a mutual focus on an interpretive, qualitative approach to research and theory. Although these trends are not new, the extent to which the "qualitative revolution" has overtaken the social sciences and related professional fields has been nothing short of amazing.

Reflecting this revolution, a host of textbooks, journals, research monographs, and readers have been published in recent years. In 1994 we published the first edition of the *Handbook of Qualitative Research* in an attempt to represent the field in its entirety, to take stock of how far it had come and how far it might yet go. The immediate success of the first edition suggested the need to offer the *Handbook* in terms of three separate volumes. So in 1998 we published a three-volume set, *The Landscape of Qualitative Research: Theories and Issues*; *Strategies of Inquiry*; and *Collecting and Interpreting Qualitative Materials*. In 2003 we offer a new three-volume set, based on the second edition of the handbook.

In 2000 we published the second edition of the *Handbook*. Although it became abundantly clear that the "field" of qualitative research is still defined primarily by tensions, contradictions, and hesitations—and that they exist in a less-than-unified arena—we believed that the handbook could and would be valuable for solidifying, interpreting, and organizing the field in spite of the essential differences that characterize it.

The first edition attempted to define the field of qualtiative research. The second edition went one step further. Building on themes in the first edition, we asked how the practices of qualitative inquiry could be used to address issues of equity and of social justice.

We have been enormously gratified and heartened by the response to the *Handbook* since its publication. Especially gratifying has been that it has been used and adapted by such a wide variety of scholars and graduate students in precisely the way we had hoped: as a starting point, a springboard for new thought and new work.

◆ The Paperback Project

The second edition of the *Landscape Series* of the *Handbook of Qualitative Research* is virtually all new. Over half of the authors from the first edition have been replaced by new contributors. Indeed, there are 33 new chapter authors or co-authors. There are six totally new chapter topics, including contributions on queer theory, performance ethnography, *testimonio*, focus groups in feminist research, applied ethnography, and anthropological poetics. All returning authors have substantially revised their original contributions, in many cases producing totally new chapters.

The second edition of the *Handbook of Qualitative Research* continues where the first edition ended. With Thomas Schwandt (Chapter 7, Volume 1), we may observe that qualitative inquiry, among other things, is the name for a "reformist movement that began in the early 1970s in the academy." The interpretive and critical paradigms, in their multiple forms, are central to this movement. Indeed, Schwandt argues that this movement encompasses multiple paradigmatic formulations. It also includes complex epistemological and ethical criticisms of traditional social science research. The movement now has its own journals, scientific associations, conferences, and faculty positions.

The transformations in the field of qualitative research that were taking place in the early 1990s continued to gain momentum as we entered the new century. Today, few in the interpretive community look back with skepticism on the narrative turn. The turn has been taken, and that is all there is to say about it. Many have now told their tales from the field. Further, today we know that men and women write culture differently, and that writing itself is not an innocent practice.

Experimental ways of writing first-person ethnographic texts are now commonplace. Sociologists and anthropologists continue to explore new ways of composing ethnography, and many write fiction, drama, performance texts, and ethnographic poetry. Social science journals hold fiction contests. Civic journalism shapes calls for a civic, or public, ethnography.

There is a pressing need to show how the practices of qualitative research can help change the world in positive ways. So, at the beginning of the twenty-first century, it is necessary to re-engage the promise of qualitative research as a generative form of inquiry (Peshkin, 1993) and as a form of radical democratic practice. This is the agenda of the second edition of the *Landscape Series*, as it is for the second edition of the *Handbook*: namely, to show how the discourses of qualitative research can be used to help imagine and create a free, democratic society. Each of the chapters in the three-volume set takes up this project, in one way or another.

A handbook, we were told by our publisher, should ideally represent the distillation of knowledge of a field, a benchmark volume that synthesizes an existing literature, helping to define and shape the present and future of that discipline. This mandate organized the second edition. In metaphoric terms, if you were to take one book on qualitative research with you to a desert island (or for a comprehensive graduate examination), a handbook would be the book.

We decided that the part structure of the *Handbook* could serve as a useful point of departure for the organization of the paperbacks. Thus Volume 1, titled *The Landscape of Qualitative Research: Theories and Issues*, takes a look at the field from a broadly theoretical perspective and is composed of the *Handbook*'s Parts I ("Locating the Field"), II ("Paradigms and Perspectives in Transition"), and VI ("The Future of Qualitative Research"). Volume 2, titled *Strategies of Qualitative Inquiry*, focuses on just that and consists of Part III of the *Handbook*. Volume 3, titled *Collecting and Interpreting Qualitative Materials*, considers the tasks of collecting, analyzing, and interpreting empirical materials and comprises the *Handbook*'s Parts IV ("Methods of Collecting and Analyzing Empirical Materials") and V ("The Art and Practices of Interpretation, Evaluation, and Representation").

As with the first edition of the *Landscape* series, we decided that nothing should be cut from the original *Handbook*. Nearly everyone we spoke to who used the *Handbook* had his or her own way of using it, leaning heavily on certain chapters and skipping others altogether. But there was consensus that this reorganization made a great deal of sense both pedagogically and economically. We and Sage are committed to making this iteration of the *Handbook* accessible for classroom use. This commitment is reflected in the size, organization, and price of the paperbacks, as well as in the addition of end-of-book bibliographies.

It also became clear in our conversations with colleagues who used the *Handbook* that the single-volume, hard-cover version has a distinct place and value, and Sage will keep the original version available until a revised edition is published.

◆ Organization of This Volume

Strategies of Qualitative Inquiry isolates the major strategies—historically, the research methods—that researchers can use in conducting concrete qualitative studies. The question of methods begins with the design of the research project, which Valerie Janesick in Chapter 2 describes in dance terms. Design issues also involve matters of money and funding, issues discussed by Julianne Cheek in Chapter 3. Questions of design always begin with a socially situated observer who moves from a research question to a paradigm or perspective, and then to the empirical world. So located, the researcher then addresses a range of methods that can be employed in any study. The history and uses of these strategies are explored extensively in this volume. The chapters move from performance ethnography to case studies, issues of ethnogaphic representation, grounded theory strategies, *testimonios*, life histories, participatory action research, and clinical research.

◆ Acknowledgments

Of course, this book would not exist without its authors or the editorial board members for the *Handbook* on which it is based. These individuals were able to offer both long-term sustained commitments to the project and short-term emergency assistance.

In addition, we would like to thank the following individuals and institutions for their assistance, support, insights, and patience: our respective universities and departments, as well as Jack Bratich, Ben Scott, Ruoyun Bai, and Francyne Huckaby, our respective graduate students. Without them, we could never have kept this project on course. There are also several people to thank at Sage Publications. We thank Margaret Seawell, our new editor; this three-volume version of the *Handbook* would not have been possible without Margaret's wisdom, support, humor, and grasp of the field in all its current diversity.

As always, we appreciate the efforts of Greg Daurelle, the director of books marketing at Sage, along with his staff, for their indefatigable efforts in getting the word out about the *Handbook* to teachers, researchers, and methodologists around the world. Claudia Hoffman was essential in moving the series through production; we are also grateful to the copy editor, Judy Selhorst, and to those whose proofreading and indexing skills were so central to the publication of the *Handbook* on which these volumes are based. Finally, as ever, we thank our spouses, Katherine Ryan and Egon Guba, for their forbearance and constant support.

The idea for this three-volume paperback version of the *Handbook* did not arise in a vacuum, and we are grateful for the feedback we received from countless teachers and students.

—Norman K. Denzin
University of Illinois at Urbana–Champaign

—Yvonna S. Lincoln
Texas A&M University

1

Introduction

The Discipline and

Practice of Qualitative Research

Norman K. Denzin and Yvonna S. Lincoln

◆ Qualitative research has a long, distinguished, and sometimes anguished history in the human disciplines. In sociology, the work of the "Chicago school" in the 1920s and 1930s established the importance of qualitative inquiry for the study of human group life. In anthropology, during the same time period, the discipline-defining studies of Boas, Mead, Benedict, Bateson, Evans-Pritchard, Radcliffe-Brown, and Malinowski charted the outlines of the fieldwork method (see Gupta & Ferguson, 1997; Stocking, 1986, 1989). The agenda was clear-cut: The observer went to a foreign setting to study the customs and habits of another society and culture (see in Volume 1, Vidich & Lyman, Chapter 2; Tedlock, this volume, Chapter 6; see also Rosaldo, 1989, pp. 25-45, for criticisms of this tradition). Soon, qualitative research would be employed in other social and behavioral science disciplines, including education (especially the work of Dewey), history, political science, business, medicine, nursing, social work, and communications.

In the opening chapter in Part I of Volume 1, Vidich and Lyman chart many key features of this history. In this now classic analysis, they note, with some irony, that qualitative research in sociology and anthropology was "born out of concern to understand the 'other.' " Furthermore, this other was the exotic other, a primitive, nonwhite person from a foreign culture judged to be less civilized than that of the researcher. Of course, there were colonialists long before there were anthropologists. Nonetheless, there would be no colonial, and now no postcolonial, history were it not for this investigative mentality that turned the dark-skinned other into the object of the ethnographer's gaze.

Thus does bell hooks (1990, pp. 126-128) read the famous photo that appears on the cover of *Writing Culture* (Clifford & Marcus, 1986) as an instance of this mentality (see also Behar, 1995, p. 8; Gordon, 1988). The photo depicts Stephen Tyler doing fieldwork in India. Tyler is seated some distance from three dark-skinned persons. A child is poking his or her head out of a basket. A woman is hidden in the shadows of a hut. A man, a checkered white-and-black shawl across his shoulder, elbow propped on his knee, hand resting along the side of his face, is staring at Tyler. Tyler is writing in a field journal. A piece of white cloth is attached to his glasses, perhaps shielding him from the sun. This patch of whiteness marks Tyler as the white male writer studying these passive brown and black persons. Indeed, the brown male's gaze signals some desire, or some attachment to Tyler. In contrast, the female's gaze is completely hidden by the shadows and by the words of the book's title, which cross her face (hooks, 1990, p. 127). And so this cover photo of perhaps the most influential book on ethnography in the last half of the 20th century reproduces "two ideas that are quite fresh in the racist imagination: the notion of the white male as writer/authority . . . and the idea of the passive brown/black man [and woman and child] who is doing nothing, merely looking on" (hooks, 1990, p. 127).

In this introductory chapter, we will define the field of qualitative research and then navigate, chart, and review the history of qualitative research in the human disciplines. This will allow us to locate this volume and its contents within their historical moments. (These historical moments are somewhat artificial; they are socially constructed, quasi-historical, and overlapping conventions. Nevertheless, they permit a "performance" of developing ideas. They also facilitate an increasing sensitivity to and sophistication about the pitfalls and promises of ethnography and qualitative research.) We will present a conceptual framework for reading the qualitative research act as a multicultural, gendered process, and then provide a brief introduction to the chapters that follow.

Returning to the observations of Vidich and Lyman as well as those of hooks, we will conclude with a brief discussion of qualitative research and critical race theory (see also in Volume 1, Ladson-Billings, Chapter 9; and in Volume 3, Denzin, Chapter 13). As we indicate in our preface, we use the metaphor of the bridge to structure what follows. We see this volume as a bridge connecting historical moments, research methods, paradigms, and communities of interpretive scholars.

◆ Definitional Issues

Qualitative research is a field of inquiry in its own right. It crosscuts disciplines, fields, and subject matters.[1] A complex, interconnected family of terms, concepts, and assumptions surround the term *qualitative research.* These include the traditions associated with foundationalism, positivism, postfoundationalism, postpositivism, poststructuralism, and the many qualitative research perspectives, and/or methods, connected to cultural and interpretive studies (the chapters in Part II of Volume 1 take up these paradigms).[2] There are separate and detailed literatures on the many methods and approaches that fall under the category of qualitative research, such as case study, politics and ethics, participatory inquiry, interviewing, participant observation, visual methods, and interpretive analysis.

In North America, qualitative research operates in a complex historical field that crosscuts seven historical moments (we discuss these moments in detail below). These seven moments overlap and simultaneously operate in the present.[3] We define them as the traditional (1900–1950); the modernist or golden age (1950–1970); blurred genres (1970–1986); the crisis of representation (1986–1990); the postmodern, a period of experimental and new ethnographies (1990–1995); postexperimental inquiry (1995–2000); and the future, which is now (2000–). The future, the seventh moment, is concerned with moral discourse, with the development of sacred textualities. The seventh moment asks that the social sciences and the humanities become sites for critical conversations about democracy, race, gender, class, nation-states, globalization, freedom, and community.

The postmodern moment was defined in part by a concern for literary and rhetorical tropes and the narrative turn, a concern for storytelling, for composing ethnographies in new ways (Ellis & Bochner, 1996). Laurel Richardson (1997) observes that this moment was shaped by a new sensibility, by doubt, by a refusal to privilege any method or theory (p. 173).

But now, at the beginning of the 21st century, the narrative turn has been taken. Many have learned how to write differently, including how to locate themselves in their texts. We now struggle to connect qualitative research to the hopes, needs, goals, and promises of a free democratic society.

Successive waves of epistemological theorizing move across these seven moments. The traditional period is associated with the positivist, foundational paradigm. The modernist or golden age and blurred genres moments are connected to the appearance of postpositivist arguments. At the same time, a variety of new interpretive, qualitative perspectives were taken up, including hermeneutics, structuralism, semiotics, phenomenology, cultural studies, and feminism.[4] In the blurred genres phase, the humanities became central resources for critical, interpretive theory, and for the qualitative research project broadly conceived. The researcher became a *bricoleur* (see below), learning how to borrow from many different disciplines.

The blurred genres phase produced the next stage, the crisis of representation. Here researchers struggled with how to locate themselves and their subjects in reflexive texts. A kind of methodological diaspora took place, a two-way exodus. Humanists migrated to the social sciences, searching for new social theory, new ways to study popular culture and its local, ethnographic contexts. Social scientists turned to the humanities, hoping to learn how to do complex structural and poststructural readings of social texts. From the humanities, social scientists also learned how to produce texts that refused to be read in simplistic, linear, incontrovertible terms. The line between text and context blurred. In the postmodern experimental moment researchers continued to move away from foundational and quasi-foundational criteria (see in Volume 3, Smith & Deemer, Chapter 12, and Richardson, Chapter 14; and in Volume 1, Gergen & Gergen, Chapter 13). Alternative evaluative criteria were sought, criteria that might prove evocative, moral, critical, and rooted in local understandings.

Any definition of qualitative research must work within this complex historical field. *Qualitative research* means different things in each of these moments. Nonetheless, an initial, generic definition can be offered: Qualitative research is a situated activity that locates the observer in the world. It consists of a set of interpretive, material practices that make the world visible. These practices transform the world. They turn the world into a series of representations, including field notes, interviews, conversations,

4

photographs, recordings, and memos to the self. At this level, qualitative research involves an interpretive, naturalistic approach to the world. This means that qualitative researchers study things in their natural settings, attempting to make sense of, or to interpret, phenomena in terms of the meanings people bring to them.[5]

Qualitative research involves the studied use and collection of a variety of empirical materials—case study; personal experience; introspection; life story; interview; artifacts; cultural texts and productions; observational, historical, interactional, and visual texts—that describe routine and problematic moments and meanings in individuals' lives. Accordingly, qualitative researchers deploy a wide range of interconnected interpretive practices, hoping always to get a better understanding of the subject matter at hand. It is understood, however, that each practice makes the world visible in a different way. Hence there is frequently a commitment to using more than one interpretive practice in any study.

The Qualitative Researcher as Bricoleur and Quilt Maker

The qualitative researcher may take on multiple and gendered images: scientist, naturalist, field-worker, journalist, social critic, artist, performer, jazz musician, filmmaker, quilt maker, essayist. The many methodological practices of qualitative research may be viewed as soft science, journalism, ethnography, bricolage, quilt making, or montage. The researcher, in turn, may be seen as a *bricoleur*, as a maker of quilts, or, as in filmmaking, a person who assembles images into montages. (On montage, see the discussion below as well as Cook, 1981, pp. 171-177; Monaco, 1981, pp. 322-328. On quilting, see hooks, 1990, pp. 115-122; Wolcott, 1995, pp. 31-33.)

Nelson, Treichler, and Grossberg (1992), Lévi-Strauss (1966), and Weinstein and Weinstein (1991) clarify the meanings of *bricolage* and *bricoleur*.[6] A *bricoleur* is a "Jack of all trades or a kind of professional do-it-yourself person" (Lévi-Strauss, 1966, p. 17). There are many kinds of *bricoleurs*—interpretive, narrative, theoretical, political (see below). The interpretive bricoleur produces a *bricolage*—that is, a pieced-together set of representations that are fitted to the specifics of a complex situation. "The solution [bricolage] which is the result of the *bricoleur's* method is an [emergent] construction" (Weinstein & Weinstein, 1991, p. 161) that changes and takes new forms as different tools, methods, and techniques of representation and interpretation are added to the puzzle. Nelson et al.

STRATEGIES OF QUALITATIVE INQUIRY

(1992) describe the methodology of cultural studies "as a bricolage. Its choice of practice, that is, is pragmatic, strategic and self-reflexive" (p. 2). This understanding can be applied, with qualifications, to qualitative research.

The qualitative researcher as *bricoleur* or maker of quilts uses the aesthetic and material tools of his or her craft, deploying whatever strategies, methods, or empirical materials are at hand (Becker, 1998, p. 2). If new tools or techniques have to be invented, or pieced together, then the researcher will do this. The choices as to which interpretive practices to employ are not necessarily set in advance. The "choice of research practices depends upon the questions that are asked, and the questions depend on their context" (Nelson et al., 1992, p. 2), what is available in the context, and what the researcher can do in that setting.

These interpretive practices involve aesthetic issues, an aesthetics of representation that goes beyond the pragmatic, or the practical. Here the concept of *montage* is useful (see Cook, 1981, p. 323; Monaco, 1981, pp. 171-172). Montage is a method of editing cinematic images. In the history of cinematography, montage is associated with the work of Sergei Eisenstein, especially his film *The Battleship Potemkin* (1925). In montage, several different images are superimposed onto one another to create a picture. In a sense, montage is like pentimento, in which something that has been painted out of a picture (an image the painter "repented," or denied) becomes visible again, creating something new. What is new is what had been obscured by a previous image.

Montage and pentimento, like jazz, which is improvisation, create the sense that images, sounds, and understandings are blending together, overlapping, forming a composite, a new creation. The images seem to shape and define one another, and an emotional, gestalt effect is produced. Often these images are combined in a swiftly run filmic sequence that produces a dizzily revolving collection of several images around a central or focused picture or sequence; such effects are often used to signify the passage of time.

Perhaps the most famous instance of montage is the Odessa Steps sequence in *The Battleship Potemkin*.[7] In the climax of the film, the citizens of Odessa are being massacred by czarist troops on the stone steps leading down to the harbor. Eisenstein cuts to a young mother as she pushes her baby in a carriage across the landing in front of the firing troops. Citizens rush past her, jolting the carriage, which she is afraid to push down to the next flight of stairs. The troops are above her firing at

6

the citizens. She is trapped between the troops and the steps. She screams. A line of rifles pointing to the sky erupt in smoke. The mother's head sways back. The wheels of the carriage teeter on the edge of the steps. The mother's hand clutches the silver buckle of her belt. Below her people are being beaten by soldiers. Blood drips over the mother's white gloves. The baby's hand reaches out of the carriage. The mother sways back and forth. The troops advance. The mother falls back against the carriage. A woman watches in horror as the rear wheels of the carriage roll off the edge of the landing. With accelerating speed the carriage bounces down the steps, past the dead citizens. The baby is jostled from side to side inside the carriage. The soldiers fire their rifles into a group of wounded citizens. A student screams as the carriage leaps across the steps, tilts, and overturns (Cook, 1981, p. 167).[8]

Montage uses brief images to create a clearly defined sense of urgency and complexity. Montage invites viewers to construct interpretations that build on one another as the scene unfolds. These interpretations are built on associations based on the contrasting images that blend into one another. The underlying assumption of montage is that viewers perceive and interpret the shots in a "montage sequence not *sequentially*, or one at a time, but rather *simultaneously*" (Cook, 1981, p. 172). The viewer puts the sequences together into a meaningful emotional whole, as if in a glance, all at once.

The qualitative researcher who uses montage is like a quilt maker or a jazz improviser. The quilter stitches, edits, and puts slices of reality together. This process creates and brings psychological and emotional unity to an interpretive experience. There are many examples of montage in current qualitative research (see Diversi, 1998; Jones, 1999; Lather & Smithies, 1997; Ronai, 1998). Using multiple voices, different textual formats, and various typefaces, Lather and Smithies (1997) weave a complex text about women who are HIV positive and women with AIDS. Jones (1999) creates a performance text using lyrics from the blues songs sung by Billie Holiday.

In texts based on the metaphors of montage, quilt making, and jazz improvisation, many different things are going on at the same time— different voices, different perspectives, points of views, angles of vision. Like performance texts, works that use montage simultaneously create and enact moral meaning. They move from the personal to the political, the local to the historical and the cultural. These are dialogical texts. They presume an active audience. They create spaces for give-and-take between reader and writer. They do more than turn the other into the object of the social science gaze (see McCall, Chapter 4, this volume.

Qualitative research is inherently multimethod in focus (Flick, 1998, p. 229). However, the use of multiple methods, or triangulation, reflects an attempt to secure an in-depth understanding of the phenomenon in question. Objective reality can never be captured. We can know a thing only through its representations. Triangulation is not a tool or a strategy of validation, but an alternative to validation (Flick, 1998, p. 230). The combination of multiple methodological practices, empirical materials, perspectives, and observers in a single study is best understood, then, as a strategy that adds rigor, breadth, complexity, richness, and depth to any inquiry (see Flick, 1998, p. 231).

In Chapter 14 of Volume 3, Richardson disputes the concept of triangulation, asserting that the central image for qualitative inquiry is the crystal, not the triangle. Mixed-genre texts in the postexperimental moment have more than three sides. Like crystals, Eisenstein's montage, the jazz solo, or the pieces that make up a quilt, the mixed-genre text, as Richardson notes, "combines symmetry and substance with an infinite variety of shapes, substances, transmutations. . . . Crystals grow, change, alter. . . . Crystals are prisms that reflect externalities *and* refract within themselves, creating different colors, patterns, and arrays, casting off in different directions."

In the crystallization process, the writer tells the same tale from different points of view. For example, in *A Thrice-Told Tale* (1992), Margery Wolf uses fiction, field notes, and a scientific article to give an accounting of the same set of experiences in a native village. Similarly, in her play *Fires in the Mirror* (1993), Anna Deavere Smith presents a series of performance pieces based on interviews with people involved in a racial conflict in Crown Heights, Brooklyn, on August, 19, 1991 (see Denzin, Chapter 13, Volume 3). The play has multiple speaking parts, including conversations with gang members, police officers, and anonymous young girls and boys. There is no "correct" telling of this event. Each telling, like light hitting a crystal, reflects a different perspective on this incident.

Viewed as a crystalline form, as a montage, or as a creative performance around a central theme, triangulation as a form of, or alternative to, validity thus can be extended. Triangulation is the display of multiple, refracted realities simultaneously. Each of the metaphors "works" to create simultaneity rather than the sequential or linear. Readers and audiences are then invited to explore competing visions of the context, to become immersed in and merge with new realities to comprehend.

The methodological *bricoleur* is adept at performing a large number of diverse tasks, ranging from interviewing to intensive self-reflection and introspection. The theoretical *bricoleur* reads widely and is knowledgeable about the many interpretive paradigms (feminism, Marxism, cultural studies, constructivism, queer theory) that can be brought to any particular problem. He or she may not, however, feel that paradigms can be mingled or synthesized. That is, one cannot easily move between paradigms as overarching philosophical systems denoting particular ontologies, epistemologies, and methodologies. They represent belief systems that attach users to particular worldviews. Perspectives, in contrast, are less well developed systems, and one can more easily move between them. The researcher-as-*bricoleur*-theorist works between and within competing and overlapping perspectives and paradigms.

The interpretive *bricoleur* understands that research is an interactive process shaped by his or her personal history, biography, gender, social class, race, and ethnicity, and by those of the people in the setting. The political *bricoleur* knows that science is power, for all research findings have political implications. There is no value-free science. A civic social science based on a politics of hope is sought (Lincoln, 1999). The gendered, narrative *bricoleur* also knows that researchers all tell stories about the worlds they have studied. Thus the narratives, or stories, scientists tell are accounts couched and framed within specific storytelling traditions, often defined as paradigms (e.g., positivism, postpositivism, constructivism).

The product of the interpretive *bricoleur*'s labor is a complex, quilt-like bricolage, a reflexive collage or montage—a set of fluid, interconnected images and representations. This interpretive structure is like a quilt, a performance text, a sequence of representations connecting the parts to the whole.

Qualitative Research as a Site of Multiple Interpretive Practices

Qualitative research, as a set of interpretive activities, privileges no single methodological practice over another. As a site of discussion, or discourse, qualitative research is difficult to define clearly. It has no theory or paradigm that is distinctly its own. As the contributions to Part II of Volume 1 reveal, multiple theoretical paradigms claim use of qualitative research methods and strategies, from constructivist to cultural studies, feminism, Marxism, and ethnic models of study. Qualitative research is used in many separate disciplines, as we will discuss below. It does not belong to a single discipline.

Nor does qualitative research have a distinct set of methods or practices that are entirely its own. Qualitative researchers use semiotics, narrative, content, discourse, archival and phonemic analysis, even statistics, tables, graphs, and numbers. They also draw upon and utilize the approaches, methods, and techniques of ethnomethodology, phenomenology, hermeneutics, feminism, rhizomatics, deconstructionism, ethnography, interviews, psychoanalysis, cultural studies, survey research, and participant observation, among others.[9] All of these research practices "can provide important insights and knowledge" (Nelson et al., 1992, p. 2). No specific method or practice can be privileged over any other.

Many of these methods, or research practices, are used in other contexts in the human disciplines. Each bears the traces of its own disciplinary history. Thus there is an extensive history of the uses and meanings of ethnography and ethnology in education (see Fine, Weis, Weseen, & Wong, Volume 1, Chapter 4); of participant observation and ethnography in anthropology (see Tedlock, this volume, Chapter 6; Ryan & Bernard, Volume 3, Chapter 7; Brady, Volume 3, Chapter 15), sociology (see Gubrium & Holstein, this volume, Chapter 7; Harper, Volume 3, Chapter 5; Fontana & Frey, Volume 3, Chapter 2; Silverman, Volume 3, Chapter 9), communication (see Ellis & Bochner, Volume 3, Chapter 6), and cultural studies (see Frow & Morris, Volume 1, Chapter 11); of textual, hermeneutic, feminist, psychoanalytic, semiotic, and narrative analysis in cinema and literary studies (see Olesen, Volume 1, Chapter 8; Brady, Volume 3, Chapter 15); of archival, material culture, historical, and document analysis in history, biography, and archaeology (see Hodder, Volume 3, Chapter 4; Tierney, this volume, Chapter 9); and of discourse and conversational analysis in medicine, communications, and education (see Miller & Crabtree, this volume, Chapter 12; Silverman, Volume 3, Chapter 9).

The many histories that surround each method or research strategy reveal how multiple uses and meanings are brought to each practice. Textual analyses in literary studies, for example, often treat texts as self-contained systems. On the other hand, a researcher taking a cultural studies or feminist perspective will read a text in terms of its location within a historical moment marked by a particular gender, race, or class ideology. A cultural studies use of ethnography would bring a set of understandings from feminism, postmodernism, and poststructuralism to the project. These understandings would not be shared by mainstream post-positivist sociologists. Similarly, postpositivist and poststructuralist historians bring different understandings and uses to the methods and findings of historical research (see Tierney, this volume, Chapter 9). These tensions and contradictions are all evident in the chapters in this volume.

These separate and multiple uses and meanings of the methods of qualitative research make it difficult for researchers to agree on any essential definition of the field, for it is never just one thing.[10] Still, we must establish a definition for our purposes here. We borrow from, and paraphrase, Nelson et al.'s (1992, p. 4) attempt to define cultural studies:

> Qualitative research is an interdisciplinary, transdisciplinary, and sometimes counterdisciplinary field. It crosscuts the humanities and the social and physical sciences. Qualitative research is many things at the same time. It is multiparadigmatic in focus. Its practitioners are sensitive to the value of the multimethod approach. They are committed to the naturalistic perspective and to the interpretive understanding of human experience. At the same time, the field is inherently political and shaped by multiple ethical and political positions.
>
> Qualitative research embraces two tensions at the same time. On the one hand, it is drawn to a broad, interpretive, postexperimental, postmodern, feminist, and critical sensibility. On the other hand, it is drawn to more narrowly defined positivist, postpositivist, humanistic, and naturalistic conceptions of human experience and its analysis. Further, these tensions can be combined in the same project, bringing both postmodern and naturalistic or both critical and humanistic perspectives to bear.

This rather complex statement means that qualitative research, as a set of practices, embraces within its own multiple disciplinary histories constant tensions and contradictions over the project itself, including its methods and the forms its findings and interpretations take. The field sprawls between and crosscuts all of the human disciplines, even including, in some cases, the physical sciences. Its practitioners are variously committed to modern, postmodern, and postexperimental sensibilities and the approaches to social research that these sensibilities imply.

Resistances to Qualitative Studies

The academic and disciplinary resistances to qualitative research illustrate the politics embedded in this field of discourse. The challenges to qualitative research are many. Qualitative researchers are called journalists, or soft scientists. Their work is termed unscientific, or only exploratory, or subjective. It is called criticism and not theory, or it is interpreted politically, as a disguised version of Marxism or secular humanism (see Huber, 1995; see also Denzin, 1997, pp. 258-261).

These resistances reflect an uneasy awareness that the traditions of qualitative research commit the researcher to a critique of the positivist or postpositivist project. But the positivist resistance to qualitative research goes beyond the "ever-present desire to maintain a distinction between hard science and soft scholarship" (Carey, 1989, p. 99; see also in Volume 1, Schwandt, Chapter 7; in Volume 3, Smith & Deemer, Chapter 12). The experimental (positivist) sciences (physics, chemistry, economics, and psychology, for example) are often seen as the crowning achievements of Western civilization, and in their practices it is assumed that "truth" can transcend opinion and personal bias (Carey, 1989, p. 99; Schwandt, 1997b, p. 309). Qualitative research is seen as an assault on this tradition, whose adherents often retreat into a "value-free objectivist science" (Carey, 1989, p. 104) model to defend their position. They seldom attempt to make explicit, or to critique, the "moral and political commitments in their own contingent work" (Carey, 1989, p. 104; see also Lincoln & Guba, Chapter 6, Volume 1).

Positivists further allege that the so-called new experimental qualitative researchers write fiction, not science, and that these researchers have no way of verifying their truth statements. Ethnographic poetry and fiction signal the death of empirical science, and there is little to be gained by attempting to engage in moral criticism. These critics presume a stable, unchanging reality that can be studied using the empirical methods of objective social science (see Huber, 1995). The province of qualitative research, accordingly, is the world of lived experience, for this is where individual belief and action intersect with culture. Under this model there is no preoccupation with discourse and method as material interpretive practices that constitute representation and description. Thus is the textual, narrative turn rejected by the positivists.

The opposition to positive science by the postpositivists (see below) and the poststructuralists is seen, then, as an attack on reason and truth. At the same time, the positivist science attack on qualitative research is regarded as an attempt to legislate one version of truth over another.

This complex political terrain defines the many traditions and strands of qualitative research: the British tradition and its presence in other national contexts; the American pragmatic, naturalistic, and interpretive traditions in sociology, anthropology, communication, and education; the German and French phenomenological, hermeneutic, semiotic, Marxist, structural, and poststructural perspectives; feminist studies, African American studies, Latino studies, queer studies, studies of indigenous and aboriginal cultures. The politics of qualitative research create a tension that informs each of the above traditions. This tension itself is constantly being reexamined and interrogated, as qualitative research confronts a changing historical world, new intellectual positions, and its own institutional and academic conditions.

To summarize: Qualitative research is many things to many people. Its essence is twofold: a commitment to some version of the naturalistic, interpretive approach to its subject matter and an ongoing critique of the politics and methods of postpositivism. We turn now to a brief discussion of the major differences between qualitative and quantitative approaches to research. We then discuss ongoing differences and tensions within qualitative inquiry.

Qualitative Versus Quantitative Research

The word *qualitative* implies an emphasis on the qualities of entities and on processes and meanings that are not experimentally examined or measured (if measured at all) in terms of quantity, amount, intensity, or frequency. Qualitative researchers stress the socially constructed nature of reality, the intimate relationship between the researcher and what is studied, and the situational constraints that shape inquiry. Such researchers emphasize the value-laden nature of inquiry. They seek answers to questions that stress how social experience is created and given meaning. In contrast, quantitative studies emphasize the measurement and analysis of causal relationships between variables, not processes. Proponents of such studies claim that their work is done from within a value-free framework.

Research Styles:
Doing the Same Things Differently?

Of course, both qualitative and quantitative researchers "think they know something about society worth telling to others, and they use a variety of forms, media and means to communicate their ideas and findings"

(Becker, 1986, p. 122). Qualitative research differs from quantitative research in five significant ways (Becker, 1996). These points of difference turn on different ways of addressing the same set of issues. They return always to the politics of research, and to who has the power to legislate correct solutions to these problems.

Uses of positivism and postpositivism. First, both perspectives are shaped by the positivist and postpositivist traditions in the physical and social sciences (see the discussion below). These two positivist science traditions hold to naïve and critical realist positions concerning reality and its perception. In the positivist version it is contended that there is a reality out there to be studied, captured, and understood, whereas the postpositivists argue that reality can never be fully apprehended, only approximated (Guba, 1990, p. 22). Postpositivism relies on multiple methods as a way of capturing as much of reality as possible. At the same time, emphasis is placed on the discovery and verification of theories. Traditional evaluation criteria, such as internal and external validity, are stressed, as is the use of qualitative procedures that lend themselves to structured (sometimes statistical) analysis. Computer-assisted methods of analysis that permit frequency counts, tabulations, and low-level statistical analyses may also be employed.

The positivist and postpositivist traditions linger like long shadows over the qualitative research project. Historically, qualitative research was defined within the positivist paradigm, where qualitative researchers attempted to do good positivist research with less rigorous methods and procedures. Some mid-20th-century qualitative researchers (e.g., Becker, Geer, Hughes, & Strauss, 1961) reported participant observation findings in terms of quasi-statistics. As recently as 1998, Strauss and Corbin, two leaders of the grounded theory approach to qualitative research, attempted to modify the usual canons of good (positivist) science to fit their own postpositivist conception of rigorous research (but see Charmaz, Chapter 8, this volume; see also Glaser, 1992). Some applied researchers, while claiming to be atheoretical, often fit within the positivist or postpositivist framework by default.

Flick (1998, pp. 2-3) usefully summarizes the differences between these two approaches to inquiry. He observes that the quantitative approach has been used for purposes of isolating "causes and effects . . . operationalizing theoretical relations . . . [and] measuring and . . . quantifying phenomena . . . allowing the generalization of findings" (p. 3). But today doubt is cast on such projects, because "Rapid social change and the resulting diversification of life worlds are increasingly confronting social researchers with new social contexts and perspectives. . . . traditional deductive methodologies . . . are failing. . . . thus research is increasingly forced to make use of inductive strategies instead of starting from theories and testing them. . . . knowledge and practice are studied as local knowledge and practice" (p. 2).

Spindler and Spindler (1992) summarize their qualitative approach to quantitative materials: "Instrumentation and quantification are simply procedures employed to extend and reinforce certain kinds of data, interpretations and test hypotheses across samples. Both must be kept in their place. One must avoid their premature or overly extensive use as a security mechanism" (p. 69).

Although many qualitative researchers in the postpositivist tradition will use statistical measures, methods, and documents as a way of locating groups of subjects within larger populations, they will seldom report their findings in terms of the kinds of complex statistical measures or methods to which quantitative researchers are drawn (i.e., path, regression, or log-linear analyses).

Acceptance of postmodern sensibilities. The use of quantitative, positivist methods and assumptions has been rejected by a new generation of qualitative researchers who are attached to poststructural and/or postmodern sensibilities (see below; see also in Volume 1, Vidich & Lyman, Chapter 2; and in Volume 3, Richardson, Chapter 14). These researchers argue that positivist methods are but one way of telling stories about society or the social world. These methods may be no better or no worse than any other methods; they just tell different kinds of stories.

This tolerant view is not shared by everyone (Huber, 1995). Many members of the critical theory, constructivist, poststructural, and postmodern schools of thought reject positivist and postpositivist criteria when evaluating their own work. They see these criteria as irrelevant to their work and contend that such criteria reproduce only a certain kind of science, a science that silences too many voices. These researchers seek alternative methods for evaluating their work, including verisimilitude, emotionality, personal responsibility, an ethic of caring, political praxis, multivoiced texts, and dialogues with subjects. In response, positivists and postpositivists argue that what they do is good science, free of individual bias and subjectivity. As noted above, they see postmodernism and poststructuralism as attacks on reason and truth.

Capturing the individual's point of view. Both qualitative and quantitative researchers are concerned with the individual's point of view. However, qualitative investigators think they can get closer to the actor's perspective through detailed interviewing and observation. They argue that quantitative researchers are seldom able to capture their subjects' perspectives because they have to rely on more remote, inferential empirical methods and materials. The empirical materials produced by interpretive methods are regarded by many quantitative researchers as unreliable, impressionistic, and not objective.

Examining the constraints of everyday life. Qualitative researchers are more likely to confront and come up against the constraints of the everyday social world. They see this world in action and embed their findings in it. Quantitative researchers abstract from this world and seldom study it directly. They seek a nomothetic or etic science based on probabilities derived from the study of large numbers of randomly selected cases. These kinds of statements stand above and outside the constraints of everyday life. Qualitative researchers, on the other hand, are committed to an emic, idiographic, case-based position, which directs their attention to the specifics of particular cases.

Securing rich descriptions. Qualitative researchers believe that rich descriptions of the social world are valuable, whereas quantitative researchers, with their etic, nomothetic commitments, are less concerned with such detail. Quantitative researchers are deliberately unconcerned with rich descriptions because such detail interrupts the process of developing generalizations.

The five points of difference described above (uses of positivism and postpositivism, postmodernism, capturing the individual's point of view, examining the constraints of everyday life, securing thick descriptions) reflect commitments to different styles of research, different epistemologies, and different forms of representation. Each work tradition is governed by its own set of genres; each has its own classics, its own preferred forms of representation, interpretation, trustworthiness, and textual evaluation (see Becker, 1986, pp. 134-135). Qualitative researchers use ethnographic prose, historical narratives, first-person accounts, still photographs, life histories, fictionalized "facts," and biographical and autobiographical materials, among others. Quantitative researchers use mathematical models, statistical tables, and graphs, and usually write about their research in impersonal, third-person prose.

Tensions Within Qualitative Research

It is erroneous to presume that all qualitative researchers share the same assumptions about the five points of difference described above. As the discussion below will reveal, positivist, postpositivist, and poststructural differences define and shape the discourses of qualitative research. Realists and postpositivists within the interpretive qualitative research tradition criticize poststructuralists for taking the textual, narrative turn. These critics contend that such work is navel gazing. It produces conditions "for a dialogue of the deaf between itself and the community" (Silverman, 1997, p. 240). Those who attempt to capture the point of view of the interacting subject in the world are accused of naive humanism, of reproducing "a Romantic impulse which elevates the experiential to the level of the authentic" (Silverman, 1997, p. 248).

Still others argue that lived experience is ignored by those who take the textual, performance turn. Snow and Morrill (1995) argue that "this performance turn, like the preoccupation with discourse and storytelling, will take us further from the field of social action and the real dramas of everyday life and thus signal the death knell of ethnography as an empirically grounded enterprise" (p. 361). Of course, we disagree.

With these differences within and between the two traditions now in hand, we must now briefly discuss the history of qualitative research. We break this history into seven historical moments, mindful that any history is always somewhat arbitrary and always at least partially a social construction.

◆ The History of Qualitative Research

The history of qualitative research reveals, as Vidich and Lyman remind us in Chapter 2 of Volume 1, that the modern social science disciplines have taken as their mission "the analysis and understanding of the patterned conduct and social processes of society." The notion that this task could be carried out presupposed that social scientists had the ability to observe this world objectively. Qualitative methods were a major tool of such observations.[11]

Throughout the history of qualitative research, investigators have always defined their work in terms of hopes and values, "religious faiths, occupational and professional ideologies" (Vidich & Lyman, Chapter 2, Volume 1). Qualitative research (like all research) has always been judged on the "standard of whether the work communicates or 'says' something to us" (Vidich & Lyman, Chapter 2, Volume 1), based on how we conceptualize our reality and our images of the world. *Epistemology* is the word that has historically defined these standards of evaluation. In the contemporary period, as we have argued above, many received discourses on epistemology are now being reevaluated.

Vidich and Lyman's history covers the following (somewhat) overlapping stages: early ethnography (to the 17th century); colonial ethnography (17th-, 18th-, and 19th-century explorers); the ethnography of the American Indian as "other" (late-19th- and early-20th-century anthropology); the ethnography of the "civic other," or community studies, and ethnographies of American immigrants (early 20th century through the 1960s); studies of ethnicity and assimilation (midcentury through the 1980s); and the present, which we call the *seventh moment*.

In each of these eras, researchers were and have been influenced by their political hopes and ideologies, discovering findings in their research that confirmed prior theories or beliefs. Early ethnographers confirmed the racial and cultural diversity of peoples throughout the globe and attempted to fit this diversity into a theory about the origins of history, the races, and civilizations. Colonial ethnographers, before the professionalization of ethnography in the 20th century, fostered a colonial pluralism that left natives on their own as long as their leaders could be co-opted by the colonial administration.

European ethnographers studied Africans, Asians, and other Third World peoples of color. Early American ethnographers studied the American Indian from the perspective of the conqueror, who saw the life world of the primitive as a window to the prehistoric past. The Calvinist mission to save the Indian was soon transferred to the mission of saving the "hordes" of immigrants who entered the United States with the beginnings of industrialization. Qualitative community studies of the ethnic other proliferated from the early 1900s to the 1960s and included the work of E. Franklin Frazier, Robert Park, and Robert Redfield and their students, as well as William Foote Whyte, the Lynds, August Hollingshead, Herbert Gans, Stanford Lyman, Arthur Vidich, and Joseph Bensman. The post-1960 ethnicity studies challenged the "melting pot" hypothesis of Park and his followers and corresponded to the emergence of ethnic studies programs that saw Native Americans, Latinos, Asian Americans, and African Americans attempting to take control over the study of their own peoples.

The postmodern and poststructural challenge emerged in the mid-1980s. It questioned the assumptions that had organized this earlier history in each of its colonializing moments. Qualitative research that crosses the "postmodern divide" requires one, Vidich and Lyman argue in Volume 1, Chapter 2, to "abandon all established and preconceived values, theories, perspectives . . . and prejudices as resources for ethnographic study." In this new era, the qualitative researcher does more than observe history; he or she plays a part in it. New tales from the field will now be written, and they will reflect the researcher's direct and personal engagement with this historical period.

Vidich and Lyman's analysis covers the full sweep of ethnographic history. Ours is confined to the 20th century and complements many of their divisions. We begin with the early foundational work of the British and French as well the Chicago, Columbia, Harvard, Berkeley, and British schools of sociology and anthropology. This early foundational period established the norms of classical qualitative and ethnographic research (see Gupta & Ferguson, 1997; Rosaldo, 1989; Stocking, 1989).

◆ The Seven Moments of Qualitative Research

As suggested above, our history of qualitative research in North America in this century divides into seven phases, each of which we describe in turn below.

The Traditional Period

We call the first moment the traditional period (this covers Vidich and Lyman's second and third phases). It begins in the early 1900s and continues until World War II. In this period, qualitative researchers wrote "objective," colonializing accounts of field experiences that were reflective of the positivist scientist paradigm. They were concerned with offering valid, reliable, and objective interpretations in their writings. The "other" who was studied was alien, foreign, and strange.

Here is Malinowski (1967) discussing his field experiences in New Guinea and the Trobriand Islands in the years 1914–1915 and 1917–1918. He is bartering his way into field data:

> Nothing whatever draws me to ethnographic studies. . . . On the whole the village struck me rather unfavorably. There is a certain disorganization . . . the rowdiness and persistence of the people who laugh and stare and lie discouraged me somewhat. . . . Went to the village hoping to photograph a few stages of the bara dance. I handed out half-sticks of tobacco, then watched a few dances; then took pictures—but results were poor. . . . they would not pose long enough for time exposures. At moments I was furious at them, particularly because after I gave them their portions of tobacco they all went away. (quoted in Geertz, 1988, pp. 73-74)

In another work, this lonely, frustrated, isolated field-worker describes his methods in the following words:

> In the field one has to face a chaos of facts. . . . in this crude form they are not scientific facts at all; they are absolutely elusive, and can only be fixed by interpretation. . . . *Only laws and generalizations are scientific facts,* and field work consists only and exclusively in the interpretation of the chaotic social reality, in subordinating it to general rules. (Malinowski, 1916/1948, p. 328; quoted in Geertz, 1988, p. 81)

Malinowski's remarks are provocative. On the one hand they disparage fieldwork, but on the other they speak of it within the glorified language of science, with laws and generalizations fashioned out of this selfsame experience.

The field-worker during this period was lionized, made into a larger-than-life figure who went into and then returned from the field with stories about strange people. Rosaldo (1989, p. 30) describes this as the period of the Lone Ethnographer, the story of the man-scientist who went off in search of his native in a distant land. There this figure "encountered the object of his quest . . . [and] underwent his rite of passage by enduring the ultimate ordeal of 'fieldwork' " (p. 30). Returning home with his data, the Lone Ethnographer wrote up an objective account of the culture studied. These accounts were structured by the norms of classical ethnography. This sacred bundle of terms (Rosaldo, 1989, p. 31) organized ethnographic texts in terms of four beliefs and commitments: a commitment to objectivism, a complicity with imperialism, a belief in monumentalism (the ethnography would create a museumlike picture of the culture studied), and a belief in timelessness (what was studied would never change). The other was an "object" to be archived. This model of the researcher, who could also write complex, dense theories about what was studied, holds to the present day.

The myth of the Lone Ethnographer depicts the birth of classic ethnography. The texts of Malinowski, Radcliffe-Brown, Margaret Mead, and Gregory Bateson are still carefully studied for what they can tell the novice about conducting fieldwork, taking field notes, and writing theory. Today this image has been shattered. The works of the classic ethnographers are seen by many as relics from the colonial past (Rosaldo, 1989, p. 44). Although many feel nostalgia for this past, others celebrate its passing. Rosaldo (1989) quotes Cora Du Bois, a retired Harvard anthropology professor, who lamented this passing at a conference in 1980, reflecting on the crisis in anthropology: "[I feel a distance] from the complexity and disarray of what I once found a justifiable and challenging discipline. . . . It has been like moving from a distinguished art museum into a garage sale" (p. 44).

Du Bois regards the classic ethnographies as pieces of timeless artwork contained in a museum. She feels uncomfortable in the chaos of the garage sale. In contrast, Rosaldo (1989) is drawn to this metaphor: "[The garage sale] provides a precise image of the postcolonial situation where cultural artifacts flow between unlikely places, and nothing is sacred, permanent, or sealed off. The image of anthropology as a garage sale depicts our present global situation" (p. 44). Indeed, many valuable treasures may be found if one is willing to look long and hard, in unexpected places. Old standards no longer hold. Ethnographies do not produce timeless truths. The commitment to objectivism is now in doubt. The complicity with imperialism is openly challenged today, and the belief in monumentalism is a thing of the past.

The legacies of this first period begin at the end of the 19th century, when the novel and the social sciences had become distinguished as separate systems of discourse (Clough, 1992, pp. 21-22; see also Clough, 1998). However, the Chicago school, with its emphasis on the life story and the "slice-of-life" approach to ethnographic materials, sought to develop an interpretive methodology that maintained the centrality of the narrated life history approach. This led to the production of texts that gave the researcher-as-author the power to represent the subject's story. Written under the mantle of straightforward, sentiment-free social realism, these texts used the language of ordinary people. They articulated a social science version of literary naturalism, which often produced the sympathetic illusion that a solution to a social problem had been found. Like the Depression-era juvenile delinquent and other "social problems" films (Roffman & Purdy, 1981), these accounts romanticized the subject. They turned the deviant into a sociological version of a screen hero. These sociological stories, like their film counterparts, usually had happy endings, as they followed individuals through the three stages of the classic morality tale: being in a state of grace, being seduced by evil and falling, and finally achieving redemption through suffering.

Modernist Phase

The modernist phase, or second moment, builds on the canonical works from the traditional period. Social realism, naturalism, and slice-of-life ethnographies are still valued. This phase extended through the post-war years to the 1970s and is still present in the work of many (for reviews, see Wolcott, 1990, 1992, 1995; see also Tedlock, Chapter 6, this volume). In this period many texts sought to formalize qualitative methods (see, for example, Bogdan & Taylor, 1975; Cicourel, 1964; Filstead, 1970; Glaser & Strauss, 1967; Lofland, 1971, 1995; Lofland & Lofland, 1984, 1995; Taylor & Bogdan, 1998).[12] The modernist ethnographer and sociological participant observer attempted rigorous qualitative studies of important social processes, including deviance and social control in the classroom and society. This was a moment of creative ferment.

A new generation of graduate students across the human disciplines encountered new interpretive theories (ethnomethodology, phenomenology, critical theory, feminism). They were drawn to qualitative research practices that would let them give a voice to society's underclass. Postpositivism functioned as a powerful epistemological paradigm. Researchers attempted to fit Campbell and Stanley's (1963) model of internal and external validity to constructionist and interactionist conceptions of the research act. They returned to the texts of the Chicago school as sources of inspiration (see Denzin, 1970, 1978).

A canonical text from this moment remains *Boys in White* (Becker et al., 1961; see also Becker, 1998). Firmly entrenched in mid-20th-century methodological discourse, this work attempted to make qualitative research as rigorous as its quantitative counterpart. Causal narratives were central to this project. This multimethod work combined open-

22

ended and quasi-structured interviewing with participant observation and the careful analysis of such materials in standardized, statistical form. In a classic article, "Problems of Inference and Proof in Participant Observation," Howard S. Becker (1958/1970) describes the use of quasi-statistics:

> Participant observations have occasionally been gathered in standardized form capable of being transformed into legitimate statistical data. But the exigencies of the field usually prevent the collection of data in such a form to meet the assumptions of statistical tests, so that the observer deals in what have been called "quasi-statistics." His conclusions, while implicitly numerical, do not require precise quantification. (p. 31)

In the analysis of data, Becker notes, the qualitative researcher takes a cue from statistical colleagues. The researcher looks for probabilities or support for arguments concerning the likelihood that, or frequency with which, a conclusion in fact applies in a specific situation (see also Becker, 1998, pp. 166-170). Thus did work in the modernist period clothe itself in the language and rhetoric of positivist and postpositivist discourse.

This was the golden age of rigorous qualitative analysis, bracketed in sociology by *Boys in White* (Becker et al., 1961) at one end and *The Discovery of Grounded Theory* (Glaser & Strauss, 1967) at the other. In education, qualitative research in this period was defined by George and Louise Spindler, Jules Henry, Harry Wolcott, and John Singleton. This form of qualitative research is still present in the work of such persons as Strauss and Corbin (1998) and Ryan and Bernard (see Chapter 7, Volume 3).

The "golden age" reinforced the picture of qualitative researchers as cultural romantics. Imbued with Promethean human powers, they valorized villains and outsiders as heroes to mainstream society. They embodied a belief in the contingency of self and society, and held to emancipatory ideals for "which one lives and dies." They put in place a tragic and often ironic view of society and self, and joined a long line of leftist cultural romantics that included Emerson, Marx, James, Dewey, Gramsci, and Martin Luther King, Jr. (West, 1989, chap. 6).

As this moment came to an end, the Vietnam War was everywhere present in American society. In 1969, alongside these political currents, Herbert Blumer and Everett Hughes met with a group of young sociologists called the "Chicago Irregulars" at the American Sociological

Association meetings held in San Francisco and shared their memories of the "Chicago years." Lyn Lofland (1980) describes the 1969 meetings as a

> moment of creative ferment—scholarly and political. The San Francisco meetings witnessed not simply the Blumer-Hughes event but a "counter-revolution." . . . a group first came to . . . talk about the problems of being a sociologist and a female. . . . the discipline seemed literally to be bursting with new . . . ideas: labelling theory, ethnomethodology, conflict theory, phenomenology, dramaturgical analysis. (p. 253)

Thus did the modernist phase come to an end.

Blurred Genres

By the beginning of the third stage (1970–1986), which we call the moment of blurred genres, qualitative researchers had a full complement of paradigms, methods, and strategies to employ in their research. Theories ranged from symbolic interactionism to constructivism, naturalistic inquiry, positivism and postpositivism, phenomenology, ethnomethodology, critical theory, neo-Marxist theory, semiotics, structuralism, feminism, and various racial/ethnic paradigms. Applied qualitative research was gaining in stature, and the politics and ethics of qualitative research—implicated as they were in various applications of this work—were topics of considerable concern. Research strategies and formats for reporting research ranged from grounded theory to the case study, to methods of historical, biographical, ethnographic, action, and clinical research. Diverse ways of collecting and analyzing empirical materials were also available, including qualitative interviewing (open-ended and quasi-structured) and observational, visual, personal experience, and documentary methods. Computers were entering the situation, to be fully developed as aids in the analysis of qualitative data in the next decade, along with narrative, content, and semiotic methods of reading interviews and cultural texts.

Two books by Geertz, *The Interpretation of Culture* (1973) and *Local Knowledge* (1983), defined the beginning and end of this moment. In these two works, Geertz argued that the old functional, positivist, behavioral, totalizing approaches to the human disciplines were giving way to a more pluralistic, interpretive, open-ended perspective. This new perspective took cultural representations and their meanings as its point of de-

24

parture. Calling for "thick descriptions" of particular events, rituals, and customs, Geertz suggested that all anthropological writings are interpretations of interpretations.[13] The observer has no privileged voice in the interpretations that are written. The central task of theory is to make sense out of a local situation.

Geertz went on to propose that the boundaries between the social sciences and the humanities had become blurred. Social scientists were now turning to the humanities for models, theories, and methods of analysis (semiotics, hermeneutics). A form of genre diaspora was occurring: documentaries that read like fiction (Mailer), parables posing as ethnographies (Castañeda), theoretical treatises that look like travelogues (Lévi-Strauss). At the same time, other new approaches were emerging: poststructuralism (Barthes), neopositivism (Philips), neo-Marxism (Althusser), micromacro descriptivism (Geertz), ritual theories of drama and culture (V. Turner), deconstructionism (Derrida), ethnomethodology (Garfinkel). The golden age of the social sciences was over, and a new age of blurred, interpretive genres was upon us. The essay as an art form was replacing the scientific article. At issue now is the author's presence in the interpretive text (Geertz, 1988). How can the researcher speak with authority in an age when there are no longer any firm rules concerning the text, including the author's place in it, its standards of evaluation, and its subject matter?

The naturalistic, postpositivist, and constructionist paradigms gained power in this period, especially in education, in the works of Harry Wolcott, Frederick Erickson, Egon Guba, Yvonna Lincoln, Robert Stake, and Elliot Eisner. By the end of the 1970s, several qualitative journals were in place, including *Urban Life and Culture* (now *Journal of Contemporary Ethnography*), *Cultural Anthropology, Anthropology and Education Quarterly, Qualitative Sociology,* and *Symbolic Interaction,* as well as the book series *Studies in Symbolic Interaction.*

Crisis of Representation

A profound rupture occurred in the mid-1980s. What we call the fourth moment, or the crisis of representation, appeared with *Anthropology as Cultural Critique* (Marcus & Fischer, 1986), *The Anthropology of Experience* (Turner & Bruner, 1986), *Writing Culture* (Clifford & Marcus, 1986), *Works and Lives* (Geertz, 1988), and *The Predicament of Culture* (Clifford, 1988). These works made research and writing more reflexive and called into question the issues of gender, class, and race. They articulated the consequences of Geertz's "blurred genres" interpretation of the field in the early 1980s.[14]

New models of truth, method, and representation were sought (Rosaldo, 1989). The erosion of classic norms in anthropology (obectivism, complicity with colonialism, social life structured by fixed rituals and customs, ethnographies as monuments to a culture) was complete (Rosaldo, 1989, pp. 44-45; see also Jackson, 1998, pp. 7-8). Critical, feminist, and epistemologies of color now competed for attention in this arena. Issues such as validity, reliability, and objectivity, previously believed settled, were once more problematic. Pattern and interpretive theories, as opposed to causal, linear theories, were now more common, as writers continued to challenge older models of truth and meaning (Rosaldo, 1989).

Stoller and Olkes (1987, pp. 227-229) describe how the crisis of representation was felt in their fieldwork among the Songhay of Niger. Stoller observes: "When I began to write anthropological texts, I followed the conventions of my training. I 'gathered data,' and once the 'data' were arranged in neat piles, I 'wrote them up.' In one case I reduced Songhay insults to a series of neat logical formulas" (p. 227). Stoller became dissatisfied with this form of writing, in part because he learned that "everyone had lied to me and . . . the data I had so painstakingly collected were worthless. I learned a lesson: Informants routinely lie to their anthropologists" (Stoller & Olkes, 1987, p. 9). This discovery led to a second—that he had, in following the conventions of ethnographic realism, edited himself out of his text. This led Stoller to produce a different type of text, a memoir, in which he became a central character in the story he told. This story, an account of his experiences in the Songhay world, became an analysis of the clash between his world and the world of Songhay sorcery. Thus Stoller's journey represents an attempt to confront the crisis of representation in the fourth moment.

Clough (1992) elaborates this crisis and criticizes those who would argue that new forms of writing represent a way out of the crisis. She argues:

While many sociologists now commenting on the criticism of ethnography view writing as "downright central to the ethnographic enterprise" [Van Maanen, 1988, p. xi], the problems of writing are still viewed as different from the problems of method or fieldwork itself. Thus the solution usually offered is experiments in writing, that is a self-consciousness about writing. (p. 136)

It is this insistence on the difference between writing and fieldwork that must be analyzed. (Richardson is quite articulate about this issue in Chapter 14, Volume 3.)

In writing, the field-worker makes a claim to moral and scientific authority. This claim allows the realist and experimental ethnographic texts to function as sources of validation for an empirical science. They show that the world of real lived experience can still be captured, if only in the writer's memoirs, or fictional experimentations, or dramatic readings. But these works have the danger of directing attention away from the ways in which the text constructs sexually situated individuals in a field of social difference. They also perpetuate "empirical science's hegemony" (Clough, 1992, p. 8), for these new writing technologies of the subject become the site "for the production of knowledge/power . . . [aligned] with . . . the capital/state axis" (Aronowitz, 1988, p. 300; quoted in Clough, 1992, p. 8). Such experiments come up against, and then back away from, the difference between empirical science and social criticism. Too often they fail to engage fully a new politics of textuality that would "refuse the identity of empirical science" (Clough, 1992, p. 135). This new social criticism "would intervene in the relationship of information economics, nation-state politics, and technologies of mass communication, especially in terms of the empirical sciences" (Clough, 1992, p. 16). This, of course, is the terrain occupied by cultural studies.

Richardson (Volume 3, Chapter 14), Tedlock (this volume, Chapter 6), Brady (Volume 3, Chapter 15), and Ellis and Bochner (Volume 3, Chapter 6) develop the above arguments, viewing writing as a method of inquiry that moves through successive stages of self-reflection. As a series of written representations, the field-worker's texts flow from the field experience, through intermediate works, to later work, and finally to the research text, which is the public presentation of the ethnographic and narrative experience. Thus fieldwork and writing blur into one another. There is, in the final analysis, no difference between writing and fieldwork. These two perspectives inform one another throughout every chapter in these volumes. In these ways the crisis of representation moves qualitative research in new and critical directions.

A Triple Crisis

The ethnographer's authority remains under assault today (Behar, 1995, p. 3; Gupta & Ferguson, 1997, p. 16; Jackson, 1998; Ortner, 1997, p. 2). A triple crisis of representation, legitimation, and praxis confronts qualitative researchers in the human disciplines. Embedded in the discourses of poststructuralism and postmodernism (see Vidich & Lyman, Volume 1, Chapter 2; and Richardson, Chapter 14, Volume 3), these three crises are coded in multiple terms, variously called and associated with *the critical, interpretive, linguistic, feminist*, and *rhetorical* turns in social theory. These new turns make problematic two key assumptions of qualitative research. The first is that qualitative researchers can no longer directly capture lived experience. Such experience, it is argued, is created in the social text written by the researcher. This is the representational crisis. It confronts the inescapable problem of representation, but does so within a framework that makes the direct link between experience and text problematic.

The second assumption makes problematic the traditional criteria for evaluating and interpreting qualitative research. This is the legitimation crisis. It involves a serious rethinking of such terms as *validity, generalizability*, and *reliability*, terms already retheorized in postpositivist (Hammersley, 1992), constructionist-naturalistic (Guba & Lincoln, 1989, pp. 163-183), feminist (Olesen, Chapter 8, Volume 1), interpretive (Denzin, 1997), poststructural (Lather, 1993; Lather & Smithies, 1997), and critical (Kincheloe & McLaren, Chapter 10, Volume 1) discourses. This crisis asks, How are qualitative studies to be evaluated in the contemporary, poststructural moment? The first two crises shape the third, which asks, Is it possible to effect change in the world if society is only and always a text? Clearly these crises intersect and blur, as do the answers to the questions they generate (see in Volume 1, Schwandt, Chapter 7; Ladson-Billings, Chapter 9; and in Volume 3, Smith & Deemer, Chapter 12).

The fifth moment, the postmodern period of experimental ethnographic writing, struggled to make sense of these crises. New ways of composing ethnography were explored (Ellis & Bochner, 1996). Theories were read as tales from the field. Writers struggled with different ways to represent the "other," although they were now joined by new representational concerns (see Fine et al., Chapter 4, Volume 1). Epistemologies from previously silenced groups emerged to offer solutions to these problems. The concept of the aloof observer has been abandoned. More action, participatory, and activist-oriented research is on the horizon. The search for grand narratives is being replaced by more local, small-scale theories fitted to specific problems and particular situations.

The sixth (postexperimental) and seventh (the future) moments are upon us. Fictional ethnographies, ethnographic poetry, and multimedia texts are today taken for granted. Postexperimental writers seek to connect their writings to the needs of a free democratic society. The demands of a moral and sacred qualitative social science are actively being explored by a host of new writers from many different disciplines (see Jackson, 1998; Lincoln & Denzin, Chapter 6, Volume 1).

Reading History

We draw four conclusions from this brief history, noting that it is, like all histories, somewhat arbitrary. First, each of the earlier historical moments is still operating in the present, either as legacy or as a set of practices that researchers continue to follow or argue against. The multiple and fractured histories of qualitative research now make it possible for any given researcher to attach a project to a canonical text from any of the above-described historical moments. Multiple criteria of evaluation compete for attention in this field (Lincoln, in press). Second, an embarrassment of choices now characterizes the field of qualitative research. There have never been so many paradigms, strategies of inquiry, or methods of analysis for researchers to draw upon and utilize. Third, we are in a moment of discovery and rediscovery, as new ways of looking, interpreting, arguing, and writing are debated and discussed. Fourth, the qualitative research act can no longer be viewed from within a neutral or objective positivist perspective. Class, race, gender, and ethnicity shape the process of inquiry, making research a multicultural process. It is to this topic that we now turn.

◆ Qualitative Research as Process

Three interconnected, generic activities define the qualitative research process. They go by a variety of different labels, including *theory, method, analysis, ontology, epistemology,* and *methodology.* Behind these terms stands the personal biography of the researcher, who speaks from a particular class, gender, racial, cultural, and ethnic community perspective. The

29

gendered, multiculturally situated researcher approaches the world with a set of ideas, a framework (theory, ontology) that specifies a set of questions (epistemology) that he or she then examines in specific ways (methodology, analysis). That is, the researcher collects empirical materials bearing on the question and then analyzes and writes about them. Every researcher speaks from within a distinct interpretive community that configures, in its special way, the multicultural, gendered components of the research act.

In this volume we treat these generic activities under five headings, or phases: the researcher and the researched as multicultural subjects, major paradigms and interpretive perspectives, research strategies, methods of collecting and analyzing empirical materials, and the art, practices, and politics of interpretation. Behind and within each of these phases stands the biographically situated researcher. This individual enters the research process from inside an interpretive community. This community has its own historical research traditions, which constitute a distinct point of view. This perspective leads the researcher to adopt particular views of the "other" who is studied. At the same time, the politics and the ethics of research must also be considered, for these concerns permeate every phase of the research process.

◆ The Other as Research Subject

Since its early-20th-century birth in modern, interpretive form, qualitative research has been haunted by a double-faced ghost. On the one hand, qualitative researchers have assumed that qualified, competent observers can, with objectivity, clarity, and precision, report on their own observations of the social world, including the experiences of others. Second, researchers have held to the belief in a real subject, or real individual, who is present in the world and able, in some form, to report on his or her experiences. So armed, researchers could blend their own observations with the self-reports provided by subjects through interviews and life story, personal experience, case study, and other documents.

These two beliefs have led qualitative researchers across disciplines to seek a method that would allow them to record accurately their own observations while also uncovering the meanings their subjects bring to their life experiences. This method would rely upon the subjective verbal and written expressions of meaning given by the individuals studied as

30

windows into the inner lives of these persons. Since Dilthey (1900/1976), this search for a method has led to a perennial focus in the human disciplines on qualitative, interpretive methods.

Recently, as noted above, this position and its beliefs have come under assault. Poststructuralists and postmodernists have contributed to the understanding that there is no clear window into the inner life of an individual. Any gaze is always filtered through the lenses of language, gender, social class, race, and ethnicity. There are no objective observations, only observations socially situated in the worlds of—and between—the observer and the observed. Subjects, or individuals, are seldom able to give full explanations of their actions or intentions; all they can offer are accounts, or stories, about what they did and why. No single method can grasp all of the subtle variations in ongoing human experience. Consequently, qualitative researchers deploy a wide range of interconnected interpretive methods, always seeking better ways to make more understandable the worlds of experience they have studied.

Table 1.1 depicts the relationships we see among the five phases that define the research process. Behind all but one of these phases stands the biographically situated researcher. These five levels of activity, or practice, work their way through the biography of the researcher. We take them up briefly in order here; we discuss these phases more fully in the introductions to the individual parts of this volume.

Phase 1: The Researcher

Our remarks above indicate the depth and complexity of the traditional and applied qualitative research perspectives into which a socially situated researcher enters. These traditions locate the researcher in history, simultaneously guiding and constraining work that will be done in any specific study. This field has been characterized constantly by diversity and conflict, and these are its most enduring traditions (see Greenwood & Levin, Chapter 3, Volume 1). As a carrier of this complex and contradictory history, the researcher must also confront the ethics and politics of research (see Christians, Chapter 5, Volume 1). The age of value-free inquiry for the human disciplines is over (see in Volume 1, Vidich & Lyman, Chapter 2; and Fine et al., Chapter 4). Today researchers struggle to develop situational and transsituational ethics that apply to all forms of the research act and its human-to-human relationships.

TABLE 1.1   The Research Process

Phase 1: The Researcher as a Multicultural Subject

    history and research traditions

    conceptions of self and the other

    ethics and politics of research

Phase 2: Theoretical Paradigms and Perspectives

    positivism, postpositivism

    interpretivism, constructivism, hermeneutics

    feminism(s)

    racialized discourses

    critical theory and Marxist models

    cultural studies models

    queer theory

Phase 3: Research Strategies

    study design

    case study

    ethnography, participant observation, performance ethnography

    phenomenology, ethnomethodology

    grounded theory

    life history, *testimonio*

    historical method

    action and applied research

    clinical research

Phase 4: Methods of Collection and Analysis

    interviewing

    observing

    artifacts, documents, and records

    visual methods

    autoethnography

    data management methods

    computer-assisted analysis

    textual analysis

    focus groups

    applied ethnography

Phase 5: The Art, Practices, and Politics of Interpretation and Presentation

    criteria for judging adequacy

    practices and politics of interpretation

    writing as interpretation

    policy analysis

    evaluation traditions

    applied research

Phase 2: Interpretive Paradigms

All qualitative researchers are philosophers in that "universal sense in which all human beings . . . are guided by highly abstract principles" (Bateson, 1972, p. 320). These principles combine beliefs about ontology (What kind of being is the human being? What is the nature of reality?), epistemology (What is the relationship between the inquirer and the known?), and methodology (How do we know the world, or gain knowledge of it?) (see Guba, 1990, p. 18; Lincoln & Guba, 1985, pp. 14-15; see also Lincoln & Guba, Chapter 6, Volume 1). These beliefs shape how the qualitative researcher sees the world and acts in it. The researcher is "bound within a net of epistemological and ontological premises which—regardless of ultimate truth or falsity—become partially self-validating" (Bateson, 1972, p. 314).

The net that contains the researcher's epistemological, ontological, and methodological premises may be termed a *paradigm*, or an interpretive framework, a "basic set of beliefs that guides action" (Guba, 1990, p. 17). All research is interpretive; it is guided by a set of beliefs and feelings about the world and how it should be understood and studied. Some beliefs may be taken for granted, invisible, only assumed, whereas others are highly problematic and controversial. Each interpretive paradigm makes particular demands on the researcher, including the questions he or she asks and the interpretations the researcher brings to them.

At the most general level, four major interpretive paradigms structure qualitative research: positivist and postpositivist, constructivist-interpretive, critical (Marxist, emancipatory), and feminist-poststructural. These four abstract paradigms become more complicated at the level of concrete specific interpretive communities. At this level it is possible to identify not only the constructivist, but also multiple versions of feminism (Afrocentric and poststructural)[15] as well as specific ethnic, Marxist, and cultural studies paradigms. These perspectives, or paradigms, are examined in Part II of Volume 1.

The paradigms examined in Part II of Volume 1 work against and alongside (and some within) the positivist and postpositivist models. They all work within relativist ontologies (multiple constructed realities), interpretive epistemologies (the knower and known interact and shape one another), and interpretive, naturalistic methods.

Table 1.2 presents these paradigms and their assumptions, including their criteria for evaluating research, and the typical form that an

TABLE 1.2   Interpretive Paradigms

Paradigm/ Theory	Criteria	Form of Theory	Type of Narration
Positivist/ postpositivist	internal, external validity	logical-deductive, grounded	scientific report
Constructivist	trustworthiness, credi- bility, transferability, confirmability	substantive-formal	interpretive case studies, ethnographic fiction
Feminist	Afrocentric, lived experience, dialogue, caring, accountability, race, class, gender, reflexivity, praxis, emotion, concrete grounding	critical, standpoint	essays, stories, experimental writing
Ethnic	Afrocentric, lived experience, dialogue, caring, accountability, race, class, gender	standpoint, critical, historical	essays, fables, dramas
Marxist	emancipatory theory, falsifiable, dialogical, race, class, gender	critical, historical, economic	historical, economic, sociocultural analyses
Cultural studies	cultural practices, praxis, social texts, subjectivities	social criticism	cultural theory as criticism
Queer theory	reflexivity, deconstruction	social criticism, his- torical analysis	theory as criticism, autobiography

interpretive or theoretical statement assumes in each paradigm.[16] These paradigms are explored in considerable detail in Volume 1, Part II by Lincoln and Guba (Chapter 6), Schwandt (Chapter 7), Olesen (Chapter 8), Ladson-Billings (Chapter 9), Kincheloe and McLaren (Chapter 10),

Frow and Morris (Chapter 11), and Gamson (Chapter 12). We have discussed the positivist and postpositivist paradigms above. They work from within a realist and critical realist ontology and objective epistemologies, and rely upon experimental, quasi-experimental, survey, and rigorously defined qualitative methodologies. Ryan and Bernard (Chapter 7, Volume 3) develop elements of this paradigm.

The constructivist paradigm assumes a relativist ontology (there are multiple realities), a subjectivist epistemology (knower and respondent cocreate understandings), and a naturalistic (in the natural world) set of methodological procedures. Findings are usually presented in terms of the criteria of grounded theory or pattern theories (see in Volume 1, Lincoln & Guba, Chapter 6; in this volume, Charmaz, Chapter 8; and in Volume 3, Ryan & Bernard, Chapter 7). Terms such as *credibility, transferability, dependability,* and *confirmability* replace the usual positivist criteria of internal and external validity, reliability, and objectivity.

Feminist, ethnic, Marxist, and cultural studies and queer theory models privilege a materialist-realist ontology; that is, the real world makes a material difference in terms of race, class, and gender. Subjectivist epistemologies and naturalistic methodologies (usually ethnographies) are also employed. Empirical materials and theoretical arguments are evaluated in terms of their emancipatory implications. Criteria from gender and racial communities (e.g., African American) may be applied (emotionality and feeling, caring, personal accountability, dialogue).

Poststructural feminist theories emphasize problems with the social text, its logic, and its inability ever to represent the world of lived experience fully. Positivist and postpositivist criteria of evaluation are replaced by other terms, including the reflexive, multivoiced text that is grounded in the experiences of oppressed people.

The cultural studies and queer theory paradigms are multifocused, with many different strands drawing from Marxism, feminism, and the postmodern sensibility (see in Volume 1, Frow & Morris, Chapter 11; Gamson, Chapter 12; and in Volume 3, Richardson, Chapter 14). There is a tension between a humanistic cultural studies, which stresses lived experiences (meaning), and a more structural cultural studies project, which stresses the structural and material determinants (race, class, gender) and effects of experience. Of course, there are two sides to every coin, and both sides are needed and are indeed critical. The cultural studies and queer theory paradigms use methods strategically—that is, as resources for understanding and for producing resistances to local structures of domination. Scholars may do close textual readings and discourse analyses of cultural texts (see in Volume 1, Olesen, Chapter 8; Frow & Morris, Chapter 11; and Silverman, Volume 3, Chapter 9) as well as conducting local ethnographies, open-ended interviewing, and participant observation. The focus is on how race, class, and gender are produced and enacted in historically specific situations.

Paradigm and personal history in hand, focused on a concrete empirical problem to examine, the researcher now moves to the next stage of the research process—namely, working with a specific strategy of inquiry.

Phase 3: Strategies of Inquiry and Interpretive Paradigms

Table 1.1 presents some of the major strategies of inquiry a researcher may use. Phase 3 begins with research design, which, broadly conceived, involves a clear focus on the research question, the purposes of the study, "what information most appropriately will answer specific research questions, and which strategies are most effective for obtaining it" (LeCompte & Preissle, 1993, p. 30; see also in this volume Janesick, Chapter 2; Cheek, Chapter 3). A research design describes a flexible set of guidelines that connect theoretical paradigms first to strategies of inquiry and second to methods for collecting empirical material. A research design situates researchers in the empirical world and connects them to specific sites, persons, groups, institutions, and bodies of relevant interpretive material, including documents and archives. A research design also specifies how the investigator will address the two critical issues of representation and legitimation.

A strategy of inquiry comprises a bundle of skills, assumptions, and practices that the researcher employs as he or she moves from paradigm to the empirical world. Strategies of inquiry put paradigms of interpretation into motion. At the same time, strategies of inquiry also connect the researcher to specific methods of collecting and analyzing empirical materials. For example, the case study relies on interviewing, observing, and document analysis. Research strategies implement and anchor paradigms in specific empirical sites, or in specific methodological practices, such as making a case an object of study. These strategies include the case study, phenomenological and ethnomethodological techniques, and the use of grounded theory, as well as biographical, autoethnographic, historical, action, and clinical methods. Each of these strategies is connected to a complex literature, and each has a separate history, exemplary works, and preferred ways for putting the strategy into motion.

Phase 4: Methods of
Collecting and Analyzing Empirical Materials

The researcher has several methods for collecting empirical materials.[17] These methods are taken up in Part I of Volume 3. They range from the interview to direct observation, the analysis of artifacts, documents, and cultural records, and the use of visual materials or personal experience. The researcher may also use a variety of different methods of reading and analyzing interviews or cultural texts, including content, narrative, and semiotic strategies. Faced with large amounts of qualitative materials, the investigator seeks ways of managing and interpreting these documents, and here data management methods and computer-assisted models of analysis may be of use. Ryan and Bernard (Volume 3, Chapter 7) and Weitzman (Volume 3, Chapter 8) discuss these techniques.

Phase 5: The Art and Politics
of Interpretation and Evaluation

Qualitative research is endlessly creative and interpretive. The researcher does not just leave the field with mountains of empirical materials and then easily write up his or her findings. Qualitative interpretations are constructed. The researcher first creates a field text consisting of field notes and documents from the field, what Roger Sanjek (1990, p. 386) calls "indexing" and David Plath (1990, p. 374) calls "filework." The writer-as-interpreter moves from this text to a research text: notes and interpretations based on the field text. This text is then re-created as a working interpretive document that contains the writer's initial attempts to make sense of what he or she has learned. Finally the writer produces the public text that comes to the reader. This final tale from the field may assume several forms: confessional, realist, impressionistic, critical, formal, literary, analytic, grounded theory, and so on (see Van Maanen, 1988).

The interpretive practice of making sense of one's findings is both artistic and political. Multiple criteria for evaluating qualitative research now exist, and those that we emphasize stress the situated, relational, and textual structures of the ethnographic experience. There is no single interpretive truth. As we argued earlier, there are multiple interpretive communities, each with its own criteria for evaluating an interpretation.

Program evaluation is a major site of qualitative research, and qualitative researchers can influence social policy in important ways. The contributions by Greenwood and Levin (Volume 1, Chapter 3), Kemmis and McTaggart (this volume, Chapter 11), Miller and Crabtree (this volume, Chapter 12), Chambers (Volume 3, Chapter 11), Greene (Volume 3, Chapter 16), and Rist (Volume 3, Chapter 17) trace and discuss the rich history of applied qualitative research in the social sciences. This is the critical site where theory, method, praxis, action, and policy all come together. Qualitative researchers can isolate target populations, show the immediate effects of certain programs on such groups, and isolate the constraints that operate against policy changes in such settings. Action-oriented and clinically oriented qualitative researchers can also create spaces for those who are studied (the other) to speak. The evaluator becomes the conduit through which such voices can be heard. Chambers, Greene, and Rist explicitly develop these topics in their chapters.

◆ Bridging the Historical Moments: What Comes Next?

Ellis and Bochner (Volume 3, Chapter 6), Gergen and Gergen (Volume 1, Chapter 13), and Richardson (Volume 3, Chapter 14) argue that we are already in the post "post" period—post-poststructuralist, post-postmodernist, post-postexperimental. What this means for interpretive ethnographic practices is still not clear, but it is certain that things will never again be the same. We are in a new age where messy, uncertain, multivoiced texts, cultural criticism, and new experimental works will become more common, as will more reflexive forms of fieldwork, analysis, and intertextual representation. We take as the subject of our final essay in Volume 1 these fifth, sixth, and seventh moments. It is true that, as the poet said, the center no longer holds. We can reflect on what should be at the new center.

Thus we come full circle. Returning to our bridge metaphor, the chapters that follow take the researcher back and forth through every phase of the research act. Like a good bridge, the chapters provide for two-way traffic, coming and going between moments, formations, and interpretive communities. Each chapter examines the relevant histories, controversies, and current practices that are associated with each paradigm, strategy, and method. Each chapter also offers projections for the future, where a specific paradigm, strategy, or method will be 10 years from now, deep into the formative years of the 21st century.

In reading the chapters that follow, it is important to remember that the field of qualitative research is defined by a series of tensions, contradictions, and hesitations. This tension works back and forth between the broad, doubting postmodern sensibility and the more certain, more traditional positivist, postpositivist, and naturalistic conceptions of this project. All of the chapters that follow are caught in and articulate this tension.

◆ Notes

1. Qualitative research has separate and distinguished histories in education, social work, communications, psychology, history, organizational studies, medical science, anthropology, and sociology.

2. Some definitions are in order here. *Positivism* asserts that objective accounts of the real world can be given. *Postpositivism* holds that only partially objective accounts of the world can be produced, because all methods for examining them are flawed. According to *foundationalism*, we can have an ultimate grounding for our knowledge claims about the world, and this involves the use of empiricist and positivist epistemologies (Schwandt, 1997a, p. 103). *Nonfoundationalism* holds that we can make statements about the world without "recourse to ultimate proof or foundations for that knowing" (p. 102). *Quasifoundationalism* holds that certain knowledge claims can be made about the world based on neorealist criteria, including the correspondence concept of truth; there is an independent reality that can be mapped (see Smith & Deemer, Chapter 12, Volume 3).

3. Jameson (1991, pp. 3-4) reminds us that any periodization hypothesis is always suspect, even one that rejects linear, stagelike models. It is never clear to what reality a stage refers, and what divides one stage from another is always debatable. Our seven moments are meant to mark discernible shifts in style, genre, epistemology, ethics, politics, and aesthetics.

4. Some further definitions are in order. *Structuralism* holds that any system is made up of a set of oppositional categories embedded in language. *Semiotics* is the science of signs or sign systems—a structuralist project. According to *poststructuralism*, language is an unstable system of referents, thus it is impossible ever to capture completely the meaning of an action, text, or intention. *Postmodernism* is a contemporary sensibility, developing since World War II, that privileges no single authority, method, or paradigm. *Hermeneutics* is an approach to the analysis of texts that stresses how prior understandings and prejudices shape the interpretive process. *Phenomenology* is a complex system of ideas associated with the works of Husserl, Heidegger, Sartre, Merleau-Ponty, and Alfred Schutz. *Cultural studies* is a complex, interdisciplinary field that merges critical theory, feminism, and poststructuralism.

5. Of course, all settings are natural—that is, places where everyday experiences take place. Qualitative researchers study people doing things together in the places where these

things are done (Becker, 1986). There is no field site or natural place where one goes to do this kind of work (see also Gupta & Ferguson, 1997, p. 8). The site is constituted through the researcher's interpretive practices. Historically, analysts have distinguished between experimental (laboratory) and field (natural) research settings, hence the argument that qualitative research is naturalistic. Activity theory erases this distinction (Keller & Keller, 1996, p. 20; Vygotsky, 1978).

6. According to Weinstein and Weinstein (1991), "The meaning of *bricoleur* in French popular speech is 'someone who works with his (or her) hands and uses devious means compared to those of the craftsman.' . . . the *bricoleur* is practical and gets the job done" (p. 161). These authors provide a history of the term, connecting it to the works of the German sociologist and social theorist Georg Simmel and, by implication, Baudelaire. Hammersley (in press) disputes our use of this term. Following Lévi-Strauss, he reads the *bricoleur* as a mythmaker. He suggests the term be replaced with the notion of the boatbuilder. Hammersley also quarrels with our "moments" model of qualitative research, contending that it implies some sense of progress.

7. Brian De Palma reproduced this baby carriage scene in his 1987 film *The Untouchables*.

8. In the harbor, the muzzles of the *Potemkin*'s two huge guns swing slowly toward the camera. Words onscreen inform us, "The brutal military power answered by guns of the battleship." A final famous three-shot montage sequence shows first a sculptured sleeping lion, then a lion rising from his sleep, and finally the lion roaring, symbolizing the rage of the Russian people (Cook, 1981, p. 167). In this sequence Eisenstein uses montage to expand time, creating a psychological duration for this horrible event. By drawing out this sequence, by showing the baby in the carriage, the soldiers firing on the citizens, the blood on the mother's glove, the descending carriage on the steps, he suggests a level of destruction of great magnitude.

9. Here it is relevant to make a distinction between techniques that are used across disciplines and methods that are used within disciplines. Ethnomethodologists, for example, employ their approach as a method, whereas others selectively borrow that method as a technique for their own applications. Harry Wolcott (personal communication, 1993) suggests this distinction. It is also relevant to make distinctions among topic, method, and resource. Methods can be studied as topics of inquiry; that is how a case study gets done. In this ironic, ethnomethodological sense, method is both a resource and a topic of inquiry.

10. Indeed, any attempt to give an essential definition of qualitative research requires a qualitative analysis of the circumstances that produce such a definition.

11. In this sense all research is qualitative, because "the observer is at the center of the research process" (Vidich & Lyman, Chapter 2, Volume 1).

12. See Lincoln and Guba (1985) for an extension and elaboration of this tradition in the mid-1980s, and for more recent extensions see Taylor and Bogdan (1998) and Creswell (1997).

13. Greenblatt (1997, pp. 15-18) offers a useful deconstructive reading of the many meanings and practices Geertz brings to the term *thick description*.

14. These works marginalized and minimized the contributions of standpoint feminist theory and research to this discourse (see Behar, 1995, p. 3; Gordon, 1995, p. 432).

15. Olesen (Chapter 8, Volume 1) identifies three strands of feminist research: mainstream empirical, standpoint and cultural studies, and poststructural, postmodern. She

places Afrocentric and other models of color under the cultural studies and postmodern categories.

16. These, of course, are our interpretations of these paradigms and interpretive styles.

17. *Empirical materials* is the preferred term for what are traditionally described as data.

◆ References

Aronowitz, S. (1988). *Science as power: Discourse and ideology in modern society.* Minneapolis: University of Minnesota Press.

Bateson, G. (1972). *Steps to an ecology of mind.* New York: Ballantine.

Becker, H. S. (1970). Problems of inference and proof in participant observation. In H. S. Becker, *Sociological work: Method and substance.* Chicago: Aldine. (Reprinted from *American Sociological Review, 1958, 23, 652-660*)

Becker, H. S. (1986). *Doing things together.* Evanston: Northwestern University Press.

Becker, H. S. (1996). The epistemology of qualitative research. In R. Jessor, A. Colby, & R. A. Shweder (Eds.), *Ethnography and human development: Context and meaning in social inquiry* (pp. 53-71). Chicago: University of Chicago Press.

Becker, H. S. (1998). *Tricks of the trade: How to think about your research while you're doing it.* Chicago: University of Chicago Press.

Becker, H. S., Geer, B., Hughes, E. C., & Strauss, A. L. (1961). *Boys in white: Student culture in medical school.* Chicago: University of Chicago Press.

Behar, R. (1995). Introduction: Out of exile. In R. Behar & D. A. Gordon (Eds.), *Women writing culture* (pp. 1-29). Berkeley: University of California Press.

Bogdan, R. C., & Taylor, S. J. (1975). *Introduction to qualitative research methods: A phenomenological approach to the social sciences.* New York: John Wiley.

Campbell, D. T., & Stanley, J. C. (1963). *Experimental and quasi-experimental designs for research.* Chicago: Rand McNally.

Carey, J. W. (1989). *Communication as culture: Essays on media and society.* Boston: Unwin Hyman.

Cicourel, A. V. (1964). *Method and measurement in sociology.* New York: Free Press.

Clifford, J. (1988). *The predicament of culture: Twentieth-century ethnography, literature, and art.* Cambridge, MA: Harvard University Press.

Clifford, J., & Marcus, G. E. (Eds.). (1986). *Writing culture: The poetics and politics of ethnography.* Berkeley: University of California Press.

Clough, P. T. (1992). *The end(s) of ethnography: From realism to social criticism.* Newbury Park, CA: Sage.

Clough, P. T. (1998). *The end(s) of ethnography: From realism to social criticism* (2nd ed.). New York: Peter Lang.

Cook, D. A. (1981). *A history of narrative film.* New York: W. W. Norton.

Creswell, J. W. (1997). *Qualitative inquiry and research design: Choosing among five traditions.* Thousand Oaks, CA: Sage.

Denzin, N. K. (1970). *The research act.* Chicago: Aldine.

Denzin, N. K. (1978). *The research act* (2nd ed.). New York: McGraw-Hill.

Denzin, N. K. (1997). *Interpretive ethnography.* Thousand Oaks, CA: Sage.

Dilthey, W. L. (1976). *Selected writings.* Cambridge: Cambridge University Press. (Original work published 1900)

Diversi, M. (1998). Glimpses of street life: Representing lived experience through short stories. *Qualitative Inquiry, 4,* 131-137.

Ellis, C., & Bochner, A. P. (Eds.). (1996). *Composing ethnography: Alternative forms of qualitative writing.* Walnut Creek, CA: AltaMira.

Filstead, W. J. (Ed.). (1970). *Qualitative methodology.* Chicago: Markham.

Flick, U. (1998). *An introduction to qualitative research: Theory, method and applications.* London: Sage.

Geertz, C. (1973). *The interpretation of cultures: Selected essays.* New York: Basic Books.

Geertz, C. (1983). *Local knowledge: Further essays in interpretive anthropology.* New York: Basic Books.

Geertz, C. (1988). *Works and lives: The anthropologist as author.* Stanford, CA: Stanford University Press.

Glaser, B. G. (1992). *Emergence vs. forcing: Basics of grounded theory.* Mill Valley, CA: Sociology Press.

Glaser, B. G., & Strauss, A. L. (1967). *The discovery of grounded theory: Strategies for qualitative research.* Chicago: Aldine.

Gordon, D. A. (1995). Culture writing women: Inscribing feminist anthropology. In R. Behar & D. A. Gordon (Eds.), *Women writing culture* (pp. 429-441). Berkeley: University of California Press.

Gordon, D. A. (1988). Writing culture, writing feminism: The poetics and politics of experimental ethnography. *Inscriptions, 3/4(8),* 21-31.

Greenblatt, S. (1997). The touch of the real. In S. B. Ortner (Ed.), The fate of "culture": Geertz and beyond [Special issue]. *Representations, 59,* 14-29.

Guba, E. G. (1990). The alternative paradigm dialog. In E. G. Guba (Ed.), *The paradigm dialog* (pp. 17-30). Newbury Park, CA: Sage.

Guba, E. G., & Lincoln, Y. S. (1989). *Fourth generation evaluation.* Newbury Park, CA: Sage.

Gupta, A., & Ferguson, J. (1997). Discipline and practice: "The field" as site, method, and location in anthropology. In A. Gupta & J. Ferguson (Eds.), *Anthropological locations: Boundaries and grounds of a field science* (pp. 1-46). Berkeley: University of California Press.

Hammersley, M. (1992). *What's wrong with ethnography? Methodological explorations.* London: Routledge.

Hammersley, M. (in press). Not bricolage but boatbuilding. *Journal of Contemporary Ethnography.*

hooks, b. (1990). *Yearning: Race, gender, and cultural politics.* Boston: South End.

Huber, J. (1995). Centennial essay: Institutional perspectives on sociology. *American Journal of Sociology, 101,* 194-216.

Jackson, M. (1998). *Minima ethnographica: Intersubjectivity and the anthropological project.* Chicago: University of Chicago Press.

Jameson, F. (1991). *Postmodernism; or, The cultural logic of late capitalism.* Durham, NC: Duke University Press.

Jones, S. H. (1999). Torch. *Qualitative Inquiry, 5,* 235-250.

Keller, C. M., & Keller, J. D. (1996). *Cognition and tool use: The blacksmith at work.* New York: Cambridge University Press.

Lather, P. (1993). Fertile obsession: Validity after poststructuralism. *Sociological Quarterly, 35,* 673-694.

Lather, P., & Smithies, C. (1997). *Troubling the angels: Women living with HIV/AIDS.* Boulder, CO: Westview.

LeCompte, M. D., & Preissle, J. (with Tesch, R.). (1993). *Ethnography and qualitative design in educational research* (2nd ed.). New York: Academic Press.

Lévi-Strauss, C. (1966). *The savage mind* (2nd ed.). Chicago: University of Chicago Press.

Lincoln, Y. S. (1999, June). Courage, vulnerability and truth. Keynote address delivered at the conference "Reclaiming Voice II: Ethnographic Inquiry and Qualitative Research in a Postmodern Age," University of California, Irvine.

Lincoln, Y. S. (in press). Varieties of validity: Quality in qualitative research. In J. S. Smart & C. Ethington (Eds.), *Higher education: Handbook of theory and research.* New York: Agathon Press.

Lincoln, Y. S., & Guba, E. G. (1985). *Naturalistic inquiry.* Beverly Hills, CA: Sage.

Lofland, J. (1971). *Analyzing social settings.* Belmont, CA: Wadsworth.

Lofland, J. (1995). Analytic ethnography: Features, failings, and futures. *Journal of Contemporary Ethnography, 24,* 30-67.

Lofland, J., & Lofland, L. H. (1984). *Analyzing social settings: A guide to qualitative observation and analysis* (2nd ed.). Belmont, CA: Wadsworth.

Lofland, J., & Lofland, L. H. (1995). *Analyzing social settings: A guide to qualitative observation and analysis* (3rd ed.). Belmont, CA: Wadsworth.

Lofland, L. (1980). The 1969 Blumer-Hughes Talk. *Urban Life and Culture, 8,* 248-260.

Malinowski, B. (1948). *Magic, science and religion, and other essays.* New York: Natural History Press. (Original work published 1916)

Malinowski, B. (1967). *A diary in the strict sense of the term* (N. Guterman, Trans.). New York: Harcourt, Brace & World.

Marcus, G. E., & Fischer, M. M. J. (1986). *Anthropology as cultural critique: An experimental moment in the human sciences.* Chicago: University of Chicago Press.

Monaco, J. (1981). *How to read a film: The art, technology, language, history and theory of film* (Rev. ed.). New York: Oxford University Press.

Nelson, C., Treichler, P. A., & Grossberg, L. (1992). Cultural studies: An introduction. In L. Grossberg, C. Nelson, & P. A. Treichler (Eds.), *Cultural studies* (pp. 1-16). New York: Routledge.

Ortner, S. B. (1997). Introduction. In S. B. Ortner (Ed.), The fate of "culture": Geertz and beyond [Special issue]. *Representations, 59,* 1-13.

Plath, D. W. (1990). Fieldnotes, filed notes, and the conferring of note. In R. Sanjek (Ed.), *Fieldnotes: The makings of anthropology* (pp. 371-384). Ithaca, NY: Cornell University Press.

Richardson, L. (1997). *Fields of play: Constructing an academic life.* New Brunswick, NJ: Rutgers University Press.

Roffman, P., & Purdy, J. (1981). *The Hollywood social problem film.* Bloomington: Indiana University Press.

Ronai, C. R. (1998). Sketching with Derrida: An ethnography of a researcher/erotic dancer. *Qualitative Inquiry, 4,* 405-420.

Rosaldo, R. (1989). *Culture and truth: The remaking of social analysis.* Boston: Beacon.

Sanjek, R. (Ed.). (1990). *Fieldnotes: The makings of anthropology.* Ithaca, NY: Cornell University Press.

Schwandt, T. A. (1997a). *Qualitative inquiry: A dictionary of terms.* Thousand Oaks, CA: Sage.

Schwandt, T. A. (1997b). Textual gymnastics, ethics and angst. In W. G. Tierney & Y. S. Lincoln (Eds.), *Representation and the text: Re-framing the narrative voice* (pp. 305-311). Albany: State University of New York Press.

Silverman, D. (1997). Towards an aesthetics of research. In D. Silverman (Ed.), *Qualitative research: Theory, method and practice* (pp. 239-253). London: Sage.

Smith, A. D. (1993). *Fires in the mirror: Crown Heights, Brooklyn, and other identities.* Garden City, NY: Anchor.

Snow, D., & Morrill, C. (1995). Ironies, puzzles, and contradictions in Denzin and Lincoln's vision of qualitative research. *Journal of Contemporary Ethnography, 22,* 358-362.

Spindler, G., & Spindler, L. (1992). Cultural process and ethnography: An anthropological perspective. In M. D. LeCompte, W. L. Millroy, & J. Preissle (Eds.), *The handbook of qualitative research in education* (pp. 53-92). New York: Academic Press.

Stocking, G. W., Jr. (1986). Anthropology and the science of the irrational: Malinowski's encounter with Freudian psychoanalysis. In G. W. Stocking, Jr.

(Ed.), Malinowski, Rivers, Benedict and others: *Essays on culture and personality* (pp. 13-49). Madison: University of Wisconsin Press.

Stocking, G. W., Jr. (1989). The ethnographic sensibility of the 1920s and the dualism of the anthropological tradition. In G. W. Stocking, Jr. (Ed.), *Romantic motives: Essays on anthropological sensibility* (pp. 208-276). Madison: University of Wisconsin Press.

Stoller, P., & Olkes, C. (1987). *In sorcery's shadow: A memoir of apprenticeship among the Songhay of Niger.* Chicago: University of Chicago Press.

Strauss, A. L., & Corbin, J. (1998). *Basics of qualitative research: Techniques and procedures for developing grounded theory* (2nd ed.). Thousand Oaks, CA: Sage.

Taylor, S. J., & Bogdan, R. (1998). *Introduction to qualitative research methods: A guidebook and resource* (3rd ed.). New York: John Wiley.

Turner, V., & Bruner, E. (Eds.). (1986). *The anthropology of experience.* Urbana: University of Illinois Press.

Van Maanen, J. (1988). *Tales of the field: On writing ethnography.* Chicago: University of Chicago Press.

Vygotsky, L. S. (1978). *Mind in society: The development of higher psychological processes* (M. Cole, V. John-Steiner, S. Scribner, & E. Souberman, Eds.). Cambridge, MA: Harvard University Press.

Weinstein, D., & Weinstein, M. A. (1991). Georg Simmel: Sociological flaneur bricoleur. *Theory, Culture & Society, 8,* 151-168.

West, C. (1989). *The American evasion of philosophy: A genealogy of pragmatism.* Madison: University of Wisconsin Press.

Wolcott, H. F. (1990). *Writing up qualitative research.* Newbury Park, CA: Sage.

Wolcott, H. F. (1992). Posturing in qualitative inquiry. In M. D. LeCompte, W. L. Millroy, & J. Preissle (Eds.), *The handbook of qualitative research in education* (pp. 3-52). New York: Academic Press.

Wolcott, H. F. (1995). *The art of fieldwork.* Walnut Creek, CA: AltaMira.

Wolf, M. A. (1992). *A thrice-told tale: Feminism, postmodernism, and ethnographic responsibility.* Stanford, CA: Stanford University Press.

2

The Choreography of Qualitative Research Design

Minuets, Improvisations, and Crystallization

Valerie J. Janesick

Movement never lies. It is a barometer telling the state of the soul—to all who can read it.

—Martha Graham

◆ Qualitative research design is very much like choreography. As Flick (1998) reminds us, the essence of good qualitative research design turns on the use of a set of procedures that are simultaneously open-ended and rigorous and that do justice to the complexity of the social setting under study. A good choreographer captures the complexity of the dance/story by using rigorous and tested procedures and in fact refuses to be limited to one approach to choreography. In this chapter, I wish to develop this metaphor through the use of two kinds of dances: a precisely set piece, a minuet, and a piece that has structure and form yet is totally free, the approach known as improvisation. Finally, I will discuss my views on crystallization as an alternative to triangulation in qualitative research design.

I have selected the metaphor of choreography to extend my earlier writing (Janesick, 1994a, 1998a) using the dance metaphor for two reasons. First, dance is the art form to which I am most devoted, having been a dancer, dance teacher, and choreographer for more than 25 years. I became a choreographer as a matter of natural evolution, following in the footsteps of many of my dear and influential teachers, and as a matter of survival. I have choreographed dances for various groups and my own dance company in three states, and I continued to study dance long after giving up my work as a choreographer. I have spent summers in New York City studying technique at the schools of Martha Graham, Merce Cunningham, Alvin Ailey, and Erick Hawkins.[1] While studying at Michigan State University at the Institute for Research on Teaching, I taught all levels of modern dance, choreography, dance history, and anatomy for the dancers at Lansing Community College in addition to my research internship. In fact, it was this simultaneous experience in dance and research studies that prepared me for my academic career as an ethnographic researcher, teacher of qualitative research methods, and designer of qualitative research projects.

Second, the metaphor of choreography is simply a tool to make the reader think about metaphor. Metaphor in general creeps up on you, surprises you. It defies the one-size-fits-all approach to a topic. I can only wholeheartedly agree with Eisner (1991) when he discusses metaphor:

> What is ironic is that in the professional socialization of educational researchers, the use of metaphor is regarded as a sign of imprecision; yet, for making public the ineffable, nothing is more precise than the artistic use of language. Metaphoric precision is the central vehicle for revealing the qualitative aspects of life. (p. 227)

Consequently, I invite the reader to embrace this metaphor of choreography, to stretch your imagination and broaden your view of qualitative research design. Choreography is about the art of making dances. Because dance and choreography are about lived experience, choreography seems to me the perfect metaphor for discussing qualitative research design. Because the qualitative researcher is the research instrument, the metaphor is even more apropos for this discussion, as the body is the instrument of dance.

The qualitative researcher is remarkably like a choreographer at various stages in the design process, in terms of situating and recontextualizing the research project within the shared experience of the researcher and the participants in the study. When choreographers are asked what they do, they typically speak of each individual piece, case by case, within the social context of the given choreographic study. This similarity with the work of qualitative researchers is striking. For example, as a choreographer, Doris Humphrey (1959/1987) was one of the first to write about choreography as a field of study. She viewed choreographic theory and the study of it as a craft. She did not eschew talent or genius, but she believed that it is not possible to teach someone to "create" a dance, for example. This is like the architect who still must know about glass and steel no matter what level of giftedness he or she possesses. For Humphrey, the craft of making dances was about learning the principles, then expanding and embroidering. Similarly, as newcomers to the field of qualitative research begin the task of designing research projects, the first stage for them is to learn the principles, so that they can then expand and embroider. This ancient concept was captured centuries ago in the writings of the Chinese master painters:

> Some set great value on method, while others pride themselves on dispensing with method. To be without method is deplorable, but to depend on method entirely is worse. You must first learn to observe the rules faithfully; afterwards, modify them according to your intelligence and capacity. The end of all method is to have no method. (Lu Ch'ai)

The qualitative researcher and the choreographer are similar in yet another way: Both refuse to separate art from ordinary experience. Choreographers and qualitative researchers can routinely benefit from the view, expressed more than 65 years ago by John Dewey (1934/1958), that art is about communication and experience. Although Dewey was roundly criticized in his time for this idea, over time many have come to see the value of his thinking. Dewey wrote about art as providing a sense of the whole of something, much like the qualitative researcher and the choreographer, who do this very thing in their work. As Dewey (1934/1958) noted, "The artist should restore continuity between the refined and intensified forms of experience that are works of art and the everyday events, doings, and sufferings that are universally recognized to constitute experience" (p. 3). This thoughtful and critical approach to everyday experience and to art as experience is very much like the approaches taken by the qualitative researcher and the choreographer.

◆ Of Minuets and Improvisations

A good choreographer refuses to be limited to just one approach or one technique from dance history. Likewise, the qualitative researcher refuses to be limited; as Flick (1998) has recently observed, the qualitative researcher uses various techniques and rigorous and tested procedures in working to capture the nuance and complexity of the social situation under study. From the amazing range of types of dances that have been described thus far in dance history, I have chosen two seemingly unrelated forms, the minuet and improvisation, to illustrate my discussion of the design process in qualitative research studies. The minuet represents the most confined approach, with a prescribed set of steps in a given dance piece. It is a dance with definite steps, definite turns, and prescribed patterns of foot and arm movements. On the other end of the spectrum is improvisational dance. Imagine yourself as a choreographer and consider how you might approach the challenge of choreographing both kinds of dances.

First, let us look at the minuet. At the risk of sounding like Forrest Gump, I must point out that dance history writers have noted that life is like a minuet: The dancer makes a few turns in order to curtsy or bow and end up in the same place where the dance began. However, the minuet is not as simple as it seems. Imagine yourself in France in the year 1650. It is a period of luxury and calm for those who are able to enjoy music and dance. Strict rules apply to manners, customs, art, music, ceremonies, life as a whole, and certainly daily dress. Millions are spent on the production of the minuet at parties and court gatherings. Costumers, choreographers, set designers, musicians, jesters, and poets are called upon to see that the perfect minuet is danced. In fact, dancing teachers and choreographers of the period are revered as angels, architects of god; all would-be dancers of the minuet bow to these teachers as they look for instruction in this dance.

Now imagine yourself in the present day, about to choreograph an improvisation. Improvisation is probably the approach to dance most unlike the minuet. It first appeared in the 1960s as part of postmodern dance in general. Improvisation is spontaneous and reflective of the social condition; it is up to the individual dancer to interpret an idea, given a set problem or context in which to work. Improvisation in dance is like any creative endeavor. It relies on (a) preparation, (b) exploration, and (c) illumination and formulation. For example, I recall one of my dance teachers saying, in an improvisation session, "Think of a favorite poem. Now listen to this music I am playing. Now *move*." This is an example of a choreographic study of an improvisation. As with any dance, one must be keenly aware of the body and kinesiology, phrasing, core imagery, and the idea to be expressed to an audience. Likewise, the choreographer is balancing all this as he or she prompts an improvisation. The point is that all dance, all choreography, begins with an idea, whether the dance is defined in an exact form or spontaneous. I see a connection to the qualitative researcher's work in Blom and Chaplin's (1988) description of improvisational dance components:

> Certainly and easily we can say that spontaneity is one of its constituent parts. At the same time it is not without direction. It is at once intentional and reactive. . . . An organic plan emerges to take us forward in time, yet it only becomes articulated as we move. Because improv is a phenomenological process, we cannot examine any product per se. But it does exist and is perceivable. What we can do is examine the route it takes and our consciousness of it, a route which is on the way to creating itself while being itself. (p. 7)

Thus the qualitative researcher may learn from the choreographic forms of both minuet and improvisation. The design of the study begins with some fixed movements: precise interviews are planned, observations are scheduled, documents are reviewed and analyzed. In this way the researcher is like the choreographer/dancer of the minuet. At the same time, within the parameters of the interviews, information is disclosed that allows the researcher to improvise, to find out more about some critical event or moment in the lives of the participants. So the researcher begins to use the techniques of the improvisational choreographer/dancer. Even the act of charting observations and interviews is sometimes improvisational. One interview may lead the researcher to find out that another individual may become part of the study for one reason or another. One document may lead to many more, and so on. Likewise, the researcher charts the progress and examines the route of the study as it proceeds by keeping track of his or her own role in the research process. A good way for the researcher to do this is to keep a reflective journal of the research process (Janesick, 1999). Like choreographers who document their thinking and work in their notes and on videotape, the researcher may do the same to contribute to the historical record.

◆ Qualitative Research Design as Choreography

All choreographers make a statement and begin, explicitly or implicitly, with the question, What do I want to say in this dance? In much the same way, the qualitative researcher begins with a similar question: What do I want to know in this study? This is a critical beginning point. Regardless of the researcher's point of view, and quite often because of that point of view, the researcher constructs and frames a question for inquiry. After this question is clear, the researcher selects the most appropriate methodology to proceed with the research project. For the qualitative researcher, the question cannot be entirely separated from the method, in the same way the dancer cannot be separated from the dance or the choreographer from what is danced. Qualitative research design, like choreography, begins with a question, or at least an intellectual curiosity if not a passion for a particular topic. Of course, a qualitative researcher designs a study with real individuals in mind, and with the intent of living in that social setting over time. The qualitative researcher studies a social setting to understand the meaning of participants' lives in the participants' own terms. This contrasts with the work of the quantitative researcher, who is perfectly comfortable with aggregating large numbers of people without communicating with them face-to-face. So the questions the qualitative researcher asks will be quite different from those asked by the quantitative researcher. In general, questions that are suited to qualitative inquiry have long been the questions of many educational researchers and theorists, sociologists, anthropologists, students of organizations, and historians. For example:

1. Questions concerning the quality of a given innovation or program;
2. Questions regarding the meaning or interpretation of some component of the context under study;

3. Questions that relate to organizations and society in terms of their socio-linguistic aspects;

4. Questions related to the whole system, as in a classroom, school, school district, city, country, organization, hospital, or prison;

5. Questions regarding the political, economic, or sociopsychological aspects of organizations and society;

6. Questions regarding the hidden curriculum or hidden agendas in an organization;

7. Questions pertaining to the social context of an organization;

8. Questions pertaining to participants' implicit theories about their work;

9. Questions about the meaning of an individual's life;

10. Questions that afflict the comfortable and comfort the afflicted.

This list is not meant to be exhaustive; it serves only to illustrate the basic areas where research has been completed and has employed qualitative techniques because of, among other things, the suitability of the technique and the question.

Just as the choreographer begins with stages of completion of a choreographic piece, I like to think of qualitative design as made up of three stages of design. First is the warm-up, preparation, or prechoreographic stage of design decisions at the beginning of the study; second is the exploration or tryout and total workout stage, when design decisions are made throughout the study; and third is the illumination and formulation or completion stage, when design decisions are made at the end or near the end of the study. At the same time, the qualitative researcher, like the choreographer, follows set routines (such as those found in the minuet) as well as improvisational moments. Likewise, just as the choreographer relies on the spine of the dancer for the power and coherence of the dance, the qualitative researcher relies on the design of the study. Both are elastic. Like the dancer who finds her center from the base of the spine and the connection between the spine and the body, the qualitative researcher is centered by a series of design decisions. A dancer who is centered may tilt forward and backward and from side to side, yet always return to the center, the core of the dancer's strength. If one thinks of the design of the study as the spine, and the base of the spine as the beginning of the warm-up in dance, one can see that the beginning decisions in a study are very much like the warm-up for the dancer and the predesign decisions made by the choreographer.

◆ Warming Up and Preparation: Design Decisions at the Beginning of the Study and Elements for Choreography

The first set of design decisions have to do with what is studied, under what circumstances, for what duration of time, and with whom. For the choreographer, motivation for movement, themes for the dance, dynamics, rhythm, and phrasing are first considerations. As a researcher, I always start any given research project with a question. For example, when I was studying deaf culture in Washington, D.C., over a 4-year period, my basic question was, How do some deaf adults manage to succeed academically and in the workplace given the stigma of deafness in our society (Janesick, 1994b)? This basic question informed all my observations and interviews and led me to use focus groups and oral history techniques later in the study. Both the focus groups and oral histories evolved after I came to know the perspectives on deafness of the twelve individuals in my study. I then used theoretical sampling techniques to select three individuals to participate in an oral history component of the study.[2] I use this example to illustrate the elasticity of qualitative design. Focus groups allowed me to moderate and observe interactions among three of my participants on their perspectives on deafness, something I could not have planned in the first days in the field. Nor could I have realized at the beginning of the study the value of incorporating these techniques, which allowed me to capture a richer interpretation of participants' perspectives on deafness as well as to experience the use of various techniques and disciplines. Choreographers must also make adjustments as they create choreographic studies. For example, questions about the use of space, the types of dancers, types of soloists, and use of movement are preperformance decisions. During rehearsals, the choreographer may reorganize and adjust many of these elements as the work proceeds.

Further examples to illustrate this point come from the qualitative research projects conducted by Judith Gouwens, Patricia Williams-Boyd, and Byron DeFreese. Gouwens (1995) studied the principals of two Chicago schools to determine their personal realities regarding their professional roles. After deciding to describe and explain how the principals do what they do, she was able to determine that interviews, observations, and document reviews were appropriate techniques for her research project. Similarly, Boyd (1996) studied a full-service school and its effects on the community in which it is located. By living in the setting, interviewing, observing, and taking photographs, Boyd documented the everyday lives of the actors involved and extracted meaning from their lived experience so as to guide prospective practitioners in this area. DeFreese (1996) studied an assistant school superintendent to find out how he made decisions and how he viewed his role. Through careful interviews over time and by reviewing documents related to this person's life, DeFreese found a way to do justice to a life of service to the community. Thus qualitative researchers have open minds, but not empty minds. They formulate questions to guide their studies, but those questions are under constant revision and are continually taking new shapes. On a regular basis, I am confronted by colleagues who state that qualitative researchers just hang around aimlessly until something pops up; or worse, they claim that there are no questions in qualitative projects. Nothing could be further from the truth.

Simultaneous with formulating the question that guides the study, the qualitative researcher needs to select a site and develop a rationale for the choice of that site. Access and entry are sensitive components in qualitative research, and the researcher must establish trust, rapport, and authentic communication patterns with participants. By establishing trust and rapport at the beginning of the study, the researcher is better able to capture the nuances and meanings of each participant's life from the participant's point of view. This also ensures that participants will be more willing to share everything, warts and all, with the researcher. Maintaining trust and rapport continues through the length of the study and long after in fact. Yet it must begin at the beginning. It would be difficult to imagine establishing trust, say, 6 months into a study. All of us who have done fieldwork know how critical the initial interactions in the field are, as a precursor to establishing trust and rapport. This holds true in dance as well. There must be trust between choreographer and dancers if they are to create a dance.

Once the researcher has a question, a site, a participant or a number of participants, and a reasonable period of time in which to undertake the study, he or she needs to decide what data collection strategies are most suited to the study. The selection of these strategies is intimately connected to how the researcher views the purpose of the work—that is, how to understand the social setting under study. Most often, qualitative researchers use some combination of participant observation, interviews, and document analysis. The use of such approaches and strategies in qualitative studies is well documented in the literature (Bogdan & Biklen, 1992; Creswell, 1997; Denzin, 1989; Goetz & LeCompte, 1984; Guba & Lincoln, 1994; Janesick, 1998a; LeCompte, Millroy, & Priessle, 1992; Lincoln &

Guba, 1985; Marshall & Rossman, 1995; Maxwell, 1996; Spradley, 1979, 1980; Strauss & Corbin, 1990; Wolcott, 1990b, 1994). For example, in education and human services over the past three decades, case study, oral history (including narrative and life history approaches), grounded theory, literary criticism, and ethnographic approaches to research have been discovered and used because of their fit with research questions. Education has, at long last, embraced the techniques of the anthropologist, the sociologist, and the historian. This makes sense, given that these are the very approaches that allow researchers to deal with individuals. Choreographers must make similar design decisions before they create their dances. First, there is usually some inspiration for the dance in the first place. In Alvin Ailey's work, for example, there is no getting away from the major idea that prompts the dance. Ailey's ability to combine music for effect, costumes, lighting, and selection of the perfect soloist can be compared with the researcher's ability to make design decisions that he or she can rely upon throughout the study.

Summary

In summary, the warm-up period, or the period of making decisions at the beginning of the study, includes decisions regarding the following:

1. The questions that guide the study;
2. Selection of a site and participants;
3. Access and entry to the site and agreements with participants;
4. Timeline for the study;
5. Selection of appropriate research strategies, which may include some of the following (this list is not meant to be inclusive of all possibilities):
   a. ethnography
   b. life history
   c. oral history
   d. ethnomethodology
   e. case study
   f. participant observation
   g. field research or field study
   h. naturalistic study
   i. phenomenological study
   j. ecological descriptive study
   k. descriptive study

  l. symbolic interactionist study
  m. microethnography
  n. interpretive research
  o. action research
  p. narrative research
  q. historiography
  r. literary criticism

6. The place of theory in the study;

7. Identification of the researcher's own beliefs and ideology;

8. Identification of appropriate informed consent procedures and willingness to deal with ethical issues as they present themselves.

Regarding the last two categories listed above, I would like to point out that qualitative researchers accept the fact that research is ideologically driven. There is no value-free or bias-free design. Early on, the qualitative researcher identifies his or her own biases and articulates the ideology or conceptual frame for the study. By identifying one's biases, one can see easily where the questions that guide the study are crafted. The researcher owns up to his or her perspective on the study and may even track its evolution by keeping a critical reflective journal on the entire research process and the particular role of the researcher. This is a big difference between paradigms. I have yet to see a study in the quantitative arena in which the researcher discusses the ideology that guided and shaped the study. The myth that research is objective in some way can no longer be taken seriously. At this point in time, all researchers should be free to challenge prevailing myths, such as this myth of objectivity. As we try to make sense of our social world and give meaning to what we do as researchers, we continually raise awareness of our own beliefs. There is no attempt to pretend that research is value-free. Likewise, qualitative researchers, because they deal with individuals face-to-face on a daily basis, are attuned to making decisions regarding ethical concerns, because this is part of life in the field. From the beginning moments of informed consent decisions, to other ethical decisions in the field, to the completion of the study, qualitative researchers need to allow for the possibility of recurring ethical dilemmas and problems in the field. Ethical issues arise regularly in the field. For example, questions regarding how much to disclose in the final report and how much to keep out of the final report are ever present. The researcher and participants in the project—or coresearchers, if you will—decide how to present the information that best captures the social setting yet will not compromise or harm any members in the study.

In addition to the decisions made at the beginning of the study, it is helpful for researchers to consider some characteristics of qualitative design (again, the following list is not meant to be exhaustive; it is meant to be used merely as a heuristic tool):

1. Qualitative design is holistic. It looks at the larger picture, the whole picture, and begins with a search for understanding of the whole. Qualitative research is not constructed to prove something or to control people.

2. Qualitative design looks at relationships within systems or cultures.

3. Qualitative design is concerned with the personal, face-to-face, and immediate.

4. Qualitative design is focused on understanding given social settings, not necessarily making predictions about those settings.

5. Qualitative design demands that the researcher stay in the setting over time.

6. Qualitative design demands time in analysis equal to the time in the field.

7. Qualitative design sometimes requires that the researcher develop a model of what occurred in the social setting. (I like to encourage this because developing a model comes close to choreographic work or artistic work and serves as a heuristic tool. I am sure there are many qualitative researchers who do not need or value model development; however, like the scene designer or architect who builds a model, the choreographer or dancer who captures the dance on film, or the artist who creates a drawing or series of drawings, the researcher can use the model as a tool for further work or it can serve as a simple historical record.)

8. Qualitative design requires the researcher to become the research instrument. This means the researcher must have the ability to observe behavior and must sharpen the skills necessary for observation and face-to-face interview. (Like the dancer and the choreographer, the qualitative researcher must be in tune with the body: The eyes must be taught to see, the ears must be taught to hear, and so on.)

9. Qualitative design incorporates informed consent decisions and is responsive to ethical concerns.

10. Qualitative design incorporates room for description of the role of the researcher as well as description of the researcher's own biases and ideological preference.

11. Qualitative design requires the construction of an authentic and compelling narrative of what occurred in the study and the various stories of the participants.

12. Qualitative design requires ongoing analysis of the data.

Other chapters in this volume discuss many of these characteristics in depth, and the reader will benefit from those discussions. Once the researcher begins the study and is in the field, another set of decision points emerges.

◆ Stage 2: Exploration and Exercises—Design Decisions Throughout the Course of the Study and Choreography as a Work in Progress

Stretching Exercises and Background Work

Before researchers devote themselves to the arduous and significant time commitments of qualitative studies, it is a good idea for them to do some background work, or what I have called "stretching exercises." (I have in the past used the term *pilot study,* but I now reject that term as far too limiting for qualitative researchers.) Stretching exercises allow prospective qualitative researchers to practice interview, observation, writing, reflection, and artistic skills to refine their research instruments, which are the researchers themselves. In dance, as I have written earlier, the dancer stretches to move beyond the current starting point (Janesick, 1998c). Likewise, qualitative researchers in training need to stretch their imaginations as well as their bodies—their eyes for observation, their ears for listening, their hands for writing, and so on. During this short period, preinterviews with selected key participants and a period of observations and document review can be helpful to researchers in a number of ways.

Also at this point, the researcher should take a trip to the library or go on-line to investigate what has been done before, historically, in his or her field. Just as the choreographer makes a dance from a historical posture, so the qualitative researcher designs a research project from some set of historical antecedents. It is a good idea for the researcher to identify those historical antecedents in the background work for the study. This background work will allow the researcher to focus on particular areas that previously may have been unclear. In addition, the researcher may use preinterviews to test certain questions.

This initial part of the process allows the researcher to begin to develop and solidify rapport with participants as well as to establish effective communication patterns. By including some time for reviewing records and documents, the researcher may uncover some insight into the shape of the study that previously was not apparent. To use another example from my study on deaf culture: Prior to my interviews with participants, I spent time in the Gallaudet University archives, reading journals, looking at newspaper clippings, and viewing videotapes, all of which helped me to understand the historical influences that led to the "Deaf President Now" movement.[3] I saw, in retrospect, common themes and categories in the subsequent interview transcripts that made perfect sense given a series of historical situations in a 125-year period prior to the selection of Gallaudet University's first deaf president. Thus the time invested in background work can be valuable and enriching for later phases of the study. In addition, graduate students who are getting ready to write the proposals for their dissertations should first and foremost check the past 10 years of *Dissertation Abstracts* to see what research projects have preceded them in their fields.

Other decisions made during the study usually concern effective use of time, participants' issues, or researcher issues. Because working in the field is unpredictable a good deal of the time, the qualitative researcher must be ready to readjust schedules and interview times, add or subtract observations or interviews, replace participants in the event of trauma or tragedy, and even rearrange terms of the original agreement. My own experiences in conducting long-term ethnographic studies have led me to refine and readjust study design constantly as I proceed, especially at this phase. While totally immersed in the immediate and local actions and statements of belief of participants, the researcher must be ready to deal with the substantive focus of the study and with his or her own presuppositions. Simply observing and interviewing do not ensure that the research is qualitative; the qualitative researcher must also interpret the beliefs and behaviors of participants. To offer an example: I was recently asked to review some proposals for research projects funded in-house. One of the proposals was for a study that the proposal author claimed would be both qualitative and quantitative. The proposal described a lengthy survey (quantitative) and journal writing (qualitative). However, the author forgot to say what was to be done with the journals. How would they be integrated into the project? How would they be protected, ethically speaking? How would they connect to the survey? So you see, this was hardly a qualitative component. It was like an extra lump of clay in the hands of an indecisive sculptor: Should he throw it on the existing piece or not? If it can be integrated into the sculpture and will make sense, of course he should consider using it. If it will not make sense and will add nothing to the integrity of the final work of art, why would he use it?

Merely employing a qualitative technique here and there does not make a study qualitative. There seems to be a prevailing misunderstanding of qualitative work, and only those of us in the field can work to rectify this through careful documentation of our work on qualitative research projects. Painstaking, detailed descriptions and explanations of the design and conduct of studies are required not only for our own use but for future generations of qualitative researchers.

In a sense, while in the field the researcher is constantly immersed in a combination of deliberate decisions about hypotheses generated and tested on the one hand and intuitive reactions on the other. The researcher can find in the vast literature of sociology, anthropology, and education some common rules of thumb on which most researchers agree:

1. Look for meaning, the perspectives of the participants in the study.
2. Look for relationships regarding the structure, occurrence, and distribution of events over time.
3. Look for points of tension: What does not fit? What are the conflicting points of evidence in the case?

It is much the same in the dance world. Although the Graham technique represented a paradigm shift from ballet into modern dance, elements of ballet are still used within the idiom of modern dance. Furthermore, modern dance has embraced multiple competing and rival techniques, such as those developed by Cunningham and Tharp. As a choreographer presents an idea for an audience, you can be sure that many adjustments were made in the tryouts and rehearsals prior to the actual performance. Even dancing the minuet, with its set style in form and steps, every body is different, and one footstep from a 4-foot body is very different from that same step made by a 6-foot body. Similarly, improvisational dance is constantly changing depending on design decisions within each case, moment by moment. Basically, the qualitative researcher as designer of the research project will be making decisions at all stages of the project. Warm-up decisions and preparations made before entering the field constitute the first set of decisions. Exercises and exploration, the second stage of decisions, occur within the period of data collection in the field. The third stage of design decisions encompasses those that are made at the end of the study, what I call cooling down, illumination and formulation, or the decisions the researcher makes after leaving the field.

◆ Cooling Down: Illumination and Formulation— Design Decisions Made at the End of the Study

Design decisions at the end of the study are similar to the cooling-down portion of the dance movement or the choreographer's decision to come to completion of the choreographic study. The researcher must decide when to actually leave the field setting, often an emotional and traumatic event because of the close rapport developed during the course of the study. I usually ease out of the setting, much as a dancer will cool down gradually. For example, in my study of a teacher's classroom perspective, after observing on a daily basis for 6 months, I started staggering my observations and interviews in the seventh month of fieldwork from the 5 days per week, to 3 days, to once a week, and then to meetings with the teacher to go over interview transcripts at his convenience (Janesick, 1982).

Following the process of leaving the field, final data analysis can begin. Of course, the qualitative researcher has been developing categories from the data, through constant comparative analysis,[4] over the entire time frame of the study. The process of reduction of data into a compelling, authentic, and meaningful statement constitutes an end goal of qualitative research design. As Richardson (1994) suggests, narrative writing is in itself a type of inquiry. Every qualitative researcher must inevitably be a good writer in order to do justice to the complexity and substance of the life stories of participants in any study. The researcher must continually reassess and refine concepts while conducting the fieldwork. As the analysis proceeds, the researcher may develop working models or theories in action that explain the behavior under study. As the analysis continues, the researcher may identify relationships that connect portions of the description with the explanations offered in the working models. The researcher can attempt to determine the significance of the various elements in the working models and then try to verify these by checking through field notes, interview transcripts, and documents. Not all qualitative researchers agree about the use of working models. I am suggesting this from the standpoint of choreography, which employs this kind of approach. The choreographer develops working models as the work proceeds in order to work toward the final artistic statement. The work is always open to discussion and critique from the dancers, the audience, and so on. Similarly, I am suggesting that in qualitative research design, researchers develop working models, because they are more like artists than they may think.

Following the fieldwork, the researcher needs to present the data in a narrative form supported by evidence from the statements and behaviors recorded in field notes, critical reflection journals, and interviews. In other words, the researcher must make empirical assertions supported by direct quotations from notes and interviews. The researcher also needs to provide some interpretive commentary framing the key findings in the study. The theoretical discussion should be traceable in the data. In addition, the researcher should describe his or her own role thoroughly, so that readers will understand the relationship between the researcher and the participants. This allows the researcher to confront the major assertions in the study with credibility while surveying the full range of evidence. Because qualitative work recognizes early on the perspective of the researcher as it evolves through the study, the description of the role of the researcher is a critical component of the written report of the study. The researcher must describe and explain his or her social, philosophical, and physical location in the study. The qualitative researcher must honestly probe his or her own biases at the onset of the study, during the study, and at the end of the study by clearly describing and explaining the precise role of the researcher in the study.

Recently, a colleague called me to ask, "Are there any textbooks or journals on qualitative methods?" As an educator I felt I had to try to explain the current rich store of superb books and journals and in fact sent him information that I thought would be helpful, such as an annotated bibliography, my course syllabus for "Qualitative Methods," and a packet of information including on-line list servers and resources. I mention this only to illustrate that the qualitative researcher, in addition to the responsibility of designing his or her own study, may have to take on the added responsibility of explaining the most basic information to individuals who are not researchers or who are unaware of the substantial discussion on qualitative research methods in written texts, professional journals, on-line dialogues and other resources, and even such progress in their own fields. In fact, every one of my students who has done a qualitative dissertation has had to start early in the proposal writing stage to educate members of their committees, who may have forgotten about reading the books and journals available in this field. Inevitably, this becomes a responsibility for the qualitative researcher, and I see this as part of the social location of the researcher.

◆ Major Considerations in Writing the Narrative and Other Points

The qualitative researcher uses inductive analysis, which means that categories, themes, and patterns come from the data. The categories that emerge from field notes, documents, and interviews are not imposed prior to data collection. Early on, the researcher must develop a system for coding and categorizing the data. There is no one best system for analysis. The researcher may follow rigorous guidelines described in the literature (see Eisner, 1991; Fetterman, 1989; Goetz & LeCompte, 1984; Lincoln & Guba, 1985; Miles & Huberman, 1994; Patton, 1990), but the ultimate decisions about the narrative reside with the researcher. Like the choreographer, the researcher must find the most effective way to tell the story and to convince the audience of the meaning of the study. Staying close to the data is the most powerful means of telling the story, just as in dance the story is told through the body itself. As in the quantitative arena, the purpose of conducting a qualitative study is to produce findings. The methods and strategies used are not ends in themselves. There is a danger in becoming so taken up with methods that the substantive findings are obscured.

In fact, a problem that concerns me in doctoral programs is obsession with method. For example, many doctoral students take a number of statistics classes and, for whatever reason, hire others to do the statistics for their studies and in fact the analysis and interpretation. Qualitative researchers do not fall into this trap. The role of the qualitative researcher, like that of the dancer or the choreographer, demands a presence, an attention to detail, and a powerful use of the researcher's own mind and body in analysis and interpretation of the data. No one can dance your dance, so to speak. No one can choreograph your dance but you. No one can interpret your data but you. Qualitative researchers do not hire people to analyze and interpret their data. This is a critical difference between the two paradigms, and it illustrates the usefulness once again of the dance metaphor. It also prompts us as researchers to begin a dialogue on methodolatry, and whether or not we are actually contributing to

63

methodolatry by either allowing others to analyze and interpret data for our studies, as in the case of many quantitative researchers, or standing by and not questioning this practice as professors of qualitative research. After all, the entire point of doing a dissertation is to pass through the rites of passage of designing a study, implementing the study, and disseminating the findings of the study. If someone else does two-thirds of that work, what rite of passage has the student completed?

◆ Methodolatry

I use the term *methodolatry*, a combination of *method* and *idolatry*, to describe a preoccupation with selecting and defending methods to the exclusion of the actual substance of the story being told. Methodolatry is the idolatry of method, or a slavish attachment and devotion to method, that so often overtakes the discourse in the education and human services fields. Methodolatry manifests itself in many ways. A good example of methodolatry at its worst is found in the cases of survey researchers who throw out survey responses that don't match the answers they are looking for in order that they might do the only statistical techniques they were taught (and this is aside from the ethical issues raised by such practices). Another great example is the dissertation that contains 30 t tests or more about no particular issue, always in good faith, of course, but with very little reflection. In my lifetime, I have witnessed an almost constant obsession with the trinity of validity, reliability, and generalizability. It is always tempting to become obsessed with methods, but when this happens, experience is separated from knowing. Methodolatry is another way to move away from understanding the actual experience of participants in the research project. In the final stage of writing up the project, it is probably wise for the qualitative researcher to avoid being overly preoccupied with method. In other words, the researcher should immediately focus on the substance of the findings. Qualitative research depends on the presentation of solid descriptive data, so that the researcher leads the reader to an understanding of the meaning of the experience under study.

In classic terms, sociologists and anthropologists have shown us that finding categories and the relationship and patterns between and among categories leads to completeness in the narrative. Spradley (1980) suggests searching for cultural themes or domains. Denzin (1989) follows

Husserl's earlier conception of bracketing, which is to hold the phenomenon up for serious inspection, and suggests the following steps:

1. Locate within the personal experience, or self-story, key phrases and statements that speak directly to the phenomenon in question.
2. Interpret the meanings of these phrases as an informed reader.
3. Obtain the participants' interpretation of these findings, if possible.
4. Inspect these meanings for what they reveal about the essential, recurring features of the phenomenon being studied.
5. Offer a tentative statement or definition of the phenomenon in terms of the essential recurring features identified in Step 4.

In the process of bracketing, the researcher has the opportunity to treat the data in all its forms equally. Then the researcher may categorize, group, and cluster the data in order to interpret the data. The researcher uses constant comparative analysis to look for statements and indices of behavior that occur over time and in a variety of periods during the study. In addition, bracketing allows the researcher to find points of tension and conflict and what doesn't fit. After total immersion in the setting, the researcher needs time for analysis and contemplation of the data. By allowing sufficient time to go over the data carefully, the researcher opens up possibilities for uncovering the meaning in participants' lives. I have found Moustakis (1990) helpful in providing a heuristic approach here. He offers room to use inductive analysis through five phases. First, immersion in the setting starts the inductive process. Second, the incubation process allows for thinking, becoming aware of nuance and meaning in the setting, and capturing intuitive insights, to achieve understanding. Third, there is a phase of illumination that allows for expanding awareness. Fourth, and most understandably, is a phase of explication that includes description and explanation to capture the experience of individuals in the study. Finally, creative synthesis enables the researcher to synthesize and bring together as a whole the individual's story, including the meaning of the lived experience. These phases are similar to what the choreographer registers through the stages of preparation, exploration, and illumination.

The purposes of these disciplined approaches to analysis are, of course, to describe and to explain the essence of experience and meaning in participants' lives. Essentially this is what dancers do in interpreting a dance, and most assuredly what choreographers do in designing choreographic studies. Patton (1990) suggests a balance between description and interpretation. Denzin (1989) elaborates further by suggesting that thick description makes thick interpretation possible. Endless description is not useful if the researcher is to present a powerful narrative. Analysis and interpretation effectively balance description. There is no one way to accomplish this balance. Many beginning students ask me, "How many interviews must I do?" or "How long should I observe?" or "How many documents should I look at?" All of these are legitimate questions, of course, and all flow out of the psychometric—How long? How many? and so on. What the qualitative researcher needs to do is begin to reframe these questions in a language of interpretation and meaning, much as dancers and choreographers do—indeed, as any artist does. Rather than ask, for example, "How many interviews should I do?" the researcher can pose the question as a choreographer might: "What type of interview and with which actors would be most sensible given the purpose of my study and the exploratory questions that guide my study?" Such a question will yield answers that are far more textured and demanding. I am always amazed at the resistance to qualitative research by fellow professors who manage only to ask the child's question, "How many?" or, even more transparent, "Where's the control group?" rather than really think as qualitative researchers and ask solid, meaningful, textured questions. I am convinced that what separates good researchers from mediocre or bad ones is the same as what separates good choreographers from mediocre ones—the basic ability to formulate a meaningful textured question or statement.

◆ Crystallization Instead of Triangulation in Research Projects

If one reviews the literature in the area of qualitative research methods and design, one sees that historically there have been periodic discussions of triangulation as an important part of the design process. In the 1970s, Denzin (1978) identified four basic types of triangulation:

1. *Data triangulation:* the use of a variety of data sources in a study;

2. *Investigator triangulation:* the use of several different researchers or evaluators;

3. *Theory triangulation:* the use of multiple perspectives to interpret a single set of data;

4. *Methodological triangulation:* the use of multiple methods to study a single problem.

In the 1990s, I initially wrote of interdisciplinary triangulation (Janesick, 1994a). Now, as we move toward the new millennium, I am in agreement with Richardson (1994), who offers the idea of crystallization as a better lens through which to view qualitative research designs and their components. Richardson elegantly explains the concept of crystallization as part of the postmodern project. Crystallization recognizes the many facets of any given approach to the social world as a fact of life. The image of the crystal replaces that of the land surveyor and the triangle. We move on from plane geometry to the new physics. The crystal "combines symmetry and substance with an infinite variety of shapes, substances, transmutations, multidimensionalities, and angles of approach. Crystals grow, change, and alter, but are not amorphous" (Richardson, 1994, p. 522). What we see when we view a crystal, for example, depends on how we view it, how we hold it up to the light or not. Richardson continues, "Crystallization provides us with a deepened, complex, thoroughly partial, understanding of the topic. Paradoxically, we know more and doubt what we know" (p. 522).

I like to think that crystallization incorporates the use of other disciplines, such as art, sociology, history, dance, architecture, and anthropology, to inform our research processes and broaden our understanding of method and substance. For example, in the discipline of history, historians rely on documents and interviews almost entirely. There is constant discussion of method, but this is connected to content. We might learn a great deal from historians on this point alone. Returning to the arts and choreography, just the awareness of the choreographer's concerns with rhythm, tempo, the use of negative space, and action, for example, may broaden our own views on our respective research projects. Too often we become comfortable in our worlds and, to paraphrase Goethe, sometimes the most obvious things are hardest to see because they are right in front of our eyes. Thus I propose that we use the notion of crystallization to include incorporation of various disciplines as part of multifaceted qualitative research design.

To illustrate, I require all my students to incorporate journal writing, in which they reflect on the research process, into their preparatory work before they go out into the field for their dissertation work. The act of journal writing is a rigorous documentary tool (Janesick, 1998b, 1999). The students keep journals as do the researcher and the participants in the study in their roles as coresearchers on the project. Often, if students elect to do so, interactive journals between researcher and participants as coresearchers are also used. These techniques, borrowed from the arts and the humanities, are extremely helpful for focusing individuals on the project at hand; they also serve as a useful tool for describing the role of the researcher. If keeping journals is not a viable option, letter writing between members of the study, actual short essays, and other written work can provide a useful data set for further understanding in the research project. I like to think of these activities as multidisciplinary. I also use other artistic techniques, such as collages, mounted constructions, and haiku and other poetry, during class activities to get prospective researchers thinking in an artistic frame and stretching that part of their brains. I ask students to dig deep into their souls to create haiku, a traditional Japanese poetry form containing only 17 syllables, about their work in their research projects. Here are two haiku examples that appear in my book *Stretching Exercises for Qualitative Researchers* (1998c); the first is my own, and the second was written by Judith Gouwens:

Willingness to fail,
Easing into Silence,
Stumbling upon secrets.

Seeing past happening,
Hearing between words,
Touching heart stories.

This is what I mean by *stretching exercises;* for me, at least, such activities fit with the idea of crystallization.

The Issue of Credibility

The qualitative research literature contains many valuable and useful treatments of the issue of credibility (see, e.g., Eisner, 1991; Lincoln & Guba, 1985; Patton, 1990). Basically, qualitative researchers have been patiently responding to questions usually formulated from a psychometric perspective. Most often, questions addressed to qualitative researchers are constructed from the psychometric paradigm and revolve around the

68

trinity of validity, reliability, and generalizability, as if there were no other linguistic representations for questions.

Replacing Validity, Generalizability, and Reliability With Qualitative Referents

Many qualitative researchers have struggled to identify more appropriately how we do what we do. So, rather than take terms from the quantitative paradigm, qualitative researchers have correctly offered alternative ways to think about descriptive validity and the unique qualities of case study work. In order to explain this, I rely on experience and the literature. The description of persons, places, and events has been the cornerstone of qualitative research. I believe it will remain the cornerstone, because this is the qualitative researcher's reason for being. What has happened recently, as Wolcott (1990a, 1995) reminds us, is that the term *validity*, for example, which is overspecified in one domain, has become confusing because it is reassigned to another. Validity in the quantitative arena has a set of technical microdefinitions, and the reader is most likely well aware of those. Validity in qualitative research has to do with description and explanation and whether or not the explanation fits the description. In other words, is the explanation credible? In addition, qualitative researchers do not claim that there is only one way of interpreting an event. There is no one "correct" interpretation.

By applying the suggestions of Lincoln and Guba (1985) and others, we may cross-check our work through member checks and audit trails. As a rule, in writing up the narrative, the qualitative researcher must decide what form the member check will take. For example, quite often, participants in a study move, leave the area, or request that they omit being part of the member check. The researcher needs to find a way to allow for the participants to review the material one way or another. For years, anthropologists and sociologists have incorporated a kind of member check by having an outsider read their field notes and interview transcripts (see Janesick, 1998b). This current variation is a good one, for educational research is always public, open to the public, and in many cases funded under federal mandates. Implicit in the member check directive, however, is the psychometric assumption that the trinity of validity, generalizability, and reliability, all terms from the quantitative paradigm, are to be adhered to in research. I think it is time to question that trinity and the use of psychometric language, and in fact to replace that language with language that more accurately captures the complexity and texture of qualitative research. The excellent suggestions of Flick (1998), Lincoln and Guba (1985), Janesick (1994a), and Wolcott (1995), to name a few, offer us heuristic tools to reconceptualize this space. There is no need for us to go over again and again those terms that more correctly apply to another paradigm.

Wolcott (1990a, 1995) presents provocative discussions about seeking and rejecting validity. He argues for understanding the absurdity of validity by developing a case for no single "correct" interpretation. Dancers and choreographers know this as well. Even, for example, if we consider the minuet, with its set movements and prescribed gestures, one dancer's arm movements may be very different from another's, even as both are dancing the same dance. Similarly, Donmoyer (1990) makes an even stronger case for rejecting traditional notions of generalizability for those researchers in education and human services who are concerned with individuals and the meaning in their lives. Donmoyer argues that traditional ways of thinking about generalizability are inadequate. He does not eschew generalizability altogether; for example, bureaucrats and policy makers seem to prefer aggregated numbers about certain social conditions, but only because no one has taken the time to offer them sensible or viable alternatives. In fact, the research community is often silent on such points. Is it time for the research community to assert itself and offer bureaucrats and policy makers some range of options for understanding the social settings under study? For the needs of the bureaucrats, the old notions of generalizability seem to make sense, if only for expediency. On the other hand, for those of us who are interested in questions of meaning and interpretation in individual cases—the kind of research done in education and human services and in the arts and humanities—traditional thinking about generalizability falls short, and in fact may do serious damage to individual persons. The traditional view of generalizability limits the ability to reconceptualize the role of social science in education and human services. In addition, the whole history of case study research in anthropology, education, sociology, and history stands solidly on its merits. In fact, the value of the case study is its uniqueness; consequently, reliability in the traditional sense of replicability is pointless here. I hope that we can move beyond discussions of this trinity of psychometrics and get on with the discussion of powerful statements from carefully done,

70

rigorous long-term studies that uncover the meanings of events in individuals' lives.

Somehow we have lost the human and passionate element of research. Becoming immersed in a study requires passion: passion for people, passion for communication, and passion for understanding people. This is the contribution of qualitative research, and it can only enhance educational and human services practice. In the other paradigm, people are taken out of the formula and, worse, are often lumped together in some undefinable aggregate as if they were not individual persons. In the qualitative arena the individual is not only inserted into the study, the individual is the backbone of the study. We can take a lesson about this from dance and choreography. It would be difficult indeed to find a dancer or choreographer who lacks passion for his or her work, or who looks away from the individual person who is part of the dance. For too long we have allowed psychometrics to rule our research and subsequently have decontextualized individual persons. By depersonalizing the most personal of social events, education and human services, we have lost our way. Now it is time to return to a discourse on the personal, on what it means to be alive. We need to capture the lived experience of individuals and their stories, much like the choreographer who crafts a dance.

◆ Meaning and Choreography: Revisiting Minuets and Improvisations

> *We had the experience but missed the meaning.*
> *And approach to the meaning restores the experience*
> *In a different form*
>
> —T. S. Eliot

Isn't it remarkable that the entire history of dance has been characterized by a deep division, the division between classical ballet and modern and postmodern forms? What might we learn from this? All arts and sciences draw upon tradition, and a first step in understanding them is to understand their past. Dance and choreography are tied to the past in a peculiar way. Dance and choreography originated from one element of society, the courts of kings and queens. However, as society developed and organized, dividing into tribes, nations, and classes, the function of dance became much more complicated. Its language, steps, and movements no longer only represented kings and queens, but included the dances of ordinary people in the form of folk dances. Dance became divided.

One form of this division survives as folk dance from the ancient primitive thread of communal dances. The other thread emerged from society's ruling class, the court, center of social power. It was not long before ballet became an official lexicon of the court and the court dances a definite class and status symbol. It was not until the 20th century that the ruling influence in dance, ballet, was challenged by a determined, frail woman from Vermont, Martha Graham. The field today in dance is well into a postmodern era, mostly due to choreographers such as Merce Cunningham. Essentially, Cunningham made the following claims (Banes, 1980, p. 6):

1. Any movement can be material for dance.
2. Any procedure can be valid.
3. Any part or parts of the body can be used, subject to nature's limitation.
4. Music, costume, lighting, and dancing have their own separate logics and identities.
5. Any dancer in a company may be a soloist.
6. Any space may be danced in.
7. Dancing can be about anything, but it is fundamentally and primarily about the human body and its movements, beginning with walking.

Cunningham's dances decentralize space and stretch out time. They do away with what is familiar and easy. They are unpredictable. They sometimes do not even turn out as planned. He may use chance methods, such as tossing coins. (Banes, 1980, points out that although this was to be random, the dancers' movements were determined by this chance event.) Chance subverts habits and allows for new combinations and interpretations. Cunningham truly makes the word *radical*, returning to the root, come alive. He preserves continuity and a physical logic to his search for meaning in movement and the desire to tell a story. In thinking about dance as a metaphor for qualitative research design, I find that the meaning for me lies in the fact that the substance of dance is the familiar; walking, running, and any movement of the body. The qualitative researcher is like the dancer or the choreographer, then, in seeking to describe, explain, and make understandable the familiar in a contextual, personal, and passionate way.

◆ Summary, Afterthoughts, and Future Directions

The qualitative researcher's design decisions can be thought of as similar to the dancer's three stages of warm-up, exercises, and cool-down, or, as the choreographer might say, preparation, exploration, and illumination/ formulation. The qualitative researcher makes a series of decisions at the beginning, middle, and end of the study. Qualitative research design has an elastic quality, much like the elasticity of the dancer's spine. Just as dance mirrors and adapts to life, qualitative design is adapted, changed, and redesigned as the study proceeds, due to the social realities of doing research among and with the living. The qualitative researcher focuses on description and explanation, and all design decisions ultimately relate to these acts. Built into qualitative research design is a system of checks and balances that include staying in a setting over time and capturing and interpreting the meaning in individual persons' lives. By staying in a setting over time, the researcher has the opportunity to use crystallization, whereby he or she may view the approaching work in the study through various facets to deepen understanding of what is going on in the study. This allows for multiple ways of framing the problem, selecting research strategies, and extending discourse across several fields of study. This is exactly the opposite of the quantitative approach, which relies on one mind-set, the psychometric, and which prefers to aggregate numbers that are one or more steps removed from social reality. The qualitative researcher is uncomfortable with methodolatry and prefers to capture the lived experience of participants in order to understand their meaning perspectives, case by case. Finally, the qualitative researcher is like the choreographer who creates a dance to make a statement. For the researcher, the story told is like the dance, in all its complexity, context, originality, and passion. In addition, the researcher is, like the dancer, always a part of the research project and, like the choreographer, an intellectual critic throughout the study. Whether or not the dancer is performing a minuet or an improvisation, like the qualitative researcher, she is involved in interpretation. Qualitative research design is an act of interpretation from beginning to end.

73

Future Directions

I am optimistic concerning the future directions in our field in general and in qualitative research design in particular. In looking over the current writings in the arts, humanities, and social sciences, one can only be optimistic. Here are my reasons for this statement.

1. We live in a postmodern world where the old boundaries, voices, and power structures are constantly being questioned. In fact, the locus of psychometric control is eroding, simply because when psychometric practices are called into question, the same old tired arguments are used—they didn't work in the first place. Look at the critics of education, for example: Many of these writers have pointed out that the past half century of educational research has yielded little in the way of results. The public, members of Congress, business executives, and leaders in the field often point out that indeed schools are no better places today than they were, say, 50 years ago, all other factors aside. In fact, the kinds of questions educational researchers have pursued are often termed trivial because they have little to do with teachers, students, and the underlying work of schools. Postmodernists and post-postmodernists (or whatever we end up calling the next wave of critics) have forced us to return to the heart of the matter: individual lives and how they are exploited in organizations on a daily basis. We should all be thankful for the postmodern questions.

2. With the hostile political context in Congress, and the consistent cutting of funds for education and educational research since the Reagan-Bush-Quayle years, researchers are finding fewer dollars for their research projects. Thus they will have to turn to research that relies on historical techniques and archival expertise; they will have to go to libraries and other repositories of information. In general, I see a return to those techniques used by artists and humanitarians. Researchers will be forced to confront historical contexts and, instead of working in big, grant-funded shops, may have to work individually in archives, libraries, and other repositories of written texts.

3. With corporate sponsors stepping in to finance artworks such as public murals, dance concerts, and symphonies, there may be an opportunity for researchers to argue persuasively for corporate sponsorship of oral history, life history, and other narrative projects to document the lived experience of community members. For example, the Disney Corporation

74

funded Julie Taymor's creation and direction of the highly original, imaginative, and successful Broadway hit *The Lion King*. At no time did Disney interfere with the project because of its utter faith in this remarkable artist. I see such developments as expanding our notion of how corporations might work with qualitative researchers at some point in the future.

4. Foundations may also be interested in partnerships with qualitative researchers. Indeed, foundations may continue their support of careful long-term case studies, as the Ford Foundation did with the case studies on immigration captured by Louise Lamphere's (1992) edited volume. The Ford Foundation also funded the research described in later work by Lamphere, Stepick, and Grenier (1994) on restructuring the U.S. economy. This is a positive and important sign that shows how foundations might work with qualitative researchers over extended periods of time to document the narratives of newcomers in the workplace.

5. With the renewed emphasis on communitarianism and the call to re-vision particular communities, individual qualitative researchers may find a growing demand for documentation of the lived experience of key members of given communities through long-term, carefully done studies. A bit of ingenuity and library time can uncover many funding sources, such as civic organizations and foundations, for research in any given community. Each semester, I am called upon to talk to community workers who would like to do oral history projects in the community and are looking for information on finding exemplars in that area.

6. Cultivation of the art of writing, and thus a return to communication, will be central to our future work: writing journals, writing letters, writing sensible e-mail messages. In fact, I teach my students to include in their final research reports written testimony from participants in their projects, in as many forms as possible. Most often, these appear as letters, short essays, and journal entries. After all, in the end, the written narrative is indeed a type of permanent insurrection. Choreographers, other artists, and qualitative researchers are also part of this permanent insurrection.

7. I think there will be a need for researchers to develop their imaginations and to use those imaginations when it comes to designing qualitative research projects. For far too long, research has been for the few, and, in the field of education at least, research is often forgotten as soon as it is reported (with a few exceptions). One of the reasons for this is that research traditionally has been reported without passion or imagination, and in many cases without wisdom. It is time to rekindle the researcher's

imagination. I foresee that those who can use imagination in their work will be a significant force in shaping future research projects.

◆ Notes

1. I went to New York because it is the center of the dance world. From Erick Hawkins I learned that creativity and the body/mind are one, and I was introduced to Eastern thought. Hawkins and all his teachers were inspiring and brilliant persons. From Merce Cunningham and the teachers at Westbeth, I learned to trust the body and to draw upon lived experience in my work as a choreographer. For Cunningham, dance is a *chance* encounter between movement, sound, and light through space. The viewer makes of it what the viewer will. Cunningham pursues the process of dance in a Zen-like manner. He has also been called the anarchist of modern dance as well as the beginning point of the postmodern movement in dance. All dances are grounded in some experience, and all stories that are told about that experience rely on the body, which is the research instrument. The body is the instrument through which life is lived. In dance, the body cannot deny the impulse to express the lived experience. It is virtually impossible for the body to tell a lie or to cover up the truth in the dance. As the painter Salvador Dalí remarked, "Drawing is the honesty of art. There is no possibility of cheating."

2. I first learned of theoretical sampling in my training as an ethnographer of the symbolic interactionist school, by reading Glaser and Strauss (1967). Theoretical sampling is the heart of grounded theory approaches to research. It allows for the use of the constant comparative method in data collection and analysis. Theoretical sampling allows for direction in the study and allows the researcher to have confidence in his or her categories, because they emerge from the data and are constantly and selectively reformulated along the way. The data in any study do not speak for themselves. The researcher must make sense of the data in a meaningful way, and any technique that allows the researcher to find an active way of searching the data is welcome. This is only one of many approaches to qualitative analysis. However, it is most helpful to students who have studied only psychometric approaches to research. This seems to be a transition tool for many who have approached research as a boilerplate activity.

3. Gallaudet University is the only liberal arts university dedicated to educating deaf individuals.

4. Constant comparative analysis allows the researcher to develop grounded theory. A grounded theory is one inductively derived from the study. Data collection, analysis, and theory are related reciprocally. The researcher grounds the theory in the data from statements of belief and behavior of participants in the study. See Glaser and Strauss (1967) and Strauss and Corbin (1990) for more detailed descriptions of grounded theory. It is basically opposite to the use of theory in the quantitative paradigm. Instead of proving a theory, the qualitative researcher studies a setting over time and develops theory grounded in the data. This is only one of many approaches to analysis, but it is a solid one and is especially useful for beginners. To move further, I suggest we look to the arts and humanities, particularly

choreography and writing, to expand our notions of how to make sense of, analyze, and interpret qualitative data.

◆ References

Banes, S. (1980). *Terpsichore in sneakers: Post-modern dance.* Boston: Houghton Mifflin.

Blom, L. A., & Chaplin, L. (1988). *The moment of movement: Dance improvisation.* Pittsburgh, PA: University of Pittsburgh Press.

Bogdan, R. C., & Biklen, S. K. (1992). *Qualitative research for education: An introduction to theory and methods* (2nd ed.). Boston: Allyn & Bacon.

Creswell, J. W. (1997). *Qualitative inquiry and research design: Choosing among five traditions.* Thousand Oaks, CA: Sage.

DeFreese, B. (1996). *A case study of an assistant superintendent.* Unpublished doctoral dissertation, University of Kansas.

Denzin, N. K. (1978). *The research act: A theoretical introduction to sociological methods* (2nd ed.). New York: McGraw-Hill.

Denzin, N. K. (1989). *Interpretive interactionism.* Newbury Park, CA: Sage.

Dewey, J. (1958). *Art as experience.* New York: Capricorn. (Original work published 1934)

Donmoyer, R. (1990). Generalizability and the single-case study. In E. W. Eisner & A. Peshkin (Eds.), *Qualitative inquiry in education: The continuing debate* (pp. 175-200). New York: Teachers College Press.

Eisner, E. (1991). *The enlightened eye: Qualitative inquiry and the enhancement of educational practices.* New York: Macmillan.

Fetterman, D. M. (1989). *Ethnography: Step by step.* Newbury Park, CA: Sage.

Flick, U. (1998). *An introduction to qualitative research: Theory, method and applications.* London: Sage.

Glaser, B. G., & Strauss, A. L. (1967). *The discovery of grounded theory: Strategies for qualitative research.* Chicago: Aldine.

Goetz, J. P., & LeCompte, M. D. (1984). *Ethnography and qualitative design in educational research.* New York: Academic Press.

Gouwens, J. A. (1995). *Leadership for school change: An interview observation study of two Chicago elementary principals.* Unpublished doctoral dissertation, University of Kansas.

Guba, E. G., & Lincoln, Y. S. (1994). Competing paradigms in qualitative research. In N. K. Denzin & Y. S. Lincoln (Eds.), *Handbook of qualitative research* (pp. 105-117). Thousand Oaks, CA: Sage.

Humphrey, D. (1987). *The art of making dances.* Penington, NJ: Princeton Book. (Original work published 1959)

Janesick, V. J. (1982). Of snakes and circles: Making sense of classroom group processes through a case study. *Curriculum Inquiry, 12,* 161-185.

Janesick, V. J. (1994a). The dance of qualitative research design: Metaphor, methodolatry, and meaning. In N. K. Denzin & Y. S. Lincoln (Eds.), *Handbook of qualitative research* (pp. 209-219). Thousand Oaks, CA: Sage.

Janesick, V. J. (1994b). *Of heart windows and utopias: A case study of deaf culture.* Paper presented at the Ethnography in Education Forum, University of Pennsylvania, Philadelphia.

Janesick, V. J. (1998a). The dance of qualitative research design: Metaphor, methodolatry, and meaning. In N. K. Denzin & Y. S. Lincoln (Eds.), *Strategies of qualitative inquiry.* Thousand Oaks, CA: Sage.

Janesick, V. J. (1998b). *Journal writing as a qualitative research technique: History, issues, and reflections.* Paper presented at the annual meeting of the American Educational Research Association, San Diego, CA.

Janesick, V. J. (1998c). *Stretching exercises for qualitative researchers.* Thousand Oaks, CA: Sage.

Janesick, V. J. (1999). A journal about journal writing as a qualitative research technique. *Qualitative Inquiry, 5*(4).

Lamphere, L. (Ed.). (1992). *Structuring diversity: Ethnographic perspectives on the new immigration.* Chicago: University of Chicago Press.

Lamphere, L., Stepick, A., & Grenier, G. (1994). *Newcomers in the workplace: Immigrants and the restructuring of the U.S. economy.* Philadelphia: Temple University Press.

LeCompte, M. D., Millroy, W. L., & Preissle, J. (Eds.). (1992). *The handbook of qualitative research in education.* New York: Academic Press.

Lincoln, Y. S., & Guba, E. G. (1985). *Naturalistic inquiry.* Beverly Hills, CA: Sage.

Marshall, C., & Rossman, G. (1995). *Designing qualitative research* (2nd ed.). Thousand Oaks, CA: Sage.

Maxwell, J. A. (1996). *Qualitative research design: An interactive approach.* Thousand Oaks, CA: Sage.

Miles, M. B., & Huberman, A. M. (1994). *Qualitative data analysis: An expanded sourcebook* (2nd ed.). Thousand Oaks, CA: Sage.

Moustakis, C. (1990). *Heuristic research design, methodology, and applications.* Newbury Park, CA: Sage.

Patton, M. Q. (1990). *Qualitative evaluation and research methods* (2nd ed.). Newbury Park, CA: Sage.

Richardson, L. (1994). Writing: A method of inquiry. In N. K. Denzin & Y. S. Lincoln (Eds.), *Handbook of qualitative research* (pp. 516-529). Thousand Oaks, CA: Sage.

Spradley, J. P. (1979). *The ethnographic interview.* New York: Holt, Rinehart & Winston.

Spradley, J. P. (1980). *Participant observation.* New York: Holt, Rinehart & Winston.

Strauss, A. L., & Corbin, J. (1990). *Basics of qualitative research: Grounded theory procedures and techniques.* Newbury Park, CA: Sage.

Williams-Boyd, P. (1996). *A case study of a full service school: A transformational dialectic of empowerment, collaboration, and commu*nitarianism. Unpublished doctoral dissertation, University of Kansas.

Wolcott, H. F. (1990a). On seeking and rejecting validity in qualitative research. In E. W. Eisner & A. Peshkin (Eds.), *Qualitative inquiry in education: The continuing debate* (pp. 121-152). New York: Teachers College Press.

Wolcott, H. F. (1990b). *Writing up qualitative research.* Newbury Park, CA: Sage.

Wolcott, H. F. (1994). *Transforming qualitative data: Description, analysis, and interpretation.* Thousand Oaks, CA: Sage.

Wolcott, H. F. (1995). *The art of fieldwork.* Walnut Creek, CA: AltaMira.

3

An Untold Story?

Doing Funded

Qualitative Research

Julianne Cheek

◆ The Untold Story

Ever-increasing numbers of articles, book chapters, and even books are available on how to "do" funded research. Although not many of these are written with qualitative research specifically in mind, much of what is stated can be applied to research using qualitative approaches. However,

AUTHOR'S NOTE: I would like to acknowledge the critical but constructive feedback on various drafts of this chapter provided by Yvonna Lincoln, Norman Denzin, Ann Austin, and William Tierney. Their comments have helped me to tighten and focus the discussion. In particular, I would like to thank Yvonna Lincoln for helping me to overcome a dilemma I faced in wanting to create a text that focuses on the practicalities of doing funded qualitative research while at the same time troubling what I perceive as the subtle (and not so subtle) commodification of research. Her suggestion of using Patti Lather's notion of writing in a different register for each perspective helped me to go some way toward meeting the competing demands of reviewers and thus, I hope, to reach the readers of this chapter.

too often the discussion begins at what I see as the middle stage in the process of doing research rather than at the start. For example, working out who to approach for funding, and how this should be done, is as important as knowing how to prepare research proposals or fill in application guidelines. Yet often it is taken for granted that researchers instinctively know how to go about identifying and approaching potential funders. Similarly, most discussions about applying for funding come to an end at the point where the proposal has been prepared and submitted, giving the impression that somehow the research process from there on is smooth sailing—which in my experience it certainly is not. Insights into the process of allocating funding, and ways in which researchers can interact with that process and learn from it, remain very much outside the major focus of conventional literature about doing funded research. Questions that need to be addressed, although more often than not they are ignored, include the following: What are some of the things researchers need to consider before accepting funds? Does accepting funding affect in any way the qualitative research process? What are the ethical issues bound up in both the search and selection process for funding and the actual research itself? What other issues might researchers face while actually conducting funded qualitative research?

Thus, for many would-be researchers, doing funded qualitative research remains shrouded in mystique. In short, it is largely "an unknown story" ("The Leading Edge," 1996). In response to this, what follows is my attempt to make known certain aspects of the story of "doing" funded qualitative research that are seldom told. Consequently, I offer no detailed information as to how to write the various sections of a research proposal. Nor do I address specific research approaches and methods. Rather, I present detailed discussion of those aspects of "doing" funded qualitative research that otherwise may not get attention yet are vitally important to the smooth conduct of a research project. At all times, I try to concentrate on points that I believe have particular relevance to *qualitative* research that is funded.

My aim in writing this chapter is thus to begin to tell a story that for whatever reason tends to remain untold. I do not claim to tell the full story or the only story possible—rather, it is my story, drawn from my experiences and the experiences and writings of others. It is also a story with no end. I hope that readers will be able to add to the story from their own experiences and from understandings they gain from either considering or "doing" funded qualitative research.

◆ Setting the Parameters for the Chapter: The Notion of Funded Qualitative Research

Funded research, particularly funded *qualitative* research, forms the focus of the discussion to follow. Funded research is research carried out with financial support, which can take various forms. The researcher could receive a certain amount of money to be used directly for salaries, equipment, travel, or other expenses identified as having been incurred in carrying out the research. In some cases, support for projects is offered "in-kind": Rather than supplying cash, the funder may choose to provide the researcher with access to specialist staff or equipment as a means of supporting the research. This type of support can be very useful, as it may give the researcher access to resources that otherwise may not be available and without which he or she could not undertake the research. Thus when we talk about *funded* qualitative research, it is not always money that we are talking about.

Each form of support for qualitative research places its own unique demands on both the researcher and the research project. In particular, the amount of freedom the researcher has in terms of the project design and the form the "products" of the research take will vary depending on what type of support is received. For example, when a researcher initiates a project, he or she is free to develop the aims and objectives as well as the general direction of the research. However, in projects that are funded as components of larger studies, such as some evaluation projects, the researcher in all probability cannot assume the freedom to develop the aims and direction of the research to be undertaken.

It is apparent from this introductory discussion that there are a range of ways in which qualitative research might be funded and a number of different purposes that such funded research might serve. Funded qualitative research is not a homogeneous category that can be reduced to a single understanding. In the same way that qualitative approaches to research are varied in focus and purpose, so are funded qualitative projects. Thus it is not possible to provide a single "recipe" to follow for researchers who wish to undertake funded qualitative research. In the remainder of this chapter, I explore some of the issues and questions that may arise for researchers either when they are "doing" funded qualitative research or when they are thinking about the notion of funded qualitative research. Of course, some of what follows is not necessarily unique to qualitative

82

approaches but applies across the board to all research, whether qualitative or not.

Following this section, in which I set the parameters for the chapter and examine the notion of funded qualitative research, the next section explores the craft of attracting funds for qualitative research. In this very practical discussion, I address how researchers can go about identifying and building relationships with funding bodies, approaching potential funders, crafting proposals to request funding, and navigating the application process, including building on initial failure, to attract funds. I then explore issues the researcher may encounter when undertaking funded qualitative research. Most of what I discuss arises from issues that I have had to confront and grapple with while either doing, or contemplating doing, funded qualitative research. Thus the discussion is grounded in the reality of doing such research. Issues to be explored include how funding can affect considerations around the ethics of the research, matters pertaining to the control of the research, and the effect funding might have on the relationships among the various parties involved in the research.

Following that discussion, I make a shift in register (Lather, 1996) to explore the notion of the research "market" and whether or not there is the potential for funded qualitative research to be privileged over unfunded research. In this exploration I aim to trouble the concept of qualitative funded research—not to set up a polemic between unfunded and funded research, but rather to encourage readers to think about their own assumptions about funded research and how such assumptions have embedded within them many taken-for-granteds about the nature of research and research "products." In the concluding section, the various threads that have been woven throughout the chapter are drawn together. I end the chapter where I began—urging readers to think deeply about all aspects of funded qualitative research, not just the "how-to," but issues such as the "use" to which research products will be put.

Finally, in terms of setting the parameters for what is to follow, I wish to state up front the positions (for they are plural) from which I am writing this chapter. To a large extent these positions provide the "con-text," that is, the "text that is 'with' " (Halliday & Hasan, 1989, p. 11) the discussion that occurs. Any analysis of what I have written in this chapter must consider, among other things, the wider processes in its development. Such an analysis must situate the text that is this chapter in terms of the texts that inform and are "with" the main text. In other words, it is important to ask what texts are framing the discussion that occurs in this chapter. On reflecting upon this question, I have identified some of the con-texts that I am aware have affected the text that you are reading now. First, I write from the position of an individual committed to qualitative approaches to research. Second, I write as someone who recognizes that funded qualitative research is not only possible, but actually opens up opportunities that otherwise may not be available to researchers in terms of types of projects, scope of projects, and simply the ability to undertake research that is as person- and time-intensive as many qualitative studies are.

However, equally I write as someone who has discovered many pitfalls when doing funded qualitative studies. Most of these pitfalls could not be predicted, and they forced me to confront some very fundamental questions about what research is for and how much, as a researcher, I am prepared to give up in order to conform to funding requirements. From another position altogether, I write as an academic who has grappled with the requirement to produce performance outcomes measured by, for instance, the amount of funding received for research. I write also as one who has faced the dilemma of whether the funding or the project should assume primary importance. Finally, I write with the aim of consciously trying to avoid setting up any form of polemic in the discussion that is to follow.

Thus I am not arguing for or against doing funded qualitative research—rather, I am exploring what "doing" funded qualitative research might mean for both the researcher and the research. In so doing, I aim to provide practical details for researchers but also to encourage readers to think carefully about the con-texts that are in operation at any point in time, including while they are doing funded qualitative research. Any text has embedded within it assumptions about the reality in question and a certain view that is being conveyed to the reader of the text. This is the subtext or "the hidden script" (Sachs, 1996, p. 633). Put another way, the subtext is "the assumptions that every text makes in presuming it will be understood" (Agger, 1991, p. 112). This chapter has embedded within it a critical subtext that aims to challenge aspects of doing funded qualitative research that can otherwise come to be taken for granted. The chapter should not be read as either for or against funded or any other type of research. Rather, it should be read as a text that takes a particular view of doing funded qualitative research. It is up to the readers how they position themselves with respect to that view.

◆ Getting Started: Turning a
Research Idea Into a Submission for Funding

One of the first things that researchers do when trying to attract funding for a research proposal, or to be in a position to know about contracts/tenders that are offered for various research projects, is to identify potential funding sources. Zagury (1997) has identified six categories of potential funding sources: local community funds, special-purpose foundations, family-sponsored foundations, national foundations, government grants, and corporate foundations and/or corporate funding. It is important to be aware that there are distinct national differences in types and patterns of funding. Hence it may well be that in certain countries some of the above categories of funders are of less significance than in others. However, regardless of the actual mix of funding sources in any particular country or part of a country (for there are regional variations in many nations), it is imperative that researchers "do their homework" with respect to uncovering potential funding sources.

One place for researchers to start is by obtaining publications that list the names of potential funders for research. For example, in Australia one such publication is *The Australian Grants Register,* whose author states that it has been compiled "to give everyone ready access to information concerning grants in Australia, and to enable forward planning so that applications are well prepared" (Summers, 1998, p. vii). It is useful for those beginning to investigate funding sources to investigate what types of grant registers exist in their local contexts. Watching advertisements in newspapers, particularly in the contract/tender section, is another way of identifying potential funding sources, as is getting on the mailing list of the university research office, for those who work in university settings. Another very useful way researchers can get to know about potential funding sources that may not be advertised or appear in any grants register or list is by talking to people who have received funding in areas similar to the proposed research. I have found that, on the whole, people are only too willing to share their experiences. Often they can provide the names of contacts who might be interested in the type of research being considered.

Once potential funding sources have been identified, the real work begins. It is important for the researcher to get as much information as possible about those funding agencies identified as potential sources of support. One way of doing this is to obtain copies of the agencies' funding

85

guidelines and/or annual reports. These documents, among other things, give a good overview of what types of projects the agencies appear to fund and the amount of funding available for projects. From this, the researcher can assess whether the proposed research seems to fit the priorities and interests of the funders concerned.

If, after the researcher has absorbed the documentation from an agency, it remains a potential funder for the research in question, then the researcher will need to approach the agency directly to discuss the research idea. How this is done will vary, depending on the type of sponsor. For example, if the funder calls for proposals on an annual basis, the researcher may initiate contact with the office that deals with those applications, so as to gain information about the process and to introduce both the research and the researcher(s) to the people who are likely to be administratively dealing with the application. Speaking with representatives of the agency can give the researcher insight into the processes and practices of the agency with respect to the way that funding is allocated. Further, it should be possible for the researcher to ascertain more information about what has been funded in the past. The agency may even supply reports of completed research and/or copies of proposals for projects that have been funded. Such documents are invaluable; from them, the researcher can ascertain the format and scope expected of a proposal, and they can help the researcher to formulate ideas in language appropriate to the funder in question. Furthermore, they can enable the researcher to locate the proposed study better in terms of work already done in the area. Situating the research in terms of what has preceded it is crucial; this enables the researcher to better address questions from the funder such as: Can this research be done? Is there a need? Will the research deliver? What is the researcher's expertise? What do others think? (See Zagury, 1997.) It is thus critical that the researcher have personal communication with potential funding bodies, as this can provide insights and advice not readily available elsewhere.

Further, depending on the agency's policy, representatives of the agency may put the researcher in contact with members of the agency's funding decision-making committee. Such contact is invaluable, particularly if members of the committee are not used to proposals oriented toward a qualitative approach to research. As Lidz and Ricci (1990) point out, reviewers and funders, like all of us, have "culturally prescribed ideas about 'real' research" (p. 114). If a particular granting committee seems to have an aversion to funding qualitative research, then it may be necessary for the researcher to look elsewhere for potential funders. At the same time, this does not mean that the researcher should not agitate for change; it is possible to get the composition of panels changed, the better to reflect an appreciation of all types of research. I recently had the experience of being invited onto a granting panel for just this purpose. I found that the other members of the panel, although not opposed to qualitative research as such, simply did not have the expertise to judge the merits of qualitative proposals, given their backgrounds. My task as a member is to provide this input.

Much of what I have discussed above also applies when a researcher approaches a funding agency that does not call for proposals, but that tends to fund research on a more ad hoc basis. One difference is that it may not be immediately obvious to the researcher which person he or she should contact in the sponsor's organization. It is important that the researcher find the right person, in the right section of the organization, to talk to about the intended research and the possibility of funding for it. In this way, the researcher becomes familiar with the organization and the members of the organization get to know the researcher. This is important, as a crucial question for any funding agency is whether it can trust a particular researcher to complete a worthwhile project successfully once the agency has committed money to it.

When speaking to the agency representative, the researcher should present a clear, simple idea that is both researchable and likely to produce valuable benefits and outcomes from the funder's perspective. The researcher might consider submitting a concept paper first, either by mail or in person, before making contact with the individual representative of the organization. The concept paper could include any preliminary work done or data already collected. This would allow the researcher to address the points identified by Bogdan and Biklen (1998) as important in the initiation of contact with funders: "1. What have you done already? 2. What themes, concerns, or topics have emerged in your preliminary work? What analytic questions are you pursuing?" (p. 70).

Accompanying the concept paper should be a statement of the researcher's track record. It is important that the researcher demonstrate that there is every likelihood, based on past experience, of his or her being able to complete the project on time and within budget. Not only is it important to sell the research idea, it is also important to sell the researcher. For instance, the advantages of being associated with a researcher situated in a particular organization may be attractive to the funder. Zagury (1997) provides a useful set of self-reflective questions for the researcher to ask in this situation: "What qualities make my organization the best at what it does? Do we offer our clients/patients/customers something that they cannot get elsewhere, what is this special offering? What strengths does my organization have over our competitors? Are there specific, identifiable and unique capabilities that the funding source can only get from my organization?" (p. 26).

One of the problems facing many researchers is the catch-22 situation of needing a track record to attract funding while not being able to get the funding needed to build up a track record. One way a researcher can get around this is to join a research team that has already established a track record in the same or a closely related area of research, and to work as part of that team. This has the advantage of allowing the researcher to establish contact with the research expertise that is collectively present. It is an ideal way for an individual to learn about the research process in a safe way and can lead to the formation of enduring research relationships between colleagues. Another strategy for building a track record is for the researcher to gain some form of seed funding from their employing organization, which may be less competitive than larger funding bodies and directed to more novice researchers. Such seed funding, although invariably modest in amount, can be enough for a researcher to begin a small research project that can lead to publications and thus provide a foundation on which other research can be built.

What should be evident by now is that gaining funding is not a quick or easy process. Much lead time is often needed for planning and for establishing research credentials and rapport with funding sources. It all takes time, a lot of energy, and, above all, courage. There will be the inevitable failures, and it is very difficult not to take these personally. However, in my experience, persistence does pay off.

Other researchers can provide valuable advice and support throughout this process. As I pointed out previously, many research textbooks begin their discussions of how to gain funding by talking about proposal writing. This, I believe, is nowhere near the beginning. The strategies I have just discussed—those the researcher must employ to get to the point where he or she can write a proposal for a specific funding agency—represent, in my opinion, the actual start of "doing" funded qualitative research.

The Next Step:
Crafting a Proposal for Funding

Having identified a potential funder, the researcher must take the next step—crafting a proposal to seek funding for the research. I use the word *crafting* deliberately here, because proposal writing is a craft requiring a unique set of skills, most of which are learned as a result of practice. Writing a proposal involves shaping and tailoring the research idea to fit the guidelines or application process imposed by the intended funding agency. Different applications, even for the same proposal, will vary depending on the characteristics and requirements of the funders being approached. When a proposal is written for a potential sponsor's consideration, it is written for a particular audience that has assumptions and expectations of the form a proposal should take and the language it should use. Thus, as I have emphasized before, it is important for the researcher to know that audience and its expectations.

Writing a proposal is to some extent a political process. The researcher will need to consider whether the approach proposed and the likely outcomes of the research "fit" the agenda of the funding body. It is quite reasonable for those who provide funding for research to ask whether or not the proposed project represents an appropriate use of the funds for which they have responsibility. The majority of funders take the allocation of monies very seriously indeed. They have to weigh up the relative merits, from their point of view, of proposals competing for limited resources. Thus it is essential that the researcher submit a proposal that is clear in terms of its purpose and rationale. Are the outcomes of the project stated? Are they important and useful—able to make a difference in people's lives? Some funding bodies may be a little self-serving in their reasons for funding specific proposals, but, on the whole, funders do make a genuine effort to fund worthy research proposals, and most treat the selection process very seriously.

In the following discussion, I draw on my own experience in preparing proposals to share some insights into the *process* of formulating the application. I place particular emphasis on issues and problems that qualitative approaches may pose for the researcher attempting to craft a proposal. Hence what follows is not about proposal writing, per se, as much has been written about this in many research textbooks (see the appendix to this chapter for information on three such books). Rather, the emphasis is on continuing to expose aspects of what otherwise may remain the untold story of the funding process.

All application forms or guidelines that are put out by research funding agencies contain often unwritten and unspoken assumptions and rules— the subtext of the guidelines. It is important that the researcher excavate these assumptions and understandings so as to work out how best to fit the research proposal to the rules. Hence the researcher must read the guidelines and application form carefully, not only for what they say but also for what they *do not* say. Further, it should go without saying that the researcher must follow these instructions carefully. I have reviewed many research funding applications, and although it may seem somewhat strange, even patronizing, for me to write this, it is all too evident that some researchers do not follow instructions when applying for support. For example, when asked to confine an application to a certain page limit or word limit, the researcher should do so. Similarly, if asked to explain something in lay terms, the researcher should do so. No one is impressed by impenetrable language.

Perhaps most crucial is that the researcher follow instructions meticulously with respect to the detail required about the research budget and the way the funds will be used. Many ambitious claims appear in proposals for amounts that are obviously well beyond, or outside, the funding parameters of the grants program in question. Put simply, the researcher must tailor the proposal to the guides, not the guides to the proposal. Asking colleagues to read their draft proposals and provide critical comment is one strategy employed by many successful researchers to ensure that their proposals closely approximate the guidelines.

One issue that faces many researchers writing applications for funding for qualitative research is that their research approaches may not fit the guidelines in terms of the language used. For instance, I have been confronted with application forms asking me to write sections on, for example, the hypotheses to be tested. My response has been to write in terms related to the qualitative approaches that I am using and to discuss why it is not appropriate to state hypotheses in this particular study. I make the point that there are issues or problems driving the research, rather than hypotheses, which assume a certain research orientation. However, I have noticed that many application guides and forms have begun to develop language that is more inclusive of different research approaches. For example, guidelines may ask that a proposal include a discussion of considerations to do with "sample size/participant selection," where once the requirement would simply have been "sample size."

Where guidelines remain inflexible in terms of the language used, this may well be a good indication that the funding body is not suitable after all to support qualitative approaches. This is another reason why it is useful for the researcher to find out as much as possible about the funding body that will be the "audience" for the proposal and to consider what that audience's expectations are likely to be. Apart from the organization itself, this also applies to the specific assessors of the proposal (who may act in a consulting role from elsewhere). What might reviewers of the proposal be looking for? If they are not particularly familiar with qualitative techniques, will they still be able to work out clearly what is actually going to happen in the proposed study, how, and why? It is vital that the researcher address any concerns they may have, especially questions pertaining to what they might term *validity* and *reliability*. The researcher must stand, as it were, on the other side of the process, looking in, to consider how assessors are likely to view the proposal. This is an important principle for the researcher to consider when he or she is asked to provide names of assessors whom the funding agency might approach. The researcher needs to put as much thought into this as he or she puts into the actual development of the proposal.

A key point for the researcher to bear in mind is that any research proposal, qualitative or not, must formulate a clear issue or question—the initial idea that provided the impetus for the research must have been transformed into a researchable focus. Schutt (1996) provides certain criteria that he believes can be used, regardless of the research approach employed, to distinguish what he terms "good research questions from mediocre ones. A good research question will be *feasible* within the time and resources available, it will be *socially important,* and it will be *scientifically relevant*" (p. 35). The rest of the proposal must unpack that research question and demonstrate how the approach to be taken will enable it to be answered. The proposed research must be contextualized in terms of what has preceded it. The study must be situated in terms of what others are doing, and how this research links to that. It must be justified in terms of approach and design, having a clear direction and focus with clearly achievable outcomes in line with the funder's priorities and stated goals. The credentials of the researcher or research team will also need to be established.

The amount of information the researcher needs to give about the research design, analysis, and data collection will be in part determined by the format of the guides or application form. However, it will also be determined by whether the reader of the proposal can clearly understand from the document what is intended for the study and why. More information does not necessarily mean a better proposal. As stated previously, one of the best ways for the researcher to get a sense of the level of detail required is by obtaining copies of proposals that have already been successful with certain funding bodies. If that is not possible, then the researcher could ask those who have gained funding to provide copies of their proposals, or at least to engage in discussion about the development process.

Once the researcher has written and submitted the proposal, it is important that he or she ascertain the timelines involved and the procedures followed by the decision-making person/committee. In other words, it is important that the researcher gain insight into the agency's process of allocating funds. Such insight will prepare the researcher to expect a response in a certain format within a set time and will inform any necessary follow-up.

When the decision about funding is finally made, there are usually three possible outcomes. The request may be successful; in this case the researcher receives funding and the research commences as soon as all appropriate permissions, such as ethics clearance, are obtained. Another possible outcome is that the researcher may be asked to add or change something—for instance, to supply more information about one or more aspects of the proposal. This should be interpreted as a positive sign; more often than not it means that the funder is considering the request seriously and feels it has some merit, but requires clarification about certain aspects of it. As another example, the decision-making committee may ask the researcher to consider linking up with another researcher or group of researchers who have applied for funding on a similar project. It is important that the researcher think carefully about such a request, for, although collaboration has many benefits, it requires much goodwill and give-and-take to work successfully.

In another version of this outcome, the researcher may be asked if the study could be conducted with a reduced budget and, if so, how. This is not unusual. Sometimes funders have set amounts to allocate; if a proposed study is toward the end of the list of projects an agency wishes to fund, it may be able to offer only a proportion of the funds requested. It is important that the researcher think carefully about whether to accept such funding. I believe that funded research should not be attempted without adequate support for the activities necessary to the research. It is very tempting to accept any funding offered, but inadequate funding can lead to all sorts of problems in actually doing the research. Clearly, the process of securing research funding poses moral issues, not only about the wise use of funds, but also about the wisdom of whether or not to accept funds in the first place.

The third possible outcome is one that is becoming all too common, given the increasing competition for grants—namely, the request for funding is rejected. If this happens, it is important that the researcher get as much feedback as possible. He or she should make an appointment to speak to the Chair of the committee or a representative of the trust/foundation making the decision and use that meeting to find out as much as possible. Copies of the reviewers' reports may be made available; these often contain very useful critiques that can help the researcher in preparing the proposal for resubmission. If it is not possible for the researcher to see these reports, then he or she may be able to request a list of the projects that *were* successful; this may shed some light on whether the researcher's idea did in fact match the funding priorities of the funder. If all this fails and no feedback at all is available, then the researcher should ask those researchers who *have* been funded to review the unsuccessful proposal and help in debriefing the process just undergone. Talking it through may help the researcher to see things he or she can do differently the next time.

In many grants programs in Australia, the success rate is below 20%. Such low success rates are increasingly the case in most countries, as the competition for shrinking funding sources grows relentlessly. This means that it is much more likely for researchers *not* to gain funding than to be successful. Researchers should not take rejection personally, but should build on it. It may simply be the case that there is not enough money; this does not necessarily reflect on the personal worthiness of the researcher. Nevertheless, research proposals do take much time and effort to complete, and it is hard to cope with constant rejection. Remember that no researcher is alone. By keeping contact with others and setting in place the strategies outlined so far in this chapter, they can maximize their chances of success.

◆ Issues That May Arise in the "Doing" of Funded Qualitative Research

I turn now to a consideration of some of the issues that may arise when the researcher is "doing" funded qualitative research. The issues discussed in this section are not the only issues that may confront the researcher; I have chosen these because they seem to me to have particular relevance to funded qualitative research. Put another way, I believe that a funded qualitative study puts a particular "spin" on the issues. The discussion to follow is structured around three interrelated sets of issues. The first group of issues have to do with the ethics of research, including some fundamental questions for the researcher to consider when thinking about accepting funding. The next group of issues pertain to the question of who controls the research and how this can pose unique dilemmas for the funded qualitative researcher. The issues in the third group focus on the effects that doing funded qualitative research can have on relationships among the various players in the research enterprise.

Ethical Considerations for Researchers "Doing" Funded Qualitative Research

The first, and central, ethical consideration for a researcher thinking about doing funded qualitative research is whether or not to apply to a particular funding agency. The researcher must consider the potentially conflicting agendas of funders, participants, and researchers. For example, at the university in which I work, we have just had a major debate over whether to accept funds from the tobacco industry. The arguments revolve around the ethics of taking money from an industry that is associated with health risks as well as questionable targeting of young people in product promotion. A question was also raised as to what would happen if funds were accepted for research whose findings did not support the tobacco industry in some way. The outcome of the debate was that the university decided, as a general principle, neither to seek nor to accept funding from the tobacco industry. This is just one example; no doubt, there are many more instances of question marks over the ethics of accepting funding from certain industries, agencies, or even governments. Considerations may include whether a particular industry is involved in questionable environmental activities or health practices, or whether it is a multinational company involved in possible exploitation of Third World workforces. Taking money from a sponsor is not a neutral activity. It links the researcher and the research inexorably with the values of that funder.

Another important issue for the researcher to consider early on is whether or not the proposed research should, in fact, be done. Do the potential benefits of the research outweigh the potential harm caused by the research? The notion of harm as interpreted by ethics committees has, at times, in my opinion, become somewhat narrow. These committees tend to place emphasis on more obvious (and still important) ethical issues to do with, for example, anonymity for participants and confidentiality of data, rather than the broader picture of the potential effects on partici-pants of the research findings and actions arising therefrom. Guba and Lincoln (1989) identify, as part of this broader picture of potential harm, "the loss of dignity, the loss of individual agency and autonomy, and the loss of self-esteem that occur upon discovering that one has been duped and objectified" (p. 121). I would argue that this is particularly the case for qualitative research, with its much closer relationship between researcher and researched. I concur with Guba and Lincoln's assertion that harm "has been construed entirely too narrowly. . . . 'harm' is a concept that needs much more consideration, and that could possibly benefit from expanded definition" (p. 121).

Elsewhere, Lincoln (1995) has explored what she terms "emerging cri-teria" for quality in qualitative and interpretive research, and has argued that "nearly all of the emerging criteria are relational, that is they recog-nize and validate relationships between the inquirer and those who partic-ipate in the inquiry" (p. 278). This does not simply mean that the re-searcher communicated well with the participants once the research got under way, or that the participants were involved in decision making once the researcher had defined the issues and the approach to be taken. It is far more than that. Quality involves the *ethics* of the research, and one of the most fundamental questions to be asked is whether or not this research should be done in relation to the broader conception of harm discussed above. Indeed, Lincoln (1995) argues that "standards for quality in inter-pretive social science are also standards for ethics" (p. 287).

When they think about the ethics involved in research, many research-ers immediately think of the process of getting the research approved by the appropriate ethics committees or institutional review boards. Most funding bodies require that evidence of ethics approval be submitted with the application as part of their approval process; or they may make fund-ing conditional upon the receipt of such approval. It is important that the researcher identify the committees he or she needs to approach for approval; there may be several. If the research involves particularly vulnerable and historically exploited groups, such as indigenous peoples, then there is a further requirement for approval from ethics committees that deal specifically with research involving these groups. Not all ethics committees will recognize the approval of other committees, so several ethics applications may be necessary if, for example, a research study spans several sites, such as a group of hospitals. More often than not, these committees require that the research application be made according to their particular guidelines.

The same principles outlined earlier in this chapter about approaching funding bodies apply to working with, and approaching, ethics boards. The researcher must find out as much as possible about the processes used by each review board, and should ask to see examples of proposals that have been accepted. These will help the researcher to get an idea of both the level of detail and the format that the committee requires. The researcher should speak to others who have applied for ethics approval to the committee in question. Ethics boards and committees usually require clear statements about informed consent, guarding from harm and deception, and ensuring the privacy of participants; their focus is usually on the confidentiality of data collected and the anonymity of participants (see Guba & Lincoln, 1989). As Guba and Lincoln (1989) note, such issues often pertain to reasonably conventional safeguards and fairly standard ways of dealing with both data and participants in research.

It is clearly important for researchers undertaking funded qualitative research to remember that they will need to secure ethics approvals. However, gaining clearances can take a great deal of time. Ethics committees may meet only monthly and may require researchers to submit modified proposals to be taken up at future meetings before they grant approval. Researchers should take into consideration the potential for delays in obtaining ethics approval when they are developing the timelines for funded projects.

One problem that is somewhat unique to qualitative research (but not necessarily to funded qualitative research) is that ethics committees often take detailed interest in exactly who participants will be, how they will be approached, and what they will be asked if, for example, interviews are being used. In some qualitative studies, it may not be possible for the researchers to be specific about such information. I have found it useful to write to ethics committees and explain how I have filled in their forms and why I have done so, especially with respect to not being able to conceptualize certain details of the research fully until the study is actually under way. It is possible to state how the initial approach will be made to participants, and to outline the general principles that will be employed regarding confidentiality, and so forth. I have also stated that, if the committee members would find it useful, I would be happy to talk about the research and discuss any concerns they might have. I have found most committees willing to listen and quite reasonable. However, sometimes compromises have been necessary. There have been instances where interim approval was given and I had to submit details progressively as they became available. Although this was tedious, I do not believe it compromised the research in any way.

Another time, a student of mine and I were dealing with an extremely traditional hospital's medical ethics committee, for which the proposal in question was the committee members' first experience of a certain approach, and thus something of a culture shock. We agreed to change the word *participant* to *patient* on the consent forms and information sheets that would be given to participants in the research. We had to think deeply about this, but in the end considered that it was more important for the research to go forward than to take a stand on this issue. However, this does raise an important point. At times, researchers may find themselves asked to modify proposals in ways that appear to compromise the approaches they wish to take. In instances like this, they must make what I would argue is a fundamentally ethical decision: Can the research proceed under these conditions? Grappling with such decisions is often another part of the untold story of doing funded qualitative research.

Who Controls the Research?

A related set of issues emerges from a consideration of who controls the qualitative research that is funded. It is a fact that, once the researcher has accepted funding for research, he or she is not an entirely free agent with respect to the direction and outcome of that research. However, depending on the policies and attitudes of the funder, the degree of freedom allowed the researcher in carrying out the research (such as changing its direction if the need arises as a result of findings, and talking and writing about the research) may vary considerably. The researcher needs to engage in careful negotiation about the issue of control in the very early stages of the research, as it is often too late once the project is well under way. Yet too often researchers either ignore or are simply unaware of the problems that can arise. Taking funding from someone in order to conduct research is not a neutral act. It implies a relationship with that funder that has certain obligations for both parties. It is important that the researcher discuss with the funder all the expectations and assumptions, spoken and unspoken, that both of them may have about the research.

As an example, one such expectation relates to what can be said about the research, and by whom. Put another way, this is an issue about who actually owns the data or findings that result from the study, and how those data can be used both during and after the study. Some researchers have found themselves in the situation of not being able to write about the research in the way they want to, if at all. For example, I carried out a funded piece of research, using qualitative approaches, that produced four main findings, each of which was accompanied by a series of recommendations. When I submitted the report, I found that the funding body was willing to act on two of the findings, as the agency believed these were within their statutory remit, but not on the others. Although this seems reasonable at one level, I was concerned that the remaining two findings were in danger of being lost. The recommendations associated with those findings were important and needed to be acted on. I was even more concerned when the funder wanted to alter the report to include only the two findings the funding body believed were relevant to it. Fortunately, a solution was found whereby the report was framed to highlight the findings considered relevant by the funder while making reference to the other findings as well. In some ways, this may seem like an uneasy compromise, but at least the whole picture was given with respect to the findings. In retrospect, I realize that I was somewhat naïve in not anticipating the issue arising as to what data and findings should or could be included in a study, or what data, conversely, might be excluded. I am now much more careful to negotiate how the findings of a study will be reported, the use of the data, and my rights to publish the study findings in full, myself, in scholarly literature.

A related issue can arise when the findings of a study do not please the funder. What happens if the findings are, or have the potential to be, beneficial to the participants but may displease the sponsor? Who has the say as to whether or not these findings will be published? As Parahoo (1991) points out, "Too often those who control the purse tend to act in their own interests when they veto the publication of research. To others this is an abuse of power and office, and a waste of public money" (p. 39). This is a particularly important question if the research involves working with groups that are relatively powerless or disenfranchised. A real dilemma is posed for qualitative researchers, in that much of their research is built on developing relationships of trust with participants. Researchers have found themselves in the position of not being able to publish or even disseminate results in any way because of contractual arrangements they have entered into when accepting funds. When a contract is finalized, the researcher should check it carefully to be sure that he or she is comfortable and can live with the conditions set down.

Issues such as these make it clear that the researcher must invest careful thought in deciding whether or not to accept money from a particular funder. Funders, just like researchers, have motives for wanting research to be done. Some bodies may be entirely altruistic, others less so. Some funders, particularly in the evaluation area, may overtly be funding research to "vindicate policies and practices" (Parahoo, 1991, p. 37). As Guba and Lincoln (1989) note in writing about evaluation studies, "Often evaluation contracts are issued as requests for proposals just as research contracts are; in this way, winning evaluators are often those whose definitions of problems, strategies, and methods exhibit 'fit' with the clients' or funders' values" (p. 124). This is why Bogdan and Biklen (1998) assert, "You can only afford to do evaluation or policy research [or, I would add, any funded form of qualitative research] if you can afford not to do so" (p. 209).

None of this is to suggest that qualitative researchers should not seek funding. Rather, what it does suggest is the need for close self-scrutiny on the part of any researcher considering taking funding for a project. It is important for the researcher to consider whether it is possible for him or her to retain integrity and independence as a researcher when paid by someone else or provided with the support to do research. Key questions for the researcher to ask are, How much freedom will I lose if someone else is paying? How do I feel about this? Funding for projects is a means to an end; it must not become an end in itself.

The final issue I want to consider concerning the control of research pertains to the need for clarity about exactly what will be "delivered" to the funder in return for the funding received. What is it that the researcher is contracting with the funder to provide? This is a very important area, as many potential problems arise if both parties involved do not understand this in the same way. It is very easy and tempting for researchers, particularly if they are inexperienced, to underestimate the amount of time and energy needed to conduct research projects. Consequently, they may "over commit" in terms of what they promise to deliver to funders. The researcher must consider carefully what it is reasonable to provide for the funding received and make this explicit to the funder. Time frames should be placed against each deliverable so that both parties are aware of what will be produced and when it can be expected.

Some funders may approach researchers to produce summaries of their research, or to present the findings for them in forums, once the final report has been submitted. It is important for the researcher to distinguish such requests from the core deliverables that form part of the research contract. When faced with such requests, which are really over and above the requirements for the research, I have negotiated with the funders concerned. If the request is to present the findings at a local meeting, then I will usually agree. If, however, I am asked to present the findings at some location further away or if the work otherwise involves expense to myself, I will then claim costs, because they are not covered by the funding received for the project. If I am asked to produce a shortened version of a research report, suitable for a particular audience for whom I had not written the original report, then I will usually agree to do so, but only if the funder provides the necessary editorial support. I make it clear that I do so as a gesture of goodwill, and that I have neither the time nor the resources to physically produce the additional report. I believe it is important to take this position, as otherwise the potential exists for researchers to be exploited, whether intentionally or not. The key to all of this is the researcher's establishment of open and clear communication with the funder from the outset. I have found working with funding bodies, on the whole, to be an enjoyable and mutually satisfying experience.

The Effect of Funding on Relationships in the Research

Qualitative approaches to research are premised on an honest and open working relationship between the researcher and the participants in the research. Inevitably in such studies the researcher spends a great deal of time with participants, getting to know aspects of their world and learning about the way they live in that world. At the center of a good working relationship in qualitative research is the development of trust. Further, as qualitative researchers, we have all dealt with issues such as participants' feeling threatened by the research and therefore concealing information, or participants' being anxious to please us and giving us the information they think we want to hear or that they think we need to know. These issues can become even more complicated for researchers who are doing funded qualitative research.

When doing funded research it is important for researchers to tell participants who is providing the funding and what that funding is being given for. Successful researchers report the importance of making their own relationship to the funder clear—for example, are they acting as paid employees of the funder or are they independent? Equally crucial to a successful relationship between researchers and participants is that the researchers ensure, and give assurances, that the participants will remain anonymous and that the confidentiality of their individual information will be safeguarded. This is a major concern for some participants, who may believe they will be identified and "punished" in some way by the funder if, for example, the funder is their employer and the participants are critical of the organization. When conducting research in specific settings among specified groups of people, it may be very difficult for researchers to ensure the anonymity of participants. It is crucial that researchers be clear about this issue and that they discuss it with participants, who need to know what will happen to specific information in the project, who will have access to that information, and how their rights to confidentiality are being assured. Individuals may choose not to participate if they have concerns about a particular funder having access to information they have given, or if they question the motives for that funding being given in the first place.

Further, if there are any restrictions on what can or cannot be said about the findings of the research and the research undertaking itself, then it is important for the researchers to make potential participants aware of this as well. Part of the constant process of giving feedback to participants must include feedback about any issues that arise about ownership of the research and the way it will be disseminated. All of this is to empower participants to make informed decisions about whether or not to participate and to give them some idea about the use to which the research is likely to be put. This enables them to be better positioned to follow up the research findings and to have a say in what happens as a result of them. It is a part of valuing all perspectives in the research, and of treating participants as more than simply research objects who are subject to the findings of a research agenda that has been imposed on them.

It is important in a research team that all team members share similar approaches to the issues that have been raised. This needs to be discussed from the outset of the formation of the team, and is just as important to the smooth functioning of the team as the particular expertise each team member brings to the project. There must be trust among team members that decisions made will be adhered to. Further, it is important for team members to talk about how team decisions will be made. Who will control the budget? What happens if there is disagreement about the way the research is proceeding? The involvement of a third party—namely, the funder—makes the need to be clear about these issues all the more imperative. Furthermore, the team needs to have clear guidelines about which member(s) will communicate with the funder and how. Working as part of a research team offers the individual researcher the advantages of a team approach that is multiskilled and often multidisciplinary in focus. However, funding increases the need for good communication in the team and clear understandings of each member's role, both in terms of the research itself and in terms of dealing with the funder. Strategies that research teams can employ to assist in the smooth functioning of funded projects include outlining all members' responsibilities, including their contributions to the final report; drawing up timelines for all members to adhere to; upholding all members' access to support and funds; and holding regular meetings for team members to discuss issues.

Obtaining funding creates another research relationship that needs to be developed during the conduct of the research—namely, that between funder and researcher. All funding bodies require reports about the progress of research projects. When communicating with and reporting to the funder, which often involves reporting to an individual nominated by the funder as a point of contact, it is important that the researcher be honest and up-front. This applies particularly if something has gone "wrong" or if for some reason the research plan has had to be changed. In my experience, funders would much rather find out about these things as they arise than be faced at the end with a project that has not met expectations.

The extent of funding bodies' involvement in research can vary considerably, ranging from researchers' submission of one or two reports a year to a very hands-on approach where a representative of the agency seeks to play an active role in the research undertaken. Whatever approach is adopted, it is important that there be clear communication as to the role each party will play in the research. It is also important for the researcher to clarify that, if research is being carried out in which participants will be known to the representative of the agency, then there may have to be restrictions on access to information put in place, so as to protect the participants' rights to confidentiality. Similarly, if a funder requires that an advisory board be established to provide guidance on the progress and direction of the research, it is important that both researcher and funder understand the parameters within which the board will operate. Often such boards can be invaluable in assisting researchers with broad issues pertaining to the substantive focus of the research. Indeed, many experienced researchers, recognizing the value of advisory boards for helping them to think through aspects of doing their projects, interpreting the findings, and considering the routes for dissemination, may constitute such boards regardless of funder requirements. However, clear understandings must be put in place as to what access, if any, the board can have to specific sets of information collected in the study, especially if board members are connected in any way to the study site and/or to participants.

Thus the funding of research can affect the nature of relationships between the research participants and the researcher. Funded research can also result in the development of a new set of relationships, especially between the researcher/research team and the funding agency, and between the researcher and any other structures the funder may wish to put in place, such as advisory boards. When there is clear communication, these relationships can enhance the research effort and assist its smooth functioning. However, such relationships cannot be taken for granted; all parties involved need to work on them actively. The development of these relationships is another part of the too often untold story of doing funded qualitative research.

◆ "The Research Market": The Potential for Privileging Funded Research

Up to this point, the discussion has focused on the everyday issues and realities confronting the funded qualitative researcher. This chapter, so far, has been unashamedly practical in orientation, but in a way that explores, not just prescribes, strategies with which to approach funded qualitative research. I wish now to change register (Lather, 1996) overtly. In so doing, I shift the focus of the discussion from the practicalities of doing funded qualitative research to a much more macro level—a kind of supercontext where the focus is on larger social issues and forces that impact on the funded qualitative researcher. The shift in register is reflected by my use of a more critical voice, one that probes, challenges, and tests assumptions about what I have termed the research market and the concomitant com-modification of research. As Lather (1996) puts it, "Here the text turns back on itself, putting the authority of its own affirmations in doubt" (p. 533). It is to this task that I now turn.

The late 1990s have seen the emergence of a climate of economic re-straint and funding cuts by governments in most Western countries. These cuts have had severe impacts on the availability of funding for research in that many funding agencies, particularly government departments, no longer have the resources to support research to the extent that they once did. At the same time, educational institutions such as universities have also experienced cuts to their funding. One of the consequences of such cuts to university operating budgets has been the imperative for staff to be able to generate income for the institution. In some cases such income has become part of academics' salaries; in others this income has been fac-tored into the operating budget of the institution to pay for the basic resources needed to continue teaching and research programs. One way in which academics are able to generate income is by winning research grants. This, in some instances, has created a whole new imperative for gaining funding—the funding itself, rather than the research, has become highly prized. Put another way, it is possible that what is becoming impor-tant to some university administrations is the amount of funding gained rather than the contribution of the research and its associated scholarship to new knowledge and problem solving. In such a climate there is the potential to privilege funded research over unfunded research.

Historically there has always been a place for both funded and un-funded research in universities and elsewhere. Some types of research sim-ply have not required funding, yet have been able to produce significant contributions to knowledge for which they have been valued. Further, re-search serves a variety of purposes. On one hand, it can be carried out to investigate a well-defined issue or problem arising in a specific area or field; on the other, it can be conducted to probe or explore what the issues might be in the first place. Research can also be carried out simply for the pleasure of investigating new and different ways of thinking about aspects of our reality. Some research projects might incorporate all of the above. In other words, just as there are a variety of research approaches and asso-ciated techniques, so there are a range of purposes for which research might be carried out. Each research project has its own intended audience who will relate to the assumptions framing the problem to be investigated, as embedded within that piece of research.

However, with the imperative for academics to generate income, there has been a subtle, and at times not so subtle, shift in thinking toward valuing research that is funded more highly than research that is not, simply on the basis of funding alone. As Keat (1991) notes about the United Kingdom, "Academics complain that . . . the value of their research is now being judged by intellectually facile considerations of 'marketability' " (p. 216). Given this, the question can be asked as to whether we are seeing the emergence of what Derrida (1976) terms a binary opposition with respect to funded/unfunded research.

Derrida holds that any positive representation of a concept in language, such as "funded research," rests on the negative representation of its "opposite"—in this case, unfunded research. In a binary opposition there is always a dominant or prior term, and, conversely, there is always a subordinate or secondary term. For example, consider such common binary oppositions as masculine/feminine and reason/emotion. In each case the first-named term is given priority over the second, which is often defined in terms of "not" the dominant. However, as I have noted elsewhere, "the definitional dynamic extends to the primary term as well in that it can only sustain its definition by reference to the secondary term. Thus the definition and status of the primary term is in fact maintained by the negation and opposition of the secondary partner" (Cheek, Shoebridge, Willis, & Zadoroznyj, 1996, p. 189). Derrida points out that binary oppositions are constructions of certain worldviews. They are not natural givens that can be taken for granted. In the instance of funded/unfunded research, it is important to recognize that there is a binary opposition in operation and to explore both how it has come to be and how it is maintained. An interesting way to commence such an exploration is to reverse the binary pairing and note the effect. What is the effect on the way research is viewed and understood if unfunded research assumes primacy and funded research becomes the secondary or derivative term?

In a climate where funded research is assuming ever-increasing importance, the power of funding agencies to set research agendas has increased markedly. As Parahoo (1991) notes: "A successful researcher is sometimes defined by the ability to attract funds, and most researchers know that in order to do so one must submit proposals on subjects which sponsors are prepared to spend money on. This can mean that the real issues that concern practitioners are sometimes ignored" (p. 37). Although it is not unreasonable that sponsors should be able to fund research that is relevant to them, a problem arises if funds are not available for researcher-initiated research in order to address questions that have arisen from the field. If funding alone drives research agendas, then this may infringe on the academic freedom of researchers to pursue topics of importance and interest. As Porter (1997) notes, "Pressure is therefore exerted on academics to tailor their work in order to meet the requirements of funders" (p. 655). Creativity may be sacrificed for expediency in that some research topics will have more currency than others in terms of their likeliness to attract funding. Drawing on Mills (1959), Stoesz (1989) observes that "to the extent that this happens, an enormous problem emerges—social science [read research] becomes a commodity, the nature of which is defined by the bureaucracies of the corporate and governmental sectors" (p. 122).

Further, a trend that is emerging in times of fiscal restraint is for some funding bodies to decline to fund chief investigators' salaries, arguing that the salaries of these researchers are already paid by the institutions at which they work (such as universities) and therefore the funders should not have to pay second, supplementary salaries. This is the case in Canada and in Australia, to give but two instances, with respect to many major grants programs. In my experience, one interesting effect of the reluctance of many funding bodies to pay investigators' salaries has been the emergence of a trend in universities, in many parts of the world, to insist that researchers put in their research budgets an amount (for example, in Australia usually somewhere between 10% and 30% of the grant total) to be paid to the university for indirect costs, such as infrastructure charges for the project. The argument is that universities should not be asked to supplement funding bodies by providing "free" research infrastructure. This has led to problems for researchers in some grants programs as funders have refused to fund such levies, agreeing to award funding only for the amount requested minus the levy. This, of course, leaves the researchers in a dilemma—should they take the reduced funds, knowing that the levy will still be taken from them, and thereby effectively ensure that the research remains underfunded?

The emerging emphasis on funded research, in terms of its ability to produce income for institutions, has, in my opinion, led to an increasing view of research as a commodity to be bought and sold on the research market. Information and data from research projects are seen as "products" to be traded on this market and sold to the highest bidders. Researchers increasingly find themselves struggling with the often competing demands of research as the generation of new knowledge and research as a commodity to be traded on the marketplace. Turpin and Hill

(1995) describe this as a boundary struggle between the different domains of research activity:

> On the one hand researchers are concerned with the generation and transfer of new knowledge through research and teaching, on the other hand they are encouraged through various policy mechanisms, to be concerned with securing and maintaining market niches for selling that knowledge. The two domains of work are dominated by different sets of reward criteria, different sets of objectives, different ways of measuring success, different modes of communication. . . . in short they are culturally distinct. (p. 185)

This struggle is exacerbated by a trend in which the act of winning funding for research is itself viewed as currency to be traded in the academic marketplace. For example, promotion and tenure committees in many universities see the amount of funding individuals have received as a measure of research success. This has the effect of maintaining the binary opposition of funded/unfunded research in that performance in terms of funded research is valued whereas the absence of funding—that is, unfunded research—is not. Further, large quantitative studies usually require more funds than do most qualitative projects, which are often on a smaller scale and do not require expensive equipment. There is a very real danger that using amount of funding to measure things for which it was never intended, such as academic performance, will have the effect of making the pursuit of funds an end in itself rather than the means to an end, as it was always intended to be.

The idea of research being perceived as a commodity, along with the trend to privilege funded research over unfunded research, poses some particular dilemmas for qualitative researchers. For instance, it is still true that, despite progress, most funding in some disciplinary fields, such as medicine, is attracted by research projects using traditional scientific methods. As Gilbert (1995) points out, "The present forms of truth and rationality determine the issues acceptable for research monies and for publication" (p. 869). This means that it is harder in these fields to gain funding for qualitative research. If success in gaining funding is used, rightly or wrongly, to measure performance and to put a value on research, then there is a real danger that qualitative research could be marginalized, because it is not as easy to attract funds for research using qualitative approaches.

All of this is to bring into sharp focus some very fundamental questions that qualitative researchers need to grapple with. These questions relate to the background assumptions about research and research performance that are driving many research agendas and researchers. Assumptions about how research performance should be measured and valued need to be exposed. They can then be considered and explored in terms of the effects they have on the two notions of what research is for and what the nature of a research product should be. Funding is important in that it enables research to be carried out that would otherwise not happen because of resource constraints. It is not funding itself that is the issue here; rather, it is the uses to which the act of gaining funding is being put, apart from enabling specific pieces of research to proceed. I am not arguing against funded qualitative research—far from it. What I am suggesting is that researchers need to think about their own assumptions about funded research and how such assumptions have embedded within them many taken-for-granteds about the nature of research and research products. Research is not, and must not be reduced to, a commodity to be sold to the highest bidder in a market driven by expediency. Resisting such reductionism poses one of the biggest challenges facing qualitative researchers—indeed, all researchers—as we enter the new millennium.

◆ Conclusion: Thinking Deeply About Doing Funded Qualitative Research

Doing funded qualitative research is more than developing a proposal or carrying out a piece of research. It is a process that a researcher undertakes, involving various stages. The process begins with the researcher's identification of potential funding sources for the project, initiation of contact with the potential funder, and development of a proposal for funding; only then does it move to the stages in which the research is carried out and the findings are disseminated. Each of these stages involves a number of issues that qualitative researchers must face in order to maintain their own integrity and that of the research. Facing these issues is as much a part of "doing" funded qualitative research as the actual fieldwork itself.

At the same time, it is imperative that researchers think deeply about all aspects of doing qualitative research, from developing the idea right through to the "use" to which the final product is put. In order to think deeply, researchers must consider the con-texts that accompany research as text and the effects that these can have on the way the research is viewed. This is particularly crucial in a climate where, increasingly, funded research is enjoying a privileged status because of the income it provides for cash-strapped institutions. Doing funded qualitative research is not a neutral and value-free activity. Researchers must constantly examine their motives for doing the research and the motives of funding bodies in funding the research.

However, given this, as I have emphasized throughout this chapter, in no way should my writing be viewed as arguing against "doing" funded qualitative research. Quite to the contrary—used well, funding can enhance and enable projects to proceed that otherwise could not do so. Satisfying relationships can be developed between funders and researchers. Participants can benefit from research that has been funded. Rather, what I have been arguing for is the ability to do funded qualitative research in a way that retains the integrity of the researcher, the participants, the research project, *and* the funding body.

At the outset of this chapter, I stated that my aim in writing about "doing" funded research was to tell a story that has largely remained untold. An accompanying aim has been my attempt to create, at least in part, a "multivoiced text that moves through different registers and that speaks to multiple audiences" (Lather, 1996, p. 525). I hope that readers of this chapter will be able to take up their own position(s) with respect to the position(s) I have taken. I have told my part of the story, it is now up to readers to add their stories to it.

♦ Appendix:
Annotated Bibliography of Works on Proposal Writing

Locke, L. F., Spirduso, W. W., & Silverman, S. J. (1993). *Proposals that work: A guide for planning dissertations and grant proposals* (3rd ed.). Newbury Park, CA: Sage.

This book has two major parts: Part I focuses on writing the proposal, and Part II contains four specimen proposals—for an experimental design, a qualitative study, a quasi-experimental design, and a funded grant. The book appears to be aimed at postgraduate students or beginning researchers. The first part covers a range of topics, including the basic elements of a proposal, ethical issues, developing a thesis/dissertation, content and form of the proposal, asking for money, and preparing a grant proposal. One chapter, subtitled "Different

Assumptions," is dedicated to the preparation of proposals for qualitative re-search. The authors state that it is written with an emphasis on experimental and quasi-experimental studies, mainly because this was the "most economical method for assisting readers who have a wide variety of research interests" (p. xii).

Ogden, T. E., & Goldberg, I. A. (1995). *Research proposals: A guide to success* (2nd ed.). New York: Raven.

This book is a how-to guide to preparing grant proposals for the National Institutes of Health (NIH). As the title suggests, it concentrates on how to obtain funding for grants, especially for experimental, scientific research proposals. It discusses topics such as the review process, enhancing proposal effectiveness, and NIH programs and procedures. It is divided into three sections: "Basic Grantsmanship," "Advanced Grantsmanship," and "Advice for New Scientists."

Reif-Lehrer, L. (1995). *Grant application writer's handbook*. Boston: Jones & Bartlett.

This volume is a comprehensive guide to preparing successful NIH and National Science Foundation grants in the United States. The author goes beyond simply detailing how to write a research grant proposal. Sections are "Getting Started," which includes where to get information about available grants; "Understanding the Review Process"; "Parts of the Grant Application"; "Planning the Research Plan"; "Writing the Research Plan"; "Submitting and Tracking the Grant Application"; "Summary Statements, Rebuttals, and Revisions"; and "Some Final Words." Finally, the book includes extensive appendices with details of specific grant awards to apply for and examples of various proposal sections.

◆ References

Agger, B. (1991). Critical theory, poststructuralism, postmodernism: Their sociological relevance. *Annual Review of Sociology, 17,* 105-131.

Bogdan, R. C., & Biklen, S. K. (1998). *Qualitative research for education: An introduction to theory and methods* (3rd ed.). Boston: Allyn & Bacon.

Cheek, J., Shoebridge, J., Willis, E., & Zadoroznyj, M. (1996). *Society and health: Social theory for health workers*. Melbourne: Longman Australia.

Derrida, J. (1976). *Of grammatology* (G. C. Spivak, Trans.). Baltimore: Johns Hopkins University Press.

Gilbert, T. (1995). Nursing: Empowerment and the problem of power. *Journal of Advanced Nursing, 21,* 865-871.

Guba, E. G., & Lincoln, Y. S. (1989). Ethics and politics: The twin failures of positivist science. In E. G. Guba & Y. S. Lincoln, *Fourth generation evaluation* (pp. 117-141). Newbury Park, CA: Sage.

Halliday, M. A. K., & Hasan, R. (1989). Context of situation. In M. A. K. Halliday & R. Hasan (Eds.), *Language, context, and text: Aspects of language in a social-semiotic perspective* (pp. 3-14). Geelong, Victoria, Australia: Deakin University Press.

Keat, R. (1991). Consumer sovereignty and the integrity of practices. In R. Keat & N. Abercrombie (Eds.), *Enterprise culture* (pp. 216-230). London: Routledge.

Lather, P. (1996). Troubling clarity: The politics of accessible language. *Harvard Educational Review, 66*, 525-545.

The leading edge. (1996). *A Closer Look, 25*(6), 4.

Lidz, C. W., & Ricci, E. (1990). Funding large scale qualitative sociology. *Qualitative Sociology, 13*(2), 113-126.

Lincoln, Y. S. (1995). Emerging criteria for quality in qualitative and interpretive inquiry. *Qualitative Inquiry, 1*, 275-289.

Mills, C. W. (1959). *The sociological imagination.* New York: Oxford University Press.

Parahoo, K. (1991). Politics and ethics in nursing research. *Nursing Standard, 6*(1), 35-39.

Porter, S. (1997). The degradation of the academic dogma. *Journal of Advanced Nursing, 25*, 655-656.

Sachs, L. (1996). Casualty, responsibility and blame: Core issues in the cultural construction and subtext of prevention. *Sociology of Health and Illness, 18*, 632-652.

Schutt, R. (1996). *Investigating the social world: The process and practice of research.* Thousand Oaks, CA: Pine Forge.

Stoesz, D. (1989). Provocation on the politics of government funded research: Part 1. *Social Epistemology, 4*(1), 121-123.

Summers, J. (1998). *The Australian grants register.* Melbourne: Australian Scholarly Publishing.

Turpin, T., & Hill, S. (1995). Researchers, cultural boundaries, and organizational change. *Research in the Sociology of Work, 5*, 179-204.

Zagury, C. S. (1997). Grant writing: The uncertain road to funding: Part V. From the other side: How reviewers look at proposals. *Alternative Health Practitioner, 3*(1), 25-29.

4

Performance Ethnography

A Brief History and Some Advice

Michal M. McCall

◆ The term *performance* entered art critical and academic discourses in the 1970s, to name a new visual art form and to distinguish dramatic scripts from particular productions of them—that is, from performances onstage.[1] Similar terms were *events* and *happ*enings in the 1950s and 1960s and *body art* and *experimental theater* in the 1970s and 1980s. Conventional histories locate the roots of performances, events, happenings, body art, and experimental theater in the futurist, dadaist, and surrealist movements of the early 20th century. Here, in excerpts from two such histories, are an overview and brief descriptions of those movements.

Overview

Members of the historic avant-garde movement throughout Europe (ca. 1900-1935) wanted to propose an "other" theatre, different in every way from what had gone before: a theatre freed from the chains of literature, constituted as an autonomous art form; a theatre which did not imitate a reality which actually existed, but which created its own reality; a theatre which nullified the radical split between stage and spectator and which developed new forms of communication between them, so that the chasm between art (theatre) and life, so typical and characteristic of bourgeois society, might be bridged. (Fischer-Lichte, 1997, p. 115)

Futurism

The launching of futurism in 1909 was a typical example, with a manifesto by Filippo Marinetti in . . . *Le Figaro.* Futurism is in fact rather better known for its manifestos than for its actual artistic achievements, but both contributed importantly to the performance tradition of this century. The interest of the futurists in movement and change drew them away from the static work of art and provided an important impetus for the general shift in modern artistic interest from product to process, turning even painters and sculptors into performance artists. (Carlson, 1996, p. 89)

Dadaism

[From the] founding of the Cabaret Voltaire in 1916 in Zurich . . . [all] dadaist activities were directed at the spectator. While at first they only aimed to "épater le bourgeois," these ventures occurred increasingly in the form of an organized assault on the audience, a "strategy of revolt" . . . aimed at challenging and reexamining the purely passive attitude of expectation and customary practices of spectator reception. In this way, they attempted to dissolve the discrepancies between art and society for the duration of the performance. (Fischer-Lichte, 1997, pp. 267-268)

Surrealism

Perhaps the most important contribution of the surrealist movement to subsequent experimental theater and performance was the theoretical writing of Antonin Artaud, which exerted an enormous influence in the 1960s and 1970s. In his visionary *The Theater and Its Double,* Artaud advanced his own powerful version of the argument found throughout the early twentieth-century avant-garde that the traditional theatre had lost contact with the deeper and more significant realms of human life by its emphasis on plot, language, and intellectual and psychological concerns. The subjugation of the theatre to the written text must be ended, to be replaced by a spectacle of "direct" and "objective" action: "cries, groans, apparitions, surprises, theatricalities of all kinds, magic beauty of costumes taken from certain ritual models; resplendent lighting, incantational beauty of voices, the charms of harmony, rare notes of music, colors of objects, physical rhythm of movements . . . masks, effigies yards high, sudden changes of light." (Carlson, 1996, pp. 91-92)

◆ Events

An *Untitled Event* produced in 1952 at Black Mountain College in North Carolina by composer John Cage, dancer Merce Cunningham, painter Robert Rauschenberg, and others "has often been cited as the model for the wave of happenings and related performance events that swept the art world in the late 1950s and early 1960s. In many respects, this event recapitulated many of the motifs and practices of earlier avant-gardes," according to one historian (Carlson, 1996, p. 95). In *Untitled Event,* performances, "each timed to the second, took place in and around an arena audience" (Carlson, 1996, p. 95):

> Each performer was given a "score" which consisted purely of "time brackets" to indicate moments of action, inaction, and silence that each individual performer was expected to fill. . . . Cage, in a black suit and tie, stood on a stepladder and read a text on "the relation of music to Zen Buddhism" and excerpts from Meister Eckhart. Later he performed a "composition with a radio." At the same time, Rauschenberg played old records on a wind-up gramophone with a trumpet while a dog sat beside it listening, and David Tudor played a "prepared piano." A little later, Tudor started to pour water from one bucket to another. . . . Cunningham and others danced through the aisles chased by the dog. . . . Rauschenberg projected abstract slides (created by colored gelatin sandwiched between the glass) and clips of film onto [his "white paintings"] on the ceiling; the film clips showed first the school cook and then, as they gradually moved from the ceiling down the walls, the setting sun. (Fischer-Lichte, 1997, pp. 233-234)

◆ Happenings

In the late 1950s, Allan Kaprow invented "happenings," and this label was applied to all sorts of experimental performances in the 1960s.

A key event in the history of modern performance was the presentation in 1959 of Allan Kaprow's *18 Happenings in 6 Parts* at the Reuben Gallery [in New York City]. This first public demonstration established the "happening" for public and press as a major new avant-garde activity, so much so that a wide range of performance work during the following years was characterized as "happenings," even when many creators of such events specifically denied the term. Audiences at Kaprow's happening were seated in three different rooms where they witnessed six fragmented events, performed simultaneously in all three spaces. The events included slides, playing of musical instruments, posed scenes, the reading of fragmentary notes from placards, and artists painting canvas walls. (Carlson, 1996, pp. 95-96)

◆ Body Art and Experimental Theater

In the 1970s and 1980s, visual and theater artists developed two different forms of "performance art": the "body art" of Vito Acconci, Chris Burden, Carolee Schneemann, Hannah Wilke, and other visual artists; and the "elaborate spectacles not based on the body or the psyche of the individual artist but devoted to the display of nonliterary aural and visual images, often involving spectacle, technology, and mixed media" (Carlson, 1996, pp. 104-105; see also Sayre, 1995) of Laurie Anderson, Lee Bruer, Richard Foreman, Robert Wilson, and, later, Spalding Gray, Bill Irwin, and other theatrical storytellers, jugglers, and clowns.

According to Amelia Jones (1998), the "body art" of the 1960s and 1970s was a "set of performative practices" that used "passionate and convulsive relationships (often explicitly sexual)" with audiences (whether physically present or viewing documentary photographs, films, videos and other texts), to "instantiate the dislocation or decentering of the Cartesian subject of modernism" (p. 1). Furthermore, and not incidentally, because it was "dramatically intersubjective," body art undercut the "masculinist and racist ideology of individualism shoring up modernist formalism" in art criticism (p. 3). For example:

> *Interior Scroll* [was] originally performed in 1975. . . . Her face and body covered in strokes of paint, [Carolee] Schneemann pulled a long, thin coil of paper from her vagina ("like a ticker tape . . . plumb line . . . the umbilicus and tongue"), unrolling it to read a narrative text to the audience. Part of this text read as follows: "I met a happy man,/a structuralist filmmaker . . . he said we are fond of you/you are charming/but don't ask us/to look at your

films/. . . we cannot look at/*the personal clutter/the persistence of feelings/the hand-touch sensibility.*" (Jones, 1998, p. 3)

In *Transference Zone* (1972), [Vito] Acconci locked himself in a room with a group of photographs and objects owned by seven significant people in his life. One at a time, he let in visitors who knocked on the door, transferring his feelings about these "prime" people onto the unsuspecting recipient. . . . Playing out Freudian notions of transference—a dynamic involving the projection of one's subconscious conflicts and desires onto another—Acconci's piece opens out the contingency and performativity of identity and subjectivity itself. (Jones, 1998, pp. 139-140)

Experimental theater performances, on the other hand, "developed the aesthetic of a new theatre through productions which picked up the program of the historical avant-garde movement . . . and seemed to fulfill it: the 'retheatricalization' of theatre which was to be a radical move away from the literary theatre predominant in Western culture since the eighteenth century" (Fischer-Lichte, 1997, p. 200). An example is Robert Wilson's visual opera of the 1970s:

His manipulation of space and time, his fusion of visual, aural, and performing arts, his utilization of chance and collage techniques in construction, his use of language for sound and evocation rather than discursive meaning, all show his close relationship to earlier experimental work in theatre, music, the visual arts, and dance. Speaking of *Einstein on the Beach* [1976], Wilson advised: "You don't have to think about the story, because there isn't any. You don't have to listen to words, because the words don't mean anything. You just enjoy the scenery, the architectural arrangements in time and space, the music, the feelings they all evoke. Listen to the pictures." (Carlson, 1996, p. 110)

◆ Performance Ethnography

In the late 1980s and early 1990s, sociologists began to turn their ethnographic field notes into performances, and theater artists and academics in performance studies began to produce or adapt ethnographies in order to perform them (see Becker, McCall, & Morris, 1989; Conquergood, 1985; Denzin, 1997; McCall, 1993; Mienczakowski, 2000; Paget, 1990; Pollock, 1990; Richardson, 1997; Siegel & Conquergood, 1985, 1990;

Smith, 1993, 1994). The performance ethnographies of theater artists and people in performance studies were surely informed by the history of "performance art" and "experimental theater" in the 20th century. Ours certainly were not—despite the veiled reference to performance art in "performance science," the name Becker, Morris, and I gave our early pieces (see McCall & Becker, 1990). Our work was very much text based: There was a story, the words did mean something, and there were very few images to "listen to."

We based three performance pieces—*Local Theatrical Communities*; *Theatres and Communities: Three Scenes*; and *Performance Science*—on "formal interviews with seventy actors, directors and other theater workers (playwrights, critics, administrators, and technical people)" in "three metropolitan areas: Chicago, San Francisco, and Minneapolis/St. Paul" (Becker et al., 1989, p. 93). In performances we carried and read from scripts, did not wear costumes or use props, sat in chairs or stood behind podiums, and moved only to exchange seats or to get from chairs to podiums and back. We played multiple characters: ourselves, as sociologists, and various people one of us had interviewed. In *Theatres and Communities: Three Scenes,* for example, we played a total of 25 characters. We shifted body positions and visual focus, and occasionally stood, to mark character and scene changes and to guide audience attention.

> For example, we addressed the audience directly when we were making analytic statements, but turned and looked at one another when we were conversing, as "sociologists" and other characters. In the body of [published] script[s], italicized stage directions indicate[d] who was being addressed in each speech; a longer stage direction at the beginning of the first scene explain[ed] where we sat and looked and how we held our scripts to focus attention on the voices of the people we interviewed. (Becker et al., 1989, p. 96)

Likewise, the parodic ethnography of performance artists Coco Fusco and Guillermo Gómez-Peña was explicitly not based in the history of "avant-garde" movements, although, like other performance art, Fusco and Gómez-Peña's work depended less on text than on visual images. As Fusco (1995) notes: "Performance Art in the West did not begin with Dadaist 'events.' Since the early days of European 'conquest,' 'aboriginal samples' of people from Africa, Asia, and the Americas were brought to Europe for aesthetic contemplation, scientific analysis, and entertainment" (p. 41). Fusco states, "My collaborator, Guillermo Gómez Peña, and I were intrigued by this legacy of performing the identity of an Other for a white audience, sensing its implications for us as performance artists dealing with cultural identity in the present" (p. 37).

> Our plan was to live in a golden cage for three days, presenting ourselves as undiscovered Amerindians from an island in the Gulf of Mexico that had somehow been overlooked by Europeans for five centuries. We called our homeland Guatinau, and ourselves Guatinauis. We performed our "traditional tasks," which ranged from sewing voodoo dolls and lifting weights to watching television and working on a laptop computer. A donation box in front of the cage indicated that, for a small fee, I would dance (to rap music), Guillermo would tell authentic Amerindian stories (in a nonsensical language), and we would pose for Polaroids with visitors. Two "zoo guards" would be on hand to speak to visitors (since we could not understand them), take us to the bathroom on leashes, and feed us sandwiches and fruit. At the Whitney Museum in New York we added sex to our spectacle, offering a peek at authentic Guatinaui male genitals for $5. A chronology with highlights from the history of exhibiting non-Western peoples was on one didactic panel and a simulated Encyclopedia Britannica entry with a fake map of the Gulf of Mexico showing our island was on another. . .
> . . . We did not anticipate that our self-conscious commentary . . . could be believable. We underestimated the public faith in museums as bastions of truth, and institutional investment in that role. Furthermore, we did not anticipate that literalism would dominate the interpretation of our work. Consistently from city to city, more than half of our visitors believed our fiction and thought we were "real." . . . As we moved our performance from public site to natural history museum, pressure mounted from institutional representatives . . . to correct audience misinterpretation. . . . we were perceived as either noble savages or evil tricksters, dissimulators who discredit museums and betray public trust. (Fusco, 1995, pp. 39, 50)

The ethnographic performances of theater artists and academics in performance studies are more theatrical than those of sociologists and more like performance art. They combine texts and visual elements such as movement, settings, costumes, and props. Emilie Beck's adaptation of a sociological text and Della Pollock's adaptation of an oral history are good examples.

Emilie Beck adapted an article that Marianne Paget (1990) wrote "about the erroneous construction of a medical diagnosis of a woman who was a cancer patient" (p. 136) and directed a performance of it titled *The*

Work of Talk: Studies in Misunderstandings. There were seven characters, played by performance studies and theater students: the narrator, the doctor, the patient, and a panel of four experts "(two women, two men)," each of whom "was a rather singular and one-dimensional type. One was rather prim, like our stereotype of the librarian. Another was young and precocious. He was constantly unmasking the doctor and enjoyed it. The third was all business and matter of fact, and the fourth was rather lewd, a guy 'on the make' " (Paget, 1990, p. 144). The narrator was Cancer.

"The doctor and patient enacted dialogue" based on a series of transcripts Paget analyzed in the article. "Sometimes they commented on what they had said or would soon say, just as I had done in the original article. Sometimes they reacted to the panel" (Paget, 1990, p. 138). They also "danced together. They tangoed. . . . Sometimes, as she sat on a small table, he examined or asked her questions. . . . The experts reported the science" of Paget's analysis. "Sometimes they also 'gossiped' about what was going on between the doctor and patient. Sometimes they mimicked their dialogue or acted like a chorus." Once the "cast acted as a machine, a many levered instrument producing work along a line. Everyone bleated or bayed a mechanical sound and moved synchronously. The machine (cast) surrounded the patient," miming "the physician's oddly mechanical talk" (pp. 139-140).

Cancer wore a long white dress, carried an evening bag and was barefooted.

> She was both lovely and flirtatious. . . . Throughout the performance, she pays close attention to the patient. She dresses her up, coming at one point to apply makeup and at another to give her a chocolate. The patient belongs to Cancer. Occasionally panel members also try to help the patient. At one point panel member #1 drops glitter on her back; at another time she massages her back. These attentions to her back foreshadow the final moments when the patient reports that she has gone to another clinic and has been told that she has cancer of the spine. (Paget, 1990, pp. 139-141)

Della Pollock directed performances of *Like a Family: The Making of a Southern Cotton Mill World* (Hall et al., 1987), an oral history based on 300 interviews with former cotton mill workers in the Carolina Piedmont region. Eleven undergraduates "were selected by application" for "an independent study project that would give [them] credit for learning mill history through performance" (Pollock, 1990, p. 4). Pollock and her students developed the script and the performances together. The students played multiple roles, including themselves, and were costumed in "the long skirts and wool pants of the early twentieth century mill worker." Sets "consisted of chairs borrowed from the audience's seating area and prop pieces (a washboard, a tin kettle) borrowed from a distinctly 'other' era" (Pollock, 1990, p. 18).

> [Performances] began with actors in costume ushering audience members to their seats while other actors set up the stage area, tuned guitars, etc. The lights remained bright. A selection of traditional songs buoyed both the actors and audience members. A general hubbub ensued until all of the actors—in both the stage and audience areas—joined in a round of "I Saw the Light." At the song's conclusion, the usher/actors took seats in the audience and one of the actors on stage came forward to introduce the performance and herself. She was followed by four others, each telling a brief story about his or her relation to the mill world. . . . As part of their introduction, the actors then recalled questions the *Like a Family* interviewers had asked former mill workers. . . In a spirit of genuine curiosity, the actors asked, How much free time did you have? Did you go to church? What happened when the union organizers came in?
>
> We then gently, playfully blurred the performance frame. Actors stood in the audience to respond to the stage actors' questions. Rather than convincing shills, these were clearly actors: they were the ushers in costume who greeted audience members at the door and then sat next to them or their neighbor. When the actor stood to declare that she was Icy Norman or that he was Hoyle McCorkle, he or she was quite explicitly acting—representing someone else, expressing a point of view not his or her own. This kind of self-conscious theatricality helped us to confuse conventional distinctions between actor and audience and yet to maintain unconventional distinctions between actor and character. In this way we invited audience members to participate. (Pollock, 1990, p. 21)

At the end of the performance,

> one of the *Like a Family* authors was invited to join the performers, to tell his or her own story and to invite, in turn, the audiences' stories and comments. Closing applause was thus postponed until after audience members had also assumed the role of performer. . . . When applause did occur, it was mutual: performers clapped for audience members and audience members for performers. Their roles were blurred in the expression of general pleasure. (p. 23)

The performance ethnographies I wrote, performed, and/or cast in the mid-1990s were influenced by Pollock's work. From 1992 through 1998, I worked with a photographer, Linda Gammell, and a sculptor, Sandra M. Taylor, on a study of midwestern women who practiced and/or advocated sustainable agriculture.[2] During that period we held seven daylong "workshops"—group interviews, really—with 52 women farmers.

We began the workshops by asking the women to answer the question "Who are you and what is your connection to the land?" After the introductions, Gammell and Taylor presented a slide lecture on stereotypes of rural women in art and advertising. Next, each woman described the object or objects she had brought to "represent farm life and/or farm women" and added it or them to a "centerpiece" on the table we sat around. Gammell photographed the centerpiece and, later, made portraits of the objects in the women's hands (see Taylor, Gammell, & McCall, 1994). We closed the workshops with open-ended questions such as, "If you were to have a very public opportunity to communicate something about women and rural life and the changes that are happening in rural culture, what would you say?" As the participants left, we gave each a roll of film and asked her to photograph her own landscape and mail the used film back to us; we had the film developed and sent the women copies of their prints. Gammell also made slides from their negatives.

A grant from the Blandin Foundation, which funded our work in the summer of 1993 and allowed us to hire three student research assistants, required that we and the students collaboratively report our findings to foundation officials and other grant recipients at an October conference. I wrote *Not "Just" a Farmer and Not Just a "Farm Wife"* (McCall, 1993) for that purpose. Only five of us could attend the conference, so I based the script on a workshop with four farm women, played by the students and me, and added the role of "questioner" and slide projector operator for Taylor. The performance began and ended with a tape recording of Patty Kakac, a workshop participant, singing "I'm Just a Farmer," a song she wrote. Throughout the performance, Taylor showed slides of the landscape photographs taken by women in four workshops. Although we read from scripts, sitting on stools, and were not costumed, the addition of music and visual images made this performance a bit less "text-bound" and more like Pollock's adaptation of *Like a Family* than my previous work with Becker and Morris.

Like Pollock, I wanted to "return the stories to the communities out of which they emerged." I understood that "telling personal, traditional and historical tales at work, on a front porch, or during an interview was itself performative action," and I "hoped we could realize their performative nature" by "re-performing these tales" (Pollock, 1990, p. 4). So I arranged three more performances in which women who participated in the workshops played the parts of Michal and Sandra; Sara, Michelle, and Liza (the students); and Patty, Alice, Gloria, and Donna (the farm women) for Minnesota Food Association Board members (our other sponsors) and workshop participants.

◆ Some Tips

Performance ethnography requires at least the following from the ethnographer or adapter: He or she must write a script and then cast and/or perform and/or stage it (adding movement, sets, costumes, props). Writing a script is the easiest task for a sociologist/ethnographer, I think, because we always turn our field notes and interview transcripts into written texts—even if these are normally meant for readers and not for performers and audiences. Emerson, Fretz, and Shaw (1995) call the texts ethnographers usually write "thematic narratives" and explain them as follows:

> In coding and memo-writing, the ethnographer has started to create and elaborate analytic themes. In writing an ethnographic text, the writer organizes some of these themes into a coherent "story" about life and events in the setting studied. Such a narrative requires selecting only some small portion of the total set of fieldnotes and then linking them into a coherent text representing some aspect or slice of the world studied. (p. 170)

Emerson et al. explain to student ethnographers how to "jot" notes in the field, how to "write them up" to create "scenes on the page," how to "discover" members' meanings in field notes, and how to "process" field notes through "open coding, focused coding and integrative memos" (pp. v-vii). In a chapter titled "Writing an Ethnography," they explain how to "build up piece by piece a coherent, fieldnote-centered story" (p. 179). They advise students to write "excerpt-commentary units" using field notes and initial memos; an "excerpt-commentary unit" includes an analytic point, orienting information (e.g., the social statuses of speakers), an excerpt from the field notes, and analytic commentary (pp. 182-183).

Next, Emerson et al. tell students to order these units within a section and to order sections within the text and, finally, to write an introduction, a "literature review," and a conclusion to the ethnography.

Writing an ethnographic performance script is very similar, except that "orienting information" and "analytic points and commentary" are unnecessary: The first is embodied, and the second can be done by the "characters." And, of course, dialogue replaces description and narration. Still, ethnographic scriptwriters must read and reread their field notes or transcripts to "create and elaborate analytic themes" and "organize some of these into a coherent story."

To write *Not "Just" a Farmer,* I read and reread the transcript of a workshop we held in St. Cloud, Minnesota, on August 21, 1993. It was approximately 120 pages long, representing 6 hours of audiotaped conversation. I needed to produce a script that would take 30 minutes to perform (the time allotted to us at the Blandin conference); as it turned out, this meant the script was 10½ pages long—only a "small portion of the total set of fieldnotes."

The St. Cloud workshop was organized by Barb Thomes, who had participated in a 1992 workshop. Barb lived on a farm and worked for Lutheran Social Services, providing crisis counseling and other services to farm families. She invited four women to participate in the 1993 workshop. Donna Johnson and her husband lost their farming operation, but not his maternal grandparents' farm, in the 1980s "farm crisis." Patty Kakac and her husband lived on a 160-acre farm, kept bees and sold honey, and grew their own food, but she earned her living as a folksinger. She and Alice Tripp were political activists; Alice was a retired dairy farmer and former candidate for governor of Minnesota. Gloria Schneider owned a 200-acre dairy farm, which she had farmed alone since 1989, when her husband died suddenly; she was hoping her son would move back and farm with her. It is not surprising, then, that the dominant themes in the workshop were the difficulties family farmers have earning a living; the vast wealth and power, by comparison, of corporate food processors, retailers, and transportation, seed, and chemical companies; the loss of farmland to urban migration, suburban sprawl, and the depressed rural economy; and our responsibilities, as urban eaters, to learn where our food comes from and, where possible, to buy it from local family farmers who grow it without chemical herbicides, pesticides, or fertilizers. Secondary themes were the importance of women's work on traditional farms, the diversity of rural women's work lives in the present, and the opportunities for women in sustainable agriculture. I organized the script around these themes.

It began with the question, "What is your connection to the land?" directed to the audience and asked in unison by four of us, seated on tall stools, onstage. Next, Sara and I, Michelle and Liza, and Sandra, who was seated in the audience near the slide projector, introduced ourselves by answering that question. Then, Sara, Michelle, Liza, and I changed places and introduced "ourselves" as Donna (Sara), Gloria (me), Patty (Michelle), and Alice (Liza). As we became the other characters, Sandra began to project the slides. She also asked questions and made comments; I used quotes from the transcript, mostly her own words, but I rearranged them to provide transitions from topic to topic and to motivate or explain comments and answers from the other participants. An example is the first segment of the script after the introductions:

Sandra: [We've] noticed that there isn't a very true picture of women and land in the media. Or the fine arts. So that's what we're going to talk about today and ask you for your help: to give us better information. About what it means to be a woman associated with the land in the 1990s and beyond. So thank you for coming to help us. . . . And now, if you could, take whatever you brought and put it in the middle [of the table].

Sandra: Linda [Gammell] brought some good stuff. [She said] she brought this little cow because she was "interested in the idea of how people depict animals. And how animals then become dolls and toys."

Patty: Somehow the cow became really popular in the, you know, cutesy art stuff. Just as farmers [were losing their farms]. . . . And it just kind of made me sick. I go to Craft Fairs, selling for my friend. And people who sold cows—you know, you can make lots of money selling cows! God this is not right! There's something screwy about this. That you can make money selling little cows but you can't make money selling food from it. . . . I've noticed, throughout the country, no matter what product you make if it's for food you can't make a living on it. But if you can entertain people . . . And that's how a lot of farmers are

124

going. Having people come out and they have vacations on the farm.

Donna: Uh-huh. Bed and Breakfasts.

Patty: To make money.

Sandra: Really?

Patty: Yeh, that's one alternative to making money [farming].

Donna: It's like supplemental income.

Patty: Yeh, people raising vegetables go to raising dried flowers. To make money. They can make money on dried flowers but not on vegetables.

Sandra: Is it that people don't see a difference between supermarket food and food that's grown on a farm?

Donna: I don't think there's any connection left.

Patty: There also is, there was a policy in this country, you know, established. That food would be cheap. Which allowed some people to make money on it, but not others.

Sandra: Which ones? Who gets to make money?

Patty: Those who

Alice: process. General Mills.

Patty: The supermarkets, the handlers.

Alice: Food processors.

[Sara]: Fertilizer people.

Patty: Yeh.

Donna: Banks, anybody. I'm not much of a TV person—much at all. But there was just an ad not too long ago, about the price of corn being, let's say, two dollars in nineteen—pick a number—twenty. And at this point it's two dollars again. And all the costs [have gone up]. Say the newspaper cost a nickel at that time, or whatever it was. Did anybody see that ad?

Patty: I didn't see that ad but I've seen similar things. Yeh.

Alice: There used to be a Department of Agriculture bulletin that said it cost three dollars a bushel to *raise* corn. So how are you going to make money? Yeh.

Donna: Yeh, but the public doesn't see that.

Alice: Yeh, right.

Patty: Umhuh.

Donna: The public will see this commercial and nice colors and . . .

Patty: Sure.

This script was less artificial than the scripts I wrote with Becker and Morris because it was based on a group interview. Those early scripts were based on individual interviews that were not tape-recorded; we used the information in them as much as we used the interviewers' and interviewees' actual words when we "made up" the dialogue. We also let the "sociologists" make the analytic points and do the commentary. In *Theatres and Communities: Three Scenes,* for example, the "sociologists" made 61% of all 165 speeches and all but 8 of 67 "analytic" speeches. I didn't have to "make up" the dialogue in *Not "Just" a Farmer*—it was already there, recorded in the transcript. The "analytic commentary" was also in the transcript, provided by the women farmers themselves. The "questioner" needed only to introduce the performance and provide context and transitions.

◆ Casting

I learned what I know about casting as a "participant observer" in the community theater world. My husband directed 23 plays, with amateur actors, in 3 years at two community theaters and, as the "director's wife," I observed auditions, rehearsals, and performances; participated in backstage activities; and listened to endless discussions about the artistic choices and decisions a director makes. I learned there is a discrepancy between actors' casting expectations and directors' casting purposes. Amateur actors think the "best" actor (sometimes simply the highest-status person in the community) should get the "biggest" part. The director, on the other hand, wants to cast a strong, balanced ensemble of actors. As my husband's teacher has explained:

> Actors at the point of auditioning should be aware that the director wants to arrive at a comfortable solution of the casting problem. The director wants to do as little work or readjustment as possible, and tries to develop an almost extrasensory awareness as to whether or not the chosen actor will be sympathetic with the character which is to be played. . . .
>
> Certainly it is helpful to have a sprinkling of previously successful experience in the cast, mainly to help create rapport and sympathetic relationships. . . . When I know the pluses and minuses of the actors and the script, it becomes my job to meld them together and put the strong people where

126

they will lend strength—not necessarily in the strongest plot roles. Often the strongest part is so well-written that a person who is adequate will develop the necessary strength while rehearsing and playing. But in the weaker sections of the play, where it could fall apart, the stronger actors may be needed more sorely. (Spayde, 1993, pp. 43-45)

For the original performance of *Not "Just" a Farmer and Not Just a "Farm Wife,"* I had to cast the five of us who conducted the research and could attend the Blandin conference. Indeed, I chose to work with the St. Cloud transcript because it had the right number of characters, including the generic "questioner." However, as I cast the five of us I did try make sure each "actor" would be "sympathetic with the character" she played. Like Donna and her husband, Sara's parents lost their farming operation but still lived on a farm. Both Patty and Michelle were singers. (Michelle's "object" was a tape recording of Minnesota musicians, and she talked about singing when she introduced herself: "My mother and my sister and I always sang. And in California it was something that just *we* did. And when we moved to Fergus Falls [Minnesota], one of the most interesting things was that singing was something that *everyone* did, together. There were so many songs that everyone knew, that we didn't know.") I cast Liza as Alice because Alice was about the same age as Liza's great-grandmother, of whom she said: "I feel like my strongest connection to the land is my great-grandma who lives in a small town in Illinois and we're pretty close. She's eighty-four and she runs greenhouses so she can sell for the Lord." I cast myself as Gloria because I thought she was the least sympathetic character—less politicized than the others and more traditional in her farming and her gender practices, she was boisterous and talked too much, before she left early. Because she was the "outsider" in the workshop the other "actors" participated in, I was afraid they might not give her a sympathetic reading. I thought perhaps I could, because I was aware of the problem.

◆ Directing and Performing

I won't presume to give the reader acting advice. Instead I will quote from one of hundreds of books of advice to actors, written by experts. According to playwright David Mamet (1997), "To act means to perform an action, to do something" (p. 72). He asserts:

127

To you, to the actor, it is not the words which carry the meaning—it is the actions. Moment to moment and night to night the play will change, as you and your adversaries onstage change, as your conflicting actions butt up against each other. That play, that interchange, is drama. But the words are set and unchanging. Any worth in them was put there by the author. His or her job is done, and the best service you can do them is accept the words as is, and speak them simply and clearly in an attempt to get what you want from another actor. (pp. 62-63)

Mamet also states:

The plane is designed to fly; the pilot is trained to direct it. Likewise, the play is designed, if correctly designed, as a series of incidents in which and through which the protagonist struggles toward his or her goal. It is the job of the actor to show up, and use the lines and his or her will and common sense, to attempt to achieve a goal similar to that of the protagonist. And that is the end of the actor's job. (p. 12)

Of course *we* were not acting; we were simply reading aloud the traces of a conversation among ourselves and four women farmers. Instead of "directing" the "actors," I tried to make the words in my script easy to speak "simply and clearly," requiring little interpretive work, by transcribing the *sounds* of words and pauses in our conversations, the music of our speech, and transferring these to the script. This way of working is consistent with Anna Deavere Smith's (1993) idea that you "find a character's psychological reality by 'inhabiting' that character's words" (p. xxvii).

Since the mid-1980s, Smith has created a series of performances "based on actual events" (Smith, 1994, p. xvii) that she calls *On the Road: A Search for American Character.* The best-known performances in the series are *Fires in the Mirror,* about 3 days of riots, marches, and demonstrations that broke out in Crown Heights, Brooklyn, after "one of the cars in a three-car procession carrying the Lubavitcher Hasidic rebbe (spiritual leader) ran a red light, hit another car, and swerved onto a sidewalk," where it "struck and killed Gavin Cato, a seven-year-old Black boy from Guyana, and seriously injured his cousin Angela" and after "a group of young Black men fatally stabbed Yankel Rosenbaum, a 29-year-old Hasidic scholar from Australia" in retaliation (Smith, 1933, p. xliii); and *Twilight: Los Angeles, 1992,* about the civil disturbances in Los Angeles in April 1992.

Each *On the Road* performance evolves from interviews I conduct with individuals directly or indirectly involved in the event I intend to explore. Basing my scripts entirely on this interview material, I perform the interviewees on stage using their own words. *Twilight: Los Angeles, 1992* is the product of my search for the character of Los Angeles in the wake of the initial Rodney King verdict. (Smith, 1994, p. xvii)

As an acting student, Smith learned "the importance of thinking on the word, rather than between the words in order to discover the character" (Smith, 1993, p. xxiv). Following her Shakespeare teacher's instructions, she said a 14-line speech from *Richard III* "over and over well into the wee hours of the morning." Because she did not try to "control the words," Smith learned "about the power of rhythm and imagery to evoke the spirit of a character, of a play, of a time" (p. xxiv). Later she realized she could "create the illusion of being another person by reenacting something they had said *as they had said it*" (p. xxvi).

Actors . . . are trained to develop aspects of our memories that are more emotional and sensory than intellectual. The general public often wonders how actors remember their lines. What's more remarkable to me, is how actors remember, recall, and reiterate feelings and sensations. The body has a memory just as the mind does. The heart has a memory, just as the mind does. The act of speech is a physical act. It is powerful enough that it can create, with the rest of the body, a kind of cooperative dance. That dance is a sketch of something that is inside a person, and not fully revealed by the words alone. I came to realize that if I were able to record part of the dance—that is, the spoken part—and reenact it, the rest of the body would follow. (Smith, 1993, pp. xxv-xxvi)

At first, Smith used published interviews to "engage" her "students in putting themselves in other people's shoes" (p. xxvi). Later, she began to conduct her own interviews and, later still, to perform them herself.

I wanted to develop an alternative to the self-based [acting] technique, a technique that would begin with the other and come to the self, a technique that would empower the other to find the actor rather than the other way around. I needed very graphic evidence that the manner of speech could be a mark of individuality. If we were to inhabit the speech pattern of another, and walk in the speech of another, we could find the individuality of the other and experience that individuality viscerally. I became increasingly convinced that the activity of reenactment could tell us as much, if not more, about another individual than the process of learning about the other by using the self as a frame of reference. The frame of reference for the other would *be* the other. (Smith, 1993, p. xxvii)

◆ Staging

Besides casting and coaching actors, the director of a performance or play also *"stages the event"* by "controlling the mise-en-scène": sets, lighting, costumes, props, and movement (Bordwell & Thompson, 1993, p. 145). As I have said, the staging has been minimal in the performances I have done, so I cannot tell the reader "how to" do it. Nor are other published descriptions of performance ethnography very helpful. Staging requires interpretive choices. Anna Deavere Smith works with professional directors, dramaturges, and set, sound, lighting, and costume designers in making these choices. And although they explain their interpretive purposes, neither Pollock nor Paget/Beck tells us how these interpretive choices were made. Pollock (1990) says that she hoped "re-performing" the oral histories of cotton mill workers would "invigorate their claim to self-representation" (p. 4) and "help to recover their historical life" (p. 5). She wanted to avoid "the illusion that the past was present" because she thought this would turn "drama's advantage of immediacy towards the end of time-warp titillation" (p. 6). The interpretive choices she made to achieve her goals included keeping costumes, sets, and props simple (to avoid "the illusion that the past was present") and casting performers in multiple roles, so that "the audience member is liberated from any particular historical position (including his or her own) but constrained within a dialectic of history-making" because the "audience member identifies . . . above all [with] the actor's power to transform him or herself and, in the process, the world" (p. 18).

Because Marianne Paget (1990) has published the description of "On the Work of Talk," we do not know how Emilie Beck, the director, made her interpretive choices. However, in discussing the alternative choices she imagined Beck might have made, Paget does provide one small clue:

> I thought of the performed text as Emilie Beck's version. Making Cancer the narrator was a stunning interpretive act which had many implications for the production of the performance's meaning. . . . Excluding the author and

investigator was another interpretive act. Including me as the investigator, Emilie Beck argued, interfered with the production of a necessary atmosphere that would engage the audience. Here is one of the conundrums of the performance. [It] made fantastic some of the facts in order to state them. (pp. 144-145)

Performance ethnography is a relatively new form. Perhaps, with time, people who are trained in theater and performance techniques will write books of advice for directors of such ethnographies. In the meantime, I can recommend a book of advice for theater directors. Titled *Backwards and Forwards: A Technical Manual for Reading Plays* and written by David Ball (1983), an experienced playwright and director, it "reveals a script not only as literature, but as raw material for theatrical performance," as director Michael Langham (1983, p. vii) says in his foreword to the book.

There is all the difference in the world between literature and drama. A play's sound, music, movement, looks, dynamics—and much more—are to be discovered deep in the script, yet cannot be detected through strictly literary methods of reading and analysis. [In] this little book . . . there is guidance and illumination about the nature of scripts [even for directors with] a lot of experience. (Langham, 1983, pp. vii-viii)

◆ Notes

1. The distinction was new to theater critics, but not to theater artists (see Mamet, 1997, pp. 62-63).
2. An agriculture more sustainable than the current agribusiness system would rely less on petrochemicals (which, in some cases, "cost" more calories than the food they produce and can cause water, soil, and air pollution and a host of health problems), less on long-distance transportation (buying and selling food locally are basic tenets of sustainable agriculture), and less on "middlemen" (buying directly from farmers at farmers' markets or through memberships in Community Supported Agriculture is also a basic tenet).

◆ References

Ball, D. (1983). *Backwards and forwards: A technical manual for reading plays.* Carbondale: Southern Illinois University Press.

Becker, H. S., McCall, M. M., & Morris, L. V. (1989). Theatres and communities: Three scenes. *Social Problems, 36,* 93-116.

Bordwell, D., & Thompson, K. (1993). *Film art: An introduction.* New York: McGraw-Hill.

Carlson, M. (1996). *Performance: A critical introduction.* New York: Routledge.

Conquergood, D. (1985). Performing as a moral act: Ethical dimensions of the ethnography of performance. *Literature in Performance, 5,* 1-13.

Denzin, N. K. (1997). *Interpretive ethnography: Ethnographic practices for the 21st century.* Thousand Oaks, CA: Sage.

Emerson, R. M., Fretz, R. I., & Shaw, L. L. (1995). *Writing ethnographic fieldnotes.* Chicago: University of Chicago Press.

Fischer-Lichte, E. (1997). *The show and the gaze of theatre: A European perspective.* Iowa City: University of Iowa Press.

Fusco, C. (1995). *English is broken here: Notes on cultural fusion in the Americas.* New York: New Press.

Hall, J. D., Leloudis, J., Korstad, R., Murphy, M., Jones, L. A., & Daly, C. B. (1987). *Like a family: The making of a southern cotton mill world.* Chapel Hill: University of North Carolina Press.

Jones, A. (1998). *Body art/performing the subject.* Minneapolis: University of Minnesota Press.

Langham, M. (1983). Foreword. In D. Ball, *Backwards and forwards: A technical manual for reading plays* (pp. vii-viii). Carbondale: Southern Illinois University Press.

Mamet, D. (1997). *True and false: Heresy and common sense for the actor.* New York: Pantheon.

McCall, M. M., & Becker, H. S. (1990). Performance science. *Social Problems, 37,* 116-132.

McCall, M. M. (1993). *Not "just" a farmer and not just a "farm wife."* Unpublished performance script.

Mienczakowski, J. (2000). Ethnodrama: Performed research—limitations and potential. In P. Atkinson, S. Delamont, & A. Coffey (Eds.), *Handbook of ethnography.* London: Sage.

Paget, M. A. (1990). Performing the text. *Journal of Contemporary Ethnography, 19,* 136-155.

Pollock, D. (1990). Telling the told: Performing like a family. *Oral History Review, 18,* 1-36.

Richardson, L. (1997). *Fields of play: Constructing an academic life.* New Brunswick, NJ: Rutgers University Press.

Sayre, H. (1995). Performance. In F. Lentricchia & T. McLaughlin (Eds.), *Critical terms for literary study* (pp. 91-104). Chicago: University of Chicago Press.

Siegel, T., & Conquergood, D. (Producers & Directors). (1985). *Between two worlds: The Hmong shaman in America* [Video documentary].

Siegel, T., & Conquergood, D. (Producers & Directors). (1990). *The heart broken in half* [Video documentary].

132

Smith, A. D. (1993). *Fires in the mirror: Crown Heights, Brooklyn, and other identities.* Garden City, NY: Anchor.

Smith, A. D. (1994). *Twilight: Los Angeles, 1992.* Garden City, NY: Anchor.

Spayde, S. H. (with Mackey, D. A.). (1993). *Doors into the play: A few practical keys for theatricians.* San Bernardino, CA: Borgo.

Taylor, S. M., Gammell, L., & McCall, M. M. (1994). *The one about the farmer's daughter: Stereotypes and self-images.* St. Paul: Minnesota Food Association.

5
Case Studies

Robert E. Stake

◆ Case studies have become one of the most common ways to do qualitative inquiry, but they are neither new nor essentially qualitative.
Case study is not a methodological choice but a choice of what is to be
studied. By whatever methods, we choose to study the case. We could
study it analytically or holistically, entirely by repeated measures or
hermeneutically, organically or culturally, and by mixed methods—but we
concentrate, at least for the time being, on the case.

The physician studies the child because the child is ill. The child's symptoms are both qualitative and quantitative. The physician's record is more
quantitative than qualitative. The social worker studies the child because
the child is neglected. The symptoms of neglect are both qualitative and
quantitative. The formal record the social worker keeps is more qualitative than quantitative.[1] In many professional and practical fields, cases are
studied and recorded. As a form of research, case study is defined by interest in individual cases, not by the methods of inquiry used.

Perhaps a majority of researchers doing casework call their studies by
some other name. Howard Becker (personal communication, 1980), for

AUTHOR'S NOTE: This revision of my chapter of the same title in the first edition of the
Handbook of Qualitative Research has been enhanced by the fine contributions to *What Is a
Case?* edited by Charles Ragin and Howard Becker (1992), as well as by the critical readings of
Norman Denzin, Yvonna Lincoln, Orlando Fals Borda, Morten Levin, Linda Mabry, and Rita
Davis.

example, when asked what he called his own studies, reluctantly said, "Fieldwork," adding that such labels contribute little to the understanding of what researchers do. Some of us emphasize the name *case study* because it draws attention to the question of what specially can be learned from the single case. That epistemological question is the driving question of this chapter: What can be learned from the single case? I will emphasize designing the study to optimize understanding of the case rather than generalization beyond.

◆ Identification of the Case

A case may be simple or complex. It may be a child, or a classroom of children, or an incident such as a mobilization of professionals to study a childhood condition. It is one among others. In any given study, we will concentrate on the one. The time we may spend concentrating our inquiry on the one may be long or short, but, while we so concentrate, we are engaged in case study.

Custom has it that not everything is a case. A child may be a case. A doctor may be a case—but *his doctoring* probably lacks the specificity, boundedness, to be called a case.[2] An agency may be a case. But the *reasons* for child neglect or the *policies* of dealing with neglectful parents will seldom be considered a case. We think of those topics as generalities rather than specificities. The case is a specific One.

If we are moved to study it, the case is almost certainly going to be a functioning specific. The case is a "bounded system" (Flood, as reported in Fals Borda, 1998). In the social sciences and human services, the case has working parts; it is purposive; it often has a self. It is an integrated system. However immature, the child is a working combination of physiological, psychological, cultural, aesthetic, and other forces. Similarly, the hospital as case, the agency as case. Functional or dysfunctional, rational or irrational, the case is a system.

Its behavior is patterned. Coherence and sequence are prominent. It is common to recognize that certain features are within the system, within the boundaries of the case, and other features outside. Some are significant as context. William Goode and Paul Hatt (1952) observe that it is not always easy for the case researcher to say where the child ends and the environment begins. But boundedness and behavior patterns are useful concepts for specifying the case (Stake, 1988).

Ultimately, we may be interested in a general phenomenon or a population of cases more than in the individual case. And we cannot understand this case without knowing about other cases. But while we are studying it, our meager resources are concentrated on trying to understand *its* complexities. For the while, we probably will not study comparison cases. We may simultaneously carry on more than one case study, but each case study is a concentrated inquiry into a single case.

Charles Ragin (1992) gives emphasis to the question of "What is it a case of?" as if "membership in" or "representation of" something else were the main consideration in case study. He makes detailed reference to the casework of Michel Wieviorka (1988) on terrorism. Ragin was writing for the social scientist seeking theoretical generalization, justifying the study of the particular only if it serves an understanding of grand issues or explanations. He recognized that even in formal experimentation and statistical survey work there is interest in the illustrative or deviant case. But historians, program evaluators, institutional researchers, practitioners in all professions are interested in the individual case without necessarily caring what it is a case of.

Even if my definition of case study were agreed upon,[3] and it is not, the terms *case* and *study* defy full specification (Kemmis, 1980). A case study is both a process of inquiry about the case and the product of that inquiry. Lawrence Stenhouse (1984) advocates calling the latter, the product, a *case record,* and occasionally we do, but the practice of calling the final report a *case study* is widely established. Here and there, researchers call a great variety of things case studies.[4] But the more the object of study is a specific, unique, bounded system, the greater the usefulness of the epistemological rationales described in this chapter.

◆ Intrinsic and Instrumental Interest in Cases

I find it useful to identify three types of case study. I call a study an *intrinsic case study* if it is undertaken because, first and last, the researcher wants better understanding of this particular case. Here, it is not undertaken primarily because the case represents other cases or because it illustrates a particular trait or problem, but because, in all its particularity *and* ordinariness, this case itself is of interest. The researcher at least temporarily subordinates other curiosities so that the stories of those "living the case" will be teased out. The purpose is not to come to understand some abstract

136

construct or generic phenomenon, such as literacy or teenage drug use or what a school principal does. The purpose is not theory building— although at other times the researcher may do just that. Study is undertaken because of an intrinsic interest in, for example, this particular child, clinic, conference, or curriculum. Writings illustrating intrinsic case study include the following:

> *The Education of Henry Adams: An Autobiography* (Adams, 1918)
> - *God's Choice* (Peshkin, 1986)
> - *Bread and Dreams: A Case Study of Bilingual Schooling in the U.S.A.* (Mac-Donald, Adelman, Kushner, & Walker, 1982) (and most program evaluation studies; see Mabry, 1998)
> - *An Aberdeenshire Village Propaganda: Forty Years Ago* (Smith, 1889)
> - *The Swedish School System* (Stenholm, 1984)

I call it *instrumental case study* if a particular case is examined mainly to provide insight into an issue or to redraw a generalization. The case is of secondary interest, it plays a supportive role, and it facilitates our understanding of something else. The case still is looked at in depth, its contexts scrutinized, its ordinary activities detailed, but all because this helps the researcher to pursue the external interest. The case may be seen as typical of other cases or not. (In a later section, I will discuss when typicality is important.) Here the choice of case is made to advance understanding of that other interest. Because the researcher simultaneously has several interests, particular and general, there is no line distinguishing intrinsic case study from instrumental; rather, a zone of combined purpose separates them. Writings illustrating instrumental case study include these:

> "Campus Response to a Student Gunman" (Asmussen & Creswell, 1995/1997)
> - *Boys in White: Student Culture in Medical School* (Becker, Geer, Hughes, & Strauss, 1961)
> - "Thrown Overboard: The Human Costs of Health Care Rationing" (Kolker, 1996)
> - *On the Border of Opportunity: Education, Community, and Language at the U.S.-Mexico Line* (Pugach, 1998)
> - "A Nonreader Becomes a Reader: A Case Study of Literacy Acquisition by a Severely Disabled Reader" (McCormick, 1994)

With even less intrinsic interest in one particular case, a researcher may jointly study a number of cases in order to investigate a phenomenon, population, or general condition. I call this *collective case study*.[5] It is instrumental study extended to several cases. Individual cases in the collection may or may not be known in advance to manifest some common characteristic. They may be similar or dissimilar, redundancy and variety each important. They are chosen because it is believed that understanding them will lead to better understanding, perhaps better theorizing, about a still larger collection of cases. Works illustrating collective case study include the following:

> *Teachers' Work* (Connell, 1985)
> - "Researching Practice Settings: A Case Study Approach" (concerning medical clinics; Crabtree & Miller, 1999)
> - *Savage Inequalities* (Kozol, 1991)
> - *Bold Ventures: Patterns Among U.S. Innovations in Science and Mathematics Education* (Raisin & Britton, 1997)
> - "The Dark Side of Organizations: Mistake, Misconduct and Disaster" (Vaughan, 1999)

Reports (and authors) often do not fit neatly into such categories. I see these three as heuristic more than determinative. Alan Peshkin (personal communication, October 1992) responded to my classification of *God's Choice* (1986) as an intrinsic case study by saying: "I mean to present my case so that it can be read with interest in the case itself, but I always have another agenda—to learn from the case about some class of things. Some of what that will be remains an emergent matter for a long time." In this work, for 3 years Peshkin studied a single school, Bethany Baptist Academy. Until the final chapter, he does not tell the reader about the emergent matters of great importance to him and to the school people and citizens broadly. The first order of business was to understand the case, and a harsh understanding it turned out to be. But the immediate, if not ultimate, interest was intrinsic. The methods Peshkin used centered on the case, only latently taking up his abiding concern for community, freedom, and survival. Yes, this work could also have been called an instrumental study.

Other types of case study have been acknowledged. Harrison White (1992) categorizes social science casework according to three purposes: case studies for identity, explanation, or control. Similarly, Yvonna Lincoln and Egon Guba (1985) discuss five functions. Ragin (1992) sorts the studies two by two, conceptualizing cases as empirical units or theoretical constructs, general or specific. Historians and political scientists regularly examine singular episodes or movements or eras, such as Norman Gottwald's (1979) study of the emergence of Jewish identity. But I choose not to call such investigations case studies when the episodes or relationships—however complex, impacting, and bounded—are not easily thought of as organic and systemic, laced with purpose and self.

Elsewhere there is a common form of cases used in teaching to illustrate a point, a condition, a category, something important for instruction (Kennedy, 1979). For decades, law school and school of business professors have gallaried these cases.[6] For staff development and management training, such reports constitute the articles of the *Journal of Case Research*, key publication of the North American Case Research Association. Used for instruction and consultation, they result from instrumental case study.

One could also make a separate category for biography. Bill Tierney's contribution to this series (Volume 2, Chapter 9) is case centered, noting that biography calls for special attention to chronological structures and to procedures for the protection of human subjects. Similarly, television documentaries, many of them easily classifiable as case studies, require their own methods. The work of ethnographers, critical theorists, institutional demographers, and many others follows conceptual and stylistic patterns that not only amplify the taxonomy but also extend the foundation for case study research in the social sciences and social services. My purpose here in categorization is not taxonomic; rather, I want to emphasize variation in concern for and methodological orientation to *the case*. Thus I focus on three types: intrinsic, instrumental, and collective.

◆ Study of the Particular

Case researchers seek both what is common and what is particular about the case, but the end result regularly portrays something of the uncommon (Stouffer, 1941), drawing from all of the following:

1. The nature of the case;
2. The case's historical background;
3. The physical setting;
4. Other contexts (e.g., economic, political, legal, and aesthetic);

5. Other cases through which this case is recognized;

6. Those informants through whom the case can be known.

To study the case, to show particularity, many researchers gather data on all of the above.

The search for particularity competes with the search for generalizability. What all should be said about a single case is quite different from what should be said about all cases. Each case has important atypical features, happenings, relationships, and situations. Pursuit of understanding of those atypicalities not only robs time from the study of the generalizable but also diminishes the value, to some extent, that we place on demographic and policy issues.

Most academic researchers are supportive of the study of cases only if there is clear expectation of generalizability to other cases. Case-by-case uniqueness is seldom an ingredient of scientific theory. Case study research has been constrained even by qualitative methodologists who grant less than full regard to study of the particular (Denzin, 1989; Glaser & Strauss, 1967; Herriott & Firestone, 1983; Yin, 1989). These and other social scientists have written about case study as if intrinsic study of a particular case is not as important as studies to obtain generalizations pertaining to a population of cases.[7] Some have emphasized case study as typification of other cases, as exploration leading up to generalization-producing studies, or as an occasional early step in theory building. At least as I see it, case study method has been too little honored as the intrinsic study of a valued particular, as it is in biography, institutional self-study, program evaluation, therapeutic practice, and many lines of work. Generalization should not be emphasized in all research (Feagin, Orum, & Sjoberg, 1991; Simons, 1980).

Reflecting upon the pertinent literature, I find case study methodology written largely by people who presume that the research should contribute to scientific generalization. The bulk of case study work, however, is done by individuals who have *intrinsic* interest in the case and little interest in the advance of science. Their designs aim the inquiry toward understanding of what is important about that case within its own world, which is seldom the same as the worlds of researchers and theorists. Those designs develop what is perceived to be the case's own issues, contexts, and interpretations, its *thick description*. In contrast, the methods of instrumental case study draw the researcher toward illustrating how the concerns of researchers and theorists are manifest in the case. Because the critical issues are more likely to be known in advance and following disciplinary expectations, such a design can take greater advantage of already developed instruments and preconceived coding schemes.

In intrinsic case study, researchers do not avoid generalization—they cannot. Certainly they generalize to happenings of their cases at times yet to come and in other situations. They expect readers to comprehend the reported interpretations but to modify their (the readers') own. Thus researchers use the methods for casework that they actually use to learn enough about their cases to encapsulate complex meanings into finite reports—and thus to describe the cases in sufficient descriptive narrative so that readers can vicariously experience these happenings and draw conclusions (which may differ from those of the researchers).

Even intrinsic case study can be seen as a small step toward grand generalization (Campbell, 1975; Vaughan, 1992), especially in the case that runs counter to the existing rule. Damage occurs when the commitment to generalize or to theorize runs so strong that the researcher's attention is drawn away from features important for understanding the case itself.[8] The case study researcher faces a strategic decision in regard to how much and how long the complexities of the case should be studied. Not everything about the case can be understood—how much needs to be? Each researcher has choices to make.

Contexts and Situations

With its own unique history, the case is a complex entity operating within a number of contexts—physical, economic, ethical, aesthetic, and so on. The case is singular, but it has subsections (e.g., production, marketing, sales departments), groups (e.g., students, teachers, parents), occasions (e.g., workdays, holidays, days near holidays), a concatenation of domains—many so complex that at best they can only be sampled.

Holistic case study calls for the examination of these complexities. As Yvonna Lincoln and Egon Guba point out in Chapter 6 of Volume 1, much qualitative research is based on a holistic view that social phenomena, human dilemmas, and the nature of cases are situational and influenced by happenings of many kinds. Qualitative researchers are sometimes disposed toward causal determination of events (Becker, 1992) but more often tend to perceive, as does Tolstoy in *War and Peace*, events not simply and singly caused. Many find the search for cause of little value, and dramatize instead the coincidence of events, seeing some events as purposive, some as situational, many of them interrelated. They favor inquiry designs that seek data describing diverse operations of the case. To do case studies does not require examination of diverse issues and contexts, but that is the way that most qualitative researchers do them.

Organizing Around Issues

A case study, like research of all kinds, has conceptual structure. It is usually organized around a small number of research questions. These are not just information questions, such as "Who influenced her career choice?" or "What was the impact of his teaching?" They are issues or thematic lines, such as "In what ways did the change in hiring policy require a change in performance standards?" or "Did the addiction therapy, originally developed for male clients, need reconceptualization for women?"

Issues are complex, situated, problematic relationships. They invite attention to ordinary experience but also to the language and understanding of the common disciplines of knowledge, such as sociology, economics, ethics, and literary criticism. Seeking a different purview from that of most crafters of experiments and testers of hypotheses, qualitative case researchers orient to complexities connecting ordinary practice in natural habitats to the abstractions and concerns of diverse academic disciplines. This broader purview is applied to the single case, but does not replace it as focus. Generalization and proof (Becker, 1992) linger in the mind of the researcher, so a tension exists.[9]

The issues mentioned two paragraphs back were aimed at a particular case, but their statement can be more general: "Does change in hiring policy away from affirmative action require change in performance standards?" or "Does addiction therapy originally developed for male clients need reconceptualization for women?" But even when stated for generalization, the issues, as organizers for case study, serve to deepen understanding of the specific case.

Starting with a topical concern, researchers may pose "foreshadowed problems,"[10] concentrate on issue-related observations, interpret patterns of data that reform the issues as assertions. The transformation I have experienced in my work in program evaluation is illustrated by the

TABLE 5.1 An Example of Issue Evolution in a Study

1. *Topical issue:* The goals of the music education program.
2. *Foreshadowed problem:* The majority of the community supports the present emphasis on band, chorus, and performances, but a few teachers and community leaders want a more intellectual emphasis, including history, literature, and critical review of music.
3. *Issue under development:* What are the pros and cons of having this teaching staff teach music theory and music as a discipline in courses required of everyone?
4. *Assertion:* This community was found (by the researcher) to be not supportive of the extra funding necessary to provide intellectual learning of music for all secondary school students.

sequence displayed in Table 5.1, issues for a hypothetical case study of a music education program.

In choosing issues to organize their studies, researchers reflect their orientations to intrinsic or instrumental study. To treat the case as an exemplar, they ask, Which issues bring out our initial concerns, the dominant theme? To maximize understanding of the case, they ask, Which issues seek out compelling uniquenesses? For an evaluation study, they ask, Which issues help reveal merit and shortcoming? But in general, they ask, Which issues facilitate the planning and activities of inquiry, including inspiring and rehabilitating the researcher? Issues are chosen partly in terms of what can be learned within the opportunities for study. They will be chosen differently depending on the purpose of the study, and differently by different researchers. One might say a contract is drawn between researcher and phenomenon. For all the devotion to science or to a client, What can be learned *here* that a researcher needs to know?

The issues used to organize the study may or may not be the ones used to report the case to others. Observing is different work from presenting the case report. At the end, it may be the anticipated issues of readers that will structure the report.

Storytelling

Some call for letting the case "tell its own story" (Carter, 1993; Coles, 1989). We cannot be sure that a case, telling its own story, will tell all or tell well—but the ethos of *interpretive* study, seeking out emic meanings held by the people within the case, is strong. The choices of presentation styles are many. John Van Maanen (1988) identifies these: realistic, impressionistic, confessional, critical, formal, literary, and jointly told. One cannot know at the outset what the issues, the perceptions, the theory will be. Case researchers enter the scene expecting, even knowing, that certain events, problems, and relationships will be important, yet they discover that some of them this time will be of little consequence (Parlett & Hamilton, 1976; Smith, 1994). Case content evolves even in the last phases of writing.

Storytelling as cultural representation and as sociological text emerges from many traditions, but nowhere more strongly than oral history and folklore, and is becoming more disciplined in a line of work called *narrative inquiry* (Clandinin & Connelly, 1999; Ellis & Bochner, 1996; Lockridge, 1988; Richardson, 1997; see also the *Journal of Narrative and Life History*).

Even when empathic and respectful of each person's realities, the researcher decides what the case's *own story* is, or at least what will be included in the report. More will be pursued than was volunteered. Less will be reported than was learned. Even though the competent researcher will be guided by what the case somehow indicates is most important, even though patrons, other researchers, and those researched will advise, what is necessary for an understanding of the case will be decided by the researcher.[11] What results may be the case's own story, but the report will be the researcher's dressing of the case's own story. This is not to dismiss the aim of finding the story that best represents the case but to remind the reader that, usually, the researcher ultimately decides criteria of representation.[12]

Many a researcher would like to tell the whole story but of course cannot; the whole story exceeds anyone's knowing, anyone's telling. Even those inclined to tell all find strong the obligation to winnow and consolidate. A continuum runs from telling lots to telling nothing. The holistic researcher, like the single-issue researcher, must choose. Criteria for selecting content are many (Van Maanen, 1988). Some are set by funding agencies, prospective readers, rhetorical convention, the researcher's career pattern, and the prospect of publication. Some criteria are set by a notion of what represents the case most fully, most appreciably for the hospitality received, most comprehensibly. These are subjective choices not unlike those all researchers make in choosing what to study. Some are made while the case study is being designed, but some continue to be made through the final hours.

◆ Learning From the Particular Case

The researcher is a teacher using at least two pedagogical methods (Eisner, 1985). Teaching *didactically,* the researcher teaches what he or she has learned. Arranging for what educationists call *discovery learning,* the researcher provides material for readers to learn, on their own, things the teacher does not know as well as those he or she does know. What can one learn from a single case? Donald Campbell (1975), David Hamilton (1980), Stephen Kemmis (1980), and Robert Yin (1989) are among those who have advanced the epistemology of the particular.[13] How we learn from the singular case is related to how the case is like and unlike other cases (i.e., comparisons). Yet, in the words of Charles Ragin, "variable oriented comparative work (e.g., quantitative cross-national research) as compared with case oriented comparative work disembodies and obscures cases" (Ragin & Becker, 1992, p. 5).

From case reports we increase both propositional and experiential knowledge (Geertz, 1983; Polanyi, 1962; Rumelhart & Ortony, 1977; von Wright, 1971). Readers assimilate certain descriptions and assertions into memory. When the researcher's narrative provides opportunity for vicarious experience, readers extend their memories of happenings. Naturalistic, ethnographic case materials, to some extent, parallel actual experience, feeding into the most fundamental processes of awareness and understanding. Deborah Trumbull and I have called these processes *naturalistic generalization* (Stake & Trumbull, 1982). The reader comes to know some things told, as if he or she had experienced it. Enduring meanings come from encounter, and are modified and reinforced by repeated encounter.

In life itself, this occurs seldom to the individual alone but in the presence of others. In a social process, together they bend, spin, consolidate, and enrich their understandings. We come to know what has happened partly in terms of what others reveal as their experience. The case researcher emerges from one social experience, the observation, to choreograph another, the report. Knowledge is socially constructed, so we constructivists believe (see Schwandt, Chapter 7, Volume 1), and, in their experiential and contextual accounts, case study researchers assist readers in the construction of knowledge.

Knowledge Transfer From Researcher to Reader

Both researcher and reader bring their conceptual structures, for example, advanced organizers (Ausubel & Fitzgerald, 1961), schemata (Anderson, 1977), and an unfolding of realization (Bohm, 1985). Some such frameworks for thought are unconscious. Communication is facilitated by carefully crafted structures. Thought itself, conversation surely, and writing especially draw phrases into paragraphs, append labels onto constructs. Meanings aggregate or attenuate. Associations become relationships; relationships become theory (Robinson, 1951). Generalization can be an unconscious process for both researcher and reader.

In private and personal ways, ideas are structured, highlighted, subordinated, connected, embedded *in* contexts, embedded *with* illustration, laced with favor and doubt. However moved to share ideas, however clever and elaborated their writings, case researchers, like others, pass along to readers some of their personal meanings of events and relationship—and fail to pass along others. They know that the reader, too, will add and subtract, invent and shape—reconstructing the knowledge in ways that leave it differently connected and more likely to be personally useful.

A researcher's knowledge of the case faces hazardous passage from writing to reading. The writer seeks ways of safeguarding the trip. Even as reading begins, often much earlier, the case assumes a place in the company of previously known cases. Conceptually for the reader, the new case cannot be but some combination of cases already known. A new case without commonality cannot be understood. Yet a new case without distinction will not be noticed. Researchers cannot know well the already known cases, the peculiarities of mind, of their readers. They seek ways to protect and substantiate the transfer of knowledge.

The researcher recognizes a need to accommodate the readers' preexisting knowledge. Although everyone deals with this need every day and draws upon a lifetime of experience, we know precious little about how new experience merges with old. According to Spiro, Vispoel, Schmitz, Samarapungavan, and Boerger (1987), most personal experience is *illstructured*, neither pedagogically nor epistemologically neat. It follows that a well-structured, propositional presentation will often not be the better way to *transfer* experiential knowledge. The reader has a certain *cognitive flexibility*, the readiness to assemble a situation-relative schema from the knowledge fragments of a new encounter. Spiro et al. contend that

> the best way to learn and instruct in order to attain the goal of cognitive flexibility in knowledge representation for future application is by a method of case-based presentations which treats a content domain as a landscape that is explored by "criss-crossing" it in many directions, by reexamining each case "site" in the varying contexts of different neighboring cases, and by using a variety of abstract dimensions for comparing cases. (p. 178)

Transfer remains difficult to understand. And even less understood is how a small aspect of the case may be found by many readers to modify an existing understanding about cases in general, even when the case is not typical.[14] In a ghetto school, I observed a teacher with one set of rules for classroom decorum—except that for Adam, a nearly expelled, indomitable youngster, a more liberal set had to be continuously invented (Stake, 1995). Reading my account, teachers from very different schools agreed with both. "Yes, you have to be strict with the rules." "Yes, sometimes you have to bend the rules." They recognized in the report an unusual but generalizable circumstance. People find in case reports certain insights into the human condition, even while being well aware of the atypicality of the case. They may be *too* quick to accept the insight. The case researcher needs to provide grounds for validating both the observation and generalization.

Triangulation

With reporting and reading both "ill-structured" (and within an atmosphere of constructivism), it is not surprising to find here a tolerance of ambiguity and the championing of multiple perspectives. Still, I have yet to meet any case researchers who are unconcerned about the clarity and validity of their own communications. Even if meanings do not transfer intact but squeeze into the conceptual space of the reader, there is no less urgency for researchers to assure that their senses of situation, observation, reporting, and reading stay within some limits of correspondence. However accuracy is construed, researchers don't want to be inaccurate, caught without confirmation. Joseph Maxwell (1992) has written of the need for thinking of validity separately for descriptions, interpretations, theories, generalizations, and evaluative judgments.

To reduce the likelihood of misinterpretation, researchers employ various procedures, two of the most common being redundancy of data gathering and procedural challenges to explanations (Denzin, 1989; Goetz & LeCompte, 1984). For qualitative casework, these procedures generally are called *triangulation*. Triangulation has been generally considered a process of using multiple perceptions to clarify meaning, verifying the repeatability of an observation or interpretation.[15] But, acknowledging that no observations or interpretations are perfectly repeatable, triangulation serves also to clarify meaning by identifying different ways the phenomenon is being seen (Flick, 1998; Silverman, 1993; see also Smith, Chapter 12, Volume 3).

Comparisons

Researchers report their cases as cases, knowing they will be compared to others. They differ as to how much they will take responsibility for making comparisons, setting up comparative cases for the reader or acknowledging reference cases different for each reader. Most naturalistic, ethnographic, phenomenological researchers will concentrate on describing the present case in sufficient detail so that the reader can make good comparisons. Sometimes the researcher will point out comparisons that might be made. Many quantitative and evaluation case researchers will try to provide some comparisons, sometimes by presenting one or more reference cases, sometimes by providing statistical norms for reference groups from which a hypothetical reference case can be imagined. Both the quantitative and qualitative approaches provide narrow grounds for strict comparison of cases, even though a tradition of grand comparison exists within comparative anthropology and related disciplines (Ragin, 1987; Sjoberg, Williams, Vaughan, & Sjoberg, 1991; Tobin, 1989).

I see comparison as actually competing with learning about and from the particular case. Comparison is a grand epistemological strategy, a powerful conceptual mechanism, fixing attention upon one or a few attributes. And it obscures case knowledge that fails to facilitate comparison. Comparative description is the opposite of what Clifford Geertz (1973) calls "thick description." Thick description of a music program, for example, would include conflicting perceptions of the staffing, recent program changes, the charisma of the choral director, the working relationship with a church organist, diverse interest in a critical vote of the school board, and the lack of student interest in taking up the clarinet. In these particularities lie the vitality, trauma, and uniqueness of the case. Comparison might be made on any of these characteristics, but it tends to be made on more general variables traditionally noted in the organization of music programs, such as staffing, budget, and tour policy. With concentration on the bases for comparison, uniquenesses and complexities will be glossed over. A research design featuring comparison substitutes (a) *the comparison* for (b) *the case* as the focus of the study.

Regardless of the type of case study—intrinsic, instrumental, or collective—readers often learn little from control or reference cases chosen only for comparison. When there are multiple cases of intrinsic interest, then, of course, it can be useful to compare them.[16] But more often than not, there is but one case of intrinsic interest, if any at all. Readers with intrinsic interest in the case learn more of it directly from the description, not ignoring comparisons with other cases but not concentrating on comparisons. Readers examining instrumental case studies are shown how the phenomenon exists within particular cases. As to accuracy, differences are fundamentally more inaccurate than simple measurements. Similarly, conclusions about the differences between any two cases are less to be trusted than conclusions about one. Still, illustration as to how a phenomenon occurs in the circumstances of several exemplars can provide valuable and trustworthy knowledge (Vaughan, in press).

Many are the ways of conceptualizing cases to maximize learning from the case. The case is expected to be something that functions, that operates; the study is the observation of operations. There is something to be described and interpreted. The conceptions of most naturalistic, holistic, ethnographic, phenomenological case studies need accurate description and subjective, yet disciplined, interpretation; a respect and curiosity for culturally different perceptions of phenomena; and empathic representation of local settings—all blending (perhaps clumped) within a constructivist epistemology.

◆ Arrangements for the Study

Perhaps the simplest rule for method in qualitative casework is this: Place your best intellect into the thick of what is going on. The brain work ostensibly is observational, but, more basically, it is *reflective*.[17] In being ever reflective, the researcher is committed to pondering the impressions, deliberating recollections and records—but not necessarily following the conceptualizations of theorists, actors, or audiences (Carr & Kemmis, 1986). Local meanings are important; foreshadowed meanings are important; and readers' consequential meanings are important. The case researcher teases out meanings of these three kinds and, for whatever reason, works on one kind more than the other two. In each case, the work is reflective.[18]

If we typify qualitative casework, we see data sometimes precoded but continuously interpreted, on first sighting and again and again. Records and tabulations are perused not only for classification and pattern recognition but also for "crisscrossed" reflection (Spiro et al., 1987). An observation is interpreted against one issue, perspective, or utility, then interpreted against others. Qualitative case study is characterized by researchers spending extended time, on site, personally in contact with activities and operations of the case, reflecting, revising meanings of what is going on.

Teaming

Naturalistic, ethnographic, phenomenological caseworkers seek to see what is *ordinary* in happenings, in settings, in expressions of value. Blumer (1969, p. 149) calls for us to accept, develop, and use the distinctive expression (of the particular case) in order to detect and study the common. What detail of life the researchers are unable to see for themselves they obtain by interviewing people who did see it or by finding documents recording it. Part IV of this *Handbook* deals extensively with the methods of qualitative research, particularly observation, interview, coding, data management, and interpretation. These pertain, of course, to qualitative case study.

Documenting the ordinary takes a lot of time for data gathering, and more for arrangements, analysis, and write-up. In many studies, there are no clear stages: Issue development continues to the end of the study; write-up begins with preliminary observations. A speculative, page-allocating outline for the report helps anticipate how issues will be handled and how the case will become visible. For most researchers, to set out upon an unstructured, open-ended study is a calamity in the making. Still, the caseworker needs to anticipate the need to recognize and develop late-emerging issues. Many qualitative field-workers invest little in instrument construction, partly because even the familiar case is too little known. And the budget is too quickly consumed by devising and field testing instruments to pursue what turn out to be too many foreshadowing questions, with some of them maturing, some dying, some moving to new levels of complexity. The ordinary is too complicated to be mastered in the time available.

When the case is too large for one researcher to know well or for a collective case study, teaming is an important option. The method requires integrated, holistic comprehension of the case, but in the larger studies, no one individual can handle the complexity. Coding can be a great help if the team is experienced in the process and with each other. But learning a detailed analytic coding system within the study period often is too great a burden (Smith & Dwyer, 1979), reducing observations to simple categories, eating up the on-site time. As much as possible, sites, key groups or actors, and issues should be assigned to single team members, including junior members. The case's parts to be studied and the research issues need to be pared down to what can be comprehended by the collection of team members. It is better to negotiate the parts to be studied and the parts not, and then do an in-depth study pursuing a few key issues. Each team member writes up his or her parts; other team members need to read and critique them. Usually the team leader needs to write the synthesis, getting critiques from the team, data sources, and selected skeptical friends.

Case Selection

Perhaps the most unique aspect of case study in the social sciences and human services is the selection of cases to study. Intrinsic casework regularly begins with cases already identified. The doctor, the social worker, the program evaluator receive their cases; they do not choose them. The cases are of prominent interest before formal study begins. Instrumental and collective casework regularly requires researchers to choose their cases. Understanding the critical phenomena depends on choosing the case well (Patton, 1990; Vaughan, 1992; Yin, 1989). Suppose we are trying to understand the behavior of people who take hostages and decide to probe the phenomenon using a case study. Hostage taking does not happen often—in the whole world there are few cases to choose. Current options, let us imagine, boil down to a bank robber, an airline hijacker, an estranged father who kidnapped his own child, and a Shi'ite Muslim group. We want to generalize about hostage-taking behavior, yet realize that each of these cases, each sample of one, weakly *represents* the larger group of interest.

When one designs a study in the manner advocated by Michael Huberman and Matthew Miles (1994) and by Gery Ryan and Russell Bernard in Chapter 7 of Volume 3, nothing is more important than making a proper selection of cases. For this design, formal sampling is needed. The cases are expected to represent some population of cases. The phenomenon of interest observable in the case represents the phenomenon writ large. For Huberman and Miles, Yin, and Malinowski, the main work is science, an enterprise to gain the best possible explanations of phenomena (von Wright, 1971). In the beginning, phenomena are given; the cases are opportunities to study the phenomena. But even in the larger collective case studies, the sample sizes are usually much too small to warrant random selection. For qualitative fieldwork, we draw a purposive sample, building in variety and acknowledging opportunities for intensive study.

The phenomenon on the table is hostage taking. We want to improve our understanding of hostage taking, to fit it into what we know about criminology, conflict resolution, human relations—that is, various *abstract dimensions*.[19] We recognize a large population of hypothetical cases, a small subpopulation of accessible cases. We want to generalize about hostage taking without special interest in any of those cases available for study. On representational grounds, the epistemological opportunity seems small, but we are optimistic that we can learn some important things from almost any case. We choose one or a small number of exemplars. Hostages usually are strangers to their captors who happen to be available. We might rule out studying a father who takes his own child as hostage. Such kidnappings may actually be more common, but we rule out the father. We are more interested in hostage taking accompanying a criminal act, hostage taking in order to gain refuge. The researcher examines various interests in the phenomenon, selecting a case of some typicality, but leaning toward those cases that seem to offer *opportunity to learn*. My choice would be to examine that case from which we feel we can learn the most.[20] That may mean taking the one most accessible, the one we can spend the most time with. Potential for learning is a different and sometimes superior criterion to representativeness. Isn't it better to learn a lot from an atypical case than a little from a seemingly typical case?

Another illustration: Suppose we are interested in the attractiveness of interactive displays (which the visitor manipulates and gets feedback from) in children's museums. We have resources to study four museums, to do a collective study of four cases. It is likely that we would set up a typology, perhaps of (a) museum types (namely, art, science, and history), (b) city types (namely, large and very large), and (c) program types (namely, exhibitory and participative), making a 12-cell matrix. Examples probably cannot be found for all 12 cells, but resources do not allow us to study 12 anyway. With four to be studied, we are likely to start out thinking we should have one art, one history, and two science museums (because interactive displays are more common in science museums), two located in large cities and two in very large cities, and two each of the program types. But when we actually look at existing cases, the logistics, the potential reception, the resources, and additional characteristics of relevance, we move toward choosing four museums to study that offer variety (falling short of structured representation) across the attributes, the four that give us the best opportunities to learn about interactive displays.[21] Any best possible selection of four museums from a balanced design would not give us compelling representation of museums as a whole, and certainly not a statistical basis for generalizing about interactions between interactivity and site characteristics. Several desirable types usually have to be omitted. Even for collective case studies, selection by sampling of attributes should not be the highest priority. Balance and variety are important; opportunity to learn is of primary importance.

Cases Within the Case

The same process of selection will occur as part of intrinsic case study. Even though the case is decided in advance (usually), there are subsequent choices to make about persons, places, and events to observe. Here again, training and intuition tell us to seek a good sample. Suppose that we are studying a program for placing computers in the homes of fourth graders for scholastic purposes.[22] The cases—that is, the school sites—have already been selected. Although there is a certain coordination of activity, each participating researcher has one case study to develop. A principal issue has to do with impact on the family, because certain expectations of computer use accompany placement in the home. (The computer should be available for word processing, record keeping, and games by family members, but certain time should be set aside for fourth-grade homework.) At one site, 50 homes now have computers. The researcher can get certain information from every home, but observation in the home can occur only in a small number. Which homes should be selected? Just as in the collective case study, the researcher notes attributes of interest: gender of the fourth grader, siblings, family structure, home discipline, previous use of computers and other technology in the home, and so on. The researcher discusses these characteristics with informants, gets recommendations, visits several homes, and gets attribute data. The choices are made, assuring variety but not necessarily representativeness, without strong argument for typicality, again weighted by considerations of access and even by hospitality, for the time is short and perhaps too little can be learned from inhospitable parents.[23] Here, too, the primary criterion is opportunity to learn.

Ethics

Ethical considerations for qualitative research are reviewed by Clifford Christians in Chapter 5 of Volume 1 (and elsewhere by such as Coles, 1997; Graue & Walsh, 1998). Case studies often deal with matters of public interest but for which there is neither public nor scholarly "right to know." Funding, scholarly intent, or a passed preliminary oral does not constitute license to invade the privacy of others. The value of the best research is not likely to outweigh injury to a person exposed. Qualitative researchers are guests in the private spaces of the world. Their manners should be good and their code of ethics strict.

Along with much qualitative work, case study research shares an intense interest in personal views and circumstances. Those whose lives and expressions are portrayed risk exposure and embarrassment, as well as loss of standing, employment, and self-esteem. Something of a contract exists between researcher and the researched, a disclosing and protective covenant, usually informal, but best not silent—a moral obligation (Schwandt, 1993).[24] Risks to well-being cannot be inventoried but should be exemplified. Issues of observation and reportage should be discussed in advance. Limits to access should be suggested and agreements heeded. It is important (but never sufficient) for targeted persons to receive drafts revealing how they are presented, quoted, and interpreted and for the researcher to listen well for signs of concern. It is important that researchers exercise great caution to minimize the risks. Even with good information, the researched cannot be expected to protect themselves against the risks inherent in participation. Researchers must follow rules for protection of human subjects (yet should protest those rules when they serve only to protect the institution from litigation). Researchers should go beyond those rules, avoiding low-priority probing of sensitive issues and drawing in advisers and reviewers to help extend the protective system.

Ethical problems arise (inside and outside the research topics) with nondisclosure of malfeasance and immorality. When rules of study are set that prevent the researcher from "whistle-blowing" or that limit the exercise of compassion, a problem exists. Where an expectation has been raised that propriety is being examined and no mention is made of serious impropriety observed, the report is deceptive. Breach of ethics is seldom a simple matter; often it occurs when two contradictory standards apply, such as withholding full disclosure (as per the contract) in order to protect a good but vulnerable agency (Mabry, 1999). Ongoing and summative review procedures are needed, with impetus from conscience, from stakeholders, and from the research community.

◆ Summary

The major conceptual responsibilities of the qualitative case researcher are as follows:

1. Bounding the case, conceptualizing the object of study;
2. Selecting phenomena, themes, or issues—that is, the research questions—to emphasize;
3. Seeking patterns of data to develop the issues;
4. Triangulating key observations and bases for interpretation;
5. Selecting alternative interpretations to pursue;
6. Developing assertions or generalizations about the case.

Except for the first of these, the steps are similar to those taken by other qualitative researchers. The more the researcher has intrinsic interest in the case, the more the focus of study will be on the case's uniqueness, particular context, issues, and story.

Some major stylistic options for case researchers include the following:

1. How much to make the report a story;
2. How much to compare with other cases;
3. How much to formalize generalizations or leave that to readers;

4. How much to include description in the report of the researcher interacting;

5. Whether or not and how much to anonymize.

Case study is a part of scientific methodology, but its purpose is not limited to the advance of science. Single or a few cases are poor representation of a population of cases and questionable grounds for advancing grand generalization. Yet, "because more than one theoretical notion may be guiding an analysis, confirmation, fuller specification, and contradiction all may result from one case study" (Vaughan, 1992, p. 175). For example, we lose confidence in the generalization that a child of separated parents is better off placed with the mother when we find a single instance of resulting injury. Case studies are of value for refining theory and suggesting complexities for further investigation, as well as helping to establish the limits of generalizability.

Case study can also be a disciplined force in public policy setting and reflection on human experience. Vicarious experience is an important basis for refining action options and expectation. Formal epistemology needs further development, but somehow people draw, from the description of an individual case, implications for other cases—not always correctly, but with a confidence shared by people of dissimilar views.

The purpose of a case report is not to represent the world, but to represent the case. Criteria for conducting the kind of research that leads to valid generalization need modification to fit the search for effective particularization. The utility of case research to practitioners and policy makers is in its extension of experience. The methods of qualitative case study are largely the methods of disciplining personal and particularized experience.

◆ Notes

1. Many case studies are both qualitative and quantitative. In search of fundamental pursuits common to both qualitative and quantitative research, Robert Yin (1992) analyzed three well-crafted research efforts: (a) a quantitative investigation to resolve disputed authorship of the *Federalist Papers,* (b) a qualitative study of Soviet intent at the time of the Cuban missile crisis, and (c) his own studies of the recognizability of human faces. He found four common commitments: to bring expert knowledge to bear upon the phenomena studied, to round up all the relevant data, to examine rival interpretations, and to ponder and probe the degree to which the findings have implication elsewhere. These commitments are as important in case research as in any other kind of research.

2. Ethnomethodologists study *methods* as topics of inquiry, examining how certain things, such as work or play, get done (Garfinkel, 1967). Coming to understand a case usually requires extensive examination of how things get done, but the prime referent in case study is the case, not the methods by which cases operate.

3. Definition of the case is not independent of interpretive paradigm or methods of inquiry. Seen from different worldviews and in different situations, the "same" case *is* different. And however we originally define the case, the working definition changes as we study. And the definition of the case changes in different ways under different methods of study. The case of Theodore Roosevelt was not just differently portrayed but differently defined as biographer Edmund Morris (1979) presented him as "the Dude from New York," "the Dear Old Beloved Brother," "the Snake in the Grass," "the Rough Rider," and "the Most Famous Man in America."

4. The history of case study, like the history of curiosity and common sense, is found throughout the library. Peeps at that history can be found in the work of Bogdan and Biklen (1982), Delamont (1992), Feagin, Orum, and Sjoberg (1991), Stake (1978), White (1992), and Wieviorka (1992), as well as throughout this volume.

5. Collective case study is essentially what Herriott and Firestone (1983) call "multisite qualitative research." Multisite program evaluation is another common example. A number of German sociologists, such as Martin Kohli and Fritz Schütze, have used collective case studies with Strauss's grounded theory approach.

6. In law, the *case* has a special definition; the practice of law itself could be called case study.

7. In a thoughtful review of a draft of this chapter, Orlando Fals Borda urged me to abandon the effort to promote intrinsic casework and the study of particularity. In persisting here, I think it important to support disciplined and scholarly study that takes up important questions but has no scientific aspiration.

8. In 1922, Bronislaw Malinowski said, "One of the first conditions of acceptable Ethnographic work certainly is that it should deal with the totality of all social, cultural and psychological aspects of the community" (1922/1984, p. xvi). Good spirit there, although totalities defy the acuity of the eye and the longevity of the watch.

9. Generalization from collective case study has been discussed by Herriott and Firestone (1983), Miles and Huberman (1994), and Vaughan (1992).

10. Malinowski (1922/1984) claims that we can distinguish between arriving with closed minds and arriving with an idea of what to look for. He notes: "Good training in theory, and acquaintance with its latest results, is not identical with being burdened with 'preconceived ideas.' If a man sets out on an expedition, determined to prove certain hypotheses, if he is incapable of changing his views constantly and casting them off ungrudgingly under the pressure of evidence, needless to say his work will be worthless. But the more problems he brings with him into the field, the more he is in the habit of moulding his theories according to facts, and of seeing facts in their bearing upon theory, the better he is equipped for the work. Preconceived ideas are pernicious in any scientific work, but *foreshadowed problems* are the main endowment of a scientific thinker, and these problems are first revealed to the observer by his theoretical studies" (p. 9).

11. It appears I claim here there is no such thing as participatory evaluation (Cousins & Earl, 1992; Greene, Chapter 16, Volume 3) or participatory action research (Fals Borda, 1998; Heron, 1996; Whyte, 1991). There is. Shared responsibility for design, data

gathering, and interpretation are to be found, and can be what is needed. Most researchers make some effort to negotiate interpretations, but ultimately decide themselves what array of interpretations to present. However interactive the researcher is, there is an abiding professional responsibility for him or her to decide what will be included under his or her byline. In those situations where the values of the study have been collaboratively set, it is important for the reader to know it.

12. The case report is a representation of the case or, more considerately, a collection of representations. The presumptuousness of representations has been a "hot topic" in postmodern discussions (Clifford, 1983). Researchers need to locate themselves somewhere between extruding description from the template of their personal experience and saying nothing.

13. Among the earlier philosophers of science providing groundwork for qualitative contributions to theory elaboration were Herbert Blumer, Barney Glaser, Bronislaw Malinowski, and Robert Merton.

14. Sociologists have used the term *micro/macro* to refer to the leap from understanding individual cases or parts to understanding the system as a whole. Even without an adequate epistemological map, sociologists do leap, and so do our readers (Collins, 1981).

15. Creative use of "member checking," submitting drafts for review by data sources, is one of the most needed forms of validation of qualitative research (Glesne & Peshkin, 1992; Lincoln & Guba, 1985).

16. Evaluation studies comparing the innovative program to a control case regularly fail to make the comparison credible. No matter how well studied, the control case too weakly represents cases currently known by the reader. By comprehensively describing the program case, the researcher should help the reader draw naturalistic generalizations.

17. I would prefer to call it *interpretive* to emphasize the production of meanings, but ethnographers have used that term to mean "learn the special views of actors, the local meanings" (see Erickson, 1986; Schwandt, Chapter 7, Volume 1).

18. Ethnographic use of the term *reflective* sometimes limits attention to the need for self-challenging the researcher's etic issues, frame of reference, cultural bias (see Tedlock, Chapter 6, this volume). That challenge is important, but, following Donald Schön (1983), I refer to a general frame of mind when I call qualitative casework *reflective*.

19. As indicated in a previous section, I call them issues or issue areas. Mary Kennedy (1979) calls them "relevant attributes." Spiro et al. (1987) call them "abstract dimensions." Malinowski (1922/1984) calls them "theories." In our research, these will be our "working theories" more than the "grand theories" of the disciplines.

20. My emphasis is on learning the most about both the individual case and the phenomenon, especially the latter if the special circumstances may yield unusual insight into an issue.

21. Firestone (1993) advises maximizing diversity and being "as like the population of interest as possible."

22. This in fact happened with the Buddy Project, a component of the Indiana public school reform effort of 1990-1993 (see Quinn & Quinn, 1992).

23. Patton (1990), Strauss and Corbin (1990), and Firestone (1993) have discussed successive selection of cases over time.

24. A special obligation exists to protect those with limited resources. Those who comply with the researcher's requests, who contribute in some way to the making of the case,

should not thus be hurt—usually. When continuing breaches of ethics or morality are discovered, or are the reason for the study, the researcher must take some ameliorative action. Exposé and critique are legitimate within case study, but luring self-indictment out of a respondent is no more legitimate in research than in the law.

◆ References

Adams, H. (1918). *The education of Henry Adams: An autobiography*. Boston: Houghton Mifflin.

Anderson, R. C. (1977). The notion of schema and the educational enterprise. In R. C. Anderson, R. J. Spiro, & W. E. Montague (Eds.), *Schooling and the acquisition of knowledge* (pp. 415-431). Hillsdale, NJ: Lawrence Erlbaum.

Asmussen, K. J., & Creswell, J. W. (1997). Campus response to a student gunman. In J. W. Creswell, *Qualitative inquiry and research design: Choosing among five traditions* (pp. 357-373). Thousand Oaks, CA: Sage. (Reprinted from *Journal of Higher Education*, 1995, 66, 575-591)

Ausubel, D. P., & Fitzgerald, D. (1961). Meaningful learning and retention: Interpersonal cognitive variables. *Review of Educational Research, 31*, 500-510.

Becker, H. S. (1992). Cases, causes, conjunctures, stories, and imagery. In C. C. Ragin & H. S. Becker (Eds.), *What is a case? Exploring the foundations of social inquiry* (pp. 205-216). Cambridge: Cambridge University Press.

Becker, H. S., Geer, B., Hughes, E. C., & Strauss, A. L. (1961). *Boys in white: Student culture in medical school*. Chicago: University of Chicago Press.

Blumer, H. (1969). *Symbolic interactionism: Perspective and method*. Englewood Cliffs, NJ: Prentice Hall.

Bogdan, R. C., & Biklen, S. K. (1982). *Qualitative research for education: An introduction to theory and methods*. Boston: Allyn & Bacon.

Bohm, D. (1985). *Unfolding meaning: A weekend of dialogue with David Bohm*. New York: Routledge.

Campbell, D. T. (1975). Degrees of freedom and case study. *Comparative Political Studies, 8*, 178-193.

Carr, W. L., & Kemmis, S. (1986). *Becoming critical: Education, knowledge and action research*. London: Falmer.

Carter, K. (1993). The place of story in the study of teaching and teacher education. *Educational Researcher, 22*(1), 5-12.

Clandinin, D. J., & Connelly, F. M. (1999). *Narrative inquiry: Experience and story in qualitative research*. San Francisco: Jossey-Bass.

Clifford, J. (1983). On anthropological authority. *Representations, 1*, 118-146.

Coles, R. (1989). *The call of stories: Teaching and the moral imagination*. Boston: Houghton Mifflin.

Coles, R. (1997). *Doing documentary work*. Oxford: Oxford University Press.

Collins, R. (1981). On the microfoundations of macrosociology. *American Journal of Sociology, 86,* 984-1014.

Connell, R. W. (1985). *Teachers' work.* Sydney: George Allen & Unwin.

Cousins, J. B., & Earl, L. M. (1992). The case for participatory evaluation. *Educational Evaluation and Policy Analysis, 14,* 397-418.

Crabtree, B. F., & Miller, W. L. (1999). Researching practice settings: A case study approach. In B. F. Crabtree & W. L. Miller (Eds.), *Doing qualitative research* (2nd ed.). Thousand Oaks, CA: Sage.

Delamont, S. (1992). *Fieldwork in educational settings: Methods, pitfalls and perspectives.* London: Falmer.

Denzin, N. K. (1989). *The research act: A theoretical introduction to sociological methods* (3rd ed.). Englewood Cliffs, NJ: Prentice Hall.

Eisner, E. W. (Ed.). (1985). *Learning and teaching the ways of knowing* (84th yearbook of the National Society for the Study of Education). Chicago: University of Chicago Press.

Erickson, F. (1986). Qualitative methods in research on teaching. In M. C. Wittrock (Ed.), *Handbook of research on teaching* (3rd ed., pp. 119-161). New York: Macmillan.

Fals Borda, O. (Ed.). (1998). *People's participation: Challenges ahead.* New York: Apex.

Feagin, J. R., Orum, A. M., & Sjoberg, G. (1991). *A case for the case study.* Chapel Hill: University of North Carolina Press.

Ellis, C., & Bochner, A. P. (Eds.). (1996). *Composing ethnography: Alternative forms of qualitative writing.* Walnut Creek, CA: AltaMira.

Firestone, W. A. (1993). Alternative arguments for generalizing from data as applied to qualitative research. *Educational Researcher, 22*(4), 16-23.

Flick, U. (1998). *An introduction to qualitative research: Theory, method and applications.* London: Sage.

Garfinkel, H. (1967). *Studies in ethnomethodology.* Englewood Cliffs, NJ: Prentice Hall.

Geertz, C. (1973). Thick description: Toward an interpretive theory of culture. In C. Geertz, *The interpretation of cultures: Selected essays* (pp. 3-30). New York: Basic Books.

Geertz, C. (1983). *Local knowledge: Further essays in interpretive anthropology.* New York: Basic Books.

Glaser, B. G., & Strauss, A. L. (1967). *The discovery of grounded theory: Strategies for qualitative research.* Chicago: Aldine.

Glesne, C., & Peshkin, A. (1992). *Becoming qualitative researchers: An introduction.* White Plains, NY: Longman.

Goetz, J. P., & LeCompte, M. D. (1984). *Ethnography and qualitative design in educational research.* New York: Academic Press.

Goode, W. J., & Hatt, P. K. (1952). The case study. In W. J. Goode & P. K. Hatt, *Methods of social research* (pp. 330-340). New York: McGraw-Hill.

Gottwald, N. K. (1979). *The tribes of Jahweh: A sociology of the religion of liberated Israel, 1250-1050 B.C.E.* Maryknoll, NY: Orbis.

Graue, M. E., & Walsh, D. J. (1998). *Studying children in context: Theories, methods, ethics.* Thousand Oaks, CA: Sage.

Hamilton, D. (1980). Some contrasting assumptions about case study research and survey analysis. In H. Simons (Ed.), *Towards a science of the singular* (pp. 76-92). Norwich, England: University of East Anglia, Centre for Applied Research in Education.

Heron, J. (1996). *Co-operative inquiry: Research into the human condition.* London: Sage.

Herriott, R. E., & Firestone, W. A. (1983). Multisite qualitative policy research: Optimizing description and generalizability. *Educational Researcher, 12*(2), 14-19.

Huberman, A. M., & Miles, M. B. (1994). Data management and analysis methods. In N. K. Denzin & Y. S. Lincoln (Eds.), *Handbook of qualitative research* (pp. 428-444). Thousand Oaks, CA: Sage.

Kemmis, S. (1980). The imagination of the case and the invention of the study. In H. Simons (Ed.), *Towards a science of the singular* (pp. 93-142). Norwich, England: University of East Anglia, Centre for Applied Research in Education.

Kennedy, M. M. (1979). Generalizing from single case studies. *Evaluation Quarterly, 3,* 661-678.

Kolker, A. (1996). Thrown overboard: The human costs of health care rationing. In C. Ellis & A. P. Bochner (Eds.), *Composing ethnography: Alternative forms of qualitative writing* (pp. 132-159). Walnut Creek, CA: AltaMira.

Kozol, J. (1991). *Savage inequalities.* New York: Harper.

Lincoln, Y. S., & Guba, E. G. (1985). *Naturalistic inquiry.* Beverly Hills, CA: Sage.

Lockridge, E. (1988). Faithful in her fashion: Catherine Barkley, the invisible Hemingway heroine. *Journal of Narrative Technique, 18,* 170-178.

Mabry, L. (1998). Case study methods. In H. J. Walberg & A. J. Reynolds (Eds.), *Advances in educational productivity: Vol. 7. Evaluation research for educational productivity* (pp. 155-170). Greenwich, CT: JAI.

Mabry, L. (1999). Circumstantial ethics. *American Journal of Evaluation, 20,* 199-212.

MacDonald, B., Adelman, C., Kushner, S., & Walker, R. (1982). *Bread and dreams: A case study in bilingual schooling in the U.S.A.* Norwich, England: University of East Anglia, Centre for Applied Research in Education.

Malinowski, B. (1984). *Argonauts of the western Pacific.* Prospect Heights, IL: Waveland. (Original work published 1922)

Maxwell, J. A. (1992). Understanding and validity in qualitative research. *Harvard Educational Review, 63,* 279-300.

McCormick, S. (1994). A nonreader becomes a reader: A case study of literacy acquisition by a severely disabled reader. *Reading Research Quarterly, 29*(2), 157-176.

Miles, M. B., & Huberman, A. M. (1994). *Qualitative data analysis: An expanded sourcebook* (2nd ed.). Thousand Oaks, CA: Sage.

Morris, E. (1979). *The rise of Theodore Roosevelt.* New York: Coward, McCann & Geognegan.

Parlett, M., & Hamilton, D. (1976). Evaluation as illumination: A new approach to the study of innovative programmes. In G. V Glass (Ed.), *Evaluation studies review annual* (Vol. 1, pp. 141-157). Beverly Hills, CA: Sage.

Patton, M. Q. (1990). *Qualitative evaluation and research methods* (2nd ed.). Newbury Park, CA: Sage.

Peshkin, A. (1986). *God's choice.* Chicago: University of Chicago Press.

Polanyi, M. (1962). *Personal knowledge: Towards a post-critical philosophy.* Chicago: University of Chicago Press.

Pugach, M. C. (1998). *On the border of opportunity: Education, community, and language at the U.S.-Mexico line.* Mahwah, NJ: Lawrence Erlbaum.

Quinn, W., & Quinn, N. (1992). *Buddy evaluation.* Oakbrook, IL: North Central Regional Educational Laboratory.

Ragin, C. C. (1987). *The comparative method.* Berkeley: University of California Press.

Ragin, C. C. (1992). Cases of "What is a case?" In C. C. Ragin & H. S. Becker (Eds.), *What is a case? Exploring the foundations of social inquiry* (pp. 1-18). Cambridge: Cambridge University Press.

Ragin, C. C., & Becker, H. S. (Eds.). (1992). *What is a case? Exploring the foundations of social inquiry.* Cambridge: Cambridge University Press.

Raisin, S., & Britton, E. D. (Eds.). (1997). *Bold ventures: Patterns among U.S. innovations in science and mathematics education.* Dordrecht, Netherlands: Kluwer Academic.

Richardson, L. (1997). *Fields of play: Constructing an academic life.* New Brunswick, NJ: Rutgers University Press.

Robinson, W. S. (1951). The logical structure of analytic induction. *American Sociological Review, 16,* 812-818.

Rumelhart, D. E., & Ortony, A. (1977). The representation of knowledge in memory. In R. C. Anderson, R. J. Spiro, & W. E. Montague (Eds.), *Schooling and the acquisition of knowledge* (pp. 99-135). Hillsdale, NJ: Lawrence Erlbaum.

Schön, D. (1983). *The reflective practitioner: How professionals think in action.* New York: Basic Books.

Schwandt, T. A. (1993). Theory for the moral sciences: Crisis of identity and purpose. In G. Mills & D. J. Flinders (Eds.), *Theory and concepts in qualitative research* (pp. 5-23). New York: Teachers College Press.

Silverman, D. (1993). *Interpreting qualitative data.* London: Sage.

Simons, H. (Ed.), (1980). *Towards a science of the singular.* Norwich, England: University of East Anglia, Centre for Applied Research in Education.

Sjoberg, G., Williams, N., Vaughan, T. R., & Sjoberg, A. (1991). The case approach in social research: Basic methodological issues. In J. R. Feagin, A. M. Orum, & G. Sjoberg, *A case for the case study* (pp. 27-79). Chapel Hill: University of North Carolina Press.

Smith, L. M. (1994). Biographical method. In N. K. Denzin & Y. S. Lincoln (Eds.), *Handbook of qualitative research* (pp. 286-305). Thousand Oaks, CA: Sage.

Smith, L. M., & Dwyer, D. (1979). *Federal policy in action: A case study of an urban education project.* Washington, DC: National Institute of Education.

Smith, R. (1889). *An Aberdeenshire village propaganda: Forty years ago.* Edinburgh: David Douglas.

Spiro, R. J., Vispoel, W. P., Schmitz, J. G., Samarapungavan, A., & Boerger, A. E. (1987). Knowledge acquisition for application: Cognitive flexibility and transfer in complex content domains. In B. C. Britton (Ed.), *Executive control processes* (pp. 177-199). Hillsdale, NJ: Lawrence Erlbaum.

Stake, R. E. (1978). The case study method of social inquiry. *Educational Researcher, 7*(2), 5-8.

Stake, R. E. (1988). Case study methods in educational research: Seeking sweet water. In R. M. Jaeger (Ed.), *Complementary methods for research in education* (pp. 253-278). Washington, DC: American Educational Research Association.

Stake, R. E. (1995). *The art of case study research.* Thousand Oaks, CA: Sage.

Stake, R. E., & Trumbull, D. J. (1982). Naturalistic generalizations. *Review Journal of Philosophy and Social Science, 7,* 1-12.

Stenholm, B. (1984). *The Swedish school system.* Stockholm: Swedish Institute.

Stenhouse, L. (1984). Library access, library use and user education in academic sixth forms: An autobiographical account. In R. G. Burgess (Ed.), *The research process in educational settings: Ten case studies* (pp. 211-234). London: Falmer.

Stouffer, S. A. (1941). Notes on the case-study and the unique case. *Sociometry, 4,* 349-357.

Strauss, A. L., & Corbin, J. (1990). *Basics of qualitative research: Grounded theory procedures and techniques.* Newbury Park, CA: Sage.

Tobin, J. (1989). *Preschool in three cultures.* New Haven, CT: Yale University Press.

Van Maanen, J. (1988). *Tales of the field: On writing ethnography.* Chicago: University of Chicago Press.

Vaughan, D. (1992). Theory elaboration: The heuristics of case analysis. In C. C. Ragin & H. S. Becker (Eds.), *What is a case? Exploring the foundations of social inquiry* (pp. 173-292). Cambridge: Cambridge University Press.

Vaughan, D. (1999). The dark side of organizations: Mistake, misconduct and disaster. *Annual Review of Sociology, 25,* 271-305.

Vaughan, D. (in press). *Theorizing: Analogy, cases, and comparative social organization.* Chicago: University of Chicago Press.

von Wright, G. H. (1971). *Explanation and understanding.* London: Routledge & Kegan Paul.

White, H. C. (1992). Cases are for identity, for explanation, or for control. In C. C. Ragin & H. S. Becker (Eds.), *What is a case? Exploring the foundations of social inquiry* (pp. 83104). Cambridge: Cambridge University Press.

Whyte, W. F. (Ed.). (1991). *Participatory action research.* London: Sage.

Wieviorka, M. (1988). *Sociétés et terrorisme.* Paris: Fayard.

Wieviorka, M. (1992). Case studies: History or sociology? In C. C. Ragin & H. S. Becker (Eds.), *What is a case? Exploring the foundations of social inquiry* (pp. 159-172). Cambridge: Cambridge University Press.

Yin, R. K. (1989). *Case study research: Design and methods* (2nd ed.). Newbury Park, CA: Sage.

Yin, R. K. (1992, November). *Evaluation: A singular craft.* Paper presented at the annual meeting of the American Evaluation Association, Seattle, WA.

6

Ethnography and Ethnographic Representation

Barbara Tedlock

◆ Ethnography involves an ongoing attempt to place specific encounters, events, and understandings into a fuller, more meaningful context. It is not simply the production of new information or research data, but rather the way in which such information or data are transformed into a written or visual form. As a result, it combines research design, fieldwork, and various methods of inquiry to produce historically, politically, and personally situated accounts, descriptions, interpretations, and representations of human lives. As an inscription practice, ethnography is a continuation of fieldwork rather than a transparent record of past experiences in the field. The ongoing nature of fieldwork connects important personal experiences with an area of knowledge; as a result, it is located between the interiority of autobiography and the exteriority of cultural analysis.

Because ethnography is both a process and a product, ethnographers' lives are embedded within their field experiences in such a way that all of their interactions involve moral choices. Experience is meaningful, and human behavior is generated from and informed by this meaningfulness. Because ethnographers traverse both territorial and semantic boundaries, fashioning cultures and cultural understandings through an intertwining of voices, they appear heroic to some and ludicrous to others. They are cross-dressers, outsiders wearing insiders' clothes while gradually acquiring the language and behaviors that go along with them.

Long enshrined as a method, a theoretical orientation, and even a philosophical paradigm within anthropology, ethnography has recently been extended (primarily as a useful methodology) to cultural studies, literary theory, folklore, women's studies, sociology, cultural geography, and social psychology. It has also proved useful in a number of applied areas, including education, counseling, organization studies, planning, clinical psychology, nursing, psychiatry, law, criminology, management, and industrial engineering. Wherever it has been adopted, a key assumption has been that by entering into close and relatively prolonged interaction with people (one's own or other) in their everyday lives, ethnographers can better understand the beliefs, motivations, and behaviors of their subjects than they can by using any other approach (Hammersley, 1992).

◆ A Brief Historical Sketch of Ethnography

Over the past two centuries, anthropologists have used a number of ethnographic methods to collect, analyze, and represent information. In the late 19th century the British Association for the Advancement of Science published *Notes and Queries on Anthropology* (1874). The purpose of this circular was to help theorists obtain "accurate anthropological observation on the part of travelers, and to enable those who are not anthropologists themselves to supply the information which is wanted for the scientific study of anthropology at home" (p. iv). This document, filled with ethnocentric ideas and leading questions, was distributed widely to travelers, merchants, missionaries, and government officials. Edward Tylor, keeper of the university museum and reader in anthropology at Oxford University, helped to revise the earlier questionnaire, but soon decided that some of the more promising results should be subject to "a personal survey" by a trained scientist (Stocking, 1983, p. 73). To that end, he established a committee "for the purpose of investigating and publishing reports on the physical characters, languages, and industrial and social condition of the North-western Tribes of the Dominion of Canada" (Tylor, 1884). A similar circular was created by James Frazer, *Questions on the Manners, Customs, Religion, Superstitions, etc. of Uncivilized or Semi-Civilized Peoples* (1887). Because his pamphlet was produced with the express aim of facilitating his own comparative research for *The Golden Bough* (1890/ 1981), it was designed to gather exactly the sort of information that would fit into his own theories (Richards, 1994, pp. 150-153). This early unsuccessful use of questionnaires as a method of inquiry resulted in a desire on the part of scholars to undertake their own fieldwork in order to gather their own, perhaps more reliable, information.

The new concept of firsthand scholarly "fieldwork" was derived from the discourse of field naturalists by Alfred Cort Haddon. In his 1903 presidential address to the Anthropological Institute in London, he spoke of the pressing need for "fresh investigations in the field." He warned against the "rapid collector" and emphasized the necessity for the researcher not simply "to gather specimens" but to take the time "to coax out of the native by patient sympathy" the deeper connections and meanings of the materials collected (quoted in Stocking, 1983, pp. 80-81). His idea of using a sympathetic method was already standard practice in North America. By the end of the 19th century, thanks to the fieldwork carried out among Native Americans by Matilda Cox Stevenson, Alice Fletcher, Franz Boas, and Frank Hamilton Cushing, the model of experientially gained knowledge of other cultures had displaced armchair methods (Visweswaran, 1998). Cushing, at Zuni Pueblo, New Mexico (1879-1884), wrote to his employer, Spencer Baird of the Smithsonian Institution: "My *method* must succeed. I live among the Indians, I eat their food, and sleep in their houses. . . . On account of this, thank God, my notes will contain much which those of all other explorers have failed to communicate" (Cushing, 1979, pp. 136-137).

Although Cushing was among the earliest ethnographers to realize that his own direct participation in the ongoing lives of his subjects was the basis of his method, it is Bronislaw Malinowski who has been credited with formulating fieldwork as a paradigm or theory (Firth, 1985). The practice of fieldwork, however, was clearly not invented by Malinowski; what he actually accomplished was the enshrinement of fieldwork as a central element of "ethnography" as a new genre (Rabinow, 1985, p. 4). Ever since Malinowski (1922) suggested that an ethnographer's goal should be to grasp the "native's point of view" (p. 25), there has been an expectation that "participant observation" would lead to human understanding through a field-worker's learning to see, think, feel, and sometimes even behave as an insider or "native." Because of the emphasis on an experiential approach, in which the researcher acquires entrance into and at least partial socialization by the society he or she studies, it has become commonplace to suggest that a field-worker adopt the stance of a "marginal native" (Freilich, 1970) or "professional stranger" (Agar, 1980). As "self-denying emissaries" (Boon, 1982), field-workers bring forward an ethnography about the social settings they study. In these roles ethnographers are expected to maintain a polite distance from those studied and to cultivate rapport, not friendship; compassion, not sympathy; respect, not belief; understanding, not identification; admiration, not love. If the researcher were to cultivate friendship, sympathy, belief, identification, and love, then, so we are told, he or she would run the risk of taking up "complete membership" (Adler & Adler, 1987) or "going native."

The negative portrayal of "going native" appeared in late-19th-century colonial fiction, in which the colonizers were created and then embraced within a deeply racialized discourse that also represented the colonial other. Although the colonizers were shown as being at the top of the evolutionary cultural and racial hierarchies, they were also imagined as capable of falling from this pinnacle. Degeneration, "going native," or, in its most excessive form, "going troppo" became a common theme in narratives of white travel and residence in tropical lands (Eves, 1999; Pick, 1989; Young, 1995). Two classic narratives of this sort are Joseph Conrad's *Heart of Darkness* and Jack London's *The Call of the Wild*. In Conrad's depiction of Kurtz's descent into savagery, he produces a narrative of degeneration that reveals the vulnerability of colonists in foreign lands. London's characters, like many ethnographers, do not live as the locals do, and they maintain the marks of colonial prestige, power, and authority vested in material objects such as clothing, watches, and radios. Their way of "going native" is through moral degeneration rather than the adoption of the surface trappings and cultural inscriptions of the native other, such as tattoos.

Early ethnographic examples of "gone-native field-workers" include Alexandra David-Neel, Curt Unkel, and Verrier Elwin. These European ethnographers (French, German, and English, respectively) went into the field early in the 20th century in order to study the cultures of indigenous peoples. They stayed for most, or all, of the rest of their lives, fluently speaking the languages of their hosts and becoming deeply identified with their cultures. David-Neel, during her more than 14 years of living in Sri Lanka, India, Nepal, Sikkim, Japan, China, and Tibet, learned to speak a number of non-European languages, including all of the Tibetan dialects. She meditated in lonely caves and on snowy mountaintops with yogi hermits and studied philosophical Buddhism as well as Tibetan Tantra (David-Neel, 1936, 1959). After her initiation, she traveled in disguise to meet the Dalai Lama in Lhasa, which was closed to all foreigners at the time (David-Neel, 1927). Although she became a devout Buddhist, proficient in creating disembodied thought forms, visions, and control of her own body heat, she retained the philosophic skepticism of René Descartes. She wrote that "psychic training, rationally and scientifically conducted, can lead to desirable results. That is why the information gained about such training . . . constitutes useful documentary evidence worthy of our attention" (David-Neel, 1932, p. vi).

Curt Unkel was formally adopted by the Guaraní Indians in Brazil and took the name Nimuendajú, but he maintained a European-style home in the city of Belém, where he wrote detailed ethnographic monographs (Nimuendajú, 1914/1978, 1939, 1942, 1946, 1952). Although he had little formal training prior to his fieldwork, he collaborated with the well-known ethnographer Robert H. Lowie in such a way that his mode of writing might be called "dialogic" (Damatta, 1994, p. 123). Verrier Elwin, an Englishman who went to India during the 1930s, married into a tribe, was naturalized an Indian citizen, and became recognized as an important pioneer Indian anthropologist (Misra, 1973). He published extraordinarily detailed ethnographies and collections of folklore much admired in both India and England (Elwin, 1932, 1942, 1946, 1947, 1954, 1961).

For these pioneer ethnographers, fieldwork was not merely a rite of passage. Rather, the lived reality of their ethnographic experience was the center of their intellectual and emotional lives. As Elwin (1964) expresses it in his autobiography: "For me anthropology did not mean 'field-work': it meant my whole life. My method was to settle down among the people, live with them, share their life as far as an outsider could and generally do several books together. . . . This meant that I did not depend merely on asking questions, but knowledge of the people gradually sank in until it was part of me" (p. 142). These individuals were so fully incorporated into their host communities that they might be described as "complete members" (Lee, 1995, p. 61). This role can be further divided into "converts," who enter the setting as outsiders but become members, and "double agents," who, although they also may be inducted into full group membership, do so with the sole intention of describing the setting and then departing. Cushing was in fact a double agent. During his fieldwork at Zuni he was adopted into a clan and initiated into the war priesthood (Cushing 1882, 1883). Because of these activities, he has been described repeatedly, and erroneously, as having "gone native" (Gronewold, 1972). However, according to his own field notes and letters, his sole purpose in seeking membership within these organizations was to gain entrance into secret meetings in order to observe, write field notes, and make sketches (Brandes, 1965, p. 48; Cushing, 1979, p. 135; Cushing, 1990, pp. 237-246, 353, 401). When he was recalled to Washington, D.C., by the Bureau of American Ethnology, he switched his research interests from ethnography to archaeological exploration and museum work, never to return to Zuni (Cushing, 1990, p. 26).

Because these early ethnographers retained key European values and philosophies while becoming (to an impressive degree) members of non-Western cultures, it might be better to bracket the question of intentionality and describe them as having become "bicultural" (Tedlock, 1991). Just as one can become "bilingual," given enough time and effort, so one can learn to behave appropriately within a different cultural setting and even acquire a second worldview. The main way this is accomplished is through direct participation in the practices of the new culture. That undertaking this experiential method is not the same thing as simply going native is made clear by the fact that many ethnographers have been able to combine the talents of scholar with those of apprentice.[1] Undergoing an apprenticeship has long been considered a way to equalize power differentials between ethnographers and their consultants. By dismantling and reorganizing the social interaction from that of an inquiring outsider to a relationship between teacher and student, apprenticeship becomes a negotiated ethnographic endeavor. It empowers consultants by allowing them to choose the topics of inquiry, the way of learning, and even the manner of writing essays or a book about the knowledge and experience shared. Apprentices and other participatory ethnographers have given their consultants the power to vet entire manuscripts, or sections of manuscripts, before publication (Simonelli & Winters, 1997). Afterward, they may invite these ethnographic subjects to become coauthors of the ethnography. These sorts of relationships have usually occurred between First World anthropologists and Third or Fourth World consultants (Bahr, Gregorio, Lopez, & Alvarez, 1974; Fischer & Abedi, 1990; Gudeman & Rivera, 1990; Humphrey, 1996; Lambek, 1997; Tehindrazanarivelo, 1997) or between middle-class social scientists and members of a lower class or a criminal subculture (Prus & Irini, 1980; Prus & Sharper, 1977).

When ethnographers began to undertake intensive long-term participant observation fieldwork in European, American, and Middle Eastern urban centers, their work involved "studying up" (concentrating on elite institutions) or "across" (working with people in a similar class or power location) rather than "down" (studying subcultures and marginal peoples).[2] In these new sorts of collaborations, with individuals who participated in highly elaborated and well-established local traditions, texts often became important sources of data and strategic sites of negotiation (Archetti, 1994, pp. 11-13; Rogers, 1997; Shryock, 1996, 1997; Terrio, 1998, pp. 27-28). In working with their cultural contemporaries, the researchers became increasingly aware not only of the dialogical understandings of the emergence of data and knowledge, but also of the political and literary issues involved in the processes of writing, publishing, and reading ethnographies.

◆ Genres of Ethnography

Although there has been some discussion concerning the different styles of ethnography—classical, modernist, postmodernist, poststructuralist—that discussion has, for the most part, been rather general and superficial.[3] What has been ignored in these debates is the fact that thousands of works written in many languages and genres have been encoded as "ethnographic." Researchers can and do inscribe the same material in many different ways, using different formats, styles, and genres. Because audiences have expectations—including overall form and organization, metaphors, and images—regarding texts they may want to read, it is important for ethnographers, like other authors, to know these parameters (Gerhart, 1992; L. Richardson, 1990). Thus, although genre is often thought of in relation to the work of authoring, it also plays an important role in the work of reading. Because the meanings readers derive from a text are shaped by the discourse communities to which they belong, an author needs a clear idea of which readers he or she wishes to address. Over the course of a career, an ethnographer typically utilizes a number of genres to create and communicate findings to and for different groups of readers.

An ethnographer may begin with an extended monograph based on either a master's thesis or a doctoral dissertation. Each chapter unfolds spatially and logically, treating a standard topic—environment, social relations, identity, or worldview—constructed by means of a repetitive accumulation of equivalent episodes and data. The chapter headings are designed to suggest exhaustive coverage, such as that found in an encyclopedia or a catalog (Thornton, 1988). Later the ethnographer may take up writing more clearly narrative genres that, because they depend on lived experience and have a strongly linear arrangement, are more accessible to the general educated public (MacClancy, 1996). These include personal documents such as biographies and life stories of consultants, memoirs and autobiographies of both consultants and ethnographers, and field diaries and chronicles. Alternative forms of documentation, such as travelogues and autoethnographies, are also popular. More self-consciously literary genres, such as novels, novellas, short stories, poems, and plays, have also been used as vehicles of ethnographic documentation and representation.

One of the earliest and most popular narrative genres to be developed by ethnographers is the biography, or "life history." Although biographies can be produced on the basis of interview materials alone, the most frequent way they emerge is from the fieldwork context itself. The use of life histories as an alternative form of ethnographic documentation goes back at least as far as Thomas and Znaniecki's publication of *The Polish Peasant in Europe and America* (1918-1920) and Paul Radin's *Crashing Thunder* (1920). At that time, ethnographers' aim in collecting life histories was to illuminate cultural, historical, and social facts rather than individual lives or aspects of personality (Shaw, 1930; Underhill, 1936). Life histories depend upon the use of the rhetorical figure of synecdoche, in which a "representative" individual is selected and made to stand for an entire culture. Thus, according to Ricardo Pozas, his biography *Juan the Chamula* (1962) "should be considered a small monograph on the culture of the Chamulas" (p. 1). It was only later that an interest in personality was added to the life history (Langness & Frank, 1981, pp. 21-23). Oscar Lewis energetically promoted the life history as primarily a cultural document. He began his family biography approach to ethnography and developed his idea of a "culture of poverty" with his now-classic book, *Five Families* (1959). In the introduction, he describes the family portraits he constructs as neither "fiction nor conventional ethnography. For want of a better term I would call them ethnographic realism, in contrast to literary realism" (p. 5). His writing technique depends upon the layering of synecdoches in which a single family stands for a common type of family and a single day stands for any day, or every day. He sets before his readers five perfectly ordinary days—days not marked by any unusual events, such as births, baptisms, or funerals—in the lives of five ordinary, representative Mexican families. This book was soon followed by more truly biographical and emotionally moving accounts: *The Children of Sánchez* (1961), *Pedro Martínez* (1964), and *La Vida* (1965).

The second type of personal document is the "memoir," in which an author takes the reader back to a corner of the author's own life in the field that was unusually vivid, full of affect, or framed by unique events. By narrowing the lens, the author provides a window into a segment of his or her life in the field. Although most ethnographers who have published memoirs have done so under their own names, some have used pseudonyms. Margaret Field published her memoir of doing ethnography among the Gâ of West Africa, *Stormy Dawn* (1947), under the name Mark Freshfield. Laura Bohannan novelized her experiences as a neophyte ethnographer in West Africa, *Return to Laughter* (1954), under the name Elenore Smith Bowen. Philip Drucker published his Mexican ethnographic memoir, *Tropical Frontier* (1969), under the name Paul Record. Karla Poewe published her memoir of African fieldwork, *Reflections of a Woman Anthropologist* (1982), under the name Manda Cesara. One reason some authors might distance themselves from their memoirs by using pseudonyms is that this enables them to publish their fieldwork experiences for a general readership and keep this activity totally separate, even secret, from their professional peers. This distancing move may indicate that these authors feel that publishing personal materials could damage their credibility as scientists. Later in life, however, as in the cases of Laura Bohannan and Karla Poewe, they might choose to reveal their pseudonyms to their profession and take credit for their books.

A third ethnographic genre, the "narrative ethnography," evolved from the overlapping of the first two genres, life history and memoir. This hybrid form was created when individuals attempted to portray accurately the subjects of biographies but also to include their own experiences in their texts. For example, Vincent Crapanzano in *Tuhami* (1980) documents the life of his Moroccan subject and his own emotional and intellectual responses in working with him. He dwells at length on the psychological and cultural tensions and yearnings present in his extended face-to-face interactions with Tuhami, showing how each of them became engrossed in the encounter as a consequence of becoming the "object of transference" to the other. Thus, although Tuhami was initially the primary focus of the biography, Crapanzano became a secondary focus, produced during the writing process. The result is a psychodynamically rich double portrait in the form of a narrative ethnography. A similar intertwining of a biography with the story of the ethnographic encounter, both in the field and in retrospect, structures Laurel Kendall's book *The Life and Hard Times of a Korean Shaman* (1988). Here, in a series of shamanic autobiographical exchanges, reproduced from memory and captured on tape, Kendall represents herself and her field assistant as sympathetic students of a woman shaman. With the addition of Kendall's personal and theoretical interludes, which occur in typographically marked sections throughout the book, we witness the multiple narrative event of a female shaman actively engaging with a female ethnographer, her female field assistant, and her readers.

An overlap between biography and personal memoir also structures Ruth Behar's *Translated Woman* (1993). Here Behar confesses how worried, yet relieved, she was when she realized that after nearly 3 years of studying what colonial women had said to their inquisitors and developing relationships with a number of townswomen, she had let one of her subjects take over her research. Throughout the text, she portrays her inner feelings by using an italic font: "*I am remembering the hurt I had felt several days before. While I was sitting in the half-open doorway reading, a boy had run past, gotten a peek at me, and yelled out with what to me sounded like venom in his voice, 'Gringa!'*" (p. 250). Because Behar is a Cuban American, she found this verbal insult from another Hispanic quite unexpected and painful.

What these psychologically rich documents contributed was an unsettling of the boundaries that had been central to the notion of a self studying an other. This form of border-zone cultural production became the new direction of ethnographic interchange and cultural inscription. At its inception, this sea change in ethnographic representation of both the self and other within a single text was lumped together with other writing strategies and labeled as part of a mythic "experimental moment in the human sciences" (Marcus & Fischer, 1986, p. 165). However, as Renato Rosaldo (1989, p. 231) indicates, this analysis embodied a facile application of Thomas Kuhn's notion of experimentalism as occurring only during scientific paradigm shifts. The ongoing historical refiguration of social thought and practice should not be described as part of a unique and radically ahistorical "experimental moment," but should be recognized for what it was: a major change in ethnographic epistemology and methodology embodying key historical, political, ethical, analytic, and authorial issues.

Just as in feminist critical theory, which denies the split between epistemology and politics, ethnographic critical theory became simultaneously reflexive and political.[4] There emerged a passionate interest in co-producing ethnographic knowledge, creating and representing it in the only way it could be, within a critical interactive self-other conversation or dialogue.[5] An extreme yearning for such a dialogic embrace is poignantly portrayed by the French ethnographer Pierre Clastres in his chronicle of fieldwork. In South America during the mid-1960s, he encountered the Atchei people in Paraguay, who had only recently been contacted by outsiders. When he met them they refused to accept his gifts or to speak with him, even though he spoke a neighboring dialect of their language. As he describes the scene, "they were still green," "hardly touched, hardly contaminated by the breezes of our civilization," a society "so healthy that it could not enter into a dialogue with me, with another world" (Clastres, 1998, p. 97). Clastres's translator, the novelist Paul Auster (1998), notes that the chronicle is "the true story of a man's experiences," that "the result is not just a portrait of the people he is studying, but a portrait of himself," and that "he writes with the cunning of a good novelist" (p. 8). In other words, his chronicle takes the form of a narrative ethnography.

That a fiction writer might recognize Clastres's novelistic cunning should not be surprising given that the most popular literary genre read or written by social scientists is the novel—especially the kind that is based on a combination of the author's personal history and background, scholarly training, and field experiences.[6] Although some of these fictive works can be categorized as science fiction, mysteries, or historical novels, most are also what have come to be called "ethnographic novels" (Buelow, 1973; Langness & Frank, 1978; Schmidt, 1981, 1984). This genre is different from other novelistic categories in that it conforms not only to the principles set up within the text itself, but also to those within the external culture the novel describes. Thus ethnographic novels combine internal textual accuracy with external cultural accuracy. For this type of novel to be considered ethnographically complete, it must contain accurate information on how the ethnic group portrayed is organized and how it relates, or refuses to relate, to the wider world.

The Swiss archaeologist Adolf F. Bandelier was the originator of this genre. His novel *The Delight Makers* (1890/1971) is set in the American Southwest among the Pueblo Indians. Bandelier noted that although the plot was his own, he was true to the geographic nature of the country as well as the indigenous architecture, traditions, manners, and customs that he and other ethnologists had observed. He actually witnessed the scenes the novel describes, and the people portrayed are complicated human beings living in a structured and regulated society. Although the novel was immediately recognized by both archaeologists and anthropologists as a classic, it failed to attract the general public for whom it was written. As Stefan Jovanovich (1971) points out, this was due to the fact that Bandelier "had taken the adventure out of the Old West; he had written about the enemy, the Indians, as if they were real (that is, white) people struggling in a muddled social world rather than mythical creatures grazing in a long-extinct forest" (p. xvii). Indeed, it would be nearly 40 years before the general public was ready to appreciate ethnographic fiction about Indians as real people. In 1929, Oliver La Farge won the Pulitzer Prize in Literature for his ethnographic novel *Laughing Boy* (1929). The main characters in the novel are Laughing Boy, a model of everything good in traditional Navajo culture, and Slim Girl, an acculturated Navajo raised in a mission school. They fall in love, and through the various social interactions that arise from their marriage we learn that the Navajo are matrilineal, matrilocal, semisedentary, horticulturists, and herders and that they consider reconciliation to be the most important positive result of legal proceedings. Inherent in Laughing Boy's actions is the importance placed by Navajo culture upon a unity of mind, body, and spirit. Because his wife lacks this integrative faculty, Laughing Boy is threatened and almost destroyed.[7]

In Latin America, at about the same time, the Peruvian ethnologist José María Arguedas became the major Indianist novelist of his time. He invented a language for his ethnographic novels using native Quechua syntax with Spanish vocabulary. In what is widely considered his best novel, *Yawar Fiesta* (1941/1985), he dramatically portrays the clash between Indian and Hispanic cultures in Puquio, the highland village where he lived during his early childhood and adolescence. A more recent literary ethnographer is John Stewart, who has taught English literature as well as anthropology. The Royal Society of Literature awarded him its Winifred Holthy Memorial Prize for his novel *Last Cool Days* (1971). Because this novel, as well as his other ethnographic fiction, is based on a combination of his West Indian birth and upbringing together with his more recent black American experience, it is as much an exercise in self-exploration as it is cultural portraiture. He shares this dual identity, resulting from a field situation in which the ethnographer is among his or her own chief informants, with Arguedas. This work is also closely associated with W. E. B. Du Bois's (1903/1969, p. 45) notion of a "double consciousness" within African American life.

Chad Oliver was 22 years old when he sold his first short story, "The Boy Next Door" (1951), to Anthony Boucher, the editor of the magazine *Fantasy and Science Fiction*. Martha Foley listed it that season on her prestigious register of "Distinctive Short Stories in American Magazines" (Nolan, 1968, p. 110). A year later, Oliver finished his master's thesis in anthropology at the University of Texas, titled *They Builded a Tower: The Story of Science Fiction* (1952), and began teaching there. He soon became a prime contender for the Heinlein-Clarke front rank of what Boucher called "genuine science fiction, in which the science is as accurately absorbing as the fiction is richly human" (Oliver, 1957, cover blurb). Oliver's science fiction novel *Shadows in the Sun* (1954), which explores the theme of humanlike aliens on earth, was cited by the *New York Times* as "tops in its field" for that year. Throughout his academic career, Oliver (1962, 1981) published ethnography and introduced anthropological themes into science fiction. His novella *Guardian Spirit*, first published in 1958, examines the ultimate definition of civilization by exploring the relation between technological man and primitive man. A later novel, *The Shores of Another Sea* (1971), is set in Kenya, where Oliver undertook his doctoral fieldwork. In this story, a scientist who runs a baboonery suddenly finds that his animals have changed. The detached look in their eyes reveals to him that they have been taken over by an alien intelligence. They are now studying him. He realizes that he is no longer the hunter, but the hunted. Oliver's combination of traditional science fiction themes—early man, lost races, and future wars—and ethnographic reflexivity resulted in classic works of ethnographic fiction.[8]

A number of social scientists have chosen other fictive genres—such as the short story, novella, and play—for representing ethnographic materials.[9] Hilda Kuper (1947, 1960), a well-known South African ethnographer, published several literary works based on her ethnographic fieldwork, including a novel, a play, and short stories (1965, 1970, 1943/ 1984). In a panel at the Africanists' meetings in 1981, she declared that her best ethnographic writing was her play, *A Witch in My Heart*. Several other plays centering on ethnographers and ethnographic field experiences have been performed and published.[10] Dennis Tedlock (1986, 1998) and Dorinne Kondo (1995, 1997, p. 22) have written ethnographic plays and worked with professional theater groups as producers and dramaturges. The ethnographer Catherine Allen and the playwright Nathan Garner collaborated in teaching a course, then wrote and coproduced an ethnographic play, *Condor Qatay* (1993). They later wrote both an essay and a book about the process, suggesting that playwriting provides an appropriate vehicle not only for ethnographic description but also for interpretation and analysis (Allen & Garner, 1995, p. 69; 1997). Robert Laughlin served as an ethnographic consultant, dramaturge, and impresario for a play written and performed by Mayans about the sociopolitical conditions behind the Zapatista uprising in Chiapas, Mexico (Laughlin, 1994; Skomal, 1995).

Another way of communicating ethnographic experiences intertwined with emotional response has been to weave them together; these works may take the form of travelogues, chronicles, or diaries.[11] Ethnographic travelogues often take on the easygoing, chatty tone of travel brochures, whereas chronicles and diaries tend to reveal the inner thoughts, bittersweet emotions, and prejudices of their authors. In *Tristes Tropiques,* Claude Lévi-Strauss (1973) writes lyrically, "The bay at Rio eats right into the heart of the city: you land in the centre, as if the other half, like the fabled town of Ys, had already been engulfed by waves" (p. 76). Zora Neale Hurston, in *Tell My Horse* (1938), uses a chatty tone: "If you go to Jamaica you are going to want to visit the Maroons of Accompong. They are under the present rule of Colonel Rowe, who is an intelligent, cheerful man. But I warn you in advance not to ride his wall-eyed, pot-bellied mule" (p. 21). Brian Moeran's *Okubo Diary: Portrait of a Japanese Valley* (1985) is a refashioning of the contents of three journals Moeran kept during his 4 years of fieldwork in rural Japan. In part because his son was seriously injured while in primary school and Moeran ended up having to sue the local school board, the diary is filled with estrangement and melancholy self-reflection: "These mountain silhouettes that I know so well, these sounds of birds calling, of the wind in the pear trees, of the bamboo swaying. They will never be mine. Perhaps they never, after all, were mine. I who am caught in this bridge of dreams" (p. 204).

There have also been tell-all ethnographic diaries. The French poet and ethnographer Michel Leiris published his rather shocking field diary *L'Afrique fantôme* (*Phantom Africa,* 1934), documenting the activities of the Dakar-Djibouti expedition to the Dogon of Sanga and the Ethiopians of Gondar, together with the activities of various African subjects (Beaujour, 1987). He revealed the strained relationships between the European members of the research team and the unethical museum collecting procedures of the expedition. These revelations were to be the cause of Leiris's permanent break with his friend and colleague Marcel Griaule. In a later work, *L'Age d'homme* (1939), translated as *Manhood*

(1983), which combines novelistic fiction with an intimate journal, Leiris goes beyond the merely chronological collection of anecdotes and snapshots to construct a story on the model of photomontage. This anthology of the self cultivates a photographic viewpoint with no attempt to speak from the heart. It is a fable of disenchantment, combining an acute sense of the futility of existence with a strong desire to salvage its meaningful details in the form of perception, quotation, and memory. By interrupting the smooth ethnographic story of an access to Africa, Leiris undermines the assumption that self and other can ever be gathered in a stable narrative coherence. He ends abruptly with words quoted from a dream: "I explain to my mistress how necessary it is to construct a wall around oneself by means of clothing" (1983, p. 146).

Perhaps the most scandalous ethnographic field diary of all time is Bronislaw Malinowski's posthumously published *A Diary in the Strict Sense of the Term* (1967). It reveals the self-proclaimed inventor of participant observation and the hidden authorial voice of *Argonauts of the Western Pacific* (1922) as a person who not only participated very little in Kiriwinian culture, but was racially prejudiced (Willis, 1969, p. 140). As a response to the controversy caused by the revelation of this secret diary, ethnographers became self-conscious about their own political, ethnic, and racial backgrounds and prejudices, as well as about the nature of their participation, or lack of participation, in the cultures they lived in and wrote about (Caulfield, 1979; Nash & Wintrob, 1972). They were shaken also by Malinowski's imperialist ideas and embarrassed by the colonialist practices within social science (Asad, 1973; Banaji, 1970; Gough, 1968; Lewis, 1973; Stavenhagen, 1971). A small group of anthropologists dared publicly to ask themselves the painful question, "If the discipline did not exist, would it have to be invented?" To which Dell Hymes and the other contributors to his edited volume *Reinventing Anthropology* (1969) answered no. To a second question, "If anthropology were reinvented, would it be the anthropology we have now?" the answer was also no. Instead, as Bob Scholte (1969) suggested, a reinvented anthropology ought to become "a critical and emancipatory discipline."

This new critical self-awareness was further enhanced by a second major controversy within social science. This time, debate surrounded the publication, in the journal *Science,* of an essay titled "On Being Sane in Insane Places" (Rosenhan, 1973). The essay describes a novel research design in which eight social scientists invented symptoms and then presented themselves to psychiatric outpatient clinics with the aim of being admitted to inpatient psychiatric wards. Upon admission to the wards, they never again referred to their symptoms and were never spotted as researchers. When the research was published, the clinicians were outraged and accused the social scientists of manufacturing the data, which they had not. Although some undercover ethnographic work continued (Rose, 1987), covert observation was deemed unethical and became unfashionable (Brink, 1993).

These controversies contributed to an exploration of both ethical and authorial issues involved in the process of generating ethnographic information and in the writing and publishing of ethnographic accounts. Some researchers began to advocate a more humanly involved and politically savvy role for ethnographers, together with the blending in single texts of epistemological and personal understandings (Dwyer, 1979, 1982; Scholte, 1969; Thomas, 1983). And it was just this combination of a new vantage point and critical practice that resulted in the shift from participant observation to "the observation of participation" (Tedlock, 1991), in which ethnographers both experience and observe their own and others' coparticipation within the ethnographic scene of encounter. The shift entailed a major representational transformation in which, instead of having to choose between writing a memoir or autobiography centering on the self or a life history or standard monograph centering on the other, the ethnographer can present both self and other together within a single narrative frame that focuses on the process and character of the ethnographic dialogue.

◆ From Participant Observation to the Observationof Participation

Participant observation was originally forged as a method in the study of small, relatively homogeneous societies. An ethnographer lived in a society for an extended period of time, learned the local language, participated in daily life, and steadily observed. The oxymoron *participant observation* implies simultaneous emotional involvement and objective detachment. Ethnographers attempted to be both engaged participants and coolly dispassionate observers of the lives of others. This strangely empathic yet impassive methodology was widely believed to produce documentary data that somehow reflected the natives' own points of view. It has even been argued that because we cannot study the social world without being a part of it, all social research is a form of participant observation (Hammersley & Atkinson, 1983).

The privileging of the trope of participant observation as a scientific method encouraged ethnographers to demonstrate both their observational skills and their social participation by producing radically different forms of writing: scholarly monographs and personal documents, such as life histories and memoirs. This dualistic approach split public from private and objective from subjective realms of experience. John Beattie (1960), for example, first published a scholarly monograph based on his doctoral thesis, which he felt was an "objective" ethnographic account. Five years later, at the suggestion of his publisher, he wrote a second version of his field research, which he described as a "subjective" first-person account (Beattie, 1965). Even though this second book emphasizes overt methodologies—the use of assistants, informants, questionnaires, house-to-house surveys, note taking, photography, keeping a diary, and writing up the research—he is nonetheless apologetic about being "autobiographical" or subjective, remarking in his preface on his "somewhat immodest undertaking."[12]

Discomfort with the act of revealing the self within a serious ethnography can also be detected in Paul Rabinow's (1977) memoir, in which he refers to his 1975 monograph as a "more traditionally anthropological treatment of the same data" (p. 7). Jean-Paul Dumont, like Rabinow, published his standard ethnographic monograph (1976) before his first-person fieldwork account (1978). However, he revealed a different attitude toward including himself in his ethnography. For him the work of self-representation was no less "traditional" than the standard representation of the ethnographic other. In fact, as Peter Rivière (1980) has pointed out, we learn rather more about the Panaré in Dumont's first-person account than we do in Dumont's monograph. Part of the reason for this is that Dumont self-consciously centered his field account around the question of who he was for the Panaré rather than who the Panaré were for him, this latter being the implicit question most ethnographies explore.

Unlike these authors, Nigel Barley released his ethnographic monograph and fieldwork account simultaneously. The monograph, *Symbolic Structures: An Exploration of the Culture of the Dowayos* (1983b), is a Lévi-Straussian structuralist study. The first-person ethnographic field account, *Adventures in a Mud Hut* (1983a), is a funny, warts-and-all, first-person narrative of Barley's West African fieldwork. The remarkable difference in tone, tenor, and material presented in these two books reveals

181

Barley's extreme discomfort with representing himself in an ethnographic account. In his experiential ethnography he comes off as a silly, sad, incompetent slapstick character who marched, limped, and finally was carried through his initiatory field research. The natives also come off as clowns; foolish old men stare at photographs of lions and leopards, turning them in all directions and saying things like, "I do not know this man" (Barley, 1983a, p. 96). Here, what purports to be a personal document ends up as a lampoon of the entire ethnographic enterprise.

Instead of focusing on the embarrassing or funny edges of the ethnographic encounter (De Vita, 1990), some ethnographers have chosen to explore the complex personal and political dimensions involved in crossing cultural boundaries. Kurt Wolff (1964) describes how, during his field research in a northern New Mexico village, he opened himself to the risk of being hurt by becoming so totally involved and identified with the community that everything he saw or experienced became relevant to him: "It was years before I understood what had happened to me: I had fallen through the web of culture patterns and assorted conceptual meshes into the chaos of love; I was looking everywhere, famished, with a ruthless glance" (p. 235). It is precisely these risks that Ruth Behar, in *The Vulnerable Observer* (1996), portrays as the central ethnographic project. No matter how much care the ethnographer devotes to the project, its success depends upon more than individual effort. It is tied to outside social forces, including local, national, and sometimes even international relationships that make the research possible as well as to a readership that accepts the endeavor as meaningful. The issues are not so much objectivity, neutrality, and distance as they are risk, the possibility of failure, and the hope of success. More recently, such intimate topics as fear of physical violence, rape, friendship, love, sexuality, and erotic fieldwork encounters—both homosexual and heterosexual—have begun to be inscribed as social science.[13]

◆ Autoethnography and Feminist Ethnography

Another key factor in ethnographers' changing choices and development of alternative topics and styles of research and representation is found in the changes in the population of individuals electing to become ethnographers. In terms of class, more ethnographers are now from middle- and lower-class backgrounds. Concerning gender and sexuality, more are now women as well as open gays and lesbians. In terms of ethnicity, more are minority, hybrid (Eurasians, *mestizos,* and so on), as well as Third and Fourth World scholars. Such transformations have spurred not only a democratization of knowledge but a new critical awareness, resulting in the suggestion that the class, race, culture, and gender beliefs and behaviors of the inquirer be placed within the same historical moment, or critical plane, as those of the subjects of inquiry.[14]

These changes have been stimulated by the emergence of an articulate population of "native" and "feminist" ethnographers, including various bicultural inside/outsiders. Although it is undoubtedly true that insiders may have easier access to certain types of information, especially in the area of daily routines (Jones, 1970; Ohnuki-Tierney, 1984), native ethnography can be distinguished from indigenous ethnography in that native ethnographers are those who have their origins in non-European or non-Western cultures and who share a history of colonialism, or an economic relationship based upon subordination. Just as being born female does not automatically result in "feminist" consciousness, being born an ethnic minority does not automatically result in "native" consciousness. Nonetheless, it has been suggested that women's binary view or "dual consciousness"—similar to the double consciousness attributed to blacks and other racial minorities—gives women a certain advantage in understanding oppressed peoples worldwide.[15]

Native ethnographers have critiqued Western ethnocentric practices in social science (Harrison, 1991; Hsu & Textor, 1978). They have pointed out the strange preoccupation with issues such as caste in South Asia (Appadurai, 1986; Daniel, 1984) and the lack of systematic portrayal of sentiments in studies of kinship, exchange, and reciprocity. Tongan anthropologist Epeli Hau'ofa (1982) notes that the scarcity of attention to emotions within these highly charged areas of human relations "has rendered most such studies in Oceania (and probably elsewhere) incomplete and therefore half-meaningful" (p. 222). He illustrates the serious moral consequences of this form of misrepresentation, noting that when Melanesian leaders were reduced to a "caricature of the quintessential Western capitalist" (Hau'ofa, 1975, p. 285), this resulted in Polynesian racist feelings against Melanesians. Native ethnographers have also objected to the application of the term *matriarchal* only to a hypothetical society completely ruled by women. The Igbo anthropologist Ifi Amadiume (1987,

p. 189) has called for the recognition of such factors as matrifocality, matricentrism, and female orientation in West Africa as aspects of matriarchal cultures.

These scholars have worked to bridge the gulf between self and other by revealing both parties as vulnerable experiencing subjects working to coproduce knowledge (Abu-Lughod, 1993). The observer and the observed are not entirely separate categories, they argue. For them, theory is not a transparent, culture-free zone, not a duty-free intellectual marketplace hovering between cultures, lacking all connection to embodied, lived experience. Knowledge and experience from outside fieldwork should be brought into ethnographic narratives; ethnographers should demonstrate how ideas matter to them, bridging the gap between their narrow academic world and wide cultural experiences. As Vietnamese ethnographer and cinematographer Trinh T. Minh-ha (1989) states, "In writing close to the other of the other, I can only choose to maintain a self-reflexively critical relationship toward the material, a relationship that defines both the subject written and the writing subject, undoing the I while asking 'what do I want wanting to know you or me?' " (p. 76). Or, as Jean-Paul Dumont (1978) says at the close of his narrative ethnography, "Who was I for them?" (p. 200).

Writing for and about the community in which one has grown up and lived, or at least achieved some degree of insider status, should produce engaged writing centering on the ongoing dialectical political-personal relationship between self and other. This is not a new idea. In 1972, Martin Yang published an important essay discussing the role of both his graduate education and what he called his "firsthand fieldwork" in the production of his highly acclaimed ethnography *A Chinese Village* (1945). His field research was conducted in the village in which he lived until he went away to college. As Yang (1972) notes, "My fieldwork was my own life and the lives of others in which I had an active part" (p. 63). This type of ethnographic experience has been called variously *ethnosociology, ethnoethnography, autoanthropology,* and *autoethnography* (Deck, 1990; Fogelson, 1984; Hayano, 1979; Reed-Danahay, 1997; Strathern, 1987a). Yang was by no means the first indigenous anthropologist to publish an ethnography about his own group. Jomo Kenyatta (1938), Fei Hsiao Tung (1939), and Chie Nakane (1970), among others, had already done so. But Yang, unlike the others, wrote a self-reflexive essay about the experience of doing an autoethnography.

What has received far too little attention to date are the political exchanges and verbal encounters between ethnographers and natives who have different interests and goals (Chilungu, 1976). Roger Keesing (1985) has provided an important example of the cross-gender micropolitics of talk. In his fieldwork among the Kwaio, a traditional group living in the Solomon Islands of the South Pacific, he found that men told their life stories eagerly and artfully, even though Kwaio lack the genre we call autobiography. At the same time, he found that he was not able to elicit autobiographical narratives from women. They spoke to him in a fragmented, inarticulate, and joking way, this in front of the elder men who had urged them to cooperate. Eight years later, during a subsequent joint field trip with a woman ethnographer, he found that in sessions in which they were both present Kwaio women took control of the encounters and even brought female friends along as audience members for their recording sessions. Unlike the men, who provided personal life stories and societal rules, the women created moral texts about the virtues of womanhood, inserting only enough personal experience to illustrate a woman's possible path through life. Clearly, the women's initial inarticulateness and subsequent "voice," as much as the men's systematization of their culture, were responses to wider fields of force that assure that some genres are more powerful than others.

Feminist scholars might have predicted the changes produced by the presence of women anthropologists. They would have understood that the genre of autobiography is problematic, not only because it is culturally specific to the West, but because it has been shaped by a gender ideology that assumes a male subject. Kwaio women's refusal to recite the personal narratives and societal rules characteristic of men's responses and their insistence on moral justifications of womanhood evoke a parallel strategy in other women's autobiographies. In these, a recurring figure of "divided consciousness" can be detected, revealing the authors' awareness that they are being read as women and thus judged differently from men in their self-constructions (Gal, 1991; Tedlock, 1995).

Women's ethnographic and autobiographical intentions are often powered by the motive to convince readers of the authors' self-worth, to clarify and authenticate their self-images. Many of these self-images are projected by understatement, the very means individuals use to distance or detach themselves from intimacy. Women ethnographers often either tend toward straightforward and objective representation of their experiences or write obliquely and elliptically, using a free-indirect or stream-of-consciousness style (DeVault, 1990; Stanley & Wise, 1983). Sometimes they poke fun at themselves as field-workers in order to camouflage their professional desires and will to power. Over and over again, women ethnographers, be they novices or experienced researchers, reveal their uncertainty about fieldwork and about ethnographic writing. Kirin Narayan, in *Storytellers, Saints and Scoundrels* (1989), undermines her own ethnographic authority by not offering a romantic insider's view of an alien culture. Instead, she subtly portrays the irony of an inside/outside woman who, while sitting among the South Asian people with whom she grew up and with whom she felt a comfortable sense of solidarity, was partly rejected as an academic outsider listening to religious teachings for material, rather than spiritual, reasons. She reports that her guru said to her: "You're taking this on tape. You'll take this and do a business. . . . In your university you'll say, I saw this, I saw that. This is what Bhagavan is. That's why you learn this: not to understand it" (p. 59).

Masculine ethnographic and autobiographical intentions, on the other hand, are often powered by the desire to unify a work by concentrating on one period of a life or a single characteristic of a personality. It is not surprising that with men socially conditioned to pursue successful careers, we find harmony and orderliness in their autobiographies. The unidirectionality of men's lives seems somehow appropriately cast into self-assured progressive narratives. Thus anthropologist Kenneth Read's (1986) self-portrayal of fieldwork is beatific: "Looking back now, I believe I was permanently elated most of the time I was there. At least this is the only name I can give to a state of mind in which certainty in my own abilities and discovery of myself joined with a compassion for others and a gratitude for the lessons in acceptance that they taught me" (p. 6).

Narratives of women's lives, by contrast, are often neither chronological nor progressive but disjointed, fragmentary, or organized into self-sustained units rather than connecting chapters (Krieger, 1983). Feminist authors and critics have been weaving autobiography into history and criticism, journals into analysis, and the spirit of poetry into interdisciplinary prose. A number of women ethnographers have used the female mode, constructing their texts of fragments: letters from the field, diary extracts, musings, poems, dreams, drawings, and stories. One of the most radical and truly successful examples of this type of experimentation is Karen McCarthy Brown's *Mama Lola* (1991), an ethnographic study of Vodou in

186

New York City. In this beautifully crafted book, Brown employs four separate vocal registers: the voice of Alourdes, the Vodou priestess who is the main character; the scholarly voice of Karen Brown, the ethnographer; the personal intimate voice of Brown, as narrator and character in the tale she herself is constructing; and the mythic voice of Gede, the teller of ancestral fictional tales. The feminine narrative is also often marked by conflicts between the personal and the professional. There may be a tension between the conventional role of wife, mother, sister, or daughter and another, unconventional role that includes ambition or a vocation. In her memoir, *Nest in the Wind* (1989), Martha Ward undermines her own authority by noting, "I have probably imparted more wisdom to myself in recounting these events than I deserve. The written accounts, letters, field notes, and reports from this period have provided a framework, but memory and shifts in my own consciousness alter my perspectives." This admittedly unreliable narrator also notes that "this book was not written for my peers or professional colleagues. It is only what John Van Maanen [1988] calls 'an impressionist tale' " (p. 3).

Women ethnographers have revealed not only lack of rapport and even bad faith during fieldwork, but also their accidental, informal, or personal rather than professional reasons for undertaking field research. Barbara Bode's stated motive for doing research in Peru was to fill the void in herself created by the loss of her baby. She explains, in the introduction to *No Bells to Toll* (1989), that she went to Peru primarily in order to catapult herself out of her own personal tragedy. Marjorie Shostak, in her biography *Nisa: The Life and Words of a !Kung Woman* (1981), admits that the impetus for her collection of personal information from Nisa arose because she herself felt lonely and hoped that more structured interactions might allow her to share in other people's lives. Judith Stacey (1995) notes that she undertook her "accidental ethnography" of the families of white working-class people in California's Silicon Valley because of the demands and delights of "delayed mothering," which confined her field research options to locations close to her San Francisco Bay Area home. She structured her trade book *Brave New Families* (1990) as two first-person documentary novellas within an overall third-person expository account of the historical changes in family life within the United States.

These gendered textual practices are learned partly through reading. In the not-too-distant past, wherever a husband and wife worked in the same region, it was the man who wrote about what were considered more centrally important topics and adopted the expository mode. The woman wrote on what were considered more peripheral topics and adopted the narrative mode.[16] An early example of this segmentation is the joint ethnographic career of Charles and Brenda Seligman. Upon marriage, Brenda Salaman gave up her premedical training to become an ethnographic field partner with her husband among the Veddahs of Ceylon and the Nuba in the Sudan (Stocking, 1995, p. 117). While she became a specialist in kinship and social organization, her husband collected data on what were considered more important topics at the time: physical types and material culture. They published their research jointly (Seligman & Seligman, 1911, 1932).

Another couple who researched and wrote jointly were the South Africans Eileen Jensen Krige and Jack Krige. In this case, Eileen was the trained ethnographer and included her lawyer husband in her research among the Lovedu of the northern Transvaal, but the result was similar. The book they published was based on fieldwork they conducted together during the 1930s. When they constructed their joint ethnography *The Realm of a Rain-Queen* (1943), she took primary responsibility for what they describe as the "more feminine" topics, including health, fertility, the family, children, drum and rain cults, and the Rain-Queen. Her husband handled what they describe as the "more masculine" topics, including subsistence, economic exchange, social groups, tribal history, politics, and law. This split reflects the gendered typification of feminine domestic versus masculine public spheres. The book is united with evocative descriptions of everyday life written by Eileen Krige (Hammond-Tooke, 1997, pp. 85-89).

A similar segmentation of writing tasks along gender lines appeared more recently in Elizabeth and Robert Fernea's coauthored ethnographies *The Arab World* (1985) and *Nubian Ethnographies* (1991). Here the wife narrates the couple's encounters in a breezy travel-diary style while the husband contributes abstractions and commentaries that are typifying and authoritative. While Elizabeth represents herself as experiencing various locations and cultures, Robert takes up a strategic location within the authoritative "heart" of Arab culture as it was known and described by earlier scholars. These textual strategies, representing alternative modes of reading and claiming very different audiences, coexist within both books. The effect of these strongly gendered accounts is to highlight the points of difference rather than the Ferneas' shared observations and interpretations.

Just as men have sometimes cast their lives into heroic molds in order to project their universal import, women can also exaggerate, mythologize, or monumentalize their own lives or those of their consultants. Judith Okely (1992) reports that her stories about fieldwork with Gypsies "naturally" became heroically embellished through numerous tellings and retellings to her male colleagues. This masculinization of an ethnographic narrative is not at all surprising, given that professional identity, like sexual identity, is acquired through a process of language learning that constitutes the social person. During the early days of anthropology, women like Audrey Richards may even have succeeded, to a certain degree, in achieving disciplinary equality by becoming "honorary males." Professional masculinization is also revealed when they claim that honorary-male status has been bestowed upon them during their fieldwork. However, most women trying to be men have actually found themselves perceived as "pseudomales," occupying neither a male nor a female role. Jean Jackson (1986), an ethnographer in South America, wrote home to her family and friends, "I am like a man from Mars here; I suppose I should say woman except that I am so foreign to the Bará they probably don't see much difference" (p. 263).

Ifi Amadiume (1987) has suggested that the ideas and practices leading to this honorary-male or pseudomale role during fieldwork ought to be examined, modified, and perhaps rejected. She points out that assuming such a role may in fact be neopatriarchal as well as neocolonialist. During ethnographic research in her own matrilineal Igbo community, when she found that an important women's council was excluded from the constitution by local male leaders, she chose not to identify with the men but rather spoke up about the unfairness of a situation that seriously diminished the status of local women. After becoming directly involved in raising the women's consciousness about this situation, however, she decided on a self-imposed exile in England, where she has reported that she plans to do research and use her pen to contribute to the political struggle back home.

Women can, and often do, enter into women's worlds during their field research, writing from a politically involved, woman-centered perspective. This movement from honorary-male ethnographer to woman-centered ethnographer is revealed in the plotting, rhetoric, and texture of writing produced through a strongly participatory feminist consciousness (Maguire, 1996). Feminist ethnographers today, although they exist within what has been described as a patriarchal discipline, are practicing

189

an antilogocentric or antiphallocentric approach to writing by speaking "otherwise"—against, even outside, paternal truth, reason, and phallic desire.

◆ Conclusions

Long enshrined as a theoretical orientation and philosophical paradigm within anthropology, ethnography has been adopted more recently as a useful methodology in cultural studies, literary theory, folklore, women's studies, nursing, law, planning, and even industrial engineering. Wherever this has happened, a key assumption has been that by entering into first-hand interaction with people in their everyday lives, ethnographers can reach a better understanding of the beliefs, motivations, and behaviors of their subjects than they can by using any other method.

In the past, the human sciences modeled themselves on the physical sciences, which emphasize the structures of reality outside the area of meaning. However, because human beings exist within the realm of meaning as well as in the material and organic realms, ethnographers now pay careful attention to this dimension. One of the most important forms for creating meaning is a narrative that attends to the temporal dimension of human existence and shapes events into a unity. Ethnographers who have recently provided models for the investigation of narrative have realized that the human sciences, instead of striving toward natural science, need to conceive of themselves as multiple sciences. The human being, the object and subject of their inquiry, exists in multiple strata of reality, which are organized in different ways. The realm of meaning is emergent from the material and organic strata rather than a product of them.

Following the controversies caused by the posthumous publication of Malinowski's diary and the repudiation of undercover observation, there was a movement away from participant observation toward the observation of participation. The shift from an objectifying methodology to an intersubjective methodology entails a representational transformation. The exploration of ethical issues involved in the process of generating ethnographic information and publishing ethnographic accounts encouraged ethnographers to combine the political, philosophical, and personal within single accounts. Instead of choosing between writing an ethnographic memoir centering on the self or a life history or standard monograph centering on the other, an ethnographer can allow both self and

190

other to appear together within a single narrative that carries a multiplicity of dialoguing voices.

Experience is intersubjective and embodied, not individual and fixed, but social and processual. Intersubjectivity and dialogue involve situations where bodies marked by the social—that is, by difference (gender, ethnicity, race)—may be presented as partial identities. The experience of being a woman, or being black, or being Muslim, can never be singular. It will always be dependent on a multiplicity of locations and positions that are socially constructed. These positionings are different for each individual, as well as for each culture that ethnographers come into contact with as field-workers, observant participants, and collectors of life stories.

In part, the shifts in the practice and construction of ethnography reflect an important change in the population of ethnographers and readers of ethnographies. With more middle- and lower-class individuals, more minority as well as Third and Fourth World scholars, and more women reading and practicing ethnography, the class, race, culture, and gender beliefs and behaviors of the inquirers have been placed within the same historical moment, or critical plane, as those of the subjects of inquiry. As a result, the doing, framing, representation, and reading of ethnography have been changed in both ethical and encoding practices. Participant observation has become the observation of participation, and the genre of narrative ethnography has emerged from the margins and moved to claim the center.

◆ Notes

1. Individuals who have taken on a strongly participatory role, and in some cases even undergone apprenticeships, include Reichard (1934), Hurston (1938), Dunham (1969), Jules-Rosette (1975), Maquet (1975), Riesman (1977), Chernoff (1980), Cooper (1980), Harner (1980), Peters (1981), Hayano (1982), Schipper (1982), Tedlock (1982), Dalby (1983), Johnson (1984), Turner (1985, 1993), Rose (1987), Coy (1989), Dilley (1989), Stoller (1989a), Wafer (1991), Seremetakis (1993), Knab (1995), Friedson (1996), Emad (1997), Tarn (1997), and Prechtel (1998).

2. Ever since Laura Nader (1969) advocated "studying up," there have been a growing number of studies of power elites, especially those involved in the most prestigious areas within Western science and biomedicine; see Latour (1987), Martin (1987), Traweek (1988), and Cassell (1991, 1998). There has also been attention to "studying horizontally" (Cassell, 1988, p. 89), in which there are only small power differences between the researcher and the research partners. For an instructive comparison of the benefits and problems involved in studying up, down, and sideways, see Schrijvers (1991).

3. For useful discussions of ethnography as a modernist, postmodernist, or non-modern endeavor, see Ardener (1985), Strathern (1987b), Ashley (1991), Crapanzano (1990), Manganaro (1990), Wolf (1992), Denzin (1993), Visweswaran (1994, pp. 85-94), Hastrup (1995, pp. 49-51), Pool (1995), and Dawson (1996).

4. Both critical feminism and critical ethnography have close ties to the critical theory of society explored by members of the Frankfurt school; see Wellmer (1971) and Geuss (1981).

5. More about the role of reflexivity in feminist and ethnographic critical theory can be found in Scholte (1969), Babcock (1980), Ruby (1982), Caplan (1988), and Stacey (1988). For examples of dialogical anthropology, discussions about dialogical approaches to ethnography, and critical dialogue, see Stavenhagen (1971), Dwyer (1977, 1979, 1982), D. Tedlock (1979, 1987), Webster (1982), Crapanzano (1985), Buckley (1987), Feld (1987), Tyler (1987a, 1987b), Page (1988), Fischer and Abedi (1990), Harrison (1991), Jordan (1991), B. Tedlock (1991), and Tedlock and Mannheim (1995). In sociology these same issues, but focusing on naturally occurring conversation rather than the trope of dialogue, are covered within symbolic interactionism, ethnomethodology, and the sociology of knowledge (Rapport, 1997).

6. Some of the novels written by ethnographers—both members of the cultures described and outsiders—are those of Bandelier (1890), Haggard and Lang (1890), Driberg (1930), Coon (1933, 1940), Griaule (1934), McNickle (1936, 1978), Hurston (1937), Elwin (1937, 1938), Underhill (1940), Arguedas (1941/1985, 1958/1978), Osgood (1953), Ekvall (1954, 1981), Miller (1959), Matthiessen (1965, 1975), Leighton (1971), Stewart (1971), Buelow (1973), Wendt (1973, 1979), Wilson (1974), Bista (1980), Salerno and Vanderburgh (1980), Jaffe (1983), Bennett (1986), Ghosh (1986, 1993, 1996), M. Jackson (1986), Thomas (1987), Deloria (1988), Courlander (1990), Gear and Gear (1990), Narayan (1995b), and Price (1998).

7. La Farge went on to write other novels that depended upon ethnographic knowledge of the indigenous peoples of the American Southwest and Guatemala (1931, 1937, 1945, 1951). He also wrote two collections of short stories based on ethnography and ethnographers (1957, 1965).

8. *The Wolf Is My Brother* (1967), which won the Golden Spur Award as best western historical novel, is set in the American Southwest, where Oliver lived. His last novel, *Broken Eagle* (1989), is an epic of the Old West with a Cheyenne warrior whose wife and child were killed at the Sand Creek Massacre as the hero. More recently, Kathy Reichs, of the University of North Carolina at Charlotte, has used her knowledge of and experiences in forensic anthropology to become a best-selling mystery writer. Her ethnographic novel *Déjà Dead* (1997) is built upon a composite of cases she actually worked on, and the novel's heroine, Temperance Brennan, is based on her own professional background. Her protagonist's personal problems with alcoholism and marital troubles, however, are "purely fictional" (Montell, 1997).

9. Ethnographic short stories and novellas include those of Stewart (1975, 1989, 1995), Nelson (1980), Frank (1981), Jaffe (1982, 1995), M. Richardson (1984, 1990), Applebaum (1985), Skafte (1986), B. Tedlock (1986), Waldorf (1986), Stacey (1990), McNickle (1992), Wolf (1992), Altork (1994), Nimmo (1994), Zedeño (1994), Goldschmidt (1995), Narayan (1995a), Reck (1995), Ruiz (1995), Springwater (1996), and Flynn (1997).

10. Some of the ethnographic plays that have been written and/or produced include those of Kuper (1970), Brook (1976), Higgins and Canan (1984), D. Tedlock (1986, 1998), Grindal and Shephard (1987), Richardson and Lockridge (1991), and Kondo (1995, 1997). The lives of ethnographers have also been at the center of theatrical productions. Kirsten Hastrup (1992) discusses her experience of being an object of dramatic representation. A play about the relationship between the feminist ethnographer Marjorie Shostak and her !Kung subject, Nisa, written by Brenda Bynum (1995) based on the ethnographer's field notes, journals, and letters home, was performed at the American Anthropological Association meeting in Atlanta, Georgia, in December 1995. The following year, at the AAA annual meeting in San Francisco, a staged reading was presented of a play, *Myth of the Docile Woman,* centering on Louise Lamphere's ethnographic research among sweatshop seamstresses and her own successful sex-discrimination lawsuit against Brown University (Schevill & Gordon, 1996).

11. Ethnographic diaries, letters, and travelogues include those of Leiris (1934), Elwin (1936), Lévi-Strauss (1955), Condominas (1957), Matthiessen (1962), Bista (1979), Ribeiro (1979), Chaffetz (1981), Brandão (1982), Moeran (1985), Good (1991), Behar (1995), Price and Price (1992), Goodale (1996), Turner (1996), Kirk (1997), Yu (1997), and Clastres (1998).

12. Colin Turnbull reversed this process by publishing an accessible first-person account of his fieldwork among the Congo pygmies (1961) and then releasing a coolly distanced, more authoritative monograph on the same topic (1965). Paul Stoller first published a jointly written memoir centering on his African fieldwork cowritten with his first wife, Cheryl Olkes (1987). Two years later, he released two solely authored books: a formal ethnography and a theoretical text (Stoller, 1989a, 1989b).

13. For examples of works touching on such topics, see Weston (1991, 1993), Scheper-Hughes (1992), Kleinman and Copp (1993), Newton (1993), Wade (1993), Blackwood (1995), Bolton (1995), Dubisch (1995), Grindal and Salomone (1995), Kulick (1995), Kulick and Willson (1995), Lewin (1995), Nordstrom and Robben (1995), Behar (1996), Daniel (1996), Kennedy and Davis (1996), Lewin and Leap (1996), Wafer (1996), and Willson (1997).

14. Important attempts to grapple with the intersections of class, gender, "race" and racism, ethnicity, nationalism, and sexuality are found in the work of Brah (1996) and Lewis (1996). Examples of feminist and native ethnographers (who often form an overlapping category) include Visweswaran (1988, 1994), Abu-Lughod (1990), Bell (1993), Narayan (1993), Hong (1994), Kanaaneh (1997), and Rang (1997). Discussion of these important changes can be found in Harding (1987, p. 9), Rose (1990, p. 10), D'Amico-Samuels (1991), Harrison (1991), Panini (1991), and Strathern (1987a).

15. For background reading in this contested area of "native" versus "indigenous" ethnographic practice, including the concept of "dual consciousness" that theoretically gives women and other subalterns a special ethnographic advantage, see Fahim (1977, 1987), Huizer (1979), Nash (1980), Fei (1981), Madan (1987), McClaurin-Allen (1989), Deck (1990), Kim (1990), Harrison (1991), Limón (1991), Driessen (1993), Jones (1995), and Motzafi-Haller (1997).

16. Compare the gendered discourse strategies used by women field-workers and their husbands: D. A. Talbot (1915) with P. A. Talbot (1923, 1969), E. W. Fernea (1965, 1975) with R. A. Fernea (1970, 1973), D. Dwyer (1978) with K. Dwyer (1982), E. Turner (1987,

1996) with V. Turner (1967, 1969), and Meyerson (1990) with Urton (1981). Family or "accompanied" fieldwork has only recently been described and theorized; see Cassell (1987), Gottlieb and Graham (1993), and Flinn, Marshall, and Armstrong (1998).

◆ References

Abu-Lughod, L. (1990). Can there be a feminist ethnography? *Women and Performance, 5*(1), 7-27.
Abu-Lughod, L. (1993). *Writing women's worlds: Bedouin stories.* Berkeley: University of California Press.
Adler, P. A., & Adler, P. (1987). *Membership roles in field research.* Newbury Park, CA: Sage.
Agar, M. H. (1980). *The professional stranger: An informal introduction to ethnography.* New York: Academic Press.
Allen, C. J., & Garner, N. (1993). *Condor Qatay* [Play]. (Produced and performed at George Washington University, Dorothy Betts Marvin Theater, March 31, 1994)
Allen, C. J., & Garner, N. (1995). *Condor Qatay*: Anthropology in performance. *American Anthropologist, 97*(1), 69-82.
Allen, C. J., & Garner, N. (1997). *Condor Qatay: Anthropology in performance.* Prospect Heights, IL: Waveland.
Altork, K. (1994). Working Norman's birthday. *Anthropology and Humanism, 19*(2), 159-162.
Amadiume, I. (1987). *Male daughters, female husbands: Gender and sex in an African society.* New York: Zed.
Appadurai, A. (1986). Theory in anthropology: Center and periphery. *Comparative Studies in Society and History, 28,* 356-361.
Applebaum, H. A. (1985). *Blue chips.* Lawrenceville, VA: Brunswick.
Archetti, E. P. (1994). Introduction. In E. P. Archetti (Ed.), *Exploring the written: Anthropology and the multiplicity of writing* (pp. 11-28). Oslo: Scandinavian University Press.
Ardener, E. W. (1985). Social anthropology and the decline of modernism. In J. Overing (Ed.), *Reason and morality.* London: Tavistock.
Arguedas, J. M. (1985). *Yawar Fiesta* (F. H. Barraclough, Trans.). Austin: University of Texas Press. (Original work published 1941)
Arguedas, J. M. (1978). *Deep rivers* (F. H. Barraclough, Trans.). Austin: University of Texas Press. (Original work published 1958)
Asad, T. (Ed.). (1973). *Anthropology and the colonial encounter.* Atlantic Highlands, NJ: Humanities Press.
Ashley, D. (1991). Critical theory, poststructuralism, postmodernism: Their sociological relevance. *Annual Review of Sociology, 17,* 105-131.

Auster, P. (1998). Translator's note. In P. Clastres, *Chronicle of the Guayaki Indians* (pp. 7-13). New York: Zone.

Babcock, B. (1980). Reflexivity: Definitions and discriminations. *Semiotica, 30*(1-2), 1-14.

Bahr, D., Gregorio, J., Lopez, D., & Alvarez, A. (1974). *Piman shamanism and staying sickness.* Tucson: University of Arizona Press.

Banaji, J. (1970). The crisis of British anthropology. *New Left Review, 64.*

Bandelier, A. F. (1971). *The delight makers: A novel of prehistoric Pueblo Indians.* New York: Harcourt Brace Jovanovich. (Original work published 1890)

Barley, N. (1983a). *Adventures in a mud hut: An innocent anthropologist abroad.* New York: Vanguard.

Barley, N. (1983b). *Symbolic structures: An exploration of the culture of the Dowayos.* Cambridge: Cambridge University Press.

Beattie, J. (1960). *Bunyoro: An African kingdom.* New York: Holt, Rinehart & Winston.

Beattie, J. (1965). *Understanding an African kingdom.* New York: Holt, Rinehart & Winston.

Beaujour, M. (1987). Michel Leiris: Ethnography or self-portrayal? *Cultural Anthropology, 2,* 470-480.

Behar, R. (1993). *Translated woman: Crossing the border with Esperanza's story.* Boston: Beacon.

Behar, R. (1995). Writing in my father's name: A diary of *Translated woman's first year. In R. Behar & D. A. Gordon (Eds.), Women writing culture* (pp. 65-82). Berkeley: University of California Press.

Behar, R. (1996). *The vulnerable observer: Anthropology that breaks your heart.* Boston: Beacon.

Bell, D. (1993). Yes Virginia, there is a feminist ethnography: Reflections from three Australian fields. In D. Bell, P. Caplan, & W. J. Karim (Eds.), *Gendered fields: Women, men and ethnography* (pp. 28-43). London: Routledge.

Bennett, J. A. W. (1986). *Downfall people.* Toronto: McClelland & Stewart.

Bista, D. B. (1979). *Report from Lhasa.* Kathmandu: Sajha Prakashan.

Bista, D. B. (1980). *Shotala.* Kathmandu, Nepal: Sajha Prakashan.

Blackwood, E. (1995). Falling in love with an-Other lesbian: Reflections on identity in fieldwork. In D. Kulick & M. Willson (Eds.), *Taboo: Sex, identity and erotic subjectivity in anthropological fieldwork* (pp. 51-75). New York: Routledge.

Bode, B. (1989). *No bells to toll: Destruction and creation in the Andes.* New York: Scribner's Sons.

Bolton, R. (1995). Tricks, friends, and lovers: Erotic encounters in the field. In D. Kulick & M. Willson (Eds.), *Taboo: Sex, identity and erotic subjectivity in anthropological fieldwork* (pp. 140-167). New York: Routledge.

Boon, J. A. (1982). *Other tribes, other scribes: Symbolic anthropology in the comparative study of cultures, histories, religions, and texts.* Cambridge: Cambridge University Press.

Bowen, E. S. (pseudonym of L. Bohannan). (1954). *Return to laughter: An anthropological novel.* New York: Harper & Row.

Brah, A. (1996). *Cartographies of diaspora: Contesting identities.* London: Routledge.

Brandão, C. R. (1982). *Diário de campo: A antropologia com alegoria.* São Paulo: Brasiliense.

Brandes, R. S. (1965). *Frank Hamilton Cushing: Pioneer Americanist.* Ann Arbor, MI: University Microfilms International.

Brink, P. J. (1993). Studying African women's secret societies. In C. M. Renzetti & R. M. Lee (Eds.), *Researching sensitive topics* (pp. 235-248). Newbury Park, CA: Sage.

British Association for the Advancement of Science. (1874). *Notes and queries on anthropology, for the use of travellers and residents in uncivilized lands.* London: CRAA.

Brook, J. P. (1976). *The Ik* [Play]. (Directed and produced by Peter Brook, Round House Theatre, London)

Brown, K. M. (1991). *Mama Lola: A Vodou priestess in Brooklyn.* Berkeley: University of California Press.

Buckley, T. (1987). Dialogue and shared authority: Informants as critics. *Central Issues in Anthropology, 7*(1), 13-23.

Buelow, G. D. (1973). *The ethnographic novel in Africa.* Unpublished doctoral dissertation, University of Oregon.

Bynum, B. (1995, December). *My heart is still shaking.* Play performed at the annual meeting of the American Anthropological Association, Atlanta, GA.

Caplan, P. (1988). Engendering knowledge: The politics of ethnography. *Anthropology Today, 4*(5), 8-12.

Cassell, J. (1987). *Children in the field: Anthropological experiences.* Philadelphia: Temple University Press.

Cassell, J. (1988). The relationship of observer to observed when studying up. In R. Burgess (Ed.), *Studies in qualitative methodology* (Vol. 1, pp. 89-108). London: JAI.

Cassell, J. (1991). *Expected miracles: Surgeons at work.* Philadelphia: Temple University Press.

Cassell, J. (1998). *The woman in the surgeon's body.* Cambridge, MA: Harvard University Press.

Caulfield, M. D. (1979). Participant observation or partisan participation? In G. Huizer & B. Mannheim (Eds.), *The politics of anthropology: From colonialism and sexism toward a view from below* (pp. 309-318). The Hague: Mouton.

Cesara, M. (pseudonym of K. Poewe). (1982). *Reflections of a woman anthropologist: No hiding place.* London: Academic Press.

Chaffetz, D. (1981). *A journey through Afghanistan: A memorial.* Chicago: University of Chicago Press.

Chernoff, J. M. (1980). *African rhythm and African sensibility.* Chicago: University of Chicago Press.

Chilungu, S. W. (1976). Issues in the ethics of research method: An interpretation of the Anglo-American perspective. *Current Anthropology, 17,* 457-481.

Clastres, P. (1998). *Chronicle of the Guayaki Indians* (P. Auster, Trans.). New York: Zone.

Condominas, G. (1957). *Nous avons mangé la forêt de la Pierre-Génie Gôo.* Paris: Mercure de France.

Coon, C. S. (1933). *The ruffian.* Boston: Little, Brown.

Coon, C. S. (1940). *Flesh of the wild ox.* New York: Morrow.

Cooper, E. (1980). *The woodcarvers of Hong Kong: Craft production in the world capitalist periphery.* New York: Cambridge University Press.

Courlander, H. (1990). *The Bordeaux narrative.* Albuquerque: University of New Mexico Press.

Coy, M. W. (1989). Being what we pretend to be: The usefulness of apprenticeship as a field method. In M. W. Coy (Ed.), *Apprenticeship: From theory to method and back again* (pp. 115-135). Albany: State University of New York Press.

Crapanzano, V. (1980). *Tuhami: Portrait of a Moroccan.* Chicago: University of Chicago Press.

Crapanzano, V. (1985). *Waiting: The whites of South Africa.* New York: Random House.

Crapanzano, V. (1990). Afterword. In M. Manganaro (Ed.), *Modernist anthropology: From fieldwork to text* (pp. 300-308). Princeton, NJ: Princeton University Press.

Cushing, F. H. (1882). My adventures in Zuñi. *Century Illustrated Monthly Magazine, 25,* 191-207, 500-511.

Cushing, F. H. (1883). My adventures in Zuñi. *Century Illustrated Monthly Magazine, 26,* 28-47.

Cushing, F. H. (1979). *Zuñi: Selected writings of Frank Hamilton Cushing* (J. Green, Ed.). Lincoln: University of Nebraska Press.

Cushing, F. H. (1990). *Cushing at Zuni: The correspondence and journals of Frank Hamilton Cushing 1879-1884* (J. Green, Ed.). Albuquerque: University of New Mexico Press.

Dalby, L. C. (1983). *Geisha.* Berkeley: University of California Press.

Damatta, R. (1994). Some biased remarks on interpretivism: A view from Brazil. In R. Borofsky (Ed.), *Assessing cultural anthropology* (pp. 119-132). New York: McGraw-Hill.

D'Amico-Samuels, D. (1991). Undoing fieldwork: Personal, political, theoretical and methodological implications. In F. V. Harrison (Ed.), *Decolonizing anthropology: Moving further toward an anthropology for liberation* (pp. 68-87). Washington, DC: Association of Black Anthropologists/American Anthropological Association.

Daniel, E. V. (1984). *Fluid signs: Being a person the Tamil way.* Berkeley: University of California Press.

Daniel, E. V. (1996). *Charred lullabies: Chapters in an anthropology of violence.* Princeton, NJ: Princeton University Press.

David-Neel, A. A. (1927). *My journey to Lhasa: The personal story of the only white woman who succeeded in entering the Forbidden City.* London: William Heinemann.

David-Neel, A. A. (1932). *Magic and mystery in Tibet.* New York: Claude Kendall.

David-Neel, A. A. (1936). *Le bouddhisme, ses doctrines et ses methodes.* Paris: Plon.

David-Neel, A. A. (1959). *Initiations and initiates in Tibet.* New York: University.

Dawson, L. L. (1996). Postmodern ethnography and the sociology of religion. *Research in the Social Scientific Study of Religion, 7,* 3-41.

Deck, A. A. (1990). Autoethnography: Zora Neale Hurston, Noni Jabavu, and cross-disciplinary discourse. *Black American Literature Forum, 24,* 237-256.

Deloria, E. C. (1988). *Waterlily.* Lincoln: University of Nebraska Press.

Denzin, N. K. (1993). The postmodern sensibility. In N. K. Denzin (Ed.), *Studies in symbolic interaction* (pp. 179-188). Greenwich, CT: JAI.

DeVault, M. L. (1990). Women write sociology: Rhetorical strategies. In A. Hunter (Ed.), *The rhetoric of social research: Understood and believed* (pp. 97-110). New Brunswick, NJ: Rutgers University Press.

De Vita, P. R. (Ed.). (1990). *The humbled anthropologist: Tales from the Pacific.* Belmont, CA: Wadsworth.

Dilley, R. M. (1989). Secrets and skills: Apprenticeship among Tukolor weavers. In M. W. Coy (Ed.), *Apprenticeship: From theory to method and back again* (pp. 181-198). Albany: State University of New York Press.

Driberg, J. H. (1930). *People of the small arrow.* New York: Payson & Clarke.

Driessen, H. (1993). *The politics of ethnographic reading and writing: Confrontations of Western and indigenous views.* Saarbrücken, Germany: Verlag.

Dubisch, J. (1995). Lovers in the field: Sex, dominance, and the female anthropologist. In D. Kulick & M. Willson (Eds.), *Taboo: Sex, identity and erotic subjectivity in anthropological fieldwork* (pp. 29-50). New York: Routledge.

Du Bois, W. E. B. (1969). *The souls of black folk: Essays and sketches.* New York: Fawcett. (Original work published 1903)

Dumont, J.-P. (1976). *Under the rainbow: Nature and supernature among the Panaré Indians.* Austin: University of Texas Press.

Dumont, J.-P. (1978). *The headman and I: Ambiguity and ambivalence in the fieldworking experience.* Austin: University of Texas Press.

Dunham, K. (1969). *Island possessed.* Chicago: University of Chicago Press.

Dwyer, D. (1978). *Images and self-images: Male and female in Morocco.* New York: Columbia University Press.

Dwyer, K. (1977). On the dialogic of fieldwork. *Dialectical Anthropology, 2,* 143-151.

Dwyer, K. (1979). The dialogic of ethnology. *Dialectical Anthropology, 4,* 205-224.

Dwyer, K. (1982). *Moroccan dialogues: Anthropology in question.* Baltimore: Johns Hopkins University Press.

Ekvall, R. B. (1954). *Tents against the sky.* London: Victor Gollancz.

Ekvall, R. B. (1981). *The lama knows.* Novato, CA: Chandler & Sharp.

Elwin, V. (1932). *Truth and India: Can we get it?* London: George Allen & Unwin.

Elwin, V. (1936). *Leaves from the jungle: Life in a Gond village.* London: Oxford University Press.

Elwin, V. (1937). *Phulmat of the hills.* London.

Elwin, V. (1938). *A cloud that is dragonish.* London.

Elwin, V. (1942). *The Agaria.* London: Oxford University Press.

Elwin, V. (1946). *Folk-songs of Chhattisgarh.* London: Oxford University Press.

Elwin, V. (1947). *The Muria and their ghotul.* Bombay: Oxford University Press.

Elwin, V. (1954). *Tribal myths of Orissa.* Bombay: Oxford University Press.

Elwin, V. (1961). *Nagaland.* Shillong: Adviser's Secretariat.

Elwin, V. (1964). *The tribal world of Verrier Elwin.* Bombay: Oxford University Press.

Emad, M. (1997). Twirling the needle: Pinning down anthropologists' emergent bodies in the disclosive field of American acupuncture. *Anthropology of Consciousness, 8*(2-3), 88-96.

Eves, R. (1999). Going troppo: Images of white savagery, degeneration and race in turn-of-the-century colonial fictions of the Pacific. *History and Anthropology, 11,* 351-385.

Fahim, H. (1977). Foreign and indigenous anthropology: The perspectives of an Egyptian anthropologist. *Human Organization, 36,* 80-86.

Fahim, H. (Ed.). (1987). *Indigenous anthropology in non-Western countries.* Durham, NC: Carolina Academic Press.

Fei H. T. (1939). *Peasant life in China.* London: Kegan Paul, Trench & Trubner.

Fei H. T. (1981). *Toward a people's anthropology.* Beijing: New World.

Feld, S. (1987). Dialogic editing: Interpreting how Kaluli read *Sound and sentiment. Cultural Anthropology, 2,* 190-210.

Fernea, E. W. (1965). *Guests of the sheik: An ethnography of an Iraqi village.* Garden City, NY: Doubleday.

Fernea, E. W. (1975). *A street in Marrakech.* Garden City, NY: Doubleday.

Fernea, E. W., & Fernea, R. A. (1985). *The Arab world: Personal encounters.* Garden City, NY: Doubleday.

Fernea, E. W., & Fernea, R. A. (1991). *Nubian ethnographies.* Prospect Heights, IL: Waveland.

Fernea, R. A. (1970). *Shaykh and effendi: Changing patterns of authority among the El Shaban of southern Iraq.* Cambridge, MA: Harvard University Press.

Fernea, R. A. (1973). *Nubians in Egypt.* Austin: University of Texas Press.

Firth, R. (1985). Degrees of intelligibility. In J. Overing (Ed.), *Reason and morality.* London: Tavistock.

Fischer, M. M., & Abedi, M. (1990). *Debating Muslims: Cultural dialogues in postmodernity and tradition.* Madison: University of Wisconsin Press.

Flinn, J., Marshall, L., & Armstrong, J. (Eds.). (1998). *Fieldwork and families: Constructing new models for ethnographic research.* Honolulu: University of Hawaii Press.

Flynn, S. I. (1997). A feast of mangoes. *Anthropology and Humanism, 22*(1), 119-124.

Fogelson, R. D. (1984). Who were the Ani-Kutani? An excursion into Cherokee historical thought. *Ethnohistory, 31,* 255-263.

Frank, G. (1981). Mercy's children. *Anthropology and Humanism Quarterly, 6*(4), 8-12.

Frazer, J. G. (1887). *Questions on the manners, customs, religion, superstitions, etc. of uncivilized or semi-civilized peoples* [Pamphlet]. London: Author.

Frazer, J. G. (1981). *The golden bough: The roots of religion and folklore.* New York: Avenel. (Original work published 1890)

Freilich, M. (1970). *Marginal natives: Anthropologists at work.* New York: Harper & Row.

Freshfield, M. (pseudonym of M. Field). (1947). *Stormy dawn.* London: Faber.

Friedson, S. M. (1996). *Dancing prophets: Musical experience in Tumbuka healing.* Chicago: University of Chicago Press.

Gal, S. (1991). Between speech and silence: The problematics of research on language and gender. In M. di Leonardo (Ed.), *Gender at the crossroads of knowledge* (pp. 175-203). Berkeley: University of California Press.

Gear, W. M., & Gear, K. O. (1990). *People of the wolf.* New York: Tor.

Gerhart, M. (1992). *Genre choices, gender questions.* Norman: University of Oklahoma Press.

Geuss, R. (1981). *The idea of a critical theory: Habermas and the Frankfurt school.* Cambridge: Cambridge University Press.

Ghosh, A. (1986). *The circle of reason.* New York: Viking.

Ghosh, A. (1993). *In an antique land.* New York: Alfred A. Knopf.

Ghosh, A. (1996). *Calcutta chromosome: A novel of fevers, delirium, and discovery.* London: Picador.

Goldschmidt, W. (1995). Pietro's house. *Anthropology and Humanism, 20*(1), 47-51.

Good, K. (with Chanoff, D.). (1991). *Into the heart: One man's pursuit of love and knowledge among the Yanomama.* New York: Simon & Schuster.

Goodale, J. C. (with Chowning, A.). (1996). *The two-party line: Conversations in the field.* Lanham, MD: Rowman & Littlefield.

Gottlieb, A., & Graham, P. (1993). *Parallel worlds: An anthropologist and a writer encounter Africa.* New York: Crown.

Gough, K. (1968). Anthropology: Child of imperialism. *Monthly Review, 19*(11).

Griaule, M. (1934). *Les flambeurs d'hommes.* Paris: Calmann-Lévy.

Grindal, B., & Salomone, F. (Eds.). (1995). *Bridges to humanity: Narratives on anthropology and friendship.* Prospect Heights, IL: Waveland.

Grindal, B., & Shephard, W. H. (1987). Redneck girl: From experience to performance. *Journal of the Steward Anthropological Society, 17*(1-2), 193-218.

Gronewold, S. (1972). Did Frank Hamilton Cushing go native? In S. T. Kimball & J. B. Watson (Eds.), *Crossing cultural boundaries: The anthropological experience* (pp. 33-50). San Francisco: Chandler.

Gudeman, S., & Rivera, A. (1990). *Conversations in Colombia: The domestic economy in life and text.* Cambridge: Cambridge University Press.

Haggard, H. R., & Lang, A. (1890). *The world's desire.* London: Longman, Green.

Hammersley, M. (1992). *What's wrong with ethnography? Methodological explorations.* London: Routledge.

Hammersley, M., & Atkinson, P. (1983). *Ethnography: Principles in practice.* London: Tavistock.

Hammond-Tooke, W. D. (1997). *Imperfect interpreters: South Africa's anthropologists 1920-1990.* Johannesburg: Witwatersrand University Press.

Harding, S. (Ed.). (1987). *Feminism and methodology: Social science issues.* Bloomington: Indiana University Press.

Harner, M. (1980). *The way of the shaman.* New York: Harper & Row.

Harrison, F. V. (1991). Ethnography as politics. In F. V. Harrison (Ed.), *Decolonizing anthropology: Moving further toward an anthropology for liberation* (pp. 88-109). Washington, DC: Association of Black Anthropologists/American Anthropological Association.

Hastrup, K. (1992). Out of anthropology: The anthropologist as an object of dramatic representation. *Cultural Anthropology, 7,* 327-345.

Hastrup, K. (1995). *A passage to anthropology: Between experience and theory.* London: Routledge.

Hau'ofa, E. (1975). Anthropology and Pacific islanders. *Oceania, 45,* 283-289.

Hau'ofa, E. (1982). Anthropology at home: A South Pacific islands experience. In H. Fahim (Ed.), *Indigenous anthropology in non-Western countries* (pp. 213-222). Durham, NC: Carolina Academic Press.

Hayano, D. M. (1979). Auto-ethnography: Paradigms, problems, and prospects. *Human Organization, 38,* 113-120.

Hayano, D. M. (1982). *Poker faces.* Berkeley: University of California Press.

Higgins, C., & Canan, D. (1984). *The Ik* [Play].

Hong, K. (1994). Experiences of being a "native": Observing anthropology. *Anthropology Today, 10*(3), 6-9.

Hsu, F. L., & Textor, R. (1978). Third World anthropologists and the reprisal of anthropological paradigms. *Anthropology Newsletter, 19*(1), 5.

Huizer, G. (1979). Anthropology and politics: From naïveté toward liberation? In G. Huizer & B. Mannheim (Eds.), *The politics of anthropology: From colonialism and sexism toward a view from below* (pp. 3-141). The Hague: Mouton.

Humphrey, C. (with Onon, U.). (1996). *Shamans and elders: Experience, knowledge, and power among the Daur Mongols.* Oxford: Clarendon.

Hurston, Z. N. (1937). *Their eyes were watching God.* New York: Collier.

Hurston, Z. N. (1938). *Tell my horse.* Philadelphia: J. B. Lippincott.

Hymes, D. (Ed.). (1969). *Reinventing anthropology.* New York: Random House.

Jackson, J. (1986). On trying to be an Amazon. In T. L. Whitehead & M. E. Conaway (Eds.), *Self, sex, and gender in cross-cultural fieldwork* (pp. 263-274). Urbana: University of Illinois Press.

Jackson, M. (1986). *Barawa and the ways birds fly in the sky.* Washington, DC: Smithsonian Institution Press.

Jaffe, H. (1982). *Mourning crazy horses: Stories.* New York: Fiction Collective.

Jaffe, H. (1983). *Dos indios.* New York: Thunder's Mouth.

Jaffe, H. (1995). *Straight razor: Stories.* Normal, IL: Black Ice.

Johnson, N. B. (1984). Sex, color, and rites of passage in ethnographic research. *Human Organization, 43,* 108-120.

Jones, D. J. (1970). Towards a native anthropology. *Human Organization, 29*(4), 1-59.

Jones, D. J. (1995). Anthropology and the oppressed: A reflection on "native" anthropology. In E. L. Cerroni-Long (Ed.), *Insider anthropology* (pp. 58-70). Washington, DC: American Anthropological Association.

Jordan, G. H. (1991). On ethnography in an intertextual situation: Reading narratives or deconstructing discourse? In F. V. Harrison (Ed.), *Decolonizing anthropology: Moving further toward an anthropology for liberation* (pp. 42-67). Washington, DC: Association of Black Anthropologists/American Anthropological Association.

Jovanovich, S. (1971). Adolf Bandelier: An introduction. In A. F. Bandelier, *The delight makers: A novel of prehistoric Pueblo Indians* (pp. v-xix). New York: Harcourt Brace Jovanovich.

Jules-Rosette, B. (1975). *African apostles: Ritual and conversion in the church of John Maranke.* Ithaca, NY: Cornell University Press.

Kanaaneh, M. (1997). The "anthropologicality" of indigenous anthropology. *Dialectical Anthropology, 22,* 23-49.

Keesing, R. (1985). "Kwaio women speak": The micropolitics of autobiography in a Solomon Island society. *American Anthropologist, 87*(12), 27-39.

Kendall, L. (1988). *The life and hard times of a Korean shaman: Of tales and the telling of tales.* Honolulu: University of Hawaii Press.

Kennedy, E. L., & Davis, M. D. (1996). *Boots of leather, slippers of gold: The history of a lesbian community.* New York: Routledge.

Kenyatta, J. (1938). *Facing Mount Kenya: The tribal life of the Gikuyu.* London: Secker & Warburg.

Kim, C. S. (1990). The role of the non-Western anthropologist reconsidered: Illusion versus reality. *Current Anthropology, 31,* 191-201.

Kirk, R. (1997). *The monkey's paw: New chronicles from Peru.* Amherst: University of Massachusetts Press.

Kleinman, S., & Copp, M. A. (1993). *Emotions and fieldwork.* Newbury Park, CA: Sage.

Knab, T. J. (1995). *A war of witches: A journey into the underworld of the contemporary Aztecs.* San Francisco: Harper.

Kondo, D. K. (1995). Bad girls: Theater, women of color, and the politics of representation. In R. Behar & D. A. Gordon (Eds.), *Women writing culture* (pp. 49-64). Berkeley: University of California Press.

Kondo, D. K. (1997). *About face: Performing race in fashion and theater.* New York: Routledge.

Krieger, S. (1983). *The mirror dance: Identity in a women's community.* Philadelphia: Temple University Press.

Krige, E. J., & Krige, J. D. (1943). *The realm of a rain-queen: A study of the pattern of Lovedu society.* London: Oxford University Press.

Kulick, D. (1995). The sexual life of anthropologists: Erotic subjectivity and ethnographic work. In D. Kulick & M. Willson (Eds.), *Taboo: Sex, identity and erotic subjectivity in anthropological fieldwork* (pp. 1-28). New York: Routledge.

Kulick, D., & Willson, M. (Eds.). (1995). *Taboo: Sex, identity and erotic subjectivity in anthropological fieldwork.* New York: Routledge.

Kuper, H. (1947). *An African aristocracy: Rank among the Swazi.* London: Oxford University Press.

Kuper, H. (1960). *Indian people in Natal.* Natal, Brazil: Natal University Press.

Kuper, H. (1965). *Bite of hunger: A novel of Africa.* New York: Harcourt, Brace & World.

Kuper, H. (1970). *A witch in my heart: A play set in Swaziland in the 1930s.* London: Oxford University Press.

Kuper, H. (1984). Work, misses? *Anthropology and Humanism Quarterly, 9,* 15-17. (Original work published 1943)

La Farge, O. (1929). *Laughing boy.* New York: Literary Guild of America.

La Farge, O. (1931). *Sparks fly upward.* Boston: Houghton Mifflin.

La Farge, O. (1937). *The enemy gods.* Boston: Houghton Mifflin.

La Farge, O. (1945). *Raw material.* Boston: Houghton Mifflin.

La Farge, O. (1951). *Behind the mountain.* Boston: Houghton Mifflin.

La Farge, O. (1957). *A pause in the desert.* Boston: Houghton Mifflin.

La Farge, O. (1965). *The door in the wall.* Boston: Houghton Mifflin.

Lambek, M. (1997). Pinching the crocodile's tongue: Affinity and the anxieties of influence in fieldwork. *Anthropology and Humanism, 22*(1), 31-53.

Langness, L. L., & Frank, G. (1978). Fact, fiction, and the ethnographic novel. *Anthropology and Humanism Quarterly, 3*(1-2), 18-22.

Langness, L. L., & Frank, G. (1981). *Lives: An anthropological approach to biography.* Novato, CA: Chandler & Sharp.

Latour, B. (1987). *Science in action.* Cambridge, MA: Harvard University Press.

Laughlin, R. (1994, March 24). *From all for all.* Play performed at the conference "La Sabiduria Maya ah Idzatil: The Wisdom of the Maya," University of Florida.

Lee, R. M. (1995). *Dangerous fieldwork.* Thousand Oaks, CA: Sage.

Leighton, A. H. (1971). *Come near.* New York: W. W. Norton.

Leiris, M. (1934). *L'Afrique fantôme.* Paris: Plon (Terre Humaine).

Leiris, M. (1939). *L'age d'homme.* Paris: Editions Gallimard.

Leiris, M. (1983). *Manhood: A journey from childhood into the fierce order of virility* (R. Howard, Trans.). Chicago: University of Chicago Press.

Lévi-Strauss, C. (1955). *Tristes tropiques.* Paris: Plon (Terre Humaine).

Lévi-Strauss, C. (1973). *Tristes tropiques.* New York: Washington Square Press.

Lewin, E. (1995). Writing lesbian ethnography. In R. Behar & D. A. Gordon (Eds.), *Women writing culture* (pp. 322-335). Berkeley: University of California Press.

Lewin, E., & Leap, W. L. (Eds.). (1996). *Out in the field: Reflections of lesbian and gay anthropologists.* Urbana: University of Illinois Press.

Lewis, D. K. (1973). Anthropology and colonialism. *Current Anthropology, 14,* 581-597.

Lewis, O. (1959). *Five families: Mexican case studies in the culture of poverty.* New York: Basic Books.

Lewis, O. (1961). *The children of Sánchez: Autobiography of a Mexican family.* New York: Random House.

Lewis, O. (1964). *Pedro Martínez: A Mexican peasant and his family.* New York: Random House.

Lewis, O. (1965). *La vida: A Puerto Rican family in the culture of poverty—San Juan and New York.* New York: Vintage.

Lewis, R. (1996). *Gendering Orientalism: Race, femininity and representation.* London: Routledge.

Limón, J. (1991). Representation, ethnicity, and the precursory ethnography: Notes of a native anthropologist. In R. G. Fox (Ed.), *Recapturing anthropol-*

ogy: Working in the present (pp. 115-135). Santa Fe, NM: School of American Research Press.

MacClancy, J. (1996). Popularizing anthropology. In J. MacClancy & C. McDonaugh (Eds.), *Popularizing anthropology* (pp. 1-57). London: Routledge.

Madan, T. N. (1987). Indigenous anthropology in non-Western counties: An overview. In H. Fahim (Ed.), *Indigenous anthropology in non-Western countries* (pp. 263-268). Durham, NC: Carolina Academic Press.

Maguire, P. (1996). Considering more feminist participatory research: What's congruency got to do with it? *Qualitative Inquiry, 2,* 106-118.

Malinowski, B. (1922). *Argonauts of the western Pacific: An account of native enterprise and adventure in the archipelagoes of Melanesian New Guinea.* New York: E. P. Dutton.

Malinowski, B. (1967). *A diary in the strict sense of the term* (N. Guterman, Trans.). New York: Harcourt, Brace & World.

Manganaro, M. (1990). Textual play, power, and cultural critique: An orientation to modernist anthropology. In M. Manganaro (Ed.), *Modernist anthropology: From fieldwork to text* (pp. 3-47). Princeton, NJ: Princeton University Press.

Maquet, J. (1975). Meditation in contemporary Sri Lanka: Idea and practice. *Journal of Transpersonal Psychology, 7*(2), 182-195.

Marcus, G. E., & Fischer, M. M. J. (1986). *Anthropology as cultural critique: An experimental moment in the human sciences.* Chicago: University of Chicago Press.

Martin, E. (1987). *The woman in the body: A cultural analysis of reproduction.* Boston: Beacon.

Matthiessen, P. (1962). *Under the mountain wall: A chronicle of two seasons in Stone Age New Guinea.* London: Penguin.

Matthiessen, P. (1965). *At play in the fields of the Lord.* New York: Random House.

Matthiessen, P. (1975). *Far Tortuga.* New York: Random House.

McClaurin-Allen, I. (1989). *Theorizing "native" anthropology: Who, what, why and how.* Unpublished manuscript.

McNickle, D. (1936). *The surrounded.* New York: Dodd, Mead.

McNickle, D. (1978). *Wind from an enemy sky.* San Francisco: Harper & Row.

McNickle, D. (1992). *The hawk is hungry and other stories.* Tucson: University of Arizona Press.

Meyerson, J. (1990). *'Tambo: Life in an Andean village.* Austin: University of Texas Press.

Miller, W. (1959). *The cool world.* New York: Fawcett.

Misra, B. (1973). *Verrier Elwin: A pioneer Indian anthropologist.* New York: Asia.

Moeran, B. (1985). *Okubo diary: Portrait of a Japanese valley.* Stanford, CA: Stanford University Press.

Montell, G. (1997, October 24). An anthropologist's best-selling thriller. *Chronicle of Higher Education,* p. A8.

Motzafi-Haller, P. (1997). Writing birthright: On native anthropologists and the politics of representation. In D. E. Reed-Danahay (Ed.), *Auto/ethnography: Rewriting the self and the social* (pp. 195-222). New York: Berg.

Nader, L. (1969). Up the anthropologist: Perspectives gained from studying up. In D. Hymes (Ed.), *Reinventing anthropology* (pp. 284-311). New York: Random House.

Nakane, C. (1970). *Japanese society.* Berkeley: University of California Press.

Narayan, K. (1989). *Storytellers, saints and scoundrels: Folk narrative in Hindu religious teaching.* Philadelphia: University of Pennsylvania Press.

Narayan, K. (1993). How native is a "native" anthropologist? *American Anthropologist, 5,* 671-686.

Narayan, K. (1995a). Come out and serve. *Anthropology and Humanism, 20*(1), 51-59.

Narayan, K. (1995b). *Love stars and all that.* New York: Washington Square.

Nash, D., & Wintrob, R. (1972). The emergence of self-consciousness in ethnography. *Current Anthropology, 13,* 527-542.

Nash, J. (1980). A critique of social science roles in Latin America. In J. Nash & H. Safa (Eds.), *Sex and class in Latin America* (pp. 1-22). South Hadley, MA: Bergin & Garvey.

Nelson, R. K. (1980). *Shadow of the hunter: Stories of Eskimo life.* Chicago: University of Chicago Press.

Newton, E. (1993). My best informant's dress: The erotic equation in fieldwork. *Cultural Anthropology, 8,* 3-23.

Nimmo, H. A. (1994). *The songs of Salanda and other stories of Sulu.* Seattle: University of Washington Press.

Nimuendajú, C. (pseudonym of C. Unkel). (1939). *The Apinayé.* Washington, DC: Catholic University of America.

Nimuendajú, C. (pseudonym of C. Unkel). (1942). *The Serente.* Boston: Frederick Webb Hodge Anniversary Publication Fund.

Nimuendajú, C. (pseudonym of C. Unkel). (1946). *The eastern Timbira* (Publications in American Archaeology and Ethnology No. 14). Berkeley: University of California.

Nimuendajú, C. (pseudonym of C. Unkel). (1952). *The Tukuna.* Berkeley: University of California Press.

Nimuendajú, C. (pseudonym of C. Unkel). (1978). *Los mitos de creación y de destrucción del mundo como fundamentos de la religión de los Apapokuva-Guarani.* Lima: Centro Amazonico de Antropología y Aplicación Practica. (Original work published 1914)

Nolan, W. F. (1968). Chad Oliver. In W. F. Nolan (Ed.), *3 to the highest power: Bradbury, Oliver, Sturgeon* (pp. 109-160). New York: Avon.

Nordstrom, C., & Robben, A. C. G. M. (Eds.). (1995). *Fieldwork under fire: Contemporary studies of violence and survival.* Berkeley: University of California Press.

Ohnuki-Tierney, E. (1984). Native anthropologists. *American Ethnologist, 3,* 584-586.

Okely, J. (1992). Anthropology and autobiography: Participatory experience and embodied knowledge. In J. Okely & H. Callaway (Eds.), *Anthropology and autobiography* (pp. 1-28). London: Routledge.

Oliver, C. (1951, June). The boy next door. *Fantasy and Science Fiction.*

Oliver, (S.) C. (1952). *They builded a tower: The story of science fiction.* Unpublished master's thesis, University of Texas.

Oliver, C. (1954). *Shadows in the sun.* New York: Ballantine.

Oliver, C. (1957). *The winds of time.* New York: Doubleday.

Oliver, C. (1962). *Ecology and cultural continuity as contributing factors in the social organization of the Plains Indians.* Berkeley: University of California Press.

Oliver, C. (1967). *The wolf is my brother.* New York: Bantam.

Oliver, C. (1971). *The shores of another sea.* New York: Crown.

Oliver, C. (1981). *The discovery of humanity: An introduction to anthropology.* New York: Bantam.

Oliver, C. (1989). *Broken eagle.* New York: Bantam.

Osgood, C. (1953). *Winter.* New York: W. W. Norton.

Page, H. E. (1988). Dialogic principles of interactive learning in the ethnographic relationship. *Journal of Anthropological Research, 44,* 163-181.

Panini, M. N. (Ed.). (1991). *From the female eye: Accounts of women fieldworkers studying their own society.* Delhi: Hindustan.

Peters, L. (1981). *Ecstasy and healing in Nepal: An ethnopsychiatric study of Tamang shamanism.* Malibu, CA: Undena.

Pick, D. (1989). *Faces of degeneration: A European disorder, c. 1848-1918.* Cambridge: Cambridge University Press.

Pool, R. (1995). Breaking the conspiracy of silence: Some reflections on fieldwork and new modes of ethnographic writing. In K. Geuijen, D. Raven, & J. de Wolf (Eds.), *Post-modernism and anthropology: Theory and practice* (pp. 108-119). Assen-Maastricht, Netherlands: Van Gorcum.

Pozas, R. (1962). *Juan the Chamula: An ethnological re-creation of the life of a Mexican Indian.* Berkeley: University of California Press.

Prechtel, M. (1998). *Secrets of the talking jaguar: A Mayan shaman's journey to the heart of the indigenous soul.* New York: Jeremy P. Tarcher.

Price, R. (1998). *The convict and the colonel.* Boston: Beacon.

Price, R., & Price, S. (1992). *Equatoria.* New York: Routledge.

Prus, R., & Irini, S. (1980). *Hookers, rounders, and desk clerks: The social organization of the hotel community.* Salem, WI: Sheffield.

207

Prus, R., & Sharper, C. R. D. (1977). *Road hustler: Career contingencies of professional card and dice hustlers.* Lexington, MA: Lexington.

Rabinow, P. (1975). *Symbolic domination: Cultural form and historical change in Morocco.* Chicago: University of Chicago Press.

Rabinow, P. (1977). *Reflections on fieldwork in Morocco.* Berkeley: University of California Press.

Rabinow, P. (1985). Discourse and power: On the limits of ethnographic texts. *Dialectical Anthropology, 10,* 1-13.

Radin, P. (1920). Crashing Thunder: The autobiography of an American Indian. *University of California Publications in American Archaeology and Ethnology, 16,* 381-473.

Rang, S. (1997). Native anthropology and other problems. *Dialectical Anthropology, 22,* 23-49.

Rapport, N. (1997). Culture as conversation: Representation as conversation. In A. James, J. Hockey, & A. Dawson (Eds.), *After writing culture: Epistemology and praxis in contemporary anthropology* (pp. 177-193). New York: Routledge.

Read, K. E. (1986). *Return to the high valley.* Berkeley: University of California Press.

Reck, G. (1995). Resurrection. *Anthropology and Humanism, 20*(2), 160-164.

Record, P. (pseudonym of P. Drucker). (1969). *Tropical frontier.* New York: Alfred A. Knopf.

Reed-Danahay, D. E. (Ed.). (1997). *Auto/ethnography: Rewriting the self and the social.* New York: Berg.

Reichard, G. A. (1934). *Spider Woman: A story of Navajo weavers and chanters.* New York: Macmillan.

Reichs, K. J. (1997). *Déjà dead.* New York: Scribner.

Ribeiro, B. G. (1979). *Diário do Xingu.* São Paulo: Editora Paz e Terra.

Richards, D. (1994). *Masks of difference: Cultural representations in literature, anthropology and art.* Cambridge: Cambridge University Press.

Richardson, L. (1990). *Writing strategies: Reaching diverse audiences.* Newbury Park, CA: Sage.

Richardson, L., & Lockridge, E. (1991). *The sea monster*: An ethnographic drama. *Symbolic Interaction, 14,* 335-340.

Richardson, M. (1984). The museum. *Southern Review, 20,* 919-927.

Richardson, M. (1990). *Cry lonesome and other accounts of the anthropologist's project.* Albany: State University of New York Press.

Riesman, P. (1977). *Freedom in Fulani social life.* Chicago: University of Chicago Press.

Rivière, P. (1980). Review of *The headman and I: Ambiguity and ambivalence in the fieldworking experience. American Ethnologist, 7,* 213.

Rogers, S. C. (1997). Explorations in terra cognita. *American Anthropologist, 99,* 717-719.

Rosaldo, R. I. (1989). *Culture and truth: The remaking of social analysis.* Boston: Beacon.

Rose, D. (1987). *Black American street life.* Philadelphia: University of Pennsylvania Press.

Rose, D. (1990). *Living the ethnographic life.* Newbury Park, CA: Sage.

Rosenhan, D. L. (1973). On being sane in insane places. *Science, 179,* 250-258.

Ruby, J. (Ed.). (1982). *A crack in the mirror: Reflexive perspectives in anthropology.* Philadelphia: University of Pennsylvania Press.

Ruiz, O. (1995). Testimony. *Anthropology and Humanism, 20*(2), 164-166.

Salerno, N. F., & Vanderburgh, R. M. (1980). *Shaman's daughter.* New York: Dell.

Scheper-Hughes, N. (1992). *Death without weeping: The violence of everyday life in Brazil.* Berkeley: University of California Press.

Schevill, J., & Gordon, A. (1996). *The myth of the docile woman.* San Francisco: California OnStage.

Schipper, K. (1982). *Le corps taoïste.* Paris: Librairie Arthème Fayard.

Schmidt, N. J. (1981). The nature of ethnographic fiction: A further inquiry. *Anthropology and Humanism Quarterly, 6*(1), 8-18.

Schmidt, N. J. (1984). Ethnographic fiction: Anthropology's hidden literary style. *Anthropology and Humanism Quarterly, 9*(4), 11-14.

Scholte, B. (1969). Toward a reflexive and critical anthropology. In D. Hymes (Ed.), *Reinventing anthropology* (pp. 430-457). New York: Random House.

Schrijvers, J. (1991). Dialectics of a dialogical ideal: Studying down, studying sideways and studying up. In L. Nencel & P. Pels (Eds.), *Constructing knowledge: Authority and critique in social science* (pp. 162-179). London: Sage.

Seligman, C. G., & Seligman, B. Z. (1911). *The Veddas.* The Hague: Osterhout.

Seligman, C. G., & Seligman, B. Z. (1932). *Pagan tribes of the Nilotic Sudan.* London.

Seremetakis, C. N. (1993). *The last word: Women, death and divination in inner Mani.* Chicago: University of Chicago Press.

Shaw, C. (1930). *The jack-roller: A delinquent boy's own story.* Chicago: University of Chicago Press.

Shostak, M. (1981). *Nisa: The life and words of a !Kung woman.* Cambridge, MA: Harvard University Press.

Shryock, A. (1996). Tribes and the print trade: Notes from the margins of literate culture in Jordan. *American Anthropologist, 98,* 26-40.

Shryock, A. (1997). *Nationalism and the genealogical imagination: Oral history and textual authority in tribal Jordan.* Berkeley: University of California Press.

Simonelli, J. M., & Winters, C. D. (1997). *Crossing between worlds: The Navajos of Canyon de Chelly.* Santa Fe, NM: School of American Research Press.

Skafte, P. (1986). Narayan's road: The wheel of change in Nepal. *Anthropology and Humanism Quarterly, 11,* 102-104.

Skomal, S. (1995). Monkey business in Chiapas. *Anthropology Newsletter, 36*(7), 41.

Springwater, C. (1996). Stories of red clay: Man of the mesa. *Anthropology and Humanism, 21*(2), 192-199.

Stacey, J. (1988). Can there be a feminist ethnography? *Women's Studies International Forum, 11,* 21-27.

Stacey, J. (1990). *Brave new families: Stories of domestic upheaval in late-twentieth-century America.* New York: Basic Books.

Stacey, J. (1995). Disloyal to the disciplines: A feminist trajectory in the borderlands. In D. C. Stanton & A. J. Steward (Eds.), *Feminisms in the academy* (pp. 311-329). Ann Arbor: University of Michigan Press.

Stanley, L., & Wise, S. (1983). *Breaking out: Feminist consciousness and feminist research.* London: Routledge & Kegan Paul.

Stavenhagen, R. (1971). Decolonizing applied social sciences. *Human Organization, 39,* 333-357.

Stewart, J. O. (1971). *Last cool days.* London: Andre Deutsch.

Stewart, J. O. (1975). *Curving road.* Urbana: University of Illinois Press.

Stewart, J. O. (1989). *Drinkers, drummers, and decent folk: Ethnographic narratives of village Trinidad.* Albany: State University of New York Press.

Stewart, J. O. (1995). Carnival mourning. In B. Grindal & F. Salamone (Eds.), *Bridges to humanity* (pp. 213-230). Prospect Heights, IL: Waveland.

Stocking, G. W., Jr. (1983). The ethnographer's magic: Fieldwork in British anthropology from Tylor to Malinowski. In G. W. Stocking, Jr. (Ed.), *Observers observed: Essays on ethnographic research* (pp. 70-120). Madison: University of Wisconsin Press.

Stocking, G. W., Jr. (1995). *After Tylor: British social anthropology 1888-1951.* Madison: University of Wisconsin Press.

Stoller, P. (1989a). *The taste of ethnographic things: The senses in anthropology.* Philadelphia: University of Pennsylvania Press.

Stoller, P. (1989b). *Fusion of the worlds: An ethnography of possession among the Songhay of Niger.* Chicago: University of Chicago Press.

Stoller, P., & Olkes, C. (1987). *In sorcery's shadow: A memoir of apprenticeship among the Songhay of Niger.* Chicago: University of Chicago Press.

Strathern, M. (1987a). The limits of auto-anthropology. In A. Jackson (Ed.), *Anthropology at home* (pp. 59-67). London: Tavistock.

Strathern, M. (1987b). Out of context: The persuasive fictions of anthropology. *Current Anthropology, 28,* 251-282.

Talbot, D. A. (1915). *Woman's mysteries of a primitive people: The Ibibios of southern Nigeria.* London: Frank Cass.

Talbot, P. A. (1923). *Life in Southern Nigeria: The magic, beliefs, and customs of the Ibibio tribe*. London: Frank Cass.

Talbot, P. A. (1969). *The peoples of southern Nigeria*. London: Frank Cass.

Tarn, N. (with Prechtel, M.). (1997). *Scandals in the house of birds: Shamans and priests on Lake Atitlan*. New York: Marsilio.

Tedlock, B. (1982). *Time and the highland Maya*. Albuquerque: University of New Mexico Press.

Tedlock, B. (1986). Keeping the breath nearby. *Anthropology and Humanism Quarterly, 11,* 92-94.

Tedlock, B. (1991). From participant observation to the observation of participation: The emergence of narrative ethnography. *Journal of Anthropological Research, 47,* 69-94.

Tedlock, B. (1995). Works and wives: On the sexual division of textual labor. In R. Behar & D. A. Gordon (Eds.), *Women writing culture* (pp. 267-286). Berkeley: University of California Press.

Tedlock, D. (1979). The analogical tradition and the emergence of a dialogical anthropology. *Journal of Anthropological Research, 35,* 387-400.

Tedlock, D. (1986). *The translator* or *Why the crocodile was not disillusioned*: A play in one act. *Translation Review, 20,* 6-8.

Tedlock, D. (1987). Questions concerning dialogical anthropology. *Journal of Anthropological Research, 43,* 325-344.

Tedlock, D. (1998, April 24-25). *Man of Rabinal: The Mayan dance of the trumpets of sacrifice*. Linguistic and cultural translation of a Mayan play produced and performed in the Katharine Cornell Theater, State University of New York at Buffalo.

Tedlock, D., & Mannheim, B. (Eds.). (1995). *The dialogic emergence of culture*. Urbana: University of Illinois Press.

Tehindrazanarivelo, E. D. (1997). Fieldwork: The dance of power. *Anthropology and Humanism, 22*(1), 54-60.

Terrio, S. J. (1998). Deconstructing fieldwork in contemporary urban France. *Anthropological Quarterly, 71*(1), 18-31.

Thomas, E. M. (1987). *Reindeer moon*. New York: Pocket Books.

Thomas, J. (1983). Toward a critical ethnography. *Urban Life, 11,* 477-490.

Thomas, W. I., & Znaniecki, G. (1918-1920). *The Polish peasant in Europe and America* (5 vols.). Boston: Richard G. Badger.

Thornton, R. J. (1988). The rhetoric of ethnographic holism. *Cultural Anthropology, 3,* 285-303.

Traweek, S. (1988). *Beamtimes and lifetimes: The world of high energy physicists*. Cambridge, MA: Harvard University Press.

Trinh T. M. (1989). *Woman, native, other: Writing postcoloniality and feminism*. Bloomington: Indiana University Press.

Turnbull, C. (1961). *The forest people: A study of the Pygmies of the Congo.* New York: Simon & Schuster.

Turnbull, C. (1965). *Wayward servants: The two worlds of the African Pygmies.* Garden City, NY: Natural History Press.

Turner, E. (1985). Prologue: From the Ndembu to Broadway. In E. Turner (Ed.), *On the edge of the bush: Anthropology as experience* (pp. 1-15). Tucson: University of Arizona Press.

Turner, E. (1987). *The Spirit and the drum: A memoir of Africa.* Tucson: University of Arizona Press.

Turner, E. (1993). The reality of spirits: A tabooed or permitted field of study? *Anthropology of Consciousness, 4*(1), 9-12.

Turner, E. (1996). *The hands feel it: Healing and spirit presence among a northern Alaskan people.* De Kalb: Northern Illinois University Press.

Turner, V. (1967). *The forest of symbols: Aspects of Ndembu ritual.* Ithaca, NY: Cornell University Press.

Turner, V. (1969). *The ritual process: Structure and anti-structure.* Ithaca, NY: Cornell University Press.

Tyler, S. A. (1987a). *The unspeakable: Discourse, dialogue, and rhetoric in the postmodern world.* Madison: University of Wisconsin Press.

Tyler, S. A. (1987b). On "writing-up/off" as "speaking-for." *Journal of Anthropological Research, 43,* 338-342.

Tylor, E. B. (1884). American aspects of anthropology. In *Report of the 54th meeting of the British Association for the Advancement of Science* (pp. 898-924). London: British Association for the Advancement of Science.

Underhill, R. (1936). *Chona, Papago woman.* Menasha, WI: American Anthropological Association.

Underhill, R. (1940). *Hawk over whirlpools.* New York: J. J. Augustin.

Urton, G. (1981). *At the crossroads of the earth and the sky: An Andean cosmology.* Austin: University of Texas Press.

Van Maanen, J. (1988). *Tales of the field: On writing ethnography.* Chicago: University of Chicago Press.

Visweswaran, K. (1988). Defining feminist ethnography. *Inscriptions, 3-4,* 7-44.

Visweswaran, K. (1994). *Fictions of feminist ethnography.* Minneapolis: University of Minnesota Press.

Visweswaran, K. (1998). "Wild West" anthropology and the disciplining of gender. In H. Silverberg (Ed.), *Gender and American social science: The formative years* (pp. 86-123). Princeton, NJ: Princeton University Press.

Wade, P. (1993). Sexuality and masculinity among Colombian blacks. In D. Bell, P. Caplan, & W. J. Karim (Eds.), *Gendered fields: Women, men and ethnography* (pp. 199-214). London: Routledge.

Wafer, J. (1991). *The taste of blood: Spirit possession in Brazilian candomblé.* Philadelphia: University of Pennsylvania Press.

Wafer, J. (1996). Out of the closet and into print: Sexual identity in the textual field. In E. Lewin & W. L. Leap (Eds.), *Out in the field: Reflections of lesbian and gay anthropologists* (pp. 261-273). Urbana: University of Illinois Press.

Waldorf, S. (1986). The pig man. *Anthropology and Humanism Quarterly, 11,* 95-101.

Ward, M. C. (1989). *Nest in the wind: Adventures in anthropology on a tropical island.* Prospect Heights, IL: Waveland.

Webster, S. (1982). Dialogue and fiction in ethnography. *Dialectical Anthropology, 7,* 91-114.

Wellmer, A. (1971). *Critical theory of society.* New York: Herder & Herder.

Wendt, A. (1973). *Sons for the return home.* Auckland, New Zealand: Longman Paul.

Wendt, A. (1979). *Leaves of the banyan tree.* Harmondsworth: Penguin.

Weston, K. (1991). *Families we choose: Lesbians, gays, kinship.* New York: Columbia University Press.

Weston, K. (1993). Lesbian/gay studies in the house of anthropology. *Annual Review of Anthropology, 22,* 339-367.

Willis, W. S. (1969). Skeletons in the anthropological closet. In D. Hymes (Ed.), *Reinventing anthropology* (pp. 121-152). New York: Random House.

Willson, M. (1997). Playing the dance, dancing the game: Race, sex and stereotype in anthropological fieldwork. *Ethnos, 62*(3-4), 24-48.

Wilson, C. (1974). *Crazy February: Death and life in the Maya highlands of Mexico.* Berkeley: University of California Press.

Wolf, M. A. (1992). *A thrice-told tale: Feminism, postmodernism, and ethnographic responsibility.* Stanford, CA: Stanford University Press.

Wolff, K. H. (1964). Surrender and community study: The study of Loma. In A. J. Vidich, J. Bensman, & M. R. Stein (Eds.), *Reflections on community studies* (pp. 233-263). New York: John Wiley.

Yang, M. M. C. (1945). *A Chinese village.* New York: Columbia University Press.

Yang, M. M. C. (1972). How *A Chinese village* was written. In S. T. Kimball & J. B. Watson (Eds.), *Crossing cultural boundaries: The anthropological experience* (pp. 63-73). San Francisco: Chandler.

Young, R. J. C. (1995). *Colonial desire: Hybridity in theory, culture and race.* London: Routledge.

Yu, P.-L. (1997). *Hungry lightning: Notes of a woman anthropologist in Venezuela.* Albuquerque: University of New Mexico Press.

Zedeño, M. N. (1994). Saint versus the hummingbird. *Anthropology and Humanism, 19*(2), 162-164.

7

Analyzing
Interpretive Practice

Jaber F. Gubrium and James A. Holstein

◆   Qualitative inquiry's analytic pendulum is constantly in motion.
There have been times when naturalism was on the upswing, when
the richly detailed description of social worlds was the goal. At other
times, analysis has shifted toward the processes by which these worlds and
their experiences are socially constructed. The pendulum has even dou-
bled back on itself as postmodern sensibilities have refocused the analytic
project on itself, viewing it as a source of social reality in its own right (see
Gubrium & Holstein, 1997). Although it can be unsettling, this oscillation
invariably clears new space for growth.

This chapter capitalizes on a momentum that is currently building
among qualitative researchers interested in the social accomplishment of
meaning and order. As social constructionist analysis expands, diversi-
fies, and claims an increasingly prominent place on the qualitative scene,
analysts are drawing new inspiration from ingenious "misreadings" and
innovative admixtures of canonical sources. Recently, ethnomethodological sensibilities have been appropriated to the constructionist move
(see Gubrium & Holstein, 1997; Holstein & Gubrium, 1994, 2000),
heightening and broadening its analytic acuity. At the same time, yet riding
a different current in the discursive and linguistic flow of the social sciences, poststructuralist discourse analysis has suffused constructionism

with cultural, institutional, and historical concerns as well. This chapter outlines one attempt to explore and extend the discursive and interactional terrain that is emerging at the intersection of ethnomethodology and Foucauldian discourse analysis.

For some time, qualitative researchers have been interested in documenting the processes by which social reality is constructed, managed, and sustained. Alfred Schutz's (1962, 1964, 1967, 1970) social phenomenology, Peter Berger and Thomas Luckmann's (1967) social constructionism, and process-oriented strains of symbolic interactionism (e.g., Blumer, 1969; Hewitt, 1997; Weigert, 1981) have all contributed to the constructionist project, but ethnomethodology arguably has been the most analytically radical and empirically productive in specifying the actual procedures through which social order is accomplished (see Garfinkel, 1967; Heritage, 1984; Holstein & Gubrium, 1994; Maynard & Clayman, 1991; Mehan & Wood, 1975; Pollner, 1987, 1991).[1] The analytic emphasis throughout has been on the question of *how* social reality is constructed, with ethnomethodology taking the lead in documenting the mechanisms by which this is accomplished in everyday life.

Recently, a new set of concerns has emerged in relation to ethnomethodology, reflecting a heretofore suspended interest in *what* is being accomplished, under *what* conditions, and out of *what* resources. Older naturalistic questions are being resurrected, but with a more analytically sophisticated, empirically sensitive mien. Analyses of reality construction are now reengaging questions concerning the broad cultural and institutional contexts of meaning making and social order. The emerging empirical horizons, although still centered on processes of social accomplishment, are increasingly viewed in terms of "interpretive practice"—the constellation of procedures, conditions, and resources through which reality is apprehended, understood, organized, and conveyed in everyday life (Gubrium & Holstein, 1997; Holstein, 1993; Holstein & Gubrium, 1994, 2000). Interpretive practice engages both the *hows* and the *whats* of social reality; it is centered both in how people methodically construct their experiences and their worlds and in the configurations of meaning and institutional life that inform and shape their reality-constituting activity. A growing attention to both the *hows* and the *whats* of the social construction process echoes Karl Marx's (1956) adage that people actively construct their worlds, but not completely on, or in, their own terms. An analytics of interpretive practice is emerging to address these dual concerns, complete with its own conceptual vocabulary. This chapter will sketch a version of this analytics, beginning from its conceptual foundations in several major sociological traditions.

◆ Foundational Matters

An analytics of interpretive practice has diverse conceptual bases. These range from Schutz's development of a social phenomenology to the related empirical concerns embodied in ethnomethodological programs of research developed in the wake of Harold Garfinkel's (1967) early studies, to studies of talk and interaction (see Sacks, 1992; Silverman, 1998), and to the contemporaneous studies of institutional and historical discourses presented by Michel Foucault (see Dreyfus & Rabinow, 1982). Let us consider these in turn as they point us toward more recent developments.

Phenomenological Background

Edmund Husserl's (1970) philosophical phenomenology provides the point of departure for Schutz and other social phenomenologists. Concerned with the experiential underpinnings of knowledge, Husserl argues that the relation between perception and its objects is not passive. Rather, human consciousness actively constitutes objects of experience. Consciousness, in other words, is always consciousness-of-something. It does not stand alone, over and above experience, more or less immaculately perceiving and conceiving objects and actions but, instead, exists always already—from the start—as a constitutive part of what it is conscious of. Although the term *construction* came into fashion much later, we might say that consciousness constructs as much as it perceives the world. Husserl's project is to investigate the structures of consciousness that make it possible to apprehend an empirical world.

Schutz (1962, 1964, 1967, 1970) turns Husserl's philosophical project toward the ways in which ordinary members of society attend to their everyday lives, introducing a set of tenets that also align with ethnomethodological studies. Schutz argues that the social sciences should focus on the ways that the life world—the world every individual takes for granted—is experienced by its members. He cautions that "the safeguarding of [this] subjective point of view is the only but sufficient guarantee that the world of social reality will not be replaced by a fictional non-existing world constructed by the scientific observer" (1964, p. 8). From this perspective, the scientific observer deals with how the social world is made meaningful. The observer's focus is on *how* members of the social world apprehend and act upon the objects of their experience as if they are things separate and distinct from themselves. Emile Durkheim's (1961, 1964) formulation of a sociology based on the emergence of categories sui generis, separate and distinct from individual thought and action, resonates with this aim.

This is a radical departure from the assumptions underlying what Schutz calls "the natural attitude," which is the stance that takes the world to be principally "out there," so to speak, categorically distinct from acts of perception or interpretation. In the natural attitude, it is assumed that the life world exists before members are present and it will be there after they depart. Schutz's recommendation for studying members' attention to this life world is to first "bracket" it for analytic purposes. That is, the analyst must temporarily set aside belief in its reality. This makes it possible to view the constitutive processes—the *hows*—by which a separate and distinct empirical world becomes an objective reality for members. Ontological judgments about the nature and essence of things and events are temporarily suspended so that the observer can focus on the ways that members of the life world subjectively constitute the objects and events they take to be real—that is, to exist independent of their attention to, and presence in, the world.

Schutz's orientation to the subjectivity of the life world pointed him to the commonsense knowledge that members use to "objectify" (make into objects) its social forms. He noted that individuals approach the life world with a stock of knowledge composed of ordinary constructs and categories that are social in origin. These images, folk theories, beliefs, values, and attitudes are applied to aspects of experience, thus making them meaningful and giving them a semblance of everyday familiarity. The stock of knowledge produces a world with which members already seem to be acquainted. In part this is because of the categorical manner by which knowledge of particular objects and events is articulated. The myriad phenomena of everyday life are subsumed under a delimited number of shared constructs (or types). These "typifications" make it possible for individuals to account rationally for experience, rendering various things and sundry occurrences recognizable as particular types of objects or events. Typification, in other words, organizes the flux of life into recognizable form, making it meaningful. In turn, as experience is given shape, the stock of knowledge is itself elaborated and altered in practice.

Ordinary language is the modus operandi. In the natural attitude, the meaning of a word is taken principally to be what it references or stands for in the real world, following a correspondence theory of meaning; in this framework, the leading task of language is to convey accurate information. Viewed as a process of typification, however, words and categories are the constitutive building blocks of the social world. Typification through ordinary language use creates the sense among users that the life world is familiarly organized and substantial, which simultaneously gives it shape and meaning. Individuals who interact with one another do so in an environment that is concurrently constructed and experienced in fundamentally the same terms by all parties, even while mistakes may be made in its particular apprehensions. Taking for granted that we intersubjectively share the same reality, we assume further that we can understand each other in its terms. Intersubjectivity is thus a social accomplishment, a set of understandings sustained in and through the shared assumptions of interaction and recurrently sustained in processes of typification.

Ethnomethodological Formulations

Although indebted to Schutz, ethnomethodology is not a mere extension of his social phenomenological program. Ethnomethodology addresses the problem of order by combining a "phenomenological sensibility" (Maynard & Clayman, 1991) with a paramount concern for everyday social practice (Garfinkel, 1967). From an ethnomethodological standpoint, the social world's facticity is accomplished by way of members' constitutive interactional work, the mechanics of which produces and maintains the accountable circumstances of their lives.[2] In a manner of speaking, ethnomethodologists focus on how members actually "do" social life, aiming in particular to document how they concretely construct and sustain social entities, such as gender, self, and family.

Although Garfinkel's studies were phenomenologically informed, his overall project also was a response to his teacher Talcott Parsons's theory of action (Heritage, 1984; Lynch, 1993). According to Parsons, social order is made possible through socially integrating systems of norms and values, a view that leaves little room for the everyday production of social order. Garfinkel sought an alternative to this approach, which in his judgment portrays actors as "cultural dopes" who automatically respond to external social forces and internalized moral imperatives. Garfinkel's

(1952) response was a vision of social order built from the socially contingent, practical reasoning of ordinary members of society. He viewed members as possessing ordinary linguistic and interactional skills through which the accountable features of everyday life are produced. This approach deeply implicates members in the production of social order. Rather than more or less playing out moral directives, Garfinkel conceptualized members as actively using them, thus *working* to give their world a sense of orderliness. Ethnomethodology's research topic became members' integral "methods" for accomplishing everyday reality.

The empirical investigation of members' methods takes its point of departure from phenomenological bracketing. Adopting the parallel policy of "ethnomethodological indifference" (Garfinkel & Sacks, 1970), the investigator temporarily suspends all commitments to a priori or privileged versions of the social world, focusing instead on how members accomplish a sense of social order. Social realities such as crime or mental illness are not taken for granted; instead, belief in them is temporarily suspended in order to make visible how they become realities for those concerned. Analysis then centers on the ordinary constitutive work that produces the locally unchallenged appearance of stable realities. This policy vigorously resists judgmental characterizations of the correctness of members' activities. Contrary to the common sociological tendency to ironicize and criticize commonsense formulations from the standpoint of ostensibly correct sociological views, ethnomethodology takes members' practical reasoning for what it is—circumstantially adequate ways of interpersonally orienting to and interpreting the world at hand. The abiding guideline is succinctly conveyed by Melvin Pollner (personal communication, May 1983): "Don't argue with the members!"

Ethnomethodologists have examined many facets of social order. One aim has been to document how recognizable structures of behavior, systems of motivation, or causal ties between motivations and social structures are evidenced in members' practical reasoning (Zimmerman & Wieder, 1970). Whereas conventional sociology orients to rules, norms, and shared meanings as exogenous explanations for members' actions, ethnomethodology turns this around to consider how members themselves orient to and use rules, norms, and shared meanings to account for the regularity of their actions. Ethnomethodology sets aside the idea that actions are externally rule governed or internally motivated in order to observe how members themselves establish and sustain social regularities. The appearance of action as being the consequence of a rule is treated as just that—the *appearance* of action as compliant or noncompliant. In "accounting" for their actions by prospectively invoking rules or retrospectively offering rule-motivated explanations for action, members convey a sense of structure and order and, in the process, cast their actions as rational, coherent, precedented, and reproducible for all practical purposes (Zimmerman, 1970).

For example, a juror in the midst of deliberation may account for her opinion by saying that the judge's instructions on how to consider the case in question compel her to think as she does. She actively uses the judge's instructions to make sense of her opinion, thereby giving it the semblance of rationality, legality, and correctness because it was formed "according to the rule" invoked (Holstein, 1983). In contrast, another juror might account for his opinion by saying that it is serving the interests of justice, citing a value or moral principle in explanation (Maynard & Manzo, 1993). From an ethnomethodological standpoint, the rationality or correctness of these opinions and the reasoning involved are not at issue. Instead, the focus is on the individuals' use of instructions, values, moral principles, and other accounts to construct a sense of coherence in social action, in this case a shared understanding among jurors of what led them to form their opinions and reach a verdict.

The accountable display of social order forms ethnomethodology's analytic horizon. Rather than assuming a priori that members share meanings and definitions of situations, ethnomethodologists consider how members achieve them by applying a native capacity to account "artfully" for their actions, rendering them orderly. Social order is not externally imposed by proverbial social forces, nor is it the expression of more or less socialized members of society; instead, ethnomethodologists view it as locally produced by way of the practices of mundane reason (Pollner, 1987). If social order is accomplished in and through its practices, then social worlds and circumstances are self-generating. Members, as we noted earlier, are continually "doing" social life in the very actions they take to communicate and make sense of it. Their language games, to borrow from Ludwig Wittgenstein (1958), virtually constitute their everyday realities; in this sense, the games are "forms of life."

This implicates two properties of ordinary social action. First, all actions and objects are "indexical"; they depend upon (or "index") context. Objects and events have equivocal or indeterminate meanings without a discernible context. It is through contextualization that practical meaning is derived. Second, the circumstances that provide meaningful contexts are themselves self-generating. Each reference to, or account for, an action—such as the juror's comment that she is expressly following the judge's directives—establishes a context (in this case, of procedural duti-fulness) for evaluating the selfsame and related actions of the juror herself and the actions of others. The account simultaneously establishes a particular context, which in turn becomes a basis for the juror's making her own and others' actions accountable. Having established this context, the juror can then virtually turn around and account for her actions by saying, for example, "That's why I feel as I do," in effect parlaying the context she has constructed for her actions into something recognizable and reasonable (accountable), if not ultimately acceptable. Practical reasoning, in other words, is simultaneously in and about the settings to which it orients, and that it describes. Social order and its practical realities are thus "reflexive." Accounts or descriptions of a setting constitute that setting while they are simultaneously being shaped by the contexts they constitute.

Procedurally, ethnomethodological research is keenly attuned to naturally occurring talk and social interaction, orienting to them as constitutive elements of the settings studied (see Atkinson & Drew, 1979; Maynard, 1984, 1989; Mehan & Wood, 1975; Sacks, 1972). This has taken different empirical directions, in part depending upon whether the interactive meanings or the structure of talk is emphasized. Ethnographic studies tend to focus on locally crafted meanings and the settings within which social interaction constitutes the practical realities in question. Such studies consider the situated content of talk in relation to local meaning making (see Gubrium, 1992; Holstein, 1993; Lynch & Bogen, 1996; Miller, 1991; Pollner, 1987; Wieder, 1988). They combine attention to how social order is built up in everyday communication with detailed descriptions of place settings as those settings and their local understandings and perspectives mediate the meaning of what is said in the course of social interaction. The texts produced from such studies are highly descriptive of everyday life, with both conversational extracts from the settings and ethnographic accounts of interaction used to convey the methodical production of the subject matter in question. To the extent the analysis of talk in relation to social interaction and setting is in place, this tends to take the form of (non-Foucauldian) discourse analysis (DA), emphasizing how talk and conversation are used to make meaning (see Potter, 1996, 1997; Potter & Wetherell, 1987).

Studies that emphasize the structure of talk itself examine the conversational "machinery" through which meaning emerges. The focus here is on the sequential, utterance-by-utterance, socially structuring features of talk or "talk-in-interaction," the now familiar bailiwick of conversation analysis (CA; see Heritage, 1984; Sacks, Schegloff, & Jefferson, 1974; Silverman, 1998; Zimmerman, 1988; see also Silverman, Chapter 9, Volume 3). The analyses produced from such studies are detailed explications of the communicative processes by which speakers methodically and sequentially construct their concerns in conversational practice. Often bereft of ethnographic detail except for brief lead-ins that describe place settings, the analytic sense conveyed is that biographical and social particulars can be understood as artifacts of the unfolding conversational machinery, although the analysis of what is called "institutional talk" or "talk at work" has struck a greater balance in this regard (see, for example, Drew & Heritage, 1992). Whereas some contend that CA's connection to ethnomethodology is tenuous because of this lack of concern with ethnographic detail (Atkinson, 1988; Lynch, 1993; Lynch & Bogen, 1994; for counterarguments, see Maynard & Clayman, 1991; ten Have, 1990), CA clearly shares ethnomethodology's interest in the local and methodical construction of social action (Maynard & Clayman, 1991).

John Heritage (1984) summarizes the fundamentals of conversation analysis in three premises. First, interaction is sequentially organized, and this may be observed in the regularities of ordinary conversation. All aspects of interaction can be found to exhibit stable and identifiable features that are independent of speakers' individual characteristics. This sets the stage for the analysis of talk as structured in and through social interaction, not by internal sources such as motives or by external determinants such as social status. Second, social interaction is contextually oriented in that talk is simultaneously productive of, and reflects, the circumstances of its production. This premise highlights both the local conditioning and the local constructiveness of talk and interaction, exhibiting the dual properties of indexicality and reflexivity noted earlier. Third, these properties characterize all social interaction, so that no form of talk or interactive detail can be dismissed as irrelevant.

Conversation analysis has come under fire from ethnomethodologists who argue that the in situ details of everyday life are ignored at the risk of reducing social life to recorded talk and conversational sequencing. Michael Lynch, for example, has drawn a parallel between CA and molecular biology. On one hand, this serves to underscore Lynch's claims about CA's basic formalism and scientism. On the other, it projects the image of conversation as a relatively predictable set of socially structured techniques through which orderly social activities are assembled. Conversation analysts, according to Lynch (1993), attempt to describe "a simple order of structural elements and rules for combining them, and thus they undertake a reductionist program not unlike molecular biology" (p. 259), which attempts to deconstruct DNA for its molecular structures and rules of combination.

As a "molecular sociology" (Lynch, 1993), CA focuses on the normative, sequential "machinery" of conversation that constitutes social action. This machinery in many ways inverts conventional understandings of human agency, substituting the demands of a moral order of conversation for psychological and motivational imperatives. Although this does not strip participants of all agency, it does place them in the midst of a "liberal economy" of conversational rights and obligations (Lynch, 1993) that tests ethnomethodological tolerance for deterministic formulations.

In contrast to what Lynch and David Bogen (1994) have labeled the "enriched positivism" of CA, Garfinkel, Lynch, and others have elaborated what they refer to as a "postanalytic" ethnomethodology that is less inclined to universalistic generalizations regarding the enduring structures or machinery of social interaction (see Garfinkel, 1988; Lynch, 1993; Lynch & Bogen, 1996). This program of research centers on the highly localized competencies that constitute specific domains of everyday "work," especially the (bench)work of astronomers (Garfinkel, Lynch, & Livingston, 1981), biologists and neurologists (Lynch, 1985), and mathematicians (Livingston, 1986). The aim is to document the "haecceity"—the "just thisness"—of social practices within circumscribed domains of knowledge and activity (Lynch, 1993). The practical details of the real-time work of these activities are viewed as *incarnate* features of the knowledges they produce. It is impossible to separate the knowledges from the highly particularized occasions of their production. The approach is theoretically minimalist in that it resists a priori conceptualization or categorization, especially historical time, while advocating detailed descriptive studies of the specific, local practices that manifest order and render it accountable (Bogen & Lynch, 1993).

Despite their success at displaying a panoply of social accomplishment practices, CA and postanalytic ethnomethodology in their separate ways tend to disregard an important balance in the conceptualizations of talk, setting, and social interaction that was evident in Garfinkel's early work and Harvey Sacks's (1992) pioneering lectures on conversational practice (see Silverman, 1998, and Chapter 9, Volume 3). Neither Garfinkel nor

Sacks envisioned the machinery of conversation as productive of recogniz-able social forms in its own right. Attention to the constitutive *hows* of social realities was balanced with attention to the meaningful *whats*. Set-tings, cultural understandings, and their everyday mediations were viewed as reflexively interwoven with talk and social interaction (see Silverman, Chapter 9, Volume 3). Sacks, in particular, understood culture to be a mat-ter of practice, something that served as a resource for discerning the pos-sible linkages of utterances and exchanges. Whether they wrote of (Garfinkel's) "good organizational reasons" or (Sacks's) "membership cat-egorization devices," both initially avoided the reduction of social practice to highly localized or momentary haecceities of any kind.

As such, some of the original promise of ethnomethodology has been short-circuited as CA and postanalytic ethnomethodology have in-creasingly restricted their investigations to the relation between social practices and the immediate accounts of those practices. If the entire goal of postanalytic and CA projects is to describe the accounting practices by which descriptions are made intelligible in the immediate circumstances of their production, then constructionists may need to formulate a new proj-ect that retains ethnomethodology's interactional sensibilities while extending its scope to both the constitutive and constituted *whats* of everyday life. Michel Foucault, among others, is a valuable resource for such a project.

Foucauldian Discourse Analysis

Whereas ethnomethodology engages the accomplishment of everyday life at the interactional level, Foucault has undertaken a parallel project in a different empirical register. Appearing on the analytic stage during the early 1960s, at about the same time ethnomethodologists did, Foucault considers how historically and culturally located systems of power/knowledge construct subjects and their worlds. Foucauldians refer to these systems as "discourses," emphasizing that they are not merely bodies of ideas, ideologies, or other symbolic formulations, but are also working attitudes, modes of address, terms of reference, and courses of action suffused into social practices. Foucault (1972) himself explains that discourses are not "a mere intersection of things and words: an obscure web of things, and a manifest, visible, colored chain of words" (p. 48). Rather, they are "practices that systematically form the objects [and sub-jects] of which they speak" (p. 49). Even the design of buildings such as prisons reveals the social logic that specifies ways of interpreting persons and the physical and social landscapes they occupy (Foucault, 1979).

As in the ethnomethodological view of social interaction, Foucault views discourse as socially reflexive, both constitutive and meaningfully descriptive of the world and its subjects. But, for him, the analytic accent is as much on the constructive *whats* that discourse constitutes as it is on the *hows* of discursive technology. While this represents a swing of the analytic pendulum toward the culturally "natural," Foucault's treatment of discourse as social practice suggests, in particular, the importance of understanding the practices of subjectivity. If he offers a vision of subjects and objects constituted through discourse, he also allows for an unwittingly active subject who shapes discourse and puts it to work (Best & Kellner, 1991). As Foucault (1988) explains:

> If now I am interested . . . in the way in which the subject constitutes himself in an active fashion, by the practices of the self, these practices are nevertheless not something that the individual invents by himself. They are patterns that he finds in his culture and which are proposed, suggested and imposed on him by his culture, his society and his social group. (p. 11)

This complements ethnomethodology's interest in documenting the accomplishment of order in the everyday practice of talk and social interaction. Foucault is particularly concerned with social locations or institutional sites—the asylum, the hospital, and the prison, for example—that specify the practical operation of discourses, linking the discourse of particular subjectivities with the construction of lived experience. As in ethnomethodology, there is an interest in the constitutive quality of systems of discourse; it is an orientation to practice that views social worlds and their subjectivities as always already embedded and embodied in its discursive conventions.

Several commentators have pointed to the striking parallel between what Foucault (1980) refers to as systems of "power/knowledge" (or discourses) and ethnomethodology's formulation of the constitutive power of language use (Atkinson, 1995; Gubrium & Holstein, 1997; Heritage, 1997; Miller, 1997b; Potter, 1996; Prior, 1997; Silverman, 1993). The apparent correspondence suggests that what Foucault documents historically as "discourses-in-practice" in varied institutional or cultural sites may be likened to what ethnomethodology traces as "discursive practice" in varied forms of social interaction.[3] We will continue to apply these terms—

225

discourses-in-practice and *discursive practice*—throughout this chapter to emphasize the parallel.

Although ethnomethodologists and Foucauldians draw from different intellectual traditions and work in distinct empirical registers, we want to emphasize their respective concerns with social practice; they both attend to the reflexivity of discourse. Neither discourse-in-practice nor discursive practice is viewed as being caused or explained by external social forces or internal motives; rather, both are taken to be the working mechanism of social life itself, as actually known or performed in time and place. For both, "power" lies in the articulation of distinctive forms of social life as such, not in the application of particular resources by some to affect the lives of others. Although discourses-in-practice are represented by "regimens/regimes" or lived patterns of action that broadly (historically and institutionally) "discipline" or encompass their adherents' lives and discursive practice is manifest in patterns of talk and interaction that constitute everyday life, the practices refer in common to the lived "doing," or ongoing accomplishment, of social worlds.

For Foucault, power operates in and through discourse as the other face of knowledge, thus the term *power/knowledge*. Discourse not only puts words to work, it gives them their meaning, constructs perceptions, and formulates understanding and ongoing courses of interaction. The "work" entailed simultaneously and reflexively constitutes the realities that words are taken otherwise merely to reference or specify. To deploy a particular discourse of subjectivity is not simply a matter of representing a subject; in practice, it simultaneously constitutes the kinds of subjects that are meaningfully embedded in the discourse itself. For example, to articulate the discourse of medicine in today's world automatically generates the roles of professional healer and patient, each of whose actions in turn articulate the application and reception of technologies of healing served by the social dominance of scientific knowledge. The taken-for-grantedness of this socially encompassing discourse makes challenges to this way of "thinking" (or speaking) seem oddly misplaced. Even the weak "powerfully" participate in the discourse that defines them as weak. This is a kind of knowledge-in-social-practice, and it is powerful because it not only represents but ineluctably puts into practice what is known and shared. Language is not just more or less correlated with what it represents, but is always already a "form of life," to again put it in Wittgenstein's (1958) terms. If ethnomethodologists attend to *how* members use everyday methods to account for their activities and their worlds, Foucault makes us aware of the related conditions of possibility for *what* the results are likely to be. For example, in a Western postindustrial world, to think seriously of medicine and voodoo as equally viable paradigms for understanding sickness and healing would seem idiosyncratic, if not amusing or preposterous, in most conventional situations. The power of the medical discourse partially lies in its ability to be "seen but unnoticed," in its ability to appear as *the* only possibility while other possibilities are outside the plausible realm.

Both ethnomethodology's and Foucault's approach to empirical material are "analytics," not theoretical frameworks in the traditional sense. Conventionally understood, theory purports to explain the state of the matters in question. It provides answers to *why* concerns, such as why the suicide rate is rising or why individuals are suffering depression. Ethnomethodology and the Foucauldian project, in contrast, aim to answer how it is that individual experience comes to be understood in particular terms such as these. They are pretheoretical in this sense, respectively seeking to arrive at an understanding of how the subject matter of theory comes into existence in the first place and of what the subject of theory might possibly become. The parallel lies in the common goal of documenting the social bases of such realities.

Still, this remains a parallel. Because Foucault's project (and most Foucauldian projects) operates in a historical register, real-time talk and social interaction are understandably missing from chosen bodies of empirical material. Although Foucault himself points to sharp turns in the discursive formations that both form and inform the shifting realities of varied institutional spheres, contrasting extant social forms with the "birth" of new ones, he provides little or no sense of the *everyday* technology by which this is achieved (see Atkinson, 1995; Holstein & Gubrium, 2000). Certainly, he elaborates the broad birth of new technologies, such as the emergence of new regimes of surveillance in medicine and modern criminal justice systems (Foucault, 1975, 1979), but he does not provide us with a view of how these operate in social interaction. Neither do latter-day Foucauldians—such as Nikolas Rose (1990), who informatively documents the birth and rise of the technical apparatus for "governing the soul" that forms a private self—offer much insight into the everyday processes through which such regimes are accomplished.

Conversely, ethnomethodology's commitment to documenting the real-time, interactive processes by which reality is built up into accountable structures precludes a broader perspective on constitutive resources, possibilities, and limitations. It is one thing to show in interactive detail that our everyday encounters with reality are an ongoing accomplishment; it is quite another matter to derive an understanding of what the general parameters of those everyday encounters might be. The machinery of talk-in-interaction tells us little about the massive work and resources that inform or guide the operation of conversation, or about the consequences of producing particular results and not others, each of which is an important ingredient of practice. Members speak their worlds and their subjectivities, but they also articulate particular forms of life as they do so. What Foucauldian considerations offer ethnomethodology in this regard is an analytic sensitivity to the discursive opportunities and possibilities at work in talk and social interaction, without making it necessary to take these up as external templates for the everyday production of social order.

◆ Toward an Analytics of Interpretive Practice

If we are concerned with interpretive practice and reality construction, we clearly need to draw ethnomethodological and Foucauldian analytics together more explicitly. This is not simply another attempt to bridge the so-called macro/micro divide. That debate usually centers on the question of how to conceptualize the relationship between preexisting larger and smaller social forms, the assumption being that these are categorically distinct and separately discernible. Issues raised in the debate perpetuate the distinction between, say, social systems on the one hand and social interaction on the other. In contrast, those who consider ethnomethodology and Foucauldian analytics to be parallel operations focus their attention instead on the interactional, institutional, and cultural variabilities of socially constituting discursive practice and discourses-in-practice, as the case might be. They are concerned with how the social construction process is shaped across various domains of everyday life, not with how separate theories of macro and micro domains can be linked together for a fuller account of social organization. Doctrinaire accounts of Garfinkel, Sacks, Foucault, and others may continue to sustain a variety of distinct projects, but these projects are not likely to inform one another, nor will they lead to profitable "conversations" between dogmatic practitioners who insist on viewing themselves as speaking different analytic languages.[4] Instead, we need a new, hybridized analytics of reality construction at the crossroads of institutions, culture, and social interaction—an analytics that "misreads" and co-opts useful insights from established traditions in order to appreciate the possible complementarity of analytic idioms without losing sight of their distinctive utilities, limitations, and contributions.

Beyond Ethnomethodology

Some conversation analysts have edged in this direction by analyzing the sequential machinery of talk-in-interaction as it is patterned by institutional context. Their studies of "talk at work" aim to specify how the "simplest systematics" of ordinary conversation (Sacks et al., 1974) is shaped in various ways by the reflexively constructed speech environments of particular interactional regimes (see Boden & Zimmerman, 1991; Drew & Heritage, 1992). Ethnomethodologically oriented ethnographers approach the problem from another direction by asking how institutions and their respective representational cultures are brought into being, managed, and sustained in and through members' social interaction (or "reality work") (see Atkinson, 1995; Dingwall, Eekelaar, & Murray, 1983; Emerson, 1969; Emerson & Messinger, 1977; Gubrium, 1992; Holstein, 1993; Mehan, 1979; Miller, 1991, 1997a). Self-consciously Foucauldian ethnographers, too, have drawn links between everyday discursive practice and discourses-in-practice to document in local detail how the formulation of everyday texts, such as psychiatric case records or coroners' reports, reproduces institutional discourses (see Prior, 1997).

In their own fashions, these efforts consider both the *hows* and the *whats* of reality construction. But this is analytically risky business. Asking *how* questions without having an integral way of getting an analytic handle on *what* questions makes concern with the *whats* arbitrary. Although talk-in-interaction is locally "artful," as Garfinkel (1967) puts it, not just anything goes. On the other hand, if we swing too far analytically in the direction of contextual or cultural imperatives, we end up with the cultural, institutional, or judgmental "dopes" that Garfinkel (1967) decries.

The admonition that "not just anything goes" has been taken seriously, but cautiously, by both ethnomethodologists and conversation analysts as they have sought to document carefully the practical contours of interaction in the varied circumstances in which it unfolds. Systematic attention to everyday reasoning and to the sequential organization of conversations has made it clear that outcomes are constructed in the interactional apparatuses within which their antecedents are made topical. But this is a very delimited approach to the constitutive *whats* of social construction, one that lacks a broad view of the institutional and cultural discourses that serve as resources for what is likely to be constructed, when, and where in everyday life.

To broaden and enrich ethnomethodology's analytic scope and repertoire, we have extended its reach into the institutional and cultural *whats* that come into play in social interaction. This need not be a historical extension, as was Foucault's metier, although that certainly should not be ruled out. Rather, we appeal to a "cautious" (and self-conscious) naturalism that addresses the practical and sited production of everyday life (Gubrium, 1993). The analytics of interpretive practice is such an effort. It centers on the *interplay*, not the synthesis, of discursive practice and discourses-in-practice, the tandem projects of ethnomethodology and Foucauldian discourse analysis. This analytics assiduously avoids theorizing social forms, lest the discursive practices associated with the construction of these forms be taken for granted. By the same token, it concertedly keeps institutional or cultural discourses in view, lest they be dissolved into localized displays of practical reasoning or forms of sequential organization for talk-in-interaction. First and foremost, an analytics of interpretive practice takes us, in real time, to the "going concerns" of everyday life, as Everett Hughes (1984) liked to call social institutions. There, we can focus on how members artfully put discourses to work as they constitute their subjectivities and related social worlds.

The emphasis on the interplay between the *hows* and *whats* of interpretive practice is paramount. Interplay connotes a dynamic relationship. We assiduously avoid analytically privileging either discursive practice or discourses-in-practice. Putting it in ethnomethodological terms, the aim of an analytics of interpretive practice is to document the interplay between the practical reasoning and conversational machinery entailed in constructing a sense of everyday reality on the one hand and the institutional conditions, resources, and related discourses that substantively nourish and interpretively mediate interaction on the other. Putting it in Foucauldian terms, the goal is to describe the interplay between institutional discourses and the "dividing practices" that constitute local subjectivities and their worlds of experience (Foucault, 1965). The symmetry of real-world practice requires that we give equal treatment to both its articulative and its substantive engagements.

Qualitative researchers are increasingly focusing on these two sides of interpretive practice, looking to both the artful processes and the substantive conditions of meaning making and social order. Douglas Maynard (1989), for example, notes that most ethnographers have traditionally asked, "How do participants see things?" whereas ethnomethodologically informed discourse studies have asked, "How do participants do things?" Although his own work typically begins with the latter question, Maynard cautions us not to ignore the former. He explains that, in the interest of studying how members *do* things, ethnomethodological studies have tended to de-emphasize factors that condition their actions. Recognizing that "external social structure is used as a resource for social interaction at the same time as it is constituted within it," Maynard suggests that ethnographic and discourse studies can be mutually informative, allowing researchers to document more fully the ways in which the "structure of interaction, while being a local production, simultaneously enacts matters whose origins are externally initiated" (p. 139). "In addition to knowing how people 'see' their workaday worlds," writes Maynard, researchers should try to understand how people "discover and exhibit features of these worlds so that they can be 'seen' " (p. 144).

Expressing similar interests and concerns, Hugh Mehan (1979) has developed a discourse-oriented program of "constitutive ethnography" that puts "structure and structuring activities on an equal footing by showing *how* the social facts of the world emerge from structuring work to become external and constraining" (p. 18). Mehan (1991) examines "contrastive" instances of interpretation in order to describe both the "distal" and "proximate" features of the reality-constituting work people do "within institutional, cultural, and historical contexts" (pp. 73, 81).

Beginning from similar ethnomethodological and discourse-analytic footings, David Silverman (1993) likewise attends to the institutional venues of talk and social construction (see also Silverman, 1985, 1997). Seeking a mode of qualitative inquiry that exhibits both constitutive and contextual sensibilities, he suggests that discourse studies that consider the varied institutional contexts of talk bring a new perspective to qualitative inquiry. Working in the same vein, Gale Miller (1994) has proposed "ethnographies of institutional discourse" that serve to document "the ways in which setting members use discursive resources in organizing their practical actions, and how members' actions are constrained by the resources available in the settings" (p. 280; see also Miller, 1997b). This approach makes explicit overtures to both conversation analysis and Foucauldian discourse analysis.

Miller's (1997a) ethnography of the discourses characterizing a therapy agency is instructive, especially as it sheds light on the discursive production of the client in therapy. His 12-year ethnographic study of Northland Clinic, an internationally prominent center of "brief therapy," describes a marked shift in client subjectivity that accompanied a conscious alteration of treatment philosophy. When Miller began his fieldwork, Northland employed "ecosystemic brief therapy," which emphasized the social contexts of clients' lives and problems. In this therapeutic environment, clients' subjectivity was linked with the systems of social relationships that were taken to form and fuel their problems. The approach required the staff to discern the state of these systems and to intervene so as to alter their dynamics and thereby effect change. Miller notes that this approach was informed by a "modern" discourse of the reality of the problems in question.

Several years into the fieldwork, Northland shifted to a more "postmodern" approach, articulating intervention in an everyday linguistic and constructivist discourse. Therapists began to apply what was called "solution-focused brief therapy," which meant viewing troubles as ways of talking about everyday life. This prompted the staff to orient to the therapy process as a set of language games, expressly appropriating Wittgenstein's sense of the term. The idea here was that troubles were as much constructions—ways of talking or forms of life—as they were real difficulties for the clients in question. This transformed clients' institutional subjectivity, from their being relatively passive agents of systems of personal troubles and negative stories to being active problem solvers with a potential to formulate positive stories about themselves and design helpful solutions. As an everyday language of solutions, not a discourse of problems, became the basis of intervention, the narrative identities of clients were transformed to reveal entirely different selves. As the therapy agency itself changed over time, so did both the discourse-in-practice and discursive practices. This resulted in the construction of distinctly different "clients" and "problems" that were institutionally formulated and addressed.

Dorothy Smith (1987, 1990) has been quite explicit in addressing a version of the interplay between the *whats* and *hows* of social life from a feminist point of view. Hers has been an analytics informed by ethnomethodological and, increasingly, Foucauldian sensibilities. Moving beyond ethnomethodology, Smith (1990) calls for what she refers to as a "dialectics of discourse and the everyday" (p. 202). Stressing the "play and interplay" of discourse, Smith articulates her view of women's "active" placement in their worlds:

> It is easy to misconstrue the discourse as having an overriding power to determine the values and interpretation of women's appearances in local settings, and see this power as essentially at the disposal of the fashion industry and media. But women are active, skilled, make choices, consider, are not fooled or foolish. Within discourse there is play and interplay. (p. 202)

Philosopher Calvin Schrag (1997) similarly emphasizes the advantage of the strategy of analytic interplay over theoretical integration. Schrag puts this in the context of the need to guard against, on the one hand, reducing what we refer to as discursive practice to mere speech acts or talk-in-interaction or, on the other, supplanting the local artfulness of social interaction with its institutional discourses. Considering the self after postmodernity, Schrag echoes our own aim to keep both the constructive *whats* and *hows* in balance at the forefront of an analytics, lest the study of lived experience neglect or overemphasize one or the other.

> We must stand guard to secure the space of discourse as temporalized event of speaking *between* the objectification of speech acts and language on the one hand and the abstractions and reifications in the structuralist designs of narratology on the other hand. The event of discourse as a saying of something by someone to someone is threatened from both "below" and "above"—from below in terms of a tendency toward an ontology of elementarism fixated on the isolable, constitutive elements of speech acts and linguistic units . . . and from above in the sense of a predilection toward an abstract holism of narratological structures that leave the event of discourse behind. Only by sticking to the terrain of the "between" will the subject as the who of discourse and the who of narrative remain visible. It is on this terrain, which we will later come to call the terrain of lived-experience, that we are able to observe the august event of a self understanding itself through the twin moments of discourse and narration. (pp. 22-23)

Indeed, we echo Schrag's warning against integrating an analytics of discursive practice with an analytics of discourse-in-practice. To integrate one with the other is to reduce the empirical purview of a common enterprise. Reducing the analytics of discourse-in-practice into discursive practice risks losing the lessons of attending to institutional differences and cultural configurations as they mediate and are not "just talked into being" through social interaction. Conversely, figuring discursive practice as the mere residue of institutional discourse risks a totalized marginalization of local artfulness.

Analytic Bracketing

Rather than attempting synthesis or integration, we view an analytics of interpretive practice as more like a skilled juggling act, concentrating alternately on the myriad *hows* and *whats* of everyday life. This requires a new form of bracketing to capture the interplay between discursive practice and discourses-in-practice. We have called this technique of oscillating indifference to the realities of everyday life *analytic bracketing* (see Gubrium & Holstein, 1997).

Recall that ethnomethodology's interest in the *hows* by which realities are constructed requires a studied, temporary indifference to those realities. Like phenomenologists, ethnomethodologists begin their analysis by setting aside belief in the real in order to bring into view the everyday practices by which subjects, objects, and events come to have a sense of being observable, rational, and orderly for those concerned. The ethnomethodological project moves forward from there, documenting how discursive practice constitutes social structures. As Wittgenstein (1958, p. 19) might put it, language is "taken off holiday" in order to make visible how language works to construct the objects it is otherwise viewed as principally describing.

Analytic bracketing works somewhat differently. It is employed throughout analysis, not just at the start. As analysis proceeds, the observer intermittently orients to everyday realities as both the *products* of members' reality-constructing procedures and the *resources* from which realities are constituted. At one moment, the analyst may be indifferent to the structures of everyday life in order to document their production through discursive practice. In the next analytic move, he or she brackets discursive practice in order to assess the local availability, distribution, and/or regulation of resources for reality construction. In Wittgensteinian terms, this translates into attending to both language-at-work and language-on-holiday, alternating considerations of how languages games, in particular institutional discourses, operate in everyday life and what games are likely to come into play at particular times and places. In

Foucauldian terms, it leads to alternating considerations of discourses-in-practice on the one hand and the locally fine-grained documentation of related discursive practices on the other.

Analytic bracketing amounts to an orienting procedure for alternately focusing on the *whats* and then the *hows* of interpretive practice (or vice versa) in order to assemble both a contextually scenic and a contextually constructive picture of everyday language-in-use. The objective is to move back and forth between discursive practice and discourses-in-practice, documenting each in turn and making informative references to the other in the process. Either discursive machinery or available discourses becomes the provisional phenomenon, while interest in the other is temporarily deferred, but not forgotten. The constant interplay between the analysis of these two sides of interpretive practice mirrors the lived interplay among social interaction, its immediate surroundings, and its going concerns.

Because discursive practice and discourses-in-practice are mutually constitutive, one cannot argue that analysis should begin or end with either one, although there are predilections in this regard. As those who are ethnographically oriented are wont to do, Smith (1987, 1990), for example, advocates beginning "where people are." We take her to mean where people are located in the institutional landscape of everyday life. Conversely, conversation analysts insist on beginning with discursive practice, even though a variety of unanalyzed *whats* typically inform their efforts.[5]

Wherever one starts, neither the cultural and institutional details of discourse nor its interpolations in social interaction predetermine the other. If we set aside the need for an indisputable resolution to the question of which comes first, last, or has priority, we can designate a suitable point of departure and proceed from there, so long as we keep firmly in mind that the interplay within interpretive practice requires that we move back and forth analytically between its leading components. Of course, we don't want to reify the components; we continuously remind ourselves that the analytic task centers on the dialectics of two fields of play, not the reproduction of one by the other.

Although we advocate no rule for where to begin, there is no need to fret that the overall task is impossible or logically incoherent. Maynard (1998), for example, compares analytic bracketing to "wanting to ride trains that are going in different directions, initially hopping on one and then somehow jumping to the other." He asks, "How do you jump from one train to another when they are going in different directions?" (p. 344). The question is, in fact, merely an elaboration of the issue of how one brackets in the first place, which is, of course, the basis for Maynard's and other ethnomethodologists' and conversation analysts' own projects. The answer is simple: Knowledge of the *principle* of bracketing (and un-bracketing) makes it possible. Those who bracket the life world or treat it indifferently, as the case might be, readily set reality aside every time they get to work on their respective corpuses of empirical material. It becomes as routine as rising in the morning, having breakfast, and going to the workplace.[6] On the other hand, the desire to operationalize bracketing of any kind, analytic bracketing included, into explicitly codified and sequenced procedural moves would turn bracketing into a set of recipe-like, analytic directives, something surely to be avoided. We would assume that no one, except the most recalcitrant operationalist, would want to substitute a recipe book for an analytics.[7]

Analytic bracketing, however, is far from undisciplined; it has distinct procedural implications. As we have noted, the primary directive is to examine alternately both sides of interpretive practice. Researchers engaging in analytic bracketing must constantly turn their attention in more than one direction. This is increasingly resulting in new methodological hybrids. Some analysts undertake a more content-oriented form of discourse analysis (see Potter, 1996; Potter & Wetherell, 1987). Others develop methods of "constitutive ethnography" (Mehan, 1979), the "ethnography of practice" (Gubrium, 1988), or other discursively sensitive ethnographic approaches (see Holstein, 1993; Miller, 1991, 1997a). The distinguishing feature of such studies is their disciplined focus on both discourse-in-practice and discursive practice.

The dual focus should remind us that, in describing the constitutive role of discourses-in-practice, we must take care not to appropriate these naïvely into our analysis. We must sustain ethnomethodology's desire to distinguish between members' resources and our own. As a result, as we consider discourses-in-practice, we must attend to how they mediate, not determine, members' socially constructive activities. Analytic bracketing is always substantively temporary. It resists full-blown attention to discourses as systems of power/knowledge, separate from how they unfold in lived experience. It also is enduringly empirical in that it does not take the operation of discourses for granted as the operating truths of a setting *tout court*.[8]

Working Against Totalization

Centered at the crossroads of discursive practice and discourses-in-practice, an analytics of interpretive practice works against totalization. It restrains the propensity of a Foucauldian analytics to view all interpretations as artifacts of particular regimes of power/ knowledge. Writing in relation to the broad sweep of his "histories of the present," Foucault was inclined to overemphasize the predominance of discourses in constructing the horizons of meaning at particular times or places, conveying the sense that discourses fully detail the nuances of everyday life. A more interactionally sensitive analytics of discourse—one tied to discursive practice—resists this tendency.

Because interpretive practice is mediated by discourse through institutional functioning, we discern the operation of power/knowledge in the separate going concerns of everyday life. Yet what one institutional site brings to bear is not necessarily what another puts into practice. Institutions constitute distinct, yet sometimes overlapping, realities. While one may deploy a gaze that confers agency or subjectivity upon individuals, for example, another may constitute subjectivity along different lines, such as the family systems that are called into question as subjects and agents of troubles in family therapy (see Gubrium, 1992; Miller, 1997a).

Still, if interpretive practice is complex and fluid, it is not socially arbitrary. In the practice of everyday life, discourse is articulated in myriad sites and is socially variegated; actors methodically build up their shared realities in diverse, locally nuanced, and biographically informed terms. Although this produces considerable slippage in how discourses do their work, it is far removed from the uniform hegemonic regimes of power/ knowledge presented in some Foucauldian readings. Social organization nonetheless is evident in the going concerns referenced by participants, to which they hold their talk and interaction accountable.

An analytics of interpretive practice must deal with the perennial question of what realities and/or subjectivities are being constructed in the myriad sites of everyday life. In practice, diverse articulations of discourse intersect, collide, and work against the construction of common or uniform subjects, agents, and social realities. Interpretations shift in relation to the institutional and cultural markers they reference, which, in turn, fluctuate with respect to the varied settings in which social interaction unfolds. Discourses-in-practice refract one another as they are methodically adapted to practical exigencies, local discursive practice serving up variation and innovation in the process (see Abu-Lughod, 1991, 1993; Chase, 1995).

From How and What to Why

Traditionally, qualitative inquiry has concerned itself with *what* and *how* questions. *Why* questions have been the hallmark of quantitative sociology, which seeks to explain and ostensibly predict behavior. Qualitative researchers typically approach *why* questions cautiously. Explanation is tricky business, one that qualitative inquiry embraces discreetly in light of its appreciation for interpretive elasticity. It is one thing to describe what is going on and how things or events take shape, but the question of why things happen the way they do can lead to inferential leaps and empirical speculations that propel qualitative analysis far from its stock-in-trade. The challenge is to respond to *why* questions in ways that are empirically and conceptually consonant with qualitative inquiry's traditional concerns.

An analytics of interpretive practice provides a limited basis for raising particular kinds of *why* question in the context of qualitative inquiry. In order to pursue *why* questions, one needs to designate a domain of explanation for that which is to be explained. The familiar distinction in sociology between macrosociological and microsociological domains, for example, specifies two kinds of explanatory footing. Most commonly, macrosociological variables are used as footing for explaining microsociological phenomena, for example, using the rural/urban or the traditional/modern distinction to explain qualities of face-to-face relationships. Parsons's (1951) social system framework was once a leading model of this kind of explanation, using macro-level systemic variables to explain functioning and variation in individual lives and actions.

One way for qualitative inquiry to approach *why* questions without endangering its traditional analytic interests is to proceed from the *whats* and *hows* of social life. Provisional explanatory footing can be found at the junction of concerns for what is going on in everyday life in relation to how that is constructed, centered in the space we have located as interpretive practice. Bracketing the *whats*, footing for explaining the constructive nuances of social patterns can be found in discursive practice. Bracketing the *hows*, footing for explaining the delimited patterns of meaning consequent to social construction processes can be found in discourses-in-practice.

The interplay between discourses-in-practice and discursive practice is a source of two kinds of answers for why things are organized as they are in everyday life. One kind stems from the explanatory footings of discursive practice, directing us to the artful talk and interaction that design and designate the local contours of our social worlds. From such footings, we learn why discourses are not templates for action. Their articulation is subject to the everyday contingencies of discursive practice. Discourses-in-practice are talked into action, so to speak; they do not dictate what is said and done from the outside or from the inside, as if they were separate and distinct sources of influence. To answer why social structures are as circumstantially nuanced as they are, one can bracket the constitutive *whats* of the matter in order to reveal how recognizable activities and systems of meaning are constituted in particular domains of everyday life. Discursive practice, in other words, provides the footing for answering why recognizable constellations of social order take on locally distinctive shapes.

We may also answer limited *why* questions that are related to discursive practice, questions such as why discursive actions unfold in specific directions or why they have particular consequences. Answers emerge when we bracket the constitutive work that shapes who and what we are and what it is that we do. By itself, the machinery of conversation gives us few clues as to when, where, or what particular patterns of meaning or action will be artfully produced and managed. The machinery is like a galloping horse, but we have little or no sense of when it began to run, where it is headed, what indeed it is up to, and what might happen when it gets there. Is it racing, fleeing, playing polo, delivering the mail, or what? Each of these possibilities requires a discourse to set its course and to tell us what messages it might be conveying. This can then inform us in delimited ways of why the machinery of speech environments is organized and propelled in the ways it is. Discourse-in-practice provides the footing for answering why discursive practice proceeds in the direction it does, toward what end, in pursuit of what goals, in relation to what meanings.

◆ Sustaining a Critical Consciousness

The interplay of discourse-in-practice and discursive practice sustains an integral critical consciousness for qualitative inquiry. Each component of interpretive practice serves as an *endogenous* basis for raising serious questions relating to the empirical assumptions of ongoing inquiry. Critical consciousness is built into the analytics; it is not external to it. Indeed, it is the other face of analytic bracketing. If, for purposes of broadening our knowledge of everyday life, analytic bracketing provides a means of combining attention to constitutive *hows* with substantive *whats*, it simultaneously enjoins us to pay attention continuously to what we may be shortchanging in the service of one of these questions or the other. The continuing enterprise of analytic bracketing does not keep us comfortably ensconced throughout the research process in a domain of indifference to the lived realities of experience, as a priori bracketing does. Nor does analytic bracketing keep us comfortably engaged in the unrepentant naturalism of documenting the world of everyday life the way it really is. Rather, it continuously jerks us out of the analytic lethargies of both endeavors.

When questions of discourse-in-practice take the stage, there are grounds for problematizing or politicizing the sum and substance of what otherwise can be too facilely viewed as arbitrarily or individualistically constructed, managed, and sustained. The persistent urgency of *what* questions cautions us not to assume that interpersonal agency, artfulness, or the machinery of social interaction is the whole story. The urgency prompts us to inquire into the broader sources of matters that are built up across time and circumstance in discursive practice, the contemporaneous conditions that inform and shape the construction process, and the personal and interpersonal consequences for those involved of having constituted their world in the way they have. Although the analytics of interpretive practice does not orient naturalistically to the "real world," neither does it take everyday life as built from the ground up in talk-in-interaction on each and every conversational or narrative occasion. The political consequence of this is an analytics that turns to matters of social organization and control, implicating a reality that doesn't rest completely on the machinery of talk or the constructive quality of social interaction. It turns us to wider contexts in search of other sources of change or stability.

When discursive practice commands the spotlight, there is a basis for critically challenging the representational security of taken-for-granted realities. The continual urgency of *how* questions warns us not to assume that the world as it now is, is the world that must be. This warning prompts us to "unsettle" realities in search of their construction to reveal the constitutive processes that produce and sustain particular realities as the processes are engaged, not for time immemorial. In an analytics of interpretive practice, *how* concerns caution us to remember that the everyday realities of our lives—whether they are being normal, abnormal, law-abiding, criminal, male, female, young, or old—are realities we *do*. Having done them, we move on to do others, producing and reproducing, time and again, the worlds we inhabit. Politically, this presents the recognition that we could enact alternate possibilities or alternative directions, although the apparent organization of our lives might appear to make that impossible. If we make visible the constructive fluidity and malleability of social forms, we also reveal a potential for change (see Gubrium & Holstein, 1990, 1994, 1995, 1998; Holstein & Gubrium, 2000).

The critical consciousness of this analytics deploys the continuous imperative to take issue with discourse or discursive practice when either one is foregrounded, thus turning the analytics on itself as it pursues its goals. Reflexively framed, the interplay of discourse and discursive practice transforms analytic bracketing into critical bracketing, offering a basis not only for documenting interpretive practice, but also for commenting critically on its own constructions, putting the analytic pendulum in motion in relation to itself.

◆ Notes

1. Some self-proclaimed ethnomethodologists, however, would reject the notion that ethnomethodology is in any sense a "constructionist" or "constructivist" enterprise (see Lynch, 1993). Some reviews of the ethnomethodological canon also clearly imply that constructionism is anathema to the ethnomethodological project (see Maynard, 1998; Maynard & Clayman, 1991).

2. While clearly reflecting Garfinkel's pioneering contributions, this characterization of the ethnomethodological project is perhaps closer to the version conveyed in the work of Melvin Pollner (1987, 1991) and D. Lawrence Wieder (1988) than some of the more recent "postanalytic" or conversation-analytic forms of ethnomethodology. Indeed, Garfinkel (1988), Lynch (1993), and others might object to how we ourselves portray ethnomethodology. We would contend, however, that there is much to be gained from a studied "misreading" of the ethnomethodological "classics," a practice that Garfinkel himself advocates for the sociological classics more generally (see Lynch, 1993). With the figurative "death of the author" (Barthes, 1977), those attached to doctrinaire readings of the canon should have little grounds for argument.

3. Other ethnomethodologists have drawn upon Foucault, but without necessarily endorsing these affinities or parallels. Lynch (1993), for example, writes that Foucault's studies can be relevant to ethnomethodological investigations in a "restricted and 'literal' way" (p. 131) and resists the generalization of discursive regimes across highly occasioned "language games." See McHoul (1986) and Lynch and Bogen (1996) for exemplary ethnomethodological appropriations of Foucauldian insights.

4. There is still considerable doctrinaire sentiment for maintaining "hard-headed, rig-orous investigation in one idiom" while recognizing its possible "incommensurability" with others (Maynard, 1998, p. 345). The benefit, according to Maynard (1998), would be "strongly reliable understanding in a particular domain of social life, and it need not imply narrowness, fragmentation, limitation, or isolation" (p. 345). Our sense is that such conver-sations do produce fragmentation and isolation (see Hill & Crittenden, 1968, for a vivid example of nonproductive conversation deriving from incompatible analytic idioms), resulting in the stale reproduction of knowledge and, of course, the equally stale representa-tion of the empirical world. In our view, reliability has never been a strong enough incentive for analysts to ignore the potential validities of new analytic horizons.

5. The CA argument for this point of departure is that ostensibly distinct patterns of talk and interaction are constitutive of particular settings, and therefore must be the point of departure. This is tricky, however. CA's practitioners routinely designate and describe par-ticular institutional contexts *before* the analysis of the conversations that those conversa-tions are said to reveal. CA would have us believe that setting, as a distinct context for talk and interaction, would be visibly (hearably) constituted *in the machinery of talk* itself (see Schegloff, 1991). This would mean that no scene setting would be necessary (or even need to be provided) for the production of the discursive context to be apparent. One wonders if what is demonstrated in these studies could have been produced in the unlikely event that no prior knowledge of the settings had been available, or if prior knowledge were rigorously bracketed.

CA studies always admit to being about conversation in *some* context. Even the myriad studies of telephone interaction make that discursive context available to readers *before* the analysis begins. Indeed, titles of research reports literally announce institutional context at the start. For example, one of Heritage's (1984) articles is titled "Analyzing News Inter-views: Aspects of the Production of Talk for an Overhearing Audience." Immediately, the reader knows and, in a manner of speaking, is prepared to get the gist of what conversation is "doing" in what follows. In a word, the *productivity* of talk relies as much on this analyti-cally underrecognized start as on what the analysis proper aims to show. In such studies, context inevitably sneaks in the front door, in titles and "incidental" stage setting. Appar-ently, analysts fail to recognize that some measure of discursive context is being imported to assist in the explanation of how context is indigenously constructed.

Strictly speaking, researchers cannot hope to attribute institutional patterns completely to the machinery of conversation. Nor can they completely disattend to discourse-in-practice and meaning while describing the sequential flow of conversation. Analytically, one must at some point reappropriate institutions and external cultural understandings in order to know what is artfully and methodically going on in that talk and interaction. Centered as analytic bracketing is on both sides of interpretive practice, there is concerted warrant for the continual return of the analytic gaze to discourse-in-practice.

6. There are other useful metaphors for describing how analytic bracketing changes the focus from discourse-in-practice to discursive practice. One can liken the operation to "shifting" gears while driving a motor vehicle equipped with a manual transmission. One mode of analysis may prove quite productive, but it will eventually strain against the resis-tance engendered by its own temporary analytic orientation. When the analyst notes that the analytic "engine" is laboring under, or being constrained by, the restraints of what it is currently "geared" to accomplish, he or she can decide to virtually "shift" analytic "gears" in

242

order to gain further purchase on the aspects of interpretive interplay that were previously bracketed. Just as there can be no prescription for shifting gears while driving (i.e., one can never specify in advance at what speed one should shift up or down), changing analytic brackets always remains an artful enterprise, awaiting the empirical circumstances it encounters. Its timing cannot be prespecified. As in shifting gears while driving, changes are not arbitrary or undisciplined. Rather, they respond to the analytic challenges at hand in a principled, if not predetermined, fashion.

7. This may be the very thing Lynch (1993) decries with respect to conversation analysts who attempt to formalize and professionalize CA as a "scientific" discipline.

8. Some critics have worried that analytic bracketing represents a selective objectivism, a form of "ontological gerrymandering" (see Denzin, 1998). These, of course, have become fighting words among constructionists. But we should soberly recall that Steve Woolgar and Dorothy Pawluch (1985) have suggested that carving out some sort of analytic footing may be a pervasive and unavoidable feature of any sociological commentary. Our own constant attention to the *interplay* between discourse-in-practice and discursive practice—as they are understood and used by members—continually reminds us of their reflexive relationship. Gerrymanderers stand their separate ground and unreflexively deconstruct; analytic bracketing, in contrast, encourages a continual and methodical deconstruction of empirical groundings themselves. This may produce a less-than-tidy picture, but it also is designed to keep reification at bay and ungrounded signification under control.

◆ References

Abu-Lughod, L. (1991). Writing against culture. In R. G. Fox (Ed.), *Recapturing anthropology: Working in the present* (pp. 137-162). Santa Fe, NM: School of American Research Press.

Abu-Lughod, L. (1993). *Writing women's worlds: Bedouin stories.* Berkeley: University of California Press.

Atkinson, J. M., & Drew, P. (1979). *Order in court.* Atlantic Highlands, NJ: Humanities Press.

Atkinson, P. A. (1988). Ethnomethodology: A critical review. *Annual Review of Sociology, 14,* 441-465.

Atkinson, P. A. (1995). *Medical talk and medical work.* London: Sage.

Barthes, R. (1977). *Image, music, text* (S. Heath, Trans.). New York: Hill & Wang.

Berger, P. L., & Luckmann, T. (1967). *The social construction of reality: A treatise in the sociology of knowledge.* Garden City, NY: Doubleday.

Best, S., & Kellner, D. (1991). *Postmodern theory: Critical interrogations.* New York: Guilford.

Blumer, H. (1969). *Symbolic interactionism: Perspective and method.* Englewood Cliffs, NJ: Prentice Hall.

Boden, D., & Zimmerman, D. (Eds.). (1991). *Talk and social structure: Studies in ethnomethodology and conversation analysis.* Cambridge: Polity.

Bogen, D., & Lynch, M. (1993). Do we need a general theory of social problems? In J. A. Holstein & G. Miller (Eds.), *Reconsidering social constructionism: Debates in social problems theory* (pp. 213-237). Hawthorne, NY: Aldine de Gruyter.

Chase, S. E. (1995). *Ambiguous empowerment: The work narratives of women school superintendents.* Amherst: University of Massachusetts Press.

Denzin, N. K. (1998). The new ethnography. *Journal of Contemporary Ethnography, 27,* 405-415.

Dingwall, R., Eekelaar, J., & Murray, T. (1983). *The protection of children: State intervention and family life.* Oxford: Blackwell.

Drew, P., & Heritage, J. C. (Eds.). (1992). *Talk at work.* Cambridge: Cambridge University Press.

Dreyfus, H. L., & Rabinow, P. (1982). *Michel Foucault: Beyond structuralism and hermeneutics.* Chicago: University of Chicago Press.

Durkheim, E. (1961). *The elementary forms of the religious life.* New York: Collier-Macmillan.

Durkheim, E. (1964). *The rules of the sociological method* (S. S. Solovay & J. H. Mueller, Trans.; G. E. G. Catlin, Ed.). New York: Free Press.

Emerson, R. M. (1969). *Judging delinquents.* Chicago: Aldine.

Emerson, R. M., & Messinger, S. (1977). The micro-politics of trouble. *Social Problems, 25,* 121-134.

Foucault, M. (1965). *Madness and civilization.* New York: Random House.

Foucault, M. (1972). *The archaeology of knowledge.* New York: Pantheon.

Foucault, M. (1975). *The birth of the clinic: An archaeology of medical perception.* New York: Vintage.

Foucault, M. (1979). *Discipline and punish: The birth of the prison* (A. Sheridan, Trans.). New York: Vintage.

Foucault, M. (1980). *Power/knowledge: Selected interviews and other writings, 1972-1977* (C. Gordon, Ed.; L. Marshall, J. Mepham, & K. Soper, Trans.). New York: Pantheon.

Foucault, M. (1988). The ethic of care for the self as a practice of freedom. In M. Foucault, *The final Foucault* (J. Bernauer & G. Rasmussen, Eds.; pp. 1-20). Cambridge: MIT Press.

Garfinkel, H. (1952). *The perception of the other: A study in social order.* Unpublished doctoral dissertation, Harvard University.

Garfinkel, H. (1967). *Studies in ethnomethodology.* Englewood Cliffs, NJ: Prentice Hall.

Garfinkel, H. (1988). Evidence for locally produced, naturally accountable phenomena of order, logic, reason, meaning, method, etc. in and as of the essential quiddity of immortal ordinary society (I of IV): An announcement of studies. *Sociological Theory, 6,* 103-109.

Garfinkel, H., Lynch, M., & Livingston, E. (1981). The work of a discovering science construed with materials from the optically discovered pulsar. *Philosophy of the Social Sciences, 11,* 131-158.

Garfinkel, H., & Sacks, H. (1970). On the formal structures of practical actions. In J. C. McKinney & E. A. Tiryakian (Eds.), *Theoretical sociology* (pp. 338-366). New York: Appleton-Century-Crofts.

Gubrium, J. F. (1988). *Analyzing field reality.* Newbury Park, CA: Sage.

Gubrium, J. F. (1992). *Out of control: Family therapy and domestic disorder.* Newbury Park, CA: Sage.

Gubrium, J. F. (1993). For a cautious naturalism. In J. A. Holstein & G. Miller (Eds.), *Reconsidering social constructionism: Debates in social problems theory* (pp. 89-101). Hawthorne, NY: Aldine de Gruyter.

Gubrium, J. F., & Holstein, J. A. (1990). *What is family?* Mountain View, CA: Mayfield.

Gubrium, J. F., & Holstein, J. A. (1994). *Constructing the life course.* Dix Hills, NY: General Hall.

Gubrium, J. F., & Holstein, J. A. (1995). Life course malleability: Biographical work and deprivatization. *Sociological Inquiry, 65,* 207-223.

Gubrium, J. F., & Holstein, J. A. (1997). *The new language of qualitative method.* New York: Oxford University Press.

Gubrium, J. F., & Holstein, J. A. (1998). Narrative practice and the coherence of personal stories. *Sociological Quarterly, 39,* 163-187.

Heritage, J. C. (1984). *Garfinkel and ethnomethodology.* Cambridge: Polity.

Heritage, J. C. (1987). Ethnomethodology. In A. Giddens & J. Turner (Eds.), *Sociological theory today* (pp. 224-271). Stanford, CA: Stanford University Press.

Heritage, J. C. (1997). Conversation analysis and institutional talk: Analysing data. In D. Silverman (Ed.), *Qualitative research: Theory, method and practice* (pp. 161-182). London: Sage.

Hewitt, J. P. (1997). *Self and society.* Boston: Allyn & Bacon.

Hill, R. J., & Crittenden, K. S. (Eds.). (1968). *Proceedings of the Purdue Symposium on Ethnomethodology.* West Lafayette, IN: Purdue Research Foundation.

Holstein, J. A. (1983). Jurors' use of judges' instructions. *Sociological Methods & Research, 11,* 501-518.

Holstein, J. A. (1993). *Court-ordered insanity: Interpretive practice and involuntary commitment.* Hawthorne, NY: Aldine de Gruyter.

Holstein, J. A., & Gubrium, J. F. (1994). Phenomenology, ethnomethodology, and interpretive practice. In N. K. Denzin & Y. S. Lincoln (Eds.), *Handbook of qualitative research* (pp. 262-272). Thousand Oaks, CA: Sage.

Holstein, J. A., & Gubrium, J. F. (2000). *The self we live by: Narrative identity in a postmodern world.* New York: Oxford University Press.

Hughes, E. C. (1984). Going concerns: The study of American institutions. In E. C. Hughes, *The sociological eye: Selected papers* (D. Riesman & H. S. Becker, Eds.; pp. 52-64). New Brunswick, NJ: Transaction.

Husserl, E. (1970). *Logical investigation.* Atlantic Highlands, NJ: Humanities Press.

Livingston, E. (1986). *The ethnomethodological foundations of mathematics.* London: Routledge & Kegan Paul.

Lynch, M. (1985). *Art and artifact in laboratory science.* London: Routledge & Kegan Paul.

Lynch, M. (1993). *Scientific practice and ordinary action.* Cambridge: Cambridge University Press.

Lynch, M., & Bogen, D. (1994). Harvey Sacks' primitive natural science. *Theory, Culture & Society, 11,* 65-104.

Lynch, M., & Bogen, D. (1996). *The spectacle of history: Speech, text, and memory at the Iran-Contra hearings.* Durham, NC: Duke University Press.

Marx, K. (1956). *Selected writings in sociology and social philosophy* (T. Bottomore, Ed.). New York: McGraw-Hill.

Maynard, D. W. (1984). *Inside plea bargaining: The language of negotiation.* New York: Plenum.

Maynard, D. W. (1989). On the ethnography and analysis of discourse in institutional settings. In J. A. Holstein & G. Miller (Eds.), *Perspectives on social problems* (Vol. 1, pp. 127-146). Greenwich, CT: JAI.

Maynard, D. W. (1998). On qualitative inquiry and extramodernity. *Contemporary Sociology, 27,* 343-345.

Maynard, D. W., & Clayman, S. E. (1991). The diversity of ethnomethodology. *Annual Review of Sociology, 17,* 385-418.

Maynard, D. W., & Manzo, J. (1993). On the sociology of justice. *Sociological Theory, 11,* 171-193.

McHoul, A. (1986). The getting of sexuality: Foucault, Garfinkel, and the analysis of sexual discourse. *Theory, Culture & Society, 3,* 65-79.

Mehan, H. (1979). *Learning lessons: Social organization in the classroom.* Cambridge, MA: Harvard University Press.

Mehan, H. (1991). The school's work of sorting students. In D. Boden & D. Zimmerman (Eds.), *Talk and social structure: Studies in ethnomethodology and conversation analysis* (pp. 71-90). Cambridge: Polity.

Mehan, H., & Wood, H. (1975). *The reality of ethnomethodology.* New York: John Wiley.

Miller, G. (1991). *Enforcing the work ethic.* Albany: State University of New York Press.

Miller, G. (1994). Toward ethnographies of institutional discourse. *Journal of Contemporary Ethnography, 23,* 280-306.

246

Miller, G. (1997a). *Becoming miracle workers: Language and meaning in brief therapy.* New York: Aldine de Gruyter.

Miller, G. (1997b). Building bridges: The possibility of analytic dialogue between ethnography, conversation analysis, and Foucault. In D. Silverman (Ed.), *Qualitative research: Theory, method and practice* (pp. 24-44). London: Sage.

Parsons, T. (1951). *The social system.* New York: Free Press.

Pollner, M. (1987). *Mundane reason.* Cambridge: Cambridge University Press.

Pollner, M. (1991). Left of ethnomethodology: The rise and decline of radical reflexivity. *American Sociological Review, 56,* 370-380.

Potter, J. (1996). *Representing reality: Discourse, rhetoric and social construction.* London: Sage.

Potter, J. (1997). Discourse analysis as a way of analysing naturally-occurring talk. In D. Silverman (Ed.), *Qualitative research: Theory, method and practice* (pp. 144-160). London: Sage.

Potter, J., & Wetherell, M. (1987). *Discourse and social psychology: Beyond attitudes and behaviour.* London: Sage.

Prior, L. (1997). Following in Foucault's footsteps: Text and context in qualitative research. In D. Silverman (Ed.), *Qualitative research: Theory, method and practice* (pp. 63-79). London: Sage.

Rose, N. (1990). *Governing the soul: The shaping of the private self.* New York: Routledge.

Sacks, H. (1972). An initial investigation of the usability of conversational data for doing sociology. In D. Sudnow (Ed.), *Studies in social interaction* (pp. 31-74). New York: Free Press.

Sacks, H. (1992). *Lectures on conversation* (Vols. 1-2). Oxford: Blackwell.

Sacks, H., Schegloff, E. A., & Jefferson, G. (1974). A simplest systematics for the organization of turn-taking for conversation. *Language, 50,* 696-735.

Schegloff, E. A. (1991). Reflections on talk and social structure. In D. Boden & D. Zimmerman (Eds.), *Talk and social structure: Studies in ethnomethodology and conversation analysis* (pp. 44-70). Cambridge: Polity.

Schrag, C. O. (1997). *The self after postmodernity.* New Haven, CT: Yale University Press.

Schutz, A. (1962). *The problem of social reality.* The Hague: Martinus Nijhoff.

Schutz, A. (1964). *Studies in social theory.* The Hague: Martinus Nijhoff.

Schutz, A. (1967). *The phenomenology of the social world.* Evanston, IL: Northwestern University Press.

Schutz, A. (1970). *On phenomenology and social relations.* Chicago: University of Chicago Press.

Silverman, D. (1985). *Qualitative methodology and sociology.* Aldershot, England: Gower.

Silverman, D. (1993). *Interpreting qualitative data: Strategies for analysing talk, text and interaction.* London: Sage.

Silverman, D. (Ed.). (1997). *Qualitative research: Theory, method and practice.* London: Sage.

Silverman, D. (1998). *Harvey Sacks: Social science and conversation analysis.* Cambridge: Polity.

Smith, D. E. (1987). *The everyday world as problematic.* Boston: Northeastern University Press.

Smith, D. E. (1990). *Texts, facts, and femininity.* London: Routledge.

ten Have, P. (1990). Methodological issues in conversation analysis. *Bulletin de Methodologie Sociologique, 27,* 23-51.

Weigert, A. J. (1981). *Sociology of everyday life.* New York: Longman.

Wieder, D. L. (1988). *Language and social reality.* Washington, DC: University Press of America.

Wittgenstein, L. (1958). *Philosophical investigations.* New York: Macmillan.

Woolgar, S., & Pawluch, D. (1985). Ontological gerrymandering. *Social Problems, 32,* 214-227.

Zimmerman, D. H. (1970). The practicalities of rule use. In J. D. Douglas (Ed.), *Understanding everyday life: Toward a reconstruction of social knowledge* (pp. 221-238). Chicago: Aldine.

Zimmerman, D. H. (1988). On conversation: The conversation analytic perspective. In J. A. Anderson (Ed.), *Communication yearbook 11* (pp. 406-432). Newbury Park, CA: Sage.

Zimmerman, D. H., & Wieder, D. L. (1970). Ethnomethodology and the problem of order. In J. D. Douglas (Ed.), *Understanding everyday life: Toward a reconstruction of social knowledge* (pp. 285-295). Chicago: Aldine.

8

Grounded Theory

Objectivist and

Constructivist Methods

Kathy Charmaz

◆ Grounded theory served at the front of the "qualitative revolution" (Denzin & Lincoln, 1994, p. ix). Barney G. Glaser and Anselm L. Strauss wrote *The Discovery of Grounded Theory* (1967) at a critical point in social science history. They defended qualitative research and countered the dominant view that quantitative studies provide the only form of systematic social scientific inquiry. Essentially, grounded theory methods consist of systematic inductive guidelines for collecting and analyzing data

AUTHOR'S NOTE: I made an earlier statement of my position on constructivism in a paper titled *Studying Lived Experience Through Grounded Theory: Objectivist and Constructivist Methods,* presented at the Qualitative Research Conference "Studying Human Lived Experience: Symbolic Interaction and Ethnographic Research '93," at the University of Waterloo, Ontario, Canada, May 19-22, 1993. I am grateful to Robert Prus, who invited me to present my ideas in the conference paper; to Lyn Lofland, who wrote a detailed review of it; and to members of my first Sonoma State University writing group, Julia Allen, Patrick Jackson, and Catherine Nelson, who encouraged me to pursue the topic. I thank Julianne Cheek, Norman K. Denzin, Udo Kelle, Kyrina Kent, and Yvonna Lincoln for their supportive and thoughtful comments on earlier drafts of this chapter.

to build middle-range theoretical frameworks that explain the collected data. Throughout the research process, grounded theorists develop analytic interpretations of their data to focus further data collection, which they use in turn to inform and refine their developing theoretical analyses. Since Glaser and Strauss developed grounded theory methods, qualitative researchers have claimed the use of these methods to legitimate their research.

Now grounded theory methods have come under attack from both within and without. Postmodernists and poststructuralists dispute obvious and subtle positivistic premises assumed by grounded theory's major proponents and within the logic of the method itself (see, e.g., Denzin, 1994, 1996, 1998; Richardson, 1993; Van Maanen, 1988). What grounded theory is and should be is contested. Barney G. Glaser and the late Anselm Strauss, with his more recent coauthor, Juliet Corbin, have moved the method in somewhat conflicting directions (Glaser, 1992; Strauss, 1987; Strauss & Corbin, 1990, 1994, 1998). Nonetheless, both their positions remain imbued with positivism, with its objectivist underpinnings (Guba & Lincoln, 1994). Glaser's (1978, 1992) position often comes close to traditional positivism, with its assumptions of an objective, external reality, a neutral observer who discovers data, reductionist inquiry of manageable research problems, and objectivist rendering of data. Strauss and Corbin's (1990, 1998) stance assumes an objective external reality, aims toward unbiased data collection, proposes a set of technical procedures, and espouses verification. Their position moves into postpositivism because they also propose giving voice to their respondents, representing them as accurately as possible, discovering and acknowledging how respondents' views of reality conflict with their own, and recognizing art as well as science in the analytic product and process (see Strauss & Corbin, 1998). By taking these points further, I add another position to the fray and another vision for future qualitative research: constructivist grounded theory.[1]

Constructivist grounded theory celebrates firsthand knowledge of empirical worlds, takes a middle ground between postmodernism and positivism, and offers accessible methods for taking qualitative research into the 21st century. Constructivism assumes the relativism of multiple social realities, recognizes the mutual creation of knowledge by the viewer and the viewed, and aims toward interpretive understanding of subjects' meanings (Guba & Lincoln, 1994; Schwandt, 1994). The power of grounded theory lies in its tools for understanding empirical worlds. We can reclaim these tools from their positivist underpinnings to form a revised, more open-ended practice of grounded theory that stresses its emergent, constructivist elements. We can use grounded theory methods as flexible, heuristic strategies rather than as formulaic procedures.

A constructivist approach to grounded theory reaffirms studying people in their natural settings and redirects qualitative research away from positivism. My argument is threefold: (a) Grounded theory strategies need not be rigid or prescriptive; (b) a focus on meaning while using grounded theory *furthers,* rather than limits, interpretive understanding; and (c) we can adopt grounded theory strategies without embracing the positivist leanings of earlier proponents of grounded theory. Certainly, a continuum can be discerned between objectivist and constructivist grounded theory. In addition, individual grounded theorists have modified their approaches over time (see, e.g., Glaser, 1994; Strauss, 1995; Strauss & Corbin, 1990, 1994, 1998). For clarity, I juxtapose objectivist and constructivist approaches throughout the following discussion, but note shifts as proponents have developed their positions.

In this chapter, I provide an overview of grounded theory methods, discuss recent debates, and describe a constructivist approach, which I illustrate with examples from my earlier studies. Researchers can use grounded theory methods with either quantitative or qualitative data, although these methods are typically associated with qualitative research. And researchers can use these methods whether they are working from an objectivist or a constructivist perspective.

The rigor of grounded theory approaches offers qualitative researchers a set of clear guidelines from which to build explanatory frameworks that specify relationships among concepts. Grounded theory methods do not detail data collection techniques; they move each step of the analytic process toward the development, refinement, and interrelation of concepts. The strategies of grounded theory include (a) simultaneous collection and analysis of data, (b) a two-step data coding process, (c) comparative methods, (d) memo writing aimed at the construction of conceptual analyses, (e) sampling to refine the researcher's emerging theoretical ideas, and (f) integration of the theoretical framework.

Glaser (1978, 1992) establishes the following criteria for evaluating a grounded theory: fit, work, relevance, and modifiability. Theoretical categories must be developed from analysis of the collected data and must fit them; these categories must explain the data they subsume. Thus grounded theorists cannot shop their disciplinary stores for preconceived concepts and dress their data in them. Any existing concept must earn its way into the analysis (Glaser, 1978). A grounded theory must work; it must provide a useful conceptual rendering and ordering of the data that explains the studied phenomena. The relevance of a grounded theory derives from its offering analytic explanations of actual problems and basic processes in the research setting. A grounded theory is durable because it accounts for variation; it is flexible because researchers can modify their emerging or established analyses as conditions change or further data are gathered.

Many grounded theory studies reflect the objectivist approaches and perspectival proclivities of the founders of grounded theory (see, e.g., Biernacki, 1986; Johnson, 1991; Reif, 1975; Swanson & Chenitz, 1993; Wiener, 1975).[2] However, researchers starting from other vantage points—feminist, Marxist, phenomenologist—can use grounded theory strategies for their empirical studies. These strategies allow for varied fundamental assumptions, data gathering approaches, analytic emphases, and theoretical levels.

Thus diverse researchers can use grounded theory methods to develop constructivist studies derived from interpretive approaches. Grounded theorists need not subscribe to positivist or objectivist assumptions. Rather, they may still study empirical worlds without presupposing narrow objectivist methods and without assuming the truth of their subsequent analyses. Hence constructivist grounded theory studies of subjective experience can bridge Blumer's (1969) call for the empirical study of meanings with current postmodernist critiques.

◆ Grounded Theory Then and Now

The Development of Grounded Theory

In their pioneering book, *The Discovery of Grounded Theory* (1967), Barney G. Glaser and Anselm L. Strauss first articulated their research strategies for their collaborative studies of dying (Glaser & Strauss, 1965, 1968). They challenged the hegemony of the quantitative research paradigm in the social sciences. Chicago school sociology (see, e.g., Park & Burgess, 1925; Shaw, 1930; Thomas & Znaniecki, 1918-1920; Thrasher, 1927/1963; Zorbaugh, 1929) had long contributed a rich ethnographic tradition to the discipline. However, the ascendancy of quantitative methods undermined and marginalized that tradition. Scientistic assumptions of objectivity and truth furthered the quest for verification through precise, standardized instruments and parsimonious quantifiable variables. Field research waned. It became viewed as a preliminary exercise through which researchers could refine quantitative instruments before the real work began, rather than as a viable endeavor in its own right. The ascendancy of quantification also led to a growing division between theory and empirical research. Theorists and researchers lived in different worlds and pursued different problems. Presumably, quantitative research tested existing theory as prescribed by the logico-deductive model. However, much of this research remained atheoretical and emphasized controlling variables rather than theory testing.

Glaser and Strauss's (1967) work was revolutionary because it challenged (a) arbitrary divisions between theory and research, (b) views of qualitative research as primarily a precursor to more "rigorous" quantitative methods, (c) claims that the quest for rigor made qualitative research illegitimate, (d) beliefs that qualitative methods are impressionistic and unsystematic, (e) separation of data collection and analysis, and (f) assumptions that qualitative research could produce only descriptive case studies rather than theory development (Charmaz, 1995c). With the publication of *Discovery*, Glaser and Strauss called for qualitative research to move toward theory development.[3] They provided a persuasive intellectual rationale for conducting qualitative research that permitted and encouraged novices to pursue it. And they gave guidelines for its successful completion.

Prior to the publication of *Discovery*, most qualitative analysis had been taught through an oral tradition of mentoring, when taught at all. Glaser and Strauss led the way in providing written guidelines for systematic qualitative data analysis with explicit analytic procedures and research strategies. Glaser applied his rigorous positivistic methodological training in quantitative research from Columbia University to the development of qualitative analysis. Grounded theory methods were founded upon Glaser's epistemological assumptions, methodological terms, inductive logic, and systematic approach. Strauss's training at the University of Chicago with Herbert Blumer and Robert Park brought Chicago school field research and symbolic interactionism to grounded theory. Hence, Strauss brought the pragmatist philosophical study of process, action, and meaning into *empirical* inquiry through grounded theory.

Glaser's 1978 book *Theoretical Sensitivity* substantially advanced explication of grounded theory methods. However, the abstract terms and dense writing Glaser employed rendered the book inaccessible to many readers. Strauss's *Qualitative Analysis for Social Scientists* (1987) made grounded theory more accessible, although perhaps more theoretically diffuse than the earlier methods texts would suggest.

Reformulation and Repudiation

Grounded theory gained a wider audience, a new spokesperson, and more disciples with the appearance of Strauss's 1990 coauthored book with Juliet Corbin, *Basics of Qualitative Research: Grounded Theory Procedures and Techniques.*[4] This book aims to specify and to develop grounded theory methodology. It takes the reader through several familiar analytic steps, illustrates procedures with examples, and stirs a new technical armamentarium into the mix. *Basics* gained readers but lost the sense of emergence and open-ended character of Strauss's earlier volume and much of his empirical work. The improved and more accessible second edition of *Basics* (Strauss & Corbin, 1998) reads as less prescriptive and aims to lead readers to a new way of thinking about their research and about the world. In both editions, the authors pose concerns (1990, p. 7; 1998, p. x) about valid and reliable data and interpretations and researcher bias consistent with "normal science" (Kuhn, 1970). Strauss and Corbin impart a behaviorist, rather than interpretive, cast to their analysis of key hypothetical examples (see 1990, pp. 63-65, 78-81, 88-90, 145-147).[5] Perhaps the scientific underpinnings of the 1990 book reflect both Corbin's earlier training and Strauss's growing insistence that grounded theory is verificational (A. L. Strauss, personal communication, February 1, 1993).[6] Whether *Basics* advances grounded theory methods or proposes different technical procedures depends on one's point of view.

Glaser (1978, 1992) emphasizes emergence of data and theory through the analysis of "basic social processes." Glaser's position (see also Melia, 1996) becomes clear in his 1992 repudiation of Strauss and Corbin (1990). He advocates gathering data without forcing either preconceived questions or frameworks upon it. In *Basics of Grounded Theory Analysis: Emergence vs. Forcing* (1992), Glaser answers Strauss and Corbin's work in *Basics*. Over and over, he finds Strauss and Corbin to be forcing data and analysis through their preconceptions, analytic questions, hypotheses, and methodological techniques (see, e.g., Glaser, 1992, pp. 33, 43, 46-47, 50-51, 58-59, 63, 78, 96-100). For Glaser, the use of systematic comparisons is enough. "Categories emerge upon comparison and properties emerge upon more comparison. And that is all there is to it" (Glaser, 1992, p. 43).

In addition to Glaser's trenchant critique, readers may find themselves caught in a maze of techniques that Strauss and Corbin propose as significant methodological advancements. Linda Robrecht (1995) asserts that the new procedures divert the researcher from the data and result in poorly integrated theoretical frameworks. Glaser declares that Strauss and Corbin invoke contrived comparisons rather than those that have emerged from analytic processes of comparing data to data, concept to concept, and category to category. He views their approach as "full conceptual description," not grounded theory. Glaser argues that the purpose of grounded theory methods is to generate theory, not to verify it. His point is consistent with quantitative research canons in which verification depends upon random sampling and standardized procedures. Strauss and Corbin do not answer Glaser directly, but, as Kath Melia (1996) notes, they do state their view of the essentials of grounded theory in their contribution to the first edition of this *Handbook,* while suggesting that the method will continue to evolve (Strauss & Corbin, 1994). Similarly, Strauss and Corbin do not respond to Glaser's charge that they abandoned grounded theory in favor of full conceptual description in their second edition of *Basics* (1998). However, they do offer an elegant statement of the significance of description and conceptual ordering for theory development (pp. 16-21).

Both Strauss and Corbin's *Basics* and Glaser's critique of it assert views of science untouched by either epistemological debates of the 1960s (Adler, Adler, & Johnson, 1992; Kleinman, 1993; Kuhn, 1970; Lofland, 1993; Snow & Morrill, 1993) or postmodern critiques (Clough, 1992; Denzin, 1991, 1992a, 1996; Marcus & Fischer, 1986). Both endorse a realist ontology and positivist epistemology, albeit with some sharp differences. Glaser remains in the positivist camp; Strauss and Corbin less so. They move between objectivist and constructivist assumptions in various works, although *Basics,* for which they are best known, stands in the objectivist terrain. For example, in their efforts to maintain objectivity, they advocate taking "appropriate measures" to minimize the intrusion of the subjectivity of the researcher into the research (Strauss & Corbin, 1998, p. 43). Both Glaser and Strauss and Corbin assume an external reality that researchers can discover and record—Glaser through discovering data, coding it, and using comparative methods step by step; Strauss and Corbin through their analytic questions, hypotheses, and methodological

255

applications. In their earlier writings, Glaser and Strauss (1967) imply that reality is independent of the observer and the methods used to produce it. Because both Glaser and Strauss and Corbin follow the canons of objective reportage, both engage in silent authorship and usually write about their data as distanced experts (Charmaz & Mitchell, 1996), thereby contributing to an objectivist stance.[7] Furthermore, the didactic, prescriptive approaches described in early statements about grounded theory coated these methods with a positivist, objectivist cast (see Charmaz, 1983; Glaser, 1992; Stern, 1994b; Strauss, 1987; Strauss & Corbin, 1990, 1994).

So who's got the real grounded theory? Glaser (1998) contends that he has the pure version of grounded theory. That's correct—if one agrees that early formulations should set the standard.[8] Different proponents assume that grounded theory essentials *ought* to include different things. Their "oughts" shape their notions of the real grounded theory. Must grounded theory be objectivist and positivist? No. Grounded theory offers a set of flexible strategies, not rigid prescriptions. Should grounded theorists adopt symbolic interactionism? Not always. Emphases on action and process and, from my constructivist view, meaning and emergence within symbolic interactionism complement grounded theory. Symbolic interactionism also offers a rich array of sensitizing concepts. However, grounded theory strategies can be used with sensitizing concepts from other perspectives. Pragmatism? Yes, because applicability and usefulness are part of the criteria for evaluating grounded theory analyses. Should we expect grounded theorists to remain committed to their written statements? Not completely. Published works become separated from the contexts of their creation. Neither their authors' original purpose nor intended audience may be apparent. Authors may write mechanistic prescriptions for beginners to get them started but compose more measured pieces for peers. New developments may influence them. But readers may reify these authors' earlier written words. Strauss and Corbin's (1994) chapter in the first edition of this *Handbook* has a considerably more flexible tone than is found in the first edition of *Basics* (1990), both in describing methods and in positioning grounded theory. For example, they note that future researchers may use grounded theory in conjunction with other approaches, which I argue here. A simplified, constructivist version of grounded theory such as outlined below can supply effective tools that can be adopted by researchers from diverse perspectives.[9]

◆ Grounded Theory Strategies

Regarding Data

Grounded theory methods specify analytic strategies, not data collection methods. These methods have become associated with limited interview studies, as if limiting grounded theory methods *to* interviews and limiting the number *of* interviews are both acceptable practices (see, e.g., Creswell, 1997). Researchers can use grounded theory techniques with varied forms of data collection (for historical analyses, see Clarke, 1998; Star, 1989). Qualitative researchers should gather extensive amounts of rich data with thick description (Charmaz, 1995c; Geertz, 1973). Grounded theorists have been accused, with some justification, of slighting data collection (Lofland & Lofland, 1984). Nonetheless, a number of grounded theorists have gathered thorough data, even those who have relied primarily on interviews (see, e.g., Baszanger, 1998; Biernacki, 1986; Charmaz, 1991, 1995b). Perhaps because grounded theory methods focus on the development of early analytic schemes, data gathering remains problematic and disputed.

Glaser (1992) raises sharp differences with Strauss and Corbin (1990) about forcing data through preconceived questions, categories, and hypotheses. Perhaps both are right, although in different ways. Glaser's comparative approach and emphasis on process provide excellent strategies for making data analysis efficient, productive, and exciting—without formulaic techniques. Every qualitative researcher should take heed of his warnings about forcing data into preconceived categories through the imposition of artificial questions. However, data collecting may demand that researchers ask questions and follow hunches, if not in direct conversation with respondents, then in the observers' notes about what to look for. Researchers construct rich data by amassing pertinent details. Strauss and Corbin's many questions and techniques may help novices improve their data gathering. Glaser (1998) assumes that data become transparent, that we researchers will see the basic social process in the field through our respondents' telling us what is significant. However, what researchers see may be neither basic nor certain (Mitchell & Charmaz, 1996). What respondents assume or do not apprehend may be much more important than what they talk about. An acontextual reliance on respondents' overt concerns can lead to narrow research problems, limited data, and trivial analyses.

Most grounded theorists write as if their data have an objective status. Strauss and Corbin (1998) write of "the reality of the data" and tell us, "The data do not lie" (p. 85). Data are narrative constructions (Maines, 1993). They are reconstructions of experience; they are not the original experience itself (see also Bond, 1990). Whether our respondents ply us with data in interview accounts they recast for our consumption or we record ethnographic stories to reflect experience as best we can recall and narrate, data remain reconstructions.

As we gather rich data, we draw from multiple sources—observations, conversations, formal interviews, autobiographies, public records, organizational reports, respondents' diaries and journals, and our own tape-recorded reflections. Grounded theory analyses of such materials begin with our coding, take form with memos, and are fashioned into conference papers and articles. Yet our statement of the ideas seldom ends with publication. Rather, we revisit our ideas and, perhaps, our data and re-create them in new form in an evolving process (Connelly & Clandinin, 1990).[10]

Coding Data

How do we do grounded theory? Analysis begins early. We grounded theorists code our emerging data as we collect it. Through coding, we start to define and categorize our data. In grounded theory coding, we create codes as we study our data. We do not, or should not, paste catchy concepts on our data. We should interact with our data and pose questions to them while coding them. Coding helps us to gain a new perspective on our material and to focus further data collection, and may lead us in unforeseen directions. Unlike quantitative research that requires data to fit into *preconceived* standardized codes, the researcher's interpretations of data shape his or her emergent codes in grounded theory.

Coding starts the chain of theory development. Codes that account for our data take form together as nascent theory that, in turn, explains these data and directs further data gathering. Initial or open coding proceeds through our examining each line of data and then defining actions or events within it—line-by-line coding (see especially Glaser, 1978). This coding keeps us studying our data. In addition to starting to build ideas inductively, we are deterred by line-by-line coding from imposing extant theories or our own beliefs on the data. This form of coding helps us to

TABLE 8.1   Example of Line-by-Line Coding of an Interview Statement

Line-by-Line Coding	Interview Statement[a]
Deciding to relinquish	And so I decided, this [pain, fatigue, and stress
Accounting for costs	accruing during her workday] isn't a way to live.
Weighing the balance	I don't have to work. . . . So it was with great
Relinquishing identity	regret, and not something I planned, I turned in
Making identity trade-offs	my resignation. It was the best thing I ever did.

a. From Charmaz (1995b, p. 671).

remain attuned to our subjects' views of their realities, rather than assume that we share the same views and worlds. Line-by-line coding sharpens our use of sensitizing concepts—that is, those background ideas that inform the overall research problem. Sensitizing concepts offer ways of seeing, organizing, and understanding experience; they are embedded in our disciplinary emphases and perspectival proclivities. Although sensitizing concepts may deepen perception, they provide starting points for building analysis, not ending points for evading it. We may use sensitizing concepts *only* as points of departure from which to study the data.

Line-by-line coding likely leads to our refining and specifying any borrowed extant concepts. Much of my work on the experience of illness has been informed by concepts of self and identity. The woman whose statement is quoted in Table 8.1 talked of having loved her job as an advocate for nursing-home residents. Through coding her statement line by line, I created the code "identity trade-offs" and later developed it into a category. Line-by-line coding keeps us thinking about what meanings we make of our data, asking ourselves questions of it, and pinpointing gaps and leads in it to focus on during subsequent data collection. Note that I kept the codes active. These action codes give us insight into what people are doing, what is happening in the setting.

Generating action codes facilitates making comparisons, a major technique in grounded theory. The constant comparative method of grounded theory means (a) comparing different people (such as their views, situations, actions, accounts, and experiences), (b) comparing data from the same individuals with themselves at different points in time, (c) comparing incident with incident, (d) comparing data with category, and (e) comparing a category with other categories (Charmaz, 1983, 1995c; Glaser, 1978, 1992).

Glaser (1978, 1992) stresses constant comparative methods. Strauss (1987) called for comparisons in his research and teaching—often hypothetical comparisons or, when he was teaching, comparisons from students' lives—at every level of analysis (see also Star, 1997).[11] Strauss and Corbin (1990) introduce new procedures: dimensionalizing, axial coding, and the conditional matrix. These procedures are intended to make researchers' emerging theories denser, more complex, and more precise. Dimensionalizing and axial coding can be done during initial coding; creating a conditional matrix comes later. Schatzman (1991) had earlier developed the concept of dimensionality to recognize and account for complexity beyond one meaning of a property or phenomenon. Strauss and Corbin (1990) build on his notion by urging researchers to divide properties into dimensions that lie along a continuum. In turn, we can develop a "dimensional profile" of the properties of a category. Strauss and Corbin further propose techniques for reassembling data in new ways through what they call "axial coding." This type of coding is aimed at making connections between a category and its subcategories. These include conditions that give rise to the category, its context, the social interactions through which it is handled, and its consequences.

Selective or focused coding uses initial codes that reappear frequently to sort large amounts of data. Thus this coding is more directed and, typically, more conceptual than line-by-line coding (Charmaz, 1983, 1995c; Glaser, 1978). These codes account for the most data and categorize them most precisely. Making explicit decisions about selecting codes gives us a check on the fit between the emerging theoretical framework and the empirical reality it explains. Of the initial codes shown in Table 8.1, "identity trade-offs" was the only one I treated analytically in the published article. When comparing respondents' interviews, I found similar statements and concerns about identity.

Our categories for synthesizing and explaining data arise from our focused codes. In turn, our categories shape our developing analytic frameworks. Categories often subsume several codes. For example, my category of "significant events" included positive events and relived negative events (Charmaz, 1991). Categories turn description into conceptual analysis by specifying properties analytically, as in the following example:

A significant event stands out in memory because it has boundaries, intensity, and emotional force. . . . The emotional reverberations of a single event echo through the present and future and therefore, however subtly, shade thoughts.

In their discussion of selective coding, Strauss and Corbin (1990) introduce the "conditional matrix," an analytic diagram that maps the range of conditions and consequences related to the phenomenon or category. They describe this matrix as a series of circles in which the outer rings represent those conditions most distant from actions and interactions and the inner rings represent those closest to actions and interactions. Strauss and Corbin propose that researchers create matrices to sensitize themselves to the range of conditions conceivably affecting the phenomena of interest and to the range of hypothetical consequences. Such matrices can sharpen researchers' explanations of and predictions about the studied phenomena.

Memo Writing

Memo writing is the intermediate step between coding and the first draft of the completed analysis. This step helps to spark our thinking and encourages us to look at our data and codes in new ways. It can help us to define leads for collecting data—both for further initial coding and later theoretical sampling. Through memo writing, we elaborate processes, assumptions, and actions that are subsumed under our codes. Memo writing leads us to explore our codes; we expand upon the processes they identify or suggest. Thus our codes take on substance as well as a structure for sorting data.

Action codes (e.g., as illustrated above) spur the writing of useful memos because they help us to see interrelated processes rather than static isolated topics. As we detail the properties of our action codes in memos, we connect categories and define how they fit into larger processes. By discussing these connections and defining processes in memos early in our research, we reduce the likelihood that we will get lost in mountains of data—memo writing keeps us focused on our analyses and involved in our research.

Memo writing aids us in linking analytic interpretation with empirical reality. We bring raw data right into our memos so that we maintain those connections and examine them directly. Raw data from different sources provide the grist for making precise comparisons, fleshing out ideas, analyzing properties of categories, and seeing patterns. The first excerpt below is the first section of an early memo. I wrote this memo quickly in 1983 after comparing data from a series of recent interviews.[12]

Developing a Dual Self

The dual self in this case is the *contrast* between the *sick self* and the *monitoring self* (actually *physical* self might be a better term [than *sick self*] since some of these people try to see themselves as "well" but still feel they must constantly monitor in order to maintain that status—they also rather easily sink into self-blame when the monitoring doesn't work).

With Sara S. we see definite conversations held between the physical and monitoring self. Through her learning time or body education, self-taught and self-validated she has not only developed a sense of what her body "needs" she has developed a finely honed *sense of timing* about how to handle those needs.

With the dual self, the monitoring self *externalizes* the internal messages from the physical self and makes them concrete. It is as if dialogue and negotiation with ultimate validation of the physical self take place between the two dimensions of the dual self. Consequently, the competent monitoring self must be able to attend to the messages given by the physical self. The learning time is the necessary amount of concentration, trial and error to become an effective monitoring self.

Mark R., for example, illustrates the kind of dialogue that takes place between the monitoring and physical selves when he talks about person to kidney talks and what is needed to sustain that new transplanted kidney in his body.

The dual self in many ways is analogous to the dialogue that Mead describes between the I and the me. The me monitors and attends to the I which is creating, experiencing, feeling. The monitoring me defines those feelings, impulses and sensations. It evaluates them and develops a line of action so that what is defined as needed is taken care of. The physical self here is then taken as an object held up to view which can be compared with past physical (or for that matter, psychological selves), with perceived statuses of others, with a defined level of health or well-being, with signals of potential crises etc.

A consequence of the monitoring self is that it may be encouraged by practitioners (after all, taking responsibility for one's body is the message these days, isn't it?) when it seems to "work," yet it may be condemned when the person's tactics for monitoring conflict with practitioners' notions of reasonable action or are unsuccessful.

The following passage shows how the memo appeared in the published version of the research (Charmaz, 1991). The combination of analytic clarity and empirical grounding makes the memo above remarkably congruent with the published excerpt. Memos record researchers' stages of analytic development. Memo writing helps researchers (a) to grapple with ideas about the data, (b) to set an analytic course, (c) to refine categories, (d) to define the relationships among various categories, and (e) to gain a sense of confidence and competence in their ability to analyze data.

Developing a Dialectical Self

The dialectical self is the contrast between the sick or physical self and the monitoring self. Keeping illness contained by impeding progression of illness, rather than merely hiding it, leads to developing a monitoring self. Developing a dialectical self means gaining a heightened awareness of one's body. People who do so believe that they perceive nuances of physical changes. By his second transplant, for example, Mark Reinertsen felt that he had learned to perceive the first signs of organ rejection.

When people no longer view themselves as "sick," they still monitor their physical selves to save themselves from further illness. To illustrate, Sara Shaw explained that she spent months of "learning time" to be able to discover what her body "needed" and how to handle those needs. She commented, "I got to know it [her ill body]; I got to understand it, and it was just me and mixed connective tissue disease [her diagnosis changed], you know, and I got to respect it and I got to know—to have a real good feeling for time elements and for what my body was doing, how my body was feeling." When I asked her what she meant by "time elements," she replied:

> There's times during the month, during the course of a month, when I'm much more susceptible, and I can feel it. I can wake up in the morning and I can feel it. . . . So I really learned what I was capable of and when I had to stop, when I had to slow down. And I learned to like—give and take with that. And I think that's all programmed in my mind now, and I don't even have to think about it now, you know; I'll know. I'll know when, no matter what's going on, I've gotta go sit

down . . . and take it easy, . . . that's a requirement of that day. And so consequently, I really don't get sick.

In the dialectical self, the monitoring self externalizes the internal messages from the physical self and makes them concrete. It is as if dialogue and negotiation with ultimate validation of the physical self take place. For example, Mark Reinertsen engaged in "person to kidney" talks to encourage the new kidney to remain with him (see also McGuire and Kantor 1987). A competent monitoring self attends to messages from the physical self and over time, as Sara Shaw's comment suggests, monitoring becomes taken for granted.

In many ways, the dialectical self is analogous to the dialogue that Mead (1934) describes between the "I" and the "me." The "me" monitors and attends to the "I" that creates, experiences, and feels. The monitoring "me" defines the "I's" behaviors, feelings, impulses, and sensations. It evaluates them and plans action to meet defined needs. Here, an ill person takes his or her physical self as an object, appraises it and compares it with past physical selves, with perceived health statuses of others, with ideals of physical or mental well-being, with signals of potential crises and so forth (cf. Gadow 1982).

The dialectical self is one of ill people's multiple selves emerging in the face of uncertainty. Whether or not ill people give the dialectical self validity significantly affects their actions. For someone like Sara Shaw, the dialectical self provided guidelines for organizing time, for taking jobs, and for developing relationships with others. With jobs, she believed that she had to guard herself from the stress of too many demands. With friends, she felt she had to place her needs first. With physicians, she resisted their control since she trusted her knowledge about her condition more than theirs.

Practitioners may encourage a monitoring self when it seems to "work," yet condemn it when unsuccessful, or when monitoring tactics conflict with their advice (cf. Kleinman 1988). The development of the dialectical self illuminates the active stance that some people take toward their illnesses and their lives. In short, the dialectical self helps people to keep illness in the background of their lives. (Charmaz, 1991, pp. 70-72)

Note the change in the title of the category in the published version. This change reflects my attempt to choose terms that best portrayed the empirical descriptions that the category subsumed. I was trying to address the liminal relationship certain respondents described with their bodies in which they gained a heightened awareness of cues that other people disavow, disregard, or do not discern. The term *dialectical self* denotes a more dynamic process than does the term *dual self.*

Although many grounded theorists concentrate on overt actions and statements, I also look for subjects' unstated assumptions and implicit meanings.[13] Then I ask myself how these assumptions and meanings relate to conditions in which a category emerges. For example, some people with chronic illnesses assumed that their bodies had become alien and hostile battlegrounds where they warred with illness. Their assumptions about having alien bodies and being at war with illness affected if and how they adapted to their situations. When I developed the category "surrendering to the sick body," I asked what conditions fostered surrendering (Charmaz, 1995b). I identified three: (a) "relinquishing the quest for control over one's body," (b) "giving up notions of victory over illness," and (c) "affirming, however implicitly, that one's self is tied to the sick body" (p. 672).

Theoretical Sampling

As we grounded theorists refine our categories and develop them as theoretical constructs, we likely find gaps in our data and holes in our theories. Then we go back to the field and collect delimited data to fill those conceptual gaps and holes—we conduct theoretical sampling. At this point, we choose to sample specific issues only; we look for precise information to shed light on the emerging theory.

Theoretical sampling represents a defining property of grounded theory and relies on the comparative methods within grounded theory. We use theoretical sampling to develop our emerging categories and to make them more definitive and useful. Thus the aim of this sampling is to refine *ideas*, not to increase the size of the original sample. Theoretical sampling helps us to identify conceptual boundaries and pinpoint the fit and relevance of our categories.

Although we often sample people, we may sample scenes, events, or documents, depending on the study and where the theory leads us. We may return to the same settings or individuals to gain further information. I filled out my initial analysis of one category, "living one day at a time," by going back to respondents with whom I had conducted earlier interviews. I had already found that people with chronic illnesses took living one day at time as a strategy to maintain some control over their uncertain lives. Only by going back to selected respondents did I learn that this strategy also had consequences for how they viewed the future when they later allowed themselves to think of it. The passage of time and the events that had filled it allowed them to give up earlier cherished plans and anticipated futures without being devastated by loss.

Theoretical sampling is a pivotal part of the development of formal theory. Here, the level of abstraction of the emerging theory has explanatory power across substantive areas because the processes and concepts within it are abstract and generic (Prus, 1987). Thus we would seek comparative data in substantive areas through theoretical sampling to help us tease out less visible properties of our concepts and the conditions and limits of their applicability. For example, I address identity loss in several analyses of the experience of illness. I could refine my concepts by looking at identity loss in other situations, such as bereavement and involuntary unemployment. Comparative analysis of people who experience unanticipated identity gains, such as unexpected job promotions, could also net conceptual refinements.

The necessity of engaging in theoretical sampling means that we researchers cannot produce a solid grounded theory through one-shot interviewing in a single data collection phase. Instead, theoretical sampling demands that we have completed the work of comparing data with data and have developed a provisional set of relevant categories for explaining our data. In turn, our categories take us back to the field to gain more insight about when, how, and to what extent they are pertinent and useful.

Theoretical sampling helps us to define the properties of our categories; to identify the contexts in which they are relevant; to specify the conditions under which they arise, are maintained, and vary; and to discover their consequences. Our emphasis on studying process combined with theoretical sampling to delineate the limits of our categories also helps us to define gaps between categories. Through using comparative methods, we specify the conditions under which they are linked to other categories. After we decide which categories best explain what is happening in our study, we treat them as concepts. In this sense, these concepts are useful for helping us to understand many incidents or issues in the data (Strauss & Corbin, 1990). Strauss (personal communication, February 1, 1993) advocates theoretical sampling early in the research. I recommend conducting it later in order that relevant data and analytic directions emerge without being forced. Otherwise, early theoretical sampling may bring premature closure to the analysis.

Grounded theory researchers take the usual criteria of "saturation" (i.e., new data fit into the categories already devised) of their categories for ending the research (Morse, 1995). But what does saturation mean? In practice, saturation seems elastic (see also Flick, 1998; Morse, 1995). Grounded theory approaches are seductive because they allow us to gain a handle on our material quickly. Is the handle we gain the best or most complete one? Does it encourage us to look deeply enough? The data in works claiming to be grounded theory pieces range from a handful of cases to sustained field research. The latter more likely fulfills the criterion of saturation and, moreover, has the resonance of intimate familiarity with the studied world.

As we define our categories as saturated (and some of us never do), we rewrite our memos in expanded, more analytic form. We put these memos to work for lectures, presentations, papers, and chapters. The analytic work continues as we sort and order memos, for we may discover gaps or new relationships.

Computer-Assisted Analysis

Computer-assisted techniques offer some shortcuts for coding, sorting, and integrating the data. Several programs, including NUD•IST and the Ethnograph, are explicitly aimed at assisting in grounded theory analyses. HyperResearch, a program designed to retrieve and group data, serves qualitative sociologists across a broad range of analytic applications.[14] Such programs can prove enormously helpful with the problem of mountains of data—that is, data management. Amanda Coffey, Beverly Holbrook, and Paul Atkinson (1996) point out that other advantages of computer coding include the ability to do multiple searches using more than one code word simultaneously and the fact that it enables researchers to place memos at points in the text. Data analysis programs are also effective for mapping relationships visually onscreen. They do not, however, think for the analyst—perhaps to chagrin of some students (see also Seidel, 1991). Nonetheless, Thomas J. Richards and Lyn Richards (1994) argue that the code-and-retrieve method supports the emergence of theory by searching the data for codes and assembling ideas. Further, Renata Tesch (1991) notes that conceptual operations follow or accompany mechanical data management.

Qualitative analysis software programs do not escape controversy. Coffey et al. (1996) and Lonkila (1995) express concern about qualitative programs based on conceptions of grounded theory methods and their uncritical adoption by users. They fear that these programs overemphasize coding and promote a superficial view of grounded theory; they also note that mechanical operations are no substitute for nuanced interpretive analysis. However, Nigel G. Fielding and Raymond M. Lee (1998) do not find substantial empirical evidence for such concerns in their systematic field study of users' experiences with computer-assisted qualitative data analysis programs.[15] I still have some reservations about these programs for four reasons: (a) Grounded theory methods are often poorly understood; (b) these methods have long been used to *legitimate,* rather than to conduct, studies; (c) these software packages appear more suited for objectivist grounded theory than constructivist approaches; and (d) the programs may unintentionally foster an illusion that interpretive work can be reduced to a set of procedures. Yvonna Lincoln (personal communication, August 21, 1998) asks her students, "Why would you want to engage in work that connects you to the deepest part of human existence and then turn it over to a machine to 'mediate'?" Part of interpretive work is gaining a sense of the whole—the whole interview, the whole story, the whole body of data. No matter how helpful computer programs may prove for managing the parts, we can see only their fragments on the screen.[16] And these fragments may seem to take on an existence of their own, as if objective and removed from their contextual origins and from our constructions and interpretations. Because objectivist grounded theory echoes positivism, computer-assisted programs based on it may promote widespread acceptance not just of the software, but of a one-dimensional view of qualitative research.

◆ Critical Challenges to Grounded Theory

As is evident from the discussion above, recent debates have resulted in reassessments of grounded theory. Objectivist grounded theory has shaped views of what the method is and where it can take qualitative research. Over the years, a perception of how leading proponents have used grounded theory has become melded with the methods themselves. Subsequently, critics make assumptions about the nature of the method and its limitations (see, e.g., Conrad, 1990; Riessman, 1990a, 1990b). Riessman (1990a) states that grounded theory methods were insufficient to respect her interviewees and to portray their stories. Richardson (1993) found prospects of completing a grounded theory analysis to be alienating and turned to literary forms. Richardson (1994) also has observed that qualitative research reports are not so straightforward as their authors represent them to be. Authors choose evidence selectively, clean up subjects' statements, unconsciously adopt value-laden metaphors, assume omniscience, and bore readers.

These criticisms challenge authors' representations of their subjects, their authority to interpret subjects' lives, and their writer's voice, criticisms ethnographers have answered (see, e.g., Best, 1995; Dawson & Prus, 1995; Kleinman, 1993; Sanders, 1995; Snow & Morrill, 1993). These criticisms imply that grounded theory methods gloss over meanings within respondents' stories.[17] Conrad (1990) and Riessman (1990b) suggest that "fracturing the data" in grounded theory research might limit understanding because grounded theorists aim for analysis rather than the portrayal of subjects' experience in its fullness. From a grounded theory perspective, fracturing the data means creating codes and categories as the researcher defines themes within the data. Glaser and Strauss (1967) propose this strategy for several reasons: (a) to help the researcher avoid remaining immersed in anecdotes and stories, and subsequently unconsciously adopting subjects' perspectives; (b) to prevent the researcher's becoming immobilized and overwhelmed by voluminous data; and (c) to create a way for the researcher to organize and interpret data. However, criticisms of fracturing the data imply that grounded theory methods lead to separating the experience from the experiencing subject, the meaning from the story, and the viewer from the viewed.[18] In short, the criticisms assume that the grounded theory method (a) limits entry into subjects' worlds, and thus reduces understanding of their experience; (b) curtails representation of both the social world and subjective experience; (c) relies upon the viewer's authority as expert observer; and (d) posits a set of objectivist procedures on which the analysis rests.[19]

Researchers can use grounded theory methods to further their knowledge of subjective experience and to expand its representation while neither remaining external from it nor accepting objectivist assumptions and procedures. A constructivist grounded theory assumes that people create and maintain meaningful worlds through dialectical processes of conferring meaning on their realities and acting within them (Bury, 1986; Mishler, 1981). Thus social reality does not exist independent of human action. Certainly, my approach contrasts with a number of grounded theory studies, methodological statements, and research texts (see, e.g., Chenitz & Swanson, 1986; Glaser, 1992; Martin & Turner, 1986; Strauss & Corbin, 1990; Turner, 1981). By adopting a constructivist grounded theory approach, the researcher can move grounded theory methods further into the realm of interpretive social science consistent with a Blumerian (1969) emphasis on meaning, without assuming the existence of a unidimensional external reality. A constructivist grounded theory recognizes the interactive nature of both data collection and analysis, resolves recent criticisms of the method, and reconciles positivist assumptions and postmodernist critiques. Moreover, a constructivist grounded theory fosters the development of qualitative traditions through the study of experience from the standpoint of those who live it.

The Place of Grounded Theory in Qualitative Research

Grounded theory research fits into the broader traditions of fieldwork and qualitative analysis. Most grounded theory studies rely on detailed qualitative materials collected through field, or ethnographic, research, but they are not ethnographies in the sense of total immersion into specific communities. Nor do grounded theorists attempt to study the social structures of whole communities. Instead, we tend to look at slices of social life. Like other forms of qualitative research, grounded theories can only portray moments in time. However, the grounded theory quest for the study of basic social processes fosters the identification of connections between events. The social world is always in process, and the lives of the research subjects shift and change as their circumstances and they themselves change. Hence a grounded theorist—or, more broadly, a qualitative researcher—constructs a picture that draws from, reassembles, and renders subjects' lives. The product is more like a painting than a photograph (Charmaz, 1995a). I come close to Atkinson's (1990, p. 2) depiction of ethnography as an "artful product" of objectivist description, careful organization, and interpretive commentary. The tendency to reify the findings and the picture of reality may result more from interpreters of the work than from its author.[20] Significantly, however, many researchers who adopt grounded theory strategies do so precisely to construct objectivist— that is, positivist—qualitative studies.

Grounded theory provides a systematic analytic approach to qualitative analysis of ethnographic materials because it consists of a set of explicit strategies. Any reasonably well-trained researcher can employ these strategies and develop an analysis. The strengths of grounded theory methods lie in (a) strategies that guide the researcher step by step through an analytic process, (b) the self-correcting nature of the data collection process, (c) the methods' inherent bent toward theory and the simultaneous turning away from acontextual description, and (d) the emphasis on comparative methods. Yet, like other qualitative approaches, grounded theory research is an emergent process rather than the product of a single research problem logically and deductively sequenced into a study—or even one logically and inductively sequenced. The initial research questions may be concrete and descriptive, but the researcher can develop deeper analytic questions by studying his or her data. Like wondrous gifts waiting to be opened, early grounded theory texts imply that categories and concepts inhere within the data, awaiting the researcher's discovery (Charmaz, 1990, 1995c). Not so. Glaser (1978, 1992) assumes that we can gather our data unfettered by bias or biography. Instead, a constructivist approach recognizes that the categories, concepts, and theoretical level of an analysis emerge from the researcher's interactions within the field and questions about the data. In short, the narrowing of research questions, the creation of concepts and categories, and the integration of the constructed theoretical framework reflect what and how the researcher thinks and does about shaping and collecting the data.

The grounded theorist's analysis tells a story about people, social processes, and situations. The researcher composes the story; it does not simply unfold before the eyes of an objective viewer. This story reflects the viewer as well as the viewed. Grounded theory studies typically lie between traditional research methodology and the recent postmodernist turn. Radical empiricists shudder at grounded theorists' contamination of the story because we shape the data collection and redirect our analyses as new issues emerge. Now postmodernists and poststructuralists castigate the story as well. They argue that we compose our stories unconsciously, deny the oedipal logic of authorial desire (Clough, 1992), and deconstruct the subject. In addition, Denzin (1992a) states that even the new interpretive approaches "privilege the researcher over the subject, method over subject matter, and maintain commitments to outmoded conceptions of validity, truth, and generalizability" (p. 20). These criticisms apply to much grounded theory research. Yet we can use them to make our empirical research more reflexive and our completed studies more contextually situated. We can claim only to have interpreted *a* reality, as we understood both our own experience and our subjects' portrayals of theirs.

A re-visioned grounded theory must take epistemological questions into account. Grounded theory can provide a path for researchers who want to continue to develop qualitative traditions without adopting the positivistic trappings of objectivism and universality. Hence the further development of a constructivist grounded theory can bridge past positivism and a revised future form of interpretive inquiry. A revised grounded theory preserves realism through gritty, empirical inquiry and sheds positivistic proclivities by becoming increasingly interpretive.

In contradistinction to Clough's (1992) critique, ethnographies can refer to a feminist vision to construct narratives that do not claim to be literal representations of the real. A feminist vision allows emotions to surface, doubts to be expressed, and relationships with subjects to grow. Data collection becomes less formal, more immediate, and subjects' concerns take precedence over researchers' questions.

A constructivist grounded theory distinguishes between the real and the true. The constructivist approach does not seek truth—single, universal, and lasting. Still, it remains realist because it addresses human *realities* and assumes the existence of real worlds. However, neither human realities nor real worlds are unidimensional. We act within and upon our realities and worlds and thus develop dialectical relations among what we do, think, and feel. The constructivist approach assumes that what we take as real, as objective knowledge and truth, is based upon our perspective (Schwandt, 1994). The pragmatist underpinnings in symbolic interactionism emerge here. W. I. Thomas and Dorothy Swaine Thomas (1928) proclaim, "If human beings define their situations as real, they are real in consequences" (p. 572). Following their theorem, we must try to find what research participants define as real and where their definitions of reality take them. The constructivist approach also fosters our self-consciousness about what we attribute to our subjects and how, when, and why researchers portray these definitions as real. Thus the research products do not constitute the reality of the respondents' reality. Rather, each is a rendering, one interpretation among multiple interpretations, of a shared or individual reality. That interpretation is objectivist only to the extent that it seeks to construct analyses that show how respondents and the social scientists who study them construct those realities—*without viewing those realities as unidimensional, universal, and immutable.* Researchers' attention to detail in the constructivist approach sensitizes them to multiple realities and the multiple viewpoints within them; it does not represent a quest to capture a single reality.

Thus we can recast the obdurate character of social life that Blumer (1969) talks about. In doing so, we change our conception of it from a real world to be discovered, tracked, and categorized to a world *made real* in the minds and through the words and actions of its members. Thus the grounded theorist constructs an image of *a* reality, not *the* reality—that is, objective, true, and external.

◆ Objectivist Versus Constructivist Grounded Theory

A constructivist grounded theory recognizes that the viewer creates the data and ensuing analysis through interaction with the viewed. Data do not provide a window on reality. Rather, the "discovered" reality arises from the interactive process and its temporal, cultural, and structural contexts. Researcher and subjects frame that interaction and confer meaning upon it. The viewer then is part of what is viewed rather than separate from it. What a viewer sees shapes what he or she will define, measure, and analyze. Because objectivist (i.e., the majority of) grounded theorists depart from this position, this crucial difference reflects the positivist leanings in their studies.[21]

Causality is suggestive, incomplete, and indeterminate in a construc- tivist grounded theory. Therefore, a grounded theory remains open to refinement. It looks at how "variables" are grounded—given meaning and played out in subjects' lives (Dawson & Prus, 1995; Prus, 1996). Their meanings and actions take priority over researchers' analytic interests and methodological technology. A constructivist grounded theory seeks to define conditional statements that interpret how subjects construct their realities. Nonetheless, these conditional statements do not approach some level of generalizable truth. Rather, they constitute a set of hypotheses and concepts that other researchers can transport to similar research problems and to other substantive fields. As such, they answer Prus's (1987) call for the development and study of generic concepts. Thus the grounded theo- rist's hypotheses and concepts offer both explanation and understanding and fulfill the pragmatist criterion of usefulness.

In contrast, objectivist grounded theorists adhere more closely to pos- itivistic canons of traditional science (see Glaser, 1978, 1992; Glaser & Strauss, 1967; Strauss & Corbin, 1990, 1994; Wilson & Hutchinson, 1991).[22] They assume that following a systematic set of methods leads them to discover reality and to construct a provisionally true, testable, and ultimately verifiable "theory" of it (Strauss, 1995; Strauss & Corbin, 1990, 1994).[23] This theory provides not only understanding but predic- tion. Three extensions of this position follow: (a) Systematic application of grounded theory strategies answers the positivist call for reliability and validity, because specifying procedures permits reproducibility;[24] (b) hypothesis testing in grounded theory leads to confirmation or disconfirmation of the emerging theory; and (c) grounded theory methods allow for the exertion of controls, and therefore make changing the studied reality possible.

Objectivist grounded theory accepts the positivistic assumption of an external world that can be described, analyzed, explained, and predicted: truth, but with a small *t*. That is, objectivist grounded theory is modifiable as conditions change. It assumes that different observers will discover this world and describe it in similar ways. That's correct—to the extent that subjects have comparable experiences (e.g., people with different chronic illnesses may experience uncertainty, intrusive regimens, medical dominance) and viewers bring similar questions, perspectives, methods, and, subsequently, concepts to analyze those experiences. Objectivist grounded theorists often share assumptions with their research participants— particularly the professional participants. Perhaps more likely, they assume that respondents share their meanings. For example, Strauss and Corbin's (1990) discussion of independence and dependence assumes that these terms hold the same meanings for patients as for researchers.

Guidelines such as those offered by Strauss and Corbin (1990) structure objectivist grounded theorists' work. These guidelines are didactic and prescriptive rather than emergent and interactive. Clinton Sanders (1995) refers to grounded theory procedures as "more rigorous than thou instructions about how information should be pressed into a mold" (p. 92). Strauss and Corbin categorize steps in the process with scientific terms such as *axial coding* and *conditional matrix* (Strauss, 1987; Strauss & Corbin, 1990, 1993). As grounded theory methods become more articulated, categorized, and elaborated, they seem to take on a life of their own. Guidelines turn into procedures and are reified into immutable rules, unlike Glaser and Strauss's (1967) original flexible strategies. By taking grounded theory methods as prescriptive scientific rules, proponents further the positivist cast to objectivist grounded theory.

Given the positivist bent in objectivist grounded theory, where might a constructivist approach take us? How might it reconcile both positivist leanings and postmodernist critiques in grounded theory? A constructivist grounded theory lies between postmodernist (Denzin, 1991; Krieger, 1991; Marcus & Fischer, 1986; Tyler, 1986) and postpositivist approaches to qualitative research (Rennie, Phillips, & Quartaro, 1988;

Turner, 1981). Researchers no longer provide a solitary voice rendering the dialogue only from their standpoints. Constructivists aim to include multiple voices, views, and visions in their rendering of lived experience. How does one accomplish this?

◆ Constructing Constructivism

What helps researchers develop a constructivist grounded theory? How might they shape the data collection and analysis phases? Gaining depth and understanding in their work means that they can fulfill Blumer's (1969) call for "intimate familiarity" with respondents and their worlds (see also Lofland & Lofland, 1984, 1995). In short, constructing constructivism means seeking meanings—both respondents' meanings and researchers' meanings.

To seek respondents' meanings, we must go further than surface meanings or presumed meanings. We must look for views and values as well as for acts and facts. We need to look for beliefs and ideologies as well as situations and structures. By studying tacit meanings, we clarify, rather than challenge, respondents' views about reality.[25]

A constructivist approach necessitates a relationship with respondents in which they can cast their stories in their terms. It means listening to their stories with openness to feeling and experience. In my studies of chronic illness, several people mentioned that they saw me as someone to whom they could express their private thoughts and feelings. Sometimes, however, researchers frame their questions in ways that cloak raw experience and mute feelings. In studies that tap suffering, we may unwittingly give off cues that we do not welcome respondents' going too deep. Furthermore, one-shot interviewing lends itself to a partial, sanitized view of experience, cleaned up for public discourse. The very structure of an interview may preclude private thoughts and feelings from emerging. Such a structure reinforces whatever proclivities a respondent has to tell only the public version of the story. Researchers' sustained involvement with research participants lessens these problems.

The conceptual level of coding, writing memos, and developing categories likely differ in objectivist and constructivist grounded theory. For example, Strauss and Corbin (1990, 1998) stick close to their depiction of overt data. I aim to understand the assumptions underlying the data by piecing them together. For example, "living one day at a time" is a taken-for-granted explanation of how one manages troubles. Everyone knows what living one day at a time is. But what does it assume? Ill people report living one day at a time or having good days and bad days as self-evident facts. Not until they are asked what these terms mean experientially—that is, how they affect their relating to time, what feelings these experiences elicit, and so on—do they start to define a form and content for "living one day at a time" or "good" and "bad" days.

Objectivist grounded theory studies may offer rich description and make conditional statements, but they may remain outside of the experience. Furthermore, objectivist grounded theory methods foster externality by invoking procedures that increase complexity at the expense of experience. Axial coding can lead to awkard scientistic terms and clumsy categories. Terms and categories take center stage and distance readers from the experience, rather than concentrate their attention upon it. Processual diagrams and conceptual maps can result in an overly complex architecture that obscures experience. Any form of grounded theory can generate jargon. Objectivist grounded theory especially risks cloaking analytic power in jargon.

Making our categories consistent with studied life helps to keep that life in the foreground. Active codes and subsequent categories preserve images of experience. For example, in my discussion of immersion in illness, my categories were "Recasting Life," "Facing Dependency," "Pulling In," "Slipping Into Illness Routines," and "Weathering a Serious Episode."[26]

Coding and categorizing processes sharpen the researcher's ability to ask questions about the data. Different questions can flow from objectivist and constructivist starting points. These questions can be concrete, as described by Strauss and Corbin (1990, 1998), or more abstract. Concrete questions are revealed in their discussion of two categories—pain experience and pain relief: "Who gives pain relief to people with arthritis?" "What gives relief?" "How is the pain experienced and handled?" "How much relief is needed?" "When does the pain occur and when does she institute relief?" "Why is pain relief important?" (1990, pp. 78-79). Here the categories take on an objective, external character—objective because these questions assume answers that reflect "facts"; objective because the answers assume that the researcher discovers what being in pain "really is all about"; objective because the topic of pain now takes on an external character that can be identified, addressed, and managed.

In contrast, I start by viewing the topic of pain subjectively as a feeling, an experience that may take a variety of forms. Then I ask these questions:

What makes pain, pain? (That is, what is essential to the phenomenon as defined by those who experience it?) What defining properties or characteristics do ill people attribute to it? When do they do so? These questions lead into a question I share with Strauss and Corbin (1990, 1998): How does the person experience this pain, and what, if anything, does he or she do about it? My questions aim to get at meaning, not at truth. As a result, a constructivist grounded theory may remain at a more intuitive, impressionistic level than an objectivist approach.

My version of grounded theory fosters the researcher's viewing the data afresh, again and again, as he or she develops new ideas. Researchers can code and recode data numerous times (see also Glaser & Strauss, 1967). Posing new questions to the data results in new analytic points. I go back and forth between data and the drafts of chapters or papers many times. I take explicit findings in certain interviews and see if they remain implicit in other interviews. Then I go back to respondents and ask specific questions around the new category. For example, when I returned to a young woman with colitis to ask how the slow, monotonous time of convalescence might seem in memory, she understood my line of questioning immediately and cut in without skipping a beat: "It seems like a wink" (Charmaz, 1991, p. 92).

Every qualitative researcher makes multiple analytic decisions. Foremost among these is how much complexity to introduce. How much is necessary to convey the story with depth and clarity? How much seems like hairsplitting that will irritate or confuse the reader? At what point does collapsing categories result in conceptual muddiness and oversimplification? To achieve the right level of complexity, we must know the potential audience and sense the appropriate style and level at which to write for it.

◆ Rendering Through Writing

The analysis of qualitative data does not cease when the grounded theorist has developed a theoretical framework; it proceeds into the writing (Mitchell & Charmaz, 1996). A grounded theorist's proclivities toward objectivism or constructivism also come through in his or her writing about the research. The image of a scientific laboratory comes to mind with objectivist grounded theory, reflected in carefully organized and stated written reports of concepts, evidence, and procedures. Constructivist grounded theory spawns an image of a writer at a desk who tries to balance theoretical interpretation with an evocative aesthetic. To illustrate how analysis proceeds into writing constructivist grounded theory, I provide several writing strategies and examples from earlier work.

As Laurel Richardson (1990) declares, writing matters. Consistent with the postmodernist turn, I attempt to evoke experiential feeling through how I render it in writing. This means taking the reader into a story and imparting its mood through linguistic style and narrative exposition. This strategy removes the writing from typical scientific format without transforming the final product into fiction, drama, or poetry. I frame key definitions and distinctions in words that reproduce the tempo and mood of the experience:

> *Existing* from day to day occurs when a person plummets into continued crises that rip life apart. (Charmaz, 1991, p. 185)

> Others wait to map a future. And wait. They monitor their bodies and their lives. They look for signs to indicate what steps to take next. They map a future or move to the next point on the map only when they feel assured that the worst of their illness is over. These people map a future or move to the next point when they feel distant enough from illness to release their emotions from it. (p. 191)

Analogies and metaphors can explicate tacit meanings and feelings subsumed within a category (see also Charmaz & Mitchell, 1996; Richardson, 1994):

> Such men and women feel coerced into living one day at a time. They force it upon themselves, almost with clenched teeth. Here, living one day at a time resembles learning an unfamiliar, disagreeable lesson in grammar school; it is an unwelcome prerequisite to staying alive. (Charmaz, 1991, p. 179)

> Drifting time, in contrast [to dragging time], spreads out. Like a fan, drifting time unfolds and expands during a serious immersion in illness. (p. 91)

Simple language and straightforward ideas make theory readable. Theory remains embedded in the narrative, in its many stories. The theory becomes more accessible but less identifiable as theory. Several strategies foster making the writing accessible. Catching experiential rhythm and timing allows the researcher to reproduce it within the writing:

> From embarrassment to mortification. From discomfort to pain. Endless uncertainty. What follows? Regimentation. (Charmaz, 1991, p. 134)

> Days slip by. The same day keeps slipping by. Durations of time lengthen since few events break up the day, week, or month. Illness seems like one long uninterrupted duration of time. (p. 88)

Questions help tie main ideas together or redirect the reader. Sometimes I adopt the role of a chronically ill person and ask questions as she would.

> Is it cancer? Could it be angina? Pangs of uncertainty spring up when current, frequently undiagnosed, symptoms could mean a serious chronic illness. (Charmaz, 1991, p. 32)

Immediacy draws the reader into the story. A story occurring in the present as if now unfolding draws the reader in. I sacrificed immediacy for accuracy by writing about respondents in the past because the events described took place in the past.[27] Where authors place their stories and how they frame them can bring experience to life or wholly obscure it.

A mix of concrete detail with analytic categories connects the familiar with the unfamiliar or even esoteric. Thus I kept material in *Good Days, Bad Days* (Charmaz, 1991) that had been covered before, such as the chapter on living with chronic illness. I took the reader through messy houses, jumbled schedules, pressures to simplify life, fragile pacing, and enormous efforts to function to the relief when remission occurs. This detail gave readers imagery on which to build when I moved into a more elusive analysis of time.

Writers use a linear logic to organize their analyses and make experience understandable. Yet experience is not necessarily linear, nor is it always readily drawn with clear boundaries. For example, experiencing illness, much less all its spiraling consequences, does not fit neatly into one general process. The grounded theory method emphasizes the analysis of a basic process the researcher discovers in the data. Although I pondered over organizing the book around one process, I could not identify an overarching theme. Experiencing illness consists of many processes, not a single process that subsumes others. Further, illness ebbs and flows.

Chronically ill people define periods of relative "health" as well as spells of sickness. Thus I chose to collapse time and experience to cover illness.

Written images portray the tone the writer takes toward the topic and reflect the writer's relationships with his or her respondents. I aim for curiosity without condescension, openness without voyeurism, and participation without domination. Maintaining balance is difficult, because I try to portray respondents' worlds and views. Throughout the research and writing of *Good Days, Bad Days,* I tried to go beyond respondents' public presentation of self in illness. Otherwise, the knotty problems, the fear and pain, the moral dilemmas and ambivalent decisions do not come through.

Writers makes moral choices about portraying respondents, designing how to tell their stories, and delineating ways to interpret them. These choices also lead to the researcher's assuming a role as the writer (Krieger, 1991). In my book, I remain in the background as a storyteller whose tales have believable characters, not as an omniscient social scientist. My tone, style, and imagery reduce omniscience. However, because I stayed with the conceptual categories and built the stories around them, my work remains consistent with grounded theory and much social scientific writing.

Revising a manuscript can result in changes in style, possibly even of genre. Carefully crafted grounded theory categories work well as signposts in professional journals. A book editor may delete all the subheadings in one quick read. As signposts go, the narrative style changes. A more straightforward scientific style recedes as a more literary style evolves. Of course, how one sees that style and whether one defines it as scientific or literary depends upon where one stands. The postmodernist may see this style as objectivist, realist, and scientific; the positivist may see it as disconcertingly literary. I agree with Atkinson (1990) that impressionist tales are often embedded in realist accounts. I try to pull readers in so they might sense and situate the feeling of the speaker in the story. Here, what Van Maanen (1988) calls impressionist tales sounds exactly what Clough (1992) calls "emotional realism." Perhaps, however, portraying moods, feelings, and views evokes an aesthetic verisimilitude of them.

◆ Summary and Conclusion

Given the analysis above, what conclusions can we draw about grounded theory studies? What might be the future of grounded theory? First, grounded theory methods evolve in different ways depending upon the perspectives and proclivities of their adherents. I aim to move researchers toward an explicitly constructivist approach. If we examine our epistemological premises, we can acknowledge the limits of our studies and the ways we shape them. In this way, adopting and refining grounded theory methods furthers the study of empirical worlds.

Second, we can reduce or resolve tensions between postmodernism and constructivist grounded theory when we use the former to illuminate and extend the latter. In short, postmodernism can *inform* realist study of experience rather than simply serve as justification for abandoning it. The postmodernist turn has forced renewed awareness of our relationships with and representation of subjects that will long influence qualitative research, possibly longer than the term *postmodernism* itself holds sway. Similarly, the importance of situating qualitative research in historical and cultural context is underscored. We grounded theorists can profit from the current trend toward linguistic and rhetorical analysis by becoming more reflexive about how we frame and write our studies. This trend supports constructivist approaches in grounded theory because it explicitly treats authors' works *as* constructions instead of as objectified products.

Third, the future of grounded theory lies with both objectivist and constructivist visions. Scientific institutions and conventions are unlikely to undergo rapid change. Granting agencies and tenure review committees may long favor objectivist work over constructivist craft. The qualitative revolution has opened up possibilities and potentials, but gatekeepers are likely to reward scholars whose work comes closest to their own. Thus, we can expect to see growing numbers of large studies with small qualitative components and more team projects in multiple sites. Does this mean that constructivist grounded theory will wither and wane? No. The trend toward interpretive study, the quest for understanding, and the challenge to the imagination impel us to take our inquiry into the world. Through sharing the worlds of our subjects, we come to conjure an image of their constructions and of our own.

◆ Notes

1. For my comparisons of objectivist and constructivist grounded theory, see the section below headed "Objectivist Versus Constructivist Grounded Theory."

2. For example, in his definitive study of natural recovery from heroin addiction, Patrick Biernacki (1986) controlled his referral chains for obtaining interviews for sam-

pling, theoretical, and verificational considerations (pp. 214-219). Some colleagues have placed Biernacki's work in the emerging postmodern ethnography. However, in our conversations before he died, it was clear that he saw his work as realist qualitative research in which the investigator tries to achieve accurate reporting of a world. We both agreed that my use of grounded theory is more phenomenological and constructivist than his own. Anselm Strauss made the same assessment of my work relative to his (Strauss's) as well.

3. Lindesmith (1947) and Cressey (1953) both attempted earlier to codify analytic methods for qualitative research through analytic induction. Their work has been preserved in the criminology and deviance literatures but has faded in general methodological discussions.

4. Juliet Corbin has a strong background and a doctorate in nursing science. She has long been a leader in the establishment of qualitative methods in nursing; since the publication of *Basics*, she has attained prominence in the social sciences and other professions as well.

5. To illustrate, when discussing conceptualizing data as the first step in analysis, Strauss and Corbin (1990) provide the following hypothetical example from a restaurant: "While waiting for your dinner, you notice a lady in red. She appears to be just standing there in the kitchen, but your common sense tells you that a restaurant wouldn't pay a lady in red just to stand there, especially in a busy kitchen. Your curiosity is piqued, so you decide to do an inductive analysis to see if you can determine just what her job is. (Once a grounded theorist, always a grounded theorist).

"You notice that she is intently looking around the kitchen area, **a work site**, focusing here and then there, taking a mental note of what is going on. *You ask yourself, what is she doing here? Then you label it* **watching**. Watching what? **Kitchen work**" (pp. 63-64).

This example continues in the same vein. It relies on careful observation of the overt behavior of the woman in the restaurant, from the objective observer's viewpoint. It does not take into account what that reality is like from the perspective of the restaurant worker. Nor do the categories develop from comparative study of other restaurants.

6. Anselm Strauss critiqued the draft of my 1995 paper on grounded theory in which I then claimed that grounded theory is not verificational (Charmaz, 1995c). He said that I was wrong.

7. For example, when writing about "mutual pretense," Glaser and Strauss (1965) state: "This particular awareness context cannot exist, of course, unless both the patient and staff are aware that he is dying. Therefore all the structural conditions which contribute to the existence of open awareness (and which are absent in closed and suspicion awareness) contribute also to the existence of mutual pretense. In addition, at least one interactant must indicate a desire to pretend that the patient is not dying and the other must agree to the pretense, acting accordingly" (p. 67). Corbin and Strauss (1987) also adopt a distanced voice in the following passage: "The impact of body failure and consequent performance failure can be measured by the impact that it has on each dimension of the BBC (biographical body conceptions). Since each dimension (biographical time, body, self conceptions) exists in a tightly bound relationship with the other, the consequences of body failure with regard to one aspect are further felt with the other two. It is the combined impact of the three aspects of the BBC that profoundly affects biographical continuity and meaning" (p. 260). Several of Corbin and Strauss's works on chronic illness, such as *Unending Work and Care* (1988), read as if much less distanced than other works. Two factors may contribute to the

difference: Strauss's experience with chronic illness and Corbin's direct involvement in data gathering.

8. Stern (1994a) agrees. She sees recent developments in grounded theory methods as eroding the method and the power of the subsequent analyses.

9. For a more developed discussion of how to do constructivist grounded theory, see Charmaz (1995c).

10. Grounded theorists work up and out from data. Not every qualitative researcher does. Rena Lederman (1990) observes that some anthropologists avoid using their field notes when developing their finished work. She writes of how anthropological field notes fulfill different functions for the researcher while he or she is away in the field and later, when the researcher is home. Ethnographers write as both close to and distant from their respondents while in the field, but their loyalties shift to the professional community when they reach home. Then the same field notes that provided a concrete grasp of reality in the field impart a sense of doubt. Lederman argues that conceptions of field notes as fixed and stable data crumble at this point. Instead, field notes can assume multiple meanings and are open to reinterpretation and contradiction.

11. Strauss's remarkably facile mind could not stop making comparisons. He taught students to compare unlikely categories of people, actions, settings, and organizations to tease out the properties of a category (see also Star, 1997).

12. The original memo was considerably longer and contained snippets of data throughout. The more distanced tone of the 1983 memo reflects my earlier socialization in writing and in grounded theory. It also reflects tensions between the relativism I adopted during my first year of graduate school and the objectivism in my grounded theory training (see Charmaz, 1983). By 1990, when *Good Days, Bad Days* went to press, this material reads as less distanced and more constructivist although it is essentially the same as the 1983 memo. In the interim, I came closer to integrating my realist intention to study empirical problems with the relativism inherent in constructivism (see Charmaz, 1990). In addition, I worked on making abstract ideas accessible.

13. I use the term *subjects* not because I view them as subordinate, or subjected to inquiry, but because the term *research participants* is so cumbersome.

14. For guidelines in choosing a data analysis software program, see Weitzman and Miles (1995).

15. However, recent listserv discussions of qualitative computer analysis indicate that some users still view the programs as too mechanical. For example, Aksel Hn Tjorca (MedSoc Listserv, November 17, 1998) found NUD•IST to be useful in sorting data initially but feared that hierarchical categories embedded in the program might work against the relational nature of the data.

16. To gain a sense of the whole on which we are working, we may need to have entire documents, if not the complete data set, before us. Yvonna Lincoln (personal communication, August 21, 1998) tells me that she works with all her data spread out on a large table. That way, she can gain a sense of the whole and, simultaneously, plan how to assemble the parts.

17. There are tensions between the constructivist assumptions of varied and problematic meaning and objectivist assumptions of the world as real, obdurate, external, and predictable. A constructivist grounded theory acknowledges realities of enduring worlds and tries to show how they are socially created through action, intention, and routine.

283

18. For a detailed report on how diverse scholars have responded to such concerns, see the 1992 debate in the *Journal of Contemporary Ethnography* about reality and interpretation in William Foote Whyte's *Street Corner Society* (Adler et al., 1992). Mariane Boelen (1992) challenges the veracity of Whyte's study and, by doing so, challenges reifications made of it (but not the notion of reifying ethnography itself). The responses to her challenge, however, range from accepting objectivist premises to questioning them (see Denzin, 1992b; Orlandella, 1992; Richardson, 1992; Vidich, 1992; Whyte, 1992). Vidich (1992) points out that Boelen assumes only one possible view of reality and that Whyte missed it. Denzin (1992b) and Richardson (1992), however, question the objectivist premises that both Whyte and Boelen share.

19. To my knowledge, those who raise these criticisms have not resolved them through using grounded theory. Their recommendations range from abandoning empirical study to moving toward narrative analysis. To the extent that narrative analysis focuses on or drifts into emphasizing the type and structure of the narrative rather than respondents' meanings, I fail to see it as a better alternative than grounded theory studies. Nor do I see recording respondents' statements in one-line stanzas as offering a better frame for meaning than interview excerpts.

20. An author may call attention to an issue, frame a manuscript on it, but assume that the one issue constitutes the entire empirical reality. For example, before my analyses of illness focused squarely on the self, I argued that loss of self is *a* fundamental form of suffering. Readers reified my argument and concluded that I erroneously saw loss of self as the only experience of illness (see Robinson, 1990).

21. Glaser and Strauss (1967; Glaser, 1992; Strauss, 1987) have long stated that the core issues become apparent in the research setting, as if any trained observer will discover them. Similarly, they write as if neither standpoint nor status affects what observers see and find.

22. For a good outline of positivist premises, see Denzin (1989).

23. Strauss and Corbin (1994) call for grounded theory advocates to abandon the quest for truth. However, they also make a strong case for aiming for verification, which assumes a quest for truth. In their 1994 chapter, they also affirm two points I raised earlier, that the researcher's analysis is an interactive product of the views of the researcher and the data, and that the early works are written as if the researcher discovers an external order in the data (see Charmaz, 1983, 1990).

24. Strauss and Corbin (1998) state that exact replication is not possible, but sufficient reproducibility is. They propose that other researchers with similar theoretical premises, data gathering procedures, and research conditions develop similar theoretical explanations.

25. By making our early drafts available to those subjects who wish to read them, we make it possible for them to challenge and correct our views.

26. It is important to distinguish when the actor has agency and when he or she is acted upon. A hazard of any inductive method such as the constructivist approach is overemphasis on the individual. The constructivist approach leads to a style that emphasizes the active, reflective actor. Yet larger social forces also act upon this actor. So the researcher needs to learn how these social forces affect the actor and what, if anything, the actor thinks, feels, and does about them.

27. See, in contrast, Catherine Riessman (1990a) for presenting stories in the present.

◆ References

Adler, P. A., Adler, P., & Johnson, J. M. (1992). New questions about old issues. *Journal of Contemporary Ethnography, 21,* 3-10.

Atkinson, P. A. (1990). *The ethnographic imagination: Textual constructions of reality.* London: Routledge.

Baszanger, I. (1998). *Inventing pain medicine: From the laboratory to the clinic.* New Brunswick, NJ: Rutgers University Press.

Best, J. (1995). Lost in the ozone again: The postmodernist fad and interactionist foibles. In N. K. Denzin (Ed.), *Studies in symbolic interaction: A research annual* (Vol. 17, pp. 125-134). Greenwich, CT: JAI.

Biernacki, P. L. (1986). *Pathways from heroin addiction: Recovery without treatment.* Philadelphia: Temple University Press.

Blumer, H. (1969). *Symbolic interactionism: Perspective and method.* Englewood Cliffs, NJ: Prentice Hall.

Boelen, W. A. M. (1992). *Street corner society*: Cornerville revisited. *Journal of Contemporary Ethnography, 21,* 11-51.

Bond, G. C. (1990). Fieldnotes: Research in past occurrences. In R. Sanjek (Ed.), *Fieldnotes: The makings of anthropology* (pp. 273-289). Ithaca, NY: Cornell University Press.

Bury, M. R. (1986). Social constructionism and the development of medical sociology. *Sociology of Health and Illness, 8,* 137-169.

Charmaz, K. (1983). The grounded theory method: An explication and interpretation. In R. M. Emerson (Ed.), *Contemporary field research* (pp. 109-126). Boston: Little, Brown.

Charmaz, K. (1990). Discovering chronic illness: Using grounded theory. *Social Science and Medicine, 30,* 1161-1172.

Charmaz, K. (1991). *Good days, bad days: The self in chronic illness and time.* New Brunswick, NJ: Rutgers University Press.

Charmaz, K. (1995a). Between positivism and postmodernism: Implications for methods. In N. K. Denzin (Ed.), *Studies in symbolic interaction: A research annual* (Vol. 17, pp. 43-72). Greenwich, CT: JAI.

Charmaz, K. (1995b). Body, identity, and self: Adapting to impairment. *Sociological Quarterly, 36,* 657-680.

Charmaz, K. (1995c). Grounded theory. In J. A. Smith, R. Harré, & L. Van Langenhove (Eds.), *Rethinking methods in psychology* (pp. 27-49). London: Sage.

Charmaz, K., & Mitchell, R. G. (1996). The myth of silent authorship: Self, substance, and style in ethnographic writing. *Symbolic Interaction, 19,* 285-302.

Chenitz, W. C., & Swanson, J. M. (Eds.). (1986). *From practice to grounded theory: Qualitative research in nursing.* Reading, MA: Addison-Wesley.

Clarke, A. E. (1998). *Disciplining reproduction: Modernity, American life sciences, and the problems of sex.* Berkeley: University of California Press.

Clough, P. T. (1992). *The end(s) of ethnography: From realism to social criticism.* Newbury Park, CA: Sage.

Coffey, A., Holbrook, B., & Atkinson, P. (1996). Qualitative data analysis: Technologies and representations. *Sociological Research Online, 1*(1). Available Internet: http://www.socresonline.org.uk/socresonline/1/1/4.html

Connelly, F. M., & Clandinin, D. J. (1990). Stories of experience and narrative inquiry. *Educational Researcher, 19*(5), 2-14.

Conrad, P. (1990). Qualitative research on chronic illness: A commentary on method and conceptual development. *Social Science and Medicine, 30,* 1257-1263.

Corbin, J., & Strauss, A. L. (1987). Accompaniments of chronic illness: Changes in body, self, biography, and biographical time. In J. A. Roth & P. Conrad (Eds.), *Research in the sociology of health care: The experience and management of chronic illness* (Vol. 6, pp. 249-282). Greenwich, CT: JAI.

Corbin, J., & Strauss, A. L. (1988). *Unending work and care: Managing chronic illness at home.* San Francisco: Jossey-Bass.

Cressey, D. R. (1953). *Other people's money: A study in the social psychology of embezzlement.* Glencoe, IL: Free Press.

Creswell, J. W. (1997). *Qualitative inquiry and research design: Choosing among five traditions.* Thousand Oaks, CA: Sage.

Dawson, L. L., & Prus, R. C. (1995). Postmodernism and linguistic reality versus symbolic interactionism and obdurate reality. In N. K. Denzin (Ed.), *Studies in symbolic interaction: A research annual* (Vol. 17, pp. 105-124). Greenwich, CT: JAI.

Denzin, N. K. (1989). *Interpretive interactionism.* Newbury Park, CA: Sage.

Denzin, N. K. (1991). *Images of postmodern society.* Newbury Park, CA: Sage.

Denzin, N. K. (1992a). The many faces of emotionality: Reading *Persona.* In C. Ellis & M. G. Flaherty (Eds.), *Investigating subjectivity: Research on lived experience* (pp. 17-30). Newbury Park, CA: Sage.

Denzin, N. K. (1992b). Whose Cornerville is it anyway? *Journal of Contemporary Ethnography, 21,* 120-132.

Denzin, N. K. (1994). The art and politics of interpretation. In N. K. Denzin & Y. S. Lincoln (Eds.), *Handbook of qualitative research* (pp. 500-515). Thousand Oaks, CA: Sage.

Denzin, N. K. (1996). Prophetic pragmatism and the postmodern: A comment on Maines. *Symbolic Interaction, 19,* 341-356.

Denzin, N. K. (1998). Review of *Pragmatism and feminism: Reweaving the social fabric. Symbolic Interaction, 21,* 221-223.

Denzin, N. K., & Lincoln, Y. S. (1994). Preface. In N. K. Denzin & Y. S. Lincoln (Eds.), *Handbook of qualitative research* (pp. ix-xii). Thousand Oaks, CA: Sage.

Fielding, N. G., & Lee, R. M. (1998). *Computer analysis and qualitative research.* London: Sage.

Flick, U. (1998). *An introduction to qualitative research: Theory, method and applications.* London: Sage.

Gadow, S. (1982). Body and self: A dialectic. In V. Kestenbaum (Ed.), *The humanity of the ill.* Knoxville: University of Tennessee Press.

Geertz, C. (1973). *The interpretation of cultures: Selected essays.* New York: Basic Books.

Glaser, B. G. (1978). *Theoretical sensitivity.* Mill Valley, CA: Sociology Press.

Glaser, B. G. (1992). *Basics of grounded theory analysis: Emergence vs. forcing.* Mill Valley, CA: Sociology Press.

Glaser, B. G. (Ed.). (1994). *More grounded theory: A reader.* Mill Valley, CA: Sociology Press.

Glaser, B. G. (1998, February 19). [Contribution to workshop]. In B. G. Glaser & P. Stern (Leaders), *Advanced grounded theory, workshop II.* Workshop conducted at the Qualitative Health Research Conference, Vancouver.

Glaser, B. G., & Strauss, A. L. (1965). *Awareness of dying.* Chicago: Aldine.

Glaser, B. G., & Strauss, A. L. (1967). *The discovery of grounded theory: Strategies for qualitative research.* Chicago: Aldine.

Glaser, B. G., & Strauss, A. L. (1968). *Time for dying.* Chicago: Aldine.

Guba, E. G., & Lincoln, Y. S. (1994). Competing paradigms in qualitative research. In N. K. Denzin & Y. S. Lincoln (Eds.), *Handbook of qualitative research* (pp. 105-117). Thousand Oaks, CA: Sage.

Johnson, J. L. (1991). Learning to live again: The process of adjustment. In J. M. Morse & J. L. Johnson (Eds.), *The illness experience: Dimensions of suffering* (pp.13-88). Newbury Park, CA: Sage.

Kleinman, A. (1988). *The illness narratives: Suffering, healing and the human condition.* New York: Basic Books.

Kleinman, S. (1993). The textual turn. *Contemporary Sociology, 22,* 11-13.

Krieger, S. (1991). *Social science and the self: Personal essays on an art form.* New Brunswick, NJ: Rutgers University Press.

Kuhn, T. S. (1970). *The structure of scientific revolutions* (2nd ed.). Chicago: University of Chicago Press.

Lederman, R. (1990). Pretexts for ethnography: On reading fieldnotes. In R. Sanjek (Ed.), *Fieldnotes: The makings of anthropology* (pp. 71-91). Ithaca, NY: Cornell University Press.

Lindesmith, A. R. (1947). *Opiate addiction.* Bloomington, IN: Principia.

Lofland, J., & Lofland, L. H. (1984). *Analyzing social settings* (2nd ed.). Belmont, CA: Wadsworth.

Lofland, J., & Lofland, L. H. (1995). *Analyzing social settings* (3rd ed.). Belmont, CA: Wadsworth.

Lofland, L. H. (1993). Fighting the good fight—again. *Contemporary Sociology, 22*, 1-3.

Lonkila, M. (1995). Grounded theory as an emerging paradigm for computer-assisted qualitative data analysis. In U. Kelle (Ed.), *Computer-aided qualitative data analysis: Theory, methods and practice* (pp. 41-51). London: Sage.

Maines, D. R. (1993). Narrative's moment and sociology's phenomena: Toward a narrative sociology. *Sociological Quarterly, 34*, 17-38.

Marcus, G. E., & Fischer, M. M. J. (1986). *Anthropology as cultural critique: An experimental moment in the human sciences.* Chicago: University of Chicago Press.

Martin, P. Y., & Turner, B. A. (1986). Grounded theory and organizational research. *Journal of Applied Behavioral Science, 22*, 141-157.

McGuire, M. B., & Kantor, D. J. (1987). Belief systems and illness experience. In J. A. Roth & P. Conrad (Eds.), *Research in the sociology of health care: The experience and management of chronic illness* (Vol. 6, pp. 241-248). Greenwich, CT: JAI.

Mead, G. H. (1934). *Mind, self, and society: From the standpoint of a social behaviorist* (C. W. Morris, Ed.). Chicago: University of Chicago Press.

Melia, K. M. (1996). Rediscovering Glaser. *Qualitative Health Research, 6*, 368-378.

Mishler, E. G. (1981). The social construction of illness. In E. G. Mishler, L. R. Amara Singham, S. T. Hauser, R. Liem, S. D. Osherson, & N. Waxler (Eds.), *Social contexts of health, illness and patient care* (pp. 141-168). New York: Cambridge University Press.

Mitchell, R. G., Jr., & Charmaz, K. (1996). Telling tales, writing stories: Postmodernist visions and realist images in ethnographic writing. *Journal of Contemporary Ethnography, 25*, 144-166.

Morse, J. M. (1995). The significance of saturation. *Qualitative Health Research, 5*, 147-149.

Orlandella, A. R. (1992). Boelen may know Holland, Boelen may know Barzini, but Boelen "doesn't know diddle about the North End!" *Journal of Contemporary Ethnography, 21*, 69-79.

Park, R. E., & Burgess, E. W. (1925). *The city.* Chicago: University of Chicago Press.

Prus, R. C. (1987). Generic social processes: Maximizing conceptual development in ethnographic research. *Journal of Contemporary Ethnography, 16*, 250-293.

Prus, R. C. (1996). *Symbolic interaction and ethnographic research: Intersubjectivity and the study of human lived experience.* Albany: State University of New York Press.

Reif, L. (1975). Ulcerative colitis: Strategies for managing life. In A. L. Strauss (Ed.), *Chronic illness and the quality of life* (pp. 81-89). St. Louis, MO: C. V. Mosby.

Rennie, D. L., Phillips, J. R., & Quartaro, G. K. (1988). Grounded theory: A promising approach to conceptualization in psychology? *Canadian Psychology, 29,* 139-150.

Richards, T. J., & Richards, L. (1994). Using computers in qualitative research. In N. K. Denzin & Y. S. Lincoln (Eds.), *Handbook of qualitative research* (pp. 445-462). Thousand Oaks, CA: Sage.

Richardson, L. (1990). *Writing strategies: Reaching diverse audiences.* Newbury Park, CA: Sage.

Richardson, L. (1992). Trash on the corner: Ethics and technography. *Journal of Contemporary Ethnography, 21,* 103-119.

Richardson, L. (1993). Interrupting discursive spaces: Consequences for the sociological self. In N. K. Denzin (Ed.), *Studies in symbolic interaction: A research annual* (Vol. 14, pp. 77-84). Greenwich, CT: JAI.

Richardson, L. (1994). Writing: A method of inquiry. In N. K. Denzin & Y. S. Lincoln (Eds.), *Handbook of qualitative research* (pp. 516-529). Thousand Oaks, CA: Sage.

Riessman, C. K. (1990a). *Divorce talk: Women and men make sense of personal relationships.* New Brunswick, NJ: Rutgers University Press.

Riessman, C. K. (1990b). Strategic uses of narrative in the presentation of self and illness: A research note. *Social Science and Medicine, 30,* 1195-1200.

Robinson, I. (1990). Personal narratives, social careers and medical courses: Analysing life trajectories in autobiographies of people with multiple sclerosis. *Social Science and Medicine, 30,* 1173-1186.

Robrecht, L. C. (1995). Grounded theory: Evolving methods. *Qualitative Health Research, 5,* 169-177.

Sanders, C. R. (1995). Stranger than fiction: Insights and pitfalls in post-modern ethnography. In N. K. Denzin (Ed.), *Studies in symbolic interaction: A research annual* (Vol. 17, pp. 89-104). Greenwich, CT: JAI.

Schatzman, L. (1991). Dimensional analysis: Notes on an alternative approach to the grounding of theory in qualitative research. In D. R. Maines (Ed.), *Social organization and social processes: Essays in honor of Anselm Strauss* (pp. 303-314). New York: Aldine de Gruyter.

Schwandt, T. A. (1994). Constructivist, interpretivist approaches to human inquiry. In N. K. Denzin & Y. S. Lincoln (Eds.), *Handbook of qualitative research* (pp. 118-137). Thousand Oaks, CA: Sage.

Seidel, J. (1991). Method and madness in the application of computer technology to qualitative data analysis. In N. G. Fielding & R. M. Lee (Eds.), *Using computers in qualitative research* (pp. 107-116). London: Sage.

Shaw, C. (1930). *The jack-roller: A delinquent boy's own story.* Chicago: University of Chicago Press.

Snow, D., & Morrill, C. (1993). Reflections upon anthropology's crisis of faith. *Contemporary Sociology, 22,* 8-11.

Star, S. L. (1989). *Regions of the mind: Brain research and the quest for scientific certainty.* Stanford, CA: Stanford University Press.

Star, S. L. (1997). Another remembrance: Anselm Strauss: An appreciation. In N. K. Denzin (Ed.), *Studies in symbolic interaction: A research annual* (Vol. 21, pp. 39-48). Greenwich, CT: JAI.

Stern, P. N. (1994a). Eroding grounded theory. In J. M. Morse (Ed.), *Critical issues in qualitative research methods* (pp. 212-223). Thousand Oaks, CA: Sage.

Stern, P. N. (1994b). The grounded theory method: Its uses and processes. In B. G. Glaser (Ed.), *More grounded theory: A reader* (pp. 116-126). Mill Valley, CA: Sociology Press.

Strauss, A. L. (1987). *Qualitative analysis for social scientists.* New York: Cambridge University Press.

Strauss, A. L. (1995). Notes on the nature and development of general theories. *Qualitative Inquiry, 1,* 7-18.

Strauss, A. L., & Corbin, J. (1990). *Basics of qualitative research: Grounded theory procedures and techniques.* Newbury Park, CA: Sage.

Strauss, A. L., & Corbin, J. (1994). Grounded theory methodology: An overview. In N. K. Denzin & Y. S. Lincoln (Eds.), *Handbook of qualitative research* (pp. 273-285). Thousand Oaks, CA: Sage.

Strauss, A. L., & Corbin, J. (1998). *Basics of qualitative research: Techniques and procedures for developing grounded theory* (2nd ed.). Thousand Oaks, CA: Sage.

Swanson, J. M., & Chenitz, C. W. (1993). Regaining a valued self: The process of adaptation to living with genital herpes. *Qualitative Health Research, 3,* 270-297.

Tesch, R. (1991). Software for qualitative researchers: Analysis needs and program capacities. In N. G. Fielding & R. M. Lee (Eds.), *Using computers in qualitative research* (pp. 16-37). London: Sage.

Thomas, W. I., & Thomas, D. S. (1928). *The child in America.* New York: Alfred A. Knopf.

Thomas, W. I., & Znaniecki, F. (1918-1920). *The Polish peasant in Europe and America* (5 vols.). Boston: Richard G. Badger.

Thrasher, F. M. (1963). *The gang: A study of 1,313 gangs in Chicago.* Chicago: University of Chicago Press. (Original work published 1927)

Turner, B. A. (1981). Some practical aspects of qualitative data analysis: One way of organizing the cognitive processes associated with the generation of grounded theory. *Quality and Quantity, 15,* 225-247.

Tyler, S. A. (1986). Post-modern ethnography: From document of the occult to occult document. In J. Clifford & G. E. Marcus (Eds.), *Writing culture: The poetics and politics of ethnography* (pp. 122-140). Berkeley: University of California Press.

Van Maanen, J. (1988). *Tales of the field: On writing ethnography.* Chicago: University of Chicago Press.

Vidich, A. J. (1992). Boston's North End: An American epic. *Journal of Contemporary Ethnography, 21,* 80-102.

Weitzman, E. A., & Miles, M. B. (1995). *Computer programs for qualitative data analysis: A software sourcebook.* Thousand Oaks, CA: Sage.

Whyte, W. F. (1992). In defense of *Street corner society. Journal of Contemporary Ethnography, 21,* 52-68.

Wiener, C. (1975). The burden of rheumatoid arthritis. In A. L. Strauss (Ed.), *Chronic illness and the quality of life* (pp. 71-80). St. Louis, MO: C. V. Mosby.

Wilson, H. S., & Hutchinson, S. A. (1991). Triangulation of qualitative methods: Heideggerian hermeneutics and grounded theory. *Qualitative Health Research, 1,* 263-276.

Zorbaugh, H. (1929). *The Cold Coast and the slum.* Chicago: University of Chicago Press.

9

Undaunted Courage

Life History and the
Postmodern Challenge

William G. Tierney

Who built Thebes of the seven gates?
In the books you will find the names of kings.
Did the kings haul up the lumps of rock? . . .

Philip of Spain wept when his armada
Went down. Was he the only one to weep?
—Bertolt Brecht, "Questions From a Worker Who Reads," 1934

◆ Almost two centuries ago, Thomas Jefferson commissioned
Meriwether Lewis to command an expedition to the Pacific. In
Undaunted Courage (1996), Stephen Ambrose writes of this journey, its
trials and tribulations. For his efforts, Ambrose won acclaim and his book
ended up a best-seller. The result of Meriwether Lewis's work was somewhat less salutary; he committed suicide in the fall of 1809.

AUTHOR'S NOTE: Michael Bamberg, Norm Denzin, Patrick Dilley, Yen Espiritu, Alexander
Jun, Yvonna Lincoln, and Michael Olivas offered helpful comments on an earlier version of
this chapter.

Although Ambrose's book includes in its subtitle *Thomas Jefferson and the Opening of the American West,* the text's major focus is on Captain Lewis. What kind of man would set off across a continent about which he knew little? Why would Lewis suggest that he share his post equally with his friend George Rogers Clark, when the military always has operated as a hierarchical chain of command? And, most tragically, why would Lewis kill himself after he had completed such a remarkable voyage and earned the praise of the country in general and of his friend Thomas Jefferson in particular?

Ambrose concludes his lyrical text by trying to guess what Lewis thought during his final moments at the hotel where he shot himself in a hamlet outside of Nashville, Tennessee. Perhaps he worried about his finances, or cursed himself for his drinking, suggests Ambrose. Or Lewis may have thought of his enemies, or he may have recalled his more heroic exploits. The reader is left really with only one conclusion—Lewis had a depressive personality and ultimately it got the better of him.

One might read *Undaunted Courage* on any number of levels. To some readers it is a rip-roaring adventure story that stretches the imagination about how anyone could possibly have navigated a crew across the North American continent—and then turned back and did it again. Jefferson's belief in Manifest Destiny and Americans' rapacious appetite for conquest provide another way to read it. Some might read the book as a map for understanding the roots of capitalism in the United States. The relationship that Lewis developed with Native Americans may be read one way by some and other ways by others. And then there is the case of Lewis himself and what the reader might make of him. Ambrose outlines a multitude of reasonable interpretations about why Lewis might have taken his life, absent one. Permit me to provide a different reading of his life.

Meriwether Lewis was a confirmed bachelor who was in love with Captain Clark. Lewis asked Clark to share his command. The book details how they were inseparable. On the trip out to the Pacific and upon the return home, every man in the party but one contracted syphilis—Lewis did not sleep with women. Lewis returned to Washington and Philadelphia but was always unsuccessful in his courtships. In fact, he more often than not wrote about the women he courted, yet his friends never met these women. Clark, on the other hand, returned home and soon married. One might plausibly conclude that Lewis killed himself a year or two later because of a broken heart.

Lewis of course may not have been gay and may not have died of heart-break. I am neither a historian of early America nor a psychologist. I raise the issue about Lewis's suicide here because it goes to the heart of the issues with which authors and readers must contend as they develop and read life histories and life stories. For example, on one level, I find it remarkable that an author as skillful as Ambrose does not even raise a question about Lewis's sexual identity. On another, I wonder how many readers who are not gay would suggest the possibility that Lewis had fallen in love with another man.

On yet another level, what would it have meant to have been homo-sexual at the beginning of the 19th century? Surely a gay identity signifies more than that Meriwether was *shtupping* George, but it also ought not mean, cannot mean, what queer theorists contend a gay man is as the 20th century ends. As Joshua Gamson comments in Chapter 12 of Volume 1, queer theory, with its roots in postmodernism, points to an "ongoing deconstruction of sexual subjectivity" such that identities—authors, sub-jects, readers—are never unified, never stable.

Some might posit that a theoretical framework that raises questions about the past (postmodernism) and a method that deals in what has hap-pened (life history) make strange bedfellows. I will argue, however, that the relationship between postmodernism and life history affords authors and readers critical insights into not so much the dead past as the develop-ing future. As Stephen Best and Douglas Kellner (1991) note:

> Postmodern theory provides a critique of representation and the modern belief that theory mirrors reality, taking instead "perspectivist" and relativ-ist positions that theories at best provide partial perspectives on their ob-jects and that all cognitive representations of the world are historically and linguistically mediated. (p. 4)

To be sure, a concrete definition of postmodernism does not ex-ist; indeed, such a definition would be ironic given postmodernism's basic tenets pertaining to indeterminacy and constant deconstruction/reconstruction. There is also a great deal of confusion between post-modernism and poststructuralism and various strands of postmodern-ism. As I will discuss later in this chapter, the framework I work from here is informed by critical theory; I oppose modernist notions of rational, autonomous subjects, totalizing discourses, and foundationalist epis-temologies. Thus a singular view of why someone acted in a particular way—Meriwether Lewis's suicide, for example—is rejected in favor of the creation of alternative interpretations that take into account the fluid nature of identity and the role of the researcher/author in the development of a text.

This chapter, then, is in many ways a history of the present. I investigate the creation of the past as a comment on the present condition. I seek neither to outline yet again the basic tenets of postmodernism nor to offer a cookbook of methodological recipes for those who wish to do life stories. Instead, in what follows I first discuss one form of life history, the *testimonio*, and outline what the project of postmodern life histories might be. I then consider the interstices of memory and history as a way to highlight the inevitable tension between fact and myth. I conclude by considering how authors might decolonize subjects by way of the construction and presentation of the narrative. My purpose here is to trouble the method, to bring into question various facets of life history work that often have gone unquestioned. In doing so, I aim to move the genre toward new projects, new relationships between the researcher and the researched, and away from previously constructed colonizations of the "Other."

◆ Life History and the Testimonio:
"I, Meriwether Lewis . . . "

Life history is a term that has meant many things to many people. Schwandt (1997) notes that it is also called "the biographical method" (p. 82). Watson and Watson-Franke (1985) state that a "life history is any retrospective account by the individual of his life in whole or part, in written or oral form, that has been elicited or prompted by another person" (p. 2). Watson (1976) argues elsewhere that the only direct purpose of life history "is as a commentary of the individual's very personal view of his own experience as he understands it" (p. 97). Dollard (1935), in a classic text, has written that the life history is "an attempt to define the growth of a person in a cultural milieu and to make theoretical sense of it" (p. 3). In a helpful table summarizing the biographical method, Denzin (1989) succinctly observes that a life history is an "account of a life based on interviews and observations" (p. 48). Hatch and Wisniewski (1995) suggest that "an analysis of the social, historical, political and economic contexts of a life story by the researcher is what turns a life story into a life history" (p. 125).

Clearly, the definition of life history varies depending on the perspective one chooses. For example, if I were to engage in life histories of Asian Americans, I might use autobiography (e.g., Lee, 1990), or perhaps oral histories (e.g., Lee, 1991) or life stories (Chow, 1998; Espiritu, 1995).

To some, the life history falls within a taxonomic biographical structure, and its emphasis is on the interactions between the researcher and the researched and on the researched's relationships to others. Life history is a culturally produced artifact in one light and an interpretive document in another. It might be defined by way of method (interviews and observations), theoretical vantage point (hermeneutics, phenomenology), or disciplinary perspective (psychology, anthropology, sociology).

I obviously am not suggesting the development of a universal definition of life history on which everyone will agree; rather, I am underscoring the multiple definitions that have surrounded the idea of life history. Often, as with the definitions I have just listed, what one finds is not so much that authors disagree but that they speak past one another.

Certainly, as the authors cited above suggest, life history is related to biography, it is a retrospective account, and it involves some form of narrative statement. However, my goal in this chapter is not to regurgitate what has been said before, but to provoke commentary on what researchers, readers, and activists might do next. I suggest that (a) the purpose of the text, (b) the truth of the text, and (c) the author of the text come into question at the end of the 20th century in ways that did not concern life historians a century ago, much less in the time of Lewis and Clark.

Although there are different formats of the life history that I might highlight in this chapter, I have chosen to feature the *testimonio*. By no means do I intend to suggest that researchers should use only the *testimonio* when attempting life history work. However, I have chosen to discuss the *testimonio* because this form of life history has the least overtly intrusive hand of an author and is the most indigenously derived of the qualitative techniques discussed in this volume. Further, as John Beverley (1992) has observed, the *testimonio* "is by nature a protean and demotic form not yet subject to legislation by a normative literary establishment" (p. 93). It is my hope that, by highlighting a literary form that is not encased by normative frames, I might contribute to our ability to consider ways to change, alter, and reconfigure other forms that are.

Perhaps the most famous *testimonio* is *I, Rigoberta Menchú: An Indian Woman in Guatemala* (1984). The book begins:

> My name is Rigoberta Menchú. I am twenty three years old. This is my testimony. I didn't learn it from a book and I didn't learn it alone. I'd like to stress that it's not only *my* life, it's also the testimony of my people. . . . My story is the story of all poor Guatemalans. My personal experience is the reality of a whole people. (p. 1)

Because I have quoted from the first page, one might reasonably conclude that I have provided the opening of the book, but actually, in a preface the volume's editor, Elisabeth Burgos-Debray (1984), writes of how the project was developed:

> When we began to use the tape recorder, I initially gave her a schematic outline, a chronology: childhood, adolescence, family involvement in the struggle. . . . As we continued, Rigoberta made more and more digressions, introduced descriptions of cultural practices into her story and generally upset my chronology. . . . I became what I really was: Rigoberta's listener. I allowed her to speak and then became her instrument, her double, by allowing her to make the transition from the spoken to the written word. (pp. xix-xx)

The *testimonio* has developed, in large part, not from Western Europe or the United States, but from Latin America. Unlike in oral history, the narrator bears witness to a social urgency; the text frequently falls within what Barbara Harlow (1987) defines as "resistance literature." The roots of *testimonio* go back to colonial *crónicas* and the war diaries of Simón Bolívar or José Martí. Over the past generation the focal points of the *testimonio* have been of those who have been silenced, excluded, and marginalized by their societies. Frequently, *testimonios* come from individuals who cannot write (e.g., Barnet, 1994; Dalton, 1982).

Some might argue (wrongly) that a *testimonio* actually erases the author function. In a traditionally defined life history or a biography, the hand of the researcher is ever present, whereas in the *testimonio* the researcher's role seems to fall to what Burgos-Debray defines as becoming the "instrument" of the individual who testifies. In this light the *testimonio* is a fundamentally different kind of document from other biographical undertakings. Whereas a life history is a written account elicited through interviews by an individual who seeks to understand a life in order to gain a greater understanding of cultural notions, the *testimonio* is developed by the one who testifies in the hope that his or her life's story will move the reader to action in concert with the group with which the testifier identifies. There is an urgency to the *testimonio* that is not always apparent in life histories or biographies and is most often absent in autoethnographies, which are more concerned with literary structures than with changing oppressive structures. In the *testimonio,* the testifier's life is directly linked to social movements and change.

Beverley (1992) defines the *testimonio* as "a novella-length narrative in book or pamphlet form, told in the first person by a narrator who is also the real protagonist or witness of the events he or she recounts, and whose unit of narration is usually a 'life' or a significant life experience" (p. 92). Thus a *testimonio* differs from an autobiography or autoethnography in that a moral or social imperative exists for the protagonist to tell his or her story. Although the *testimonio* might be circumscribed by everyday events that have happened to the individual, the centerpieces of the text pertain to issues such as torture, imprisonment, social upheaval, and the struggle for survival.

According to Beverley (1992), "Testimonio represents an affirmation of the individual subject, . . . but in connection with a group or class situation marked by marginality, oppression, and struggle. If it loses this connection, it ceases to be testimonio and becomes autobiography" (p. 103). The author of a *testimonio* is usually defined not as an author, but as an activist who is centrally tied to the struggle about which he or she writes. The individual has not risen "above" or "beyond" the struggle. Autobiography frequently looks back at a life, with the author speaking about life's challenges from a distance. The struggles may have been overcome or not, but the recollections are more reminiscence than call to action. Thus, if we return to my earlier concerns, we might initially summarize what a *testimonio* is by suggesting that (a) the *purpose* is social change, (b) the *truth* is created through the telling of an individual's events that have otherwise been occluded or ignored, and (c) the *author* is he or she who testifies, and not a researcher. Unfortunately, in a postmodern world, tidy summaries such as this are not so easy.

Textual Purpose

What is the purpose of the creation of a text? Clearly, the "disengaged" modernist who presumes him- or herself to be discovering knowledge has a very different purpose from the interlocutor of a *testimonio*. Indeed, the purpose of a text is dependent on any number of contextual issues.

Would it have been possible, for example, for Meriwether Lewis to pen a *testimonio* about his longings for Clark and bring into question the nature of sexual orientation in 1809? Presumably, even a white man of privilege who is able to write might develop a *testimonio* in the late 20th century about the oppression that gay and lesbian individuals face, or the marginalization someone who is disabled must deal with. But social constructs, Michel Foucault (1973) has taught us, are contextually and historically framed. As Jeffrey Weeks (1995, p. 5) and others have noted (e.g., Halperin, 1997; Sedgwick, 1990; see also Gamson, Chapter 12, this volume), it is deeply problematic to think of sexuality as a purely natural phenomenon, outside the boundaries of society and culture. If homosexuality was not "invented" in the manner that we have come to think of it today until the late 20th century, then Lewis could not have written a testimony to its oppression. He either would have been unable to understand his longings for George Clark or would not have had a name for them. As Montero (1997) has pointed out, gender definition is less a rigid identity than a series of repeated performances that intersect at various times with other identities—social, cultural, racial, ethnic, and so on.

Similarly, Ray McDermott and Herve Varenne (1995, p. 344) have observed that the idea of "disability" is not an individual condition but a cultural construct determined by the individual and group relations in which people function and develop meaning. I am suggesting that we cannot use the ways we define identity today to define identities of yesterday or of cultures different from those of us who do the defining.

The point, of course, is not to deny or downplay the horrific episodes that someone like Rigoberta Menchú relates, but instead to acknowledge that the individual is not an autonomous, essentialized agent capable of independently inventing him- or herself. Individual lives are constant constructs embedded in societal and cultural forces that seek to constrain some and enable others. However critical a *testimonio* is at a specific moment, and however much I urge our work to be more involved in social change, I am arguing that authors run the risk of re-creating a modernist fallacy if they assume that individual identity is not constrained by specific power relations.

I surely am not suggesting that researchers must forgo the struggle to overcome inequities. Instead, as Popkewitz (1998) has pointed out, all such work is defined by "effects of power which, when they go unnoticed in contemporary research and policy, may inter and enclose the possibility of change by reinscribing the very rules of reason and practice that need to be struggled against" (p. 3). The challenge is not to dismiss the *testimonio*, but to engage the text in ways that enable authors to enact change by acknowledging the relations of speaker, writer, and reader to truth.

Textual Truth

Recently, there has been a brouhaha about Rigoberta Menchú's version of truth. David Stoll (1999), an anthropologist who has spent a great deal of time in Central America, charges that Menchú's text is mistaken on several counts. Menchú says she never went to school, but Stoll's research reveals that her neighbors say she was sent away to a Catholic school. The point is not merely a geographic disagreement about her whereabouts: She could not have been an eyewitness to the events she relates if she was attending boarding school. Further, Menchú paints her father as a victim of *ladino* landlords and the state; Stoll (1998) interviewed Menchú's family and argues that actually her father's in-laws, cousins, and uncles had beaten him up because they thought he was stealing their land (p. 9).

Such charges have created a maelstrom. Stoll's point is more than a simple demand for veracity; rather, he turns the *testimonio* (and, by implication, life history, biography, and other such methods) back on itself. The determiner of truth becomes not the text and the reader. Instead, "we would have to acknowledge that there is no substitute for our capacity to judge competing versions of events, to exercise our authority as scholars" (Stoll, 1998, p. 11). On the face of it, what Stoll suggests has merit. One ought not believe that someone died at the hands of X when Y was actually responsible. One ought not say, "I saw a murder happen," if one did not. Certainly, analyses of contradictions between narrative and experience need to be explored and examined in any document.

However, one wonders if "truth" in a *testimonio* is to be defined in the manner that Stoll does, especially in a postmodern world where such terms are inevitably contested, argued over, and perspectival. Greg Grandin (1998) disagrees with Stoll: "I have no doubt that Menchú's testimony contains exaggerations, contradictions, if not outright fabrications. But can this come as a surprise to anyone who treats Mayans as political actors, capable of developing their own political agenda?" (p. 52). The concern here is that Stoll would have readers judge narratives as seamless and hermetically sealed, rather than through multiple filters. *Testimonio*—as well as life history, life story, autoethnography, and the like—is situated within a series of complex and ambiguous political and cultural relations. Texts are surely to be interrogated in the manner that Stoll has done, but for the interrogators the end result should not be the declamation of a scholarly "gotcha" when they find contradictions; rather, they should try to piece together how these multiple presentations account for contested versions of reality.

In her text about five women, Mary Catherine Bateson (1990) matter-of-factly states, "I have not tried to verify these narratives, beyond attending to issues of internal consistency and checking them against my knowledge of the individuals. . . . The accounts are shaped by each person's choice and selective memory. . . . These are stories I have used to think with" (p. 33). Such a statement stands in contradistinction to the empiricism of Stoll's fact checking. Again, the point here is not that facts of the kind Stoll has examined are wrong or irrelevant, but that how we use facts determines how we think about truth and how we read a text.

Lewis's omission of any discussion of his homosexuality in his journals, for example, does not necessarily mean that he was lying; at the same time, the lack of such information also ought not suggest that therefore he was a heterosexual. The heterosexual reader may not even have considered such "facts." Proponents of Stoll's position might rightfully argue that if we were able to transport ourselves back to the early 19th century and we then found evidence of Lewis's homosexuality, then it needs to be reported—and I concur. But what makes a fact a fact is not merely the act one sees or does, but the interconnections between who sees what when and how it gets reported by whom. "A fact is like a sack which won't stand up when it is empty," says Pirandello (1921/1952). "In order that it may stand up, one has to put into it the reason and sentiment which have caused it to exist" (p. 230).

The Author of the Text

From the earliest life histories to the most recent texts, such as those by Menchú, Domitila Barrios de Chungara (1978), Fernandez and Gutierrez (1996), and Elvira Alvarado (1987), the role of the author has been in question. As noted, individuals such as Burgos-Debray (1984) claim that they are their interviewees' "instruments," as if their role is little more than that of human tape recorder. However, we must disavow the notion that any text is singularly created, even in a genre that is perhaps the most responsive to the individual who provides his or her "testimony."

Listen, for example, to Alfred Kroeber's (1908) presentation of Black-Wolf's description of war: "When I was a boy, I heard about great deeds in war, and resolved to follow in the tracks of such men" (p. 197). Kroeber also had Watches-All comment on supernatural powers by observing, "Medicine-men cured the sick by sucking the body and by brushing it. As is customary among Indians, they were believed to suck through the skin without biting, cutting or puncturing it" (p. 222). Does anyone seriously believe that a native speaker—or anyone—talks in that way? Here we have an interviewer gathering a story in a language different from his own, and the reader discovers that Native Americans speak in a manner akin to the reader's.

Further, authors often interpret the spoken words of others in various ways, in large part because the speakers' language is different from theirs. Translation is always provisional; different translators translate the same texts in different ways. Conversely, authors increasingly are studying individuals and groups with whom they share much in common; that is, an African American author might study African Americans, or a lesbian might investigate a lesbian community. Once again, we cannot presume that because an author is similar to those he or she studies that the author function is irrelevant. From a postmodern perspective, all authors, all narrators, are situated; the challenge is to come to terms with the positions in which authors locate themselves.

A text is always created not simply by the speaker of the narrative and the individual who owns the tape recorder, but also by the multiple editorial decision makers who oversee the story's production. On the one hand are the questions of the interviewer. Susan Chase (1995) notes that the questions she asked framed how her interviewee thought about what to say: "Despite my repeated statements of interest in her experience, [the interviewee] heard that my primary interest lay in the connection between her experience and sociological ideas" (p. 7). One cannot escape that the individual who collects the data is doing more than merely collecting them. As Gelles (1998) asks, "What [would] Menchú's narrative have looked like if it had been solicited by a sympathetic and politically attuned Maya-speaking *ladino* or indigenous intellectual from Guatemala?" (p. 17). His observation is not that Burgos-Debray had sinister or mistaken motives, but that any text is coproduced. As researchers we are participants in the creation of the data.

And on the other hand, the editor or author also shapes the data on the written page. For example, Hones (1998) has suggested that "the rhythmic repetitions and formulaic language present in traditional oral cultures such as the Hmong should be represented in the form of poetry instead of prose" (p. 240; see also Tedlock, 1983; Tierney & Lincoln, 1997). The forms that have been employed throughout the 20th century in what constitutes academic scholarship exist in large part because of formulas derived from modernism and the Western mind. Themes, with beginnings and ends, populate texts—but not all people construct their lives in such a manner. Greg Sarris (1994) makes precisely such a point in his instructions to a medicine woman with whom he was doing a life history: "When you write a book there has to be a story, or idea, a theme." She replied, "Well, theme I don't know nothing about. That's somebody else's rule" (p. 5).

People speak expressively, with body and facial movements that help explain and extend the words they use, but usually such movements do not make it into texts dependent upon language. If we are to believe the vast majority of life histories that exist, those individuals whose lives have been reported are among the most grammatically correct and logical speakers we know; they speak in complete sentences and they develop ideas in chronological sequence. Academic rules help to shape life stories to such an extent that narrative texts cannot be seen as other than cocreated.

As Rinehart (1998) nicely summarizes: "How we choose to name other people and groups—how we categorize them—often tells more about us, about our stance on how things are, than it does about any truth of who they are. It tells more about that which is true to the namer" (p. 201). Even in a *testimonio*, then, we must accept that the document is mediated in any number of ways.

Such acceptance will raise concerns on the part of those who are wedded to a modernist framework. Indeed, much of what I have raised here should be of concern to the modernist. One might wrongly assume that in a world where facts are not facts and authors are always involved in the creation of data, I am suggesting anything goes. However, no one I know who subscribes to postmodernism suggests that the veracity of a statement should go unchecked, or that because all life histories are cocreated, one is as good as another. To be sure, one challenge that I leave for a later text is to delineate how one might evaluate the kinds of texts I am discussing here.

For now, the challenge in a world that we view as constructed on multiple levels by multiple parties is to seek some sense of voice and agency that enables action. "The autobiographical occasion," write Smith and Watson (1992), "becomes a site on which cultural ideologies intersect and dissect one another, in contradiction, consonance, and adjacency" (p. xix). The narrative site is full of potential. Our struggle is to enact that potential—and to this challenge I now turn.

◆ Between Memory and History

"History is perpetually suspicious of memory," writes Pierre Nora (1989), "and its true mission is to suppress and destroy it" (p. 9). Those who utilize the life history, the *testimonio,* the life story, the autoethnography, all begin with the assumption that it is helpful to remember. The written text, a narrative archive, on a material level seeks to assert what has occurred—that, in fact, a past existed and humanity is not always in the present. Such a statement may seem matter-of-fact—Who could argue that a past does not exist?—except that in an age consumed by the present, individuals develop historical amnesia; they are unable to grasp histories of groups and individuals except as these are constructed (or not) by current ideological forces. History, in this sense, has been hidden from memory. The past is a foreign country where a different language is spoken; too often, historians have simply assumed that history is discovery of patterns, places, and people.

Relatedly, Marjorie Becker (1997) points out that "the linear approach to historical writing so frequently employed in the twentieth century gives the impression that human experience moves sequentially, act by act, with each experience slightly more significant than the last" (p. 344). The problem with such an approach is that no two individuals engage time in the same manner. No one temporal structure can express the multitude of experiences for all people, across all times.

Scholars traditionally have attached importance to the life history for any number of reasons—perhaps to create a sense of nostalgia ("the way we were"), to develop ideological images (the "noble savage"), to re-create symbolic virtue in a world that ostensibly has been deritualized. A society such as exists at the end of the 20th century, which has been so deeply absorbed in transformation and renewal, generally has used life history as fleeting memory. Those who suggest that history is little more than collective memory overlook how ideology frames, constructs, and defines what is seen and/or obscured. Memory is assuredly not outside of history; rather, the two are conjoined in mutual constructions.

In an earlier work, I observed that discussions about the purpose of life history revolve around the twin concepts of *portal* and *process* (Tierney, 1998). A life history might be done as a portal, an entryway, through which the author and reader might understand a culture different from their own. The assumption is that a life history's purpose is to enable the reader to come to terms with different social phenomena, perhaps, or to learn vicariously about a world quite different from his or her own.

The portal approach to life history generally assumes that the author and the reader are different from the person whose story is told. A *testimonio,* obviously, is in contradistinction to the portal approach with regard to the author. However mediated a testimonio might be, the individual whose story is heard is directly involved in its construction. The purpose of the text is not merely for a foreign reader to gain a sense of an alien culture, but for an individual to testify about a compelling social problem. The portal approach to life history exoticizes the Other and tries to enable the reader to understand the life fantastic. An undertaking of this kind inevitably privileges the researcher and reinforces social relations circumscribed by power insofar as a dynamic is created in which the author has control over the final production of a text about someone else's life story.

A life history also may represent a process whereby the researcher and reader come to understand the semiotic means by which someone else makes sense of the world. "Life story researchers," explains Gelya Frank (1995), "examine the cultural scripts and narrative devices speakers use to make sense of their own life experiences" (p. 255). Through this use of the life history, the researcher and reader hopefully are able to reflect on their own lives. They achieve some understanding of one another and of the multiple realities involved in the creation of meaning. I am suggesting that the text—a life history, a life story, a *testimonio*—be seen as a personal narrative whose ontological status as a spoken interaction between two (or more) individuals helps create, define, reinforce, or change reality. Thus the process approach to life history more easily fits within a postmodern framework and enables the development and encouragement of texts such as *testimonios.*

The life history text, then, exists somewhere between history and memory. Memory is not a spontaneous word association. Speakers and researchers build memory from the shared perspective of the present. Memories are recalled for reasons that are important to someone—the speaker, the interviewer—in large part because of present contextual definitions of what constitutes identity, society, and culture. The life history not only represents the memory of an individual, it also produces identity. The challenge to us as researchers is to ensure that individuals are not the object of our discourses, but rather the agents of complex, partial, and contradictory identities that help transform the worlds they and we inhabit.

A handful of years ago, the challenge might have been to "name silenced lives" (McLaughlin & Tierney, 1993) as a way to provide voice for those who had been left out of history's picture. If one were to read only formalized histories, one might mistakenly presume, for example, that African Americans, American Indians, gay and lesbian people, and other marginalized groups did not exist prior to a generation ago. Certainly the women's movement is significantly responsible for enabling us to realize that a history of a particular epoch that speaks only of men's work is partial and incomplete.

However, the simple "naming" of silenced lives is insufficient. Yes, histories in general, and life histories in particular, are helpful for enabling societies to come to terms with individuals and groups who have been omitted from official versions of the past. But we ought not fool ourselves into thinking that simply by adding a few voices here and there our work is done if we have proven that omitted characters from official histories have representational value. Life histories are helpful not merely because they add to the mix of what already exists, but because of their ability to refashion identities. Rather than a conservative goal based on nostalgia for a paradise lost, or a liberal one of enabling more people to take their places at humanity's table, a goal of life history work in a postmodern age is to break the stranglehold of metanarratives that establishes rules of truth, legitimacy, and identity. The work of life history becomes the investigation of the mediating aspects of culture, the interrogation of its grammar, and the decentering of its norms (Tierney, 1997). In doing such work, life histories are successful in a liberal fashion—groups previously excluded from official versions of history get included—but more important, those previously excluded groups as well as other individuals and groups become redefined and redescribed. Smith and Watson (1992) are worth quoting at length here:

Western autobiography colludes in cultural mythmaking. . . . It functions as an exclusionary genre against which the utterances of other subjects are measured and misread. While inviting all subjects to participate in its practices, it provides the constraining template or the generic "law" against which those subjects and their diverse forms of self-narrative are judged and found wanting. In order to unstick both this Man and his meanings, we need to adjust, to reframe, our understanding of traditional and counter-traditional autobiographical practices. (p. xviii)

In his analysis of Menchú's *testimonio,* Stoll (1998) argues that the text is more mythopoesis than history. He defines mythopoesis as "the act of mythmaking in which people tell certain stories to justify their preferred interpretation of the world" (p. 9). One senses, of course, Stoll's very real concern that myth is not the stuff of history. Active mythmaking is intellectual fraud; myths that develop where the speaker is simply mistaken are one reason researchers must exercise their authority as scholars.

On the other hand, Beverley (1992) approvingly comments that Menchú's work "is a kind of testimonial expressionism, or magic realism" (p. 101). Lincoln and Denzin (1994) might define such a tactic as "deconstructive verisimilitude" (p. 580) insofar as Stoll accepts the idea of a singular reality that can be proved/not proved. What Beverley is trying to convey is the sense that a text is a site of political struggle over the "real" and its meanings. The challenge set forth, as Lincoln and Denzin (1994) note, is "to reproduce and deconstruct the reproductions and simulations that structure the real" (p. 580).

Susan Krieger (1996) and Carolyn Steedman (1986) offer texts that operate within the interstices of history and memory. Steedman (1986) writes, "This book is about interpretations, about the places where we rework what has already happened to give current events meaning" (p. 5); she continues, "Personal interpretations of past time . . . are often in deep and ambiguous conflict with the official interpretative devices of a culture" (p. 6). Steedman's word choice is purposive, specific. She is not simply saying that her work is about a reconfiguration of the past—a naming of a silenced life—she is saying that the text takes issue with the "interpretive devices" of that past. One of those key devices is history. The researcher's work, however, needs to be more than the stimulation of memory that reaches for easy reminiscence, for if all the researcher is doing is evoking a nostalgia for the past irrespective of ideology, then he or she has stripped the work of any possibility for change. Thus the site for a researcher's work is between memory and history, lost in the interstices.

◆ **Decolonizing Meriwether**

At the close of the 20th century, we have seen a variety of experiments with the writing of life histories. Autoethnography is one form that is being used in which the author is more explicitly involved within the text. The life story utilizes specific moments in a speaker's life that are conveyed through a story; less attention is paid to textual veracity than to what the implicit semiotic meanings of the text may be. Ruth Behar (1996) has written that "the genres of life history and life story are merging with the testimonio, which speaks to the role of witnessing in our time as a key form of approaching and transforming reality" (p. 27). Heretofore, scholars of the *testimonio* would have disagreed that an overtly mediated text such as a life history could approximate what a *testimonio* struggles to do. Obviously, there will be differences of tone, style, and urgency between the *testimonio* and some life histories and autoethnographies, but the recent past has brought forth a significant number of texts that utilize recent advances in postmodernism in a manner akin to the narrative structure of *testimonio* (Behar, 1993; Brown, 1991).

Rather than texts by distant observers who interview subjects to glean facts about their lives in order to make "objective" assertions, we have postmodern texts that work from different assumptions and frameworks. They have three different conditions from life histories of the past and follow from the overarching comments made earlier. The first is that the reality of the exchange, the data collected, is constructed. The second condition pertains to the nature of the voice and the vulnerability necessary for such a voice, what Soderqvist (1991) calls "embodied construction and reflexivity" (p. 145). The third condition involves why we write what we write. These three conditions, relating back to the discussion in the first section of this chapter, combine in a way that creates the possibility for researchers to decolonize subjects and to open up avenues for change. Researchers disavow any idea of "discovering" data as if it were waiting "out there" to be found; instead, data are created. A danger is that each condition is not well understood, and a certain authorial narcissism is capable of overpowering a text so that, rather than create a dynamic for democratic change, authors re-create a different version of the imperialist author. Because writers are embarking on uncharted methodological terrain, they do not have a map of the research design; nevertheless, a sense of general direction becomes apparent from the postmodern conditions noted above.

Storytelling

Life histories that worked from a modernist framework assumed that an underlying goal was to present verifiable information about different phenomena. Given what I have argued for, the postmodern challenge is to accept the multiple mediations at work in the creation of the text and expose them, rather than try to hide them, wish them away, or assume that they can be resolved. In this light, how to categorize and frame a life becomes of central import. The naming of individuals and groups structures how we see them.

Barely over a generation ago, for example, a life history of a gay man might well have been framed as an exploration of deviance, or a life story of a homeless person might have left unexamined the structural conditions that enable the idea of homelessness to get enacted. Similarly, a life history of a Native American would have been attempted as a way to understand the exotic "Other," but a life history of a white male who was a corporate executive would have been overlooked insofar as he was not the "Other." Life histories informed by postmodernism will begin with the assumption that identity is partial, contested, and, at times, contradictory. Such a position enables the possibility for the decolonization of previously colonized peoples—be they Native Americans, the disabled, or gay men who commit suicide because of their sexual orientation.

Well-meaning modernists may shake their heads at the implications of what I am suggesting. On the one hand, I criticize the observer who seeks to record the lives of those individuals on the border—Native Americans, lesbian and gay individuals, and the like—as an ethnographic voyeur. On the other hand, I have criticized the absence from traditional texts of those of us on the border. Am I not, some might ask, placing life historians in an untenable double bind in which they are intellectually dammed if they do (life histories) and dammed if they don't?

The answer depends on the framework employed. The point is surely not that one must eschew life histories of colonized peoples, or that the attempt to understand the Other is a fruitless undertaking. Rather, the researcher must begin with an understanding of the fragmented nature of identity and build a text that enables readers to see how the author/ narrator/speaker has created a particular identity that is fraught with contested meanings.

Toward the end of his elegiac memoir *Before Night Falls* (1993), Reinaldo Arenas writes, "Witches have played an important part in my life" (p. 294). The empiricist would try to prove whether witches actually exist or, more likely, examine Arenas's mental condition and explain why Arenas could believe such a magical idea. I am suggesting, as with the earlier comments about Menchú's testimony, that if such empiricism goes unquestioned, researchers miss a great deal by simply answering whether or not witches exist. The postmodern challenge is in part for the researcher to come to terms with alternative realities different from his or her own, not to exoticize them so that the researcher might put them on display, but instead to help create the conditions for decolonization whereby the researcher tries to understand the life of a gay Cuban man dying of AIDS in an empathic manner. Such a position resituates the research endeavor of the life historian. The researcher does not simply try to find or explain away witches, but reflects back on why such a question is important and others are not. The relationship of the researcher/author to the individual and to the text of necessity comes in for questioning and analysis.

Embodied Construction and Vulnerability

Over the past generation there has been a sea change concerning the use of the first person in texts. Although representation still exists within a quite narrow context, at least qualitative researchers have moved beyond the assumption that the only tenable way to present themselves in life histories is by authorial absence or through the third person. Indeed, a good deal of recent work in ethnographic research either advocates using or utilizes the first person (Denzin, 1994; Ellis & Bochner, 1996; Ellis & Flaherty, 1992; Richardson, 1998; Tierney & Lincoln, 1997). I welcome such a stance. Nevertheless, I also wish to suggest that writers need to extend the authorial role yet again. There needs to be greater vulnerability to the author's voice and work. Permit me to elaborate, and to do so on a personal level.

Western epistemology was shaped by the belief that emotion needed to be cut out of the process of knowledge production. The authorial response of the postmodernist has been to insert the first person into the text. And yet one need not be a postmodernist to recognize that there are multiple ways an author might utilize the voice of the first person. Indeed, as a gay man I am only too well aware of how I utilize my voice as an out gay academic. There is the "I" who can say, "I am gay—do you want to make something out of it?" as a defiant assertion in a peremptory manner, for I know that there are individuals—academics, readers—who hate me for no reason other than that I am gay. I have employed such a narrative strategy at times in my own work and in my life; I assume that anyone who has faced similar oppression and marginalization understands the defensive posture that brings forth such a voice.

Another way to use the voice of the "I" is in the manner in which I use it initially in this text. If the reader will return to the introduction to the chapter, he or she will find that I do not say there that I am gay; instead, I suggest it when I raise a question about Meriwether's sexual orientation. In this way, I employ the first person in a cool, stripped-down academic manner akin to what might be used by modernists who employ the omniscient narrator. The "I" is used presumably to move the text along, and the author is not overly intrusive. There are, of course, multiple additional possibilities for the use of the first person.

I suggest here that we also become able to make our work and ourselves vulnerable. Yes, there are times when I should be a defiant queer man; yes, there are moments when a return to the voice of the cerebral gay academic is sufficient—but there also ought to be a place where my voice is vulnerable and passionate. As we enter the new century, for example, I am only too aware of how many friends I have lost to AIDS; such loss has unalterably tinged my life—all of it, personal, political, academic. At times in our work such vulnerability also needs to be heard, for without it, we hold on to a unified voice that is power laden and dominant.

I agree with Ruth Behar (1996) when she writes: "Since I have put myself in the ethnographic picture, readers feel they have come to know me. They have poured their own feelings into their construction of me and in that way come to identify with me, or at least their fictional image of who I am" (p. 16). When we write vulnerably, we invite others to respond vulnerably. Surely not every qualitative text that is written needs to provoke a vulnerable response in the reader; just as surely, however, some texts should.

If we are to shed the role of the disengaged observer who records data from afar, then our voices must reflect our own vulnerabilities. At times I am troubled that the recent use of the first person is often akin to what I have pointed out about my own voice as a gay man. Sometimes I hear in a text the author symbolically saying, "There. I've used the first person. I've done it!" Perhaps the voice is first person, but it remains cool and disengaged. Again, I understand why as researchers and authors we have used such a voice, and I am in agreement that at times we are correct in its employment. After all, as Jane Tompkins (1993) has noted, "to break with the convention is to risk not being heard at all" (p. 26). We want to be listened to, and we have a good deal of justification about feeling defensive. However, the vulnerability of our work, our identities, and our voices also needs to be heard if we are to create the conditions for decolonization.

Praxis and the Other

We ought not lose sight of the fact that, however flawed the research endeavor, the possibility exists that in some of our work we might be able to bring about change with those with whom we work. While we employ the first person and make ourselves vulnerable, we have yet another task and obligation, and that concerns those individuals whose life histories, stories, and *testimonios* we help create.

When a text is done, one goal the writer ought to have is that the reader will have a sense of who the author is. Such a goal should not be, cannot be, the only goal. Again, if I mentioned earlier that I am troubled by the maintenance of a power-laden voice even if it is in the first person, I am equally troubled by a narcissistic voice that eschews a concern for those with whom the author works. The work of life history has to be more than the celebration of my authorial voice, for if nothing else has been accomplished, all that I have achieved is a narrative trick, a linguistic sleight of hand. I have employed the first person in a manner akin to what modernists have done with other voices. The researcher/author remains in control, and the individual with whom he or she has worked yet again takes a textual backseat to the academic narrator.

Not all research will have the social urgency of a Guatemalan peasant's *testimonio* about her people being murdered. Nevertheless, there is a strand of postmodernism that assumes change is impossible, or not a worthy goal. The focus of that form of postmodernism centers on irony and wordplay. The version of postmodernism I have worked from here, however, is informed by critical theory (Tierney, 1993, 1997). The challenge becomes the desire to change the more oppressive aspects of life that silence and marginalize some and privilege others. One certainly cannot wish away power. But the work of life history ought to try to understand the conditions in which people live and work and die, so that everyone engaged in the life history—researcher, storyteller, reader—has the possibility of reconfiguring his or her life.

◆ Conclusion

I began this chapter with a discussion of Meriwether Lewis and the possibility that he was gay. As I have suggested, some readers may well be unconvinced by the "evidence" that Lewis was gay. My point in using the example of Lewis, however, was to highlight the multiple interpretations that researchers and readers bring to events and people of the past. Lewis may have been gay, and certainly that thought will cross the minds of many gay readers as they work their way through Ambrose's text. The empiricist will demand proof, and I have suggested that such proof is a modernist fallacy.

I then turned to a discussion of life history in general and the *testimonio* in particular. Many readers may be unfamiliar with the *testimonio;* my choice of life history strategy is not simply to suggest yet another tool to add to our methodological kit. And I certainly have had no desire to convince all life historians that henceforth the *testimonio* is the only valid way to construct life's stories. Rather, in large part because it has not yet been subjected to normalizing frameworks, the *testimonio* enables a particularly compelling discussion about what I have termed three turning points in life history. As one undertakes a life history, one needs to consider (a) the purpose of the text (What is the author trying to do and why?), (b) the veracity of the text (How does one deal with the truth of what is presented?), and (c) the author of the text (Who pens a story?). Although I have not suggested that there are hard-and-fast rules that must be observed regardless of context or situation, I have argued that one needs to consider these issues as one interprets, constructs, and reads texts.

I have elaborated on these points by considering the relationship between history and memory. I have suggested that life history is something more than collective memory. Ideology and social and cultural frames help define how we see the past and construct its stories. Identity is not something fixed and predetermined; rather, it is constantly re-created. In this re-creation, the past's histories help construct the future. I have also suggested that, like the *testimonio* in particular, life histories in general cannot be simply the unearthing of untold stories. Rather, informed by the critical postmodern framework that I have employed, I have argued that texts fail if they are little more than literary experiments or the telling of untold tales.

Of consequence, life histories of the kind I have discussed here eschew the paternalism that has imbued so much social science research in the 20th century, and instead seek to create ways to decolonize those who have been silenced, forgotten, or mangled by life's forces. Such a task, I have argued, demands not only new ways of thinking about constructing texts but different relationships with those who are studied and a different stance with regard to the "Other." Instead of a disengaged empiricism, we need a greater sense of vulnerability on the part of the new life historian and an elaborated sense of social responsibility with regard to those with whom we work.

Some might argue that I have made fundamental errors in logic. I have titled this text "Undaunted Courage," which suggests that writing a life history is as difficult and daunting as crossing the continent was two centuries ago. I also have suggested that Meriwether Lewis was gay and that he be decolonized; thus a man who helped colonize America is now himself a candidate for decolonization. Those who subscribe to postmodernism also might criticize the use of the word *courage* in the title of this chapter insofar as I have borrowed it from Stephen Ambrose's book on Meriwether Lewis. Ambrose works from a modernist construction of a hero. The hero carries "courage" with him across the continent.

Courage, like voice, comes in different forms. The modernist definition of courage that explores unexplored external terrain is one viewpoint. The courage I have suggested here is of a form that allows the author to reach across boundaries and within him- or herself. The author forgoes romantic notions about truth or knowledge, but also accepts the task of trying to bridge differences. The modernist courage of Meriwether Lewis is that he reached the Pacific Ocean and then turned around and returned home.

The postmodern life historian helps create texts that are voyages of creation—for the historian, the person who speaks, and the person who ultimately reads the final product. Texts have been used to colonize people by framing individuals and groups in one light and silencing them in another. The project of decolonization is not a simple task of authorial enlightenment, nor can it be divorced from the daily situations in which authors, speakers, and readers find themselves. Indeed, a next step in the project outlined here might be further development of the parameters of what makes for a good text.

The power the author has is the ability to develop a reflexive text. Such a text enables readers to understand the author a bit better, to come to grips with the individual whose life is retold, and to reflect back on their own lives. A reflexive work of the kind I have argued for leaves a writer and speaker and reader vulnerable. Vulnerability is not a position of weakness, but one from which to attempt change and social fellowship.

◆ References

Alvarado, E. (1987). Foreword. In M. Benjamin (Ed.), *Don't be afraid, gringo: A Honduran woman speaks from the heart*. San Francisco: Institute for Food and Development Policy.

Ambrose, S. E. (1996). *Undaunted courage: Meriwether Lewis, Thomas Jefferson, and the opening of the American West*. New York: Simon & Schuster.

Arenas, R. (1993). *Before night falls: A memoir*. New York: Penguin.

Barnet, M. (1994). *Biography of a runaway slave* (W. N. Hill, Trans.). Willimantic, CT: Curbstone.

Barrios de Chungara, D. (1978). *Let me speak! Testimony of Domitila, a woman of the Bolivian mines*. New York: Monthly Review Press.

Bateson, M. C. (1990). *Composing a life: Life as a work in progress*. New York: Penguin.

Becker, M. (1997). When I was a child, I danced as a child, but now that I am old, I think about salvation. *Rethinking History, 1*, 343-355.

Behar, R. (1993). *Translated woman: Crossing the border with Esperanza's story*. Boston: Beacon.

Behar, R. (1996). *The vulnerable observer: Anthropology that breaks your heart*. Boston: Beacon.

Best, S., & Kellner, D. (1991). *Postmodern theory: Critical interrogations*. New York: Guilford.

Beverley, J. (1992). The margin at the center: On testimonio (testimonial narrative). In S. Smith & J. Watson (Eds.), *De/colonizing the subject: The politics of gender in women's autobiography* (pp. 91-114). Minneapolis: University of Minnesota Press.

Brown, K. M. (1991). *Mama Lola: A Vodou priestess in Brooklyn*. Berkeley: University of California Press.

Burgos-Debray, E. (1984). Preface. In R. Menchú, *I, Rigoberta Menchú: An Indian woman in Guatemala* (E. Burgos-Debray, Ed. & Trans.). New York: Verso.

Chase, S. E. (1995). Taking narrative seriously: Consequences for method and theory in interview studies. In R. Josselson & A. Liebech (Eds.), *Interpreting experience: The narrative study of lives* (pp. 1-26). Thousand Oaks, CA: Sage.

Chow, C. S. (1998). *Leaving deep water: The lives of Asian American women at the crossroads of two cultures.* New York: E. P. Dutton.

Dalton, R. (1982). *Miguel Marmol* (M. Randall & M. Argueta, Trans.). Willimantic, CT: Curbstone.

Denzin, N. K. (1989). *Interpretive biography.* Newbury Park, CA: Sage.

Denzin, N. K. (1994). The art and politics of interpretation. In N. K. Denzin & Y. S. Lincoln (Eds.), *Handbook of qualitative research* (pp. 500-515). Thousand Oaks, CA: Sage.

Dollard, J. (1935). *Criteria for the life history: With analysis of six notable documents.* New Haven, CT: Yale University Press.

Ellis, C., & Bochner, A. P. (Eds.). (1996). *Composing ethnography: Alternative forms of qualitative writing.* Walnut Creek, CA: AltaMira.

Ellis, C., & Flaherty, M. G. (Eds.). (1992). *Investigating subjectivity: Research on lived experience.* Newbury Park, CA: Sage.

Espiritu, Y. L. (1995). *Filipino American lives.* Philadelphia: Temple University Press.

Fernandez, R. V., & Gutierrez, C. E. (Eds.). (1996). *Andean lives: Gregario Condori Mamani and Asunta Quispe Huamán* (P. H. Gelles & G. M. Escobar, Trans.). Austin: University of Texas Press.

Frank, G. (1995). Life histories in occupational therapy clinical practice. *American Journal of Occupational Therapy, 50,* 251-264.

Foucault, M. (1973). *The order of things: An archaeology of the human sciences* (E. Gallimard, Trans.). New York: Vintage.

Gelles, P. H. (1998, April). Testimonio, ethnography, and processes of authorship. *Anthropology Newsletter,* pp. 16-17.

Grandin, G. (1998, April). She said, he said. *Anthropology Newsletter,* p. 52.

Halperin, D. (1997). Questions of evidence. In M. Duberman (Ed.), *Queer representations: Reading lives, reading cultures* (pp. 39-55). New York: New York University Press.

Harlow, B. (1987). *Resistance literature.* New York: Methuen.

Hatch, J. A., & Wisniewski, R. (1995). Life history and narrative: Questions, issues, and exemplary works. In J. A. Hatch & R. Wisniewski (Eds.), *Life history and the narrative* (pp. 113-136). Philadelphia: Taylor & Francis.

Hones, D. F. (1998). Known in part: The transformational power of narrative inquiry. *Qualitative Inquiry, 4,* 225-248.

Krieger, S. (1996). *The family silver: Essays on relationships among women.* Berkeley: University of California Press.

Kroeber, A. (1908). Ethnology of the Gros Ventre. *Anthropological Papers of the American Museum of Natural History, 1*(4), 196-222.

Lee, J. F. (1991). *Asian American experiences in the United States: Oral histories of first to fourth generation Americans from China, the Philippines, Japan, India, the Pacific islands, Vietnam and Cambodia.* Jefferson, NC: McFarland.

Lee, M. P. (1990). *Quiet odyssey: A pioneer Korean woman in America* (S. Chan, Ed.). Seattle: University of Washington Press.

Lincoln, Y. S., & Denzin, N. K. (1994). The fifth moment. In N. K. Denzin & Y. S. Lincoln (Eds.), *Handbook of qualitative research* (pp. 575-586). Thousand Oaks, CA: Sage.

McDermott, R., & Varenne, H. (1995). Culture as disability. *Anthropology and Education Quarterly, 26,* 324-348.

McLaughlin, D., & Tierney, W. G. (1993). *Naming silenced lives: Personal narratives and the process of educational change.* New York: Routledge.

Menchú, R. (1984). *I, Rigoberta Menchú: An Indian woman in Guatemala* (E. Burgos-Debray, Ed.; A. Wright, Trans.). London: Verso.

Montero, O. (1997). Notes for a queer reading of Latin American Literature. In M. Duberman (Ed.), *Queer representations: Reading lives, reading cultures* (pp. 216-225). New York: New York University Press.

Nora, P. (1989). Between memory and history: Les lieux de memoire. *Representations, 26,* 7-25.

Pirandello, L. (1952). Six characters in search of an author. In E. Bentley (Ed.), *Naked masks: Five plays by Luigi Pirandello.* New York: Meridian. (Original work published 1921)

Popkewitz, T. S. (1998). The culture of redemption and the administration of freedom as research. *Review of Educational Research, 68,* 1-34.

Richardson, L. (1998). The politics of location: Where am I now? *Qualitative Inquiry, 4,* 41-48.

Rinehart, R. (1998). Fictional methods in ethnography: Believability, specks of glass, and Chekhov. *Qualitative Inquiry, 4,* 200-224.

Sarris, G. (1994). *Mabel McKay: Weaving the dream.* Berkeley: University of California Press.

Schwandt, T. A. (1997). *Qualitative inquiry: A dictionary of terms.* Thousand Oaks, CA: Sage.

Sedgwick, E. K. (1990). *Epistemology of the closet.* Berkeley: University of California Press.

Smith, S., & Watson, J. (1992). Introduction: De/colonization and the politics of discourse in women's autobiographical practices. In S. Smith & J. Watson (Eds.), *De/colonizing the subject: The politics of gender in women's autobiography.* Minneapolis: University of Minnesota Press.

Soderqvist, T. (1991). Biography or ethnobiography or both? Embodied reflexivity and the deconstruction of knowledge-power. In F. Steier (Ed.), *Method and reflexivity: Knowing as systemic social construction* (pp. 143-162). London: Sage.

Steedman, C. (1986). *Landscape for a good woman: A story of two lives.* London: Virago.

Stoll, D. (1998, April). Life history as mythopoesis. *Anthropology Newsletter*, pp. 9-11.

Stoll, D. (1999). *Rigoberta Menchú and the story of all poor Guatemalans.* Boulder, CO: Westview.

Tedlock, D. (1983). *The spoken word and the work of interpretation.* Philadelphia: University of Pennsylvania Press.

Tierney, W. G. (1993). *Building communities of difference: Higher education in the twenty-first century.* South Hadley, MA: Bergin & Garvey.

Tierney, W. G. (1997). *Academic outlaws: Queer theory and cultural studies in the academy.* Thousand Oaks, CA: Sage.

Tierney, W. G. (1998). Life history's history: Subjects foretold. *Qualitative Inquiry, 4*, 49-70.

Tierney, W. G., & Lincoln, Y. S. (Eds.). (1997). *Representation and the text: Reframing the narrative voice.* Albany: State University of New York Press.

Tompkins, J. (1993). Me and my shadow. In D. P. Freedman, O. Frey, & F. M. Zauhar (Eds.), *The intimate critique: Autobiographical literary criticism.* Durham, NC: Duke University Press.

Watson, L. C. (1976). Understanding a life history as a subjective document: Hermeneutical and phenomenological perspectives. *Ethos, 4*(1), 95-131.

Watson, L. C., & Watson-Franke, M. (1985). *Interpreting life histories.* New Brunswick, NJ: Rutgers University Press.

Weeks, J. (1995). *Invented moralities: Sexual values in an age of uncertainty.* New York: Columbia University Press.

10

Testimonio, Subalternity, and Narrative Authority

John Beverley

◆ In a justly famous essay, Richard Rorty (1985) distinguishes between what he calls the "desire for solidarity" and the "desire for objectivity" as cognitive modes:

> There are two principal ways in which reflective human beings try, by placing their lives in a larger context, to give sense to those lives. The first is by telling the story of their contribution to a community. This community may be the actual historical one in which they live, or another actual one, distant in time or place, or a quite imaginary one, consisting perhaps of a dozen heroes and heroines selected from history or fiction or both. The second way is to describe themselves as standing in an immediate relation to a non-human reality. This relation is immediate in the sense that it does not derive from a relation between such a reality and their tribe, or their nation, or their imagined band of comrades. I shall say that stories of the former kind exemplify the desire for solidarity, and that stories of the latter kind exemplify the desire for objectivity. (p. 3)[1]

The question of *testimonio*—testimonial narrative—has come prominently onto the agenda of the human and social sciences in recent years in part because *testimonio* intertwines the "desire for objectivity" and "the desire for solidarity" in its very situation of production, circulation, and reception.

Testimonio is by nature a demotic and heterogeneous form, so any formal definition of it is bound to be too limiting.[2] But the following might serve provisionally: A *testimonio* is a novel or novella-length narrative, produced in the form of a printed text, told in the first person by a narrator who is also the real protagonist or witness of the events she or he recounts. Its unit of narration is usually a "life" or a significant life experience. Because in many cases the direct narrator is someone who is either functionally illiterate or, if literate, not a professional writer, the production of a *testimonio* generally involves the tape-recording and then the transcription and editing of an oral account by an interlocutor who is a journalist, ethnographer, or literary author.

Although one of the antecedents of *testimonio* is undoubtedly the ethnographic life history of the *Children of Sánchez* sort, *testimonio* is not exactly commensurable with the category of life history (or oral history). In the life history it is the intention of the interlocutor-recorder (the ethnographer or journalist) that is paramount; in *testimonio*, by contrast, it is the intention of the direct narrator, who *uses* (in a pragmatic sense) the possibility the ethnographic interlocutor offers to bring his or her situation to the attention of an audience—the bourgeois public sphere—to which he or she would normally not have access because of the very conditions of subalternity to which the *testimonio* bears witness.[3] *Testimonio* is not intended, in other words, as a reenactment of the anthropological function of the native informant. In René Jara's (1986, p. 3) phrase, it is rather a "narración de urgencia"—an "emergency" narrative—involving a problem of repression, poverty, marginality, exploitation, or simply survival that is implicated in the act of narration itself. In general, *testimonio* could be said to coincide with the feminist slogan "The personal is the political." The contemporary appeal of *testimonio* for educated, middle-class, transnational publics is perhaps related to the importance given in various forms of 1960s counterculture to oral testimony as a form of personal and/or collective catharsis and liberation in (for example) the consciousness-raising sessions of the early women's movement, the practice of "speaking bitterness" in the Chinese Cultural Revolution, or psychotherapeutic encounter groups.

The predominant formal aspect of the *testimonio* is the voice that speaks to the reader through the text in the form of an I that demands to be recognized, that wants or needs to stake a claim on our attention. Eliana Rivero (1984-1985) notes that "the act of speaking faithfully recorded on the tape, transcribed and then 'written' remains in the *testimonio* punctuated by a repeated series of interlocutive and conversational markers . . . which constantly put the reader on the alert, so to speak: True? Are you following me? OK? So?" (pp. 220-221). The result, she argues, is a "snail-like" discourse (*discurso encaracolado*) that keeps turning in on itself and that in the process invokes the complicity of the reader through the medium of his or her counterpart in the text, the direct interlocutor.

This presence of the voice, which the reader is meant to experience as the voice of a *real* rather than fictional person, is the mark of a desire not to be silenced or defeated, to impose oneself on an institution of power and privilege from the position of the excluded, the marginal, the subaltern. Hence the insistence on the importance of personal name or identity evident sometimes in titles of *testimonios,* such as *I, Rigoberta Menchú* (even more strongly in the Spanish: *Me llamo Rigoberta Menchú y así me nació la conciencia*), *I'm a Juvenile Delinquent* (*Soy un delincuente*), and *Let Me Speak* (*Si me permiten hablar*).

This insistence suggests an affinity between testimony and autobiography (and related forms, such as the autobiographical *bildungsroman,* the memoir, and the diary). Like autobiography, *testimonio* is an affirmation of the authority of personal experience but, unlike autobiography, it cannot affirm a self-identity that is separate from the subaltern group or class situation that it narrates. *Testimonio* involves an erasure of the function and thus also of the textual presence of the "author" that is so powerfully present in all major forms of Western literary and academic writing.[4] By contrast, in autobiography or the autobiographical *bildungsroman,* the very possibility of "writing one's life" implies necessarily that the narrator is no longer in the situation of marginality and subalternity that his or her narrative describes, but has now attained precisely the cultural status of an author (and, generally speaking, middle- or upper-class economic status). Put another way, the transition from storyteller to author implies a parallel transition from *gemeinschaft* to *gesellschaft,* from a culture of primary and secondary orality to writing, from a traditional group identity to the privatized, modern identity that forms the subject of liberal political and economic theory.

The metonymic character of testimonial discourse—the sense that the voice that is addressing us is a part that stands for a larger whole—is a crucial aspect of what literary critics would call the convention of the form:

the narrative contract with the reader it establishes. Because it does not require or establish a hierarchy of narrative authority, *testimonio* is a fundamentally democratic and egalitarian narrative form. It implies that *any* life so narrated can have a symbolic and cognitive value. Each individual *testimonio* evokes an absent polyphony of other voices, other possible lives and experiences (one common formal variation on the first-person singular *testimonio* is the polyphonic *testimonio* made up of accounts by different participants in the same event).

If the novel is a closed form, in the sense that both the story and the characters it involves end with the end of the text, in *testimonio*, by contrast, the distinctions between text and history, representation and real life, public and private spheres, objectivity and solidarity (to recall Rorty's alternatives) are transgressed. It is, to borrow Umberto Eco's expression, an "open work." The narrator in *testimonio* is an actual person who continues living and acting in an actual social space and time, which also continue. *Testimonio* can never create the illusion—fundamental to formalist methods of textual analysis—of the text as autonomous, set against and above the practical domain of everyday life and struggle. The emergence of *testimonios*, for the form to have become more and more popular in recent years, means that there are experiences in the world today (there always have been) that cannot be expressed adequately in the dominant forms of historical, ethnographic, or literary representation, that would be betrayed or misrepresented by these forms.

Because of its reliance on voice, *testimonio* implies in particular a challenge to the loss of the authority of orality in the context of processes of cultural modernization that privilege literacy and literature as a norm of expression. The inequalities and contradictions of gender, class, race, ethnicity, nationality, and cultural authority that determine the "urgent" situation of the testimonial narrator may also reproduce themselves in the relation of the narrator to the interlocutor, especially when (as is generally the case) that narrator requires to produce the *testimonio* a "lettered" interlocutor from a different ethnic and/or class background in order first to elicit and record the narrative, and then to transform it into a printed text and see to its publication and circulation as such. But it is equally important to understand that the testimonial narrator is not the subaltern as such either; rather, she or he functions as an organic intellectual (in Antonio Gramsci's sense of this term) of the subaltern, who speaks to the hegemony by means of a metonymy of self in the name and in the place of the subaltern.

By the same token, the presence of subaltern voice in the *testimonio* is in part a literary illusion—something akin to what the Russian formalists called *skaz*: the textual simulacrum of direct oral expression. We are dealing here, in other words, not with reality itself but with what semioticians call a "reality effect" that has been produced by both the testimonial narrator—using popular speech and the devices of oral storytelling—and the interlocutor-compiler, who, according to hegemonic norms of narrative form and expression, transcribes, edits, and makes a story out of the narrator's discourse. Elzbieta Sklodowska (1982) cautions in this regard that

> it would be naïve to assume a direct homology between text and history [in testimonio]. The discourse of a witness cannot be a reflection of his or her experience, but rather a refraction determined by the vicissitudes of memory, intention, ideology. The intention and the ideology of the author-editor further superimposes the original text, creating more ambiguities, silences, and absences in the process of selecting and editing the material in a way consonant with norms of literary form. Thus, although the testimonio uses a series of devices to gain a sense of veracity and authenticity—among them the point of view of the first-person witness-narrator—the play between fiction and history reappears inexorably as a problem. (p. 379, my translation; see also Sklodowska, 1996)

The point is well-taken, but perhaps overstated. Like the identification of *testimonio* with life history (which Sklodowska shares), it concedes agency to the interlocutor-editor of the testimonial text rather than to its direct narrator. It would be better to say that what is at stake in *testimonio* is the *particular* nature of the reality effect it produces. Because of its character as a narrative told in the first person to an actual interlocutor, *testimonio* interpellates the reader in a way that literary fiction or third-person journalism or ethnographic writing does not. The word *testimonio* carries the connotation in Spanish of the act of testifying or bearing witness in a legal or religious sense. Conversely, the situation of the reader of *testimonio* is akin to that of a jury member in a courtroom. *Something* is asked of us by *testimonio*, in other words. In this sense, *testimonio* might be seen as a kind of speech act that sets up special ethical and epistemological demands. (When we are addressed directly by an actual person, in such a way as to make a demand on our attention and capacity for judgment, we are under an obligation to respond in some way or other; we can act or not on that obligation, but we cannot ignore it.)

What *testimonio* asks of its readers is in effect what Rorty means by solidarity—that is, the capacity to identify their own identities, expectations, and values with those of another. To understand how this happens is to understand how *testimonio works* ideologically as discourse, rather than what it *is*.

In one of the most powerful sections of her famous *testimonio I, Rigoberta Menchú* (1984), which has come to be something like a paradigm of the genre, Menchú describes the torture and execution of her brother Petrocinio by elements of the Guatemalan army in the plaza of a small highland town called Chajul, which is the site of an annual pilgrimage by worshipers of the local saint. Here is part of that account:

> After he'd finished talking the officer ordered the squad to take away those who'd been "punished," naked and swollen as they were. They dragged them along, they could no longer walk. Dragged them to this place, where they lined them up all together within sight of everyone. The officer called to the worst of the criminals—the *Kaibiles,* who wear different clothes from other soldiers. They're the ones with the most training, the most power. Well, he called the *Kaibiles* and they poured petrol over each of the tortured. The captain said, "This isn't the last of their punishments, there's another one yet. This is what we've done with all the subversives we catch, because they have to die by violence. And if this doesn't teach you a lesson, this is what'll happen to you too. The problem is that the Indians let themselves be led by the communists. Since no-one's told the Indians anything, they go along with the communists." He was trying to convince the people but at the same time he was insulting them by what he said. Anyway, they [the soldiers] lined up the tortured and poured petrol on them; and then the soldiers set fire to each one of them. Many of them begged for mercy. Some of them screamed, many of them leapt but uttered no sound—of course, that was because their breathing was cut off. But—and to me this was incredible—many of the people had weapons with them, the ones who'd been on their way to work had machetes, others had nothing in their hands, but when they saw the army setting fire to the victims, everyone wanted to strike back, to risk their lives doing it, despite all the soldiers' arms. . . . Faced with its own cowardice, the army itself realized that the whole people were prepared to fight. You could see that even the children were enraged, but they didn't know how to express their rage. (pp. 178-179)

This passage is undoubtedly compelling and powerful. It invites the reader into the situation it describes through the medium of the eyewitness narrator, and it is the sharing of the experience through the medium of

Menchú's account that constitutes the possibility of solidarity. But "what if much of Rigoberta's story is not true?" the anthropologist David Stoll (1999, p. viii) asks. On the basis of interviews in the area where the massacre was supposed to have occurred, Stoll concludes that the killing of Menchú's brother did not happen in exactly this way, that Menchú could not have been a direct witness to the event as her account suggests, and that therefore this account, along with other details of her *testimonio*, amounts to, in Stoll's words, a "mythic inflation" (pp. 63-70, 232).

It would be more accurate to say that what Stoll is able to show is that *some* rather than "much" of Menchú's story is not true. He does not contest the fact of the murder of Menchú's brother by the army, and he stipulates that "there is no doubt about the most important points [in her story]: that a dictatorship massacred thousands of indigenous peasants, that the victims included half of Rigoberta's immediate family, that she fled to Mexico to save her life, and that she joined a revolutionary movement to liberate her country" (p. viii). But he does argue that the inaccuracies or omissions in her narrative make her less than a reliable spokesperson for the interests and beliefs of the people for whom she claims to speak. In response to Stoll, Menchú herself has publicly conceded that she grafted elements of other people's experiences and stories onto her own account. In particular, she has admitted that she was not herself present at the massacre of her brother and his companions in Chajul, and that the account of the event quoted in part above came instead from her mother, who (Menchú claims) was there. She says that this and similar interpolations were a way of making her story a collective one, rather than a personal autobiography. But the point remains: If the epistemological and ethical authority of testimonial narratives depends on the assumption that they are based on personal experience and direct witness, then it might appear that, as Stoll puts it, "*I, Rigoberta Menchú* does not belong in the genre of which it is the most famous example, because it is not the eyewitness account it purports to be" (p. 242).

In a way, however, the argument between Menchú and Stoll is not so much about what really happened as it is about who has the authority to narrate. (Stoll's quarrel with Menchú and *testimonio* is a *political* quarrel that masquerades as an epistemological one.) And that question, rather than the question of "what really happened," is crucial to an understanding of how *testimonio* works. What seems to bother Stoll above all is that Menchú *has* an agenda. He wants her to be in effect a native informant who will lend herself to *his* purposes (of ethnographic information gathering and evaluation), but she is instead functioning in her narrative as an organic intellectual, concerned with producing a text of local history—that is, with elaborating hegemony.

The basic idea of Gayatri Spivak's famous, but notoriously difficult, essay "Can the Subaltern Speak?" (1988) might be reformulated in this way: If the subaltern could speak—that is, speak in a way that really *matters* to us, that we would feel compelled to listen to, then it would not be subaltern. Spivak is trying to show that behind the gesture of the ethnographer or solidarity activist committed to the cause of the subaltern in allowing or enabling the subaltern to speak is the trace of the construction of an other who is available to speak to us (with whom we *can* speak or with whom we would feel comfortable speaking), neutralizing thus the force of the reality of difference and antagonism to which our own relatively privileged position in the global system might give rise. She is saying that one of the things being subaltern means is not mattering, not being worth listening to, or not being understood when one is "heard."

By contrast, Stoll's argument with Rigoberta Menchú is precisely with how her *testimonio* comes to matter. He is bothered by the way it was used by academics and solidarity activists to mobilize international support for the Guatemalan armed struggle in the 1980s, long after (in Stoll's view) that movement had lost whatever support it may have initially enjoyed among the indigenous peasants for whom Menchú claims to speak. That issue—"how outsiders were using Rigoberta's story to justify continuing a war at the expense of peasants who did not support it" (Stoll, 1999, p. 241)—is the main problem for Stoll, rather than the inaccuracies or omissions themselves. From Stoll's viewpoint, by making Menchú's story seem (in her own words) "the story of all poor Guatemalans"—that is, by its participating in the very metonymic logic of *testimonio*—*I, Rigoberta Menchú* misrepresents a more complex and ideologically contradictory situation among the indigenous peasants. It reflects back to the reader not the subaltern as such, but a narcissistic image of what the subaltern *should be:*

Books like *I, Rigoberta Menchú* will be exalted because they tell academics what they want to hear. . . . What makes *I, Rigoberta Menchú* so attractive in universities is what makes it misleading about the struggle for survival in Guatemala. We think we are getting closer to understanding Guatemalan peasants when actually we are being borne away by the mystifications wrapped up in an iconic figure. (Stoll, 1999, p. 227)

In one sense, of course, there is a coincidence between Spivak's concern with the production in metropolitan ethnographic and literary discourse of what she calls a "domesticated Other" and Stoll's concern with the conversion of Menchú into an icon of academic political correctness. But Stoll's argument is also explicitly *with* Spivak, as a representative of the very kind of "postmodern scholarship" that would privilege a text like *I, Rigoberta Menchú,* even to the extent of wanting to deconstruct its metaphysics of presence. Thus, Stoll states, for example:

Following the thinking of literary theorists such as Edward Said and Gayatri Spivak, anthropologists have become very interested in problems of narrative, voice, and representation, especially the problem of how we misrepresent voices other than our own. In reaction, some anthropologists argue that the resulting fascination with texts threatens the claim of anthropology to be a science, by replacing hypothesis, evidence, and generalization with stylish forms of introspection. (p. 247)

Or: "Under the influence of postmodernism (which has undermined confidence in a single set of facts) and identity politics (which demands acceptance of claims to victimhood), scholars are increasingly hesitant to challenge certain kinds of rhetoric" (p. 244). Or: "With postmodern critiques of representation and authority, many scholars are tempted to abandon the task of verification, especially when they construe the narrator as a victim worthy of their support" (p. 274).

Where Spivak is concerned with the way in which hegemonic literary or scientific representation effaces the effective presence and agency of the subaltern, Stoll's case against Menchú is precisely that: a way of, so to speak, *resubalternizing* a narrative that aspired to (and to some extent achieved) cultural authority. For in the process of constructing her narrative and articulating herself as a political icon around its circulation, Menchú is becoming not-subaltern, in the sense that she is functioning as what Spivak calls a subject of history. Her *testimonio* is a *performative* rather than simply descriptive or denotative discourse. Her narrative choices, and silences and evasions, entail that there are versions of "what really happened" that she does not or cannot represent without relativizing the authority of her own account.

It goes without saying that in any social situation, indeed even within a given class or group identity, it is always possible to find a variety of points of view or ways of telling that reflect contradictory, or simply differing, agendas and interests. "Obviously," Stoll (1999) observes, "Rigoberta is a legitimate Mayan voice. So are all the young Mayas who want to move to Los Angeles or Houston. So is the man with a large family who owns three worn-out acres and wants me to buy him a chain saw so he can cut down the last forest more quickly. Any of these people can be picked to make misleading generalizations about Mayas" (p. 247). The presence of these other voices makes Guatemalan indigenous communities—indeed even Menchú's own immediate family—seem irremediably driven by internal rivalries, contradictions, and disagreements.

But to insist on this is, in a way, to deny the possibility of subaltern agency as such, because a hegemonic project by definition points to a possibility of collective will and action that depends precisely on the transformation of the conditions of cultural and political disenfranchisement, alienation, and oppression that underlie these rivalries and contradictions. The appeal to diversity ("any of these people") leaves intact the authority of the outside observer (the ethnographer or social scientist) who is alone in the position of being able to both hear and sort through all the various conflicting testimonies.

The concern about the connection between *testimonio* and identity politics that Stoll evinces is predicated on the fact that multicultural rights claims carry with them what Canadian philosopher Charles Taylor (1994) has called a "presumption of equal worth" (and *I, Rigoberta Menchú* is, among other things, a strong argument for seeing the nature of American societies as irrevocably multicultural and ethnically heterogeneous). That presumption in turn implies an epistemological relativism that coincides with the postmodernist critique of the Enlightenment paradigm of scientific objectivity. If there is no one universal standard for truth, then claims about truth are contextual: They have to do with how people construct different understandings of the world and historical memory from the same sets of facts in situations of gender, ethnic, and class inequality, exploitation, and repression. The truth claims for a testimonial narrative like *I, Rigoberta Menchú* depend on conferring on the form a special kind of epistemological authority as embodying subaltern voice and experience. Against the authority of that voice—and, in particular, against the assumption that it can represent adequately a collective subject ("all poor Guatemalans")—Stoll wants to affirm the authority of the fact-gathering and -testing procedures of anthropology and journalism, in which accounts like Menchú's will be treated simply as ethnographic data that must be processed by more objective techniques of assessment, which, by definition, are not available to the direct narrator. But, in the final analysis, what Stoll is able to present as evidence against the validity of Menchú's account are, precisely, *other testimonio*s: other voices, narratives, points of view, in which, it will come as no surprise, he can find something *he* wants to hear.

We know something about the nature of this problem. There is not, outside the realm of human discourse itself, a level of facticity that can guarantee the truth of this or that representation, given that society itself is not an essence prior to representation, but rather the consequence of struggles to represent and over representation. That is the deeper meaning of Walter Benjamin's aphorism "Even the dead are not safe": Even the historical memory of the past is conjunctural, relative, perishable. *Testimonio* is both an art and a strategy of subaltern memory.

We would create yet another version of the native informant of classical anthropology if we were to grant testimonial narrators like Rigoberta Menchú only the possibility of being witnesses, and not the power to create their own narrative authority and negotiate its conditions of truth and representativity. This would amount to saying that the subaltern can of course speak, but only through *us*, through our institutionally sanctioned authority and pretended objectivity as intellectuals, which give us the power to decide what counts in the narrator's raw material. But it is precisely that institutionally sanctioned authority and objectivity that, in a less benevolent form, but still claiming to speak from the place of truth, the subaltern must confront every day in the forms of war, economic exploitation, development schemes, obligatory acculturation, police and military repression, destruction of habitat, forced sterilization, and the like.[5]

There is a question of agency here. What *testimonio* obliges us to confront is not only the subaltern as a (self-) represented victim, but also as the agent—in that very act of representation—of a transformative project that aspires to become hegemonic in its own right. In terms of this project, which is not our own in any immediate sense and which may in fact imply structurally a contradiction with our own position of relative privilege and authority in the global system, the testimonial text is a *means* rather than an end in itself. Menchú and the persons who collaborated with her in the creation of *I, Rigoberta Menchú* were certainly aware that the text would be an important tool in human rights and solidarity work that might have a positive effect on the genocidal conditions the text itself describes. But *her* interest in the text is not to have it become an object for us, our means of

329

getting the "whole truth"—"toda la realidad"—of her experience. It is rather to act tactically in a way she hopes and expects will advance the interests of the community and social groups and classes her *testimonio* represents: "poor" (in her own description) Guatemalans. That is as it should be, however, because it is not only *our* desires and purposes that count in relation to *testimonio*.

This seems obvious enough, but it is a hard lesson to absorb fully, because it forces us to, in Spivak's phrase, "unlearn privilege." And unlearning privilege means recognizing that it is not the intention of subaltern cultural practice simply to signify its subalternity to us. If that is what *testimonio* does, then critics like Sklodowska are right in seeing it as a form of the status quo, a kind of postmodernist *costumbrismo*.

The force of a *testimonio* such as *I, Rigoberta Menchú* is to displace the centrality of intellectuals and what they recognize as culture—including history, literature, journalism, and ethnographic writing. Like any testimonial narrator (like anybody), Menchú is of course also an intellectual, but in a sense she is clearly different from what Gramsci meant by a traditional intellectual—that is, someone who meets the standards and carries the authority of humanistic and/or scientific high culture. The concern with the question of subaltern agency and authority in *testimonio* depends, rather, on the suspicion that intellectuals and writing practices are themselves complicit in maintaining relations of domination and subalternity.

The question is relevant to the claim made by Dinesh D'Souza (1991) in the debate over the Stanford Western Culture undergraduate requirement (which centered on the adoption of *I, Rigoberta Menchú* as a text in one of the course sections) that *I, Rigoberta Menchú* is not good or great literature. D'Souza writes, "To celebrate the works of the oppressed, apart from the standard of merit by which other art and history and literature is judged, is to romanticize their suffering, to pretend that it is naturally creative, and to give it an aesthetic status that is not shared or appreciated by those who actually endure the oppression" (p. 87). It could be argued that *I, Rigoberta Menchú* is one of the most powerful works of *literature* produced in Latin America in the past several decades; but there is also some point in seeing it as a provocation in the academy, as D'Souza feels it to be. The subaltern, by definition, is a social position that is not, and cannot be, adequately represented in the human sciences or the university, if only because the human sciences and the university are among the institutional constellations of power/knowledge that create and sustain subalternity.

This is not, however, to draw a line between the world of the academy and the subaltern, because the point of *testimonio* is, in the first place, to intervene in that world—that is, in a place where the subaltern is not. In its very situation of enunciation, which juxtaposes radically the subject positions of the narrator and interlocutor, *testimonio* is involved in and constructed out of the opposing terms of a master/slave dialectic: metropolis/periphery, nation/region, European/indigenous, creole/mestizo, elite/popular, urban/rural, intellectual/manual, male/female, "lettered"/illiterate or semiliterate. *Testimonio* is no more capable of transcending these oppositions than are more purely literary or scientific forms of writing or narrative; that would require something like a cultural revolution that would abolish or invert the conditions that produce relations of subordination, exploitation, and inequality in the first place. But *testimonio* does involve a new way of articulating these oppositions and a new, collaborative model for the relationship between the intelligentsia and the popular classes.

To return to Rorty's point about the "desire for solidarity," a good part of the appeal of *testimonio* must lie in the fact that it both represents symbolically and enacts in its production and reception a relation of solidarity between ourselves—as members of the professional middle class and practitioners of the human sciences—and subaltern social subjects like Menchú. *Testimonio* gives voice to a previously anonymous and voiceless popular-democratic subject, but in such a way that the intellectual or professional is interpellated, in his or her function as interlocutor/reader of the testimonial account, as being in alliance with (and to some extent dependent on) this subject, without at the same time losing his or her identity as an intellectual.

If first-generation *testimonio*s such as *I, Rigoberta Menchú* effaced textually in the manner of the ethnographic life story (except in their introductory presentations) the presence of the interlocutor, it is becoming increasingly common in what is sometimes called the "new ethnography" to put the interlocutor into the account, to make the dynamic of interaction and negotiation between interlocutor and narrator part of what *testimonio* testifies to. Ruth Behar's *Translated Woman: Crossing the Border with Esperanza's Story* (1993), for example, is often mentioned as a model for the sort of ethnographic text in which the authority (and identity) of the ethnographer is counterpointed against the voice and authority of the subject whose life history the ethnographer is concerned with eliciting. In a similar vein, Philippe Bourgois's innovative ethnography of

Puerto Rican crack dealers in East Harlem, *In Search of Respect* (1995), often pits the values of the investigator—Bourgois—against those of the dealers he befriends and whose stories and conversations he transcribes and reproduces in his text. In *Event, Metaphor, Memory: Chauri Chaura, 1922-1992* (1995), the subaltern studies historian Shahid Amin is concerned with retrieving the "local memory" of an uprising in 1922 in a small town in northern India in the course of which peasants surrounded and burned down a police station, leading to the deaths of 23 policemen. But he is also concerned with finding ways to incorporate formally the narratives that embody that memory into his own history of the event, abandoning thus the usual stance of the historian as omniscient narrator and making the heterogeneous voices of the community itself the historian(s).

These ways of constructing testimonial material (obviously, the examples could be multiplied many times over) make visible that what happens in *testimonio* is not only the textual staging of a "domesticated Other," to recall Spivak's telling objection, but the confrontation through the text of one person (the reader and/or immediate interlocutor) with another (the direct narrator or narrators) at the level of a *possible* solidarity. In this sense, *testimonio* also embodies a new possibility of political agency (it is essentially that possibility to which Stoll objects). But that possibility—a postmodernist form of Popular Front-style alliance politics, if you will—is necessarily built on the recognition of and respect for the radical incommensurability of the situation of the parties involved. More than empathic liberal guilt or political correctness, what *testimonio* seeks to elicit is *coalition*. As Doris Sommer (1996) puts it succinctly, *testimonio* "is an invitation to a tête-à-tête, not to a heart to heart" (p. 143).

◆ Bibliographic Note

Margaret Randall, who has organized testimonial workshops in Cuba and Nicaragua (and who has herself edited a number of *testimonio*s on the roles of women in the Cuban and Nicaraguan revolutions), is the author of a very good, albeit hard to find, handbook on how to prepare a *testimonio* titled *Testimonios: A Guide to Oral History* (1985). The first significant academic discussion of *testimonio* that I am aware of was published in the 1986 collection *Testimonio y literatura,* edited by René Jara and Hernán Vidal at the University of Minnesota's Institute for the Study of Ideologies

332

and Literature. The most comprehensive representation of the debate around *testimonio* in the literary humanities in the ensuing decade or so is the collection edited by Georg Gugelberger titled *The Real Thing: Testimonial Discourse and Latin America* (1996), which incorporates two earlier collections: one by Gugelberger and Michael Kearney for a special issue of *Latin American Perspectives* (vols. 18-19, 1991), and the other by myself and Hugo Achugar titled *La voz del otro: Testimonio, subalternidad, y verdad narrativa,* which appeared as a special issue of *Revista de Crítica Literaria Latinoamericana* (1992). The initial literary "manifesto" of *testimonio* was the essay by the Cuban novelist-ethnographer Miguel Barnet (*apropos* his own *Biography of a Runaway Slave*), "La novela-testimonio: Socioliteratura" (1986), originally published in the late 1960s in the Cuban journal *Unión*. On the academic incorporation of *testimonio* and its consequences for pedagogy, see Carey-Webb and Benz (1996).

Jara and Vidal's (1986) collection happened to coincide with the famous collection on ethnographic authority and writing practices edited by James Clifford and George Marcus, *Writing Culture* (1986), which exercised a wide influence in the fields of anthropology and history. One should note also in this respect the pertinence of the work of the South Asian Subaltern Studies Group (see, e.g., Guha, 1997; Guha & Spivak, 1988) and of the Latin American Subaltern Studies Group (see Rabasa, Sanjinés, & Carr, 1994/1996). For both social scientists and literary critics, a touchstone for conceptualizing *testimonio* should be Walter Benjamin's great essay from the 1930s, "The Storyteller" (see Benjamin, 1969).

◆ Notes

1. Rorty's (1985) distinction may recall for some readers Marvin Harris's well-known distinction between *emic* and *etic* accounts (where the former are personal or collective "stories" and the latter are representations given by a supposedly objective observer based on empirical evidence).

2. Widely different sorts of narrative texts could in given circumstances function as *testimonio*s: confession, court testimony, oral history, memoir, autobiography, autobiographical novel, chronicle, confession, life story, *novela-testimonio,* "nonfiction novel" (Truman Capote), or "literature of fact" (Roque Dalton).

3. Mary Louise Pratt (1986) describes the *testimonio* usefully in this respect as "autoethnography."

4. In Miguel Barnet's (1986) phrase, the author has been replaced in *testimonio* by the function of a "compiler" (*compilador*) or "activator" (*gestante*), somewhat on the model of the film producer.

5. "Any statement of authority has no other guarantee than its very enunciation, and it is pointless for it to seek another signifier, which could not appear outside this locus in any way. Which is what I mean when I say that no metalanguage can be spoken, or, more aphoristically, that there is no Other of the Other. And when the Legislator (he who claims to lay down the Law) presents himself to fill the gap, he does so as an impostor" (Lacan, 1977, pp. 310-311).

◆ References

Amin, S. (1995). *Event, metaphor, memory: Chauri Chaura 1922-1992.* Berkeley: University of California Press.

Barnet, M. (1986). La novela-*testimonio*: Socioliteratura. In R. Jara & H. Vidal (Eds.), *Testimonio y literatura.* Minneapolis: University of Minnesota, Institute for the Study of Ideologies and Literatures.

Behar, R. (1993). *Translated woman: Crossing the border with Esperanza's story.* Boston: Beacon.

Benjamin, W. (1969). *Illuminations* (H. Zohn, Trans.). New York: Schocken.

Beverley, J., & Achugar, H. (Eds.). (1992). *La voz del otro: Testimonio, subalternidad, y verdad narrativa* [Special issue]. *Revista de Crítica Literaria Latinoamericana, 36.*

Bourgois, P. (1995). *In search of respect.* Cambridge: Cambridge University Press.

Carey-Webb, A., & Benz, S. (Eds.). (1996). *Teaching and testimony.* Albany: State University of New York Press.

Clifford, J, & Marcus, G. E. (Eds.). (1986). *Writing culture: The poetics and politics of ethnography.* Berkeley: University of California Press.

D'Souza, D. (1991). *Illiberal education.* New York: Free Press.

Gugelberger, G. M. (Ed.). (1996). *The real thing: Testimonial discourse and Latin America.* Durham, NC: Duke University Press.

Gugelberger, G. M., & Kearney, M. (Eds.). (1991). [Special issue]. *Latin American Perspectives, 18-19.*

Guha, R. (Ed.). (1997). *A subaltern studies reader.* Minneapolis: University of Minnesota Press.

Guha, R., & Spivak, G. C. (Eds.). (1988). *Selected subaltern studies.,* New York: Oxford University Press.

Jara, R. (1986). Prólogo. In R. Jara & H. Vidal (Eds.), *Testimonio y literatura* (pp. 1-3). Minneapolis: University of Minnesota, Institute for the Study of Ideologies and Literatures.

Jara, R., & Vidal, H. (Eds.). (1986). *Testimonio y literatura.* Minneapolis: University of Minnesota, Institute for the Study of Ideologies and Literatures.

Lacan, J. A. (1977). *Écrits: A selection.* New York: W. W. Norton.

Menchú, R. (1984). *I, Rigoberta Menchú: An Indian woman in Guatemala* (E. Burgos-Debray, Ed.; A. Wright, Trans.). London: Verso.

Pratt, M. L. (1986). Fieldwork in common places. In J. Clifford & G. E. Marcus (Eds.), *Writing culture: The poetics and politics of ethnography*. Berkeley: University of California Press.

Rabasa, J., Sanjinés, J., & Carr, R. (Eds.). (1996). Subaltern studies in the Americas [Special issue]. *dispositio/n, 19*(46). (Contributions written in 1994)

Randall, M. (1985). *Testimonios: A guide to oral history*. Toronto: Participatory Research Group.

Rivero, E. (1984-1985). *Testimonio* y conversaciones como discurso literario: Cuba y Nicaragua. *Literature and Contemporary Revolutionary Culture, 1.*

Rorty, R. (1985). Solidarity or objectivity? In J. Rajchman & C. West (Eds.), *Postanalytic philosophy* (pp. 3-19). New York: Columbia University Press.

Sklodowska, E. (1982). La forma testimonial y la novelística de Miguel Barnet. *Revista/Review Interamericana, 12*, 368-380.

Sklodowska, E. (1996). Spanish American testimonial novel: Some afterthoughts. In G. M. Gugelberger (Ed.), *The real thing: Testimonial discourse and Latin America* (pp. 84-100). Durham, NC: Duke University Press.

Sommer, D. (1996). No secrets. In G. M. Gugelberger (Ed.), *The real thing: Testimonial discourse and Latin America* (pp. 130-160). Durham, NC: Duke University Press.

Spivak, G. C. (1988). Can the subaltern speak? In C. Nelson & L. Grossberg (Eds.), *Marxism and the interpretation of culture* (pp. 280-316). Urbana: University of Illinois Press.

Stoll, D. (1999). *Rigoberta Menchú and the story of all poor Guatemalans*. Boulder, CO: Westview.

Taylor, C. (1994). The politics of recognition. In C. Taylor, K. A. Appiah, J. Habermas, S. C. Rockefeller, M. Walzer, & S. Wolf, *Multiculturalism: Examining the politics of recognition* (A. Gutmann, Ed.). Princeton, NJ: Princeton University Press.

11

Participatory
Action Research

Stephen Kemmis and Robin McTaggart

◆   Participatory action research is a contested concept applied to a variety of research approaches employed in a diversity of fields and settings. The nomenclature itself reflects the contestation, with the rubric *action research* perhaps best encompassing most of the approaches, with *participatory research* overlapping to include the rest. In our own work we initially used the term *collaborative action research* to emphasize the interdependence of the activities of university academics and educators in particular. More recently we have used the term *participatory action research*, in recognition of practical and theoretical convergences between our work and the activities of people engaged in "participatory research" in several different fields.

We begin by briefly describing some key approaches and some typical criticisms of them, but our aim in this chapter is to set out a particular view of participatory action research developed in our own theory and practice in recent years.

◆ The Field of "Participatory Action Research"

In this section, we outline several different approaches to inquiry for which the term *participatory action research* is sometimes used. Our synopsis includes only those kinds of inquiry that have attracted some support in relevant research literature.[1] Of course, there is considerable contestation between and within the approaches identified here, usually around questions such as the following: (a) Is this defensible as research? (b) How crucial is participation and how is it expressed here? (c) Is this research really about social improvement, or is it only about efficiency, with basic values unquestioned? (d) What are the appropriate roles for researchers, research, and other social agents in the enhancement of the human condition?

Despite the contestation, there is some convergence of interest among researchers in each of the approaches identified, and the vitality of the debates provides evidence of some shared views as well as differences. We present each approach beginning with a basic outline; we then indicate the sites and settings where the approach has been practiced most explicitly and identify what we see as some key criticisms of the approach. We present the criticisms somewhat naturalistically, expressed informally as we see them emerging in the field. In later sections we provide a more developed theoretical perspective that is useful for reflection on the nature of these criticisms.

Participatory Research

Participatory research (often called PR) is an alternative philosophy of social research (and social life, *vivencia*) often associated with social transformation in the Third World. It has roots in liberation theology and neo-Marxist approaches to community development (in Latin America, for example), but also has rather liberal origins in human rights activism (in Asia, for example). Three particular attributes are often used to distinguish PR from conventional research: shared ownership of research projects, community-based analysis of social problems, and an orientation toward community action. Given PR's commitment to social, economic, and political development responsive to the needs and opinions of ordinary people, proponents of this approach have highlighted the politics of conventional social research, arguing that orthodox social science, despite its claim to value neutrality, normally serves the ideological function of justifying the position and interests of the wealthy and powerful (Fals Borda & Rahman, 1991; Forester, Pitt, & Welsh, 1993; Freire, 1982/1988; Hall, Gillette, & Tandon, 1982; Horton, 1990; McTaggart, 1997a; Oliveira & Darcy, 1975; Park, Brydon-Miller, Hall, & Jackson, 1993).

Sites and settings. In developing countries, PR is typically undertaken by members of urban communities in *barrios* and *favellas,* remote and resource-poor rural areas, unregulated industries, and neighborhoods with high levels of unemployment, and by street dwellers. Its proponents are often the poorest of the poor, deprived and exploited people working in collaboration with *animateurs* from universities, agricultural extension agencies, community development organizations, churches, and labor unions. In "developed countries," many of those who have adopted PR approaches have been academics committed to integrating university responsibilities with community work. PR has been conducted in a variety of settings and with a variety of groups in education, social work, health care, natural resource management, and urban planning.

Criticisms. Criticisms leveled against PR include that it lacks scientific rigor, confusing social activism and community development with research. Such practices may employ desirable means and serve desirable ends, but to confuse them with research—or, worse still, to disguise or dignify them as research—is a fundamental form of deception and manipulation, in this view. Proponents of PR are sometimes accused of such close identification with the communities they study that they see themselves as special and different and they alienate potential allies among alternative research proponents in the academy.

The association of the practice of PR with activists occasionally leads to accusations that it is politically motivated outsiders, not the poor, deprived, and exploited themselves, who take the initiative in identifying problems to be investigated. This in turn may lead to the charge that the welfare, livelihoods, and, in some cases, lives of disadvantaged people are put at risk as a consequence of their involvement in PR. Further, in extreme cases, proponents of PR may be dismissed as malcontents, subversives, and "communists."

Critical Action Research

Critical action research expresses a commitment to bring together broad social analyses: the self-reflective collective self-study of practice, the way language is used, organization and power in a local situation, and action to improve things. Critical action research is strongly represented in the literatures of educational action research, and emerges from dissatisfactions with classroom action research, which typically does not take a broad view of the role of the relationship between education and social change. Critical action research has a strong commitment to participation as well as to the social analyses in the critical social science tradition that reveal the disempowerment and injustice created in industrialized societies. In recent times it has attempted also to take account of disadvantage attributable to gender and ethnicity as well as to social class, its initial point of reference (Carr & Kemmis, 1986; Fay, 1987; Henry, 1991; Kemmis, 1991; Marika, Ngurruwutthun, & White, 1992; McTaggart, 1991a, 1991b, 1991c, 1997a, 1997b; Zuber-Skerritt, 1996).

Sites and settings. Critical action research projects typically include mixed groups of participants, for example, university researchers, teachers and principals, curriculum consultants, community members, and others with interests and expertise in the area of action and inquiry. Networking is important as participants are aware that change and innovation requires broad-based support. Groups may seek input from others to help inform, initiate, and sustain changes and improvements.

Criticisms. Criticisms of critical action research echo some of the criticisms of participatory research. Critical action research may be regarded as a "dangerous" vehicle for importing "radical" ideology into social settings. This view suggests that critical action research makes social participants dependent on "radical theorists" and denies that social participants' self-understandings can alone constitute a source of critical self-reflection and emancipation. In other words, critical action research may simply be yet another vehicle for the imperialism of academic (patriarchal) discourses over participants' own ways of describing and engaging their experience. In the same vein, but perhaps more generously, critical action research may be considered a "romantic" aspiration, overemphasizing people's willingness and capacity to participate in programs of reform.

Classroom Action Research

Classroom action research typically involves the use of qualitative, interpretive modes of inquiry and data collection by teachers (often with help from academics) with a view to teachers' making judgments about how to improve their own practices. The practice of classroom action research has a long tradition but has swung in and out of favor, principally because the theoretical work that justified it lagged behind the progressive educational movements that breathed life into it at certain historical moments (McTaggart, 1991a; Noffke, 1990, 1997a, 1997b). Primacy is given to teachers' self-understandings and judgments. The emphasis is "practical"—that is, on the interpretations teachers and students are making and acting on in the situation. That is, classroom action research is practical not just idealistically, in a utopian way, or just about how interpretations might be different "in theory," but practical in Aristotle's sense of practical reasoning about how to act rightly and properly in a situation with which one is confronted. If university researchers are involved, their role is a service role to the teachers. Such university researchers are often advocates for "teachers' knowledge" and may disavow or seek to diminish the relevance of more theoretical discourses such as critical theory (Dadds, 1995; Elliott, 1976-1977/1988; Sagor, 1992; Stenhouse, 1975; Weiner, 1989).

Sites and settings. As the name implies, key participants in classroom action research are teachers, and sites are typically school settings (although action research is becoming more common in university classrooms). Other participants may be university researchers and occasionally curriculum consultants and students, but generally the professional ethics and substantive responsibilities of teachers take center stage.

Criticisms. Classroom action research is sometimes criticized for the prominence it gives to teachers' knowledge in comparison with other views of what is happening in schools. This privileging of teachers' knowledge masks the assumption that significant improvement in classrooms can be accomplished in the absence of broader patterns of community support and social change (thereby ignoring the literature on educational change; Fullan, 1982, 1991). Further, it implies that consciousness-raising among teachers is possible without the theoretical resources of traditions of feminism, racism, critical theory, postcolonialist, and other such discourses (movements that more often arose in universities and communities, not schools).

Action Learning

Action learning has its origins in the work of advocate Reg Revans, who saw traditional approaches to management inquiry as unhelpful in solving the problems of organizations. Revans's early work with colliery managers attempting to improve workplace safety marks a significant turning point for the role of professors—engaging them directly in management problems in organizations.

The fundamental idea of action learning is bringing people together to learn from each other's experience. There is emphasis on studying one's own situation, clarifying what the organization is trying to achieve, and working to remove obstacles. Key aspirations are organization efficacy and efficiency, although advocates of action learning affirm the moral purpose and content of their own work and of the managers they seek to engage in the process (Clark, 1972; Pedler, 1991; Revans, 1980, 1982).

Sites and settings. Action learning began as an approach to management (and manager) development and still has that focus. However, broader participation has been used with good effect in some settings. It is used most often in business settings (early work was with colliery managers), but has been employed in the public sector (hospitals and public housing estates), especially where organizations were seeking to emulate what were perceived to be (and are in many circumstances) successful collaborative business management practices.

Criticisms. The early work on action learning began with the practice of colliery management. Some argue that its emphasis on management and on the common practice of composing action learning "sets" (groups) primarily of managers restricts its capacity to bring about change and to respond to different workplace participants' concerns. Its tendency toward an emphasis on "efficiency" (or potential co-optability) ignores the broader questions of the values and social purposes of the organization and the different values and concerns of participants at different levels and in different parts of organizations. The emphasis on "workplace learning" and on individual organizational development is argued to deny a critical perspective—reducing "learning" to simply applying routines invented by others, believing reasons invented by others, servicing aspirations invented by others, realizing goals invented by others, and giving expression to values advocated by others. An emphasis on "problem solving" distracts attention from what is going on in the literature about similar workplaces and restricts the coherence aspired to in generating a theoretical rationale for the work of the organization or industry.

Action Science

Action science emphasizes the study of practice in organizational settings as a source of new understandings and improved practice. The field of action science systematically builds the relationship between academic organizational psychology and practical problems as they are experienced in organizations. It identifies two aspects to professional knowledge: the formal knowledge that all competent members of the profession are thought to share and into which professionals are inducted during their initial training, and the professional knowledge of interpretation and enactment. A distinction is also made between the professional's "espoused theory" and "theories in use," and "gaps" between these are used as points of reference for change. A key factor in analyzing these gaps between theory and practice is helping the professional to unmask the "cover-ups" that are put in place, especially when participants are feeling anxious or threatened. The approach aspires to the development of the "reflective practitioner" (Argyris, 1990; Argyris, Putnam, & Smith, 1985; Argyris & Schön, 1974, 1978; Reason, 1988; Schön, 1983, 1987, 1991).

Sites and settings. The action science approach has been used in a wide variety of professional occupations. Educators have often espoused it, perhaps most notably in advocacies for more symmetrical and reciprocal versions of "clinical supervision" and for "reflective practice."

Criticisms. Action science faces criticisms similar to those aimed at action learning, encompassed by the term *technicism.* Participants are exposed to the judgment that an "espoused theory" does not match a *researcher-*described "theory in use." Implicit is the assumption that an espoused theory could ever adequately specify action, basically a flaw in the cognitivist position on the relationship between theory and practice. The identified gap between theory and practice then automatically exposes the participant to the intervention of the outsider, especially his or her role in "unmasking" the defenses of participants. Further, the approach can be somewhat individualistic, making each participant subject to outsider intervention and vulnerable after the intervention. The criticism also suggests unclear specification of the role and composition of the "group" of

342

participants and the relationship between the group and researchers and consultants.

Soft Systems Approaches

Soft systems approaches have their origins in organizations that use so-called hard systems of engineering especially for industrial production. Soft systems methodology is the human "systems" analogy for systems engineering that has developed as the science of product and information flow. It is defined as oppositional to positivistic science, with its emphasis on hypothesis testing. The researcher (typically an outside consultant) assumes a role as discussion partner or trainer in a real problem situation. The researcher works with participants to generate some (systems) models of the situation and uses the models to question the situation and to suggest a revised course of action (Checkland, 1981; Checkland & Scholes, 1990; Davies & Ledington, 1991; Flood & Jackson, 1991; Jackson, 1991; Kolb, 1984).

Sites and settings. Soft systems methodologies have been used in a variety of industrial and public sector organizational settings. Participants usually include an external management consultant who assumes a key role in making meaning from the attempts to bring about improvement. The consultant explicitly defers to the values of the organization avowed by participants and presents as a "neutral" process management consultant.

Criticisms. Criticisms of soft systems methodology include the ambiguous notion of participation and the potentially influential role played by the consultant. The association (typically contractual) between the consultant and the management of the organization leads to concerns about the interests underlying the role played by the consultant. The consultant is often described as "facilitator" or "process manager," and the assumption that this is a value-free, neutral, or politically inert role is strongly contested. It is suggested that there is a weak relationship between the process of inquiry and the literature and critique of the organization from a theoretically informed position. There is deference to the view that organizational reform is a "process" (and a one-off process) that requires an emphasis on processual input and consultant diagnosis at the expense of substantive input or input from sources other than the consultant.

Industrial Action Research

Industrial action research has an extended history, dating back to the post-Lewinian influence in organizational psychology and organizational development at the Tavistock Institute of Human Relations in Britain and the Research Center for Group Dynamics in the United States. It is typically consultant driven, with very strong advocacies for collaboration between social scientists and members of different levels of the organization. The work is often couched in the language of workplace democratization, but more recent explorations have aspired more explicitly to the democratization of the research act itself, following the theory and practice of the participatory research movement. Especially in its more recent manifestations, industrial action research is differentiated from "action science" and its emphasis on cognition, taking a preferred focus on reflection and the need for broader organizational and social change. Some advocacies have used critical theory as a resource to express aspirations for more participatory forms of work and evaluation, but more usually the style is somewhat humanistic and individualistic rather than "critical." Emphases on social systems in organizations, such as improving organizational effectiveness and employee relations, are common, and the Lewinian aspiration to learn from trying to bring about change is a strong theme (Bravette, 1996; Elden, 1983; Emery & Thorsrud, 1976; Emery, Thorsrud, & Trist, 1969; Foster, 1972; Levin, 1985; Pasmore & Friedlander, 1982; Sandkull, 1980; Torbert, 1991; Warmington, 1980; Whyte, 1989, 1991).

Sites and settings. Participants in industrial action research are typically shop-floor employees, middle managers, and professional consultants from outside the organization working in collaboration. The approach has been documented in a wide variety of industrial (and service) settings, and persuasive evidence of the broad positive effect of workplace "democratization" using action research approaches is widespread.

Criticisms. It is suggested that industrial action research has not adequately engaged the problem of the hierarchies and goals of industrial settings. In this view, "participation" is too limited to the lower echelons of organizations, and thereby senior management, company directors, and shareholders are insulated from questions about basic organizational values and directions. The work draws more thoughtfully on social theory than do other forms of action research in industrial settings, but criticisms from the participatory research movement indicate a profound wariness about the adoption of that movement's cherished ideas and hard-won practices in the very transnational corporations that have created serious dysfunction and poverty in Third World settings. Although industrial action research may constitute organizational development and an expression of democracy in some parts of the organization, it is feared that it may too easily drift back into technicist, co-optive, and control practices such as quality circles and quality assurance.

◆ Research and Social Practice

Much contemporary participatory action research has evolved as an extension of applied research into practical social settings, with participants taking on roles formerly occupied by social researchers from outside the settings (Adelman, 1997; Altrichter & Gstettner, 1997). By contrast, participatory research and collaborative action research emerged more or less deliberately as forms of resistance to conventional research practices that were perceived by particular kinds of participants as acts of colonization—that is, as a means of normalizing or domesticating people to research and policy agendas imposed on a local group or community from central agencies often far removed from local concerns and interests.

This switch of perspective is not just of "political" or historical interest. It challenges some fundamental presuppositions about the nature of research as a social practice, including (for example) presuppositions about the nature of social life and about who can be a researcher (we discuss some of these issues later in this chapter). Theorizing participatory action research requires articulating and—to an extent—formalizing what is implied when participants in a social setting decide to take the construction and reconstruction of their social reality into their own hands, knowing that they are not alone in constructing or reconstructing it, but nevertheless taking an active, agential role in changing the processes of construction of social realities.

One way to understand this shift in perspective is to see it historically. Some histories of this kind are available (Fals Borda, 1979, 1988; McTaggart, 1991a, 1997a; Noffke, 1990, 1997a, 1997b). It is also possible to understand it (auto-)biographically or phenomenologically, from the perspectives of some of the people who have advocated and undertaken participatory action research as part of their engagement in a politics of resistance nourished by research undertaken by and for groups experiencing one or another form of oppression. Works of this kind also exist (Horton, 1990; McTaggart, 1999), some related to the histories of participatory research. In this chapter, we would like to take a different approach, partly to draw out some of the logic of what is implied by participatory research and partly to build some bridges between the participant perspective and the conventional literature of social research methodology—as a contribution to going beyond the "paradigm wars" that have bedeviled social research over much of the past century.

As Anthony Giddens (1979, p. 71) pointed out some years ago, participants in social settings are not "cultural dopes"—they can give cogent reasons for their intentions and actions, and generally demonstrate a sophisticated (although not necessarily social scientific) understanding of the situations they inhabit. Moreover, unlike social theorists attempting theoretical constructions of a setting from within a particular tradition of social theory, they are not obliged to foreclose options about how to "see" their situation—that is, to "see" it theoretically, in a way that can be construed as a contribution to a particular tradition of theorizing. Indeed, participants frequently shift from one way of seeing something to another, not only to see it from their own points of view and from the points of view of relevant others, but also to see it both from the perspective of individuals and from a "big-picture" perspective on the setting, which means seeing the local setting as connected to wider social and historical conditions.

There is also a sense in which, when participants are dissatisfied with the way things are, they do not just want things to be different; they understand that things have to be made different by themselves and others. To the extent that this is so, it indicates that participants are generally aware that social settings are constituted through social practices, and that making change is itself a practice.

Participatory action research (not always by that name) frequently emerges in situations where people want to make changes thoughtfully—that is, after critical reflection. It emerges when people want to think "realistically" about where they are now, how things came to be that way, and, from these starting points, how, in practice, things might be changed.

Taking a "realistic" perspective on changing social practices in a setting usually means that participants have to take a multifaceted view of practice—not seeing it in a narrow way. In this, participants are sometimes regarded as "naïve" or "primitive" from the point of view of social theory, but we cannot accept these descriptions. On the contrary, we want to assert that participants are far from naïve. The participant perspective poses a substantial challenge to social theory: to articulate "common" sense in a way that will be regarded as authentic and compelling by participants themselves, without converting participants to the imposed perspective of a specialist social theorist. This process of making the familiar unfamiliar (and making the unfamiliar familiar) involves treading a fine line between taking an attitude toward the situation that aims to "uncover" or "unmask" hidden forces at work in the situation (the attitude of the outsider who claims special insight into the setting) and illuminating and clarifying interconnections and tensions between elements of a setting in terms that participants themselves regard as authentic (which may include giving more weight to relationships participants had previously discounted or devalued in their deliberations). The criterion of authenticity involves a dialectic sometimes described in terms of "the melting of horizons" (Gadamer, 1975)—seeing things intersubjectively, from one's own point of view and from the point of view of others (from the inside and the outside).

In the following subsections we briefly examine the notion of "practice" as a way to build a bridge between a participant perspective on practice and different theoretical traditions in the study of practice, and then briefly examine the participant perspective as a distinctive standpoint in terms of the social relations of social research.

Different Traditions in the Study of Practice

Despite its ubiquity and familiarity, what the term *practice* means is by no means self-explanatory. In theory and research, it turns out to mean very different things to different people. Perhaps one reason for this is that researchers who examine practice from different intellectual traditions tend to focus on different aspects of practice when they investigate it. The result is confusion. On the basis of their different views about how practice itself should be understood, different theorists take different views on how it can and should be improved.

To make a start in clearing up some of these confusions, it may help if we distinguish five different aspects of practice emphasized in different investigations of practice:

1. The individual performances, events, and effects that constitute practice as it is viewed from the "objective," external perspective of an outsider (the way the practitioner's individual behavior appears to an outside observer);

2. The wider social and material conditions and interactions that constitute practice as it is viewed from the "objective," external perspective of an outsider (the way the patterns of social interaction among those involved in the practice appear to an outside observer);

3. The intentions, meanings, and values that constitute practice as it is viewed from the "subjective," internal perspective of individual practitioners themselves (the way individual practitioners' intentional actions appear to them as individual cognitive subjects);

4. The language, discourses, and traditions that constitute practice as it is viewed from the "subjective," internal social perspective of members of the participants' own discourse community who must represent (describe, interpret, evaluate) practices in order to talk about and develop them, as happens, for example, in the discourse communities of professions (the way the language of practice appears to communities of practitioners as they represent their practices to themselves and others);

5. The change and evolution of practice—taking into account all four of the aspects of practice just mentioned—that comes into view when it is understood as reflexively restructured and transformed over time, in its historical dimension.

Different approaches to the study of practice have tended to focus on one or another of these different aspects of practice, with the result that, over time, different traditions in the study of practice have emerged. Some regard these different traditions as mutually exclusive and competing, based on their view that just one is the "correct" way to view practice. Others regard these different traditions pluralistically, seeing them as different but not necessarily in competition with one another, based on their view that each will simply go its own way in the research literature. Still others regard these different traditions as talking past one another—as failing to engage with one another in reciprocal critique and debate that could permit the exploration of complementarities and points of connection between them. And still others take the view that the different traditions can be interrelated within broader, perhaps synthetic, frameworks of theory and practice. There is merit in exploring the possibilities of complementarity and connection among these different approaches, even if for the time being it seems premature to say how a broad and unifying synthesis of the different perspectives can be achieved.

Epistemological Perspectives

Although different schools of thought in theorizing and research about practice in different fields are very diverse in terms of the problems and phenomena they study and the methods they employ, it is possible to bring some of their presuppositions about problems, phenomena, and methods to the fore by making some distinctions around which these differences can be arrayed. Generally speaking, these are regarded as epistemological questions—questions about the nature of the "truth" in the human and social sciences—in the case we are considering here, the "truth" about practice. For the moment, we will focus on just two dichotomies that have divided approaches to the human and social sciences: first, the division between (a) those approaches that see human and social life largely in *individualistic* terms and (b) those that see human and social life largely in terms of the *social realm;* and second, the division between (a) those approaches that conceive of their problems, phenomena, and methods largely in *objective* terms (from an "external" perspective, as it were) and (b) those that conceive their problems, phenomena, and methods largely in *subjective* terms (from an "internal" perspective, as it were). In each case, we want to suggest that these are false dichotomies, and that we can escape from the partiality of each by seeing the two sides of the dichotomies not as opposites, only one of which can be true, but as dialectically related—that is, as mutually constitutive aspects of one another, both of which are necessary to achieve a more comprehensive perspective on practice.

The move from thinking in terms of dichotomies to thinking in dialectical terms might be characterized as a move from "either/or" thinking to "never either, always both" thinking. (The logic of what these figures of speech imply will become clearer in what follows.) For the time being, however, it suffices to say that we can transcend each of these two dichotomies—individual-social and objective-subjective—by seeing both in dialectical terms. We can use these two distinctions as a basis for a taxonomy of different approaches to the study of practice (see Figure 11.1).

1. *Practice as individual behavior, to be studied objectively.* The first perspective on practice sees it primarily "from the outside," as individual behavior. Those adopting this perspective frequently understand the science of behavior as "objective" and apply this view to their understanding

Focus:	The individual	The social	Both: Reflexive-dialectical view of individual-social relations and connections
Perspective			
Objective	(1) Practice as individual behavior, seen in terms of performances, events & effects: behaviorist and most cognitivist approaches in psychology	(2) Practice as social interaction (e.g., ritual, system-structured: structure-fuctionalist and social systems approaches	
Subjective	(3) Practice as intentional action, shaped by meaning and values: psychological *verstehen* (empathetic understanding) and most contructivist approaches	(4) Practice as socially structured, shaped by discourses, tradition: interpretive, aesthetic-historical *verstehen* & poststructuralist approaches	
Both: Reflexive-dialectical view of subjective-objective relations and connections			(5) Practice as socially and historically constituted, and as reconstituted by human agency and social action: critical theory, critical social science

Figure 11.1. Relationships Among Different Traditions in the Study of Practice

of practice. A variety of traditions in psychology, including the behaviorist and the cognitivist, adopt this view of practice.

Research on practice from this perspective adopts correlational or quasi-experimental methods; it is likely to use descriptive and inferential statistics and to adopt an instrumental view of the relationship between the researcher and the researched, in which the field being studied is understood in the "third person" (as objects whose behavior is to be changed). This approach to the study of practice is likely to be adopted when the research question is one asked by people administering organizations who want to provoke change by changing the inputs, processes, and outputs of the organization as a system (in which people are seen as elements of the system).

2. *Practice as group behavior or ritual, to be studied objectively.* The second perspective also views practice "from the outside," but sees it in terms of the social group. Those adopting this perspective also understand the study of group behavior as "objective." A variety of social psychological perspectives, and structural-functionalist perspectives in sociology, adopt this view of practice, as do some forms of systems theory in the social sciences.

Research on practice from this perspective is also likely to adopt correlational or quasi-experimental methods; it is also likely to use descriptive and inferential statistics and to adopt an instrumental view of the relationship between the researcher and the researched, in which the field being studied is understood in the "third person" (as objects whose behavior is to be changed). And, like the first perspective, this perspective would also be likely to be adopted when the research question is one asked by people administering systems who want to change them by changing system inputs, processes, and outputs.

3. *Practice as individual action, to be studied from the perspective of the subjective.* The third perspective attempts to understand practice "from the inside"—from the perspective of the individual practitioner. In this view, human action (including practice) cannot be understood as "mere" behavior; it must be seen as shaped by the values, intentions, and judgments of the practitioner. Because this view takes into account these elements of practice, as far as possible, from the perspective of the practitioner, it is frequently said to be a "subjective" view of practice (although it should be recognized that describing it as "subjective" is not to say that it is any less capable of laying claim to being scientific in its approach to the study of practice—indeed, there is a very strong tradition in the human and social sciences based on just this view). A variety of approaches in psychology take this view of practice (among them some clinical, some "humanistic," and some "gestalt" approaches, to give just a few examples). A much older and stronger tradition in the study of people and their

351

actions—one that can be traced directly back to Aristotle in the Western philosophical tradition—is also based on understanding motives, intentions, values, and notions of virtue, and it understands practice (in the sense of praxis) as the exercise of human judgment by people acting in (practical) situations in which they are obliged to act, knowing that action in real historical circumstances is always uncertain and never fully justified by appeal to technical rules or principles, but must always reflect the best judgment of the actor. As well as being found in certain kinds of humanistic philosophy, this view of practice is found in some theological writings on practice.

Research on practice from this perspective generally adopts qualitative methods (including autobiographical, idiographic, and phenomenological methods), is likely to make only limited use of statistics, and is likely to adopt a "practical" view of the relationship between the researcher and the researched, in which the field being studied is understood in the "second person" (that is, as knowing, responsible, and autonomous subjects—persons who, like the researcher her- or himself, must make their own decisions about how to act in the situations in which they find themselves). This perspective is likely to be adopted when the research question is one asked by people who understand themselves to be autonomous and responsible persons acting in life worlds of human relationships and interactions, who believe that changing these life worlds requires engaging, and perhaps re-forming, selves and relationships in shared life-world settings.

4. *Practice as social action or tradition, to be understood from the perspective of the subjective.* A fourth perspective on practice also attempts to view it "from the inside," but understands it not from the perspective of the individual acting alone, but as part of a social structure that contributes to forming the way in which action (practice) is understood by people in the situation. It also takes a "subjective" view, but it takes into account that people and the way they act are also formed historically—that they always come to situations that have been preformed, and in which only certain kinds of action are now appropriate or possible. Moreover, this view is also conscious that it must take into account that people's own perspectives, and their very words, have all been formed historically and in the interactions of social life—they are historically, socially, and discursively constituted. Much social theory, much social and moral philosophy, and much theology is based on this view of practice.

Such a view is captured in Alasdair MacIntyre's (1983) careful definition of a practice as

> any coherent and complex form of socially-established cooperative human
> activity through which goods internal to that activity are realized, in the
> course of trying to achieve those standards of excellence which are appro-
> priate to, and partially definitive of, that form of activity, with the result that
> human powers to achieve excellence, and human conceptions of the ends
> and goods involved, are systematically extended. (p. 175)

MacIntyre gives some examples of practices and distinguishes practices
from institutions:

> Practices must not be confused with institutions. Chess, physics and medi-
> cine are practices; chess clubs, laboratories, universities and hospitals are
> institutions. Institutions are characteristically and necessarily concerned
> with . . . external goods. They are involved in acquiring money and other
> material goods; they are structured in terms of power and status, and they
> distribute money, power and status as rewards. Nor could they do otherwise
> if they are to sustain not only themselves, but also the practices of which
> they are bearers. For no practices can survive any length of time unsustained
> by institutions. . . . institutions and practices characteristically form a single
> causal order in which the ideals and the creativity of the practice are always
> vulnerable to the acquisitiveness of the institution, in which the cooperative
> care for common goods of the practice is always vulnerable to the competi-
> tiveness of the institution. (p. 181)

Research on practice from this perspective is similar to the third perspective in its likely research methods (although it may also adopt clinical
or critical ethnography as a research method, or particular kinds of methods that are very explicit about the role of the researcher in the research—
as in advocacies for some feminist approaches to research), its view about
practical reasoning, and its view of the standpoint of the researcher in relation to others in the situation being studied. In this case, however, the researcher would understand her- or himself not only as another actor in a
social situation, but also as a human agent who, with others, must act at
any particular moment in a situation that is already socially, historically,
and discursively formed, and in which he or she is also, to some extent, a
representative of a tradition that contests the ground with other traditions

353

(because different and competing traditions about different things typically are simultaneously at play in any particular situation). In this sense, research in this tradition is likely to understand itself as in some sense "political"—just as the situations it studies are "political."

5. *Practice as reflexive, to be studied dialectically.* The fifth view of practice understands that it is "political" in an even more self-conscious sense: It understands that to study practice is to change it, that the process of studying it is also "political," and that its own standpoint is liable to change through the process of action—that it is a process of enlightenment about the standpoint from which one studies practice as well as about the practice itself.

This view of practice challenges the dichotomies or dualisms that separate the first four views from one another: the dualisms of the individual versus the social and the objective versus the subjective. It attempts to see each of these dimensions not in terms of polar opposites, but in terms of the mutuality and relationship between these different aspects of things. Thus it sees the individual and the social, and the objective and the subjective, as related aspects of human life and practice, to be understood dialectically—that is, as mutually opposed (and often contradictory) but mutually necessary aspects of human, social, and historical reality, in which each aspect helps to constitute the other.

In this view, it is necessary to understand practice as enacted by individuals who act in the context of history and in ways constituted by a vast historical web of social interactions among people. Similarly, it is necessary to understand practice as having both objective (externally given) and subjective (internally understood and interpreted) aspects, both of which are necessary to understand how any practice is really practiced, how it is constituted historically and socially, and how it can be transformed. This view of the relationship between the objective and the subjective is sometimes also described as "reflexive," because changing the objective conditions changes the way in which a situation is interpretively understood, which in turn changes how people act on the "external," "objective" world, which means that what they do is understood and interpreted differently, and that others also act differently, and so on. This dynamic process of reflection and self-reflection gives human action in history its dynamic, fluid, and reflexive character. In this view of practice, practitioners regard themselves explicitly as engaged in action that makes history, and they are likely to regard research as a process of learning from action and history—a

354

process conducted within action and history, not standing outside it in the role of recorder or commentator, or above it in the role of conductor or controller.

The reflexive-dialectical perspective on practice thus attempts to find a place for the four previous perspectives in a broader framework of historical, social, and discursive construction and reconstruction, and does its best to recognize not only that people's actions are caused by their intentions and circumstances, but also that people cause intentions and circumstances—that is, that people are made by action in the world, and that they also make action and history. And it aims to see how these processes occur within the ambit of the research process itself.

Research on practice from this perspective is likely to adopt research methods that are reflexive—methods like those used in critical social science (Carr & Kemmis, 1986; Fay, 1987), collaborative action research (Kemmis & McTaggart, 1988), and "memory work" (Haug, 1987). They are reflexive in the sense that they engage participants in a collaborative process of social transformation in which they learn from, and change the way they engage in, the process of transformation. Research conducted from this perspective adopts an "emancipatory" view of the point and purpose of the research, in which coparticipants attempt to remake and improve their own practice to overcome distortions, incoherence, contradictions, and injustices. It adopts a "first-person" perspective in which people construct the research process as a way of collaborating in the process of transforming their practices, their understanding of their practices, and the situations in which they practice. Like the fourth perspective on practice, it understands that research is "political," but it aims to make the research process into a politics that will in some definite ways supersede and reconstruct the preexisting politics of the settings in which it is conducted—indeed, it aims to be a process in which various aspects of social life in the setting (cultural, economic, and political) can be transformed through collaborative action (although recognizing that the internal social processes of the setting and the research are connected to, and sometimes conflict with, wider social and historical processes that the coresearchers cannot suspend or change simply by changing themselves, so they work in relation to these wider forces rather than simply "for" or "against" them).

Although the other four traditions are all necessary in their own ways, and for particular kinds of purposes, this fifth tradition is of special interest to those who want to change practices through their own efforts, and especially by their efforts in participatory, collaborative research. It is a tradition in the study of practice that aims to make explicit connections across the dimensions of "objective" and "subjective," the focus on the individual and the focus on the social, the aspects of structure and agency, and the connections between the past and the future.

The significance of the word *connections* here deserves special notice. The study of a practice as complex as the practice of education, or nursing, or public administration (to give just a few examples) is a study of connections—of many different kinds of communicative, productive, and organizational relationships among people in socially, historically, and discursively constituted media of language (discourse), work, and power—all of which must be understood dynamically and relationally. And we should recognize that there are research approaches that aim to explore these connections and relationships by participating in them and, through changing the forms in which people participate in them, to change the practice, the way it is understood, and the situations in which the practice is conducted. At its best, such a research tradition aims to help people understand themselves both as "objective" forces impinging on others and as subjects who have intentions and commitments they share with others, and both as people who act in ways framed by discourses formed beyond any one of us individually and as people who make meaning for ourselves in communication with the others alongside whom we stand, and whose fates—one way or another—we share.

Traditions of Research Into Practice as Constructed Through Social and Material Practices

Research practices are constituted in social and material relationships. To take a tough materialist stance, we might even want to think of research practices in terms of Louis Althusser's (1971) definition of a practice: "By practice in general, I shall mean any process of transformation of a determinate given raw material into a determinate product, a transformation effected by determinate human labor, using determinate means of production" (quoted in Bennett, 1979, p. 111). This definition of a practice probably rests most comfortably in the second of the five traditions outlined earlier (with the particular partialities of that perspective). It nevertheless draws attention to the concreteness of the social and material relationships that constitute practice—concrete relationships between people and things (which may include symbolic kinds of relationships and relationships between people's interpretations of people and things). Althusser nominates processes of transformation involving "raw materials," "products," "human labor," and "means of production"—all of which are determinate in any given case. We might ask ourselves what elements of the social and material relationships of any particular piece of research on practice (in education, nursing, or public administration, for example) can be described using each of these terms, and about the nature of the relationships among them.

Methodological Perspectives

At one level, considering the means of production involved in different traditions of research into practice, we may examine the kinds of research techniques these traditions typically employ. Different researchers into practice emphasize different aspects of practice in their investigations and rely on different research methods and techniques that seem appropriate in the study of practice viewed from the particular perspectives they adopt. That is, different methodological perspectives in research on practice are related to different epistemological perspectives on the nature of practice; from this it follows that different research techniques "construct" the objects of their study (practices) as phenomena of rather different kinds. Figure 11.2 outlines some of the kinds of methods and techniques that have characteristically been employed in different traditions in the study of practice.

These remarks have implications for the contemporary debate between "quantitative" and "qualitative" approaches in social and educational science. They suggest that it would be a mistake to conclude that truth and certainty reside with quantitative methods, or that they reside with qualitative methods. It is an illusion to believe that research methods and techniques provide secure paths to truth and certainty. Sadly, however, there are some who still cling to these illusions. At another extreme, however, are those who believe that, because truth and certainty cannot be attained, there is no sense in science except aesthetic or poetic sense—in short, that social science is just words, symbols, and images that can claim no power to represent the social world in any compelling way, except, perhaps, with the compulsion of narrative or myth (for example, Lyotard, 1984). These views share the mistaken assumption that truth is certain or it cannot be truth at all. There is a path between this Scylla and Charybdis, however: the view that what we call "truth" is always and only provisional, that it is always fallible, that it is always shaped by particular views

Focus:	The individual	The social	Both: Reflexive-dialectical view of individual-social relations and connections
Perspective			
Objective	(1) Practice as individual behavior: Quantitative, correlational-experimental methods. Psychometric and observational techniques, tests, interaction schedules.	(2) Practice as social and systems behavior: Quantitative, correlational-experimental methods. Observational techniques, sociometrics, systems analysis, social ecology.	
Subjective	(3) Practice as intentional action: Qualitative, interpretive methods. Clinical analysis, interview, questionnaire, diaries, journals, self-report, introspection	(4) Practice as socially structured, shaped by discourses and tradition: Qualitative, interpretive, historical methods. Discourse analysis, document analysis.	
Both: Reflexive-dialectical view of subjective-objective relations and connections			(5) Practice as socially and historically constituted, and as reconstituted by human agency and social action: Critical methods. Dialectical analysis (multiple methods).

Figure 11.2. Methods and Techniques Characteristic of Different Approaches to the Study of Practice

and material-social-historical circumstances, and that it can be approached only intersubjectively—through exploration of the extent to which it seems accurate, morally right and appropriate, and authentic in

358

the light of our lived experience. From this view, it is the task of a social or educational science to create the conditions under which provisional, fallible, intersubjectively based claims to truth can be explored. In our view, this is the rich and complex work required in theorizing practice.

There is a kind of self-fulfilling prophecy, then, in research methods and techniques that construct practices in different ways. They do produce "pictures" of practice, but, like all pictures, they construct the world from a particular observational standpoint or perspective, in the particular terms and observational categories of the media (or discourse) of the particular observational techniques employed. Thus, for example, one tradition sees practice in terms of behavior, another sees it in terms of participants' values and interests, and another sees it in terms of discursive formation. For some, these perspectives are simply incommensurable;[2] for others, they may be complementary. At the level of research methods and techniques, we must certainly concede that there is a plurality of perspectives. The question is whether this plurality can be understood as suggesting a higher-order perspective in which we can triangulate these different perspectives against one another to arrive at a more multifaceted perspective that, even if it does not promise completeness, wholeness, or a higher-level unification of the perspectives it gathers together, at least poses a problem of how the different perspectives can be interrelated.

◆ Participatory Action Research as Practice

Like other forms of social research, participatory action research is sometimes conducted principally from within one or another of the traditions outlined in this taxonomy. More generally, however, it takes a more encompassing view of practice, simply because participants in most settings cannot readily exclude one or another of these perspectives on the grounds that it is not relevant to the way participants—and others with whom they interact in the setting—see things. And, even more significant, participatory action research generally occurs very much in the dimension of historical time (Perspective 5): Participants make, and learn from, changes they make as they go.

Our own work in Aboriginal teacher education in the Northern Territory of Australia provides an example. Aboriginal teachers wanted to explore practices that made the schools in which they taught more expressive of Aboriginal culture. Western domination expressed itself in curriculum, pedagogy, and organization, and Aboriginal resistance to this domination is encapsulated in the words of Wesley Lanhupuy, Northern Territory parliamentarian representing the electorate of Arnhem and an Aboriginal elder from northeast Arnhemland, who described the problem Aboriginal teachers face in this way:

> Schools have been part of the process of the colonisation of Australia and its original inhabitants. Schools were introduced and imposed on Aborigines following the fierce struggles for the land between Aborigines and the new white settlers. This occurred in a predictable pattern as each state and territory of Australia was progressively colonised over the past two hundred years.
>
> This colonisation process has taken place within living memory in the Northern Territory and unfortunately continues in many of our schools today. These have been difficult times, in which schools have been used quite openly to capture the minds of Aboriginal children and to turn them towards the dominant balanda culture. So schools have been most significant in the attempt by non-Aboriginal Australians to assimilate Aborigines into the balanda society. . . .
>
> The strong balanda cultural orientation of the [school] and the dominating position of balanda teachers and administrators inevitably work to influence the minds of children in ways that undervalue the Aboriginal heritage. Aboriginal people now understand that if schools are to serve the political social and economic purposes of their own people, the school, as an institution, needs to be accommodated within Aboriginal society itself. Only when the cultural orientation of the school becomes Yolngu [Aboriginal], will schools become integral to the movement of Aborigines toward self-determination. The decolonisation of schools in Aboriginal communities is the challenge for Aborigines now. (Lanhupuy, 1987, p. 31)[3]

In the teacher education program we developed with help from Aboriginal teachers upgrading qualifications and from colleagues at Batchelor College in the Northern Territory of Australia, several aspects of practice were engaged and transformed: curriculum practices, teaching practices, administrative practices, practices of relating to communities, and the research practices we worked through with Aboriginal teachers to inform our work.

The curriculum, teaching, and organizational practices of both schools and Deakin University were changed as teachers and teacher educators began to understand the aspirations of Aboriginal communities. As teacher educators in this setting, we followed the lead of the Aboriginal teachers, who were changing their own teaching, curricular, and organizational practices to express more faithfully their emergent understandings of what they came to call "Aboriginal pedagogies," or, in four of their own languages, *Blekbala Wei, Deme Nayin, Yolngu Rom,* and *Ngini Nginingawula Ngawurranungurumagi* (Bunbury, Hastings, Henry, & McTaggart, 1991; Marika et al., 1992; Yirrkala Homeland Schools, 1996). Aboriginal teachers' reflections on their changing work was paralleled by documentation of the emergent rationale and critique of non-Aboriginal teacher educators' own practice (Kemmis, 1988; McTaggart, 1987, 1988, 1991b, 1991c). The enhancement of practice was informed by the principles of participatory action research expressed in various ways (Carr & Kemmis, 1986; Kemmis & McTaggart, 1988) and by an understanding of the ways the ideology, institutionalization, and practices of colonialism were insinuated into the lives of Aboriginal people and into our own lives. Only by understanding the historical location of our own work and by examining these understandings with Aboriginal people could we participate adequately in changing the work. It was an attempt to express what we now term Perspective 5: to articulate simultaneously a theory of educational practice and a theory of educational research practice that mutually support, inform, and challenge each other.

Social Relationships in the Study of Practice

A science of practice must itself be a practice. It will be describable in terms of the five kinds of aspects of practice mentioned earlier. Moreover, like other practices, a science of practice will be constructed in social relations and will involve elements of technical, practical, and critical reasoning about practice. How it understands itself in terms of the social relations of the research act is important for an understanding of what kind of a science of practice it will be.

The differences among research perspectives are not due to questions of the machinery of research (research techniques) alone; they are also differences of standpoint that reveal something of the location of the researcher in the research act—as Habermas's (1972, 1974) attempt to articulate the politics of knowledge production and distribution as well as his theory of knowledge-constitutive interests have shown. Different kinds of research serve different kinds of knowledge-constitutive interests (the reasons that frame and justify the search for knowledge through research), and they are based in different kinds of reasoning, sometimes described as "instrumental" or "technical" reason, "practical" reason, and "critical" or "emancipatory" reason (Carr & Kemmis, 1986; Grundy, 1987; Habermas, 1972, 1974).

Since Aristotle, technical reason has been understood as the kind of reason employed when we aim to improve the efficacy or efficiency of a means (for example, a strategy, a method, or a policy) in achieving pre-given and accepted goals. The ends are not in question, only the means to those ends. According to some views of educational and social science, this form of reason is at the heart of the scientific enterprise: improving the ways things are done in order to achieve established ends. Proponents of these forms of educational and social science frequently see their work as essentially continuous with the work of the natural and physical sciences, and thus adopt the attitude of those sciences toward their objects—as if these were physical phenomena rather than knowing subjects like the researchers themselves.

Practical reason, by contrast, treats both ends and means as problematic. In science, it frequently takes the view that the physical and social sciences are discontinuous, and thus require different methods. It recognizes that the objects of its studies are knowing subjects whose actions are not entirely determined by physical laws, but shaped by actors' reasons and perspectives—reasons and perspectives that can change, reflexively changing what they do. More particularly, however, practical reason is to be understood as the form of reason we employ when we have to act in complex situations, knowing that our actions and their consequences will be judged in terms of complex and sometimes conflicting values. Practical reason is at its most evident in situations described as "tragic"—that is, in situations where actors are forced to choose between conflicting sets of values, knowing that to succeed in terms of one set is to fail in terms of another. Reid (1978) gives an excellent description of the kinds of situations that require practical reasoning—practical problems, or what he calls "uncertain practical questions":

> First of all, they are questions that have to be answered—even if the answer is to decide to do nothing. In this, they differ from academic, or theoretic, questions which do not demand an answer at any particular time, or indeed any answer at all. Second, the grounds on which decisions should be made are uncertain. Nothing can tell us infallibly whose interests should be consulted, what evidence should be taken into account, or what kinds of argu-

> ments should be given precedence. Third, in answering practical questions, we always have to take some existing state of affairs into account. We are never in a position to make a completely fresh start, free from the legacy of past history and present arrangements. Fourth, and following from this, each question is in some ways unique, belonging to a specific time and context, the particulars of which we can never exhaustively describe. Fifth, our question will certainly compel us to adjudicate between competing goals and values. We may choose a solution that maximises our satisfaction across a range of possible goals, but some will suffer at the expense of others. Sixth, we can never predict the outcome of the particular solution we choose, still less know what the outcome would have been had we made a different choice. Finally, the grounds on which we decide to answer a practical question in a particular way are not grounds that point to the desirability of the action chosen as an act in itself, but grounds that lead us to suppose that the action will result in some desirable state of affairs. (p. 42)

Practical reason is what we do many times every day when we are confronted with choices about what to do, knowing that our decisions and their consequences are open to evaluation in terms of our own and others' values.

A science—and forms of research—that aims to support and strengthen practical reason is necessarily addressed to actors as people who will confront practical questions and must make decisions about what to do. It addresses these actors as persons—knowing subjects—who could make wiser and more prudent decisions in the light of a richer understanding of the situations in which they find themselves. Unlike a science aiming to support and inform technical reason, it does not aim to achieve control (in the sense of improving the means to known ends) but to educate actors or practitioners in ways that will help those persons to understand the nature and consequences of their actions more fully, and to assist them in weighing what should be done as a guide to (but not a prescription for) action.

Critical reason in some ways extends both technical and practical reason. It recognizes the primacy of practical reason—the necessity of deciding what to do when confronted with uncertain practical questions—but it does not address the problem from the perspective of the individual actor deciding alone. It aims to comprehend how a situation has come about as a result of human choices (see the third of the characteristics of uncertain practical questions that Reid mentions) and to consider how things might be reconstructed so that they could be different in the future—so that actors may have different choices from the ones forced upon them by "the way things are" currently. In a sense, this is to say that critical reason also involves an element of technical reasoning about the means to given ends, but it involves considering the kinds of ends that have shaped the way things are, judging the suitability of those ends in the light of their consequences (for example, considering whether the way educational goals have been interpreted and the way the means to those goals have been realized are adequate in terms of their historical consequences). In particular, critical reason involves evaluating situations in the light of their consequences—in terms of the extent to which, in practice, their consequences are irrational, unjust, alienating, or unsatisfying for those involved in and affected by what happens in the situation. On this basis, it aims to assist people involved in and affected by the situation in identifying, confronting, and collectively overcoming the conditions that produce these untoward consequences—even though, as in practical reasoning, it is impossible for them to describe the situation exhaustively or predict with certainty what the outcomes of their transformative action will be.

Technical, practical, and critical reasoning are realized in different patterns of social relationships between the person doing the reasoning and the people—or social systems or institutions—reasoned about. Although there is no smooth one-to-one correspondence about this, in contemporary contexts where people are interested in developing, reforming, transforming, or otherwise changing practices, instrumental (technical) approaches to practice presuppose what might be described as a "third-person" relationship between the person thinking about the practice and the practitioners of the practice (and other people inhabiting the systems or settings to be changed); practical approaches presuppose a "second-person" relationship, and critical (and especially emancipatory) approaches presuppose a "first-person" relationship.

In technical reasoning about practice, the researcher adopts an objectifying stance toward the others involved in the practice setting, perhaps treating them as elements of a "system." The researcher is therefore predisposed to regard these others, in a sense, as "them"—that is, in the third person. As in social research more generally, some kinds of action research (for example, some cases of action learning and action science) adopt this third-person perspective on practice. They treat practice as a form of strategic action—a means to an end. In this view, the point of conducting research into practice is to modify and improve it as a means to some given end—that is, it adopts a technical or instrumental view of the purpose of the research.

In practical reasoning about practice, the researcher adopts a more "subjective" stance to the practice setting, treating the practitioners and others involved as members of a shared life world—as persons who, like the researcher him- or herself, deserve the respect due to knowing subjects who are not only "others" but also autonomous and responsible agents. The researcher is therefore predisposed to regard these others as "you"— that is, in the second person. Also as in social research more generally, some kinds of action research adopt this second-person perspective (for example, some cases of classroom research). They treat practice as intentional action informed by the values and meanings of practitioners. In this view, the point of conducting research into practice is to educate practitioners and to inform practitioners' practical deliberation about the nature and conduct of their practice in particular cases. It adopts a practical view of the purpose of the research.

In critical reasoning about practice, the researcher adopts a more dialectical stance with respect to the "objective" and "subjective" and the individual and social aspects of the setting. From such a stance, the researcher treats the others involved in the setting as coparticipants who, through their participation in the practices that daily constitute and reconstitute the setting, can work together collaboratively to change the ways in which they constitute it. The researcher is therefore predisposed to regard such people as members of a group understood as "us"—that is, in the first person. As in social research more generally, some kinds of action research (for example, some cases of critical action research and participatory research) adopt this first-person (especially first-person plural) perspective. They treat practice as discursively, socially, and historically constructed, in addition to being realized in the behavior and intentional actions of practitioners. But they do not treat practice as produced only by participants— they also understand that, to a greater or lesser extent, participants enter practices that are partly preformed by discourses, social relationships, and the histories of the settings they inhabit. In this view, the purpose of research into practice is to change practice, practitioner, and practice setting (or, we might say, the work, the worker, and the workplace)—because changing practices requires changing not only behavior or intentional action (including the way the practitioner understands the practice and the practice setting) but also the situation in which the practice is conducted.

Insofar as they imply different moral and political stances toward the people in the social systems and life worlds involved, these forms of

365

reasoning, loosely correlated with third-person, second-person, and first-person standpoints on the social relationships of the setting, manifest themselves in quite different attitudes toward the process of change. In general, instrumental (technical) reasoning manifests itself in attitudes of systematization, regulation, and control—focusing on the "system" aspects of the social settings involved (which are regarded in a rather abstract, generalized, and disembedded way). By contrast, practical reason manifests itself in attitudes that value wise and prudent judgment about what to do in shared social contexts (understood in a more localized, concrete, and historically specific way). And critical-emancipatory reasoning manifests itself in attitudes of collaborative reflection, theorizing, and political action directed toward emancipatory reconstruction of the setting (understood more dialectically as both constituting and constituted by the personal as well as the political, the local as well as the global).

Arguably, the first two approaches, the instrumental and the practical, were more intertwined and interrelated in social theory, policy, and practice in the West at the end of the 19th century, and they diverged in sharply opposed theories, policies, and practices in the 20th. The third, the critical approach, emerged early in the 20th century (in response to emerging problems of Marxist theory) as some researchers' self-conscious attempt to overcome the increasing polarization between instrumental and practical tendencies in social and political theory and practice. It would be wrong to conclude, however, that critical approaches have actually been successful, in any practical sense, in overcoming such polarizations—far from it. At the beginning of the 21st century, all three approaches have their advocates, many apparently implacably opposed to one another, so that contemporary debates over the nature and objectives of social reform are consistently confused and politicized (in the narrow sense) as advocates of the different approaches contest the ground in theory, policy, and practice.

We could extend the "map" of different research traditions in the study of practice by including their general affinities with different kinds knowledge-constitutive interests, as in Figure 11.3.

Reconciling Different Traditions in the Study of Practice

Different traditions of research on practice emphasize different aspects of practice. Earlier, we suggested that it might be possible to explore complementarities and connections among these traditions, although not nec-

Traditions in the study of practice			Knowledge-constitutive interests		
Perspective:	Focus:	View of practice	*Technical*	*Practical*	*Critical-emancipatory*
Objective	*The individual*	(1) Practice as individual behavior			
	The social	(2) Practice as social behavior - e.g., ritual, system- structured			
Subjective	*The individual*	(3) Practice as intentional action, shaped by values			
	The social	(4) Practice as socially-structured, shaped by discourses and tradition			
Reflexive/dialectical view of relationships between subjective-objective and individual-social		(5) Practice as socially-, historically- and discursively constituted by human agency and social action			

Figure 11.3. General Relationships Among Different Research Traditions and Different Knowledge-Constitutive Interests

essarily by combining the research methods and techniques characteristically employed by these different traditions, because each has built-in limitations and blindnesses as well as particular ways of illuminating practice. Instead, we suggested that we would need to find more encompassing ways of theorizing practice. We want now to suggest one possible way of doing this theorizing.

In Figures 11.1 and 11.2, we have outlined some relationships among different traditions in the study of practice. In Figure 11.4, we represent these relationships in terms of dimensions of practice to be interrelated in a more encompassing perspective on practice. In the view of practice presented here, real practices can be understood more richly, and in more complex ways, if they are understood in terms of all of the five aspects of practice outlined earlier—or, to put it another way, by reference to all of the three dimensions in the space described in Figure 11.4. (As we shall see, it is in this space that we might be said to be "orienting ourselves in the process of changing practices" through action research.)

In volume 2 of his *Theory of Communicative Action*, titled *Lifeworld and System: A Critique of Functionalist Reason*, Habermas (1987b) makes a point about the lack of connections among different streams of social theory. Habermas does not make the point in the form of a plea for tolerance across theoretical perspectives and paradigms, however, but in an argument for a new view in social theory that can bring together perspectives that are currently at odds with one another in addressing "the phenomenon of modern societies."[4] His argument leads him to propose a

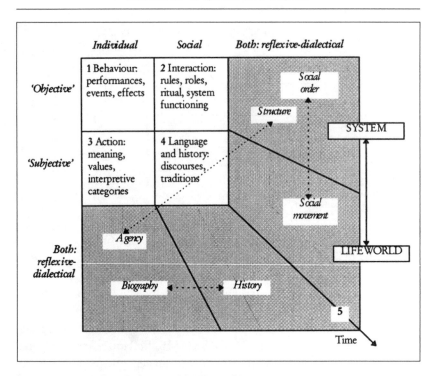

Figure 11.4. A More Encompassing View of Practice

"two-level" social theory that can overcome the one-sidedness of existing positions:

> If we leave to one side the insufficiently complex approac11of behaviorism, there are today three main lines of inquiry occupied with the phenomenon of modern societies. [Here he is referring to (a) theories of structural differentiation, which aim to give a more or less descriptive, rather than explanatory, account of the ways modern societies developed their characteristic elaborate divisions of labor, structure, and functioning; (b) the systems-theoretical approach, which sets out to explain the functioning of modern societies in terms of systems functions and their consequences; and (c) the action-theoretical approach, characteristic of interpretive sociology, which sets out to explain modern societies in terms of the way they are experienced by participants—at worst, from the viewpoint of the "victims" of modern society.] We cannot even say that they are in competition, for they scarcely have anything to say to one another.
>
> Efforts at theory comparison do not issue in reciprocal critique; fruitful critique that might foster a common understanding can hardly be developed

across these differences, but at most within one or another camp. There is good reason for this mutual incomprehension: the object domains of the competing approaches do not come into contact, for they are the result of one-sided abstractions that unconsciously cut the ties between system and lifeworld constitutive for modern societies. (pp. 375-376)

Different approaches and traditions in the study of practice suffer from mutual incomprehension of the kind Habermas observes in social theory—an incomprehension is similarly founded in different views about the object domains of research into practice. The object domains constituted by different research paradigms and traditions in the study of practice are the expressions of different views about the problems and phenomena to be addressed by theory and research, characteristically employing different research methods that they regard as appropriate to the problems and phenomena with which they are concerned.

We have described this diversity in terms of a three-dimensional matrix within which different traditions in the study of practice may be located: (a) the dimension of the individual versus the social, versus a reflexive-dialectical perspective embracing both; (b) the dimension of the objective versus the subjective, versus a reflexive-dialectical perspective embracing both; and (c) the dimension of time and history (which could be elaborated in terms of the synchronic versus the diachronic, versus a reflexive-dialectical perspective embracing both). Although Habermas does not describe the different kinds of theories he discusses in terms of this three-dimensional space, his formulation of the relationship between system and life world offers a new way of conceptualizing social change and the process of changing social and educational practices.

For reasons he makes clear in *The Theory of Communicative Action* (especially 1987b, pp. 113-198, 374-403), Habermas believes that the three approaches he discusses (the theory of structural differentiation, the systems-theoretical approach, and the action-theoretical approach) are all partial, with the result that each is inadequate to the task of explaining the character and problems of modern society. Theories of structural differentiation, Habermas says, fail to distinguish dynamics of differentiation in two different arenas of modern society, both of which are crucial to understanding it: society seen from the perspective of system (loosely speaking, as we see it from the perspective of its institutions, structures, and functions—as when we consider our work in terms of roles and functions) and society seen from the perspective of life worlds (loosely speaking, as we

369

see it from the perspective of the local settings in which we relate to others, making sense of ourselves, our coparticipants, and our relationships in the settings of family, workplace, neighborhood, and so on). Theories of structural differentiation confuse and confound these aspects in a general descriptive approach that attempts to make sense of the whole without adequately distinguishing and then interconnecting patterns or dynamics of differentiation seen from the interacting perspectives of system and life world.

The two other main approaches suffer from complementary partialities—one might even say "blindnesses." The systems-theoretical approach deals with the social life of modern societies very much from the perspective of systems integration (see also Giddens, 1979) and in terms of various kinds of functions of social systems of increasing complexity. In doing so, it neglects participants' perspectives on the social life it describes. Habermas believes that the protagonists of systems-theoretical approaches have developed their formulations in ways that have suppressed or abandoned some of the central problems that have traditionally occupied social theory, with the result that,

> once systems functionalism is cleansed of the dross of the sociological tradition, it becomes insensitive to social pathologies that can be discerned chiefly in the structural features of socially integrated domains of action. It hoists the vicissitudes of communicatively structured lifeworlds up to the level of media dynamics; by assimilating them, from the observer perspective, to disequilibria in intersystemic exchange relations, it robs them of the significance of identity-threatening deformations, which is how they are experienced from the participant perspective. (p. 377)

The action-theoretical approach, by contrast, sees social life very much from the perspective of social integration and in terms of the ways participants in social life interpret and experience their world, occasionally

> condens[ing] to fragments of history written from the point of view of its victims. Then modernization appears as the sufferings of those who had to pay for the establishment of the new mode of production and the new system of states in the coin of disintegrating traditions and forms of life. Research of this type sharpens our perception of historical asynchronicities; they provide a stimulus to critical recollection. . . . But it has as little place for the internal systemic dynamics of economic development, of nation and state building, as it does for the structural logics of rationalized

lifeworlds. As a result, the subcultural mirrorings in which the socio-pathologies of modernity are refracted and reflected retain the subjective and accidental character of uncomprehended events. (p. 377)

The task Habermas sets himself in *The Theory of Communicative Action* is to develop a "two-level" theory that can escape the limitations of formulations that either confuse system and life-world dynamics or give precedence to either the systems perspective or the life-world perspective (Habermas, 1984, 1987a, 1987b, 1990, 1992; for critical views, see also Bernstein, 1985, 1992; Fraser & Nicholson, 1988; Honneth & Joas, 1991; Honneth, McCarthy, Offe, & Wellmer, 1992; Rorty, 1985, 1989; Thompson & Held, 1982). This is a complex task, and Habermas undertakes it by reconstructing key conceptual choices made by precursor social theorists, including Marx, Weber, Durkheim, Parsons, and George Herbert Mead.

We find compelling Habermas's argument that the three major contemporary approaches to the study of "the phenomenon of modern society" are unable to offer one another the possibility of reciprocal critique—indeed, they could hardly be said even to be competitors—because they take such different views of the object domain of their inquiries. Earlier, we sought to show that different traditions in the study of practice take similarly different views of practice as an object domain of study. For Habermas, one way of overcoming the partiality of the major approaches in social theory is to concede that the relationship between system and life world is a crucial constituent of the phenomenon of modern society, and that the resources of each of the three principal approaches he mentions (theories of structural differentiation, systems theory, and action theory) can be reconstructed in the light of the distinction between system and life world, so that each may bring relevant resources to the overall problem of understanding and explaining modern society.

It is our view that educational theory and research can also learn from the system/life-world distinction, because it illuminates some of the burning issues of contemporary educational practice and policy—perhaps it even throws light on some of the characteristic differences in approach that separate the study of educational practice (which is frequently, although not invariably, conducted from an action-theoretical perspective) from the study of educational policy (which is frequently, although not invariably, conducted from a systems-theoretical perspective). It might also be true to say that some contemporary theories in education (such as those concerned with the history and social formation of education and those concerned with the conditioning of contemporary educational policies and practices by particular metadiscourses and power-knowledge configurations) offer parallels to the approach taken by theories of structural differentiation, and—following Habermas—it might be argued that they also fail to discriminate adequately between social dynamics rooted in system functioning and those rooted in life-world processes.

The social formation of education—in practice and in policy—seems to us to be an important arena in which the larger dynamics of system and life world are played out. The theory of communicative action seems to us to be a promising source for a more encompassing approach to problems of practice and policy in educational theory and research in the future.

In our view, the theory also provides a basis on which to understand the nature and work of participatory action research. Although few participants would put it in these terms, we contend that, on the one side, participants understand themselves and their practices as formed by system structures and functions that shape and constrain their actions, and that their efforts to change their practices necessarily involve encountering and reconstructing the system aspect of their social world. On the other side, we contend, participants also understand themselves and their practices as formed through the life-world processes of cultural reproduction, social integration, and socialization-individuation, and that their efforts to change their practices necessarily involve changing the substance of these processes. In addition, we contend, participants understand that there are tensions and interconnections between these two aspects of their social world, each shaping and constraining the other, and they recognize that changing their practices necessarily involves taking into account the nature and substance of these tensions and interconnections.

Participatory action research is a form of "insider research" in which participants move between two thought positions: on the one side, seeing themselves, their understandings, their practices, and the settings in which they practice from the perspective of insiders who see these things in an intimate, even "natural" way that may be subject to the partiality of view characteristic of the insider perspective; and, on the other side, seeing themselves, their understandings, their practices, and the setting from the perspective of an outsider (sometimes by adopting the perspective of an abstract, imagined outsider, and sometimes by trying to see things from the perspective of real individuals or role incumbents in and around the setting) who do not share the partiality of the inside view but who also do not have the benefit of "inside knowledge." Alternating between these perspectives gives the insider critical distance—the seed of the critical perspective that allows insiders to consider the possible as well as the actual in their social world.

For many research methodologists, this alternation of perspective is too fallible to be regarded as a secure methodological grounding for social research; for them, participatory action research will never be a method of choice. Our view is the contrary: Because only the insider has access to "inside knowledge" and can thus counterpose inside knowledge with the external view, the method of choice in social research will often be participatory action research—although it necessarily involves the development of processes of education and self-education among participants that make critical enlightenment possible. This is not to say that the aim of the process is to produce social researchers qualified in the usual academic terms; rather, it is to say that participants can develop skill and sophistication in shifting between the perspectives illustrated in Figure 11.1: seeing themselves, their understandings, their practices, and their settings from the perspective of *individuals* in and around the setting, and then from the perspective of *the social* (in terms of both system integration and social integration, under the aspect of both system and life world); from the *"subjective"/insider* perspective, and from the *"objective"/outsider* perspective; and from the *synchronic* perspective of "how things are" and from the *diachronic* perspective of "how they came to be" or "can come to be." In short, in participatory action research, participants can and do develop the skills and sophistication necessary and sufficient to explore their social world in terms of the three dimensions represented schematically in Figure 11.4 as a more encompassing perspective on social life.

The participant perspective is not only a privileged perspective on a setting; it is also the perspective in terms of which much—but not all—of the social life of the setting is constituted. Although changes to external structures and functions may also be required if participants, their understandings, their practices, and the setting are to change, change cannot be secured if participants do not change themselves, their understandings, their practices, or their constitution of the setting. Participant change is the *sine qua non* of social change (social movement), and it is for this reason we conclude that participatory action research is the preferred approach to social and educational research aimed at social and educational change—although we concede that resources and circumstances are not always available to do it and do it well. On the other hand, it seems to us that research other than participatory action research that *does* contribute to social and educational change frequently approximates participatory action research in the way it engages participants in rethinking themselves, their understandings, their practices, and their settings. To the extent that it does so, social and educational research is likely to be regarded by participants as legitimate and thus to secure their consent and commitment. To the extent that social research ignores the participant view, or imposes itself (in process or findings) on participants, it is likely to be regarded as illegitimate, to foster alienation or hostility, and thus to provoke resistance.

Is Participatory Action Research "Good" Research?

In earlier sections, we outlined some epistemological perspectives (Figure 11.1) and methodological perspectives (Figure 11.2) characteristic of different traditions in the study of practice and related these to different research purposes (knowledge-constitutive interests; Figure 11.3). We indicated that different views of research on practice in the human and social sciences occupy different locations in these tables, and that different kinds of action research similarly take different views of the nature of practice and the purpose of research into practice. We proposed a more comprehensive view of the nature of practice (Figure 11.4) that could interconnect and interrelate different aspects of practice (dialectically interrelating objective and subjective, individual and social, and synchronic and diachronic aspects of practice).

Adopting this perspective is a tall order. In our view, it requires more of what might be called *symposium research*—interrelated studies by researchers specializing in different traditions in the study of social practice, working together to investigate the formation and transformation of practices, in particular historical circumstances and conditions.

In the case of participatory action research, the task appears even more difficult—is it possible for local participants in a particular setting to develop the specialist epistemological and methodological knowledge that seems necessary to conduct this kind of symposium research in a way that could satisfy the criteria of excellence appropriate in evaluating research in every one of the traditions of research we have described? We know of no cases where participatory action researchers have attempted this task *explicitly,* and of only a few where researchers have attempted anything like it—and then only *implicitly*—as in the case of the project conducted by Gloria Maria Braga Blanco, Jose María Rozada Martínez, César Cascánte Fernández, and their colleagues (1995) in Asturias in Northern Spain. In this case, groups of teachers working in early childhood education, primary education, secondary education (one group in humanities and one group in science and mathematics), and university education have investigated their practice over many years, exploring the theme of democracy in and for education (see also Kemmis, 1998). The research group has used a variety of specialized research methods and techniques as part of an overall participatory action research project, although even in this case the researchers have not used all of the approaches to research on practice summarized in Figure 11.2.

In most action research, including participatory action research, the researchers make sacrifices in methodological and technical rigor in exchange for more immediate gains in face validity: whether the evidence they collect makes sense *to them, in their contexts.* For this reason, we sometimes characterize participatory action research as "low-tech" research: It sacrifices methodological sophistication in order to generate timely evidence that can be used and further developed in a real-time process of transformation (of practices, practitioners, and practice settings).

Some researchers wonder whether this tendency toward being low-tech makes participatory action research "bad" research—even if it may be "good" in terms of practical contributions to democratic processes of transformation in a setting. This concern presupposes that what makes research "good" can be determined on grounds of *methodology* rather than epistemology (what counts as good evidence in terms of what participants—using the evidence critically—think is accurate, relevant, appropriate, and pertinent to their purposes). It turns out that there may be a trade-off between methodological sophistication and "truth" in the sense of timely evidence capable of giving participants critical purchase on a real situation in which they find themselves. Of course, this is not to argue that validity is not an important issue for participatory action research, or to accept that the conventional canons of validity do not require revision (McTaggart, 1998).

It seems to us that some loss of methodological sophistication is a price worth paying in most practical contexts of transformative social action. Methodological sophistication is a primary concern most often when the research being conducted is of a third-person or second-person kind, where interpretation and analysis generally occur away from the setting under investigation, and where findings need to withstand scrutiny from people (generally other researchers) who have little interest in the particular case under investigation—people who are interested in more general or universalized phenomena. Frequently, too, such other audiences have no significant connection with the lived realities of participants, whereas *participants live with the consequences of the transformations they make.* The inevitability—for participants—of having to live with the consequences of transformation provides a very concrete "reality check" on the quality of their transformative work, in terms of whether their practices are more efficacious, their understandings are clearer, and the settings in which they practice are more rational, just, and productive of the kinds of consequences they are intended to achieve. For participants, the point of collecting compelling evidence is to achieve these goals, or, more precisely, to avoid subverting them intentionally or unintentionally by their action. Evidence sufficient for this kind of "reality checking" can often be low-tech (in terms of research methods and techniques) or impressionistic (from the perspective of an outsider who lacks the contextual knowledge that the insider draws on in interpreting the evidence). But it may still be "high-fidelity" evidence from the perspective of understanding the nature and consequences of particular interventions and transformations made by participants, in their own contexts—where they are privileged observers (not "cultural dopes," to use Giddens's phrase).

Most action research (and most participatory action research) is, in our view, correct to choose practical significance over methodological sophistication in the trade-off between epistemological and methodological gains—the choice between what evidence makes critical sense to participants and what evidence would satisfy the contextually nonspecific methodological criteria likely to satisfy external researchers. On the other hand, we suggest, most action research would be strengthened—for participants, not just outsiders—if more evidence were collected from across the range of different perspectives represented in Figures 11.2 and 11.3. That is, most action researchers would be well-advised to collect and consider evidence about practice as individual performance viewed as others see the practitioner (tradition 1 in Figures 11.2 and 11.3); evidence about practice as ritual and system, viewed from an external perspective (tradition 2); evidence about practice as meaningful and significant intentional action viewed from the perspectives of those involved (tradition 3); evidence about practice as discursively, socially, and historically constructed viewed from within the history and traditions of the practice (tradition 4);

and evidence of all of these kinds seen as in a continuing process of historical formation and critical transformation shaped by participants themselves (tradition 5).

Orlando Fals Borda (1979) has written of action research as "investigating reality in order to transform it." We agree, but add that action research also transforms reality in order to investigate it. Here we are speaking not of some metaphysical "Reality" that stands above and beyond any particular local context, but about the day-to-day lived realities of participants in their ordinary work and lives. The aim of action research is to make a difference in these day-to-day lived realities—the ordinary settings in which people live and work, in which some thrive and some suffer. Action research aims to set in motion processes by which participants collectively make critical analyses of the nature of their practices, their understandings, and the settings in which they practice in order to confront and overcome irrationality, injustice, alienation, and suffering *in these practice settings* and *in relation to the consequences of their practices in these settings.* In our view, this—more than a metaphysical Truth or methodological sophistication—is the criterion against which the quality of action research is to be evaluated *as research.* Research cannot be regarded as self-justifying, or as justified solely by reference to internal criteria (for example, methodological criteria); research is also a social practice, to be evaluated against criteria of the kind we have listed as the aims of action research—that is, in terms of the extent to which it contributes to confronting and overcoming irrationality, injustice, alienation, and suffering, both in the research setting and more generally in terms of its broader consequences.

Participatory Action Research: The Future

As we suggested at the beginning of this chapter, action research takes a variety of forms. It is not a unitary approach. In our view, its evolution has owed more to the press of the contexts in which it has been practiced than to the working out of some set of problems immanent in action research understood as a research *method.*

On the other hand, what most distinguishes action from other approaches to research is a kind of shared resistance to some conventional views about research, including views of the researcher (for example, notions about who can be a researcher) and the relationship of research to social practice (for example, the notion that theory—

especially "academic" theory—and research methodology stand in a mediating role between research and social practice, as if transforming practice can be warranted only by reference to grand claims to "Truth" or methodological purity). Much action research insists that the practitioner can be a researcher, with or without specialized training, and that research conducted within—not just on—practice can yield evidence and insights that can and do assist in the critical transformation of practice.

The press of the different contexts in which action research occurs will continue to shape its future. Some forms of action research will continue to develop as a species of field research by which practitioners aim to improve their practice principally in technical terms; some forms will continue to develop as an approach by which practitioners aim to improve their practice in practical terms (for example, through continuing development of the notion of the self-reflective practitioner, or the reflective professional; Schön, 1983, 1987); and some will continue to develop as a form of critical social science aimed at collective transformation of practices, practitioners, and practice settings.

Perhaps paradoxically, we believe that *participatory* action research will become both more practical and more theoretically sophisticated in the decade ahead. It will become more practical in the sense that it will be more widespread, more convivial as a form of social practice, and more congenial to practitioners in terms of the kinds of research techniques it employs. It will become more theoretically sophisticated in the sense that it will involve a more complex view of what social practice is, how particular social practices are shaped, and how they can be transformed by collective social action.

Already, participatory action researchers (along with some other kinds of action researchers) have successfully challenged the relative monopoly of "academic" researchers over the social practice of research. To some extent, they have been abetted by the modernist beliefs of a variety of state and other authorities who have insisted that practitioners must play an increasingly significant role in improving their practices (especially, but not only, in the technical terms favored by advocates of quality improvement). Research, as a social practice, has to some extent been "liberated" from the control of the academy and other highly specialized institutes and agencies. At the same time, there is a growing awareness among these practice-based practitioners of participatory action research that the social conditions that shape their practice cannot be swept away by purely local ideas and interventions. The obstacles to transformation are not just technical circumstances that participants can alter at will; they include so-cial structures and media that may yield—and sometimes only gradually—to sustained collective effort. Social transformation is not just a technical matter, it is also political, cultural, social, and cognitive.

For this reason, we expect a continuing development of participatory action research as a form of involved and committed critique. In future, it may be less wedded to the specific modernist forms of critique characte-ristic of the forms of Marxian theory that informed some versions of par-ticipatory action research in the past; instead, it is likely to become more theoretically eclectic while still sustaining the hope that through collective action people can transform circumstances that oppress them. Similarly, it may be less bound to operating within established institutional frame-works (such as the school, the hospital, or the government agency) of the social order; instead, in a kind of "flanking" move, it is likely to become more explicit about its connections to social movements that challenge and test the taken-for-granted assumptions and presuppositions that shape practice in many of our key social institutions.

It follows from this that we expect participatory action research in the future to take a more complex view of practice of the kind represented schematically in Figure 11.4. The "paradigm wars" in social research were waged primarily on methodological grounds, based on competing views about the nature of truth in the human sciences. The competition between these positions has become fruitless; it is clear that they are incommensu-rable, and that "Truth" sides with no one view. What is now required is more extensive interchange between these rival positions, undertaken with the aim of exploring the extent to which together they can contribute to greater intersubjective understanding and agreement about the nature, dynamics, and consequences of specific practices under specific condi-tions and historical circumstances.

Participatory action research will provide especially fertile ground for this kind of cooperation and collaboration—the kind of cooperation and collaboration characteristic of what we have described as symposium re-search. It will do so for a reason given earlier—because what constitutes a "reality check" for its protagonists is making a difference in terms of prac-tical actions and their consequences, not the esoteric demands of episte-mology or methodology. Despite the conditions of late modernity, where participants increasingly feel that life and work are risky, uncertain, and alienating, and where the legitimacy of social systems is increasingly in doubt, participatory action research offers practitioners a collective way of reconnecting with questions of meaning, value, and significance, and of exercising personal and collective agency for the common good. It revives practical and critical reason despite the ubiquity of the functional reason characteristic of the social systems that structure great tracts of our social realities. And it revives a kind of humanism that was displaced by the rationalism of Descartes and the scientism (the belief in science as a privileged way of knowing) of the past century (Toulmin, 1990).

Toulmin (1990) dates modernity from the end of the period of "Renaissance humanism" at the end of the 16th century. He argues that the early-modern shift from Renaissance humanism to Cartesian rationalism can best be understood in terms of four subsidiary shifts: (a) from an *oral* culture in which the theory and practice of rhetoric played a central role to a *written* culture in which formal logic played a central role in establishing the credentials of an argument; (b) from a practical concern with understanding and acting on *particular* cases to a more theoretical concern with the development of *universal* principles; (c) from a concern with the *local*, in all its concrete diversity, to the *general*, understood in terms of abstract axioms; and (d) from the *timely* (a concern with making wise and prudent decisions in the transitory situations of everyday life and society) to the *timeless* (a concern with understanding and explaining the enduring, perhaps eternal, nature of things). In the late-modern period, there is renewed interest in what has been occluded in these shifts—renewed interest in oral culture and the theory and practice of rhetoric, in understanding and acting on particular cases, in the local as against the general and abstract, and in the timely as against the timeless. Whether or not these interests signal a more general revival in the humanism of the Renaissance, they do seem to be characteristic of many groups conducting participatory action research in their local settings and circumstances. And this more humanistic approach fosters the kind of practicality and cooperative spirit likely to counter the dogmatism of the era of the paradigm wars and to encourage the kind of symposium research that we believe will be found in the participatory action research of the future.

If we are correct in thinking that participatory action research will continue to thrive because of its commitment to making a difference, it also seems to us likely that established authorities (including the state and in some entrenched areas of the academy) will make more strenuous efforts to co-opt and domesticate participatory action research. To the extent that these efforts are *not* successful, it is likely that participatory action research will be eschewed and rejected as "unscientific"—even treated as renegade. For this reason, we expect that the debate about whether participatory action research is or should be regarded as research (or "good research") will continue, and will continue to strengthen participatory action research in theory and in practice.

◆ Key Features of Participatory Action Research

Although the process of participatory action research is only poorly described in terms of a mechanical sequence of steps, it is generally thought to involve a spiral of self-reflective cycles of

> planning a change,
> acting and observing the process and consequences of the change,
> reflecting on these processes and consequences, and then
>> replanning,
>> acting and observing,
>> reflecting, and so on . . .

In reality, the process may not be as neat as the spiral of self-contained cycles of planning, acting and observing, and reflecting suggests. The stages overlap, and initial plans quickly become obsolete in the light of learning from experience. In reality, the process is likely to be more fluid, open, and responsive. The criterion of success is not whether participants have followed the steps faithfully, but whether they have a strong and authentic sense of development and evolution in their practices, their understandings of their practices, and the situations in which they practice.

Each of the steps outlined in the spiral of self-reflection is best undertaken collaboratively by coparticipants in the participatory action research process. Not all theorists of participatory action research place this emphasis on participatory action research as a collaborative process; they argue that it is frequently a solitary process of systematic self-reflection. We concede that it is often so, but nevertheless hold that participatory action research is best conceptualized in collaborative terms. One reason we say this is that participatory action research is itself a social—and educational—process. A second and more compelling reason is that participatory action research is directed toward studying, reframing, and reconstructing practices that are, by their very nature, social. If practices

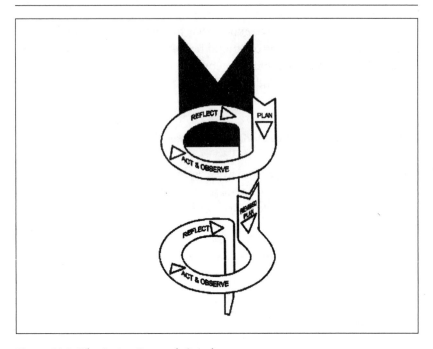

Figure 11.5. The Action Research Spiral

are constituted in social interactions among people, then changing prac-tices is a social process. To be sure, one person may change so that others are obliged to react or respond differently to that individual's changed behavior, but the willing and committed involvement of those whose interactions constitute the practice is necessary, in the end, to secure the change. Participatory action research offers an opportunity to create forums in which people can join one another as coparticipants in the strug-gle to remake the practices in which they interact—forums in which ratio-nality and democracy can be pursued together, without an artificial sepa-ration ultimately hostile to both. In his 1996 book *Between Facts and Norms,* Habermas describes this process in terms of "opening communi-cative space." At its best, this is a collaborative social process of learning, realized by groups of people who join together in changing the practices through which they interact in a shared social world—a shared social world in which, for better or for worse, we live with the consequences of one another's actions.

We should also stress that action research concerns actual, not abstract, practices. It involves learning about the real, material, concrete, particular practices of particular people in particular places. Although of course it is not possible to suspend the inevitable abstraction that occurs whenever we use language to name, describe, interpret, and evaluate things, action research differs from other forms of research in that it is more obstinate about changing particular practitioners' particular practices, rather than focusing on practices in general or in the abstract. In our view, action researchers need make no apology for seeing their work as mundane and mired in history; there are philosophical and practical dangers in the idealism that suggests that a more abstract view of practice might make it possible to transcend or rise above history, and delusions in the view that it is possible to find safe haven in abstract propositions that construe but do not themselves constitute practice. Action research is a learning process, the fruits of which are the real and material changes in (a) what people do, (b) how they interact with the world and with others, (c) what they mean and what they value, and (d) the discourses in which they understand and interpret their world.

Through action research, people can come to understand their social and educational practices as located in particular material, social, and historical circumstances that produced (and reproduce) them—and in which it may be possible to transform them. Focusing on practices in a concrete and specific way makes those practices accessible for reflection, discussion, and reconstruction as products of past circumstances that are capable of being modified in and for present and future circumstances. While recognizing that every practice is transient and evanescent, and that it can be conceptualized only in the inevitably abstract (although comfortingly imprecise) terms that language provides, action researchers aim to understand their own particular practices as they emerge in their own particular circumstances, without reducing them to the ghostly status of the general, the abstract, or the ideal—or, perhaps one should say, the unreal.

If action research is understood in such terms, then, through their investigations, action researchers may want to become especially sensitive to the ways in which their particular practices involve

> social practices of material, symbolic, and social
>> production,
>> communication, and
>> social organization;
> which shape and are shaped by social structures in
>> the cultural,

the economic, and
the political realms;
which shape and are shaped by the social media of
language/discourses,
work, and
power;
which largely shape, but can also be shaped by, participants' own knowledge,
expressed in participants'
understandings,
skills, and
values;
which, in turn, shape and are shaped by their acts of material, symbolic, and
social
production,
communication, and
social organization . . .

Action researchers might consider, for example, how their acts of communication, production, and social organization are intertwined and interrelated in the real and particular practices that connect them to others in the real situations in which they find themselves (such as communities, neighborhoods, families, schools, and other workplaces). They might consider how, by collaboratively changing the ways they participate with others in these practices, they can change the practices, their understandings of these practices, and the situations in which they live and work.

For many people, the image of the spiral of cycles of self-reflection (planning, acting and observing, reflecting, replanning, and so on) has become the dominant feature of action research as an approach. In our view, participatory action research has seven other key features that are at least as important as the self-reflective spiral. They are as follows:

1. *Participatory action research is a social process.* Participatory action research deliberately explores *the relationship between the realms of the individual and the social.* It recognizes that "no individuation is possible without socialization, and no socialization is possible without individuation" (Habermas, 1992, p. 26), and that the processes of individuation and socialization continue to shape individuals and social relationships in all the settings in which we find ourselves. Participatory action research is a process followed in research in settings, such as those of education and community development, where people, individually and collectively, try

to understand how they are formed and re-formed as individuals and in relation to one another in a variety of settings—for example, when teachers work together or with students to improve processes of teaching and learning in the classroom.

2. *Participatory action research is participatory.* Participatory action research engages people in examining their *knowledge* (understandings, skills, and values) and interpretive categories (the ways they interpret themselves and their action in the social and material world). It is a process in which each individual in a group tries to get a handle on the ways his or her knowledge shapes his or her sense of identity and agency and reflects critically on how that present knowledge frames and constrains his or her action. It is also participatory in the sense that people can do action research only "on" themselves, individually or collectively. It is not research done "on" others.

3. *Participatory action research is practical and collaborative.* Participatory action research engages people in examining the *social practices* that link them with others in social interaction. It is a process in which people explore their practices of communication, production, and social organization and try to explore how to improve their interactions by changing the acts that constitute them—to reduce the extent to which participants experience these interactions (and their longer-term consequences) as irrational, unproductive (or inefficient), unjust, and/or unsatisfying (alienating). Participatory action researchers aim to work together in reconstructing their social interactions by reconstructing the acts that constitute them.

4. *Participatory action research is emancipatory.* Participatory action research aims to help people recover, and release themselves, from the constraints of irrational, unproductive, unjust, and unsatisfying *social structures* that limit their self-development and self-determination. It is a process in which people explore the ways in which their practices are shaped and constrained by wider social (cultural, economic, and political) structures and consider whether they can intervene to release themselves from these constraints—or, if they can't, how best to work within and around them to minimize the extent to which they contribute to irrationality, lack of productivity (inefficiency), injustice, and dissatisfactions

(alienation) among people whose work and lives contribute to the structuring of a shared social life.

5. *Participatory action research is critical.* Participatory action research aims to help people recover, and release themselves, from the constraints embedded in the *social media* through which they interact: their language (discourses), their modes of work, and the social relationships of power (in which they experience affiliation and difference, inclusion and exclusion—relationships in which, grammatically speaking, they interact with others in the third, second, or first person). It is a process in which people deliberately set out to contest and to reconstitute irrational, unproductive (or inefficient), unjust, and/or unsatisfying (alienating) ways of interpreting and describing their world (language/discourses), ways of working (work), and ways of relating to others (power).

6. *Participatory action research is recursive (reflexive, dialectical).* Participatory action research aims to help people to investigate reality in order to change it (Fals Borda, 1979) and (we might add) to change reality in order to investigate it—in particular by changing their practices through a spiral of cycles of critical and self-critical action and reflection, as a deliberate social process designed to help them learn more about (and theorize) their practices, their knowledge of their practices, the social structures that shape and constrain their practices, and the social media in which their practices are expressed. In our view, this is what theorizing practice means. Participatory action research does not take an armchair view of theorizing, however; it is a process of learning, with others, by doing—changing the ways we interact in a shared social world in which, for better or for worse, we live with the consequences of our own and one another's actions. Figure 11.6 represents an attempt to sketch the recursive character of the relationships among knowledge, social practices, social structures, social media.

7. *Participatory action research aims to transform both theory and practice.* Participatory action research does not regard either theory or practice as preeminent in the relationship between theory and practice; it aims to articulate and develop each in relation to the other through critical reasoning about both theory and practice and their consequences. It does not aim to develop forms of theory that can stand above and beyond practice, as if practice could be controlled and determined without regard to the

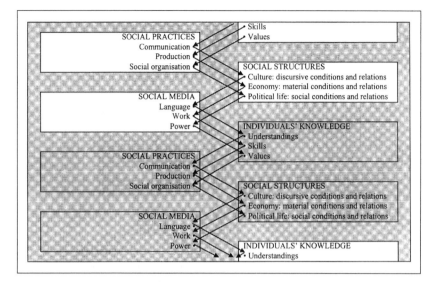

Figure 11.6. Recursive Relationships of Social Mediation That Action Research Aims to Transform

particulars of the practical situations that confront practitioners in their ordinary lives and work. Nor does it aim to develop forms of practice that might be regarded as self-justifying, as if practice could be judged in the absence of theoretical frameworks that give them their value and significance and that provide substantive criteria for exploring the extent to which practices and their consequences turn out to be irrational, unjust, alienating, or unsatisfying for the people involved in and affected by them. Participatory action research thus involves "reaching out" from the specifics of particular situations, as understood by the people within them, to explore the potential of different perspectives, theories, and discourses that might help to illuminate particular practices and practical settings as a basis for developing critical insights and ideas about how things might be transformed. Equally, it involves "reaching in" from the standpoints provided by different perspectives, theories, and discourses to explore the extent to which these provide practitioners themselves with a critical grasp of the problems and issues they actually confront in specific local situations. Participatory action research thus aims to transform *both* practitioners' theories and their practices *and* the theories and practices of others whose perspectives and practices may help to shape the conditions of life and work in particular local settings. In this way, participatory action research aims to connect the local and the global, and to live out the slogan, "The personal is the political."

These seven are the principal features of participatory action research as we see it. We take a particular, and perhaps partisan, view. There are writers on action research who prefer to move immediately from a general description of the action research process (especially the self-reflective spiral) to questions of methodology and research technique—a discussion of the ways and means for collecting data in different social and educational settings. This is a somewhat methodologically driven view of action research; it suggests that research methods are what makes action research "research."

In terms of the five aspects of practice and the five traditions in the study of practice outlined earlier, however, it seems to us that a methodologically driven view of participatory action research finds itself mired in the assumptions about practice to which one or another of the different traditions of research on practice is committed. Depending on which of these sets of presuppositions it adopts, it may find itself unable to approach (the study of) practice in a sufficiently rich and multifaceted way—that is, in terms that recognize different aspects of practice and do justice to its social, historical, and discursive construction.

If participatory action research is to explore practice in terms of each of the five aspects outlined earlier, it will need to consider how different traditions in the study of practice, and different research methods and techniques, can provide multiple resources for the task. It must also avoid accepting the assumptions and limitations of particular methods and techniques. For example, the participatory action researcher may legitimately eschew the narrow empiricism of those approaches that attempt to construe practice entirely "objectively," as if it were possible to exclude consideration of participants' intentions, meanings, values, and interpretive categories from an understanding of practice, or as if it were possible to exclude consideration of the frameworks of language, discourse, and tradition by which people in different groups construe their practices. It does not follow from this that quantitative approaches are never relevant in participatory action research; on the contrary, they may be—but without the constraints many quantitative researchers put on these methods and techniques. Indeed, when quantitative researchers use questionnaires to convert participants' views into numerical data, they tacitly concede that they cannot understand practice without taking participants' views into account. Participatory researchers will differ from one-sidedly quantitative researchers in the ways they collect and use such data, because the participatory action researcher will regard the data as crude approximations to the ways participants understand themselves, not (as quantitative researchers may assert) as more rigorous (valid, reliable) because they are scaled.

On the other hand, participatory action research will differ from the one-sidedly qualitative approach that asserts that action can be understood only from a qualitative perspective—for example, through close clinical or phenomenological analysis of an individual's views or close analysis of the discourses and traditions that shape the way a particular practice is understood by participants. The participatory action researcher will also want to explore how changing "objective" circumstances (performances, events, effects; patterns of interaction, rules, roles, and system functioning) shape and are shaped by the "subjective" conditions of participants' perspectives.

In our view, questions of research methods should not be regarded as unimportant, but (by contrast with the methodologically driven view) we would want to assert that what makes participatory action research "research" is not the machinery of research techniques but an abiding concern with the relationships between social and educational theory and practice. In our view, before we can decide questions about what kinds of research methods are appropriate, we must decide what kinds of things "practice" and "theory" are—for only then can we decide what kinds of data or evidence might be relevant in describing practice and what kinds of analyses are relevant in interpreting and evaluating people's real practices in the real situations in which they work. In this view of participatory action research, a central question is how practices are to be understood "in the field," as it were, so they become available for more systematic theorizing; once we have arrived at a general view of what it means to understand (theorize) practice in the field, we can work out what kinds of evidence, and hence what kinds of research methods and techniques, might be appropriate for advancing our understanding of practice at any particular time.

The theoretical scheme depicted in Figure 22.6 takes a view of what theorizing a practice might be like: locating practice within frameworks of participants' knowledge, in relation to social structures, and in terms of social media. By adopting a more encompassing view of practice such as the one outlined earlier (in Figure 11.4), we may be able to understand and theorize it more richly, and in more complex ways, so that powerful social dynamics (like the tensions and interconnections between system and life world) can be construed and reconstituted through a critical social practice like participatory action research.

◆ Notes

1. Dr. Colin Henry of Deakin University assisted with the compilation of an earlier version of this synopsis.

2. Describing two of the great traditions in 20th-century philosophy of social science, positivism (which he relates to a Galilean worldview) and hermeneutics (which he relates to an Aristotelian worldview), Georg Henrik von Wright (1971) draws the conclusion that they are incommensurable—but with the reservation that there is a kind of dialogue between them that might suggest that some progress is possible: "I have tried to relate some developments in the philosophy of social science to two great traditions in the history of ideas. We have seen how in the last hundred years philosophy of science has successively clung to one or the other of two basically opposed positions. After Hegel came positivism; after the antipositivist and partly neohegelian reaction around the turn of the century came neopositivism; now the pendulum is again swinging toward the Aristotelian thematics that Hegel revived.

"It would surely be an illusion to think that truth itself unequivocally sided with one of the two opposed positions. In saying this I am not thinking of the triviality that both positions contain some truth and that a compromise can be achieved on some questions. This may be so. But there is also a basic opposition, removed from the possibility both of reconciliation and of refutation—even, in a sense, removed from truth. It is built into the choice of primitives, of basic concepts for the whole argumentation. This choice, one could say, is 'existential.' It is a choice of a point of view that cannot be further grounded.

"There is nevertheless dialogue between the positions, and a kind of progress. The temporary dominance of one of the two trends is usually the result of a breakthrough following a period of criticism of the other trend. What emerges after the breakthrough is never merely a restoration of something that was there before, but also bears the impress of the ideas through whose criticism it emerged. The process illustrates what Hegel described with the words *aufgehoben* and *aufbewart,* perhaps best rendered in English as 'superseded' and 'retained.' The position which is in a process of becoming superseded usually wastes its polemical energies on fighting already outmoded features in the opposed view, and tends to see what is retained in the emerging position as only a deformed shadow of its own self. This is what happens, for example, when positivist philosophers of science in our days object to *Verstehen* with arguments perhaps valid against Dilthey or Collingwood, or when they mistake Wittgenstein's philosophy of psychology for just another form of behaviorism" (pp. 32-33).

3. The term *balanda* is used by the Yolngu Matha language group of Aboriginal people in northeast Arnhemland—the northeast corner of the "top end" of Australia's Northern Territory—in speaking of Caucasians. The origin of the term in Yolngu-matha (the language of the Yolngu) has its roots in the word for "Hollanders" used by indigenous Indonesians

(Malaccans) to refer to the Dutch colonial invaders of Indonesia. (In like manner, apparently, *Holland* was rendered by the Malaccans as *Beland*.) Indigenous Indonesians visited the coastal waters of northeast Arnhemland in search of trepang (bêche-de-mer) for hundreds of years before white settlement of Australia and, according to the Yolngu, gave the Yolngu this word for white people long before white people arrived in Arnhemland. The early cross-cultural contact between indigenous peoples of Indonesia and Australia was quite benign by comparison with the savagery of white invasion of the 18th and 19th centuries.

4. Note that Habermas speaks here of "the phenomenon," not "the phenomena" of modern societies, as he is interested in theories that make "modern society" comprehensible as a particular kind of social form—the product of particular processes of social formation and the framework that shapes particular patterns and dynamics of social life.

◆ References

Adelman, C. (1997). Action research and the problem of participation. In R. McTaggart (Ed.), *Participatory action research: International contexts and consequences* (pp. 79-106). Albany: State University of New York Press.

Althusser, L. (1971). *Lenin and philosophy and other essays* (B. Brewster, Trans.). London: New Left.

Altrichter, H., & Gstettner, P. (1997). Action research: A closed chapter in the history of German social science? In R. McTaggart (Ed.), *Participatory action research: International contexts and consequences* (pp. 45-78). Albany: State University of New York Press.

Argyris, C. (1990). *Overcoming organizational defenses: Facilitating organizational learning.* Boston: Allyn & Bacon.

Argyris, C., Putnam, R., & Smith, D. M. (1985). *Action science: Concepts, methods, and skills for research and intervention.* San Francisco: Jossey-Bass.

Argyris, C., & Schön, D. A. (1974). *Theory in practice: Increasing professional effectiveness.* San Francisco: Jossey-Bass.

Argyris, C., & Schön, D. A. (1978). *Organizational learning: A theory of action perspective.* Reading, MA: Addison-Wesley.

Bennett, T. (1979). *Formalism and Marxism.* London: Methuen.

Bernstein, R. J. (Ed.). (1985). *Habermas and modernity.* Cambridge: MIT Press.

Bernstein, R. J. (1992). *The new constellation: The ethical-political horizons of modernity/postmodernity.* Cambridge: MIT Press.

Braga Blanco, G. M., Rozada Martínez, J. M., Cascánte Fernández, C., et al. (1995). Hacia un modelo dialectico-critico en la enseñanza: Grupos asociados para la investigación-acción. In Departamento de Didáctica y Organización Escolar (Ed.), *Teoría crítica e investigación acción* (pp. 162-172). Madrid: Departamento de Didáctica y Organización Escolar.

Bravette, G. (1996). Reflection on a black woman's management learning. *Women in Management Review, 11*(3), 3-11.

Bunbury, R., Hastings, W., Henry, J., & McTaggart, R. (Eds.). (1991). *Towards Aboriginal pedagogy: Aboriginal teachers speak out, Blekbala Wei, Deme Nayin, Yolngu Rom, and Ngini Nginingawula Ngawurranungurumagi.* Geelong, Victoria, Australia: Deakin University Press.

Carr, W., & Kemmis, S. (1986). *Becoming critical: Education, knowledge and action research.* London: Falmer.

Checkland, P. (1981). *Systems thinking, systems practice.* Chichester: John Wiley.

Checkland, P., & Scholes, J. (1990). *Soft systems methodology in action.* Chichester: John Wiley.

Clark, P. A. (1972). *Action research and organisational change.* London: Harper & Row.

Dadds, M. (1995). *Passionate enquiry and school development: A story about teacher action research.* London: Falmer.

Davies, L., & Ledington, P. (1991). *Information in action: Soft systems methodology.* Basingstoke, Hampshire, England: Macmillan.

Elden, M. (1983). Participatory research at work. *Journal of Occupational Behavior, 4*(1), 21-34.

Elliott, J. (1988). Developing hypotheses about classrooms from teachers' practical constructs: An account of the work of the Ford Teaching Project. In S. Kemmis & R. McTaggart (Eds.), *The action research reader* (3rd ed., pp. 195-213). Geelong, Victoria, Australia: Deakin University Press. (Reprinted from *Interchange,* 7[2], 1976-1977, 2-22)

Emery, F. E., & Thorsrud, E. (1976). *Democracy at work : The report of the Norwegian Industrial Democracy Program.* Leiden, Netherlands: Martinus Nijhoff.

Emery, F. E., Thorsrud, E., & Trist, E. (1969). *Form and content in industrial democracy: Some experiences from Norway and other European countries.* London: Tavistock.

Fals Borda, O. (1979). Investigating reality in order to transform it: The Colombian experience. *Dialectical Anthropology, 4,* 33-55.

Fals Borda, O. (1988). *Knowledge and people's power.* New Delhi: Indian Social Institute.

Fals Borda, O., & Rahman, M. A. (Eds.). (1991). *Action and knowledge: Breaking the monopoly with participatory action-research.* New York: Apex.

Fay, B. (1987). *Critical social science: Liberation and its limits.* Cambridge: Polity.

Flood, R. L., & Jackson, M. C. (1991). *Creative problem solving: Total systems intervention.* Chichester: John Wiley.

Forester, J., Pitt, J., & Welsh, J. (Eds.). (1993). *Profiles of participatory action researchers.* Ithaca, NY: Cornell University, Department of Urban and Regional Planning.

Foster, M. (1972). An introduction to the theory and practice of action research in work organizations. *Human Relations, 25,* 529-566.

Fraser, N., & Nicholson, L. J. (1988). Social criticism without philosophy: An encounter between feminism and postmodernism. *Theory, Culture & Society, 5,* 373-394.

Freire, P. (1988). Creating alternative research methods: Learning to do it by doing it. In S. Kemmis & R. McTaggart (Eds.), *The action research reader* (3rd ed., pp. 291-313). Geelong, Victoria, Australia: Deakin University Press. (Reprinted from *Creating knowledge: A monopoly?* pp. 29-37, by B. Hall, A. Gillette, & R. Tandon, Eds., 1982, New Delhi: Society for Participatory Research in Asia)

Fullan, M. (1982). *The meaning of educational change.* New York: Teachers College Press.

Fullan, M. (1991). The new meaning of educational change. London: Cassell.

Gadamer, H.-G. (1975). *Truth and method* (2nd rev. ed.; J. Weinsheimer & D. G. Marshall, Eds. & Trans.). New York: Crossroad.

Giddens, A. (1979). *Central problems in social theory: Action, structure, and contradiction in social analysis.* London: Macmillan.

Grundy, S. (1987). *Curriculum: Product or praxis?* London: Falmer.

Habermas, J. (1972). *Knowledge and human interests* (J. J. Shapiro, Trans.). London: Heinemann.

Habermas, J. (1974). *Theory and practice* (J. Viertel, Trans.). London: Heinemann.

Habermas, J. (1984). *Theory of communicative action: Vol. 1. Reason and the rationalization of society* (T. McCarthy, Trans.). Boston: Beacon.

Habermas, J. (1987a). *The philosophical discourse of modernity: Twelve lectures* (F. G. Lawrence, Trans.). Cambridge: MIT Press.

Habermas, J. (1987b). *Theory of communicative action: Vol. 2. Lifeworld and system: A critique of functionalist reason* (T. McCarthy, Trans.). Boston: Beacon.

Habermas, J. (1990). *Moral consciousness and communicative action* (C. Lenhardt & S. W. Nicholson, Trans.). Cambridge: MIT Press.

Habermas, J. (1992). *Postmetaphysical thinking: Philosophical essays* (W. M. Hohengarten, Trans.). Cambridge: MIT Press.

Habermas, J. (1996). *Between facts and norms: Contributions to a discourse theory of law and democracy* (W. Rehg, Trans.). Cambridge: MIT Press.

Hall, B., Gillette, A., & Tandon, R. (Eds.). (1982). *Creating knowledge: A monopoly?* New Delhi: Society for Participatory Research in Asia.

Haug, F. (1987). *Female sexualization: A collective work of memory.* London: Verso.

Henry, C. (1991). If action research were tennis. In O. Zuber-Skerritt (Ed.), *Action learning for improved performance* (pp. 102-114). Brisbane: AEBIS.

Honneth, A., & Joas, H. (Ed.). (1991). *Communicative action.* Cambridge: MIT Press.

Honneth, A., McCarthy, T., Offe, C., & Wellmer, A. (Eds.). (1992). *Philosophical interventions in the unfinished project of enlightenment.* Cambridge: MIT Press.

Horton, M. (with Kohl, J., & Kohl, H.). (1990). *The long haul: An autobiography.* Garden City, NY: Doubleday.

Jackson, M. C. (1991). *Systems methodology for the management sciences.* New York: Plenum.

Kemmis, S. (1988, May). *Critical educational research.* Paper prepared for the Critical Theory Preconference of the North American Adult Education Association Research Conference, University of Calgary, Alberta, Canada.

Kemmis, S. (1991). Action research and post-modernisms. *Curriculum Perspectives, 11*(4), 59-66.

Kemmis, S. (1998). Action research exemplary projects: The Asturias project. In J. Angwin (Ed.), *The essence of action research.* Geelong, Victoria, Australia: Deakin University, Centre for Education and Change.

Kemmis, S., & McTaggart, R. (1988). *The action research planner* (3rd ed.). Geelong, Victoria, Australia: Deakin University Press.

Kolb, D. (1984). *Experiential learning: Experience as the source of learning and development.* Englewood Cliffs, NJ: Prentice Hall.

Lanhupuy, W. (1987). Balanda education: A mixed blessing for Aborigines. *Aboriginal Child at School, 15*(3), 31-36.

Levin, M. (1985). *Participatory action research in Norway.* Trondheim: ORAL.

Lyotard, J.-F. (1984). *The postmodern condition: A report on knowledge* (G. Bennington & B. Massumi, Trans.). Minneapolis: University of Minnesota Press.

MacIntyre, A. (1983). *After virtue: A study in moral theory* (2nd ed.). London: Duckworth.

Marika, R., Ngurruwutthun, D., & White, L. (1992). Always together, Yaka gäna: Participatory research at Yirrkala as part of the development of Yolngu education. *Convergence, 25*(1), 23-39.

McTaggart, R. (1987). Pedagogical principles for Aboriginal teacher education. *Aboriginal Child at School, 15*(4), 21-33.

McTaggart, R. (1988). Aboriginal pedagogy versus colonisation of the mind. *Curriculum Perspectives, 8*(2), 83-92.

McTaggart, R. (1991a). *Action research: A short modern history.* Geelong, Victoria, Australia: Deakin University Press.

McTaggart, R. (1991b). Principles for participatory action research. *Adult Education Quarterly, 4*(3), 168-187.

McTaggart, R. (1991c). Western institutional impediments to Aboriginal education. *Journal of Curriculum Studies, 23,* 297-325.

McTaggart, R. (Ed.). (1997a). *Participatory action research: International contexts and consequences.* Albany: State University of New York Press.

McTaggart, R. (1997b). Revitalising management as a scientific activity. *Management Learning, 28*(2), 177-195.

McTaggart, R. (1998). Is validity really an issue for action research? *Studies in Cultures, Organizations and Societies, 4,* 211-236.

McTaggart, R. (1999). Reflection on the purposes of research, action and scholarship: A case of cross-cultural participatory action research. *Systemic Practice and Action Research, 12*(5).

Noffke, S. E. (1990). *Action research: A multidimensional analysis.* Unpublished doctoral dissertation, University of Wisconsin–Madison.

Noffke, S. E. (1997a). Professional, personal, and political dimensions of action research. In M. W. Apple (Ed.), *Review of research in education* (Vol. 22, pp. 305-343). Washington, DC: American Educational Research Association.

Noffke, S. E. (1997b). Themes and tensions in US action research: Towards historical analysis. In S. Hollinsworth (Ed.), *International action research: A casebook for educational reform* (pp. 2-16). London: Falmer.

Oliveira, R., & Darcy, M. (1975). *The militant observer: A sociological alternative.* Geneva: IDAC.

Park, P., Brydon-Miller, M., Hall, B., & Jackson, T. (Eds.). (1993). *Voices of change: Participatory research in the United States and Canada.* Toronto: OISE.

Pasmore, W., & Friedlander, F. (1982). An action-research program for increasing employee involvement in problem-solving. *Administrative Science Quarterly, 27,* 342-362.

Pedler, M. (Ed.). (1991). *Action learning in practice.* Aldershot, England: Gower.

Reason, P. (Ed.). (1988). *Human inquiry in action: Developments in new paradigm research.* London: Sage.

Reid, W. A. (1978). *Thinking about the curriculum: The nature and treatment of curriculum problems.* London: Routledge & Kegan Paul.

Revans, R. W. (1980). *Action learning: New techniques for management.* London: Blond & Briggs.

Revans, R. W. (1982). *The origins and growth of action learning.* Bromley, England: Chartwell-Bratt.

Rorty, R. (1985). Habermas and Lyotard on modernity. In R. J. Bernstein (Ed.), *Habermas and modernity.* Cambridge: MIT Press.

Rorty, R. (1989). *Contingency, irony and solidarity.* Cambridge: Cambridge University Press.

Sagor, R. (1992). *How to conduct collaborative action research.* Alexandria, VA: ASCD.

Sandkull, B. (1980). Practice of industry: Mismanagement of people. *Human Systems Management, 1,* 159-167.

Schön, D. A. (1983). *The reflective practitioner: How professionals think in action.* New York: Basic Books.

Schön, D. A. (1987). *Educating the reflective practitioner.* San Francisco: Jossey-Bass.

Schön, D. A. (Ed.). (1991). *The reflective turn: Case studies in and on educational practice.* New York: Teachers College Press.

Stenhouse, L. (1975). *An introduction to curriculum research and development.* London: Heinemann.

Thompson, J. B., & Held, D. (Eds.). (1982). *Habermas: Critical debates.* Cambridge: MIT Press.

Torbert, W. R. (1991). *The power of balance: Transforming self, society, and scientific inquiry.* Newbury Park, CA: Sage.

Toulmin, S. (1990). *Cosmopolis: The hidden agenda of modernity.* New York: Free Press.

von Wright, G. H. (1971). *Explanation and understanding.* London: Routledge & Kegan Paul.

Warmington, A. (1980). Action research: Its methods and its implications. *Journal of Applied Systems Analysis, 7,* 23-39.

Weiner, G. (1989). Professional self-knowledge versus social justice: A critical analysis of the teacher-researcher movement. *British Educational Research Journal, 15*(1), 41-51.

Whyte, W. F. (1989). Introduction to action research for the twenty-first century: Participation, reflection, and practice. *American Behavioral Scientist, 32,* 502-512.

Whyte, W. F. (Ed.). (1991). *Participatory action research.* London: Sage.

Yirrkala Homeland Schools. (1996, May). Linking business. *Big Link, 5,* 2-6.

Zuber-Skerritt, O. (Ed.). (1996). *New directions in action research.* London: Falmer.

12

Clinical Research

William L. Miller and Benjamin F. Crabtree

◆ Conversing at the Wall

We are closer to Eden. The war against breast cancer advances and the local and national media stage another heroic celebration of the latest miracle. A drug prevents breast cancer. At multiple sites in the United States in 1992, 13,388 hopeful women with risk factors for breast cancer enrolled in an explanatory, double-blind, randomized controlled trial designed to demonstrate the efficacy of tamoxifen for preventing breast cancer. Several years later, the trial ended early because success appeared evident to the investigators (Fisher et al., 1998). Despite serious concerns about the drug's short-term side effects, two conflicting European studies (Powles et al., 1998; Veronesi et al., 1998), and no knowledge of the drug's social, emotional, or long-term consequences, a successful national marketing effort was launched to convince the Food and Drug Administration, physicians, and women to consider seriously the large-scale use of tamoxifen.

These are the complex interactions of many well-intentioned individuals, an expectant and frightened public, and institutional dynamics. There are intense escalating pressures for academic health centers to get research grant money as a way of surviving, with the vast majority of those moneys being spent for basic biomolecular/genetic "bench" research and randomized clinical trials. The large pharmaceutical conglomerates are driven to identify new markets for drugs requiring enormous investment to develop and test. Career pathways and success are linked to these same pressures. Special interest groups, the media, and cultural forces continue to push, with intense urgency, for cures and fixes, for immortality inside the genome. The research imperative to find universal (i.e., generalizable) interventions or drugs that work in preplanned, standardized ways and that sell is overwhelming. "Just give me the evidence" means "Give me the numbers," which means "Demonstrate a good profit line," which means "Assure my endangered, privileged status." Welcome to the clinical research space.

Meanwhile, amid a Middle Atlantic landscape of small farms, crowded urban streets, and rigid walls of private property, Camille joins the clan of one-breasted women (Williams, 1991). She is confused and worried. Poor, frightened, and 50, she knows the breast cancer is spreading. Her life, composed of memories, children, career, lovers, and anticipated hopes, appears shredded; she fears no one is listening. She was in the Breast Cancer Prevention Trial (Fisher et al., 1998), took the drug and still got cancer. She feels punished and ignored. Her doctors hide their fears and lose their empathy behind liver enzyme tests and offers of experimental chemotherapy clinical trial protocols. They feel tired, overregulated, angry at the continued emphasis on cost cutting, and inadequate in the face of death, but they conceal their emotions behind a wall of professional "objectivity" and the afterglow of the tamoxifen breakthrough. Camille's friend Gloria was also in the study and did well, but is not sure the drug is worth it. She didn't like taking a pill every day; it made her feel like something was wrong with her body. She worries more about everything since she joined the study, and she's stopped taking the pill. Alice is outright angry about the study. She also got the tamoxifen and not the placebo, but she developed a large blood clot in her leg and now has chronic leg and back pain and can barely walk. Meanwhile, marketing researchers for Zeneca Pharmaceuticals are conducting focus groups to learn more effective ways to convince women and physicians of tamoxifen's value. But these are not the stories known by the "public." These stories are hidden, if known at all, by conscious concealment and by the forces of unconscious cultural preference. They are also hidden behind academic walls of qualitative jargon and disciplinary tradition. Thus potential openings in the walls that barricade us all are lost in obscurity.

This is a typical tale in medical research. The story of interest and of hope for qualitative clinical researchers is in what is missing and how the story is framed. *Suffering is standardized.* The suffering related to breast cancer in "typical medical research" is framed as a universal need for some marketable product that prevents. The complexities and individualities of suffering are suppressed within this frame. Important voices and evidence are missing. Knowing the efficacy of the drug, its internal validity, is sufficient to approve using all means necessary to convince all women to "choose" the pill as a requirement for healthy life. Camille's experience of taking a daily pill that labels her formerly healthy self and body as endangered is missing. The voices of her husband and children and parents are missing. Relationships and moral discourse are missing. Feeling, spirituality, and ecology are missing. The "victory," the illusion of Eden, is possible only because depth and context have been reduced or eliminated and relationships have been isolated and alienated. But the victory is not total. As the drug enters the world of lived experience, its flaws will be exposed, its market value will fall, and disappointment will rise until the next "breakthrough." Fortunately, public discontent also continues to rise and manifests itself as growing interest in alternative and complementary healing approaches, spirituality and/or fundamentalisms, and anger with health care reform efforts and services.

This is the clinical research space we have witnessed—many conversations behind walls, but increased suffering, confusion, and searching in the clinical world despite technological "advances." The public discontent and the missing evidence are the hope upon which this chapter builds. We imagine a clinical research space where Camille, her doctors, the biomedical products industry, and the researchers meet and seek transformation. This chapter imagines a conversation at the walls (Brueggemann, 1991)— at the place where the walls meet clinical reality. At the walls separating clinician from patient, qualitative from quantitative, academy from practice, very different ways or cultures of knowing can meet and converse. This *Handbook* celebrates the qualitative research community's conversation behind the wall—the internal discourse about who we are and what we do, and about the faith and hope for our own transformation that are sustained there. The opportunity to translate this conversation outside the wall and into the clinical research space has never been better. Calls made a decade ago for a shift away from a strictly positivist position and for greater methodological diversity, including the use of qualitative research methods (e.g., Freymann, 1989; McWhinney, 1986, 1989; Waitzkin, 1991), are being answered, and qualitative approaches are finding their way into funding agency agendas, especially in primary health care, health services, and nursing. The use of qualitative methods and multiple paradigms is expanding, but such endeavors are still only a patch-work, found more in the tributaries of clinical research than in the main-stream. Patients and clinicians are increasingly being invited into the re-search conversations.[1] The methods are also evolving, beginning to separate from their parent traditions (such as ethnography, phenomenol-ogy, and grounded theory) and generating new hybrids in the clinical re-search space.

This chapter is about continuing and accelerating the flow, the explora-tion, the conversations at the walls. The understanding of clinical research that we present arises from the nexus of applied anthropology and the practice of primary health care, family practice in particular. Both of us have appointments in family medicine, and both are trained in anthro-pology; we are each on both sides of several walls. Our social science roots were fed by the development of clinically applied anthropology (Chrisman, 1977; Chrisman & Maretzki, 1982; Fabrega, 1976, 1979; Foster, 1974; Foster & Anderson, 1978; Polgar, 1962) in the 1970s, nur-tured by the later work of Kleinman (1988, 1992, 1995; Kleinman, Eisenberg, & Good, 1978), Good and Good (1981; Good, 1994), Lock (1982, 1986, 1993), Pelto and Pelto (1978, 1990), and Young (1982a, 1982b), and currently challenged by the poststructuralist debate (Burawoy et al., 1991; Clifford & Marcus, 1986; Haraway, 1993; Jackson, 1989) and critical theory (Baer, 1993; Morsy, 1996; Singer, 1995). One of us (WLM) has a busy urban family practice, directs a resi-dency program, and chairs a clinical department; the other (BFC) directs a family practice research division and is a national research consultant. We are both active participants in the politics and discourse of academic biomedicine and academic social science. The biomedical influence, with its perceived therapeutic imperative, steers toward pragmatic interven-tions and the desire for explicitness and coherence in information gather-ing and decision making and highlights the appeal of positivism and tech-nology. The actual relationships that emerge within patient care reveal the uncertainty and particularity (McWhinney, 1989) of clinical praxis and turn one toward storytelling, relationship, and interpretation. Trying to get grants funded, to publish storied knowledge in biomedical journals, and to change dominant behaviors exposes the realities of power and hegemony.

Our guiding premise is that the questions emerging from clinical expe-rience frame conversation and determine research design (Brewer & Hunter, 1989; Diers, 1979; Miller & Crabtree, 1999b). Clinical researchers have at least six discernible research styles available: experimental, survey, documentary-historical, field (qualitative), philosophical, and action/participatory (Lather, 1991, chap. 23). The clinical research space needs to be open to all of these possible sources and types of knowledge. Thus we structure this chapter around the following three goals: (a) *creating a space* for research that is open and celebrates qualitative and multiparadigmatic approaches to the clinical world, (b) *providing the tools and translations* necessary for the discovery and interpretation of the clinical stories and knowledge within this space, and (c) identifying and describing the means for *telling the stories* and sharing the knowledge. Our emphasis is on the clinical text of Western biomedicine and the particular subtext of primary health care because of our own location in that place, but the discussion is easily transferred to other clinical contexts, such as nursing care, education, and organizational management (see also Berg & Smith, 1988; Bogdan & Biklen, 1992; Morse & Field, 1997; Sapsford & Abbott, 1992; Schein, 1987; Symon & Cassell, 1998).

◆ Creating a Space

The dominant biomedical world and the smaller qualitative research community both tend to maintain methodological and academic rigidity. Creating a clinical research space requires bringing both groups outside their walls and finding common ground and common language. *The clinical questions at the wall are the common ground* (Taylor, 1993). These questions call us to rediscover the missing evidence (the people, experiences, and contexts), the richness and depth of what "effectiveness" means; to explore the human implications of rationing and cost issues, biotechnology and genetic engineering; and to enter the conflicted landscape of alternative and conventional medicine, the world between the "garden" and the "machine" (Beinfield & Korngold, 1991). We describe two core strategies for creating and entering this common ground and transforming clinical research. The first of these consists of stepping directly into the biomedical world as it is now; the second involves joining the evidence-based medicine (EBM) space. We also mention four additional strategies: using theory more explicitly; expanding cross-disciplinary collaborations; thinking in more open, multimethod, and longitudinal ways; and doing more participatory research and advocacy. These strategies assume that change is more experience based than rational and that clinical participants must actively try methods if they are to adopt them. Thus there is an emphasis on clinical participants, including patients, answering their own questions using methods appropriate for those questions.

Entering Biomedicine

Walking and working inside the walls of technocratic biomedicine is daunting and frequently challenges intellectual and personal integrity. Thriving in this world requires understanding the biomedical cultural context while also clearly articulating a model that highlights the clinical implications of qualitative clinical research. This knowledge, if also joined by patients and other community participants, facilitates bargaining, mediation, and the formation of common language that makes possible the creation of a new research space just outside the walls. This is where, in languages the existing clinical world and patients understand, a space for more expansive imagination is created, tools for listening and seeing are shared, and transforming stories are enacted.

The dominant biomedical paradigm is rooted in a patriarchal positivism; *control through rationality and separation is the overriding theme.* The biomedical model is typified by the following nine basic premises:

1. Scientific *rationality;*
2. Emphasis on *individual autonomy,* rather than on family or community;
3. The *body as machine,* with emphasis on physiochemical data and objective, numerical measurement;
4. *Mind/body separation* and dualism;
5. *Diseases as entities;*
6. *Patient as object* and the resultant alienation of physician from patient;
7. Emphasis on the *visual;*
8. Diagnosis and treatment from the *outside;*
9. *Reductionism* and the seeking of *universals* (Davis-Floyd & St. John, 1998; Gordon, 1988).

The everyday characteristics of the clinical medical world that follow from this model include these:

1. Male-centeredness;
2. Physician-centeredness;

3. Specialist orientation;

4. Emphasis on credentials;

5. High value on memory;

6. A process orientation accentuating ritual, with supervaluation on "science" and technology;

7. Therapeutic activism with emphasis on short-term results;

8. Death seen as defeat;

9. Division of the clinical space into "front" (receptionists, billing clerks, and office managers) and "back" (doctors, nurses, and phlebotomists);

10. The definition, importance, and sanctity of "medical time";

11. Emphasis on patient satisfaction;

12. Profit-driven system;

13. Reverence for the privacy of the doctor-patient relationship;

14. Intolerance of other modalities (Davis-Floyd & St. John, 1998; Helman, 1994; Pfifferling, 1981; Stein, 1990).

These are the assumptions, values, and beliefs that characterize the dominant voice of the medical clinic and that currently define the preferred boundaries of clinical research. Biomedical culture is reinforced and sustained by its comfortable fit within the prevailing cultural norms of the United States. These "normalizing ideologies" include control over the environment, rational determinism, future orientation, life as an ordered and continuous whole, and individualism with emphasis on productivity, perseverance, self-determination, and self-reliance. They are manifested in daily discourses about family, self, gender identity, and aging. Both patients and physicians refer to these ideologies and their associated discourses to help them restore order and normalcy to the disruptions of sickness (Becker, 1997).

This reigning voice of biomedicine has now been successfully corporatized in the United States, and its apparent goal is the elimination of pain, suffering, and disease. The research tends to be atheoretical, hospital based, and disease oriented. In many ways, the present situation represents the triumph of commodification and universalism, with its emphasis on cost, customers, products, outcomes, effectiveness, standardization, and evidence. The reasons for focusing on outcomes are to inform choices (market approach), to provide accountability (regulatory approach), and to improve care (management approach). Fortunately for qualitative researchers, the clinic has many additional, usually unheard, voices. If

403

these voices are entered into the conversation as evidence, the clinical research space is expanded and potentially transformed.

Successfully entering the biomedical world as a qualitative clinical researcher requires a many-eyed *model of mediation*. The biomedical model views the world through its one eye of "objectivity." Qualitative clinical researchers need to learn the discipline of seeing with three eyes—the biomedical eye, the inward searching eye of reflexivity, and a third eye that looks for the multiple, nested contexts that hold and shape the research questions. Like the shamanistic tricksters of mythology (Hyde, 1998; Hynes & Doty, 1993; Radin, 1955), we enter the biomedical world as eye jugglers (Frey, 1994), skilled at mediating multiple perspectives. This qualitative clinical model of mediation features the following nine premises:

1. Center yourself in the *clinical world,* in the eye of the storm.
2. Focus on the *questions* that dawn there.
3. Assume *both/and;* acknowledge what is of value in biomedicine *and* highlight what is missing, what is silent, invisible, ignored; expand on the already existing tension between care and competence (Good & Good, 1993); hold quantitative objectivisms in one hand and qualitative revelations in the other.
4. Follow a *natural history* path that characterizes indigenous medical traditions and the early history of Western medicine and is still an important aspect of primary health care (Harris, 1989).
5. Be *participatory;* include patients and clinicians in your inquiry work.
6. Preserve and celebrate *anomalies,* the discoveries and data that do not fit; anomalies are the levers for transformation.
7. Allow "truth" to be *emergent* and not preconceived, defensive, or forceful.
8. Respect the plea for *clinical action* and the perceived need for coherence voiced by nearly all participants in the clinical world.
9. Practice *humility and patience;* these will enable everything else.

Qualitative clinical researchers can bring several powerful perspectives to the clinical encounter that can help surface the unseen and unheard and add depth to what is already present. These include an understanding of disease as a cultural construction (Berger & Luckmann, 1967); knowledge of additional medical models, such as the biopsychosocial or humanistic model (Engels, 1977; Smith, 1996), the holistic model (Gordon, 1996; Weil, 1988), and homeopathy (Swayne, 1998), and non-Western models such as traditional Chinese (Beinfield & Korngold, 1991), Ayurvedic (Sharma & Clark, 1998), and shamanism (Drury, 1996); and recognition of faith and the importance of spirituality in human life. Qualitative researchers also recognize that the therapeutic or healing process occurs not only in the clinical moment, but also in the everyday life between clinical events. Thus the study of everyday life offers additional perspectives, additional voices to the research space being created outside the walls. Carrying the staff of your many-eyed model of mediation, you are ready to enter the clinic.

The clinic is a public sanctuary for the voicing of trouble and dispensation of relief.[2] Each clinic participant crafts meaning out of the "facts" and "feelings" inherent in each clinical encounter and seeks to weave a comforting cloth of *support*. Camille and her family, Alice and her friend, and Gloria and her family all come and meet their clinician and her staff at the clinic. These participants bring into the clinic all of their past ghosts; the emotional, physical, conceptual, sociocultural, and spiritual contingencies and competing demands of their presents; and their hopes and fears for their futures. This is the real world of clinical practice involving material bodies, intentions, meanings, intersubjectivity, values, personal knowledge, physical ecology, and ethics. Yet most published clinical research consists of observational epidemiology (Feinstein, 1985; Kelsey, Thompson, & Evans, 1986; Kleinbaum, Kupper, & Morgenstern, 1982; Sackett, 1991) and clinical trial designs (Meinert, 1986; Pocock, 1983). These studies involve separating variables of interest from their local, everyday milieu, entering them into a controlled research environment, and then trying to fit the results back into the original context. For example, Alice's clinician is aware of randomized controlled trials demonstrating clinical efficacy for short-term bed rest in patients with back pain (Deyo, Diehl, & Rosenthal, 1986; Wiesel et al., 1980). But the practitioner encounters difficulty in applying this information to the particular back pain and disability Alice is experiencing. The evidences needed to inform this encounter are many. Ideally, the clinical participants will study themselves and thus challenge their own situated knowledges and empower their own transformations. This requires that they bring qualitative methods to the clinical experience. Let's join the evidence-based medicine research space.

Joining Evidence-Based Medicine

Evidence-based medicine (EBM) is the new wonder child in clinical care and in clinical research. The premise is that individual clinical expertise must be integrated "with the best available external clinical evidence from systematic research" (Sackett, Richardson, Rosenberg, & Haynes, 1997, p. 2). Randomized clinical trials (RCTs) and meta-analyses (systematic reviews of multiple RCTs) are considered to produce the best external evidence for use in answering questions about therapeutic interventions. An international group of clinicians, methodologists, and consumers have formed the Cochrane Collaboration as a means of facilitating the collection, implementation, and dissemination of such systematic reviews (Fullerton-Smith, 1995). They have created the Cochrane Library, which is available on CD-ROM, on the Internet, and in secondary publications through the *British Medical Journal.* Major initiatives are under way to assure that all physicians, especially at the primary care level, use this evidence to guide their clinical decision making (Shaughnessy, Slawson, & Bennett, 1994; Slawson, Shaughnessy, & Bennett, 1994). The proliferation of clinical practice guidelines is one result of these initiatives. Another result is the relative reduced value of qualitative studies. But EBM actually offers qualitative clinical investigators multiple opportunities for creating a space outside the walls—there is so much *missing evidence!*

The double-blind (closed) RCT has high internal validity but often dubious external validity and almost no information about *context,* as noted in our introductory discussion of the Breast Cancer Prevention Trial. Read any RCT report, and the only voice you hear is the cold sound of the intervention and faint echoes of the investigator's biases. The cacophonous music of patients, clinicians, insurance companies, lawyers, government regulatory bodies, consumer interest groups, community agencies, office staff, corporate interests, and family turmoil is mute. Local politics and contradictory demands become the sound of thin hush. There has also been little research into the *individual clinical expertise* side of the EBM equation and the associated areas of relationship dynamics, communication, and patient preference; there is much to be learned about how patients and clinicians actually implement "best evidence." Additionally, there are many gray zones of clinical practice where the evidence about competing clinical options is incomplete or contradictory (Naylor, 1995). Breast cancer prevention is a good example. Should women at high risk of developing breast cancer undergo prophylactic mastectomy, take tamoxifen for life, have more frequent screening mammography with or without regular physician examination and rigorous breast self-examination, eat macrobiotic food and take antioxidant vitamins, and/or live life as it comes? Where is the helpful qualitative clinical research? Here are the openings for clinical researchers. We can join the EBM and RCT space and expand its vision.

The new gold standard, if there should be any at all, needs to include qualitative methods along with the RCT. In addition to those areas noted above, qualitative methods can help formalize the learning curve, test theory, inform hypothesis testing and future work, and enhance the transferability of the clinical trial into clinical practice. We propose conceptualizing the *multimethod RCT* as a double-stranded helix of DNA. On one strand are qualitative methods addressing issues of context, meaning, power, and complexity, and on the other are quantitative methods providing measurement and a focused anchor. The two strands are connected by the research questions. The qualitative and quantitative strands twist and spiral around the questions in an ongoing interaction, creating codes of understanding that get expressed in better clinical care. We hope that clinical researchers will seek out those doing clinical trials on symptom management, treatments, clinical processes, and community interventions and advocate for adding the qualitative strand. This work will also help to identify new outcomes that transpose the emphasis on individual cure and elimination of pain and disease toward care, growth, quality of life, healthier relationships, and more sustainable communities and ecosystems.

Examples showing the way already exist. Jolly, Bradley, Sharp, Smith, and Mant (1998), using RCT technology, tested a nurse-led intervention to help patients who had survived heart attacks maintain a rehabilitation program and improve health habits. The quantitative RCT strand yielded statistically insignificant results; fortunately, Wiles (1998) also conducted a qualitative depth interview study with 25 of the participants at 2 weeks and 5 months during the trial and uncovered several clinically valuable findings. At 2 weeks, most of the patients trusted the official accounts of what had happened to them and what they needed to do to prevent future problems. By 5 months, most of the patients had lost that trust because the official accounts had not adequately addressed the experienced random nature of their heart attacks, their severity, and the patients' levels of recovery. Many of the patients perceived their survival to mean that their heart attacks were mild, and, because the doctors had reassured them everything would be normal in 6 weeks, the patients assumed they could return to their original "normal" lifestyles in 6 weeks. Another example of the DNA model for RCTs concerns smoking cessation interventions and is found in the work of Willms and Wilson and their colleagues at McMaster

University. These researchers learned that the meanings patients attributed to their cigarettes had more influence on their stopping smoking than did the use of nicotine gum and counseling (Willms, 1991; Willms et al., 1990; Wilson et al., 1988). Let us join in opening the imagination inside the genome with qualitative questions and approaches.

What are the clinically grounded questions that serve as windows for opening imagination at the walls? Clinicians and patients seeking *support* in the health care setting confront four fundamental questions of clinical praxis:

1. What is going on with our *bodies?*
2. What is happening with our *lives?*
3. Who has what *power?*
4. What are the complex *relationships* among our bodies, our lives, and power?

Each of these questions has emotional, physical/behavioral, conceptual/attributional, cultural/social/historical, and spiritual/energetic ramifications. For example, from the stories of Camille, Gloria, and Alice, there are body questions about support. What are the emotions of living with a high risk for breast cancer? Is tamoxifen more effective than lifestyle change at preventing breast cancer? How will either affect my family and social bodies? What is the lived experience and meaning of breast cancer risk for patients and clinicians? What is happening in the practice or clinic as "organizational body" that helps or hinders Camille's, Gloria's, or Alice's care? There are questions concerning the support of one's life or biography. Do explanatory models of breast cancer relate to the experience and outcome of risk? How does one's self-concept relate to breast cancer risk and response to tamoxifen? What are patients' and clinicians' hopes, despairs, fears, and insecurities concerning breast cancer? How does past experience connect to the immediate experience of breast cancer risk or participation in a clinical trial? There are questions of power about how people are supported. What is happening when patients with high risk of breast cancer present to clinicians in different organizational contexts of care? How is emotional distress surfaced or suppressed? What patterns exist in these different settings? Who influences whom? How is the patient or clinician's power undermined or enhanced (Fahy & Smith, 1999)? What are the local politics? There are questions about the support of relationships. What actions in the clinical encounter enhance family relationships? How do the individuals, the families, and the clinic function as complex adaptive systems? Many of these questions are addressed adequately only if qualitative methods enter into the clinical research space.

This is the evidence needed! We need to apply these four question categories to the critically important issues of the next decade, such as rationing and cost, biotechnology and genetic products, and the often conflicted landscape where alternative medicine and biomedicine meet. How does rationing of health care affect our bodies? What are the emotional, physical, conceptual, social, and spiritual consequences? The same questions can be asked of the many new (and old) products of biotechnology. What are their impacts on our lives? Where is the power and how is it used and resisted? What are the relationships and complex systems that are affected and through which the technologies are deployed? What are the unanticipated consequences? How do patients decide about therapies? How do they juggle seeing their bodies both as gardens and as machines? What other metaphors are used, and when and how do these change outcomes? The questions are infinite and challenging. Primary care, at its core, is a context-dependent craft. EBM lacks context in its present form; it cries out for qualitative methods. Let's get to work!

Using Theory

The multimethod RCT also creates an opportunity for clinical researchers to reintroduce theory into clinical research. Theory is frequently missing from standard quantitative clinical studies, and this often results in ungrounded a posteriori speculation. Qualitative data help to surface hidden theoretical assumptions and suggest new possibilities and connections. Theory can also help bridge the dominant biomedical and other cultural worlds. Recent theoretical discussions among medical anthropologists, phenomenologists, semioticians, and sociologists concerning the metaphor of the "body" challenge biomedical assumptions about the human body and its boundaries and highlight the culturally and socially constructed aspects of the "body" that extend far beyond its corporeality (Csordas, 1994; Gordon, 1990; Johnson, 1987; Kirmayer, 1992; Martin, 1994; Scheper-Hughes & Locke, 1987; Shildrick, 1997; Turner, 1992). There is an individual body, a social body, and a body politic. There are medical bodies, the earth as body, and communicative bodies. Bodies are imagined as flexible, leaky, or effervescent, as machines or gardens, and these imaginations both shape and are shaped by the social body, the body politic, and the world body. Arthur Frank (1995), for example, has described the use of storytelling as a means of restoring voice to the body. Bodily symptoms are understood as the infolding of cultural traumas into the body; as these bodies create history, the symptoms outfold into social space. Because of their complexity, social bodies such as practice organizations are often best characterized through the use of metaphors; they might be described as *brains, machines, organisms,* or *ugly faces* (Morgan, 1998). Qualitative methods become a primary source for hearing these stories and their associated metaphors, caring in relationships, and resisting the colonizing narrative of institutionalized medicine. The study of bodies and their place in the production and expression of sickness and health becomes a core strategy for clinical research that enables the bridging of paradigms and opens the clinical research space.

Collaborating Across Disciplines

This opened clinical research space requires collaboration that emphasizes multiple linkages and different types of cross-disciplinary relationships. Linkages can occur vertically, where one moves up and down through different levels or scales, such as the molecular, individual, local, and regional levels, or linkages can be horizontal, across different sectors at the same level of social organizations such as medical practices, schools, and local businesses. Linkages also occur over time or at different times. Finally, there are multiple academic linkages, including those with the "public," with practitioners, with policy makers, and with research participants (Miller, 1994).

Multimethod and Longitudinal Strategies

Orchestrating this type of multimethod, cross-disciplinary research requires the skills and mind-set of a generalist researcher using a framework of critical multiplism (Coward, 1990; Miller, 1994). The skills and perspectives of the generalist researcher consist of negotiation, translation, theoretical pluralism, methodological pluralism, a community orientation, and comfort with and rootedness in clinical practices. These skills and attitudes are successfully implemented through a critical multiplist framework. Critical multiplism assumes that multiple ways of knowing are necessary and that these options require critical thought and choice. *Multiplism* refers not only to multiple methods but also to multiple triangulation, multiple stakeholders, multiple studies, and multiple paradigms and perspectives. *Critical* refers to the critical selection of these options based on local history, the role of power and patterns of domination, and how the different methods complement each other. Six principles help to guide the complex work of the critical multiplist: (a) Know why you choose to do something, (b) preserve method and paradigm integrity, (c) pay attention to units of analysis, (d) remember the research questions, (e) select options whose strengths and weaknesses complement each other, and (f) continually evaluate methodology throughout the study. Critical multiplism is a particularly powerful framework for doing participatory clinical research.

Participatory and Advocacy Strategies

Participatory research (Macaulay et al., 1998, chap. 23; Thesen & Kuzel, 1999) provides another entry into transforming the research space and brings us around, full circle, to the research questions. We propose that clinical researchers investigate questions emerging from the clinical experience with the clinical participants, pay attention to and reveal any underlying values and assumptions, and direct the results toward clinical participants and policy makers. This refocuses the gaze of clinical research onto the clinical experience and redefines its boundaries so as to answer three questions: Whose question is it? Are hidden assumptions of the clinical world revealed? For whom are the research results intended? (That is, who is the stakeholder or audience?) Patients and clinicians are invited to explore their own and/or each other's questions and concerns with whatever methods are necessary. Clinical researchers share ownership of the research with clinical participants, thus undermining the patriarchal bias of the dominant paradigm and opening its assumptions to investigation. This is the situated knowledge, the "somewhere in particular" (Haraway, 1991, p. 196), where space is created to find a larger, more inclusive vision of clinical research.

Getting these many kinds of evidence will require the clinical researcher to join the evidence-based medicine space, to develop cross-disciplinary collaborations, to use multiple methods with a critical multiplist conceptualization, to use bridging metaphors and theories such as the "body," and, often, to emphasize participatory and advocacy approaches. With these strategies, the clinical research space opens for the tools of the generalist clinical researcher. Qualitative researchers have seen and heard the stories and sufferings of Camille, Gloria, and Alice, but they have been retold in a language that patients and clinicians don't understand (e.g., Fisher, 1986; Fisher & Todd, 1983; Lazarus, 1988; Mishler, 1984; West, 1984; Williams, 1984). Neither clinicians nor patients know the languages of "ethnomethodology," "hermeneutics," "phenomenology," "semiotics," and "interpretive interactionism." Most qualitative clinical research is published in a language and in places that benefit researchers, not the patients and practitioners. Qualitative researchers have asked that clinicians join, listen to, and speak the "voice of the lifeworld" (Mishler, 1984). We ask clinical qualitative researchers to do the same.

◆ Providing the Tools and Translations

In this section we present the tools and translations necessary for bringing qualitative methods and traditions into the clinical research space. We begin by comparing the qualitative research process with the clinical process. The almost direct correspondence enables the clinical researcher to make qualitative methods transparent to clinicians and patients. This is followed by a brief overview of qualitative methods and how to create mixed-method research designs in the clinical setting. Finally, we put it all together with an example of clinical research that uses some of the strategies discussed.

Research Process

The clinical research space is created when the researcher focuses on the questions arising from the clinical experience, thus opening many possibilities for using the full range of qualitative data gathering and analysis methods. (Many of these qualitative approaches are presented elsewhere in this volume, and we discuss them in more detail in a text for primary care qualitative researchers; see Crabtree & Miller, 1999a.) The challenge for the researcher is to translate qualitative collection and analysis methods into clear, jargon-free language without sacrificing the methods' integrity rooted in the disciplinary conversations behind the wall. A fundamental tenet of the proposed translation is that *the question and clinical context are primary; methods must adjust to the clinical setting and the clinical questions.* Interpretive social science has traditionally feared mixed methods because this has usually meant treating qualitative research as

412

only a method subservient to the positivist paradigm or materialistic inquiry. We imagine a clinical research space where qualitative methods are empowered and constructivist and critical/ecological paradigms are included. The key is to recognize the similarity between the qualitative research process and the clinical process, particularly as it presents itself in primary health care.

Figure 12.1 is a diagram of the relationship-centered clinical method (RCCM), an emerging tool for teaching and doing the primary care clinical encounter (Stewart et al., 1995; Tresolini & Pew-Fetzer Task Force, 1994). Notice that the overall approach consists of four separate processes—exploring, understanding, finding common ground, and self-reflection. These four processes flow sequentially, but all iterate with each other during any particular encounter, and the whole process usually cycles multiple times for any given illness episode. Chronic illness care, for example, will occur over a lifetime of visits, whereas an episode of ear infection may require only one to three visits (i.e., one, two, or three iterations of the clinical method cycle).

For example, when Camille presents her embodied story of spreading breast cancer, she and her clinician begin their encounter by *exploring* specific disease issues, such as a newly discovered lump. But they also share Camille's fears and expectations and weave these into the fabric of her ongoing health story. Meanwhile, the clinician is seeking to *understand* how all of this relates to Camille's family, community, and ecological context. New information from the exploration and from *self-reflection* inform the emerging understanding, which, in turn, suggests new questions to ask. Shortly after the encounter begins, Camille and her clinician also start *finding common ground* about the issues of most concern, the goals of care, and their respective roles. This process also is informed by and informs the other three.

Doing this clinical method feels like doing qualitative research in fast-forward mode—and it is. The four clinical processes of the RCCM correspond directly to the four processes of qualitative research: gathering, analysis, interpretation, and reflexivity. These parallel processes are illustrated in Figure 12.2 (the clinical equivalents appear in parentheses above the research processes). If we use qualitative research language to describe the clinical process, the parallels and the translation of qualitative jargon become clearer. Clinicians begin their encounters by gathering data using purposeful or information-rich sampling. They focus their interviewing, participant observing, and touching on possible explanations related to

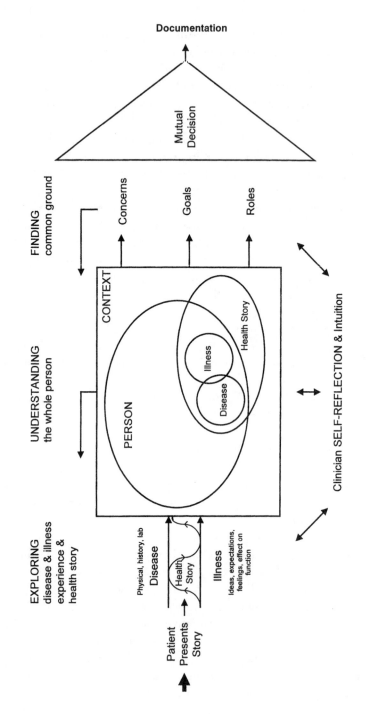

Figure 12.1. Relationship-Centered Clinical Method

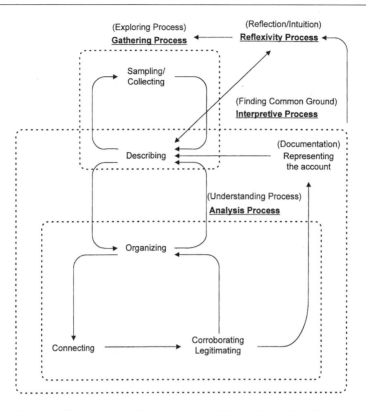

Figure 12.2. Qualitative Research Processes and Their Clinical Parallels

the patient's presenting concern or opening story. The exploration seeks "disease" information, following the biomedical model, but the process also searches for understanding of the patient's health story and his or her illness experience, especially the patient's ideas, expectations, and feelings about the health concern and its effects on the patient's everyday living. The clinician almost immediately begins analyzing the data while continuing to gather additional information. This analysis seeks to understand the patient's concern within the context of his or her life world—the patient's personal, family, community, and ecological stories. This understanding is organized around sensitizing concepts, diagnostic categories, personal experience templates or scripts, and connections looked for and then corroborated against the known evidence. Using a participatory framework, the clinician periodically shares the emerging understanding with the patient (or others) and, together, they seek a common interpretation.

Throughout this iterative process, the clinician is using self-reflection, personal feelings, and intuition to inform the gathering, analyzing, and interpreting. The visit ends when the practitioner and patient agree they have sufficient data (i.e., saturation) to implement an initial course of action. The outcomes are a course of action for the patient and a report describing the encounter written (or dictated) by the clinician. The clinician's reports occasionally undergo peer review. This sounds like, looks like, and feels like qualitative research—only most clinicians don't know it. Researchers need to use clinical language to translate qualitative methods and standards.

It is helpful to notice how clinical care also mirrors the DNA-like, multimethod RCT described earlier. In both, simplified coherence for action ("disease") is in dynamic tension with personal/social/cultural complexity ("illness" and "health story"), and the tension is held through the quest for care, through the research questions. This is most possible when participatory and cognizant of the power imbalances inherent in the relationships and in the greater health care system (such as the system is). All of the many voices must be surfaced, and attention must be paid to them. Out of this tapestry of relational forces, within given biocultural boundaries, are woven senses. The methods must parallel the clinical process and provide self-critique and correction. This is where doing science and reflexivity intersect.

Research Design

Research designs in clinical research inherently require multimethod thinking, or critical multiplism, with the particular combinations of data gathering, analysis, and interpretation approaches being driven by the research question and the clinical context. There are infinite possibilities for integrating qualitative and quantitative methods, with the design being created for each study and often evolving as a study progresses in response to the emerging questions. In clinical research, the design may be wholly qualitative or quantitative, including the use of a single method, but increasingly designs are employing combinations of these, in what have been referred to as mixed methods (Tashakkori & Teddlie, 1998). Clinical researchers must maintain multimethod thinking and remain free to mix and match methods as driven by particular clinically based questions.

There are many questions and contexts that require only a single method; however, these single-method designs should still be considered within a multimethod context. When the investigator starts with the question and considers all possible methods before deciding that a single method is appropriate for the question, he or she is maintaining multimethod thinking. Most clinical research questions are complex and require multiple approaches. Particular mixed-method combinations of qualitative and quantitative methods are generally presented in terms of typologies of multimethod designs (Stange, Miller, Crabtree, O'Connor, & Zyzanski, 1994). In actual practice, condensing these into typologies is too prescriptive and tends to oversimplify the complex dance of the research process. In conceptualizing a study, the clinical investigator creates a design from the full range of data collection and analysis tools, much as a child (or Will Miller) makes creations from the sticks and wheels of Tinkertoys or from Lego bricks. A child may make multiple airplanes, cars, windmills, and buildings, but rarely are any two exactly alike.

An important dimension of multimethod designs is the longitudinal nature of the research process. Most clinical research questions are complex and multifaceted and cannot be addressed in a single study. In constructing the design, the clinical researcher is constantly balancing the desire to address the question fully with the feasibility of being able to complete the study. Narrowing the focus potentially compromises the integrity of the question, whereas trying to accomplish too much can be overwhelming and possibly unfundable. Thus, in conceptualizing study designs, the researcher may decide to do a series of studies in a longitudinal process that fits the larger research agenda. How a design is finally put together depends on the questions and the setting. Snadden and Brown (1991) wondered about the impact of stigmatization on adults with asthma. Answering this question required them to take two steps. First, they had to identify patients with asthma who felt they were stigmatized; then, they had to explore the perceived effects of that stigmatization in the patients' lives. The researchers solved these issues by initially using a questionnaire measuring attitudes concerning asthma to identify respondents reporting high levels of stigma. They then interviewed these individuals using qualitative interview and analysis methods.

Multiple methods can also be directly integrated within a single study in a number of ways. For example, sometimes it may be helpful if two independent studies are conducted concurrently on the same study population and the results then converged. This is the approach recommended for the multimethod RCT (see Wiles, 1998; Willms, 1991). Another widely used approach to designing multimethod research involves the more intimate integration of multiple methods within a single research study. For example, Borkan, Quirk, and Sullivan (1991) had noticed that breaking a hip was often a turning point toward death for many elderly patients. They puzzled about what distinguished those patients from others who recovered with minimal complications, as the research literature did not reveal any obvious traditional biomedical factors. The researchers wondered if patients' stories about their fractures had any connection with their outcomes. They used an epidemiological cross-sectional design with a sample of hospitalized elderly patients with hip fractures. Multiple biomedical indicators were measured as independent variables, along with rehabilitation outcome measures as the dependent variable. There is nothing unusual here—this design would assure acceptance by the intended clinical audience. What distinguished this study was that the researchers also conducted in-depth interviews with each patient concerning how the patient understood the hip fracture within his or her life story. Several distinguishable injury narratives emerged. The researchers organized the narratives according to type and then entered these as another independent variable in the statistical outcome modeling. They found narrative type to be the most powerful predictor of rehabilitation outcome.

When discussing qualitative research design with clinicians and patients, we simplify the jargon. We divide data gathering methods into interviewing, observing, and document review (which includes videotapes). We further subdivide interviews into depth, focus group, and ethnographic (or key informant; see Mitchell, 1998). We describe participant observation as either short-term or prolonged. We frame the many traditions, techniques, and "confusing" jargon of qualitative analysis as a "dance of interpretation" in which three idealized organizing styles—immersion/crystallization, editing, and template (for details, see Figure 12.3; see also Miller & Crabtree, 1999a)—promote the dynamic, creative, iterative, yet disciplined craft of qualitative interpretation. All three organizing styles may be used at some time during the different gathering/interpreting iterations of a particular research project.

Putting It Together

We will now review a case study focusing on family medicine practice patterns to further demonstrate the use of a multimethod framework

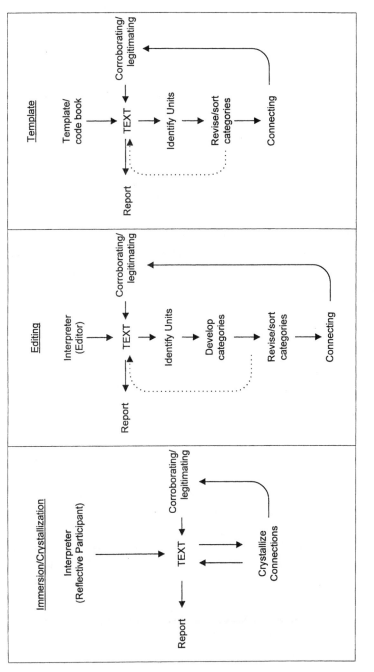

Figure 12.3. Three Organizing Styles of Analysis

(Crabtree, Miller, Aita, Flocke, & Stange, 1998; Stange et al., 1998). This study was funded by a large federal grant—a fact that provides evidence for the widening acceptance of the multimethod approach.

The Direct Observation of Primary Care (DOPC) study was designed to illuminate the "black box" of clinical practice by describing patient visits to family physicians in community practices with a special emphasis on the delivery of preventive health services. This largely quantitative cross-sectional descriptive study focused on the content and context of the out-patient visit through the direct observation of patient visits using a variation on the highly structured Davis Observation Code (Callahan & Bertakis, 1991) along with checklists of patient visits, patient exit questionnaires, medical record reviews, billing data abstractions, and physician questionnaires. To supplement and enhance these quantitative data, the research nurses dictated observational field notes immediately after each visit to provide richer descriptions of the variables under study. These ethnographic data were impressionistic and focused on describing the practices in terms of key features, such as the practice location, office relationships, and how the practice functioned. The data eventually totaled more than 2,000 pages of field notes from observations of 138 physicians in 84 different family practices. The quantitative descriptions provided valuable insights into the overall content of family medicine practice (Stange et al., 1998) as well as into many other facets of family practice (see the entire May 1998 issue of *Journal of Family Practice*). The qualitative field notes identified a long list of key features that appear to be important for understanding how practices operate on a day-to-day basis, particularly in the delivery of preventive services (Crabtree et al., 1998). The qualitative data were also used to formulate a new theoretical model of practice organization based on complexity theory. This model now provides the basis for two subsequent, federally funded studies (Miller, Crabtree, McDaniel, & Stange, 1998). These new studies include in-depth comparative case studies of family practices using ethnographic techniques (see Crabtree & Miller, 1999b) and a multimethod clinical trial using complexity theory as an intervention strategy for improving preventive health services delivery in family practices. In addition, these two studies are more participatory and directly involve the practices in analysis and feedback. These three large studies are providing data-based insights into family practice that extend well beyond their prevention focus. The progression from a multimethod observational study to an in-depth

420

comparative case study to an intervention trial grounded in insights from the previous work shows the potential for multisite, multimethod, collaborative study.

An important aspect of all of these studies is their use of a collaborative research team. The team included physicians, epidemiologists, statisticians, a psychologist, anthropologists, an economist, and a sociologist. We designed the study together, met frequently during the study to review the qualitative data and make adjustments in the study, and did intensive reflexivity work (Barry, Britten, Barber, Bradley, & Stevenson, 1999). This long-term collaborative teamwork has enabled the group to expand its use of qualitative methods and its operating paradigms.

◆ Telling the Stories

Writing Strategies

Some specific writing strategies can be useful in facilitating communication of and receptivity to qualitative clinical research (Richardson, 1990; Wolcott, 1990). The most important of these is for the writer to *avoid jargon*; the language should be kept simple and concrete. Using typologies and continua as rhetorical frames is helpful because these initially appear rational and measurable, qualities valued by traditional clinical researchers. Researchers can maintain the interpretive aspects of their work by emphasizing their studies' cultural/historical and/or inductive construction and grounding in lived clinical experience. It is also useful for researchers to communicate either in the biomedically dominant visual mode (through the use of tables, charts, diagrams, and data matrices) or in the clinically familiar narrative mode of case reports. The latter often take the form of first-person voice pathographies (Hawkins, 1993) or first-person accounts by physicians of their patient encounters (Loxterkamp, 1997; Sacks, 1984).

The dominant audience for clinical research perceives the issues of "validity," "reliability," and "generalizability" as scientific fundamentalist dogma, resulting in heightened concerns about bias. In reporting on their collaborative multimethod study, Daly and McDonald (1992) describe the impact of echocardiography on patients' perceptions of self. Their story describes how difficult it can be to have a conversation at the wall: "The biggest problem was that physicians saw qualitative research methods as . . . prone to bias. Highly structured methods of analyzing qualitative data were effectively used . . . and are probably necessary for 'covering one's back' in multidisciplinary teams" (p. 416). Daly and McDonald present strategies that qualitative researchers can use to translate their wisdom from behind the wall and engage in conversations at the wall. The methodological guidelines for quantitative methods are not relevant for qualitative clinical researchers. The rules of evidence for qualitative clinical research can be translated for clinical audiences as telling methodologically, rhetorically, and clinically convincing stories.

Telling Convincing Stories

A *methodologically convincing story* answers the question, How was the research designed and done? It is important that the researcher make explicit how and why the research design, sampling strategies, and data collection and analysis techniques fit the question and research context, as discussed earlier in this chapter. It is helpful for the researcher to mention when the research design is cross-sectional, prospective, case control, or similar to some other design from observational epidemiology (Ward, 1993). He or she should also address specific techniques, such as triangulation, member checking, and searching for disconfirming evidence (Guba & Lincoln, 1989; Kuzel & Like, 1991), when applicable.

Relationship is essential to the clinical experience. Kahn (1993) has proposed that a language of relationship be used to judge the methodological adequacy of clinical qualitative research. A methodologically convincing story addresses three different relationships: the investigator's *relationship with informants,* noting how each influenced the other during the research process; the investigator's *relationship with the data,* particularly the circularity or iterative aspects of the research experience; and the investigator's *relationship with the readers,* so that authorial intent is clear.

Methodological issues are especially important if the researcher is entering the EBM space. One popular approach for helping primary care clinicians become "information masters," or EBM experts, involves teaching them to recognize POEMS, or "patient-oriented evidence that matters" (Slawson et al., 1994). In the first step, the clinician scans an article's abstract and determines if the results relate to outcomes that are common or important in everyday clinical practice and matter to patients, and if the results might potentially change what he or she currently does in practice. If the answers are yes, the clinician takes the second step: He or she reads the article and decides whether the conclusions are methodologically sound. There are simple one-page checklists for quantitative studies. The following checklist, which we have developed, is currently being used in the evaluation of qualitative articles:

1. Is the method appropriate for the question?
2. Is the sampling adequate and information rich?
3. Is the research process iterative?
4. Is the interpretive process thorough and clearly described?
5. Is reflexivity addressed?

A methodologically convincing story is not one that pleases a positivist; rather, it is one that pleases qualitative research peers, clinicians, and patients. Thus the use of explicit guidelines and checklists is helpful, but must be tempered with a large dose of flexibility so as not to put off the doing of qualitative research (Chapple & Rogers, 1998). The approach described above is consistent with Altheide and Johnson's (1998) idea of "validity-as-reflexive-accounting," where researcher or team, the sense-making processes, and the question or topic are in interaction, with a focus on how meanings are constructed. This is a good description of the validity process in clinical care.

A *rhetorically convincing story* answers the question, How believable is this text? Readers are drawn into the story and begin imagining that the story is about them. When this occurs, the conclusions make more sense for them. The language and style of writing need to be familiar to the audience. Some of the quotations and observations selected to illustrate interpretations also need to reflect the readers' experience and/or values. A rhetorically convincing story assures readers that the writer has walked in their shoes. Bunge (1961) reviews some of the features that characterize a believable story.

A *clinically convincing story* answers the question, Does this study make clinical sense? A story is clinically convincing if it successfully addresses three features important in the clinical research space. The *question* must matter to clinical participants and the results must specifically address that question. This usually means attention is directed to the pragmatic intervention and policy focus of the clinical world. The *audience* or stakeholder is also a clinical participant for whom the results matter, and this should be obvious in the text. Finally, the manuscript reveals *assumptions* about the physical/behavioral, social/emotional, cultural/ historical, or spiritual aspects of clinical participants' bodies, lives, and/or power.

Qualitative clinical research is convincing if the methods are appropriate for the question and the investigator's relationships with informants, data, and audience are clearly addressed; if the audience recognizes itself in the findings; and if the question and results matter to clinical participants. All of these criteria are more easily satisfied if a collaborative team does the research. When this team includes clinical participants, a community of discourse is created where conversations at the walls can begin (see Denz-Penhey & Murdoch, 1993).

Where to Tell the Stories

Qualitative clinical research is widely presented and published in primary care internal medicine and family medicine, nursing, social work, and educational research books and journals. Much of this success over the past decade is owed to specific efforts to translate and introduce qualitative research in workshops within professional meetings, through newsletters, and through methods' publications emphasizing clinical usefulness. Qualitative clinical research is now appearing in clinical journals, especially in the field of primary care. *Qualitative Health Research, Qualitative Inquiry,* and *Culture, Medicine, and Psychiatry* serve as bridgebuilding publications with an almost exclusive emphasis on qualitative clinical research. All of the primary care journals have reviewers trained in qualitative research and readily publish qualitative studies. The *Journal of Family Practice* now provides space on its Web site to "publish" supplementary materials, thus making it possible for authors to condense articles into the space requirements of medical journals. The next steps are to expand presentations to the larger general medical journals, such as the *New England Journal of Medicine* and the *Journal of the American Medical Association,* and to improve ways for communicating results with the patient population. The use of the World Wide Web may become a valuable means of presenting findings to patients and the broader community.

◆ Summary

There are many clinical worlds. Each of them is a place where support is sought and power invoked. The clinical world and people's needs for support occur in nursing, primary health care, specialized medical care, administration and management, education, social work, family therapy, mental health care, public health, engineering, and law. In each of these worlds, there are questions emerging from practice. These are the questions, the settings, and the participants for doing qualitative clinical research. This is where the conversation starts. The research is judged by the clinical difference it makes.

People continue to meet in clinics, hoping to weave a comforting cloth of support, but the created relationships and patterns are now more varied, more confusing, and often too expensive. Concerns about access and cost do matter, but we cannot address them adequately without facing the abusive and dismembering experience of being a woman in the medical clinic, the pervasive delegitimation of patient experience, clinicians' increasing sense of helpless imprisonment, and the mounting problems, discontinuities, cultural conflicts, and ecological degradation within local communities. Knowing the probabilities is not enough and is often inappropriate. The stories, uniquenesses, and contexts are also essential threads in the fabric. Without them, care and moral discourse remain narrowly defined; our bodies and lives remain fragmented and power is imposed. Camille remains isolated within the clan of one-breasted women. She, and we, need the breath of qualitative research. She, and we, need *relationship* restored to the clinical world.

Ten years have passed. Camille, Gloria, and Alice are now members of a community health advisory group that provides counsel for several local primary care practices and a regional health network and hospital system. They are meeting with an interdisciplinary team of researchers, clinicians, local employers, pharmaceutical industry representatives, and a fellow from the National Institutes of Health. This group is designing a new regional research initiative jointly funded by the NIH and a local foundation that will test a promising new drug for the prevention of breast cancer using a multimethod RCT design that includes the extensive use of qualitative methods. The women's daughters will be in the locally controlled study. The analysis of the qualitative data will occur independent of the RCT analysis and will be ongoing throughout the trial. Camille, Gloria, and Alice are members of the qualitative analysis team. They have authority to end the study for any reason, at any time.

Qualitative methods are needed now more than ever, but with a participatory, collaborative, multimethod twist. Qualitative clinical researchers must move from behind their walls, engage the clinical experience and its questions, and practice humility and fidelity within a community of discourse at the walls. This is a dangerous, but exciting, conversation because it promises that no one can stay the same. Beware the idolatry of control, the idolatry of measurement. If measurement is required, insist on inviting the patients and the clinicians into the research process; insist on measuring suffering and love. Include the local ecology. Complicate the outcomes. Measure the dance of life's attachments and detachments, of mystery and grace, of breathing and the rhythms of life. Measure the process of healing. Our research needs to risk restoring relationship to the clinical world. Clinical research can heal by transforming into praxis. In time, all walls crumble, power shifts, and healing begins. We are not any closer to that dangerous and unconscious Eden. Thank heavens. It is much better than that—we are beginning to make sense of life together.

◆ Notes

1. The word *patient* derives from the Latin word *patiens,* meaning "to suffer," and from the Latin *paene,* meaning "almost," and *penuria,* meaning "need." People seek clinicians because they have need and are suffering. They are no longer complete; they lack adequate support; they are merely "almost human." People go to clinicians because they do not perceive themselves as equal and/or whole. They are "patients" in need of movement toward wholeness.

2. The word *clinic* derives from the Greek words *klinikos,* meaning "of a bed," and *klinein,"* meaning "to lean" or "to recline." From this sense, a clinic is a physical and social place for those in need of support (this support can be medical, managerial, educational, legal, economic, religious, nursing, social, or psychological). This understanding defines clinic as a bounded text for research.

◆ References

Altheide, D.L., & Johnson, J. M. (1998). Criteria for assessing interpretive validity in qualitative research. In N. K. Denzin & Y. S. Lincoln (Eds.), *Collecting and interpreting qualitative materials* (pp. 283-312). Thousand Oaks, CA: Sage.

Baer, H. A. (1993). How critical can clinical anthropology be? *Medical Anthropology, 15,* 299-317.

Barry, C. A., Britten, N., Barber, N., Bradley, C., & Stevenson, F. (1999). Using reflexivity to optimize teamwork in qualitative research. *Qualitative Health Research, 9,* 26-44.

Becker, G. (1997). *Disrupted lives: How people create meaning in a chaotic world.* Berkeley: University of California Press.

Beinfield, H., & Korngold, E. (1991). *Between heaven and earth: A guide to Chinese medicine.* New York: Ballantine.

Berg, D. N., & Smith, K. K. (Eds.). (1988). *The self in social inquiry: Researching methods.* Newbury Park, CA: Sage.

Berger, P. L., & Luckmann, T. (1967). *The social construction of reality: A treatise in the sociology of knowledge.* Garden City, NY: Anchor.

Bogdan, R. C., & Biklen, S. K. (1992). *Qualitative research for education: An introduction to theory and methods* (2nd ed.). Boston: Allyn & Bacon.

Borkan, J. M., Quirk, M., & Sullivan, M. (1991). Finding meaning after the fall: Injury narratives from elderly hip fracture patients. *Social Science and Medicine, 33,* 947-957.

Brewer, J., & Hunter, A. (1989). *Multimethod research: A synthesis of styles.* Newbury Park, CA: Sage.

Brueggemann, W. (1991). *Interpretation and obedience: From faithful reading to faithful living.* Minneapolis: Fortress.

Bunge, M. (1961). The weight of simplicity in the construction and assaying of scientific theories. *Philosophy of Science, 28,* 120-149.

Burawoy, M., Burton, A., Ferguson, A. A., Fox, K. J., Gamson, J., Gartrell, N., Hurst, L., Kurzman, C., Salzinger, L., Schiffman, J., & Ui, S. (1991). *Ethnography unbound: Power and resistance in the modern metropolis.* Berkeley: University of California Press.

Callahan, E. J., & Bertakis, K. D. (1991). Development and validation of the Davis observation code. *Family Medicine, 23,* 19-24.

Chapple, A., & Rogers, A. (1998). Explicit guidelines for qualitative research: A step in the right direction, a defense of the "soft" option, or a form of sociological imperialism? *Family Practice, 15,* 556-561.

Chrisman, N. J. (1977). The health seeking process: An approach to the natural history of illness. *Culture, Medicine, and Psychiatry, 1,* 351-377.

Chrisman, N. J., & Maretzki, T. W. (Eds.). (1982). *Clinically applied anthropology: Anthropologists in health science settings.* Boston: D. Reidel.

Clifford, J., & Marcus, G. E. (Eds.). (1986). *Writing culture: The poetics and politics of ethnography.* Berkeley: University of California Press.

Coward, D. D. (1990). Critical multiplism: A research strategy for nursing science. *Image: Journal of Nursing Scholarship, 22*(3), 163-167.

Crabtree, B. F., & Miller, W. L. (Eds.). (1999a). *Doing qualitative research* (2nd ed.). Thousand Oaks, CA: Sage.

Crabtree, B. F., & Miller, W. L. (1999b). Researching practice settings: The case study approach. In B. F. Crabtree & W. L. Miller (Eds.), *Doing qualitative research* (2nd ed.). Thousand Oaks, CA: Sage.

Crabtree, B. F., Miller, W. L., Aita, V., Flocke, S. A., & Stange, K. C. (1998). Primary care practice organization and preventive services delivery: A qualitative analysis. *Journal of Family Practice, 46,* 403-409.

Csordas, T. (Ed.). (1994). *Embodiment and experience: The existential ground of culture and self.* Cambridge: Cambridge University Press.

Daly, J., & McDonald, I. (1992). Covering your back: Strategies for qualitative research in clinical settings. *Qualitative Health Research, 2,* 416-438.

Davis-Floyd, R., & St. John, G. (1998). *From doctor to healer: The transformative journey.* New Brunswick, NJ: Rutgers University Press.

Denz-Penhey, H., & Murdoch, J. C. (1993). Service delivery for people with chronic fatigue syndrome: A pilot action research study. *Family Practice, 10,* 14-18.

Deyo, R. A., Diehl, A. K., & Rosenthal, M. (1986). How many days of bedrest for acute low back pain? A randomized clinical trial. *New England Journal of Medicine, 315,* 1064-1070.

Diers, D. (1979). *Research in nursing practice.* Philadelphia: J. B. Lippincott.

Drury, N. (1996). *Shamanism.* Shaftesbury, England: Element.

Engels, G. L. (1977). The need for a new medical model: A challenge for biomedicine. *Science, 196,* 129-136.

Fabrega, H., Jr. (1976). The function of medical care systems: A logical analysis. *Perspectives in Biology and Medicine, 20,* 108-119.

Fabrega, H., Jr. (1979). The ethnography of illness. *Social Science and Medicine, 13A,* 565-575.

Fahy, K., & Smith, P. (1999). From the sick role to subject positions: A new approach to the medical encounter. *Health, 3*(1), 71-93.

Feinstein, A. R. (1985). *Clinical epidemiology: The architecture of clinical research.* Philadelphia: W. B. Saunders.

Fisher, B., Costantino, J. P., Wickerham, D. L., Redmond, C. K., Kavanah, M., Cronin, W. M., Vogel, V., Robidoux, A., Dimitrov, N., Atkins, J., Daly, M., Wieand, S., Tan-Chiu, E., Ford, L., & Wolmark, N. (1998). Tamoxifen for prevention of breast cancer: Report of the National Surgical Adjuvant Breast and Bowel Project P-1 Study. *Journal of the National Cancer Institute, 90,* 1371-1388.

Fisher, S. (1986). *In the patient's best interest: Women and the politics of medical decisions.* New Brunswick, NJ: Rutgers University Press.

Fisher, S., & Todd, A. D. (Eds.). (1983). *The social organization of doctor-patient communication.* Washington, DC: Center for Applied Linguistics.

Foster, G. M. (1974). Medical anthropology: Some contrasts with medical sociology. *Medical Anthropology Newsletter, 6,* 1-6.

Foster, G. M., & Anderson, B. G. (1978). *Medical anthropology.* New York: John Wiley.

Frank, A. W. (1995). *The wounded storyteller: Body, illness, and ethics.* Chicago: University of Chicago Press.

Frey, R. (1994). *Eye juggling: Seeing the world through a looking glass and a glass pane.* Lanham, MD: University Press of America.

Freymann, J. G. (1989). The public's health care paradigm is shifting: Medicine must swing with it. *Journal of General Internal Medicine, 4,* 313-319.

Fullerton-Smith, I. (1995). How members of the Cochrane Collaboration prepare and maintain systematic reviews of the effects of health care. *Evidence-Based Medicine, 1,* 7-8.

Good, B. J. (1994). *Medicine, rationality, and experience.* Cambridge: Cambridge University Press.

Good, B. J., & Good, M. D. (1981). The meaning of symptoms: A cultural hermeneutic model for clinical practice. In L. Eisenberg & A. M. Kleinman (Eds.), *The relevance of social science for medicine* (pp. 165-196). Boston: D. Reidel.

Good, B. J., & Good, M. D. (1993). "Learning medicine": The constructing of medical knowledge at Harvard Medical School. In S. Lindenbaum & M. Lock (Eds.), *Knowledge, power, and practice: The anthropology of medicine and everyday life* (pp. 81-107). Berkeley: University of California Press.

Gordon, D. R. (1988). Tenacious assumptions in Western medicine. In M. Lock & D. R. Gordon (Eds.), *Biomedicine examined* (pp. 19-56). Boston: D. Reidel.

Gordon, D. R. (1990). Embodying illness, embodying cancer. *Culture, Medicine, and Psychiatry, 14,* 275-297.

Gordon, J. (1996). *Manifesto for a new medicine: Your guide to healing partnerships and the wise use of alternative therapies.* Reading, MA: Addison-Wesley.

Guba, E. G., & Lincoln, Y. S. (1989). *Fourth generation evaluation.* Newbury Park, CA: Sage.

Haraway, D. J. (1991). *Simians, cyborgs, and women: The reinvention of nature.* New York: Routledge.

Haraway, D. J. (1993). The biopolitics of postmodern bodies: Determinations of self in immune system discourse. In S. Lindenbaum & M. Lock (Eds.), *Knowledge, power, and practice: The anthropology of medicine and everyday life* (pp. 364-410). Berkeley: University of California Press.

Harris, C. M. (1989). Seeing sunflowers. *Journal of the Royal College of General Practitioners, 39,* 313-319.

Hawkins, A. H. (1993). *Reconstructing illness: Studies in pathography.* West Lafayette, IN: Purdue University Press.

Helman, C. G. (1994). *Culture, health and illness.* Oxford: Butterworth Heinemann.

Hyde, L. (1998). *Trickster makes this world: Mischief, myth, and art*. New York: Farrar, Straus & Giroux.

Hynes, W. J., & Doty, W. G. (Eds.). (1993). *Mythical trickster figures: Contours, contexts, and criticisms*. Tuscaloosa: University of Alabama Press.

Jackson, M. (1989). *Paths toward a clearing: Radical empiricism and ethnographic inquiry*. Bloomington: Indiana University Press.

Johnson, M. (1987). *The body in the mind*. Chicago: University of Chicago Press.

Jolly, K., Bradley, F., Sharp, S., Smith, H., & Mant, D. (1998). Follow-up care in general practice of patients with myocardial infarction or angina pectoris: Initial results of the SHIP trial. *Family practice, 15,* 548-555.

Kahn, D. L. (1993). Ways of discussing validity in qualitative nursing research. *Western Journal of Nursing Research, 15,* 122-126.

Kelsey, J. L., Thompson, W. D., & Evans, A. S. (1986). *Methods in observational epidemiology*. New York: Oxford University Press.

Kirmayer, L. J. (1992). The body's insistence on meaning: Metaphor as presentation and representation in illness experience. *Medical Anthropology Quarterly, 6,* 323-346.

Kleinbaum, D. G., Kupper, L. L., & Morgenstern, H. (1982). *Epidemiologic research: Principles and quantitative methods*. Belmont, CA: Lifetime Learning.

Kleinman, A. M. (1988). *The illness narratives: Suffering, healing, and the human condition*. New York: Basic Books.

Kleinman, A. M. (1992). Local worlds of suffering: An interpersonal focus for ethnographies of illness experience. *Qualitative Health Research, 2,* 127-134.

Kleinman, A. M. (1995). *Writing at the margin: Discourse between anthropology and medicine*. Berkeley: University of California Press.

Kleinman, A. M., Eisenberg, L., & Good, B. (1978). Culture, illness, and care: Clinical lessons from anthropologic and cross-cultural research. *Annals of Internal Medicine, 88,* 251-258.

Kuzel, A. J., & Like, R. C. (1991). Standards of trustworthiness for qualitative studies in primary care. In P. G. Norton, M. Stewart, F. Tudiver, M. J. Bass, & E. V. Dunn (Eds.), *Primary care research: Traditional and innovative approaches* (pp. 138-158). Newbury Park, CA: Sage.

Lather, P. (1991). *Getting smart: Feminist research and pedagogy with/in the postmodern*. New York: Routledge.

Lazarus, E. S. (1988). Theoretical considerations for the study of the doctor-patient relationship: Implications of a perinatal study. *Medical Anthropology Quarterly, 2,* 34-58.

Lock, M. (1982). On revealing the hidden curriculum. *Medical Anthropology Quarterly, 14,* 19-21.

Lock, M. (1986). The anthropological study of the American medical system: Center and periphery. *Social Science and Medicine, 22,* 931-932.

Lock, M. (1993). Cultivating the body: Anthropology and epistemologies of bodily practice and knowledge. *Annual Reviews of Anthropology, 22,* 133-156.

Loxterkamp, D. (1997). *A measure of my days: The journal of a country doctor.* Hanover, NH: University Press of New England.

Macaulay, A., Gibson, N., Commander, L., McCabe, M., Robbins, C., & Twohig, P. (1998). *Responsible research with communities: Participatory research in primary care* [On-line publication of the North American Primary Care Research Group]. Available Internet: http://views.vcu.edu/views/fap/napcrg.html

Martin, E. (1994). *Flexible bodies: The role of immunity in American culture from the days of polio to the age of AIDS.* Boston: Beacon.

McWhinney, I. R. (1986). Are we on the brink of a major transformation of clinical method? *Canadian Medical Association Journal, 135,* 873-878.

McWhinney, I. R. (1989). An acquaintance with particulars . . . . *Family Medicine, 21,* 296-298.

Meinert, C. L. (1986). *Clinical trials: Design, conduct, and analysis.* New York: Oxford University Press.

Miller, W. L. (1994). Common space: Creating a collaborative research conversation. In B. F. Crabtree, W. L. Miller, R. B. Addison, V. J. Gilchrist, & A. Kuzel (Eds.), *Exploring collaborative research in primary care* (pp. 265-288). Thousand Oaks, CA: Sage.

Miller, W. L., & Crabtree, B. F. (1999a). The dance of interpretation. In B. F. Crabtree & W. L. Miller (Eds.), *Doing qualitative research* (2nd ed.). Thousand Oaks, CA: Sage.

Miller, W. L., & Crabtree, B. F. (1999b). Primary care research: A multimethod typology and qualitative roadmap. In B. F. Crabtree & W. L. Miller (Eds.), *Doing qualitative research* (2nd ed.). Thousand Oaks, CA: Sage.

Miller, W. L., Crabtree, B. F., McDaniel, R., & Stange, K. C. (1998). Understanding change in primary care practice using complexity theory. *Journal of Family Practice, 46,* 369-376.

Mishler, E. G. (1984). *The discourse of medicine: Dialectics of medical interviews.* Norwood, NJ: Ablex.

Mitchell, M. L. (1998). *Employing qualitative methods in the private sector.* Thousand Oaks, CA: Sage.

Morgan, G. (1998). *Images of organization: The executive edition.* San Francisco: Berrett-Koehler.

Morse, J. M., & Field, P. A. (1997). *Principles of qualitative methods.* Thousand Oaks, CA: Sage.

Morsy, S. A. (1996). Political economy in medical anthropology. In C. F. Sargent & T. M. Johnson (Eds.), *Medical anthropology: Contemporary theory and method* (Rev. ed., pp. 21-40). Westport, CT: Praeger.

Naylor, C. D. (1995). Grey zones of clinical practice: Some limits to evidence-based medicine. *Lancet, 345,* 840-842.

Pelto, P. J., & Pelto, G. H. (1978). *Anthropological research: The structure of inquiry* (2nd ed.). New York: Cambridge University Press.

Pelto, P. J., & Pelto, G. H. (1990). Field methods in medical anthropology. In T. M. Johnson & C. F. Sargent (Eds.), *Medical anthropology: Contemporary theory and method* (pp. 269-297). New York: Praeger.

Pfifferling, J. H. (1981). A cultural prescription for medicocentrism. In L. Eisenberg & A. M. Kleinman (Eds.), *The relevance of social science for medicine* (pp. 197-222). Boston: D. Reidel.

Pocock, S. J. (1983). *Clinical trials: A practical approach.* New York: John Wiley.

Polgar, S. (1962). Health and human behavior: Areas of interest common to the social and medical sciences. *Current Anthropology, 3,* 159-205.

Powles, T., Eeles, R., Ashley, S., Easton, D., Chang, J., Dowsett, M., Tidy, A., Viggers, J., & Davey, J. (1998). Interim analysis of the incidence of breast cancer in the Royal Marsden Hospital tamoxifen randomised chemoprevention trial. *Lancet, 352,* 98-101.

Radin, P. (1955). *The trickster: A study in American Indian mythology.* New York: Schocken.

Richardson, L. (1990). *Writing strategies: Reaching diverse audiences.* Newbury Park, CA: Sage.

Sackett, D. L. (1991). *Clinical epidemiology: A basic science for clinical medicine* (2nd ed.). Boston: Little, Brown.

Sackett, D. L., Richardson, W. S., Rosenberg, W., & Haynes, R. B. (1997). *Evidence-based medicine: How to practice and teach EBM.* London: Churchill Livingstone.

Sacks, O. (1984). *A leg to stand on.* New York: Summit.

Sapsford, R., & Abbott, P. (1992). *Research methods for nurses and the caring professions.* Bristol, PA: Open University Press.

Schein, E. H. (1987). *The clinical perspective in fieldwork.* Newbury Park, CA: Sage.

Scheper-Hughes, N., & Locke, M. (1987). The mindful body: A prolegomenon to future work in medical anthropology. *Medical Anthropology Quarterly, 1,* 6-41.

Sharma, H., & Clark, C. (1998). *Contemporary ayurveda: Medicine and research in maharishi ayur-veda.* Philadelphia: Churchill Livingstone.

Shaughnessy, A. F., Slawson, D. C., & Bennett, J. H. (1994). Becoming an information master: A guidebook to the medical information jungle. *Journal of Family Practice, 39,* 489-499.

Shildrick, M. (1997). *Leaky bodies and boundaries: Feminism, postmodernism and (bio) ethics.* London: Routledge.

Singer, M. (1995). Beyond the ivory tower: Critical praxis in medical anthropology. *Medical Anthropology Quarterly, 9,* 80-106.

Slawson, D. C., Shaughnessy, A. F., & Bennett, J. H. (1994). Becoming a medical information master: Feeling good about not knowing everything. *Journal of Family Practice, 38,* 505-513.

Smith, R. C. (1996). *The patient's story: Integrated patient-doctor interviewing.* Boston: Little, Brown.

Snadden, D., & Brown, J. B. (1991). Asthma and stigma. *Family Practice, 8,* 329-335.

Stange, K. C., Miller, W. L., Crabtree, B. F., O'Connor, P. J., & Zyzanski, S. J. (1994). Multimethod research: Approaches for integrating qualitative and quantitative methods. *Journal of General Internal Medicine, 9*(5), 278-282.

Stange, K. C., Zyzanski, S. J., Jaen, C. R., Callahan, E. J., Kelly, R. B., Gillanders, W. R., Shank, J. C., Chao, J., Medalie, J. H., Miller, W. L., Crabtree, B. F., Flocke, S. A., Gilchrist, V. J., Langa, D. M., & Goodwin, M. A. (1998). Illuminating the "black box": A description of 4454 patient visits to 138 family physicians. *Journal of Family Practice, 46,* 377-389.

Stein, H. F. (1990). *American medicine as culture.* Boulder, CO: Westview.

Stewart, M., Brown, J. B., Weston, W. W., McWhinney, I. R., McWilliam, C. L., & Freeman, T. R. (1995). *Patient-centered medicine: Transforming the clinical method.* Thousand Oaks, CA: Sage.

Swayne, J. (1998). *Homeopathic method: Implications for clinical practice and medical science.* London: Churchill Livingstone.

Symon, G., & Cassell, C. (Eds.). (1998). *Qualitative methods and analysis in organizational research: A practical guide.* London: Sage.

Tashakkori, A., & Teddlie, C. (1998). *Mixed methodology: Combining qualitative and quantitative approaches.* Thousand Oaks, CA: Sage.

Taylor, B. (1993). Phenomenology: One way to understand nursing practice. *International Journal of Nursing Studies, 30,* 171-179.

Thesen, J., & Kuzel, A. (1999). Participatory inquiry. In B. F. Crabtree & W. L. Miller (Eds.), *Doing qualitative research* (2nd ed.). Thousand Oaks, CA: Sage.

Tresolini, C. P., & Pew-Fetzer Task Force. (1994). *Health professions education and relationship-centered care.* San Francisco: Pew Health Professions Commission.

Turner, B. (1992). *Regulating bodies: Essays in medical sociology.* New York: Routledge.

Veronesi, U., Maisonneuve, P., Costa, A., Sacchini, V., Maltoni, C., Robertson, C., Rotmensz, N., & Boyle, P. (on behalf of the Italian Tamoxifen Prevention Study). (1998). Prevention of breast cancer with tamoxifen: Preliminary findings from the Italian randomised trial among hysterectomised women. *Lancet, 352,* 93-97.

Waitzkin, H. (1991). *The politics of medical encounters: How patients and doctors deal with social problems.* New Haven, CT: Yale University Press.

Ward, M. M. (1993). Study design in qualitative research: A guide to assessing quality. *Journal of General Internal Medicine, 8,* 107-109.

Weil, A. (1988). *Health and healing.* Boston: Houghton Mifflin.

West, C. (1984). *Routine complications: Troubles with talk between doctors and patients.* Bloomington: Indiana University Press.

Wiesel, S. W., Cuckler, J. M., DeLuca, F., Jones, F., Zeide, M. S., & Rothman, R. H. (1980). Acute low back pain: An objective analysis of conservative therapy. *Spine, 5,* 324-330.

Wiles, R. (1998). Patients' perceptions of their heart attack and recovery: The influence of epidemiological "evidence" and personal experience. *Social Science and Medicine, 46,* 1477-1486.

Williams, G. (1984). The genesis of chronic illness: Narrative re-construction. *Sociology of Health and Illness, 6,* 175-200.

Williams, T. T. (1991). *Refuge: An unnatural history of family and place.* New York: Pantheon.

Willms, D. G. (1991). A new stage, a new life: Individual success in quitting smoking. *Social Science and Medicine, 33,* 1365-1371.

Willms, D. G., Best, J. A., Taylor, D. W., Gilbert, J. R., Wilson, D. M. C., Lindsay, E. A., & Singer, J. (1990). A systematic approach for using qualitative methods in primary prevention research. *Medical Anthropology Quarterly, 4,* 391-409.

Wilson, D. M. C., Taylor, D. W., Gilbert, J. R., Best, J. A., Lindsay, E. A., Willms, D. G., & Singer, J. (1988). A randomized trial of a family physician intervention for smoking cessation. *Journal of the American Medical Association, 260,* 1570-1574.

Wolcott, H. F. (1990). *Writing up qualitative research.* Newbury Park, CA: Sage.

Young, A. (1982a). The anthropologies of illness and sickness. In B. Siegel, A. Beals, & S. Tyler (Eds.), *Annual review of anthropology* (Vol. 11, pp. 257-285). Palo Alto, CA: Annual Reviews.

Young, A. (1982b). When rational men fall sick: An inquiry into some assumptions made by medical anthropologists. *Culture, Medicine, and Psychiatry, 5,* 317-335.

Suggested Readings

◆ Chapter 2

Berg, B. L. (2001). *Qualitative research methods for the social sciences, fourth edition.* Boston: Allyn and Bacon.

Cole, A. L., & Knowles, J. G. (Eds.). (2001). *Lives in context: The art of life history research.* Walnut Creek, CA: AltaMira.

Piantinida, M., & Garman, N. B. (1999). *The qualitative dissertation: A guide for students and faculty.* Thousand Oaks, CA: Corwin Press.

Silverman, D. (2000). *Doing qualitative research: A practical handbook.* Thousand Oaks, CA: Sage.

◆ Chapter 3

Bradley, D. B. (2001). Developing research questions through grant proposal development. *Educational Gerontology, 27,* 569-581.

Devers, K. J., & Frankel, R. M. (2001). Getting qualitative research published. *Education for Health, 14(1),* 109-117.

Gotley, D. C. (2000). Grantsmanship: Achieving success in research funding. *Australian & New Zealand Journal of Surgery, 70,* 297-301.

Martin, B. (2000). Research grants: Problems and options. *Australian Universities Review, 43(2),* 17-22.

Street, A. (2001). The criteria of appropriateness and feasibility. *Nursing Inquiry, 8,* 1-2.

◆ Chapter 4

Alexander, B. K. (2002). Fading, twisting and weaving: An interpretive ethnography of the black barbershop as a cultural space. *Qualitative Inquiry, 9*(1), 12-30.

◆ Chapter 5

Travers, M. (2001). *Qualitative research through case studies.* London: Sage.

◆ Chapter 6

Atkinson, P, Coffey, A, Delamont, S, Lofland, J., & Loflands, L. (Eds.) (2001). *Handbook of ethnography.* London: Sage.

James, A., Hockey, J., & Andrew Dawson, A. (Eds.). (1997). *After writing culture: Epistemology and praxis in contemporary anthropology.* London: Routledge.

◆ Chapter 7

Gubrium, J. F. (1992). *Out of control: Family therapy and domestic disorder.* Thousand Oaks, CA: Sage.

Gubrium, J. F., & Holstein, J. A. (Eds.). (2001). *Institutional selves: Troubled identity in a postmodern world.* New York: Oxford University Press.

Gubrium, J. F., & Holstein, J. A. (1997). *The new language of qualitative method.* New York: Oxford University Press.

Holstein, J. A. (1993). *Court-ordered insanity: Interpretive practice and involuntary commitment.* New York: Aldine de Gruyter.

Holstein, J. A. & Gubrium, J. F. (2000). *The self we live by: Narrative identity in a postmodern world.* New York: Oxford University Press.

◆ Chapter 8

Charmaz, K. (2001). Grounded theory analysis. In J. F. Gubrium & J. A. Holstein (Eds.), *Handbook of interviewing,* pp. 675-694. Thousand Oaks, CA: Sage.

Charmaz, K. (2001). Grounded theory: Methodology and theory construction. In N. J. Smelser & P. B. Baltes (Eds.), *International encyclopedia of the social and behavioral sciences,* pp. 6396-6399. Amsterdam: Pergamon.

Charmaz, K., & Mitchell, R. G. (2001). Grounded theory in ethnography. In P. Atkinson, A. Coffey, S. Delamont, J. Lofland, & L. H. Lofland (Eds.), *Handbook of ethnography,* pp. 160-174. London: Sage.

Dey, I. (1999). *Grounding grounded theory: Guidelines for qualitative inquiry.* San Diego: Academic Press.

Glaser, B. G. (1978). *Theoretical sensitivity.* Mill Valley, CA: Sociology Press.

Glaser, B. G. (1992). *Emergence vs. forcing: Basics of grounded theory analysis.* Mill Valley, CA: Sociology Press.

Glaser, B. G. (1998). *Doing grounded theory: Issues and discussions.* Mill Valley, CA: Sociology Press.

Glaser, B. G., & Strauss, A. L. (1967). *The discovery of grounded theory.* Chicago: Aldine.

Strauss, A. L. (1987). *Qualitative analysis for social scientists.* New York: Cambridge University Press.

Strauss, A. L., & Corbin, J. A. (1998). *Basics of qualitative research: Grounded theory procedures and techniques, 2nd ed.* Thousand Oaks, CA: Sage.

◆ Chapter 9

Jones, S. H. (2002). Emotional space: Performing the resistive possibilities of torch singing. *Qualitative Inquiry, 8,* 738-759.

Wolcott, H. F. (2002). *Sneaky Kid and Its Aftermath: Ethics and intimacy in fieldwork.* Walnut Creek, CA: AltaMira.

◆ Chapter 10

Gugelberger, G. M. (Ed.) (1996). *The real thing: Testimonial discourse and Latin America,* pp. 287-304. Durham: Duke University Press.

◆ Chapter 11

Reason, P. & Bradbury, H. (Eds.). (2001). *Handbook of action research: Participative inquiry and practice.* London: Sage.

◆ Chapter 12

Barbour, R. S. (2001). Checklists for improving rigour in qualitative research: A case of the tail wagging the dog? *British Medical Journal, 322,* 1115-1117.

Crabtree, B. F., Miller, W. L., & Stange, K. (Eds.). (2001). Results from the prevention and competing demands in primary care study. *The Journal of Family Practice, 50*(10), 837-889.

Giacomini, M. K., & Cook, D. J. (2000). Qualitative research in health care: What are the results and how do they help me care for my patients? *JAMA, 284,* 478-482.

Macaulay, A. C., Commanda, L. E., Freeman, W. L., Gibson, N., et al. (1998). Responsible research with communities: Participatory research in primary care. [On-line publication of the *North American Primary Care Research Group*.] Available Internet: http//napcrg.org/exec.html

Malterud, K. (2001). The art and science of clinical knowledge: Evidence beyond measures and numbers. *Lancet, 358,* 397-400.

Malterud, K. (2001). Qualitative research: Standards, challenges, and guidelines. *Lancet, 358,* 483-488.

Sandelowski, M. (2002). Reembodying qualitative inquiry. *Qualitative Health Research, 12,* 104-115.

Shepherd, M., Hattersley, A. T., & Sparkes, A. C. (2000). Predictive genetic testing in diabetes: A case study of multiple perspectives. *Qualitative Health Research, 10,* 242-259.

Author Index

442

Subject Index

About the Authors

John Beverley is Professor of Spanish and Latin American literature and cultural studies at the University of Pittsburgh. He has taught at the University of California at San Diego, Stanford University, University of Minnesota, University of Washington, and Universidad Andina in Quito, Ecuador. His 1989 essay "The Margin at the Center: On Testimonio" helped inaugurate the extensive critical discussion of testimonio in Latin American studies in the 1990s. His publications related to the theme of testimonio include *Literature and Politics in the Central American Revolutions* (with Marc Zimmerman; 1990), *Against Literature* (1993), *Una modernidad obsoleta: Estudios sobre el barroco* (1999), *Subalternity and Representation: Arguments in Cultural Theory* (forthcoming), and two coedited collections: *La voz del otro: Testimonio, subalternidad y verdad narrativa* (1992) and *The Postmodernism Debate in Latin America* (1995). He is one of the founding members of the Latin American Subaltern Studies Group.

Kathy Charmaz is Professor of Sociology and Faculty Writing Coordinator at Sonoma State University. Her recent works have concerned qualitative research methods, suffering chronic illness, and professional writing. She serves as the editor of *Symbolic Interaction* and is the 1999-2000 President of the Pacific Sociological Association.

Julianne Cheek is internationally recognized for her expertise in qualitative research in health-related areas. She is currently Director of the Centre for Research into Nursing and Health Care at the University of South

Australia, a university-funded, performance-based research center. She has an outstanding track record of attracting funding for qualitative research projects, with some 16 projects funded in the past 4 years. She has also attracted large sums of funding for projects related to teaching that have qualitative principles embedded within them. She currently has a book in press and has coauthored two others. She has published more than 40 refereed book chapters and journal articles and has presented more than 40 papers at international and national conferences, including keynote addresses in Vancouver, Kuala Lumpur, and Queensland, Australia.

Benjamin F. Crabtree, Ph.D., is Professor and Director of Research, Department of Family Medicine, University of Nebraska Medical Center, where he is also a medical anthropologist. He has written and contributed to numerous articles and chapters on both qualitative and quantitative methods, covering topics ranging from time-series analysis and log-linear models to in-depth interviews, case study research, and qualitative analysis strategies. He is coeditor of *Exploring Collaborative Research in Primary Care* (1994) and *Doing Qualitative Research* (second edition, 1999).

Norman K. Denzin is Distinguished Professor of Communications, College of Communications Scholar, and Research Professor of Communications, Sociology and Humanities at the University of Illinois, Urbana-Champaign. He is the author of numerous books, including *Interpretive Ethnography: Ethnographic Practices for the 21st Century, The Cinematic Society: The Voyeur's Gaze, Images of Postmodern Society, The Research Act: A Theoretical Introduction to Sociological Methods, Interpretive Interactionism, Hollywood Shot by Shot, The Recovering Alcoholic,* and *The Alcoholic Self,* which won the Charles Cooley Award from the Society for the Study of Symbolic Interaction in 1988. In 1997 he was awarded the George Herbert Award from the Study of Symbolic Interaction. He is the editor of the *Sociological Quarterly,* coeditor of *Qualitative Inquiry,* and editor of the book series *Cultural Studies: A Research Annual and Studies in Symbolic Interaction.*

Jaber F. Gubrium is Professor of Sociology at the University of Florida. He is the author of several research monographs, including *Living and Dying at Murray Manor* (1975), *Caretakers* (1979), *Describing Care* (1982), *Oldtimers and Alzheimer's* (1986), *Out of Control* (1992), and *Speaking of Life* (1993). He is the editor of the *Journal of Aging Studies* and has coedited a number of volumes dealing with time, experience, and method in old age. In collaboration with Jim Holstein, he continues to examine empirically the interpretive horizons of social forms, including the self, family, the life course, aging, normality, health, and illness. Their most recent project is *Institutional Selves: Troubled Identities in a Postmodern World.*

James A. Holstein is Professor of Sociology at Marquette University. He has published numerous books, including *Court-Ordered Insanity* (1993), and, with Gale Miller, *Reconsidering Social Constructionism* (1993), *Dispute Domains and Welfare Claims* (1996), and *Social Problems in Everyday Life* (1997). He is coauthor with Jay Gubrium of *The New Language of Qualitative Method* (1997) and *The Active Interview* (1995). Their most recent book, *The Self We Live By*, is a qualitative examination of self-construction in a postmodern world.

Valerie J. Janesick, Ph.D., is Professor of Educational Leadership and Policy Studies and Director of the Broward Doctoral Program at Florida International University in Miami and Fort Lauderdale. She teaches classes in qualitative research methods, participatory action research, narrative methods of research, curriculum planning and evaluation, curriculum theory and inquiry, and ethics in the professions. Her research interests include qualitative research methods, ethics in research and evaluation, and comparative curriculum issues. She incorporates the arts and humanities into her research and writing projects. Her text *Stretching Exercises for Qualitative Researchers* (1998) and other writings use dance as a metaphor for clarifying and expanding our notions of qualitative inquiry. Her next project is focused on ethics and qualitative research. She is taking French gourmet cooking classes in her spare time.

Stephen Kemmis is Director of Stephen Kemmis Research & Consulting Pty Ltd; Professor Emeritus, University of Ballarat; Honorary Associate, Faculty of Education, Monash University; and Adjunct Professor, School of Education and Professional Studies, Griffith University. He is coauthor, with Wilfred Carr, of *Becoming Critical: Education, Knowledge and Action Research* (1986); and, with Robin McTaggart, of *The Action Research Planner* (1986). His research and consultancy interests include the development of critical theory and critical social scientific approaches in educational research and evaluation, participatory action research, curriculum theory, university development (especially research development), and indigenous education.

Yvonna S. Lincoln is Professor of Higher Education, Texas A&M University, and coeditor of this volume and the first edition of the *Handbook of Qualitative Research* (1994). She is also coeditor of the journal *Qualitative Inquiry*, with Norman K. Denzin. She is, with her husband Egon G. Guba, coauthor of *Effective Evaluation* (1981), *Naturalistic Inquiry* (1985), and *Fourth Generation Evaluation* (1989); she is also the editor of *Organizational Theory and Inquiry* (1985) and coeditor of *Representation and the Text* (1997). She has been the recipient of numerous awards for research, including the AERA-Division J Research Achievement Award, the AIR Sidney Suslow Award for Research Contributions to Institutional Research, and the American Evaluation Association's Paul Lazarsfeld Award for Contributions to Evaluation Theory. She is the author of numerous journal articles, chapters, and conference presentations on constructivist and interpretive inquiry, and also on higher education.

Michal M. McCall is Professor of Sociology at Macalester College in St. Paul, Minnesota, where she teaches courses on consumer society, sustainable agriculture, and social theory. Whenever possible, she lives with her husband, Paul Meshejian, on their 4.6-acre farm in Birchrunville, Pennsylvania.

Robin McTaggart is Professor and Executive Dean of Education and Indigenous Studies at James Cook University, Townsville and Cairns, Queensland, Australia, and Adjunct Professor in the International Graduate School of Management of the University of South Australia. A former high school chemistry and biology teacher, he completed his Ph.D. at the Center for Instructional Research and Curriculum Evaluation at the University of Illinois. Formerly Head of the School of Administration and Curriculum Studies and Chair of the Education Studies Centre at Deakin University in Geelong, he has conducted evaluation and research studies of action research by educators, discipline-based arts education, arts programs for disadvantaged youth, instructional computing programs for intellectually disabled adults, coeducation and gender equity in private schooling, AIDS/HIV professional development for rural health workers, Aboriginal education in traditionally oriented remote communities, scientific literacy, and distance education provision in technical and further education. He has also conducted research training workshops for a variety of professions and community groups in the United States, Canada, Thailand, Indonesia, Hong Kong, Malaysia, Indonesia, New Zealand, and Singapore.

William L. Miller, M.D., M.A., is Chair and Program Director, Department of Family Medicine, Lehigh Valley Hospital, Allentown, Pennsylvania; he is also a family physician anthropologist. He is active in an effort to make qualitative research more accessible to health care researchers. He has written and contributed to book chapters and articles detailing step-by-step applications of qualitative methods. His research interests center on the role of the patient-physician relationship in health care, on physician and patient understanding of pain and pain management, and on hypertension. In his current work, he is using case study designs to model primary care practices as nonlinear complex adaptive systems.

Robert E. Stake is Professor of Education and Director of the Center for Instructional Research and Curriculum Evaluation at the University of Illinois. Since 1963 he has been a specialist in the evaluation of educational programs. Among the evaluative studies directed were works in science and mathematics in elementary and secondary schools, model programs and conventional teaching of the arts in schools, development of teaching with sensitivity to gender equity, education of teachers for the deaf and for youth in transition from school to work settings, environmental education and special programs for gifted students, and the reform of urban education. He is the author of *Quieting Reform*, a book on Charles Murray's evaluation of Cities-in-Schools; two books on methodology, *Evaluating the Arts in Education* and *The Art of Case Study Research*; and, with Liora Bresler and Linda Mabry, *Custom and Cherishing*, a book on teaching the arts in ordinary elementary school classrooms in the United States. Recently, he led a multiyear evaluation study of the Chicago Teachers Academy for Mathematics and Science. For his evaluation work, in 1988 he received the Lazarsfeld Award from the American Evaluation Association, and in 1994 he received an honorary doctorate from the University of Uppsala.

Barbara Tedlock is Full Professor and Chair of the Anthropology Department, State University of New York at Buffalo. She has served as editor in chief of the *American Anthropologist* (1993-1998), the flagship journal of the American Anthropological Association. Her publications include four ethnographies and more than 60 articles and essays. She has done extensive ethnographic research with Mayan peoples in Guatemala and Belize, the Zuni of Arizona and New Mexico, and most recently with the Roycrofters-At-Large, an arts and crafts community (a capitalist utopia of sorts) in East Aurora, New York.

William G. Tierney (Ph.D., Stanford University) is Wilbur Kieffer Professor of Higher Education and Director of the Center for Higher Education Policy Analysis at the University of Southern California. His research interests pertain to issues of access, equity, and organizational effectiveness in higher education. He has recently edited a special issue on life histories for *Qualitative Inquiry*, and he is coeditor, with Yvonna S. Lincoln, of *Representation and the Text: Re-framing the Narrative Voice*. Some of his other works include *Academic Outlaws: Queer Theory and Cultural Studies in the Academy; Naming Silenced Lives: Personal Narratives and the Process of Educational Change* (with Daniel McLaughlin), and *Building Communities of Difference: Higher Education in the 21st Century*.